WileyPLUS Learning Space

An easy way to help your students **learn, collaborate,** and **grow**.

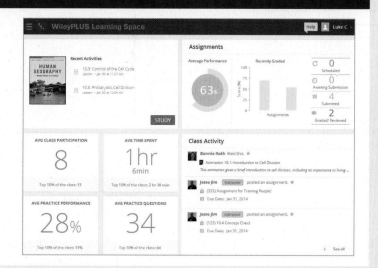

Personalized Experience

Students create their own study guide while they interact with course content and work on learning activities.

Flexible Course Design

Educators can quickly organize learning activities, manage student collaboration, and customize their course—giving them full control over content as well as the amount of interactivity among students.

Clear Path to Action

With visual reports, it's easy for both students and educators to gauge problem areas and act on what's most important.

Instructor Benefits

- Assign activities and add your own materials
- Guide students through what's important in the interactive e-textbook by easily assigning specific content
- Set up and monitor collaborative learning groups
- Assess learner engagement
- Gain immediate insights to help inform teaching

Student Benefits

- Instantly know what you need to work on
- Create a personal study plan
- Assess progress along the way
- Participate in class discussions
- Remember what you have learned because you have made deeper connections to the content

We are dedicated to supporting you from idea to outcome.

WILEY

HUMAN GEOGRAPHY

11TH EDITION

PEOPLE, PLACE, AND CULTURE

HUMAN GEOGRAPHY

11TH EDITION

PEOPLE, PLACE, AND CULTURE

Erin H. Fouberg

Northern State University

Alexander B. Murphy

University of Oregon

H. J. de Blij

Michigan State University

WILEY

Vice President & Director	Petra Recter
Executive Editor	Ryan Flahive
Assistant Editor	Julia Nollen
Editorial Assistant	Kathryn Hancox
Senior Content Manager	Kevin Holm
Aptara Project Manager	Jackie Henry
Marketing Manager	Suzanne Bochet
Senior Photo Editor	Billy Ray
Production Services	Aptara
Cover & Interior Design	Wendy Lai
Front Cover Photo	Alexander B. Murphy
Back Cover Photo (left)	btrenkel/E+/Getty Images
Back Cover Photo (right)	Dori Moreno/Gallo Images/Getty Images

This book was set in Jansen by Aptara, Inc., and printed and bound by Quad Graphics. The cover was printed by Quad Graphics.

This book is printed on acid-free paper. ∞

Founded in 1807, John Wiley & Sons, Inc. has been a valued source of knowledge and understanding for more than 200 years, helping people around the world meet their needs and fulfill their aspirations. Our company is built on a foundation of principles that include responsibility to the communities we serve and where we live and work. In 2008, we launched a Corporate Citizenship Initiative, a global effort to address the environmental, social, economic, and ethical challenges we face in our business. Among the issues we are addressing are carbon impact, paper specifications and procurement, ethical conduct within our business and among our vendors, and community and charitable support. For more information, please visit our website: www.wiley.com/go/citizenship.

Evaluation copies are provided to qualified academics and professionals for review purposes only, for use in their courses during the next academic year. These copies are licensed and may not be sold or transferred to a third party. Upon completion of the review period, please return the evaluation copy to Wiley. Return instructions and a free-of-charge return shipping label are available at www.wiley.com/go/returnlabel. If you have chosen to adopt this book for use in your course, please accept this book as your complimentary desk copy. Outside of the United States, please contact your local representative.

Main Book ISBN 978-1-118-79314-5

Binder-Ready Version ISBN 978-1-118-99538-9

AP Edition ISBN 978-1-119-04314-0

Printed in the United States of America

10 9 8 7 6 5 4 3 2 1

The noted geographer Yi-Fu Tuan once said, "People make places." People create cultures, values, aesthetics, politics, economics, and more, and each of these affects and shapes places. Places do not exist in a vacuum, as places are constantly being changed from within and in the context of the broader world. The study of human geography constantly reminds us of how people shape their world and of how people and places vary across space.

People build homes and buildings, establish economic and political systems, interact with one other, construct cultures, and shape physical environments. In the process, they create and transform places. On the front cover, the floating village on the shores of Southeast Asia's largest fresh-water lake, the Tonlé Sap in Cambodia, represents an extraordinary human adaption to a lake that rises and falls by as much as eight meters (26 feet) between the wet and dry seasons. For more than a thousand years, people have lived in floating villages and in homes built on stilts, drawing their living by fishing in the lake.

Just a short drive north, more than 1.5 million tourists visit the temple of Angkor Wat each year. Built by the Khmer Empire as a Hindu temple in the tenth century, designs on walls in the temple complex show people fishing in the Tonlé Sap. A later emperor converted to Buddhism and transformed Angkor Wat into a Buddhist temple. Empires shifted again, and the site of Angkor Wat was covered by forests by early 1500. When Europeans came to Southeast Asia in the centuries after 1500, some heard about the massive temple complex and followed local guides through the dense forest to the site.

In the 1990s Cambodia emerged from a period of great political and social upheaval, and the country was opened to tourists who began to flock to see Angkor Wat. The nearby city of Siem Reap now houses more than 170 hotels. The 30 most luxurious are in particularly high demand as Westerners, Japanese, South Koreans, and a growing number of Chinese tour the region. Every morning, tourists come in droves to witness the remarkable sunrise at Angkor Wat, each trying to capture the perfect photo, as the back cover illustrates. After visiting the temple, some choose to journey south to the shores of Tonlé Sap, where they now find children in floating villages selling trinkets and holding snakes in the hope of being photographed for money.

Tourism is an aspect of globalization that is changing places in dramatic ways. In the Eleventh Edition of *Human Geography: People, Place, and Culture*, students will learn to appreciate the pace of change unfolding in the wake of globalization and to expand their understanding of the causes and consequences of the deepening interconnections among places.

Through this course in human geography, and with the help of this book, students will learn to appreciate the types of changes taking place and to think critically about what they see, read, and hear about their world. Globalization factors heavily into the many ways people influence places. Globalization is a set of processes that flow and pulsate across and through country boundaries with varying outcomes in different places and across scales. Improvements in transportation and communication allow ideas and people to move quickly, creating an environment suitable for change.

Our goals in writing the Eleventh Edition of *Human Geography: People, Place, and Culture* were, first, to help students appreciate the diversity of the planet and the role people play in shaping that diversity; second, to provide context for the issues we address so that students can better understand their world; third, to give students the tools to grapple with the complexities of globalization; and fourth, to help students think geographically and critically about their world.

Sadly, Harm de Blij, the book's originator, died shortly before we began work on this edition. We experienced a great sense of loss in planning, researching, and writing without him, but we were buoyed by the extensive collaborations we had with Harm through the years. One of us (Erin) studied with Harm as an undergraduate and became a co-author of this book beginning with the Eighth Edition. The other of us (Alec) became a co-author on the Sixth Edition and worked with Harm on a variety of professional matters. We both had the opportunity to soak up Harm's extraordinary passion for geography, and we continue to draw inspiration from someone who was truly a master of his craft. We dedicate this edition to Harm.

ADVANCED PLACEMENT® HUMAN GEOGRAPHY

In the late 1990s, co-author Alexander B. Murphy led the campaign to add human geography to the College Board's Advanced Placement® (AP) Program. *Human Geography: People, Place and Culture* and John Wiley & Sons have supported students and instructors in AP® Human Geography since the very beginning by offering high-quality content and pedagogy that help teachers teach and students learn the concepts, ideas, and terms that they need to perform at the college level. With the Eleventh Edition of *Human Geography*, we continue that legacy of support by offering a special AP® version of the book, along with a revised AP® Student Study Guide and new student resources on the student companion website.

Students who are taking AP® Human Geography can use the "Thinking Geographically" questions found at the end of each section in each chapter as practice for the Free Response Questions (FRQs) on the AP® exam. The 2013 AP® Human Geography exam asked students to compare and contrast Rostow and Wallerstein's theories, which was the second "Thinking

Geographically" question in Chapter 10 in the Tenth Edition of *Human Geography: People, Place, and Culture*. Use the "Thinking Geographically" questions to test whether you can define key concepts and models, compare and contrast related concepts and similar models, and use specific examples or case studies to demonstrate the concepts and models. We wrote more detailed captions for maps and photographs in the Eleventh Edition to help students learn to see patterns on maps and recognize geographic concepts in photographs. Several of the captions ask readers to compare and contrast maps, which will help prepare students for FRQs and multiple-choice questions (MCQs) on the AP® exam. Key geographic concepts are defined and explained with examples and context throughout the book, which will help students understand rather than simply memorize geographic concepts that appear in the MCQs.

With the needs of AP® instructors and teachers in mind, we have highlighted a few key issues that are often emphasized on AP® exams. We expanded our coverage of basic concepts such as central place theory. We developed boxes setting forth classic geographic approaches to understanding the political organization of space and the spatial organization of cities, and we evaluate the relevance of these approaches today. We brought in new material on subjects that receive attention in AP® Human Geography outlines, including human trafficking and refugees, threats to human health, biotechnology, genetically modified organisms, impacts of new extractive industries, fair trade movement, development of the galactic city, role of social networks and opinion leaders in the diffusion of popular culture, global sourcing and flexible production of goods, location theory, first mover advantages in new technologies, and interface areas in religion (including a case study on Boko Haram in Nigeria). We also included new graphics that help illustrate core geographic concepts and ideas. Our 3-D models of the spatial organization of cities in in Southeast Asia, Latin America, and Subsaharan Africa will help students quickly grasp the types of urban arrangements that are characteristic of different world regions. Our maps and case studies of Ikea and Nike in the production and distribution of goods will help students better understand theories in economic geography. To learn more about the AP® Edition of *Human Geography: People, Place and Culture 11th Edition,* please contact your Wiley High School Solutions representative at WileyHSAP@Wiley.com or 1-855-827-4630.

NEW IN THE ELEVENTH EDITION

In writing the Eleventh Edition of *Human Geography: People, Place, and Culture*, we developed a new layout in an effort to promote the book's visual appeal and to facilitate the integration of text, photos, and illustrations. Our goals are to help students understand the role people play in shaping the world, to provide geographic context to the issues we discuss, to teach students to think geographically and critically, and

to explain how the complexities of globalization are changing the planet. As in past editions, we drew from our own field experiences as well as the research and fieldwork of hundreds of others in an effort to enrich the text.

The Eleventh Edition of *Human Geography* includes significant revision to and reorganization of the material on population (Chapter 2), popular culture (Chapter 4), political geography (Chapter 8), urban geography (Chapter 9), agriculture (Chapter 11), industry and services (Chapter 12), and the humanized environment (Chapter 13). We also updated examples throughout the book to relate to the existing body of knowledge many college students have before taking human geography. Drawing from current research in human geography, we expanded the number of terms and concepts covered to include the young and old-age dependency ratios, the proto-Eurasiatic linguistic hypothesis, galactic cities, urbicide, economies of scale, first mover advantage, location theory, global sourcing, flexible production, global social networks, and opinion leaders.

The field notes in the Eleventh Edition provide context and help the reader learn to think geographically. As in the past, each chapter in this edition starts with an *opening field note*, written by one of us, which describes an experience from the field and pulls the reader into the chapter. Several of the opening field notes in the Eleventh Edition are new.

Each chapter also includes one or more *author field notes*, in addition to the opening field note. The author field notes serve as models of how to think geographically. We took a significant majority of the approximately 200 photographs in this edition. In addition to the author field notes, we include a number of *guest field notes* written by geographers who have spent time in the field, researching a place that they profile. All guest field notes include a photograph and a paragraph focusing on how the guest field note author's observations in the field influenced his or her research.

In the Eleventh Edition, we continue to offer "Key Questions" and "Thinking Geographically" prompts to promote learning. The Key Questions are listed after the opening field note of each chapter and serve as the outline for the chapter. After each Key Question is answered in the chapter, the reader will find a Thinking Geographically prompt. These prompts ask the reader to apply a geographic concept to a real-life example. Readers who complete the Thinking Geographically prompts will learn to think geographically and to think critically. Instructors can also use the Thinking Geographically prompts as lecture launchers and as the basis for class discussions.

THE TEACHING AND LEARNING PACKAGE

The Eleventh Edition of *Human Geography: People, Place, and Culture* is supported by a comprehensive supplements package that includes an extensive selection of print, visual, and electronic materials.

Resources That Help Teachers Teach

Geography On-Location Videos. Because of their enduring popularity, we have digitized many of the videos from the original series. This rich collection of original and relevant footage was taken during H. J. de Blij's travels. The videos cover a wide range of themes and are available on the companion websites.

The *Human Geography: People, Place, and Culture* Instructor Companion Website. This comprehensive website includes numerous resources to help you enhance your current presentations, create new presentations, and employ our premade PowerPoint presentations. Resources include the following:

- **Image Gallery.** We provide online electronic files for the line illustrations and maps in the book, which the instructor can customize for presenting in class.

- A complete collection of **PowerPoint presentations.** These presentations are available in beautifully rendered, four-color format, and images are sized and edited for maximum effectiveness in large lecture halls. The high-resolution photos, maps, and figures provide a set of strong, clear images that are ready to be projected in the classroom.

- A comprehensive **Test Bank** includes multiple-choice, fill-in-the-blank, matching, and essay questions. The Test Bank is available on the secure Instructor's website as electronic files and can be saved into all major word-processing programs.

- A comprehensive collection of **animations and videos**.

- **ConceptCaching.com** is an online collection of photographs that explores places, regions, people, and their activities. Photographs, GPS coordinates, and explanations of core geographic concepts are "cached" for viewing by professors and students alike. Professors can access the images or submit their own by visiting the website.

Wiley Faculty Network. This peer-to-peer network of faculty is ready to support your use of online course management tools and discipline-specific software/learning systems in the classroom. The Wiley Faculty Network will help you apply innovative classroom techniques, implement software packages, and tailor the technology experience to the needs of each individual class, and will provide you with virtual training sessions led by faculty for faculty.

Course Management. Online course management assets are available to accompany the Eleventh Edition of *Human Geography: People, Place, and Culture*.

Resources That Help Students Learn

Student Companion Website. The easy-to-use and student-focused website helps reinforce and illustrate key geographic concepts. It also provides interactive media content to prepare for tests. This website provides additional resources to complement the book and enhance student understanding of geography:

- **Videos** provide a first-hand look at life in other parts of the world.

- **Map Quizzes** help students master the place-names that are building blocks for their success in this course. Three game-formatted place-name activities are provided for each chapter.

- **Chapter Review Quizzes** provide immediate feedback to true/false, multiple-choice, and short-answer questions.

- **Annotated Web Links** put useful electronic resources into context.

- **Area and Demographic Data** are provided for every country and world region.

- **ConceptCaching.com** is an online collection of photographs that explores places, regions, people, and their activities. Photographs, GPS coordinates, and explanations of core geographic concepts are "cached" for viewing by professors and students alike. Professors can access the images or submit their own by visiting the website.

ACKNOWLEDGMENTS

In preparing the Eleventh Edition of **Human Geography**, we benefited immensely from the advice and assistance of many of our colleagues in geography. We thank AP Human Geography teachers, professors, instructors, and students from around the country who emailed us questions and gave us suggestions. Some told us of their experiences using other editions, and others provided insightful comments on individual chapters. The list that follows acknowledges their support, but it cannot begin to measure our gratitude for all of the ways they helped shape this book:

Ian Ackroyd-Kelly	*East Stroudsburg University*
Frank Ainsley	*University of North Carolina, Wilmington*
Jennifer Altenhofel	*California State University, Bakersfield*
Charles Amissah	*Hampton University*
Alan Arbogast	*Michigan State University*
James Ashley	*University of Toledo*
Scharmaistha Bagchi-Sen	*SUNY Buffalo*
Nancy Bain	*Ohio University*
Brad Bays	*Oklahoma State University*
Sarah W. Bednarz	*Texas A&M University*
Sari Bennett	*University of Maryland, Baltimore County*
J. Best	*Frostburg State University*

Brian Blouet — *College of William & Mary*
Mark Bockenhauer — *St. Norbert College*
Margaret Boorstein — *C.W. Post College of Long Island University*
Patricia Boudinot — *George Mason University*
Michael Broadway — *Northern Michigan University*
Michaele Ann Buell — *Northwest Arkansas Community College*
Scott Carlin — *Long Island University*
Fiona M. Davidson — *University of Arkansas*
L. Scott Deaner — *Owens Community College*
Evan Denney — *University of Montana*
Ramesha Dhussa — *Drake University*
Dimitar Dimitrov — *Virginia Commonwealth University*
Dawn Drake — *University of Tennessee, Knoxville*
Steve Driever — *University of Missouri, Kansas City*
Anna Dvorak — *West Los Angeles College*
James Dyer — *Mount St. Mary's College*
Adrian X. Esparza — *University of Arizona*
Stephen Frenkel — *University of Washington, Seattle*
Juanita Gaston — *Florida A&M University*
Matthew J. Gerike — *Kansas State University*
Lay James Gibson — *University of Arizona*
Sarah Goggin — *Santa Ana College*
Abe Goldman — *University of Florida*
Richard Grant — *University of Miami*
Alyson Greiner — *Oklahoma State University*
Jeffrey A. Gritzner — *University of Montana*
Qian Guo — *Northern Michigan University*
John Heppen — *University of Wisconsin, River Falls*
John Hickey — *Inver Hills Community College*
Miriam Helen Hill — *Jacksonville State University*
Peter R. Hoffmann — *Loyola Marymount University*
Peter Hugill — *Texas A&M University*
Francis Hutchins — *Bellarmine University*
Jay Johnson — *University of Nebraska, Lincoln*
Tarek A. Joseph — *Central Michigan University*
Melinda Kashuba — *Shasta College*
Artimus Keiffer — *Wittenberg University*
Les King — *McMaster University*
Paul Kingsbury — *Miami University, Ohio*
Frances Kostarelos — *Governors State University*
Darrell P. Kruger — *Illinois State University*
Paul Larson — *Southern Utah University*
Jess A. Le Vine — *Brookdale Community College*
Ann Legreid — *Central Missouri State University*
Jose Lopez — *Minnesota State University*
David Lyons — *University of Minnesota, Duluth*

Patricia Matthews-Salazar — *Borough of Manhattan Community College*
Darrell McDonald — *Stephen F. Austin State University*
Wayne McKim — *Towson University*
Ian MacLachlan — *University of Lethbridge*
Glenn Miller — *Bridgewater State College*
Katharyne Mitchell — *University of Washington, Seattle*
John M. Morris — *University of Texas, San Antonio*
Garth A. Myers — *University of Kansas*
Darrell Norris — *SUNY Geneseo*
Ann Oberhauser — *West Virginia University*
Kenji Oshiro — *Wright State University*
Bimal K. Paul — *Kansas State University*
Gene Paull — *University of Texas at Brownsville*
Daniel R. Pavese — *Wor-Wic Community College*
Walter Peace — *McMaster University*
Sonja Porter — *Central Oregon Community College*
Virginia Ragan — *Maple Woods Community College*
Jeffrey Richetto — *University of Alabama*
Rob Ritchie — *Liberty University*
Mika Roinila — *State University of New York, New Paltz*
Karl Ryavec — *University of Wisconsin*
James Saku — *Frostburg State University*
Richard Alan Sambrook — *Eastern Kentucky University*
Joseph E. Schwartzberg — *University of Minnesota*
Allen Scott — *University of California Los Angeles*
Gary W. Shannon — *University of Kentucky*
Betty Shimshak — *Towson University*
Nancy Shirley — *Southern Connecticut State University*
Susan Slowey — *Blinn College*
Andrew Sluyter — *Pennsylvania State University*
Janet Smith — *Shippensberg University*
Herschel Stern — *Mira Costa College*
Neva Duncan Tabb — *University of South Florida*
Thomas Terich — *Western Washington University*
Donald Thieme — *Georgia Southern University*
James A. Tyner — *University of Southern California*
David Unterman — *Sierra and Yuba Community Colleges*
Barry Wauldron — *University of Michigan, Dearborn*
David Wishart — *University of Nebraska, Lincoln*
George W. White — *South Dakota State University*
Leon Yacher — *Southern Connecticut State University*
Donald Zeigler — *Old Dominion University*
Robert C. Ziegenfus — *Kutztown University*

In the Eleventh Edition, several of our colleagues in geography provided guest field notes. The stories these colleagues tell and the brilliant photos they provide will help students better appreciate the role of fieldwork in geographic research:

Jonathan Leib	*Old Dominion University*
Korine Kolivras	*Virginia Tech*
Elsbeth Robson	*Keele University*
Jason Dittmer	*University College London*
Steven M. Schnell	*Kutztown University of Pennsylvania*
Richard Francaviglia	*Geo. Graphic Designs*
Ines Miyares	*Hunter College of the City University of New York*
Sarah Halvorson	*University of Montana*
Derek Alderman	*University of Tennessee*
Mary Lee Nolan	*Oregon State University*
Paul Gray	*Russellville High School*
George White	*South Dakota State University*
Johnathan Walker	*James Madison University*
Rachel Silvey	*University of Toronto*
Judith Carney	*University of California, Los Angeles*
Fiona M. Davidson	*University of Arkansas*
William Moseley	*Macalester College*
Kenneth E. Foote	*University of Connecticut*

On a day-to-day basis, many people in the extended John Wiley & Sons family provided support and guidance. We thank Vice President and Publisher Petra Recter for her guidance with this edition of *Human Geography*. Ryan Flahive, Executive Editor for Geography, is a champion of geography, and we are fortunate to work with such a knowledgeable and involved editor. In 2014, the National Council for Geographic Education recognized Ryan Flahive with a well-deserved Presidential Award for his contributions to geography. Kathryn Hancox, Editorial Assistant, organized reviews and oversaw the art manuscripts, which helped us meet several deadlines along the way. Darnell Sessoms, Permissions Editor, tracked down sources around the world to obtain permissions for the Tenth Edition, and he continued his work on permissions with the Eleventh Edition, enabling us to create several new maps and diagrams for this edition. Julia Nollen, Assistant Editor, also organized reviews and helped get the revisions started for this edition. Billy Ray, Photo Editor, gleaned from our sometimes cryptic descriptions the visions we had for several new photos, and his ability to find beautiful images to meet our specifications directly benefits students, as each picture demonstrates geographic concepts and patterns to a tee. Don Larson, Terry Bush, and Beth Robertson from Mapping Specialists are outstanding cartographers who used their design aesthetic and skills in cartography and GIS to update or create more than 60 maps and figures in this edition. We owe a special debt of gratitude to Paula Robbins at Mapping Specialists who researched and hand-drew three-dimensional models of cities for Chapter 9. Her painstaking attention to detail makes the Latin American, Subsaharan African, and Southeast Asian city models come to life. We benefited from two exceptional Production Editors on this edition. Janet Foxman gracefully kept us on track with a tight schedule. Jackie Henry juggled the production of two titles simultaneously and was indispensable to Erin in keeping the book on schedule. Betty Pessagno, Copy Editor, gave careful attention to each word in the book and thoughtful feedback. Katrina Avery, Copy Editor, demonstrated incredible attention to detail, which benefited every chapter of the book. Kim Johnson researched and provided data for dozens of new and revised maps and figures. Marketing Manager Suzanne Bochet worked with the author team to translate our vision for *Human Geography: People, Place, and Culture* into an effective marketing message.

We thank Erin's writing mentor, David Wishart of the University of Nebraska-Lincoln, whose suggestions are found in many new topics discussed in the Eleventh Edition. We thank Paul Gray and Greg Sherwin, both AP Human Geography teachers, whose constructive reviews and feedback helped us plan portions of the content and the mapping program for this edition. Erin appreciates the support and ideas shared by geography educators at the National Council for Geographic Education Conference, as their passion for teaching students and their excitement for the field of human geography inspired her to find new ways to explain several complicated geographic concepts in the Eleventh Edition. Erin also thanks Tino Mendez for his unwavering support and encouragement and Julie Backous for her organizational skills and willingness to help. This edition also benefited greatly from research assistance and editorial input provided by Anna Moore, a doctoral student in geography at the University of Oregon, and by Richard Murphy, Alec's older son.

We are grateful to our family and friends who supported us faithfully through this edition. Special thanks from Erin to Maggie and Henry for tolerating the constant presence of her laptop, giving feedback on photo options and captions, and reading edits to explain what they took from different passages. As always, our greatest thanks go to our spouses, Robert Fouberg and Susan Gary, who through their support, understanding, and patience make us better people and better authors.

Erin H. Fouberg
Aberdeen, South Dakota

Alexander B. Murphy
Eugene, Oregon

ABOUT THE AUTHORS

ERIN HOGAN FOUBERG grew up in eastern South Dakota. She moved to Washington, D.C., to attend Georgetown University's School of Foreign Service, where she took a class in Human Geography from Harm de Blij. At Georgetown, Erin found her International Relations classes lacking in context and discovered a keen interest in political geography. She earned her master's and Ph.D. at the University of Nebraska-Lincoln (1997). After graduating, Dr. Fouberg taught for several years at the University of Mary Washington in Fredericksburg, Virginia, where the graduating class of 2001 bestowed on her the Mary Pinschmidt Award, given to the faculty member who made the biggest impact on their lives.

Dr. Fouberg is Professor of Geography and Director of the Honors Program at Northern State University in Aberdeen, South Dakota, where she won the Outstanding Faculty Award in 2011. Her research and publications focus on the governance and sovereignty of American Indian tribes, geography education, and the geography of elections. Professor Fouberg served as Vice President of Publications and Products of the National Council for Geographic Education. Dr. Fouberg co-authors *Understanding World Regional Geography* with William G. Moseley, also published by Wiley. She is active in her community, serving leadership roles on the soccer board, PTA, and fundraising campaigns for children's charities. She enjoys traveling, reading, golfing, and watching athletic and theater events at Northern State.

ALEC MURPHY grew up in the western United States, but he spent several of his early years in Europe and Japan. He obtained his undergraduate degree at Yale University, studied law at the Columbia University School of Law, practiced law for a short time in Chicago, and then pursued a doctoral degree in geography (Ph.D. University of Chicago, 1987). After graduating, Dr. Murphy joined the faculty of the University of Oregon, where he is now Professor of Geography and holder of the James F. and Shirley K. Rippey Chair in Liberal Arts and Sciences. Professor Murphy is a widely published scholar in the fields of political, cultural, and environmental geography. His work has been supported by the National Science Foundation, the National Endowment for the Humanities, the Rockefeller Foundation, and the Fulbright-Hays foreign fellowship program.

Professor Murphy served as the President of the Association of American Geographers in 2003–2004. He is currently Senior Vice President of the American Geographical Society. In the late 1990s, he led the effort to add geography to the College Board's Advanced Placement Program. He recently chaired a National Academy of Sciences study charged with identifying strategic directions for the geographical sciences. In 2014 he received the Association of American Geographers' highest honor, its Lifetime Achievement Award. His interests include hiking, skiing, camping, music, and of course exploring the diverse places that make up our planet.

HARM DE BLIJ received his early schooling in Europe, his college education in Africa, and his higher degrees in the United States (Ph.D. Northwestern, 1959). He published more than 30 books and over 100 articles, and received five honorary degrees. Several of his books were translated into foreign languages.

Dr. de Blij held the position of John A. Hannah Professor of Geography at Michigan State University. He also held the George Landegger Chair at Georgetown University's School of Foreign Service, the John Deaver Drinko Chair of Geography at Marshall University, and faculty positions at the Colorado School of Mines and the University of Miami. He served as the Geography Editor on ABC-TV's "Good Morning America" program for seven years and later served as Geography Analyst for NBC News. He was for more than 20 years a member of the National Geographic Society's Committee for Research and Exploration and was the founding editor of its scholarly journal, *National Geographic Research*. In recognition of his service, he became an honorary lifetime member of the Society.

Professor de Blij was a renaissance man. He was a soccer fan, an avid wine collector, an amateur violinist, and an inveterate traveler.

We dedicate this book to

Harm de Blij:

colleague, friend, mentor,

and indefatigable

champion of geography

BRIEF CONTENTS

CONTENTS

INTRODUCTION TO HUMAN GEOGRAPHY

Awakening to World Hunger

Dragging myself out of bed for a 9:00 A.M. lecture, I decide I need to make a stop at Starbucks. "Grande coffee of the day, please, and leave room for cream." I rub my eyes and look at the sign to see where my coffee was grown. Kenya. Ironically, I am about to lecture on Kenya's coffee plantations. Just the wake-up call I need.

When I visited Kenya in eastern Africa, I drove from Masai Mara to Kericho and I noticed that nearly all of the agricultural fields I could see were planted with coffee or tea (Fig. 1.1). I also saw the poor of Kenya, clearly hungry, living in substandard housing. I questioned, "Why do farmers in Kenya grow coffee and tea when they could grow food to feed the hungry?" Trying to answer such a question sheds light on the complexities of globalization. In a globalized world, connections are many and simple answers are few.

© H. J. de Blij

◼ Figure 1.1

Kericho, Kenya. Tea plantations established by British colonists in western Kenya. The impact of colonialism was pervasive—not just on the political institutions and social relations, but on the landscape as well.

On its face, such a huge problem might seem easy to solve. Take the total annual food production in the world, divide it by the world's population, and we have plenty of food for everyone. Yet one-seventh of the world's population is seriously malnourished. The vast majority of the 1 billion malnourished people on Earth are women and children, who have little money and even less power.

Figure 1.2 shows how food consumption is currently distributed—unevenly. Comparing Figure 1.2 with Figure 1.3 shows that the wealthier countries also are the best fed and that Subsaharan Africa (the part of Africa south of the Sahara Desert) is currently in the worst position, with numerous countries in the highest categories of hunger and malnourishment.

The major causes of malnourishment are poverty (inability to pay for food), the failure of food distribution systems, and cultural and political practices that favor some groups over others. Where food does reach the needy, its price may be unaffordable. Two billion people subsist

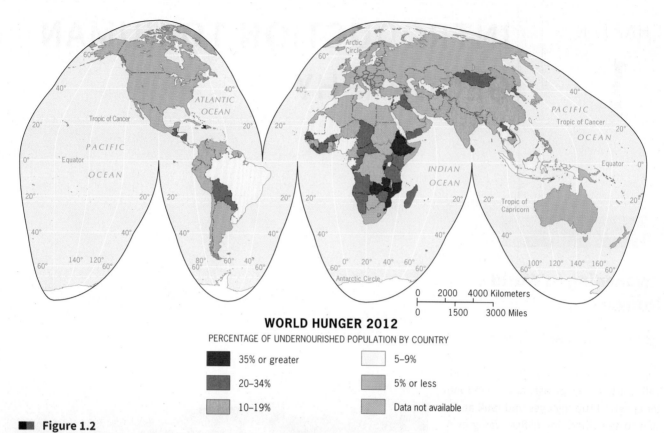

WORLD HUNGER 2012

PERCENTAGE OF UNDERNOURISHED POPULATION BY COUNTRY

■	35% or greater	□	5–9%
■	20–34%	▨	5% or less
▤	10–19%	▨	Data not available

■■ **Figure 1.2**

World Food Program Hunger Map, 2012.   Classifications designate the proportion of the population malnourished. The World Food Program estimates that just under one billion people worldwide are malnourished.   *Data from:* United Nations World Food Program 2012.

on the equivalent of two dollars a day, and many in the vast shantytowns encircling some of the world's largest cities must pay rent to landlords who own the plots on which their shacks are built. Too little is left for food, and it is the children who suffer most.

Is solving hunger as simple as each country growing enough food to feed its people? Do the best-fed countries have the most arable (farmable) land? Only 4 percent of Norway is arable land, and more than 70 percent of Bangladesh is arable land (Fig. 1.4). Despite this disparity, Norway is wealthy and well fed, whereas Bangladesh is poor and malnourished. Norway overcomes its inadequate food production by importing food. Bangladesh depends on rice as its staple crop, and the monsoon rains that flood two-thirds of the country each year during monsoon season are good for rice production, but they make survival a daily challenge for some.

If a poor country has a small proportion of arable land, does that destine its population to a lifetime of malnourishment? It depends on the place. Of all the land classified as arable, some is much more productive than others. For example, only 8 percent of Kenya's land is arable, but areas in the western highlands are some of the most productive agricultural land in the world. Do the Kenyans simply not produce enough food on their lands? Is that what accounts for their malnutrition rate of over 30 percent? No, hunger in Kenya depends much more on what it produces, who owns the land, and how Kenya is tied into the global economy.

Kenya's most productive lands, those in the western highlands, are owned by foreign coffee and tea corporations. Driving through the open, luxury-crop-covered slopes, I saw mostly Kenyan women working the plantations. The lowland plains are dotted by small farms, many of which have been subdivided to the point of making the land unviable. Here, an even higher proportion of the people working the lands are women, but the lands are registered to their husbands or sons because, by law, they cannot own them.

As I drove through the contrasting landscapes, I continued to question whether it would be better for the fertile highlands to carry food crops that could be consumed by the people in

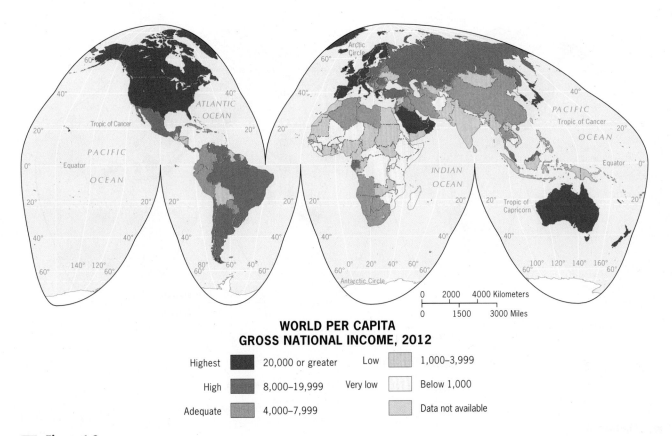

**WORLD PER CAPITA
GROSS NATIONAL INCOME, 2012**

Highest	20,000 or greater	Low		1,000–3,999
High	8,000–19,999	Very low		Below 1,000
Adequate	4,000–7,999			Data not available

■■ **Figure 1.3**

Per Capita Gross National Income (in U.S. Dollars) (GNI), 2012.   From a socioeconomic standpoint, we live in an unequal world, but this map only shows the formal economy because the GNI per capita does not estimate the informal economy. Maps, like this, that shade each country a different color report data by country and tell us nothing about the variation within countries.   *Data from*: World Bank, World Development Indicators, 2012.

Kenya. I drove to the tea processing center and talked to the manager, a member of the Kikuyu ethnic group, and asked him my question. He said that his country needed foreign income and that apart from tourism, exporting coffee and tea was the main opportunity for foreign income.

As part of an increasingly globalized economy, Kenya suffers from the complexities of globalization. With foreign corporations owning Kenya's best lands, a globalized economy that thrives on foreign income, tiny farms that are unproductive, and a gendered legal system that disenfranchises the agricultural labor force and disempowers the caregivers of the country's children, Kenya has multiple factors contributing to poverty and malnutrition in the country. In addition to these structural concerns, Kenyan agro-pastoralists, especially in the northeast, have suffered higher rates of famine since a drought began in the region in 2006. Agro-pastoralists raise crops and have livestock; therefore, they struggle against drought as well as livestock diseases and political conflict.

To solve one of the structural problems in Kenya raises another. If Kenyans converted the richest lands to cash crop production, how would the poor people be able to afford the crops? What would happen to the rest of Kenya's economy and the government itself if it lost the export revenue from tea and coffee? If Kenya lost its export revenue, how could the country pay loans it owes to global financial and development institutions?

Answering each of these questions requires geographic inquiry because the answers are rooted in the characteristics of places and the connections those places have to other places. Moreover, geographic **fieldwork** can provide tremendous insights into such questions. Geographers have a long tradition of fieldwork. They go out in the field and see what people are doing, they observe how people's actions and reactions vary across space, and they develop maps and other visualizations that help them situate and analyze what they see. We, the authors,

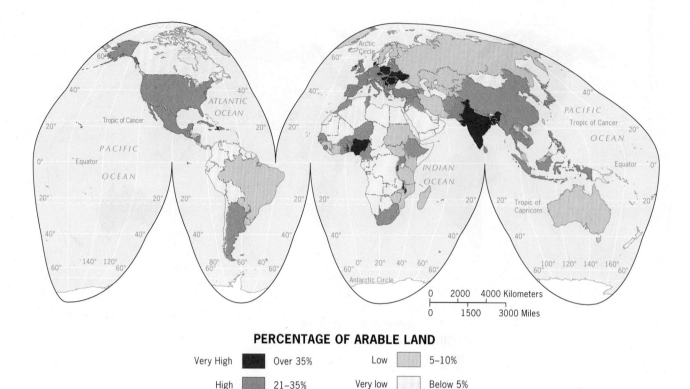

PERCENTAGE OF ARABLE LAND

Very High	■	Over 35%	Low	▢	5–10%
High	■	21–35%	Very low	▢	Below 5%
Adequate	■	11–20%		▢	Data not available

■■ **Figure 1.4**

Percent of Land that is Arable (Farmable), 2008.   Arable land is an important resource for countries, but in our globalized world, many countries with limited land suitable for agriculture are able to import the food they need to feed their population.   *Data from*: United Nations Food and Agriculture Organization, 2011.

have countless field experiences, and we share many with you to help you understand the diversity of Earth's surface and show how global processes have unique outcomes in different places.

Solving major global problems such as hunger or HIV-AIDS is complicated in our interconnected world. Each solution has its own ramifications not only in one place, but also across regions, nations, and the world. Our goals in this book are to help you see the multitude of interconnections in our world, enable you to recognize the patterns of human geographic phenomena that shape the world, give you an appreciation for the uniqueness of place, and teach you to ask and answer your own geographic questions about this world we call home.

Key Questions FOR CHAPTER 1

1. What is human geography?
2. What are geographic questions?
3. Why do geographers use maps, and what do maps tell us?
4. Why are geographers concerned with scale and connectedness?
5. What are geographic concepts, and how are they used in answering geographic questions?

WHAT IS HUMAN GEOGRAPHY?

Human geographers study people and places. The field of **human geography** focuses on how people make places, how we organize space and society, how we interact with each other in places and across space, and how we make sense of others and ourselves in our localities, regions, and the world.

Advances in communication and transportation technologies are making places and people more interconnected. Only 100 years ago the fastest modes of transportation were the steamship, the railroad, and the horse and buggy. Today, people can cross the globe in a matter of days, with easy access to automobiles, high-speed railroads, airplanes, and ships.

Economic globalization and the rapid diffusion of elements of popular culture, including fashion and architecture, are making many people and places look more alike. Despite the push toward homogeneity, our world still encompasses a multitude of ways in which people identify themselves and others. The world consists of nearly 200 countries, a diversity of religions, thousands of languages, and a wide variety of settlement types, ranging from small villages to enormous global cities. All of these attributes come together in different ways around the globe to create a world of endlessly diverse places and people. Understanding and explaining this diversity is the mission of human geography.

Places all over the world are fundamentally affected by globalization. **Globalization** is a set of processes that are increasing interactions, deepening relationships, and accelerating interdependence across national borders. Globalization is also a set of outcomes that are felt from these global processes—outcomes that are unevenly distributed and differently manifested across the world.

All too often, discussions of globalization focus on the pull between the global, seen as a blanket covering the world, and the local, seen as a continuation of the traditional despite the blanket of globalization. Geographers are well placed to recognize globalization as something significantly more complex. Geographers employ the concept of "scale" to understand individual, local, regional, national, and global interrelationships. What happens at the global scale affects the local, but it also affects the individual, regional, and national, and similarly the processes at these scales influence the global. Reducing the world to "local" and "global" risks losing sight of the complexity that characterizes modern life. In this book, we study globalization, and as geographers we are sensitive to the fact that the same globalized process has different impacts in different places because no two places are the same. Moreover, whenever we look at something at one scale, we always try to think about how processes that exist at other scales may affect what we are looking at, and vice versa (see the discussion of scale later in this chapter).

Globalizing processes occur at the world scale; these processes bypass country borders and include global financial markets and global environmental change. However, the processes of globalization do not magically appear at the global scale: What happens at other scales (individual, local, regional, national) helps create the processes of globalization and shape the outcomes of globalization.

Some argue that the impacts of globalization are exaggerated, but as geographers Ron Johnston, Peter Taylor, and Michael Watts (2002) explain, "Whatever your opinion may be, any intellectual engagement with social change in the twenty-first century has to address this concept seriously, and assess its capacity to explain the world we currently inhabit." We integrate the concept of globalization into this textbook because processes at the global scale, processes that are not confined to local places or national borders, are clearly changing the human geography of the planet. At the same time, as we travel the world and continue to engage in fieldwork and research, we are constantly reminded of how different places and people are from one another—processes at the individual, local, regional, and national scales continue to change human geography and shape globalization.

No place on Earth is untouched by people. As people explore, travel, migrate, interact, play, live, and work, they make places. People organize themselves into communities, nations, and broader societal networks, establishing political, economic, religious, linguistic, and cultural systems that enable them to function in space. People adapt to, alter, manipulate, and cope with their physical geographic environment. No environment stands apart from human action. Each place we see is affected by and created by people, and each place reflects the culture of the people in that place over time.

Imagine and describe the most remote place on Earth you can think of 100 years ago. Now, describe how globalization has changed that place and how the people there continue to shape it and make it the place it is today.

WHAT ARE GEOGRAPHIC QUESTIONS?

Geographers study human phenomena, including language, religion, and identity, as well as physical phenomena, including landforms, climate, and environmental change. Geographers also examine the interactions between humans and environment. Human geography is the study of the spatial and material characteristics of the human-made places and people, and **physical geography** is the study of spatial and material characteristics of physical environment. Human and physical geographers adopt a similar perspective but focus on different phenomena.

Geographer Marvin Mikesell once gave a shorthand definition of geography as the "why of where." Why and how do things come together in certain places to produce particular outcomes? Why are some things found in certain places but not in others? How do the characteristics of particular places shape what happens? To what extent do things in one place influence those in other places? To these questions, we add "so what?" Why do differences across geographic space matter? What role does a place play in its region and in the world, and what does that mean for people there and elsewhere? Questions like these are at the core of geographic inquiry—whether human or physical—and they are of critical importance in any effort to make sense of our world.

If geography deals with so many aspects of our world, ranging from people and places to coastlines and climates, what do the various facets of this wide-ranging discipline have in common? The answer lies in a perspective that both human and physical geographers bring to their studies: a spatial perspective. Whether they are human geographers or physical geographers, virtually all geographers are interested in the **spatial** arrangement of places and phenomena, how they are laid out, organized, and arranged on Earth, and how they appear on the landscape.

Mapping the **spatial distribution** of a phenomenon can be the first step to understanding it. By looking at a map of how something is distributed across space, a geographer can raise questions about how the arrangement came about, what processes create and sustain the particular distributions or **patterns**, and what relationships exist among different places and things.

Maps in the Time of Cholera Pandemics

In **medical geography**, mapping the distribution of a disease is the first step to finding its cause. In 1854, Dr. John Snow, a noted anesthesiologist in London, mapped cases of cholera in London's Soho District.

Cholera is an ancient disease associated with diarrhea and dehydration. It was confined to India until the beginning of the nineteenth century. In 1816 it spread to China, Japan, East Africa, and Mediterranean Europe in the first of several **pandemics**, that is, worldwide outbreaks of the disease. This initial wave abated by 1823, but by then cholera was feared throughout the world, for it had killed people everywhere by the hundreds, even thousands. Death was horribly convulsive and would come in a matter of days, perhaps a week, and no one knew what caused the disease or how to avoid it.

Soon a second cholera pandemic struck. It lasted from 1826 to 1837, when cholera crossed the Atlantic and attacked North America. During the third pandemic, from 1842 to 1862, England was severely hit, and cholera again spread into North America.

When the pandemic that began in 1842 reached England in the 1850s, cholera swept through the Soho District of London. Dr. Snow mapped the Soho District, marking all the area's water pumps—from which people got their water supply for home use—with a P and marking the residence of each person who died from cholera with a dot (Fig. 1.5). Approximately 500 deaths occurred in Soho, and as the map took shape, Snow noticed that an especially large number of those deaths clustered around the water pump on Broad Street. At the doctor's request, city authorities removed the handle from the Broad Street pump, making it impossible to get water from it. The result was dramatic: Almost immediately the number of reported new cases fell to nearly zero, confirming Snow's theory about the role of water in the spread of cholera.

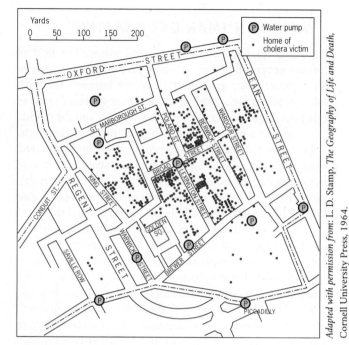

Adapted with permission from: L. D. Stamp, The Geography of Life and Death, Cornell University Press, 1964.

■ **Figure 1.5**

Deaths from Cholera in the Soho District of London, England, 1854.   Dr. Snow mapped the deaths caused by cholera in the Soho neighborhood of London along with the locations of the water pumps and noticed a spatial correlation. Most of the deaths were clustered around a single water pump. As Dr. Snow's experience showed, maps are not just attractive or interesting representations of the world; they also help us understand and confront problems.

Dr. Snow and his colleagues advised people to boil their water, but it would be a long time before his advice reached all those who might be affected, and in any case many people simply did not have the ability to boil water or wash hands with soap.

Cholera has not been defeated completely, and in some ways the risks have been rising in recent years rather than falling (Fig. 1.6). People contract cholera by eating food or water contaminated with cholera bacteria. Cholera bacteria diffuse to broader areas because once one person has cholera it can be spread via his or her feces. In an impoverished area with no sanitary sewer system, the person's feces can easily contaminate the water supply. Even in places with sanitary sewer systems, cholera contamination occurs when rivers, which are typically the water supply, flood the sanitary sewer system.

We expect to find cholera in places that lack sanitary sewer systems and in places that are flood prone. In many of the teeming shantytowns of the growing cities of the developing world, and in some of the refugee camps of Africa and Asia, cholera remains a threat. Until the 1990s, major outbreaks remained few and limited. After remaining cholera-free for a half century, Europe had its first reappearance of cholera in Naples in 1972. In 2006, a cholera outbreak in Angola, in southern Africa, spread quickly throughout the country. When heavy rains came to West Africa in 2010, an outbreak of cholera killed 1500 people in Nigeria alone.

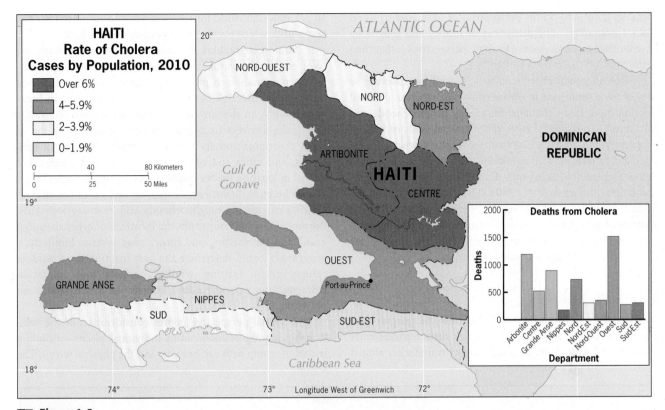

■ Figure 1.6

Cholera in Haiti, 2010. Artibonite and Centre departments were hit hard by a cholera outbreak in Haiti just after the 2010 earthquake, in part because the Artibonite River is contaminated by cholera bacteria and also because a large number of Haitians displaced from Port-au-Prince fled to camps in Artibonite and Centre. *Data from*: Centers for Disease Control, 2011. http://www.bt.cdc.gov/situationawareness/haiticholera/map_1.asp.

A cholera outbreak in the slums of Lima, Peru, in January 1991 became a fast-spreading **epidemic** (regional outbreak of a disease) that touched every country in the Americas, infected more than 1 million people, and killed over 10,000 in the region. The outbreak in Peru began when ocean waters warmed off the coast. Cholera bacteria live on plankton in the ocean, and the warming of the ocean allowed both the plankton and cholera to multiply. Fish ate the plankton, and people ate raw fish, thus bringing cholera to Peru.

In the slums of Peru, the disease diffused quickly. The slums are densely populated and lack a sanitary sewer system large enough to handle the waste of the population. An estimated 14 million Peruvians were infected with cholera, 350,000 were hospitalized, and 3500 Peruvians died during the outbreak in the 1990s. Peruvians who accessed health care received clean water, salts, and antibiotics, which combat the disease.

In January 2010, an earthquake that registered 7.0 on the Richter scale hit Haiti, near the capital of Port au Prince. Months later there was a cholera outbreak in the Artibonite region of Haiti (Fig. 1.6). Health officials are not certain exactly how cholera reached Haiti, but the disease diffused quickly through refugee camps and by October 2010 reached the capital city of Port au Prince. Scientists worry that the cholera outbreak in Haiti will be long lasting because the bacteria have contaminated the Artibonite River, which is the water supply for a large region. Although purifying water through boiling and thoroughly washing hands prevents the spread of cholera, water contaminated with cholera and a lack of access to soap abound in many neighborhoods of world cities. A vaccine exists, but its effectiveness is limited, and it is costly. Dr. Snow achieved a victory through the application of geographical reasoning, but the war against cholera is not yet won.

The fruits of geographical inquiry were lifesaving in Snow's case, and the example illustrates the general advantage that comes from looking at the geographic context of events and circumstances. Geographers want to understand how and why places are similar or different, why people do different things in different places, and how the relationship between people and the physical world varies across space.

The Spatial Perspective

Geographic literacy involves much more than memorizing places on a map. Place locations are to geography what dates are to history. History is not merely about memorizing dates. To understand history is to appreciate how events, circumstances, and ideas came together at particular times to produce certain outcomes. Knowledge of how events have developed over time is thought to be critical to understanding who we are and where we are going.

Understanding change across space is equally important to understanding change over time. The great German philosopher Immanuel Kant argued that we need disciplines focused not only on particular phenomena (such as economics and sociology), but also on the perspectives of time (history) and space (geography). The disciplines of history and geography have intellectual cores defined by these perspectives rather than being confined to a subject matter.

Human geographers employ a **spatial perspective** as they study a multitude of phenomena ranging from political elections and urban shantytowns to gay neighborhoods and folk music. To bring together the many subfields of human geography and to explain to nongeographers what geographers do, four major geographical organizations in the United States formed the Geography Educational National Implementation Project in the 1980s. The National Geographic Society published their findings in 1986, introducing the **five themes** of geography: location, human–environment interactions, region, place, and movement. The five themes are derived from geography's spatial concerns.

THE FIVE THEMES

The first theme, **location**, highlights how the geographical position of people and things on Earth's surface affects what happens and why. A concern with location underlies almost all geographical work, for location helps to establish the context within which events and processes are situated.

Some geographers develop elaborate (often quantitative) models describing the locational properties of particular phenomena—even predicting where things are likely to occur. Such undertakings have fostered an interest in **location theory**, an element of contemporary human geography that seeks answers to a wide range of questions, some of them theoretical, others highly practical: Why are villages, towns, and cities spaced the way they are? A geographer versed in location theory might assess whether a SuperTarget should be built downtown or in a suburb, given the characteristics of existing neighborhoods and new developments, the median income of people, the locations of other shopping areas, and the existing and future road system. Similarly, a geographer could determine the best location for a wildlife refuge, given existing wildlife habitats and migration patterns, human settlement patterns, land use, and road networks.

A spatial perspective invites consideration of the relationship among phenomena in individual places—including the relationship between humans and the physical world. The

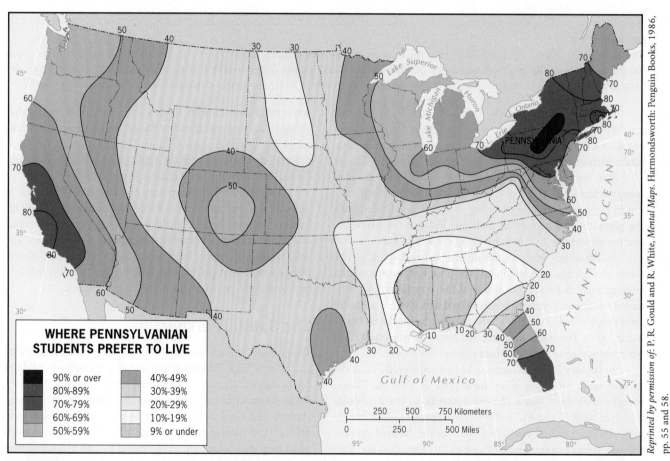

Reprinted by permission of: P. R. Gould and R. White, Mental Maps. Harmondsworth: Penguin Books, 1986, pp. 55 and 58.

■ **Figure 1.7**

Desirable Places to Live.   Where Pennsylvanian and Californian college students would prefer to live, based on questionnaires completed by college students. Proximity affects the impressions students have of other places—but so do stereotypes about certain parts of the country. How would this map look if we took a survey of Pennsylvanian and Californian college students now? Would the South be more desirable with the growth of Atlanta and other cities in the region? Would the availability of jobs in North Dakota's oil region make it a more desirable place to live?

second of the five themes concerns **human–environment interactions**. Why did the Army Corps of Engineers alter Florida's physical environment so drastically when it drained part of the Everglades? Have the changes in Florida's environment created an easier path of destruction for hurricanes? Why is the Army Corps of Engineers again changing the course of the Kissimmee River, and what does that mean for farmers around the river and residential developments in the south of Florida? Asking locational questions often means looking at the reciprocal relationship between humans and environments.

The third theme of geography is the **region**. Phenomena are not evenly distributed on Earth's surface. Instead, features tend to be concentrated in particular areas, which we call regions. Geographers use fieldwork and both quantitative and qualitative methods to develop insightful descriptions of different regions of the world. Novelist James Michener once wrote that whenever he started writing a new book, he first prepared himself by turning to books written by regional geographers about the area where the action was to occur. Understanding the regional geography of a place allows us to make sense of much of the

information we have about places and digest new place-based information as well.

The fourth theme is represented by the seemingly simple word **place**. All places on the surface of Earth have unique human and physical characteristics, and one of the purposes of geography is to study the special character and meaning of places. People develop a **sense of place** by infusing a place with meaning and emotion, by remembering important events that occurred in a place, or by labeling a place with a certain character. Because we experience and give meaning to places, we can have a feeling of "home" when we are in a certain place.

We also develop **perceptions of places** where we have never been through books, movies, stories, and pictures. Geographers Peter Gould and Rodney White asked college students in California and Pennsylvania: "If you could move to any place of your choice, without any of the usual financial and other obstacles, where would you like to live?" Their responses showed a strong bias for their home region and revealed that students from both regions had negative perceptions of the South, Appalachia, the Great Plains, and Utah (Fig. 1.7). What we know shapes our perceptions of places.

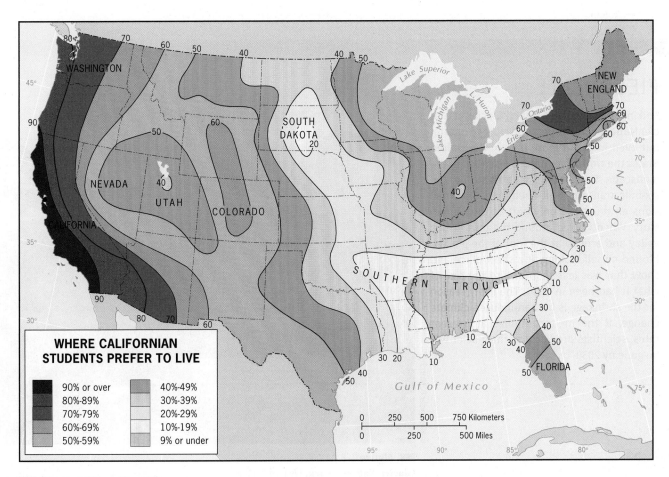

WHERE CALIFORNIAN STUDENTS PREFER TO LIVE

- 90% or over
- 80%-89%
- 70%-79%
- 60%-69%
- 50%-59%
- 40%-49%
- 30%-39%
- 20%-29%
- 10%-19%
- 9% or under

■ **Figure 1.7 (continued)**

The fifth theme, **movement**, refers to the mobility of people, goods, and ideas. Movement is an expression of the interconnectedness of places. **Spatial interaction** between places depends on the **distances** (the measured physical space between two places) among places, the **accessibility** (the ease of reaching one location from another) of places, and the transportation and communication **connectivity** (the degree of linkage between locations in a network) among places. Interactions of many kinds shape human geography.

CULTURAL LANDSCAPE

In addition to the five themes—location, human–environment, region, place, and movement—**landscape** is a core element of geography. Geographers use the term *landscape* to refer to the material character of a place, the complex of natural features, human structures, and other tangible objects that give a place a particular form.

Human geographers are particularly concerned with the **cultural landscape**, the visible imprint of human activity on the landscape. The geographer whose name is most closely identified with this concept is former University of California at Berkeley professor Carl Sauer. In Sauer's words, cultural landscapes are comprised of the "forms superimposed on the physical landscape" by human activity.

No place on Earth is in a "pristine" condition; humans have made an imprint on every place on the planet (Fig. 1.8). The cultural landscape is the visible imprint of human activity and culture on the landscape. We can see the cultural landscape in the layers of buildings, roads, memorials, churches, fields, and homes that human activities over time have stamped on the landscape.

Cultural landscapes have layers of impressions from compounded years of human activity. As each group of people arrives and occupies a place, they carry their own technological and cultural traditions and transform the landscape accordingly. Imprints made by a sequence of occupants, whose impacts are layered one on top of the other, were described as a cultural landscape of **sequent occupance** in 1929 by Derwent Whittlesey. The Tanzanian city of Dar es Salaam provides an interesting urban example of sequent occupance. Arabs from Zanzibar first chose the African site in 1866 as a summer retreat. Next, German

FIELD NOTE

"Hiking to the famed Grinnell Glacier in Glacier National Park brings one close to nature, but even in this remote part of the United States the work of humans is inscribed in the landscape. The parking lot at the start of the six-mile trail, the trail itself, and the small signs en route are only part of the human story. When I hiked around the turn in this valley and arrived at the foot of the glacier, I found myself looking at a sheet of ice and snow that was less than a third the size of what it had been in 1850. The likely reason for the shrinkage is human-induced climate change. If the melt continues at present rates, scientists predict that the glacier will be gone by 2030."

© Alexander B. Murphy.

■ **Figure 1.8**
Glacier National Park, United States.

■ **Figure 1.9 A and B**

Mumbai, India (A) and Dar-es-Salaam, Tanzania (B).   Apartment buildings throughout Mumbai (formerly Bombay), India, are typically four stories with balconies. In Dar-es-Salaam, Tanzania, this four-story walkup with balconies (right) stands where single-family African dwellings once stood, reflecting the sequent occupance of the city, as migrants from India have arrived in Dar-es-Salaam.

colonizers imprinted a new layout and architectural style (wood-beamed Teutonic) when they chose the city as the center of their East African colonies in 1891. After World War I, when the Germans were ousted, a British administration took over the city and began yet another period of transformation. The British encouraged immigration from their colony in India to Tanzania. The new migrant Asian population created a zone of three- and four-story apartment houses, which look as if they were transplanted from Bombay (now Mumbai), India (Fig. 1.9 A and B). Then, in the early 1960s, Dar es Salaam became the capital of newly independent Tanzania. Thus, the city experienced four stages of cultural dominance in less than one century, and each stage of the sequence remains imprinted on the cultural landscape.

A cultural landscape can be seen as a kind of book offering clues into each chapter of the cultural practices, values, and priorities of its various occupiers. As geographer Peirce Lewis explained in *Axioms for Reading the Landscape* (1979), "Our human landscape is our unwitting autobiography, reflecting our tastes, our values, our aspirations, and even our fears, in tangible, visible form." Like Whittlesey, Lewis recommended looking for layers of history and cultural practice in cultural landscapes, adding that most major changes in the cultural landscape occur after a major event, such as a war, an invention, or an economic depression.

 Geographers who practice fieldwork keep their eyes open to the world around them and through practice become adept at reading cultural landscapes. Take a walk around your campus or town and try reading the cultural landscape. Choose one thing in the landscape and ask yourself, "What is that and why is it there?" Take the time to find out the answers!

WHY DO GEOGRAPHERS USE MAPS, AND WHAT DO MAPS TELL US?

Maps are incredibly powerful tools in geography, and **cartography**, which is the art and science of making maps, is as old as geography itself. (For details on cartography, see Appendix A on the Wiley website.) Maps are used for countless purposes, including waging war, promoting political positions, solving medical problems, locating shopping centers, bringing relief to refugees, and warning of natural hazards. **Reference maps** show locations of places and geographic features. **Thematic maps** tell stories, typically showing the degree of some attribute or the movement of a geographic phenomenon.

Reference maps accurately show the **absolute locations** of places, using a coordinate system that allows for the precise plotting of where on Earth something is. Imagine taking an orange, drawing a dot on it with a marker, and then trying to describe the exact location of that dot to someone who is holding another orange so she can mark the same spot on her orange. If you draw and number the same coordinate system on both oranges, the task of drawing the absolute location on each orange is not only doable but simple. The coordinate system most frequently used on maps is based on latitude and longitude. For example, the absolute location of Chicago is 41 degrees, 53 minutes north latitude and 87 degrees, 38 minutes west longitude. Using these coordinates, you can plot Chicago on any globe or map that is marked with latitude and longitude lines.

Establishment of the satellite-based **global positioning system** (GPS) allows us to locate features on Earth with extraordinary accuracy. Researchers collect data quickly and easily in the field, and low-priced units encourage fishers, hunters, runners, and hikers to use GPS in their activities. New cars are equipped with GPS units, and dashboard map displays help commuters navigate traffic and travelers find their way. **Geocaching** is a popular hobby based on the use of GPS. Geocachers use their GPS units to play a treasure hunt game all over the world. People leave the treasures ("caches") somewhere, mark the coordinates on their GPS, and post clues on the Internet. If you find the cache, you take the treasure and leave a new one. Smartphones are equipped with GPS units, helping spread the use of GPS even further.

Relative location describes the location of a place in relation to other human and physical features. Descriptors such as "Chicago is on Lake Michigan, south of Milwaukee" or "Chicago is located where the cross-country railroads met in the 1800s" or "Chicago is the hub of the corn and soybean markets in the Midwest" are all descriptors of Chicago relative to other features. In the southern Wisconsin, northern Illinois, and western Indiana region, all major roads lead to Chicago (Fig. 1.10). Within this region, people define much of their lives relative to Chicago because of the tight interconnectedness between Chicago and the region. Northwest Indiana is so connected to Chicago that it has a time zone separate from the rest of Indiana,

allowing people in northwestern Indiana to stay in the same time zone as Chicago.

Absolute locations do not change, but relative locations are constantly modified and change over time. Fredericksburg, Virginia, is located halfway between Washington, D.C., and Richmond, Virginia. Today, it is a suburb of Washington, D.C., with commuter trains, van pools, buses, and cars moving commuters between their homes in Fredericksburg and their workplaces in metropolitan Washington. During the Civil War, several bloody battles took place in Fredericksburg as the North and South fought halfway between their wartime capitals. The absolute location of Fredericksburg has not changed, but its place in the world around it, its relative location, certainly has.

Mental Maps

We all carry maps in our minds of places we have been and places we have merely heard of; these are called **mental maps**. Even if you have never been to the Great Plains of the United States, you may have studied wall maps and atlases or come across the region in books, magazines, and newspapers frequently enough to envision the states of the region (North Dakota, South Dakota, Nebraska, Kansas, Oklahoma, and

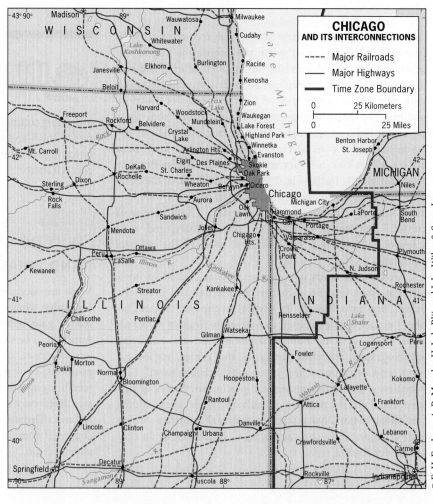

■ **Figure 1.10**
All Major Roads Lead to Chicago. The network of Midwestern roads that lead to Chicago reflects the dominance of the city in the region.

Texas) in your mind. Even if your mental map is not accurate, you still use it to process information about the Great Plains. If you hear on the news that a tornado destroyed a town in Oklahoma, you use your mental map of the Great Plains region and Oklahoma to make sense of where the tornado occurred and who was affected by it.

Our mental maps of the places within our **activity spaces**, the places we travel to routinely in our rounds of daily activity, are more accurate and detailed than our mental maps of places where we have never been. If your friend calls and asks you to meet her at the movie theater you go to frequently, your mental map will engage automatically. You will envision the hallway, the front door, the walk to your car, the lane to choose in order to be prepared for the left turn you must make, where you will park your car, and your path into the theater and up to the popcorn stand.

Geographers who study human-environment behavior have made extensive studies of how people develop mental maps. The earliest humans, who were nomadic, had incredibly accurate mental maps of where to find food and seek shelter. Today, people need mental maps to find their way through the concrete jungles of cities and suburbs.

Geographers have studied the mental map formation of children, the blind, new residents to cities, men, and women, all of whom exhibit differences in the formation of mental maps. To learn new places, women, for example, tend to use landmarks, whereas men tend to use paths. Activity spaces vary by age, and the extent of peoples' mental maps depends in part on their ages. Mental maps include **terra incognita**, unknown lands that are off-limits. If your path to the movie theater includes driving past a school that you do not attend, your map on paper may label the school, but no details will be shown regarding the place. However, if you have access to the school and you are instead drawing a mental map of how to get to the school's cafeteria, your mental map of the school will be quite detailed. Thus, mental maps reflect a person's activity space, including what is accessible to the person in his or her rounds of daily activity and what is not.

Generalization in Maps

All maps simplify the world. A reference map of the world cannot show every place in the world, and a thematic map of hurricane tracks in the Atlantic Ocean cannot pinpoint the precise path of every hurricane for the last 50 years. When mapping data, whether human or physical, cartographers, the geographers who make maps, generalize the information they present on maps. Many of the maps in this book are thematic maps of the world. Shadings show how much or how little of a phenomenon is present, and symbols show where specific phenomena are located.

Generalized maps help us see general trends, but we cannot see all cases of a given phenomenon. The map of world precipitation (Fig. 1.11) is a generalized map of mean annual precipitation received around the world. The areas shaded in burgundy, dark blue, and vibrant green are places

that receive the most rain, and those shaded in orange receive the least rain on average. Take a pen and trace along the equator on the map. Notice how many of the high-precipitation areas on the map are along the equator. The consistent heating of the equator over the course of the year brings precipitation to the equatorial region. At the scale of the world, we can see general trends in precipitation, such as this, but it is difficult to see the microscale climates of intense precipitation areas that are found throughout the world.

Remote Sensing and GIS

Geographic studies include both long- and short-term environmental change. Geographers monitor Earth from a distance, using **remote sensing** technology. Remotely sensed data are collected by satellites and aircraft and are often almost instantaneously available.

After a major weather or hazard event, such as the 2011 floods in the Mississippi River Valley, the unprecedented hurricane season in the Gulf of Mexico in 2005 (which included Hurricane Katrina), or the 2010 earthquakes in Haiti and Chile, remotely sensed data show us the major areas of impact (Fig. 1.12). A remotely sensed image surveys the damage of the earthquake, and photos taken on the ground show the impact and destruction (Fig. 1.13).

In states that restrict foreign access or that do not reliably allow foreign aid to enter the country, remote sensing can help geographers understand the physical and human geography of the place. ArcGIS Online is a free, web-based user-friendly GIS. You can create a map in ArcGIS Online and set the background to world imagery, which is composed of satellite and aerial images from a variety of sources. The images are accurate to .3 meters in the continental United States and western Europe and to 1 meter in the rest of the world.

Remotely sensed images can be incorporated in a map, and absolute locations can be studied by plotting change in remotely sensed imagery over time. Advances in computer technology and data storage, increasing accessibility to locationally based data and GPS technology, and software corporations that tailor products to specific uses have all driven incredible advances in geographic analysis based on **geographic information systems** (GIS) over the last two decades. Geographers use GIS to compare a variety of spatial data by creating digitized representations of the environment (Fig. 1.14), combining layers of spatial data, and creating maps in which patterns and processes are superimposed. Geographers also use GIS to analyze data, which can give us new insights into geographic patterns and relationships.

Geographers use GIS in both human and physical geographic research. For example, political geographers use GIS to map layers showing voters, party registration, race and ethnicity, likelihood of voting, and income in order to determine how to draw voting districts in congressional and state legislative elections. In this case, a geographer can draw a line around a group of people and ask the computer program to tally how

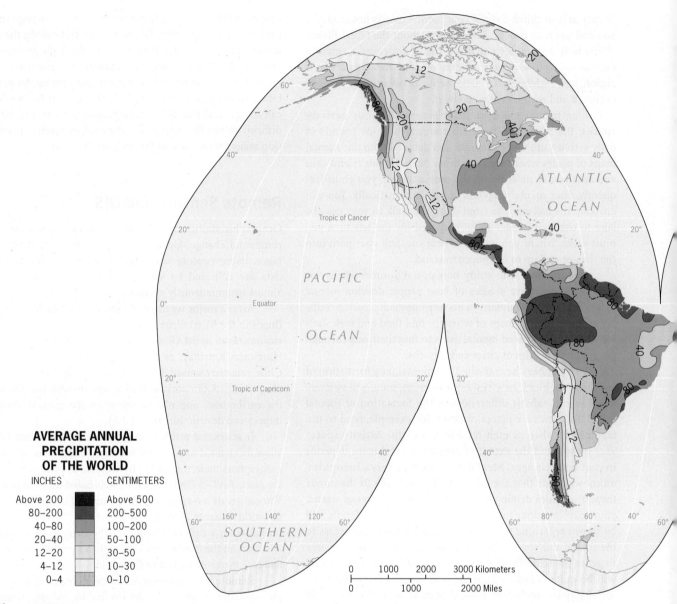

**AVERAGE ANNUAL
PRECIPITATION
OF THE WORLD**

INCHES		CENTIMETERS
Above 200		Above 500
80–200		200–500
40–80		100–200
20–40		50–100
12–20		30–50
4–12		10–30
0–4		0–10

■ **Figure 1.11**

Average Annual Precipitation of the World.   A generalized map of the mean annual precipitation received around the world. The pattern on the map shows high precipitation along the equator, where consistent heating from the sun over the year means more incoming solar radiation is absorbed and released as warm air. When warm, moist air rises and reaches its dew point, condensation and precipitation follow. The rainforest climates are found along the equator. Locations that receive little precipitation are deserts, which are found in areas of Earth dominated by high-pressure cells. In a high-pressure cell, air descends from aloft to the ground and then goes outward, making it impossible for warm air to rise. Deserts receive rain when storms pass through them, not from the solar radiation they receive each day.

many voters are inside the region, determine the racial composition of the district, and show how many of the current political representatives live within the new district's boundaries.

Geographers trained in GIS employ the technology in countless undertakings. Students who earn undergraduate degrees in geography are employed by software companies, government agencies, and businesses to use GIS to survey wildlife, map soils, analyze natural disasters, track diseases, assist first responders, plan cities, plot transportation improvements, and follow weather systems. For example, a group of

geographers working for one GIS company tailors the GIS software to serve the branches of the military and the defense intelligence community. The vast amounts of intelligence data gathered by the various intelligence agencies can be integrated into a GIS and then analyzed spatially. Geographers working in the defense intelligence community can use GIS to query a vast amount of intelligence, interpret spatial data, and make recommendations on issues of security and defense.

The amount of data digestible in a GIS, the power of the location analysis that can be undertaken on a computer

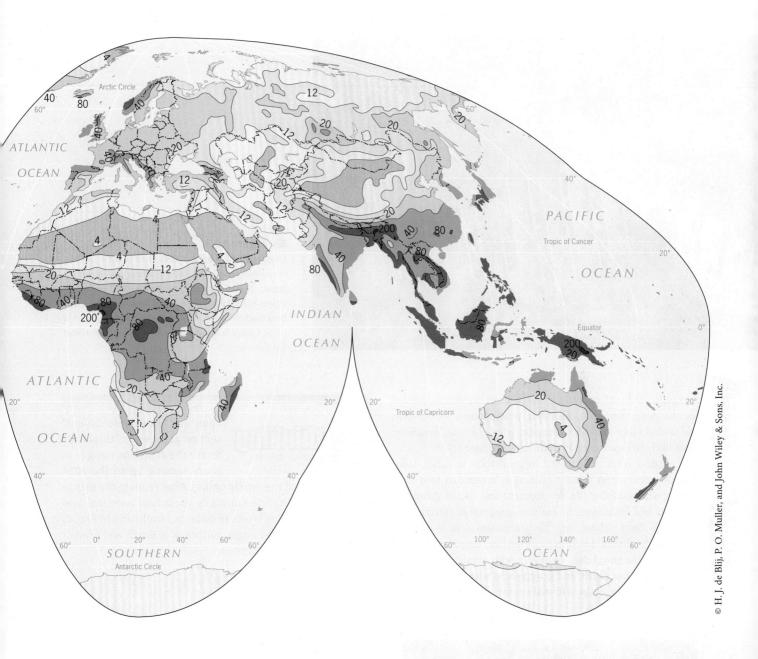

platform, and the ease of analysis that is possible using GIS software applications allow geographers to answer complicated questions. For example, geographer Korine Kolivras analyzed the probability of dengue fever outbreaks in Hawaii using GIS (Fig. 1.15). The maps Kolivras produced may look as simple and straightforward as the cholera maps produced by Dr. John Snow in the 1800s, but the amount of data that went into Kolivras's analysis is staggering in comparison. Dengue fever is carried by a particular kind of mosquito called the *Aedes*

▪▪ Figure 1.12

Concepción, Chile. Satellite image of the cities of Concepción and Hualpén, Chile, hours after an 8.8 magnitude earthquake occurred in 2010. The damage to the city is not noticeable in this satellite image except for the smoke plume from an oil refinery in the lower left corner.

© NASA/Science Source/Photo Researchers, Inc.

© H. J. de Blij, P. O. Muller, and John Wiley & Sons, Inc.

■■ Figure 1.13
Concepción, Chile. Chile has broadly adopted engineering and architecture practices that lessen the impact of earthquakes. Although the 2010 earthquake caused over $30 billion worth of damage, it could have been much worse without these building practices. Most of the damage in Concepción was to residential buildings like this one.

mosquito. Kolivras analyzed the breeding conditions needed for the *Aedes* mosquito, including precipitation, topography, and several other variables, to predict what places in Hawaii are most likely to experience an outbreak of dengue fever.

A new term of art used in geography is GISci. Geographic information science (GISci) is a research field concerned with studying the development and use of geospatial concepts and techniques to examine geographic patterns and processes. Your school may have a program in GISci that draws across disciplines, bringing together computer scientists who write the programs, engineers who create sensors that gather data about Earth, and geographers who combine layers of data and interpret them to make sense of our world.

thinking *geographically*

Look at "Learn More Online" section at the end of this chapter for the article on dengue in Brazil leading up to the 2014 World Cup. Find the article online. After reading the article and looking at Korine Kolivras's guest field note, list and explain at least five layers of data you could add in ArcGIS Online to study the dengue outbreak in Brazil and predict where an outbreak will occur.

A

B

■■ Figure 1.14
Two Representations of St. Francis, South Dakota.   1.14A is a panchromatic raster satellite image collected in 2002 at 10 m resolution during a grassland wildfire; 1.14B displays vector data—rivers, roads, cities, and land use/land cover—digitalized from the image 1.14A.

GUEST FIELD NOTE

The diffusion of diseases carried by vectors, such as the *Aedes* mosquito that transmits dengue, is not solely a result of the environmental factors in a place. I use disease ecology to understand the ways in which environmental, social, and cultural factors interact to produce disease in a place. Through a combination of fieldwork and geographic information systems (GIS) modeling, I studied the environmental habitat of the *Aedes* mosquito in Hawaii and the social and cultural factors that stimulated the outbreak of dengue in Hawaii.

When I went into the field in Hawaii, I observed the diversity of the physical geography of Hawaii, from deserts to rainforests. I saw the specific local environments of the dengue outbreak area, and I examined the puddles in streams (Fig. 1.15A) in which the mosquitoes likely bred during the 2001–2002 dengue outbreak. I talked to public health officials who worked so hard to control the dengue outbreak so that I better understood the local environmental factors contributing to the disease. I visited a family that had been heavily affected by dengue, and I saw their home, which, by their choice, lacked walls or screens on all sides. In talking with the family, I came to understand the social and cultural factors that affected the outbreak of dengue in Hawaii.

I created a GIS model of mosquito habitat that considered not only total precipitation in Hawaii (Fig. 1.15B), but also seasonal variations in precipitation (Fig. 1.15C) and temperature (Fig. 1.15D), to help explain where the *Aedes* mosquito

Korine N. Kolivras, Virginia Tech

■■ **Figure 1.15 A**

Maui, Hawaii. *Aedes* mosquitoes breed in artificial and natural water containers, including standing puddles left behind when streams dry up during a drought as shown in this photograph along the northeast coast of Maui.

is able to breed and survive on the islands. I also studied seasonal fluctuations in streams and population distributions in creating my model of dengue potential areas (Fig. 1.15E).

The GIS model I created can now be altered by public officials in Hawaii to reflect precipitation and temperature variations each year or to incorporate new layers of environmental, social, and cultural data. Officials will be able to better predict locations of dengue outbreaks so they can focus their efforts to combat the spread of the disease.

Credit: Korine N. Kolivras, Virginia Tech

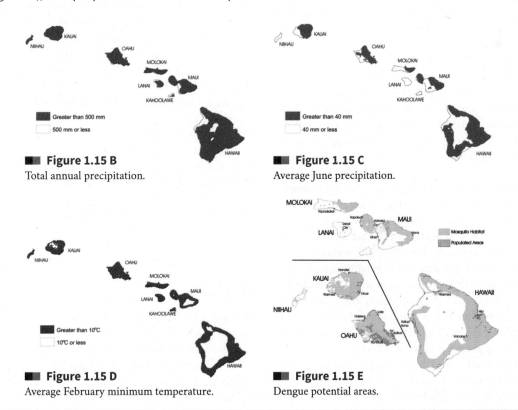

■■ **Figure 1.15 B**
Total annual precipitation.

Greater than 500 mm
500 mm or less

■■ **Figure 1.15 C**
Average June precipitation.

Greater than 40 mm
40 mm or less

■■ **Figure 1.15 D**
Average February minimum temperature.

Greater than 10°C
10°C or less

■■ **Figure 1.15 E**
Dengue potential areas.

Mosquito Habitat
Populated Areas

WHY ARE GEOGRAPHERS CONCERNED WITH SCALE AND CONNECTEDNESS?

Geographers study places and patterns across scales, including local, regional, national, and global. Scale has two meanings in geography: the first is the distance on a map compared to the distance on Earth, and the second is the spatial extent of something. When we refer to scale we are using the second of these definitions. Geographers' interest in this type of scale derives from the fact that phenomena found at one scale are usually influenced by what is happening at other scales. Explaining a geographic pattern or process requires looking across scales. Moreover, the scale of our research or analysis matters because we can make different observations at different scales. We can study a single phenomenon across different scales in order to see how what is happening at the global scale affects localities and how what is happening at a local scale affects the globe. Or we can study a phenomenon at a particular scale and then ask how processes at other scales affect what we are studying.

The scale at which we study a geographic phenomenon tells us what level of detail we can expect to see. We also see different patterns at different scales. For example, when we study the distribution of material wealth at the scale of the globe (see Fig. 1.3), we see that the countries in western Europe, Canada, the United States, Japan, and Australia are the wealthiest, and the countries of Subsaharan Africa and Southeast Asia are the poorest. Does that mean everyone in the United States is wealthy and everyone in Indonesia is poor? Certainly not, but on a global-scale map of states, that is how the data appear.

When you shift scales to North America and examine the data for States of the United States and the provinces of Canada (Fig. 1.16), you see that the wealthiest areas are on the coasts and the poorest are in the interior and in the extreme Northeast and South. The State of Alaska and the province of the Northwest Territories have high gross per capita incomes, supplemented by oil revenues shared among the residents.

By shifting scales again to just one city, for example, metropolitan Washington, D.C. (Fig. 1.17), you observe that suburbs west, northwest, and southwest of the city are the wealthiest and that suburbs to the east and southeast have lower income levels. In the city itself, a clear dichotomy of wealth divides the northwest neighborhoods from the rest of the city. Shifting scales again to the individual, if we conducted fieldwork in Washington, D.C., and interviewed people who live below the poverty line, we would quickly find that each person's experience of poverty and reasons for being in poverty vary, making it difficult to generalize. We would find some trends, such as how women in poverty who have children cope differently from single men or how immigrants with visas cope differently from paperless immigrants, but no two individual cases are exactly the same.

Because the level of detail and the patterns observed change as the scale changes, geographers must be sensitive to their scale of analysis and also be wary of researchers who make generalizations about a people or a place at a particular scale without considering other scales of analysis.

Geographers study how processes operating at different scales influence one another. If you want to understand the conflict between the Tutsi and the Hutu people in Rwanda, for example, you cannot look solely at this African country. Developments at a variety of different scales, including patterns of migration and interaction in Central Africa, the economic and political relations between Rwanda and parts of Europe, and the variable impacts of globalization—economic, political, and cultural—all influenced Rwanda and help to explain the context of the conflict.

Geographers are also interested in how people use scale politically. Locally based political movements, like the Zapatistas in southern Mexico, have learned to **rescale** their actions to involve players at other scales and create a global outcry of support for their position. By taking their political campaign from the local scale to the national scale through protests against the North American Free Trade Agreement (NAFTA), and then effectively using the Internet to wage a global campaign, the Zapatistas gained attention from the world media, a feat relatively few local political movements achieve.

Geographer Victoria Lawson uses the term *jumping scale* to describe such rescaling activities. She compares the ways in which Western countries, multinational corporations, and the World Trade Organization take products and ideas created in Western places and by Western corporations and globalize all rights to profits from them through intellectual property law. Efforts to push Western views of intellectual property challenge other local and regional views of products and ideas. To the West, rice is a product that can be owned, privatized, and bought and sold. To East Asians, rice is integral to culture, and new rice strains and new ideas about growing rice can help build community, not just profit. Lawson explains that taking a single regional view and jumping scale to globalize it can serve to legitimate that view and negate other regional and local views.

Regions

A region constitutes an area that shares similar characteristics and as a whole is distinct from other regions. Geographers define regions as formal, functional, or perceptual.

A **formal region** has a shared trait, either physical or cultural. A formal physical region is based on a shared physical geographic criterion, such as the karst region of

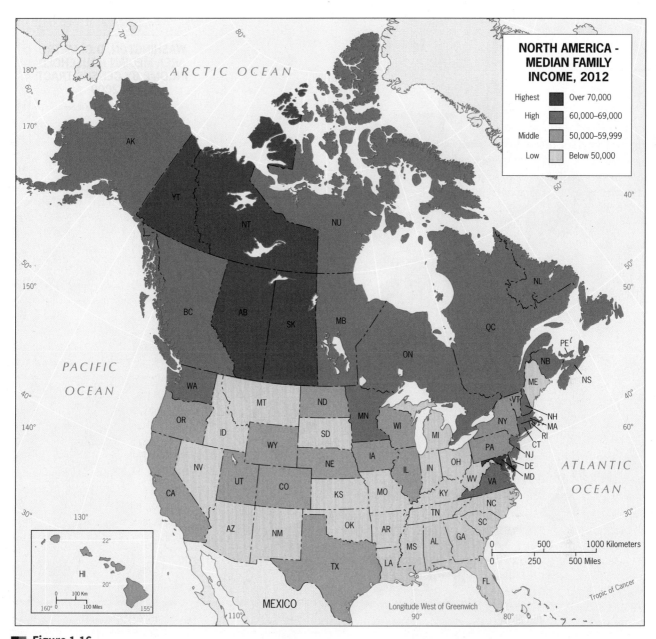

■ **Figure 1.16**

Median Family Income (in U.S. Dollars), 2011.   The relatively greater wealth of the East Coast, from New Hampshire through Virginia, stands out.   *Data from*: United States Census Bureau and Census Canada, 2010.

China (Fig. 1.18). In a formal cultural region, people share one or more cultural traits. For example, the region of Europe where French is spoken by a majority of the people can be thought of as a French-speaking region. Whether physical or cultural, when the scale of analysis shifts, the formal region changes. If we shift scales to the world, the karst region expands to lands that were previously underwater and are now covered in limestone, and the French-speaking formal region expands beyond France into former French colonies of Africa and into the overseas departments that are still under French jurisdiction.

A **functional region** is defined by a particular set of activities or interactions that occur within it. Places (also called nodes) that are part of the same functional region interact to create connections. Functional regions have a shared political, social, or economic purpose. For example, a city has a surrounding region within which workers commute, either to the downtown area or to office parks in suburbs. That entire urban area, defined by people moving toward and within it, is a functional region. A functional region is a spatial connection among nodes, and the extent of the connections defines the boundaries of the region.

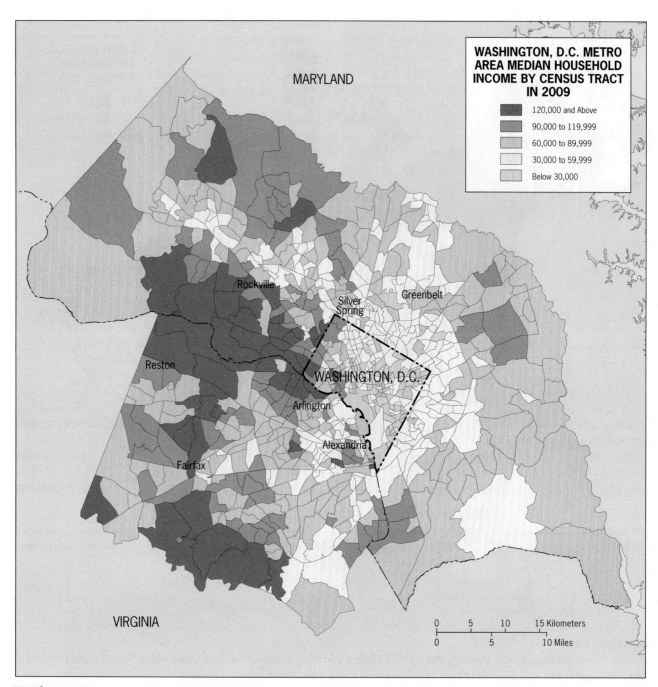

Figure 1.17

Median Family Income (in U.S. Dollars), 2009. Notice the sharp contrast between the western and eastern parts of the nation's capital, which shows up clearly on a map at this scale. *Data from*: United States Census Bureau, 2010.

Functional regions are not necessarily culturally homogeneous; instead, the people within the region function together politically, socially, or economically. The City of Chicago is a functional region and is itself part of hundreds of functional regions—from the State of Illinois to the seventh Federal Reserve district.

Regions may be perceptual, intellectual constructs that help people order their knowledge and understanding of the world. Each person carries **perceptual regions** in their mind based on accumulated knowledge of regions and cultures (Fig. 1.19). Perceptual regions can include people and their cultural traits (dress, food, language, and religion), places and their physical traits (mountains, plains, or coasts), and built environments (windmills, barns, skyscrapers, or beach houses).

Major news events help us create our perceptual regions by defining certain countries or areas of countries as part of a region. Before September 11, 2001, most Americans thought

© Alexander B. Murphy.

■■ **Figure 1.18**

Guilin, China.   The South China Karst region, bisected here by the Li River outside Guilin, is a UNESCO World Heritage Site. The landforms of the region clearly distinguish it from surrounding areas.

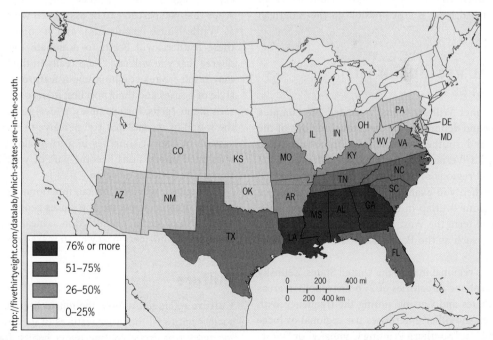

http://fivethirtyeight.com/datalab/which-states-are-in-the-south.

76% or more

51–75%

26–50%

0–25%

■■ **Figure 1.19**

The South.   The boundaries of perceptual regions are difficult to define precisely. Nate Silver's blog FiveThirtyEight (owned by ESPN) teamed up with SurveyMonkey to poll people on the web who identified themselves as a Midwesterner or Southerner "a lot" or "some" and generated maps of the perceptual regions of those who identify with the regions. Lifestyle Editor Walt Hickey analyzed the data and found Midwesterners have less agreement on what states are in the region (Illinois was chosen most frequently, with 80 percent agreeing it's part of the Midwest), whereas Southerners have a clearer idea of the states definitively in the South (about 90 percent agreed Georgia and Alabama are in the South and more than 80 percent put Louisiana and Mississippi in the South).

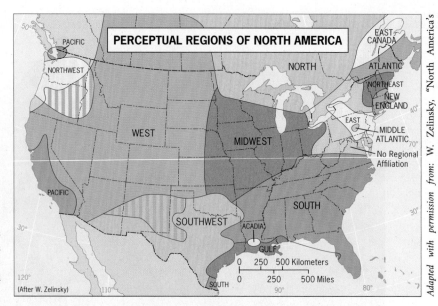

Figure 1.20
Perceptual Regions of North America. This map represents a composite of many people's ideas as to what constitute major cultural-geographic regions in the United States and southern Canada.

Adapted with permission from: W. Zelinsky, "North America's Vernacular Regions," Annals of the Association of American Geographers, 1980, p. 14.

the Middle East region included Iraq and Iran but stretched no farther east. As the hunt for Osama bin Laden began and the media focused attention on the harsh rule of the Taliban in Afghanistan, regional perceptions of the Middle East changed; for many, the region now stretched to encompass Afghanistan and Pakistan. Scholars who specialize in this part of the globe had long studied the relationship between parts of Southwest Asia and the traditional "Middle East," but the connections between Afghanistan and Pakistan and the rest of the Middle East had been almost invisible to the American population.

PERCEPTUAL REGIONS IN THE UNITED STATES

Cultural geographer Wilbur Zelinsky tackled the complex task of defining and delimiting the perceptual regions of the United States and southern Canada. In an article titled "North America's Vernacular Regions," he identified 12 major perceptual regions on a series of maps (summarized in Fig. 1.20). When you examine the map, you will notice some of the regions overlap in certain places. For example, the more general term the West actually incorporates more specific regions, such as the Pacific Region and part of the Northwest.

To make his regional map of the United States, Zelinsky analyzed the telephone directories of 276 metropolitan areas in the United States and Canada, noting the frequency with which businesses and other enterprises use regional or locational terms (such as "Southern Printing Company" or "Western Printing") in their listings. The resulting maps show a close similarity between these perceptual regions and culture regions identified by geographers.

The perceptual region of the South, shown in both Figures 1.19 and 1.20, has changed markedly since the civil rights movement of the 1960s (Fig. 1.21). A "New South"

has emerged, forged by Hispanic immigration, urbanization, movement of people from other parts of the United States to the South, and other processes. At the same time, the South continues to carry imprints of a culture with deep historical roots through language, religion, music, food preferences, and other traditions and customs.

If you drive southward from, say, Pittsburgh or Detroit, you will not pass a specific place where you enter this perceptual region. You will note features in the cultural landscape that you perceive to be associated with the South (such as Waffle House restaurants), and at some stage of the trip these features will begin to dominate the area to such a degree that you will say, "I am really in the South now." This may result from a combination of features in the culture: the style of houses and their porches, items on a roadside restaurant menu (grits, for example), a local radio station's music, the sound of accents that you perceive to be Southern, a succession of Baptist churches in a town along the way. These combined impressions become part of your overall perception of the South as a region.

Regions, whether formal, functional, or perceptual, are ways of organizing people and places geographically. Regions are a form of spatial classification, a means of handling large amounts of information so we can make sense of it.

Culture

Culture refers not only to the music, literature, and arts of a society but to all the other features of its way of life: prevailing modes of dress; routine living habits; food preferences; the architecture of houses and public buildings; the layout of fields and farms; and systems of education, government, and law. Culture is an all-encompassing term that identifies not only the whole tangible lifestyle of peoples, but also their prevailing values and beliefs. Culture lies at the heart of human geography.

GUEST FIELD NOTE

Montgomery, Alabama

Located in a predominately African American neighborhood in Montgomery, Alabama, the street intersection of Jeff Davis and Rosa Parks is symbolic of the debates and disputes in the American South over how the past is to be commemorated on the region's landscape. The Civil War and civil rights movement are the two most important events in the history of the region. The street names commemorate Montgomery's central role in both eras, and they do so in the same public space. Montgomery was the site of the first capital of the Confederacy in 1861 while Jefferson Davis was president. The Alabama capital was also the site of the 1955–1956 Montgomery bus boycott that launched the civil rights movement. The boycott was sparked by Rosa Parks's arrest after she refused to give up her seat on a city bus when ordered to do so by a white person. Most of my research examines the politics of how the region's white and African Americans portray these separate heroic eras within the region's public spaces, ranging from support for and against

Jonathan Leib, Old Dominion University

■ **Figure 1.21**

flying the Confederate flag to disputes over placing statues and murals honoring the Civil War and the civil rights movement on the South's landscape.

Credit: Jonathan Leib, Old Dominion University

Academics, from human geographers to anthropologists, have sought to define culture. Some have stressed the contributions of humans to the environment, whereas others have emphasized learned behaviors and ways of thinking. Several decades ago the noted anthropologist E. Adamson Hoebel defined culture as:

> [the] *integrated system of learned behavior patterns which are characteristic of the members of a society and which are not the result of biological inheritance . . . culture is not genetically predetermined; it is noninstinctive . . .* [Culture] *is wholly the result of social invention and is transmitted and maintained solely through communication and learning.*

Hoebel's emphasis on communication and learning anticipated the current view of culture as a system of meaning, not just a set of acts, customs, or material products. Clifford Geertz advanced this view in his classic work, *The Interpretation of Cultures* (1973), which has influenced much recent work in human geography. Human geographers are interested not just in the different patterns and landscapes associated with different culture groups, but in the ways in which cultural understandings affect both the creation and significance of those patterns and landscapes.

Cultural geographers identify a single attribute of a culture as a **culture trait**. For example, wearing a turban is a culture trait in certain societies. Many men in the semiarid and desert areas of North Africa, Southwest Asia, and South Asia wore turbans before the birth of Islam. The turbans

protected the wearers from sunlight and also helped distinguish tribes. Not all Muslim men wear turbans, but in some Muslim countries, including Afghanistan, wearing turbans is popular because either religious or political leaders prescribe it for men. Today, turbans often distinguish a man's status in society or are worn as a sign of faithfulness to God. In some Muslim countries, including Egypt and Turkey, men rarely wear turbans. When men in other Muslim countries do wear turbans, the appearance of the turban varies a great deal. For instance, in Yemen men who cover their heads typically wear kalansuwa, which are caps wrapped in fabric. In Palestine, Jordan, and Saudi Arabia, men who cover their heads typically wear kaffiyeh, which are rectangular pieces of cloth draped and secured on the head.

Wearing turbans is not a cultural trait limited to Muslims. In the United States, most men who cover their heads with a turban are Sikhs, which is a different religion from Islam. In the Sikh religion, men are required to keep their hair uncut. The common practice is to twist the hair and knot it on top of one's head and then cover it with a turban. The Sikh religion began in the 1500s, and in the late 1600s, the tenth guru of the religion taught that wearing a turban was a way to demonstrate one's faithfulness to God.

As the turban example exhibits, a culture trait is not always confined to a single culture. More than one culture may exhibit a particular culture trait, like turbans. A distinct combination of cultural traits is a **culture complex**. Herding of cattle is a cultural trait shared by many cultures. Across cultures, cattle are regarded and used in different ways.

The Maasai of East Africa, for example, follow their herds along seasonal migration paths, consuming blood and milk as important ingredients of a unique diet. Cattle occupy a central place in Maasai existence; they are the essence of survival, security, and prestige. Although the Maasai culture complex is only one of many cattle-keeping complexes, no other culture complex exhibits exactly the same combination of traits. In Europe, cattle are milked, and dairy products, such as butter, yogurt, and cheese, are consumed as part of a diet very different from that of the Maasai.

A **cultural hearth** is an area where cultural traits develop and from which cultural traits diffuse. Culture traits, for example the religion of Islam, can be traced to a single place and time. Muhammad founded Islam in the 600s C.E. (common era) in and around the cities of Mecca and Medina on the Arabian Peninsula. Other culture traits, such as agriculture, can be traced to several hearths thousands of years apart. When such a trait develops in more than one hearth without being influenced by its development elsewhere, each hearth operates as a case of **independent invention**.

Connectedness Through Diffusion

Historians believe the innovation of agriculture began independently in hearths in Europe, Africa, and Asia. Drawing from archaeological evidence, geographer Carl Sauer established that Mesoamerica was also a hearth for agriculture, another case of independent invention. From these hearths of agriculture, the ideas of purposefully planting and caring for seeds and feeding and raising livestock spread throughout the world in a process called diffusion.

In 1970, Swedish geographer Torsten Hägerstrand published pioneering research on the role of time in diffusion. Hägerstrand's research revealed how time, as well as distance, affects individual human behavior and the dissemination of people and ideas. Sauer and Hägerstrand's fascinating research attracted many geographers to the study of **diffusion**.

Geographers are still using principles of diffusion to create models of movement in GIS.

Whether a cultural trait diffuses to a place depends, in part, on the time and distance from the hearth. The farther a place is from the hearth, the less likely an innovation will be adopted. Similarly, the acceptance of an innovation becomes less likely the longer it takes to reach its potential adopters. In combination, time and distance cause **time–distance decay** in the diffusion process.

Not all cultural traits or innovations diffuse. Prevailing attitudes or cultural taboos can mean that certain innovations, ideas, or practices are not acceptable or adoptable in particular cultures. Religious teachings may prohibit certain practices or ideas, such as divorce, abortion, or contraceptive use, on the grounds of theology or morality. Some cultures or religions prohibit consumption of alcoholic beverages, and others prohibit consuming certain kinds of meat or other foods. Prescriptions cultures make about behavior act as **cultural barriers** and can pose powerful obstacles to the spread of ideas or innovations.

EXPANSION DIFFUSION

When a culture trait, such as a religion, spreads, it does so from a hearth. Islam's hearth was on the Arabian Peninsula, and from there, Islam diffused to Egypt and North Africa, through Southwest Asia, and into West Africa. This is a case of expansion diffusion, when an innovation or idea develops in a hearth and remains strong there while also spreading outward. Geographers classify diffusion into two broad categories: expansion diffusion and relocation diffusion. In the case of **expansion diffusion**, an innovation or idea develops in a hearth and remains strong there while also spreading outward (Fig. 1.22).

When a trend or innovation diffuses quickly, it seems to come out of nowhere and then can "explode" and be seen virtually everywhere you look. In 1996, Kevin Plank, a recent graduate of the University of Maryland who played football as

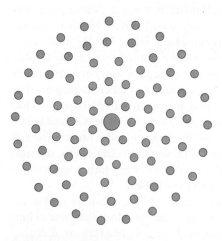

A. Contagious Diffusion

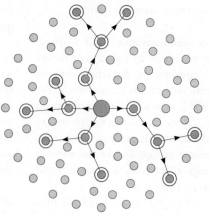

B. Hierarchical Diffusion

LEGEND

- Hearth
- Early diffusion
- Later diffusion
- ○ Important person or place
- No diffusion

■ **Figure 1.22**
Contagious and Hierarchical Diffusion.

a walk-on for the Terrapins, invented a heat gear shirt that would wick sweat away and be a cooling layer under football gear. Plank called his new body-hugging gear Under Armour. He gave samples of polyester heat gear Under Armour shirts to his friends at the University of Maryland and to friends at other football teams in the East Coast Conference. The first "knowers" of the new Under Armour brand were football players connected to Kevin Plank or to college teams on the east coast.

The spread of Under Armour heat gear is a case of **hierarchical diffusion**, a pattern in which the main channel of diffusion is some segment of those who are susceptible to (or are already adopting) what is being diffused. Under Armour diffused from college and professional football players who were trying to stay cool and keep their clothing light while practicing in the hot sun twice a day, to lacrosse players and other athletes who were friends of the football players, then to young athletes around the United States who, as fans, took note of the Under Armour logo on their favorite players' sportswear and wanted to wear what their idols were wearing, and finally to those who saw people they knew wearing Under Armour clothing and bought the gear as a fashion trend. The hierarchy of football players, other athletes, and then the **contagious diffusion** among school-age children that followed helps explain the rapid growth of the Under Armour brand, which had revenues of $200 million in 2004 and $2 billion in 2013.

Plank started giving away Under Armour heat gear, sold the shirts out of the trunk of his car from a base at his grandmother's home in Washington, D.C., and then set up headquarters for the company in Baltimore, Maryland. As is the case in expansion diffusion, the hearth of Under Armour has remained strong. The University of Maryland has close ties to Under Armour, which designed an innovative (some thought it was cool and some thought it was garish) new football uniform in 2011 (Fig. 1.23). In 2014, the University of Maryland signed a ten-year sponsorship agreement with Under Armour, one of 19 sponsorships Under Armour has with universities.

College and professional athletes whose teams had contracts with Nike or Adidas wanted to wear heat gear clothing, and some wore Under Armour beneath their Nike and Adidas uniforms. This prompted Nike, Adidas, and other athletic companies to offer their own performance gear, including compression shirts, compression shorts, and sports bras bearing their logo. Under Armour acted as a stimulus to Nike's Pro Performance line and Adidas's Clima Ultimate line. Under Armour's performance line prompted **stimulus diffusion** or local experimentation and change in the Nike and Adidas brands. The performance apparel market alone was expected to reach $7.6 billion by 2014, and Forbes estimates the entire global sports apparel market will reach $178 billion by 2019. According to Forbes, 70 percent of Under Armour's stock revenue in 2014 was generated by sales of performance apparel, and Under Armour captured 14.7 percent of the global sports apparel market, second to Nike with 27 percent of the market.

Culture traits, rather than economics, can prohibit contagious diffusion and encourage stimulus diffusion as well. Not all ideas can be readily and directly adopted by a receiving population; some are simply too vague, too unattainable, too different, or too impractical for immediate adoption. Yet, these ideas can still have an impact. They may indirectly promote local experimentation and eventual changes in ways of doing things. For example, the diffusion of fast, mass-produced food in the late twentieth century led to the introduction of the hamburger to India. Yet the Hindu religion in India prohibits consumption of beef, which is a major cultural obstacle to adoption of the hamburger (Fig. 1.24). Instead, retailers began selling burgers made of vegetable products. The diffusion of the hamburger took on a new form in the cultural context of India. With expansion diffusion, whether contagious or hierarchical, the people stay in place and the innovation, idea, trait, or disease does the moving.

■ **Figure 1.23**

College Park, Maryland. Under Armour designed controversial football uniforms for their flagship university partner, the University of Maryland. The State of Maryland's red, black, gold, and white flag is incorporated throughout the uniforms from helmets to jerseys to football gloves. Maryland's flag is divided into four quarters with the upper left and lower right gold and black checkers representing the family crest of the founder of Maryland, Lord Baltimore, and the upper right and lower left red and white cross representing the family crest of George Calvert, who is also credited with founding the State of Maryland.

Rob Carr/Getty Images

■ Figure 1.24 A and B
New Delhi, India (A) and Jodhpur, India (B).   Hindus believe cows are holy, and in India, evidence of that can be seen everywhere from cows roaming the streets to the menu at McDonald's. In 1996, the first McDonald's restaurant opened in New Delhi, India, serving Maharaja Macs and Vegetable Burgers with Cheese. In Indian towns, such as Jodhpur, cows are protected and share the streets with pedestrians, bicyclists, and motorists.

RELOCATION DIFFUSION

Relocation diffusion occurs most frequently through migration. When migrants move from their homeland, they take their culture traits with them. Developing an ethnic neighborhood in a new country helps immigrants maintain their culture in the midst of an unfamiliar one. **Relocation diffusion** involves the actual movement of individuals who have already adopted the idea or innovation, and who carry it to a new, perhaps distant, locale, where they proceed to disseminate it (Fig. 1.22). If the homeland of the immigrants loses enough of its population, the cultural customs may fade in the hearth while gaining strength in the ethnic neighborhoods abroad.

Knowing that any good, idea, or disease can diffuse in more than one way, look in your closet for a brand of clothing, a genre of music, or a religious symbol and then research and describe how it diffused from its hearth across the globe, using at least three different types of diffusion in your answer.

WHAT ARE GEOGRAPHIC CONCEPTS, AND HOW ARE THEY USED IN ANSWERING GEOGRAPHIC QUESTIONS?

To think geographically, start by asking a geographic question, one with a spatial or landscape component. Then choose the scale(s) of analysis for your research and apply one or more geographic concepts to answer the question. **Geographic concepts** give us insight and help us understand people, place, space, location, and landscape.

Geographers use fieldwork, remote sensing, GIS, GPS, and qualitative and quantitative techniques to explore linkages among people and places and to explain differences across people, places, scales, and times. Research in human geography today stems from a variety of theories and philosophies and incorporates a broad range of geographic concepts.

Rejection of Environmental Determinism

To understand what geographers do and how they do it, it is easiest to start by defining what geography is not. The ancient Greeks noticed that some of the peoples subjugated by their expanding empire were relatively docile while others were rebellious; they attributed such differences to variations in climate. Over 2000 years ago, Aristotle described northern European people as "full of spirit . . . but incapable of ruling others," and he characterized Asian people (by which he meant the inhabitants of modern-day Turkey) as "intelligent and inventive . . . [but] always in a state of subjection and slavery." Aristotle attributed peoples' response to being taken over by an outside power to the respective climates of the regions. In his mind, the cold northern European environment encouraged people to rebel and the warmer climate of Southwest Asia forced people to become enslaved.

Aristotle's views on this topic were long-lasting. As recently as the first half of the twentieth century, similar notions still had strong support. In 1940, in the *Principles of*

Human Geography, Ellsworth Huntington and C. W. Cushing wrote:

> The well-known contrast between the energetic people of the most progressive parts of the temperate zone and the inert inhabitants of the tropics and even of intermediate regions, such as Persia, is largely due to climate . . . the people of the cyclonic regions rank so far above those of the other parts of the world that they are the natural leaders.

Huntington and Cushing claim climate is the critical factor in how humans behave. Yet what constitutes an "ideal" climate lies in the eyes of the beholder. For Aristotle, it was the Mediterranean climate of Greece. Through the eyes of more recent commentators from western Europe and North America, the climates most suited to progress and productiveness in culture, politics, and technology are (you guessed it) those of western Europe and the northeastern United States. Each of these theories can be classified as **environmental determinism**, which holds that human behavior, individually and collectively, is strongly affected by, even controlled or determined by, the physical environment.

Environmentally deterministic theories that explain Europe as "superior" to the rest of the world because of the climate and location of the region ignore the fact that for thousands of years, the most technologically advanced civilizations were not in Europe. The hearths of the agricultural and urban revolutions and the hearths of all of the world's major religions were in North Africa, Southwest Asia, Southeast Asia, and East Asia, not Europe.

Chipping away at deterministic explanations helped move the geographic study of the relationships between human society and the environment in different directions. Everyone agrees that the natural environment affects human activity in some ways, but people are the decision makers and the modifiers—not just the slaves of environmental forces. People, motivated primarily by cultural traits, economics, and politics, shape environments, constantly altering the landscape and impacting environmental systems.

Possibilism

In response to environmental determinism, geographers argued that the natural environment merely serves to limit the range of choices available to a culture. The choices that a society makes depend on what its members need and on what technology is available to them. Geographers called this doctrine **possibilism**.

Even possibilism, however, has its limitations, partly because it encourages a line of inquiry that starts with the physical environment and asks what it allows. Human cultures, however, frequently push the boundaries of what is "environmentally possible" through their own ideas and ingenuity, and advances in technology. In the interconnected, technologically dependent world, it is possible to transcend many of the limitations imposed by the natural environment.

Today, much research in human geography focuses on how and why humans have altered their environment, and on the sustainability of their practices. In the process, the interest in **cultural ecology**, an area of inquiry concerned with culture as a system of adaptation to and alteration of environment, has been supplemented by interest in **political ecology**, an area of inquiry fundamentally concerned with the environmental consequences of dominant political-economic arrangements and understandings (see Chapter 13). The fundamental point is that human societies are diverse and the human will is too powerful to be determined by environment.

Today's Human Geography

Human geography today seeks to make sense of the spatial organization of humanity and human institutions on Earth, the character of the places and regions created by people, and the relationships between humans and the physical environment. Human geography encompasses many subdisciplines, including political geography, economic geography, population geography, and urban geography. Human geography also encompasses cultural geography, which incorporates a concern with culture traits such as religion, language, and ethnicity.

Cultural geography is both part of human geography and also its own approach to all aspects of human geography. Cultural geography looks at the ways culture is implicated in the full spectrum of topics addressed in human geography. As such, cultural geography can be seen as a perspective on human geography as much as a component of it.

To appreciate more fully the vast topics researched by human geographers, we can examine the multitude of careers human geographers pursue. Human geographers have varying titles: location analyst, urban planner, diplomat, remote sensing analyst, geographic information scientist, area specialist, travel consultant, political analyst, intelligence officer, cartographer, educator, soil scientist, transportation planner, park ranger, and environmental consultant. All of these careers and more are open to geographers because each of these fields is grounded in the understanding of places and is advanced through spatial analysis.

Choose a geographic concept introduced in this chapter. Think about something that is of personal interest to you (music, literature, politics, science, sports), and consider how your chosen field could be studied from a geographical perspective. Think about space, landscape, and place. Write a geographic question that could be the foundation for a geographic study of the subject you have chosen.

Summary

Our study of human geography will analyze people and places and explain how they interact across space and time to create our world. Chapters 2 and 3 lay the basis for our study of human geography by looking at where people live. Chapters 4–7 focus on aspects of culture and how people use culture and identity to make sense of themselves in their world. The remaining chapters examine how people have created a world in which they function economically, politically, and socially, and how their activities in those realms recreate themselves and their world.

Geographic Concepts

human geography	accessibility	functional region
globalization	connectivity	perceptual region
physical geography	landscape	culture
spatial	cultural landscape	culture trait
spatial distribution	sequent occupance	culture complex
pattern	cartography	cultural hearth
medical geography	reference maps	independent invention
pandemic	thematic maps	diffusion
epidemic	absolute location	time-distance decay
spatial perspective	global positioning system	cultural barrier
five themes	geocaching	expansion diffusion
location	relative location	hierarchical diffusion
location theory	mental map	contagious diffusion
human-environment	activity space	stimulus diffusion
region	terra incognita	relocation diffusion
place	generalized maps	geographic concept
sense of place	remote sensing	environmental
perception of place	geographic information	determinism
movement	systems	possibilism
spatial interaction	rescale	cultural ecology
distance	formal region	political ecology

Learn More Online

About Careers in Geography
www.aag.org/cs/careerswww.bls.gov/opub/ooq/2005/spring/art01.pdf

About Geocaching
www.geocaching.org

About Globalization and Geography
www.lut.ac.uk/gawc/rb/rb40.html

About John Snow and His Work on Cholera
http://www.ph.ucla.edu/epi/snow.html

About the State of Food Insecurity in the World
www.fao.org

About World Hunger
www.wfp.org

About Dengue in Brazil and the World Cup
www.elsevier.com/connect/scientists-predict-dengue-fever-risk-during-world-cup-in-brazil

Watch It Online

About Globalization
www.learner.org/resources/series180.html#program_descriptions
click on Video On Demand for "One Earth, Many Scales"

POPULATION AND HEALTH

Basic Infrastructure

The words wafted in the air as my colleague and I took a minute to process them. We were in Shanghai, China, visiting with a Chinese student who had spent a semester at our small college in a town of 26,000 in rural South Dakota. My colleague had asked the student what he missed most about our small town of Aberdeen. He replied without hesitating, "Basic infrastructure."

I thought about brand-new subway lines in Shanghai and Beijing, new airports throughout China, and high-speed trains being built to connect China's cities. I visualized the miles of gleaming new concrete we had driven on that afternoon on the ring highway on the outskirts of Shanghai (Fig. 2.1) and the empty fields where houses or other buildings had been leveled to make room for new high-density housing, more concrete, and more infrastructure. Shanghai's metro system only dates to 1995. Shanghai now has the most extensive metro system on Earth—a system capable of transporting 5 million people a day. I

© Erin H. Fouberg

▪ Figure 2.1
Shanghai, China. Air pollution fills the sky above a new transit center and highway interchange. The U.S. Department of State collects its own data and has its own air quality measurement system to inform Americans living in China about unhealthy air quality in major Chinese cities.

thought about the lack of public transportation in my small town. I remembered that in 2010, China made a commitment to spend an additional $1 trillion on urban infrastructure by 2015. I considered the words United States President Barack Obama used as he described, enviously, the infrastructure in China, "their ports, their train systems their airports are all vastly superior to us now."

I looked at the student and said, "Basic infrastructure? But you have better subway lines, high-speed railroads, roads, and airports than we do in the States." "Yes," he said, "But I don't have hot water." He also doesn't have clean drinking water coming from the tap.

A 2010 report in *Foreign Policy* agreed: "China's biggest urban challenge may be water; already, it has little to spare. Some 70 percent of water use today traces back to agriculture, but demand from urban consumers and commercial enterprise is on the rise. Even if the sheer amount of water isn't the problem, location will be; the country will need to spend more than $120 billion on water systems in the coming years to transport, store, and manage supplies." A graduate student in Beijing also pointed out the water problem in China's cities. Her dormitory houses about 1000 students, but they all must leave the building and walk to a central facility to shower, and she reported that they are only allowed to shower between 2 and 4 PM or between 9 and 11 PM.

China's population of 1.36 billion people has been migrating to cities in droves since economic reforms began in 1978. In 2011, the population of the world hit 7 billion people, with rising populations in China and India accounting for 40 percent of the population growth. China has undergone incredibly rapid expansion in its mining and manufacturing sectors, resulting in economic growth rates that have approached 10 percent in some years. But rapid economic growth took its toll on water quality in China, exacerbating water shortages in the country.

Providing services for 1.36 billion people is no small feat. Even though demographers now predict China's population will stabilize at 1.4 billion by 2025 and begin to decline after that, shifts in the composition of the population will continue to challenge the provision of basic infrastructure to the country's people.

Southern, coastal China has a moist climate, much like the southeastern United States, but the climate in northern China is drier. With only 7 percent of the world's fresh water supply, China faces an uphill battle in its efforts to provide water resources for its expanding population. This challenge is compounded by the fact that southern China has 80 percent of the country's water (*Foreign Policy*, 2011). To remedy the imbalance, China is now building a $60 billion canal system called the South–North Water Transfer Project that will include three different routes to divert water from the Yangtze River in southern China to the cities in the north (Fig. 2.2).

In this chapter, we examine the distribution of the world's population at several scales in order to understand where people live and why they live where they do. We also look at global population growth rates, noting that they vary widely across our planet. Even as population growth rates in wealthier parts of the world often fall below zero, the population of poorer regions continues to expand, in some countries at rates far above the global average. No discussion of population would be complete without considering the social conditions prevailing across the world: Health, well-being, and population growth tend to be closely related. Governments play a role in shaping these factors—an issue we explore at the end of the chapter.

Frederic J. Brown/AFP/Getty Images

■■ Figure 2.2
Yixian, China. This canal is part of the South–North Water Transfer Project. The $60 billion project will divert water from southern China to northern China along three different routes.

Key Questions FOR CHAPTER 2

1. Where in the world do people live and why?
2. Why do populations rise or fall in particular places?
3. Why does population composition matter?
4. How does the geography of health influence population dynamics?
5. How do governments affect population change?

WHERE IN THE WORLD DO PEOPLE LIVE AND WHY?

When geographers study population, they focus on the variability of demographic features and factors across space. *Demography* is the study of population in general perspective. Population geographers work in tandem with demographers, seeking answers to the problems posed by these variations. The concept of scale is crucial to studies of population because population dynamics that are evident at small scales (cities, intrastate regions) cannot necessarily be seen when one looks at the country or world regional scale. The reverse is true as well.

Demographers report the **population density** of a country as a measure of total population relative to land size (Fig. 2.3). Population density assumes an even distribution of people over the land. The United States, for example, with a territory of 5,692,815 square miles or 9,161,966 square kilometers (excluding the surfaces of lakes and ponds and coastal waters up to three nautical miles from shore) had a population of 316 million in 2013. This yields an average population density for the United States of just over 83 per square mile (33 per sq km). This density figure is also known as the country's **arithmetic population density**, and in a very general way it emphasizes the contrasts between the United States and such countries as Bangladesh (2817 per sq mi or 1087 per sq km), the Netherlands (1046 per sq mi or 404 per sq km), and Japan (872 per sq mi or 337 per sq km).

No country has an evenly distributed population, and arithmetic population figures do not reflect the emptiness of most of Alaska and the sparseness of population in much of

FIELD NOTE

"An overpass across one of Yangon's busy streets provides a good perspective on the press of humanity in lowland Southeast Asia. Whether in urban areas or on small back roads in the countryside, people are everywhere—young and old, fit and infirm. When population densities are high in areas of poverty and unsophisticated infrastructure, vulnerabilities to natural hazards can be particularly great. This phenomenon became stunningly evident in 2008 when a tropical cyclone devastated a significant swath of the Irrawaddy Delta south of Yangon, killing some 100,000 people and leaving millions homeless."

© Alexander B. Murphy

Figure 2.3
Yangon, Myanmar (Burma).

FIELD NOTE

"The contrasting character of the Egyptian landscape could not be more striking. Along the Nile River, the landscape is one of green fields, scattered trees, and modest houses, as along this stretch of the river's west bank near Luxor (Fig. 2.4A). But anytime I wander away from the river, brown, wind-sculpted sand dominates the scene as far as the eye can see (Fig. 2.4B). Where people live and what they do is not just a product of culture; it is shaped by the physical environment as well."

■ **Figure 2.4A**
Luxor, Egypt.

■ **Figure 2.4B**
Luxor, Egypt.

the West. In other cases, it is actually quite misleading. Egypt, with a population of 84.7 million in 2013, has a seemingly moderate arithmetic population density of 85 per square kilometer (220 per sq mi). Egypt's territory of 995,450 square kilometers (384,345 sq mi) however, is mostly desert, and the vast majority of the population is crowded into the valley and delta of the Nile River. An estimated 98 percent of all Egyptians live on just 3 percent of the country's land, so the arithmetic population density figure is meaningless in this case (Fig. 2.4A, B).

Physiologic Population Density

A more insightful index of population density relates the total population of a country or region to the area of *arable* (farmable) land it contains. This approach yields a **physiologic population density figure**, which specifies the number of people per unit area of agriculturally productive land. Take again the case of Egypt. Although millions of people live in its great cities (Cairo and Alexandria) and smaller urban centers, the irrigated farmland is densely peopled as well. When we measure the entire population of Egypt relative to the arable land in the country, the resulting physiologic density figure for Egypt in the year 2013 is 2628 per square kilometer (6808 per sq mi). This number is far more reflective of Egypt's population pressure, and it continues to rise rapidly despite Egypt's efforts to expand its irrigated farmlands.

Appendix B (available at www.wiley.com/college/fouberg) provides complete data on both arithmetic and physiologic population densities, and some of the data stand out markedly. Mountainous Switzerland's physiologic density is 10 times as high as its arithmetic density because only 1 out of every 10 acres in Switzerland is arable. Ukraine's population is 45,500,000 and its arithmetic density (population per sq km) is 75 (195 per sq mi). Ukraine has vast farmlands, which make its physiologic density 145 people per square kilometer of arable land (368 per sq mi). The difference in arithmetic density and physiologic density for a single country reveals the proportion of arable land to all land. In the case of Ukraine, the physiologic density is 1.68 times as high as the arithmetic density because 1 out of every 1.68 acres of land in Ukraine is arable.

In Appendix B, the countries and territories of Middle America and the Caribbean stand out as having high physiologic densities compared to the moderate physiologic densities for South America. India's physiologic density is the lowest in South Asia despite its huge population. Both China and India have populations well over 1 billion, but according to the physiologic density, India has much more arable land per person than China.

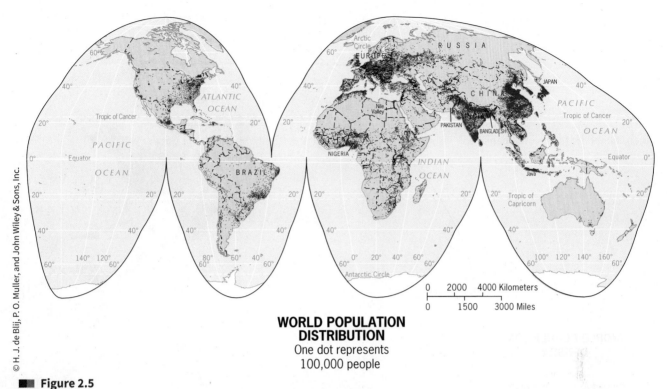

© H. J. de Blij, P. O. Muller, and John Wiley & Sons, Inc.

WORLD POPULATION DISTRIBUTION
One dot represents
100,000 people

■■ **Figure 2.5**
World Population Distribution.   Practice reading a thematic map by asking where people are most concentrated. The largest clusters of people globally are in East Asia, South Asia, and Europe. Throughout the world, people are concentrated along coastlines, major rivers, and in cities.

Population Distribution

People are not distributed evenly across the world or within a country. One-third of the world's population lives in China and India. Yet, each country has large expanses of land (the Himalayas in India and a vast interior desert in China) where people are absent or sparsely distributed. In addition to studying population densities, geographers study **population distributions**—the arrangement of people on the Earth's surface. Geographers often represent population distributions using **dot maps**, with each dot representing a certain number of people. At the local scale, a dot map of population can show each individual farm in a sparsely populated rural area. At the global scale, the data are much more generalized (e.g., Fig. 2.5). In the following section of this chapter, we study world population distribution and density.

World Population Distribution and Density

From humanity's beginnings, people have been unevenly distributed across the land. Today, contrasts between crowded countrysides and bustling cities on the one hand and empty areas on the other hand have only intensified. Historically, people tended to congregate in places where they could grow food—making for a high correlation between arable land and population density. Cities generally began in agricultural areas, and for most of history, people lived closest to the most agriculturally productive areas. In recent times, advances in agricultural technology and in the transportation of agricultural goods have begun to change this pattern.

At the global scale, where one dot on a map represents 100,000 people, three major clusters of population jump out (Fig. 2.5). Each of the three largest population clusters is on the Eurasian (Europe and Asia combined) landmass. The fourth largest is in North America.

EAST ASIA

Although the distribution map (Fig. 2.5) requires no color contrasts, Figure 2.6 depicts population density through shading: The darker the color, the larger the number of people per unit area. The most extensive area of dark shading lies in East Asia, primarily in China but also in Korea and Japan. Almost one-quarter of the world's population is concentrated here—over 1.36 billion people in China alone.

In addition to high population density in China's large cities, ribbons of high population density extend into the interior along the Yangtze and Yellow River valleys. Farmers along China's major river valleys produce crops of wheat and rice to feed not only themselves, but also the population of major Chinese cities such as Shanghai and Beijing.

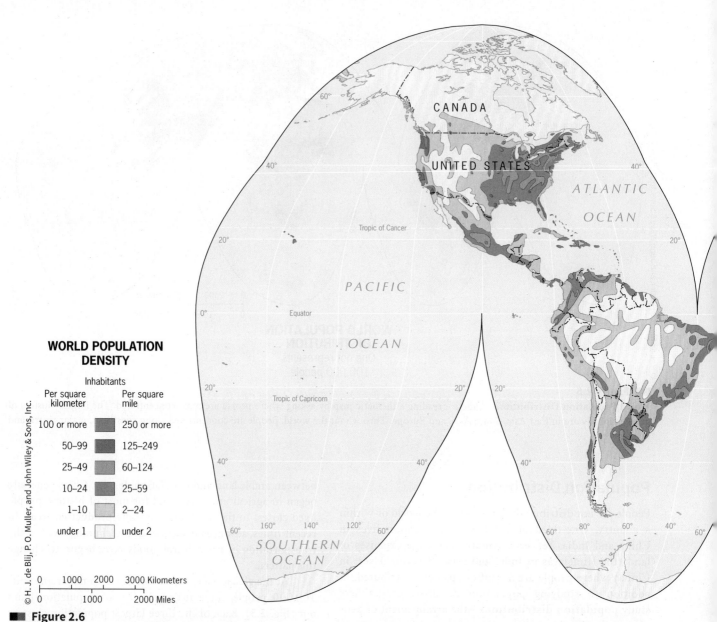

WORLD POPULATION DENSITY

Inhabitants

Per square kilometer	Per square mile
100 or more	250 or more
50–99	125–249
25–49	60–124
10–24	25–59
1–10	2–24
under 1	under 2

0   1000   2000   3000 Kilometers
0   1000   2000 Miles

© H. J. de Blij, P. O. Muller, and John Wiley & Sons, Inc.

■ **Figure 2.6**

World Population Density. Classifying population density into levels and using colors to represent levels of density, this map allows comparison between areas. The common color among East Asia, South Asia, and Europe shows these regions have similar population densities. The density level of the east coast of the United States is similar to France and other areas in blue on the map. The sparse density of much of Canada is similar to interior Australia, western China, the interior of South America, and the Sahara in Africa.

SOUTH ASIA

The second major population concentration also lies in Asia and is similar in many ways to that of East Asia. At the heart of this cluster of more than 1.5 billion people lies India. The concentration extends into Pakistan and Bangladesh and onto the island of Sri Lanka. Here, people again cluster in major cities, on the coasts, and in major river basins, such as those created by the Ganges and Indus. The South Asia population cluster is growing more rapidly than the others as a result of China's declining total fertility rate (TFR). Demographers predict that by 2030, 1 out of 6 people in the world will live in India.

Two physical geography barriers create the boundaries of the South Asia population cluster: the Himalaya Mountains to the north and the mountains west of the Indus River Valley in Pakistan. This is a confined region with a rapidly growing population. As in East Asia, the overwhelming majority of the people here are farmers, but in South Asia the pressure on the land is even greater. In Bangladesh, over 156 million people, almost all of them farmers, are crowded into an area about the size of Iowa. Over large parts of Bangladesh the rural population density is between 3000 and 5000 people per square mile. By comparison, in 2010 the population of Iowa was just

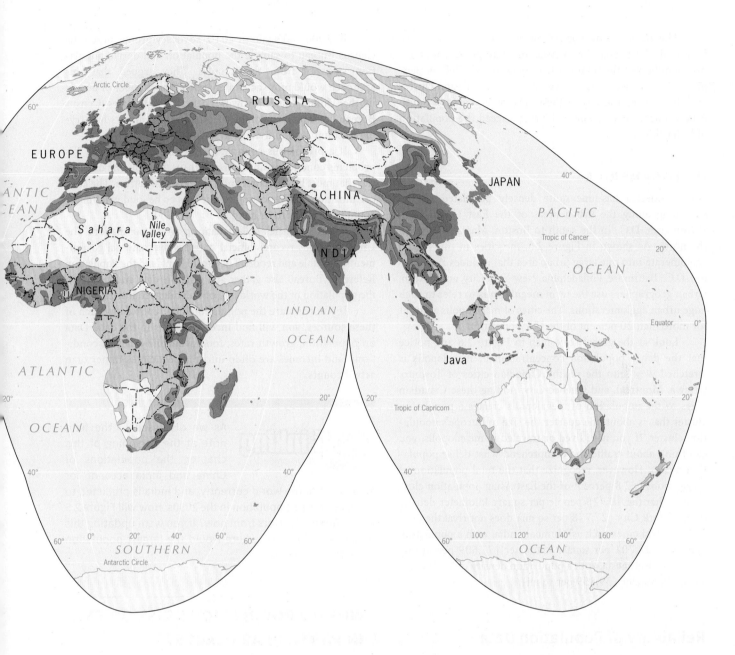

about 3 million people, and the rural population density was 53 people per square mile.

EUROPE

An axis of dense population extends from Ireland and the United Kingdom into Russia and includes large parts of Germany, Poland, Ukraine, and Belarus. It also includes the Netherlands and Belgium, parts of France, and northern Italy. This European cluster contains over 715 million inhabitants, less than half the population of the South Asia cluster. A comparison of the population and physical maps indicates that in Europe terrain and environment are not as closely related to population distribution as they are in East and South Asia. For example, note the lengthy extension in Figure 2.5, which protrudes far into Russia. Unlike the Asian extensions, which reflect fertile river valleys, the European extension reflects the orientation of Europe's coal fields. If you look closely at the physical map, you will note that comparatively dense population occurs even in mountainous, rugged country, such as the boundary zone between Poland and its neighbors to the south. A much greater correspondence exists between coastal and river lowlands and high population density in Asia than in Europe generally.

Another contrast can be seen in the number of Europeans who live in cities and towns. The European population cluster includes numerous cities and towns, many of which developed as a result of the Industrial Revolution. In Germany, 73 percent of the people live in urban places; in the United Kingdom, 80 percent; and in France, 78 percent. With so many people concentrated in the cities, the rural countryside is more open and sparsely populated than in East and South Asia (where only about 45 percent of the people reside in cities and towns).

The three major population concentrations we have discussed—East Asia, South Asia, and Europe—account for over 4 billion of the total world population of 7 billion people. Nowhere else on the globe is there a population cluster even half as great as any of these. The populations of South America and Africa combined barely exceed the population of India alone.

NORTH AMERICA

North America has one quite densely populated region, stretching along the urban areas of the East Coast, from Washington, D.C., in the south to Boston, Massachusetts, in the north. As shown in Figure 2.5, the cities in this region agglomerate into one large urban area that includes Washington, D.C., Baltimore, Philadelphia, New York City, and Boston. Urban geographers use the term **megalopolis** to refer to such huge urban agglomerations. The cities of megalopolis account for more than 20 percent of the U.S. population.

Look at the global-scale map in Figure 2.6 and notice that the dense population concentration of megalopolis is stretched west into the nearby Canadian cities of Toronto, Ottawa, Montreal, and Quebec City. Adding these Canadian cities to the population of megalopolis creates a population cluster that is about one quarter the size of Europe's population cluster. If you have lived or traveled in megalopolis, you can think about traffic and comprehend what dense population means. However, recognize that the total population of megalopolis is 2.8 percent of the East Asian population cluster and that the 10,725 people per square kilometer density of New York City (27,778 per sq mi) does not rival the density in world cities such as Mumbai, India, with a population density of 28,701 per square kilometer (77,609 per sq mi) or Jakarta, Indonesia, with a population density of 15,398 per square kilometer (39,859 per sq mi).

Reliability of Population Data

When the United States planned and conducted its 2010 population **census**, the government ran advertisements on television and sent mailings encouraging every person in the country to be counted. State and city governments also recognized the importance of having their citizens counted in order to gain more federal dollars in per capita outlays because much federal government funding depends on population data. If the population of a disadvantaged group is undercounted, it translates into a loss of dollars for city governments that rely on federal government funding to pay for social services to disadvantaged groups. As a result, advocates for disadvantaged groups encourage people to fill out their census forms; they are concerned that the people already in disadvantaged groups suffer when they are undercounted in the census. Being undercounted also translates into less government representation because the number of congressional seats allotted to each state is based on the census counts.

In 2000 and again in 2010, advocacy groups urged the Census Bureau to sample the population and derive population statistics from the samples. They argued that this approach would more accurately reflect the number of people in the United States. However, the United States Census Bureau continued to conduct its census as it always has, trying to count each individual in its borders.

If a prosperous country such as the United States has problems conducting an accurate census, imagine the difficulties that must be overcome in less well-off countries. The cost, organization, and reporting of a census go beyond what many countries can afford or handle.

Several agencies collect data on world population. The United Nations records official statistics that national governments assemble and report. The World Bank and the Population Reference Bureau also gather and generate data and report on the population of the world and of individual countries.

If you compare the population data reported by each of these sources, you will find inconsistencies in the data. Data on population, growth rates, food availability, health conditions, and incomes are often informed estimates rather than actual counts.

 As we discussed in the field note at the beginning of this chapter, the populations of China and India account for 40 percent of the world currently, and India is predicted to outpace China's population in the 2030s. How will Figure 2.5 look different 50 years from now? If you were updating this textbook in 50 years, where would the largest population clusters in the world be?

WHY DO POPULATIONS RISE OR FALL IN PARTICULAR PLACES?

In the late 1960s, alarms sounded throughout the world with the publication of Paul Ehrlich's *The Population Bomb*. Ehrlich and others warned that the world's population was increasing too quickly—and was outpacing our food production! We can trace alarms over the burgeoning world population back to 1798, when British economist Thomas Malthus published *An Essay on the Principles of Population*. In this work Malthus warned that the world's population was increasing faster than the food supplies needed to sustain it. His reasoning was that food supplies grew *linearly*, adding acreage and crops incrementally by year, whereas population grew *exponentially*, compounding on the year before. From 1803 to 1826, Malthus issued revised editions of his essay and responded vigorously to a barrage of criticism.

Malthus's predictions assumed that food production is confined spatially, that what people can eat within a country depends on what is grown in the country. We now know his assumption does not hold true; countries are not closed systems. Malthus did not foresee how globalization would aid the exchange of agricultural goods across the world. Mercantilism, colonialism, and capitalism brought interaction among the Americas, Europe, Africa, Asia, and the Pacific. Through global interaction, new agricultural methods developed, and commodities and livestock diffused across oceans. In the 1700s, farmers in Ireland grew dependent on a South American crop that was well suited for its rocky soils: the potato. Today, wealthier countries that lack arable land, such as Norway, can import the majority of their food, circumventing the limitations on food production there.

Malthus also assumed that the growth of food production was linear, but food production has grown exponentially as the acreage under cultivation expands, mechanization of agricultural production diffuses, improved strains of seed are developed, and more fertilizers are used. In the twenty-first century, bioengineering continues to bring new hybrids, genetically modified organisms, and countless herbicides and pesticides that enable exponential growth in food production.

Because of the environmental costs of modern farming techniques, serious questions have arisen about future limitations on the exponential expansion of agriculture. However, that is not why Malthus's ideas continue to attract followers. Instead, most neo-Malthusians focus on the continuing rise in the world's population, which they see as a direct cause of human suffering. Although many demographers predict the world's population will stabilize later in the twenty-first century, neo-Malthusians argue that overpopulation is a real problem that must be addressed now.

Population Growth at World, Regional, National, and Local Scales

Population change in one place is often affected by developments in neighboring places, but to understand the population picture, it is useful to start by looking at the demographic characteristics of individual places. One basic demographic indicator is the **natural increase** of the population in a given place—calculated by subtracting the total number of deaths from the total number of births. Focusing solely on natural increase, however, misses two other key pieces of the demographic picture: immigration, which along with births adds to the total population, and emigration (outmigration), which along with deaths reduces the total population. Using these four components, we can calculate demographic change within a territory.

Figure 2.7 shows natural increase rates by country but does not take into account emigration and immigration. Other maps and tables of population growth you may see

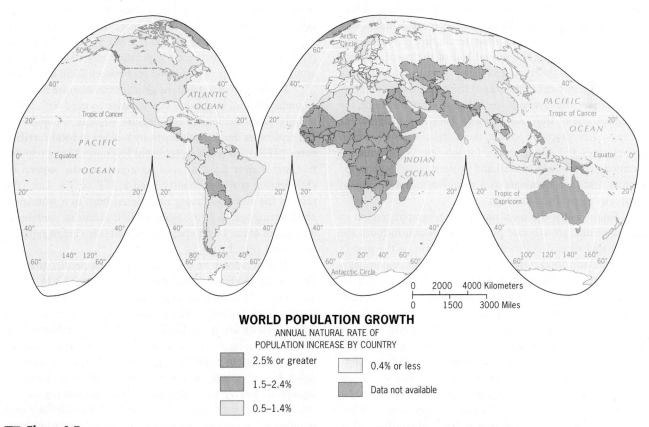

WORLD POPULATION GROWTH

ANNUAL NATURAL RATE OF
POPULATION INCREASE BY COUNTRY

- 2.5% or greater
- 1.5–2.4%
- 0.5–1.4%
- 0.4% or less
- Data not available

■■■ **Figure 2.7**
World Population Growth, 2012.   Annual natural rate of population increase by country. Population growth rates in Subsaharan Africa remain relatively high, and population growth rates in Europe and Russia remain relatively low.   *Data from*: Population Reference Bureau, 2012.

consider emigration and immigration. Statistics for each population trait can be calculated globally, by region, by country, or even by smaller locale—each telling a somewhat different story. When studying population data across scales and across the world, we must constantly remind ourselves of exactly what is being calculated and what places are being represented. Otherwise, many of the statistics we read will appear to be contradictory.

POPULATION GROWTH AT THE REGIONAL AND NATIONAL SCALES

The world map of population growth rates (Fig. 2.7), displayed by country, confirms the wide range of natural increases in different geographic regions. These variations have existed as long as records have been kept: Countries and regions go through stages of expansion and decline at varying times. In the mid-twentieth century, the population of the former Soviet Union was growing vigorously. Thirty years ago, India's population was growing at nearly 3.0 percent, more than most African countries; then India's growth rate fell below that of Subsaharan Africa. Today, Africa's rate of natural increase still is higher than India's (2.6 percent to 1.5 percent), but parts of Subsaharan Africa are still reeling from the impact of the AIDS epidemic, which killed millions, orphaned children, reduced life expectancies, and curtailed growth rates.

The map also reveals continuing high growth rates in Muslim countries of North Africa and Southwest Asia, including Sudan (2.6 percent), Yemen (2.7 percent), Afghanistan (2.8 percent) and the Palestinian territories (2.9 percent). For some time during the second half of the twentieth century, countries in this region saw their growth rates increase even as those in most of the rest of the world were declining. But more recently several of the fast-growing populations, for example, those of Iran and Morocco, have shown significant declines. Demographers point to the correlation between high growth rates and opportunities for women: Where cultural traditions restrict educational and professional prospects for women, and men dominate as a matter of custom, rates of natural increase tend to be high.

South Asia is the most important geographic region in the population growth rate picture. The region includes the country that appears destined to overtake China as the world's most populous: India. Only one country in this region has a growth rate lower than the world average: Sri Lanka. But Sri Lanka's total population is only 20.8 million, whereas the fast-growing countries, Pakistan and Bangladesh, have a combined population exceeding 347 million. India, as the map shows, is still growing at a rate well above the world average. The situation in East Asia, the world's most populous region, is different. China's official rate of natural growth has fallen well below 1.0 percent (0.5 in 2010), and Japan's population is no longer growing. Southeast Asia's natural growth rates remain higher, but this region's total population is much lower than either East or South Asia; key countries, such as Indonesia, Thailand, and Vietnam, have declining growth rates.

South America, whose natural population growth rates were alarmingly high just a generation ago, is experiencing significant reductions in their growth rates. The region as a whole is still growing at 1.1 percent, but Brazil's population growth rate, for example, has declined from 2.9 percent in the mid-1960s to 0.9 percent today. And the populations of Argentina, Chile, and Uruguay are growing at rates well below the world average.

As Figure 2.7 shows, the slowest growing countries—including those with declining rates of natural population increase—lie in the economically wealthier areas of the world extending from the United States and Canada across Europe and Japan. In the Southern Hemisphere, Australia, New Zealand, and Uruguay are in this category. Wealth is not the only reason for negative population growth rates. Russia's population is declining because of the social dislocation that took place in the wake of the collapse of the Soviet Union: Deteriorating health conditions, high rates of alcoholism and drug use, and economic problems combined to shorten life expectancies (especially among males) and to lower birth rates. In recent years, Russia's economy has improved, but its birth rate has remained low. Similar problems afflict Ukraine and Kazakhstan, two of Russia's neighbors, which also show slow or negative growth.

Between 1900 and 2000, the world's population rose from 1.6 billion people to 6.1 billion, and in 2011, it reached 7 billion. This growth is not simply a result of women having more children. Instead, the last century of population growth saw greatly expanded life expectancies. In 1900, global life expectancy was 30 years; by 2000, it was 65 years. Demographers now predict that world population may well stabilize at around 10 billion people somewhere between 2050 and 2100.

Predictions of a stabilized global population are based on a combination of longer life expectancies coupled with lower fertility rates. Demographers measure whether a population can replace its deaths with births by looking at **total fertility rates** (TFRs). To reach replacement levels—to keep a population stable over time without immigration—the women of childbearing age in a country need a TFR of 2.1. The TFR reports the average number of children born to a woman of childbearing age. In 2000, more than 60 countries, containing 45 percent of the world's population, had fallen below replacement level (Fig. 2.8).

Demographers at the United Nations predict that the TFR of the combined world will fall to around 2.2 by 2050. The world TFR combines regions including Europe, where fertility levels are low (Fig. 2.8), and regions including Africa, where fertility levels are high. In 2013, the worldwide TFR was 2.5, ranging from 1.2 in Bosnia-Herzegovina to 7.6 in Niger. Predicting population growth is difficult because so much depends on the decisions made by women of childbearing age. Demographers and population geographers agree that two major current trends will influence how much the world population continues to grow: the aging population of Europe, China, and Japan, and the declining fertility rate in many developing countries, including Brazil and Iran.

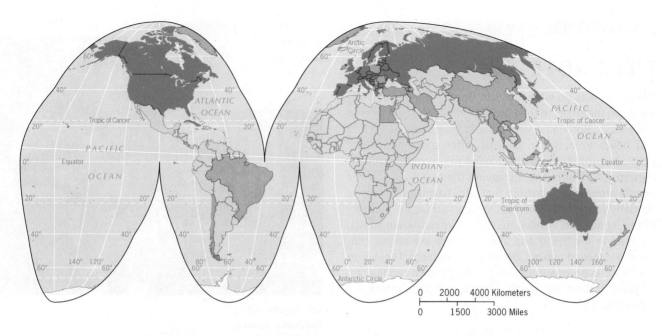

COUNTRIES WITH TOTAL FERTILITY RATE BELOW REPLACEMENT LEVEL

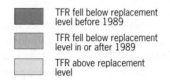

TFR fell below replacement level before 1989

TFR fell below replacement level in or after 1989

TFR above replacement level

■ **Figure 2.8**
Year That Total Fertility Rate (TFR) Among Women Fell Below Replacement Levels.   The wealthiest parts of the world were the first to see TFRs fall below replacement levels.   *Data from*: World Bank, World Development Indicators, 2012.

Both the aging population of developed countries and the declining fertility rates in developing countries lead to predictions that the global population will continue to grow but at a lower rate. In wealthier countries, more women are choosing to stay in school, work on their careers, and marry later, delaying childbirth. The impact of the aging population of Europe can be seen in its **old-age dependency ratio**, which reports the relationship between the number of people over the age of 65 and the working-age population between 15 and 64. Europe had 24 old-age dependents for every 100 working-age people in 2010, and that figure is expected to rise to 47 by 2050. The old-age dependency ratio for Africa, by contrast, was 6 in 2010. For that continent, the challenge is a high **child dependency ratio** (74 in 2010 compared to just 23 in Europe).

An aging population requires substantial social adjustments. Older people retire and eventually suffer health problems, so they need pensions and medical care. The younger workers in the population must work in order to provide the tax revenues that enable the state to pay for these services. As the proportion of older people in a country increases, the proportion of younger people decreases. Thus, fewer young workers are providing tax revenues to support programs for more retired people. To change the age distribution of an aging country and provide more taxpayers, the only answer is immigration: influxes of younger workers to do the work locals are unable or unwilling to do.

What will happen when a country resists immigration despite an aging population? Over the next half-century, Japan will be an interesting case study. Japan's population is no longer growing, and it is projected that the Japanese population will decline as it ages. The population fell from a peak of 127.84 million in 2004 to 127.3 million in 2013. Japan predicts its population will fall to around 100 million by 2050, a loss of 20 percent of its current population. Japan was a closed society for hundreds of years, and even today the Japanese government discourages immigration. More than 98 percent of the country's population is Japanese, according to government statistics. In August 1999, the British newspaper *The Guardian* reported that the Japanese government's efforts to maintain the homogeneity of the population are often "lauded domestically as a reason for the country's low crime rate" and strong industrial economy. In developing countries, a combination of government and nongovernment organizational programs encourage women to have fewer children. Some women are also choosing to have fewer children because of economic and social uncertainty. Today, TFRs are falling almost everywhere on Earth, in large part because of family planning. In some countries, fertility rates are declining dramatically. Kenya's TFR is now

FIELD NOTE

"My mind was on wine. I was in Bordeaux, France, walking down the street to the Bordeaux Wines Museum (Musée des Vins de Bordeaux) with a friend from the city. Having just flown from Dakar, Senegal, after spending several weeks in Subsaharan Africa, I found my current surroundings strikingly different. Observing the buildings and the people around me, I noticed that after having been among so many young children in Subsaharan Africa, the majority of the inhabitants I encountered in Bordeaux were adults. I turned to my friend and asked, 'Where are all the children?' He looked around, pointed, and replied, 'There goes one now!' In Bordeaux, in Paris, in all of France and the rest of Europe, there are fewer children and populations are aging (Fig. 2.9)."

© H. J. de Blij

■ **Figure 2.9**
Bordeaux, France.

down to 4.5; China's fell from 6.1 to 1.75 in just 35 years and in 2010 dropped to 1.5, which it maintains today. Once the government of Iran began to allow family planning, the TFR fell from 6.8 in 1980 to 1.9 in 2013.

At one time a low TFR seemed to be a desirable national objective, something that all governments would surely want. However, long-term economic implications and demographic projections gave many governments pause. Countries need a young, vigorous, working-age population who work and pay taxes to support the long-term needs of an aging population. When governments saw their population growth rates decline sharply, many took countermeasures. China softened its one-child only policy; Sweden, Russia, and other European countries provided financial incentives like long maternity leaves and state-paid daycare to prospective mothers; and even the Japanese found themselves in a national debate over family size and immigration. Still, such programs and debates have so far had limited success in encouraging sustained population growth.

How can the worldwide population continue to increase when so many countries are experiencing low TFRs and population decline? Despite declining population growth rates and even negative growth rates (growth rates below 0.0) in a number of the world's countries, the global population continues to rise. The worldwide TFR was 2.5 in 2013, above the replacement level of 2.1. Although the population bomb Ehrlich warned of is no longer ticking at the same rapid pace, the worldwide population continues to grow. The low TFRs and low population growth rates enumerated in this chapter are dwarfed by continued additions to the population in

countries where growth rates are still relatively high, such as India, Indonesia, Bangladesh, Pakistan, and Nigeria.

One way to explain the growth rate in world population is to compare the population's rate of growth to its doubling time. Every rate of growth has a **doubling time**; for example, if you invested $100 at 10 percent, compounded annually

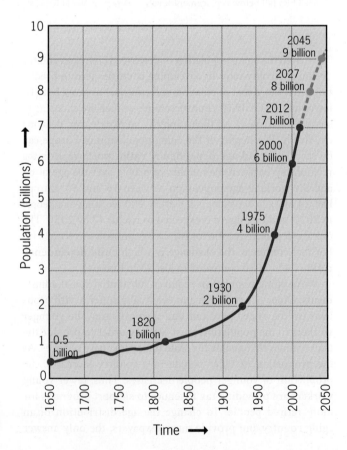

■ **Figure 2.10**
Population Growth, 1650 to 2050. The dashed line indicates one estimate of global population growth until 2050. *Data from*: United States Census Bureau, International Data Base, 2011.

(exponentially), it would take about seven years to double to $200, and then another seven years to become $400, and then another seven years to become $800. Therefore, when the growth rate is 10 percent, the doubling time is around seven years.

Two thousand years ago, the world's population was an estimated 250 million. More than 16 centuries passed before this total had doubled to 500 million, the estimated population in 1650. Just 170 years later, in 1820 (when Malthus was still writing), the population had doubled again, to 1 billion (Fig. 2.10). And barely more than a century after this, in 1930, it reached 2 billion. The doubling time was down to 100 years and dropping fast; the **population explosion** was in full gear. Only 45 years elapsed for the next doubling to take place, to 4 billion (1975). In the mid-1980s, doubling time was only 39 years. Since then, population policies designed to slow growth, including China's One Child Policy, have lengthened the word population's doubling time to 54 years.

For demographers and population geographers who study global population growth today, the concept of doubling time is losing much of its punch. With populations falling in many places, fears of global population doubling quickly are subsiding. Many indicators, such as the slowing of the doubling time, suggest that the worst may be over, that the explosive population growth of the twentieth century will be followed by a marked and accelerating slowdown during the twenty-first century. The global growth rate is now down to 1.4 percent, perhaps slightly lower. But today the world's population is 7 billion, yielding an increase in world population that still exceeds 80 million annually at this growth rate.

As a result of falling TFRs in both the developing and developed world, demographers no longer caution about doubling time. With women having fewer children, many demographers are predicting the world may reach **zero population growth** in the next 50 years. In fact, current predictions point to zero population growth globally by the end of the century, with population rising to 9.3 billion by 2050 and then leveling off to around 10 billion people.

No single factor can explain the variations shown in Figure 2.7. Economic prosperity as well as social dislocation reduce natural population growth rates. Economic well-being, associated with urbanization, higher levels of education, later marriage, family planning, and other factors, lowers population growth. In the table presented in Appendix B, compare the indices for natural population increase and the percentage of the population that is urbanized. In general, the higher the population's level of urbanization, the lower its natural increase. Cultural traditions also influence rates of population growth. Religion, for example, has a powerful impact on family planning and thus on growth rates, not only in Islamic countries but also in traditional Christian societies (such as the Philippines) and in Hindu-dominated communities (such as India).

POPULATION GROWTH WITHIN COUNTRIES

The information provided in Figure 2.7 is based on countrywide statistics. Significant demographic variations also occur *within* countries. Political geographers call countries states. Governments partition their countries into administrative units called States (United States), provinces (Canada), departments (France) or the like. In India, for example, States in the north record population growth rates far above the national average (Fig. 2.11).

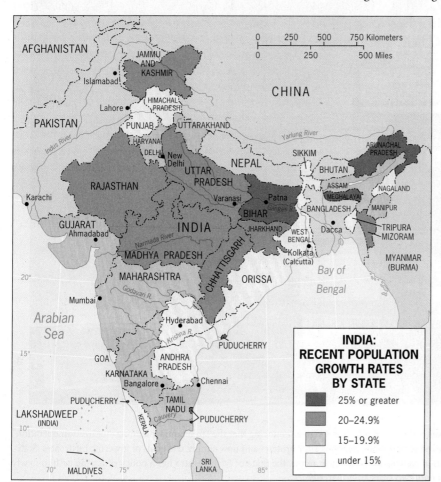

INDIA: RECENT POPULATION GROWTH RATES BY STATE

- 25% or greater
- 20–24.9%
- 15–19.9%
- under 15%

■ **Figure 2.11**
Population Growth Rates in India, 2001–2011. The agriculturally rich Ganges plain in northern India, the most densely populated part of the country, continues to have the highest growth rates. Population growth rates are lower in southern India, where women have higher literacy rates, better access to health care and birth control, and higher land ownership rates than in northern India. *Data from*: India Census Bureau, 2011.

But other States, in the west and southwest region, have populations that are growing much more slowly. Women in southern India have higher literacy rates, greater land ownership rates, better access to health care, and more access to birth control methods. All of these factors keep the growth rates lower in the south than the north of India.

In the 1950s, India became the first country in the world to institute a population planning program, before the fear of worldwide overpopulation and a global population bomb spread. In the 1960s, when census numbers revealed the extreme growth rates in the north, the Indian government instituted a national population planning program, encouraging States to join.

Despite the federal effort, rapid population growth continues, especially in the northern and eastern States. India is a federation of 28 States and 7 union territories, and the individual States differ greatly both culturally and politically. Social problems arose in some of the States where governments pursued the population planning campaign vigorously. During the 1970s, the Indian government began a policy of forced sterilization of any man with three or more children. The State of Maharashtra sterilized 3.7 million people before public opposition led to rioting, and the govern-

ment abandoned the program (Fig. 2.12). Other States also engaged in compulsory sterilization programs, with heavy social and political costs. Eventually, 22.5 million people were sterilized.

Federal sterilization programs have ended in India, but States are free to pursue their own family planning programs, including sterilization. In 2004, three districts in the State of Uttar Pradesh (India's most populous State with over 204 million people) instituted a policy of exchanging gun licenses for sterilization. The policy allowed for a shotgun license in exchange for the sterilization of two people and a revolver license in exchange for the sterilization of five people. Abuse began almost immediately, with wealthy landowners sterilizing their laborers in exchange for gun licenses. Uttar Pradesh now encourages sterilization with incentives including housing and food. Far more women than men have been sterilized. A 2008 survey of households found 19.5 percent of women had been sterilized by tubal ligations and only .3 percent of men had been sterilized by vasectomies in Uttar Pradesh.

Today, most Indian State governments are using advertising and persuasion to encourage families to have fewer children. Posters urging people to have small families are everywhere, and the government supports a network of

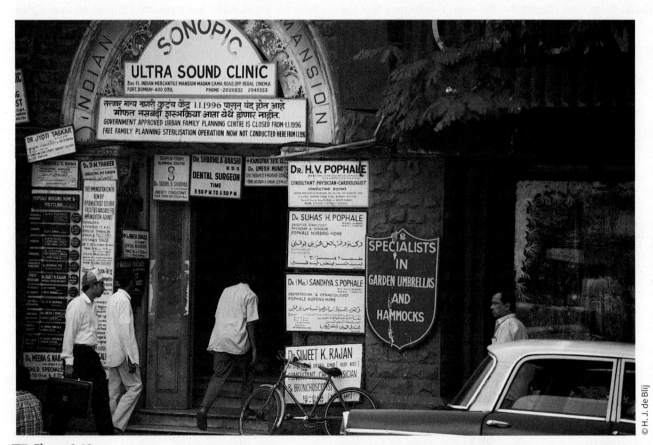

■■■ **Figure 2.12**

Maharashtra, India.   Above the entrance to a suite of medical offices is a sign announcing that the "free family planning sterilization operation" closed in 1996. The Indian government ended forced sterilization programs after protests and now simply sets goals of lowering birth rates. States in India are at liberty to create their own population control policies. For example, the State of Maharashtra has a policy of paying cash to newly married couples who delay having their first child until two years after marriage.

family planning clinics even in the remotest villages. The southern States continue to report the lowest growth rates, correlating with higher wealth and higher education levels as well as higher literacy rates of females in these States. The eastern and northern States, the poorer regions of India, continue to report the highest growth rates.

Our world map of growth rates is a global overview, a mere introduction to the complexities of the geography of population. The example of India demonstrates that what we see at the scale of a world map does not give us the complete story of what is happening within each country or region of the world. Both India and China have over 1 billion people, but as a result of the higher growth rates in India (1.64) and declining growth rates in China (.5), demographers predict India will become the most populated country in the world in 2030.

The Demographic Transition

The high population growth rates now occurring in many poorer countries are not necessarily permanent. In Europe, population growth has changed dramatically during the last three centuries. Demographers have used data on baptisms and funerals from churches in Great Britain to study changes in birth and death rates of the population. They calculated the **crude birth rate** (CBR)—the number of live births per year per thousand people in the population (Fig. 2.13)—and the

crude death rate (CDR)—the number of deaths per year per thousand people (Fig. 2.14). The difference between these two yields the rate of natural increase of a population.

The church data revealed that before the Industrial Revolution began in Great Britain in the 1750s, the country experienced high birth rates and high death rates, with small differences between the two. The result was low population growth. After industrialization began, the death rates in Great Britain began to fall as a result of better and more stable access to food and improved access to increasingly effective medicines. With a rapidly falling death rate and a birth rate that remained high, Britain's population explosion took place. From the late 1800s through two world wars in the 1900s, death rates continued to fall and birth rates began to fall, but stayed higher than death rates, resulting in continued population growth but at a slower rate. Finally, in recent history, both the birth rate and the death rate in Great Britain declined to low levels, resulting in slow or stabilized population growth.

Demographers call the shift in population growth the **demographic transition**. The transition is typically modeled as shown in Figure 2.15. The model is based on the kind of shift that Britain experienced, but other places either have gone through a similar shift or are in the process of doing so. The initial low-growth phase, which in all places endured for most of human history, is marked by high birth rates and

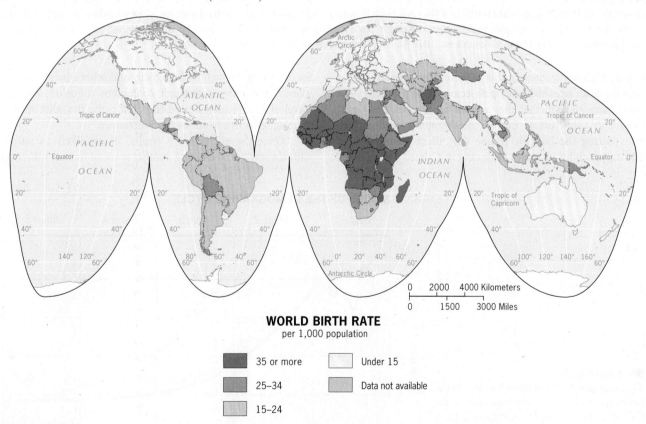

WORLD BIRTH RATE
per 1,000 population

- 35 or more
- 25–34
- 15–24
- Under 15
- Data not available

■ **Figure 2.13**
Crude Birth Rate. Number of Births in a Year per 1000 People.   A fairly distinct north–south pattern is evident, as northern countries have lower crude birth rates than southern countries. The global south has a few clear outliers with low crude birth rates, notably Australia, New Zealand, Chile, and Uruguay.   *Data from:* Population Reference Bureau 2013.

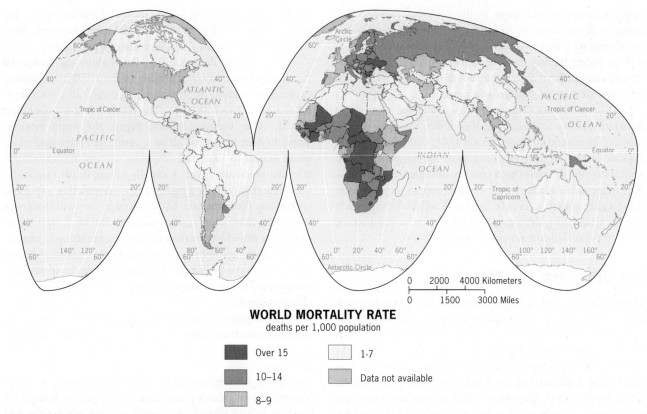

WORLD MORTALITY RATE
deaths per 1,000 population

Over 15

10–14

8–9

1–7

Data not available

■ **Figure 2.14**
Crude Death Rate: Number of Deaths in a Year per 1000 People. The death rate has declined globally as countries have transitioned into the third stage of the demographic transition and beyond. A few countries in the global north have relatively high death rates, including Russia and a number of eastern European countries. *Data from*: Population Reference Bureau, 2013.

equally high death rates. In this phase, epidemics and plagues keep the death rates high among all sectors of the population—in some cases so high that they exceed birth rates. For Great Britain and the rest of Europe, death rates exceeded birth rates during the bubonic plague (the Black Death) of the 1300s, which hit in waves beginning in Crimea on the Black Sea, diffusing through trade to Sicily and other Mediterranean islands, and moving through contagious diffusion and the travel of rats (which hosted the vector, the flea, that spread the plague) north from the Mediterranean.

Once the plague hit a region, it was likely to return within a few years, creating another wave of human suffering.

MODEL OF THE DEMOGRAPHIC CYCLE

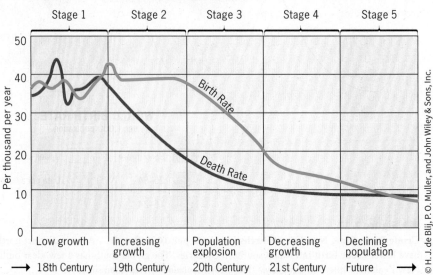

■ **Figure 2.15**
The Demographic Transition Model. Population growth is particularly high between the middle of stage 2 and the middle of stage 4, when death rates have declined due to better food supply and access to medicine but birth rates have stayed relatively high before later declining.

Estimates of plague deaths vary between one-quarter and one-half of the population, with the highest death rates recorded in the West (where trade among regions was the greatest) and the lowest in the East (where cooler climates and less connected populations delayed diffusion). Across Europe, many cities and towns were left decimated. Historians estimate the population of Great Britain fell from nearly 4 million when the plague began to just over 2 million when it ended.

Famines also limited population growth. A famine in Europe just prior to the plague likely facilitated the diffusion of the disease by weakening the people. Records of famines in India and China during the eighteenth and nineteenth centuries document millions of people perishing. At other times, destructive wars largely wiped out population gains. Charts of world population growth show an increase in the world's population from 250 million people 2000 years ago to 500 million people in 1650 and 1 billion people in 1820. However, the lines connecting these points in time should not trend steadily upward. Rather, they turn up and down frequently, reflecting the impacts of disease, crop failures, and wars.

The beginning of the Industrial Revolution ushered in a period of accelerating population growth in Europe. Before workers could move from farms to factories, a revolution in agriculture had to occur. The eighteenth century marked the Second Agricultural Revolution, so named because the first occurred thousands of years earlier (see Chapter 11). During the Second Agricultural Revolution, farmers improved seed selection, practiced new methods of crop rotation, selectively bred livestock to increase production and quality, employed new technology such as the seed drill, expanded storage capacities, and consolidated landholdings for greater efficiencies. With more efficient farming methods, the number of people needed in farming decreased and the food supply increased, thereby supporting a higher population overall.

In the 1800s, as the Industrial Revolution diffused through continental Europe, other advances also helped lower death rates. Sanitation facilities made towns and cities safer from epidemics, soap came to be more widely used, and modern medical practices began to take hold. Disease prevention through vaccination introduced a new era in public health in the twentieth century. The combined improvements in food supply and medical practice resulted in a drastic reduction in death rates. Before 1750, death rates in Europe probably averaged 35 per 1000 (birth rates averaged under 40), but by 1850 the death rate was down to about 16 per 1000.

Birth rates fell at a slower rate, leading to a population explosion. The increase in the rate of population growth in Europe spurred waves of migration. Millions of people left the squalid, crowded industrial cities (and farms as well) to emigrate to other parts of the world. They were not the first to make this journey. Adventurers, explorers, merchants, and colonists had gone before them. In a major wave of colonization from 1500 through the 1700s, European migrants decimated native populations through conquest, slavery, and the introduction of diseases against which the local people had no natural immunity.

When a second wave of European colonization began in Africa and Asia during the late 1800s, the Europeans brought with them their newfound methods of sanitation and medical techniques, but these had the opposite effect. By the mid-1900s, declining death rates in Africa, India, and South America brought rapid population increases to these regions. At this point, new alarms and cautions of worldwide overpopulation rang.

Although the global alarms continued to ring, they subsided for populations in Europe and North America when population growth rates began to decline in the first half of the 1900s. The cause was a significant decline in birth rates. Populations continued to grow but at a much slower rate. Many countries in Central and South America and in Asia experienced falling birth rates later in the twentieth century, which helped slow the global population growth rate.

Why have birth rates declined? Throughout the 1900s, lower birth rates occurred first in countries with greater urbanization, wealth, and medical advances. As more and more people moved to cities, both the economics and the culture of large families changed. Instead of lending a hand on the family farm, children in urban areas became a drain on the family finances. At the same time, new opportunities—especially for women—were not always compatible with large families. Hence, many women delayed marriage and childbearing. Medical advances lowered infant and child mortality rates, lessening the sense that multiple children were necessary to sustain a family. In recent history, the diffusion of contraceptives, the accessibility of abortions, and conscious decisions by many women to have fewer or no children or to start having children at a later age have all lowered birth rates within a country.

In some parts of the world, countries are now experiencing exceptionally low TFRs. Low birth rates along with low death rates put the countries in a position of negligible, or even negative, population growth. Birth rates are lowest in the countries where women are the most educated and most involved in the labor force.

Future Population Growth

It may be unwise to assume that the demographic cycles of all countries will follow the sequence that occurred in industrializing Europe or to believe that the still-significant population growth currently taking place in Bangladesh, Mexico, and numerous other countries will simply subside. Nonetheless, many agencies monitoring global population suggest that the populations of most (if not all) countries will stop growing at some time during the twenty-first century, reaching a so-called **stationary population level** (SPL).

Such predictions require frequent revision, however, and anticipated dates for population stabilization are often moved back. Only a few years ago, the United Nations predicted world population would stabilize at 10 billion in 200 years. The United Nations changed its predictions based on lower fertility rates in many countries. All agencies reporting population predictions have to revise their predictions periodically. In the late 1980s, for example, the World Bank predicted that the United States would reach SPL in 2035 with 276 million inhabitants. Brazil's population would stabilize at 353 million in 2070, Mexico's at 254 million in 2075, and China's at 1.4 billion in 2090. India, destined to become the world's most populous country, would reach SPL at 1.6 billion in 2150.

These figures have proven unrealistic. China's population passed the 1.2 billion mark in 1994, and India's reached 1 billion in 1998. If we were to project an optimistic decline in growth rates for both countries, China's population would "stabilize" at 1.4 billion in 2025 and India's at 1.7 billion in 2060, according to a 2011 United Nations report. But population increase is a cyclical phenomenon, and overall declines mask lags and spurts as well as regional disparities.

Examine Appendix B at www.wiley.com/college/fouberg. Study the growth rate column. Which countries have the highest growth rates? Determine what stage of the demographic transition these countries are in, and hypothesize what may lead them to the next stage.

WHY DOES POPULATION COMPOSITION MATTER?

Maps showing the regional distribution and density of populations tell us about the number of people in countries or regions, but they cannot reveal other aspects of those populations: the number of men and women and their ages. These aspects of population, the **population composition**, are important because a populous country in which half the population is very young has quite different problems from a populous country in which a large proportion of the population is elderly. When geographers study populations, they are concerned not only with spatial distribution and growth rates but also with composition: the structure of a population in terms of age, sex, and other properties such as marital status and education. Age and sex are key indicators of population composition, and demographers and geographers use **population pyramids** to represent these traits visually (Fig. 2.16).

Population pyramids are used to display the percentages of each age group in a total population (normally five-year increments) by a horizontal bar whose length represents its share. Males in the group are to the left of the center line, females to the right.

A population pyramid can instantly convey the demographic situation in a country. In poorer countries, where birth and death rates generally remain high, the pyramid looks like an evergreen tree, with wide branches at the base and short ones near the top. The youngest age groups have the largest share of the population. In the pyramid for all poorer countries, the three groups up to age 14 account for more than 40 percent of the population. Older people, in the three highest age groups, represent less than 10 percent of the total. Slight variations of this pyramidal shape mark the population structure of such countries as Pakistan, Yemen, Guatemala, The Congo, and Laos. From age group 15 to 19 upward, each group is smaller than the one below it.

Wealthy countries have population pyramids that do not look like pyramids at all. Families become smaller, children fewer. The "pyramid" looks like a slightly lopsided vase, with the largest components of the population not at the bottom

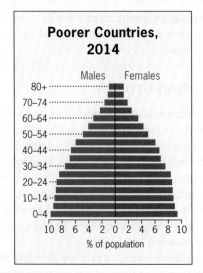

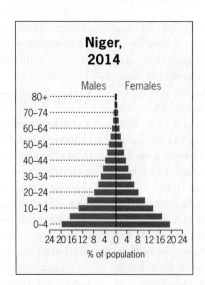

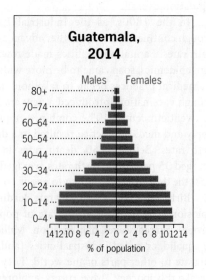

■ **Figure 2.16**

Age–Sex Population Pyramids for Countries with High Population Growth Rates.   Countries with high total fertility rates, high infant mortality rates, and low life expectancies will have population pyramids with wide bases and narrow tops.   *Data from*: United States Census Bureau, International Data Base, 2014.

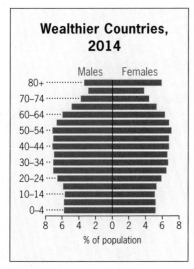

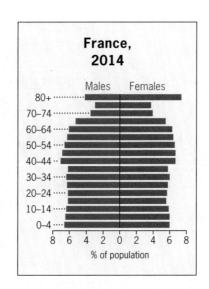

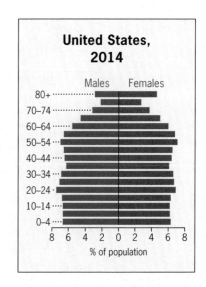

■■ **Figure 2.17**

Age–Sex Population Pyramids for Countries with Low Population Growth Rates.   Countries with lower total fertility rates and longer life expectancies have population pyramids shaped more uniformly throughout.   *Data from*: United States Census Bureau, International Data Base, 2014.

but in the middle. The middle-age bulge is moving upward, reflecting the aging of the population (Fig. 2.17) and the declining TFR. Countries with low TFR and high wealth, such as Italy, France, and Sweden, fit into this pyramid model.

HOW DOES THE GEOGRAPHY OF HEALTH INFLUENCE POPULATION DYNAMICS?

The condition of a country's population requires much more than simply knowing the total population or growth rate. Also of significance is the welfare of the country's people across regions, ethnicities, or social classes. Among the most important influences on population dynamics are geographical differences in sanitation, the prevalence of diseases, and the availability of health care. These factors are influenced in significant part by levels of socioeconomic development—an issue we will consider in Chapter 10. Health plays such a central role in population dynamics, however, that we will consider some basic aspects of the health picture here.

Infant Mortality

One of the leading measures of the condition of a country's population is the **infant mortality rate** (IMR). Infant mortality is recorded as a baby's death during the first year following its birth (unlike child mortality, which records death between ages 1 and 5). Infant mortality is normally given as the number of cases per thousand live births.

Infant and child mortality reflect the overall health of a society. High infant mortality has a variety of causes, the

physical health of the mother being a key factor. In societies where most women bear a large number of babies, the women also tend to be inadequately nourished, exhausted from overwork, suffering from disease, and poorly educated. Often, infants die because they are improperly weaned. Many children die because of diarrhea. This condition, together with malnutrition, is the leading killer of children throughout the world. Poor sanitation is yet another major threat to infants and children. More than one-fifth of the world's population is estimated to lack ready access to clean drinking water or hygienic human waste-disposal facilities.

The lowest infant mortality rate among larger populations has long been reported by Japan, with 2.2 deaths per 1000 live births in a country of over 127 million people. Some less populated countries show even lower IMRs. Singapore has over 5.4 million people and an incredibly low IMR of 1.8, and Sweden's 9.6 million people record an IMR of 2.6.

In 2013, four countries still reported an IMR of 100 or more—Sierra Leone, Central African Republic, Chad, and Democratic Republic of the Congo. Sierra Leone's IMR of 128, the highest in the world, reflects one death or more among every eight newborns. Dreadful as these figures are, they are a substantial improvement over the situation just five years ago, when 22 countries reported IMRs of 100 or more. Globally, infant mortality has been declining, even in the poverty-stricken regions of the world. Afghanistan's IMR, for example, declined from 165 in 2008, the highest in the world at the time, to 71 in 2013.

Each of these observations about infant mortality rates considers what is happening, on average, in a country. The IMR varies within countries and gives us a lens into variations in access to health care and health education depending on region, ethnicity, social class, or other criteria. The IMR of South Africa is 48 per 1000, an average of all the people within the country's borders. The IMR for South African

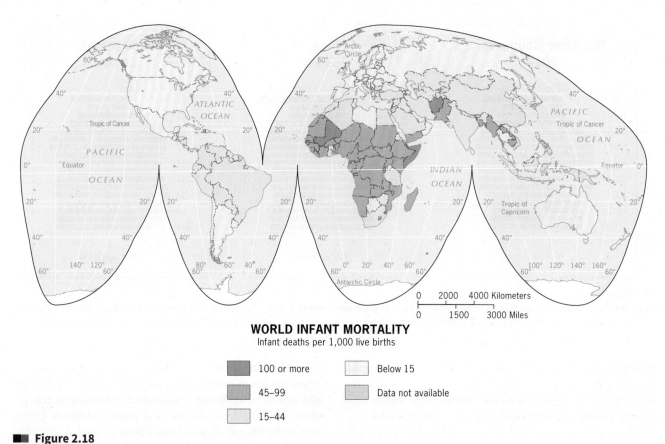

WORLD INFANT MORTALITY
Infant deaths per 1,000 live births

■ 100 or more		□ Below 15	
■ 45–99		□ Data not available	
□ 15–44			

■ **Figure 2.18**

Infant Mortality Rate, 2014.   The map shows infant mortality patterns at five levels ranging from 100 or more per thousand (one death for every eight live births) to fewer than 15. Compare this map to that of overall crude death rate (CDR) in Figure 2.14, and the correlation between high infant mortality rates and high death rates is evident.   *Data from*: CIA World Fact Book, 2014 estimate.

whites is near the European average; for black Africans it is nearer the African average; and for the Coloured and Asian population sectors it lies between these two figures. The reported average for South Africa does not reflect ethnic and class differences within South Africa.

In the United States, in 2010, the IMR for African Americans was 11.5, above the countrywide average of 6.1 and the IMR of 5.2 for non-Hispanic whites. The risk factors that lead to a high IMR afflict African Americans at a much higher rate than non-Hispanic whites in the United States. According to the Centers for Disease Control, in 2010, 85.7 percent of non-Hispanic whites but only 80.9 percent of African Americans received prenatal care starting in the first trimester of their pregnancy. Lower education levels for African American women also contributed to the higher IMR. However, one risk factor that contributes to high IMR, smoking during pregnancy, was higher for non-Hispanic whites. The Centers for Disease Control found that 22 percent of non-Hispanic whites smoked cigarettes during pregnancy in 2004, and 6.9 percent of African American women smoked during pregnancy.

The IMR in the United States also varies by region, with the highest IMR in the South and the lowest in the Northeast (Fig. 2.19). Race, ethnicity, social class, education levels, and access to health care also vary by region in the United States;

these correlations are found for many health problems ranging from diabetes to heart disease.

According to the Office of Minority Health and Health Disparities at the Department of Health and Human Services in the United States, "The leading causes of infant death include congenital abnormalities, pre-term/low birth weight, Sudden Infant Death Syndrome (SIDS), problems related to complications of pregnancy, and respiratory distress syndrome. SIDS deaths among American Indian and Alaska Natives is 2.3 times the rate for non-Hispanic white mothers."

Another measurement of children's health early in life is the newborn death rate—a measurement of the number of children who die in the first month of life out of every 1000 live births. Save the Children's annual State of the World's Mothers report explains that the high newborn death rate in the United States and in other wealthy countries is typically from premature births and low-birth-weight babies. In the poorer countries of the world, diarrhea and infections cause half of newborn deaths.

Figure 2.20 maps the Mothers' Index from the State of the World's Mothers report. The Mothers' Index measures barometers of well-being for mothers and children. Although the United States has a high newborn death rate, its position on the Mothers' Index is high. The overwhelmingly low measurements

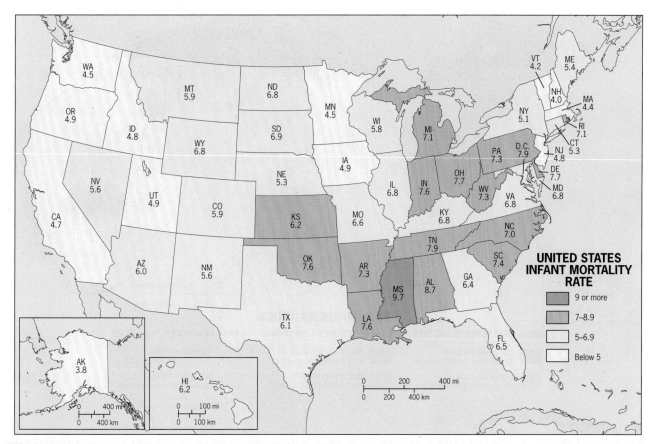

■■ Figure 2.19

Infant Mortality Rate in the United States.   Infant deaths per 1000 live births. In Figure 2.18, the entire United States is in the lowest class on the map. Shifting scales to States within the United States, the infant mortality rate shows variation, with high infant mortality rates in the South and low infant mortality rates in Washington and Massachusetts.   *Data from*: Centers for Disease Control, National Vital Statistics Reports, 2010.

for Subsaharan Africa on the Mothers' Index confirms that poverty is a major factor in the health of women and children. Specifically, 99 percent of newborn deaths and 98 percent of maternal deaths (deaths from giving birth) occur in the poorer countries of the world.

In the countries in the world experiencing violent conflict, the Mothers' Index plunges, and the chances of newborn survival fall. Examine Figure 2.20 again and note the position of countries that have violent conflict or a recent history of conflict: Iraq, Afghanistan, Liberia, Sierra Leone, and Angola.

Child Mortality

Infants who survive their first year of life still do not have a long life expectancy in the poorer areas of the world. The **child mortality rate**, which records the deaths of children between the ages of 1 and 5, remains staggeringly high in much of Africa and Asia, notably in the protein-deficient tropical and subtropical zones. *Kwashiorkor* (also known as protein malnutrition), a malady resulting from a lack of protein early in life, afflicts millions of children; *marasmus*, a condition that results from inadequate protein and insufficient calories, causes the deaths of millions more. In some countries, more

than one in five children still die between their first and fifth birthdays, a terrible record in the twenty-first century.

Life Expectancy

Yet another indicator of a society's well-being lies in the **life expectancy** of its members at birth, that is, the number of years, on average, someone may expect to remain alive. Figure 2.21 shows the average life expectancies of populations by country and thus does not take into account gender differences. Women outlive men by about four years in Europe and East Asia, by three years in Subsaharan Africa, by six years in North America, and by seven years in South America. In Russia today, the difference is approximately 12 years.

The map does reveal huge regional contrasts. At the start of the century, world average life expectancy was 68 for women and 64 for men. Not only are these levels exceeded in the wealthy countries of the Western world, but great progress has also been made in East Asia, where Japan's life expectancies are the highest in the world. With its low infant and child mortality rates and low fertility rates, Japan's life expectancy is predicted to rise to 106 by the year 2300. By contrast, tropical Subsaharan African countries have the lowest life expectancies. In Subsaharan Africa, the spread of AIDS

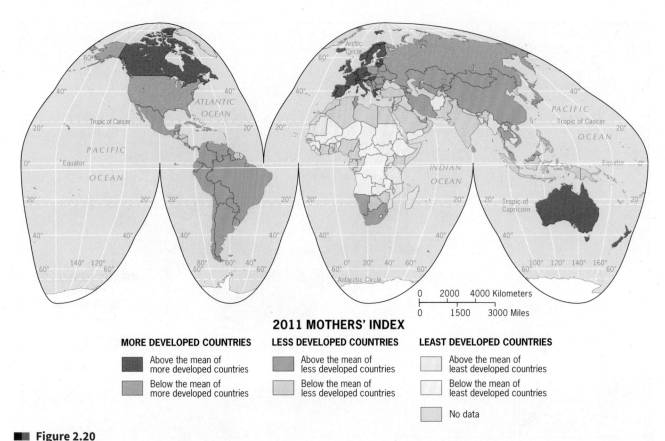

2011 MOTHERS' INDEX

MORE DEVELOPED COUNTRIES	LESS DEVELOPED COUNTRIES	LEAST DEVELOPED COUNTRIES
Above the mean of more developed countries	Above the mean of less developed countries	Above the mean of least developed countries
Below the mean of more developed countries	Below the mean of less developed countries	Below the mean of least developed countries
		No data

■■ **Figure 2.20**

The Mothers' Index, 2011.   Save the Children calculates the Mothers' Index annually, based on 13 indicators, to gauge the overall well-being of mothers and their children by country.   *Data from*: Save the Children.

over the past three decades lowered life expectancies in some countries below age 40. Today, the lowest life expectancies are closer to 50 due to access to antiretroviral treatments and programs to prevent mother-to-child transmission.

Life expectancies can change in relatively short order. For example, in South Africa, one of the countries hardest hit by the AIDS epidemic, the life expectancy rose from 56.6 to 60 years between 2009 and 2011 as a result of treatment and education programs. In the former Soviet Union, and especially in Russia, the life expectancies of males dropped quite precipitously following the collapse of communism, from 68 to 62 years. In 2010, the United Nations estimated the life expectancy for males in Russia was 63. In 2014, the BBC, reporting on an article in a medical journal, stated 25 percent "of Russian men die before they are 55" and that most of the deaths are due to alcohol. In 2013, the Population Reference Bureau estimated Russia's life expectancy for females was 76, twelve years longer than the life expectancy of Russian men.

Life expectancy figures do not mean everyone lives to a certain age. The figure is an average that takes account of the children who die young and the people who survive well beyond the average. The dramatically lower figures for the world's poorer countries primarily reflect high infant mortality. A person who has survived beyond childhood can survive well beyond the recorded life expectancy. The low life expectancy figures for the malnourished countries remind us again how hard hit children are in poorer parts of the world.

Disease

As we have seen, health is fundamentally influenced by local sanitation conditions. The availability of clean water plays a particularly critical role. Human-driven environmental pollution is also a factor; polluted water and air, and degraded lands, undermine health and well-being. Disease also has a great impact on human health. It is impossible to understand diseases without some understanding of geography because where people live affects what types of diseases they may contract, and where they move affects disease transmission. People who live in Iceland (where mosquitoes are rare) do not need to worry about contracting malaria, unless they travel to parts of the tropics where malaria prevails. Those who live in close proximity to animals, including livestock, run a greater risk of contracting certain diseases than those who live in cities. The importance of "where" questions to the study of disease has given rise to an important geographic subdiscipline known as medical geography.

Medical geographers study diseases, and they also use locational analysis to predict diffusion and to prescribe

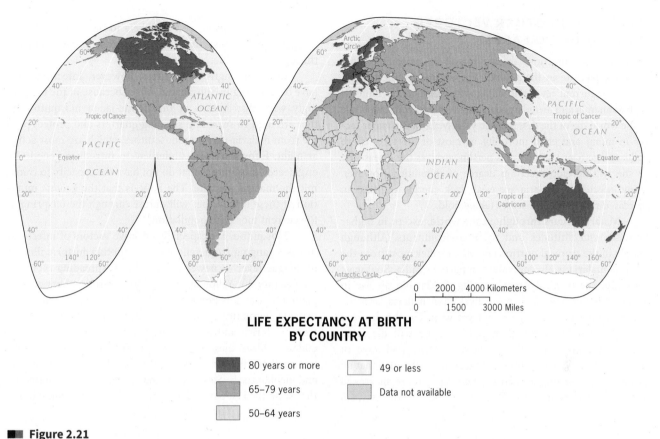

**LIFE EXPECTANCY AT BIRTH
BY COUNTRY**

- 80 years or more
- 65–79 years
- 50–64 years
- 49 or less
- Data not available

■■ **Figure 2.21**
Life Expectancy at Birth in Years, 2013.   This map highlights global inequalities in life expectancies. Someone born in Japan has a life expectancy that is three decades longer than someone born in Afghanistan or Angola.   *Data from*: Population Reference Bureau, 2013.

prevention strategies. A medical geographer can answer questions such as: Where is the bird flu most likely to diffuse and under what time line if an outbreak occurs in New York City? If a country receives enough funding to build 25 clinics for people in rural areas, what locations will allow a maximum of patients to be able to reach them?

Diseases can be grouped into categories to make it easier to understand the risks they pose. Some 65 percent of all diseases are known as **infectious diseases**, resulting from an invasion of parasites and their multiplication in the body. Malaria is an infectious disease. The remainder can be divided into the **chronic** or **degenerative diseases**, the maladies of longevity and old age such as heart disease, and the **genetic** or **inherited diseases** we can trace to our ancestry, that is, the chromosomes and genes that define our makeup. Sickle-cell anemia, hemophilia, and lactose intolerance are among these genetic diseases. These can be of special geographic interest because they tend to appear in certain areas and in particular populations, suggesting the need for special, local treatment.

Three geographic terms are used to describe the spatial extent of a disease. A disease is **endemic** when it prevails over a small area. A disease is **epidemic** when it spreads over a large region. A **pandemic** disease is global in scope.

Infectious Diseases

Infectious diseases continue to sicken and kill millions of people annually. Malaria, an old tropical disease, alone still takes more than a million lives annually and infects about 300 million people today. HIV/AIDS, an affliction that erupted in Africa just a few decades ago, has killed about 25 million people since that time. These two maladies illustrate two kinds of infectious disease: *vectored* and *nonvectored*.

A vectored infectious disease such as malaria is transmitted by an intermediary *vector*—in malaria's case a mosquito. What happens is that the mosquito stings an already-infected person or animal, called a *host*, and sucks up some blood carrying the parasites. These parasites then reproduce and multiply in the mosquito's body and reach its saliva. The next time that mosquito stings someone, some of the parasites are injected into that person's bloodstream. Now that person develops malaria as the parasites multiply in his or her body, and he or she is a host.

Nonvectored infectious diseases are transmitted by direct contact between host and victim. A kiss, a handshake, or even contact with someone's breath can transmit influenza, a cold, or some other familiar malady. HIV/AIDS is a nonvectored infectious disease that is transmitted primarily through sexual contact and secondarily through needle sharing.

MALARIA AND OTHER VECTORED INFECTIOUS DISEASES

Malaria is an infectious disease spread by mosquitoes that carry the parasite in their saliva. The disease manifests itself through recurrent fever and chills, with associated symptoms such as anemia and an enlarged spleen. Nearly 1 million people in the world die of the disease each year. Malaria is a major factor in infant and child mortality, as most of the victims are children age 5 or younger. If a person survives the disease, he or she will develop a certain degree of immunity. However, many infected by malaria are weak, lack energy, and face an increased risk of other diseases taking hold.

Malaria occurs throughout the world, except in higher latitudes and altitudes and drier environments. Although people in the tropical portions of Africa suffer most from the disease, malaria is also prevalent in parts of India, Southeast Asia, and the tropical Americas (Fig. 2.22). No disease in human history has taken more lives than malaria, and the battle against this scourge is not yet won. On the day you read this chapter, more than 2700 people will die from malaria, the great majority of them in Africa and most of them children. What these numbers do not tell you is that an estimated 3 to 5 million people live lives that are shortened and weakened by malaria infection. If you do not die from malaria as a youngster, you are likely to be incapacitated or struggle in exhaustion with chronically severe anemia throughout your life.

There are signs of progress, however. Infection rates have been falling in Subsaharan Africa because of the increasingly wide distribution of insecticide-laden mosquito nets that are used to surround sleeping quarters and protect people from malaria-carrying mosquitoes, which are most active at night. Efforts are also underway to introduce genetically engineered mosquitoes that do not have the capacity to transmit the malaria parasite. The hope is that the genetic mutation of these mosquitoes will diffuse through the offspring of the current mosquito population.

Mosquitoes are especially effective vectors of infectious diseases ranging from yellow fever (another historic illness) to dengue fever (a newer disease that is spreading rapidly—see Chapter 1). Yellow fever has killed vast numbers of people in the past. It is being driven back by a vaccine, which can provide immunity for ten years. But it is still prevalent in tropical Africa and South America where it has long been endemic, Fleas, flies, worms, snails, and other vectors transmit such terrible diseases as river blindness, guinea worm, and elephantiasis. Sleeping sickness, which is transmitted by the tsetse fly, is a particular scourge. The fly sucks the blood

Adapted with permission from: World Health Organization, Roll Back Malaria Department and United Nations Children's Fund. World Malaria Report, 2005. http://rbm.who.int/wmr2005/html/map1.htm

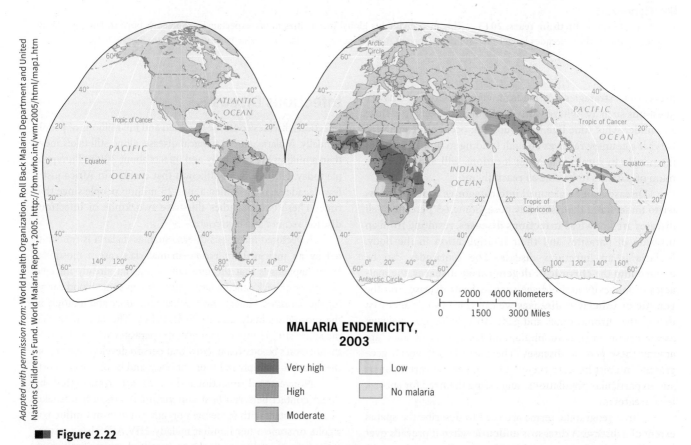

MALARIA ENDEMICITY, 2003

- Very high
- High
- Moderate
- Low
- No malaria

■ **Figure 2.22**

Global Distribution of Malaria Transmission Risk, 2003.   Malaria was once more widespread, but it is now concentrated primarily in the Tropics where moisture allows higher breeding rates for mosquitos.

from an infected animal or individual and then infects others with its bite. Sleeping sickness began around 1400 in West Africa, but it spread throughout much of Subsaharan Africa in the succeeding centuries. Both people and animals infected by the disease come down with a fever, followed by the swelling of lymph nodes and inflammation of the brain. Death is not uncommon. Progress has been made in combatting the disease through tsetse-fly eradication campaigns, but much of Subsaharan Africa is still affected. Tropical climates, where warm, moist conditions allow vectors to thrive, are the worst-afflicted areas of the world, but vectored infectious diseases are a global phenomenon.

HIV/AIDS AND OTHER NONVECTORED DISEASES

Low life expectancies in some parts of the world are caused by the ravages of **AIDS** (Acquired Immune Deficiency Syndrome)—a disease identified in Africa in the early 1980s. Undoubtedly, AIDS had taken hold in Africa years earlier, perhaps decades earlier. But its rapid diffusion worldwide began in the 1980s, creating one of the greatest health catastrophes of the past century. Nowhere has its impact been greater than in Africa itself.

Medical geographers estimate that in 1980 about 200,000 people were infected with HIV (Human Immunodeficiency Virus, which causes AIDS), all of them Africans. By 2012, the number worldwide exceeded 75 million, according to the United Nations AIDS Program, with 70 percent (25 million) of all cases in Subsaharan Africa! The infection rate worldwide has fallen 33 percent since 2001 and is continuing to slow, but eastern Europe and Central Asia have recently seen a surge in HIV infection.

The impact of the scourge of AIDS on Subsaharan Africa is striking. In 2013, some 23 percent of people aged 15 to 49 were infected in Botswana, 15.2 percent in Zimbabwe, almost 16 percent in South Africa, and 12.5 percent in Zambia. These are the official data; medical geographers estimate that as much as 20 percent of the entire population of several tropical African countries may be infected. The United Nations AIDS program reports that more than 1.6 million people died of AIDS in Subsaharan Africa in 2012 alone. Geographer Peter Gould, in his book *The Slow Plague* (1993), called Africa a "continent in catastrophe," and the demographic statistics support his viewpoint. In a continent already ravaged by other diseases, AIDS is still the leading cause of death for adults. It has reshaped the population structure of the countries hardest hit by the disease. Demographers look at the projected population pyramids for countries with high rates of infection and no longer see population pyramids; they see population chimneys—reflecting the major impact of AIDS on the younger population in the country (Fig. 2.23).

Over the past three decades, the AIDS pandemic has reached virtually all parts of the world. China is reporting at least 650,000 infected, with 70,000 new cases in 2013 alone, and the number in India may well exceed 5 million. Estimates of the number of cases in the United States surpass

1 million; in Middle and South America, nearly 2 million are infected. Southeast Asia now has as many as 6 million cases. People infected by HIV do not immediately display visible symptoms of the disease; they can carry the virus for years without being aware of it, and during that period they can unwittingly transmit it to others. Add to this the social stigma many people attach to this malady, and it is evident that official statistics on AIDS do not give a full picture of the toll the disease takes.

Fieldwork conducted by geographers is shedding light on the human toll of AIDS locally and within families. Geographer Elsbeth Robson has studied the impact of AIDS in hard-hit Zimbabwe. She found that the diffusion of AIDS and reductions in spending on health care (often mandated by structural adjustment programs) "shape young people's home lives and structure their wider experiences." In Subsaharan Africa, the number of children orphaned when parents die from AIDS is growing rapidly (Fig. 2.24). In 2004, UNICEF reported that in just two years, between 2001 and 2003, the number of global AIDS orphans (children who have lost a parent to AIDS) rose from 11.5 million to 15 million. Robson found that in addition to the rising number of AIDS orphans, many young children, especially

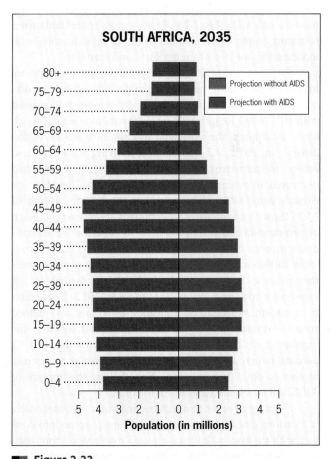

SOUTH AFRICA, 2035

Projection without AIDS
Projection with AIDS

Population (in millions)

■ **Figure 2.23**

Effect of AIDS on the Total Population Pyramid for South Africa, Predicted 2035. Estimated population, male and female, with AIDS and without AIDS. *Data from*: United States Census Bureau, 2005.

FIELD NOTE

"The day was so beautiful and the children's faces so expressive I could hardly believe I was visiting an AIDS hospice village set up for children. The Sparrow Rainbow Village on the edges of Johannesburg, South Africa, is the product of an internationally funded effort to provide children with HIV/AIDS the opportunity to live in a clean, safe environment. Playing with the children brought home the fragility of human life and the extraordinary impacts of a modern plague that has spread relentlessly across significant parts of Subsaharan Africa."

© Alexander B. Murphy

Figure 2.24
Johannesburg, South Africa.

girls, are taken out of school to serve as caregivers for their relatives with AIDS (Fig. 2.25). In her words, "more children are becoming young carers as households struggle to cope with income and labor losses through illness and mortality."

Despite the magnitude of the problem, enormous strides have been made in the past decade in the fight against the disease. Medical advancements have allowed people infected with HIV to live longer with antiretroviral treatments, which work to suppress the virus and halt the progression of the disease. In 2012, 9.7 million people living with HIV had access to antiretrovirals, and AIDS-related deaths had decreased 30 percent from their peak in 2005. Uganda, once Africa's worst-afflicted country, has slowed the growth of AIDS through an intensive, government-sponsored campaign of propaganda and action—notably the distribution of condoms in even the remotest part of the country. Life expectancy in Botswana and Swaziland, at 34 during the worst of the epidemic, has risen to the high 40s. In Zimbabwe, life expectancy rose from 36 in 2007 to 56 in 2013. In addition to treatment, reproductive education programs have helped stem the transmission of the virus. From 2001 to 2012, the number of children with HIV/AIDS worldwide dropped 52 percent, largely as a result of programs aimed at preventing mother-to-child transmission. Nonetheless, the impact of AIDS will be felt for generations to come.

Turning to other nonvectored infectious diseases, ebola is a serious disease that starts when humans come into contact with the bodily fluids of infected monkeys or fruit bats, and it is then spread from person to person through bodily fluids. Outbreaks in Subsaharan Africa are deadly, as the outbreak in West Africa in 2014 killed more than 3,000 people. The international health community mobilized to help stop the spread of ebola in West Africa. The origin of Middle East respiratory syndrome (MERS) is suggested by the name. A more recent disease, and less deadly than ebola, MERS has spread well beyond its source region, with cases appearing as far away as the United States by 2014.

Every year millions of people succumb to influenza—the "flu"—making it the most common nonvectored infectious disease. Most infected individuals recover, but hundreds of thousands do not. Influenza epidemics often start when humans come into contact with infected pigs, which in turn contract the virus from birds and waterfowl. Southern China is a particularly common source region. In some years the spread of the virus reaches pandemic proportions. The most famous pandemic occurred in 1918–1919, leading to some 50–100 million deaths around the world. More recent pandemics have been less serious, but approximately 500,000 people succumbed to one in 2009–2010 (the so-called swine flu pandemic). Vaccines have served to slow the spread of influenza, but staying ahead of virus mutations is an ongoing challenge.

Chronic and Genetic Diseases

Chronic diseases (also called degenerative diseases) are the afflictions of middle and old age, reflecting higher life expectancies. Among the chronic diseases, heart disease, cancers, and strokes rank as the leading diseases in this category, but pneumonia, diabetes, and liver diseases also take their toll. In the United States 100 years ago, tuberculosis, pneumonia, diarrheal diseases, and heart diseases (in that order) were the chief killers. Today, heart disease and cancer head the list, with stroke (cerebral hemorrhage) next and accidents also high on the list (Table 2.1). In the early 1900s, tuberculosis

GUEST FIELD NOTE

Marich Village, Kenya

"This drawing was done by a Pokot boy in a remote primary school in northwestern Kenya. He agreed to take part in my fieldwork some years after I had started researching young carers in Subsaharan Africa. Since those early interviews in Zimbabwe, I have been acutely aware of young carers' invisibility—you can't tell who are young carers just by looking at them. Indeed, invisibility is a characteristic of many aspects of the social impacts of HIV/AIDS. This young person drew himself working in the fields and taking care of cattle. African young people help with farming and herding for many reasons, but for young caregivers, assisting their sick family members in this way is especially important."

Elsbeth Robson, Keele University

■ **Figure 2.25**

and pneumonia caused 20 percent of all deaths; today, they cause fewer than 5 percent. The diarrheal diseases, which were so high on the old list, are now primarily children's maladies. Today, the diarrheal diseases are not even on the list of the 10 leading causes of death.

At the global scale, infectious diseases such as tuberculosis and pneumonia are less serious threats than they once were, but cancer and heart disease take a high toll. Recent decades have brought new lifestyles, new pressures, new consumption patterns, and exposure to new chemicals, and we do not yet know how these are affecting our health. The health impacts of the preservatives that are added to many foods are not fully understood. We substitute artificial flavoring for sugar and other calorie-rich substances, but some of those substitutes have been proven to be dangerous. Moreover, obesity plagues a significant percentage of the U.S. population, bringing with it heart disease and diabetes. Even the treatment of drinking water with chemicals is rather recent in the scheme of global population change, and we do not know its long-term effects. Future chronic diseases may come from practices we now take for granted.

Genetic diseases are of particular interest to medical geographers because they are disorders that tend to be transferred from one generation to the next and display clustering that raises questions about the environment and long-term adaptation. Prominent among these are metabolic

TABLE 2.1

Leading Causes of Death in the United States, 2010.

LEADING CAUSES OF DEATH IN THE UNTED STATES, 2010	
Cause	Percent
1. Heart Disease	25%
2. Cancer	23%
3. Stroke	6%
4. Chronic Lower Respiratory Disease	5%
5. Accidents	5%
6. Diabetes	3%
7. Alzheimer's Disease	3%

Data from: Centers for Disease Control, National Center for Health Statistics, 2010 and U.S. Census Statistical Abstract 2011.

diseases—the body's inability to process all elements of the diet—in which enzymes play a key role. If the body fails to produce enough (or any) of a particular enzyme, the result can be serious metabolic malfunction. For example, some people suffer from a malady called primary lactose intolerance. If you suffer from this disorder, you do not have an adequate supply of one (or a set) of enzymes that you need to break down the milk sugar lactose.

Geographic Influences on Health

Looking at health questions through a geographic lens means understanding some of the general spatial aspects of health indicators and disease outbreaks discussed above—what places are more or less advantaged or threatened, where diseases are found, and where and how diseases spread. But geographical analysis can contribute to an understanding of health and disease issues in other ways as well. Humans are constantly altering Earth's surface in ways that have the potential to influence health and the spread of diseases. There is growing evidence, for example, that climate-change-induced increases in precipitation and flooding, along with rising temperatures, are expanding the geographic reach of diseases that are transmitted by mosquitoes. Addressing this problem requires geographic studies that look at the impacts of ecosystem changes on health issues in particular places.

Critical social geographic factors also affect health. Medical geographers are increasingly studying not just disease patterns, but issues such as access to medical care and the ways in which place-based social norms affect disease transmission. For many people, access to medical care is fundamentally a geographic matter because access is a function of distance to medical facilities and available transportation infrastructure. As such, understanding geographical inequalities in the distribution of health-care facilities or the ways in which infrastructure impedes or facilitates access to such facilities are matters of great importance. On the social norms front, the transmission of HIV/AIDS is not just influenced by distance and population numbers; it is also a product of attitudes toward the use of condoms, mobility patterns, socioeconomic status, and other place-specific social variables. Understanding the role of such factors requires looking at the geographic context within which health challenges are situated.

Study Figure 2.19, the infant mortality rate (IMR) by State in the United States. Hypothesize why the IMR is low in some regions of the country and high in others. Shift scales in your mind, and choose one State to consider: How do you think IMR varies within this State? What other factors involved at this scale and this level of generalization explain the pattern of IMRs? Use the population Internet sites available at www.wiley.com/college/fouberg to determine whether your hypotheses are correct.

HOW DO GOVERNMENTS IMPACT POPULATION CHANGE?

Over the past century, many of the world's governments have instituted policies designed to influence the overall growth rate or ethnic ratios within the population. Certain policies directly affect the birth rate via laws ranging from subsidized abortions to forced sterilization. Others influence family size through taxation or subvention. These policies fall into three groups: expansive, eugenic, and restrictive.

The former Soviet Union and China under Mao Zedong led other communist societies in **expansive population policies**, which encourage large families and raise the rate of natural increase. Although such policies have been abandoned in China, some countries are again pursuing expansive population policies—because their populations are aging and declining. The aging population in Europe has encouraged some countries to embark on policies to encourage families (through tax incentives and the expansion of family-friendly social services) to have more children.

As noted earlier, birth rates in Russia plummeted after the 1991 collapse of the Soviet Union. The TFR in Russia, which was 2.04 in 1980, had fallen to 1.34 by the mid-2000s, though it has now rebounded somewhat to 1.7. Then Prime Minister of Russia Vladimir Putin called the demographic crisis Russia's greatest problem. The Russian government began to offer cash subsidies of $10,000 to women who give birth to a second or third child.

In response to concerns over Russia's aging population, the government of Ulyanovsk Province has held a National Day of Conception each September 12 since 2005. In 2007, government and businesses in Ulyanovsk offered the afternoon off for people to participate in the National Day of Conception. The government planned to award a free car to the proud parents of one of the children born 9 months later, on June 12—the Russian National Day. On June 12, 2008, eighty-seven children were born in the province, about 4 times its average daily birth rate. Between 2005 and 2011, the number of births in the province rose by 19.5 percent. Although Russia's birth rate has rebounded, its ability to sustain a high TFR will depend on many factors, including alleviating social problems, stabilizing incomes, and continued government support.

In the past, some governments engaged in **eugenic population policies**, which were designed to favor one racial or cultural sector of the population over others. Nazi Germany was a drastic case in point, but other countries also have pursued eugenic strategies, though in more subtle ways. Until the time of the civil rights movement in the 1960s, some observers accused the United States of pursuing social policies tinged with eugenics that worked against the interests of African Americans. Many countries have a history of forced sterilization of lesbian, gay, transgender, and bisexual individuals; some even maintain those policies today despite the efforts of some organizations to label such programs as human rights abuse. Eugenic population policies can be practiced covertly through discriminatory taxation, biased allocation of resources, and other forms of racial favoritism.

Today many of the world's governments seek to reduce the rate of natural increase through various forms of **restrictive population policies**. These policies range from toleration of officially unapproved means of birth control to outright prohibition of large families. China's **one-child policy**, instituted after the end of the Maoist period in the 1970s, drastically reduced China's growth rate from one of the world's fastest to one of the world's slowest (Fig. 2.26). Under the one-child policy, families that had more than one child were penalized financially, and educational opportunities and housing privileges were kept from families who broke the one-child mandate.

© H. J. de Blij

■ **Figure 2.26**

Chengdu, China.   A large billboard warning readers to follow China's one-child policy.

Population growth rates in China fell quickly under the one-child policy. In the 1970s, China's growth rate was 3 percent; in the mid-1980s, it was 1.2 percent; and today it is 0.5 percent (Fig. 2.27). The main goal of the one-child policy was achieved, but the policy had several unintended consequences, including an increased abortion rate, an increase in female infanticide, and a high rate of abandoned girls (many of whom were adopted in the United States and Canada).

During the 1990s, under pressure to improve its human rights records and also with the realization that the population was quickly becoming gender and age imbalanced, China

relaxed its one-child policy. Several exemptions now allow families to have more than one child. For example, if you live in a rural area and your first child is a girl, you can have a second child, and if both parents of the child are only children, they can have a second child. In late 2013, China's top legislature officially amended the one-child policy to allow all couples to have two children provided both parents are only children. With these changes, the National Bureau of Statistics of China now estimates that the population growth rate in China will climb again over the next 10 years. Although the one-child policy has begun to ease, China could see its impact for decades to come. The program has been blamed for what some older Chinese see as a generation of self-centered, financially dependent adults. The members of the so-called

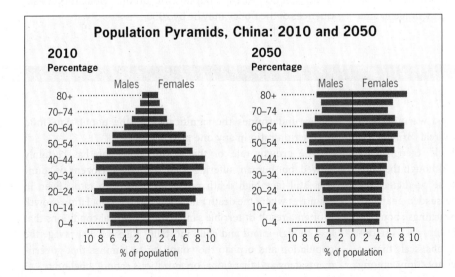

■ **Figure 2.27**

Population Pyramids, China: 2010 and 2050. The 2050 pyramid assumes present growth rates continue into the future. A continued relaxation of the one-child policy might change what the 2050 pyramid will look like. *Data from:* Population Reference Bureau, 2010.

me generation are quick to marry, have staggeringly high divorce rates, and often prefer to have only one child.

Limitations

Population policies are not independent of circumstances that can influence growth and decline. In the 1980s, the government of Sweden adopted family-friendly policies designed to promote gender equality and boost fertility rates. The programs focused on alleviating much of the cost of having and raising children. In Sweden, couples that work and have small children receive cash payments, tax incentives, job leaves, and work flexibility that last up to eight years after the birth of a child. The policies led to a mini-birth-rate-boom by the early 1990s.

When the Swedish economy slowed shortly thereafter, however, so did the birth rate. The children born in 1991 made up a class of 130,000 students in the Swedish education system. But the children born three years later, in 1994, made up a class of only 75,000 students. The government had to build new classrooms for the temporary population boom, but then faced excess capacity when the boom subsided. The birth rate fell to 1.5 children by the end of the 1990s, and the country had to think anew about how to support families and promote fertility. One imaginative approach was suggested by a spokeswoman for the Christian Democrat Party, who urged Swedish television to show racier programming at night in hopes of returning the population to a higher birth rate! Over the last 15 years, increases in child allowances and parental benefits helped to produce a natural rate of increase that is a little higher than that in many other European countries and a TFR of 1.9, the third highest in Europe behind Iceland and the United Kingdom. And in 2013, the population saw its largest annual increase in 70 years, a result of family-friendly policies but also record-high immigration.

Similarly, Singapore implemented restrictive policies only to see its population fall too rapidly. The small country's "economic miracle" in the 1960s contributed to a population boom, illustrated by a TFR of 3.5 in 1965. The population increase was seen as unsustainable, and Singapore's government implemented measures designed to decrease family size. Today Singapore's TFR of 1.3 is troubling, and the government is working to increase the birth rate among citizens while also encouraging immigration and intermarriage.

Contradictions

Some areas of the world with low population growth rates (Fig. 2.9) are in the very heart of the Roman Catholic world. Roman Catholic doctrine opposes birth control and abortion. Adherence to this doctrine appears to be stronger in areas remote from the Vatican (headquarters of the Catholic Church). For example, the Philippines, thousands of miles from the Vatican, is Asia's only Roman Catholic-majority country. The Church and the Philippine state agree on abortion, as the Philippine constitution prohibits abortion. However, the Philippine government disagrees with the Church on the issue of artificial contraceptives: The government supports birth control in order to stem population growth.

Among Islamic countries, the geographic pattern is the opposite. Saudi Arabia, home to Mecca—the hearth of Islam—has a relatively high population growth rate, with the population increasing at 1.8 percent each year. But in Indonesia, thousands of miles from Mecca, the government began a nationwide family planning program in 1970 when the population growth rate was 2.6 percent. Fundamentalist Muslim leaders objected, but the government used a combination of coercion and inducement to continue their program. By 2000, Indonesia's family planning program had lowered the growth rate to 1.6 percent, and in 2012 it stood at 1.2 percent.

When studying government policies on population, one of the most important things to remember is unintended consequences. Choose a government population policy discussed in this section of the chapter and predict what the consequences of the policy may be by 2050.

Summary

In the late 1700s, Thomas Malthus sounded warning bells about the rapidly growing population in Great Britain. He feared a massive famine would soon "check" the growing population, bringing widespread suffering. Although the famine in Great Britain did not take place as he predicted, the rapidly growing worldwide population persuaded many to embrace Malthusian ideas, issuing similar warnings about the population explosion of the preceding two centuries. A stronger case can be made for these ideas at the global scale than at smaller scales, however, because the interconnections among places undermines the significance of the population–food production ratio in any one place.

The growth rate of the world population has certainly slowed, but human suffering is far from over. Dozens of countries still face high death rates and high birth rates. Even in countries where the death rate is low, slowed population growth is often a result of terrible sanitary and medical conditions that lead to high infant and child mortality, diseases that ravage the population and orphan the young, or to famines that governments deny and that global organizations cannot ameliorate.

Population pyramids illustrate that as wealthier countries worry about supporting their aging populations, poorer countries have problems of their own. A high birth rate in a poor country does not necessarily mean overpopulation; some of the highest population densities in the world are found in wealthy countries. Even poor countries that have lowered their birth rates and their death rates are constantly negotiating what is morally acceptable to their people and their cultures.

Geography offers much to the study of population. Through geography we can see differences in population problems across space; we can also see how what happens at one scale affects developments at other scales, and how different cultures and countries approach population questions.

Geographic Concepts

population density
arithmetic population density
physiological population density
population distribution
dot map
megalopolis
census
total fertility rate (TFR)
old-age dependency ratio
child dependency ratio
doubling time
population explosion

zero population growth
crude birth rate
crude death rate
natural increase
demographic transition
stationary population level (SPL)
population composition
population pyramids
infant mortality rate
child mortality rate
life expectancy
infectious diseases

chronic or degenerative diseases
genetic or inherited diseases
endemic
epidemic
pandemic
malaria
AIDS
expansive population policies
eugenic population policies
restrictive population policies
one-child policy

Learn More Online

About China's South–North Water Transfer Project
news.bbc.co.uk/2/hi/programmes/from_our_own_
correspondent/9132843.stm

About Population Growth in the World
www.prb.org
www.pbs.org/wgbh/nova/earth/global-population-growth.html

About the Composition of the Population of the United States
www.census.gov

About the Global AIDS Crisis
www.unaids.org/en/
www.npr.org/healthscience/aids2004/

About International Population Programs
www.unfpa.org

Watch It Online

About the Population Transition in Italy
www.learner.org/resources/series85.html#program_descriptions

MIGRATION

Expanding Slums

From the top of a building in the heart of one of India's great cities—Mumbai—I look down on a massive slum settlement nestled amidst modern high rises. In almost every direction I can see other slums—and even larger ones were in evidence as I drove in from the airport.

More than 60 percent of the people in Mumbai live in slums or shanties like the one shown in Figure 3.1. The settlements are concrete manifestations of one of the great human geographic changes to have occurred in India since the 1970s: massive migration of people from rural areas to cities. The 1971 Indian census reported 5.9 million people living in the city limits of Mumbai. By 2011, the population in the city more than doubled to 12.5 million, and the larger urban area has a population of more than 20 million.

Starting in the 1970s, Indians left rural areas and migrated to urban areas in large numbers because in rural areas landholdings are often too small to support growing families and employment opportunities outside the agricultural sector are few. Cities offer at least the possibility of improved job prospects and a better life.

The Indian government did little to dissuade rural residents from migrating to cities. Rakshar Kumar described the development of slum-shanties in Mumbai in the *New York Times* (2011): "Amid unchecked migration, Mumbai's slums often began as clusters of illegal dwellings on public property, including parks, roads and pavements. Local and state governments, seeing potential votes in the slums, helped to make them permanent by providing them with electricity and drinking water." As population rose and the number of shanties built in Mumbai's slums grew, politicians gave shanty owners papers saying they owned their shanties, in hopes of garnering more votes. At times, governments have extended electrical lines to the slums, but access to utilities, including electric and sewer, is limited.

With the population of the Mumbai urban area now topping 20 million, the city is experiencing a dramatic housing shortage. The value of shanties in Mumbai has increased, particularly for those located close to the city center or close to major transportation routes.

© Alexander B. Murphy

■ **Figure 3.1**

Mumbai, India. A view from the top of a high-rise building in the central city, looking down on one of the slums found throughout the city. The 2011 census of India reported that 60 percent of Mumbai's population live in slums.

By 2025, more than 40 percent of India's population (expected to be 1.45 billion by then) will live in cities—a stark testament to the importance of migration to the human geographic story.

At the global scale, rural-to-urban migration represents one of the most dramatic shifts in the human geography of the planet over the last century. In 1900, only 13 percent of the world's people lived in cities; now the figure exceeds 50 percent, and it is on the rise. Other types of migration are increasingly important as well. Across the world, hundreds of thousands of people have fled their homelands in recent decades for opportunities in North America, Australia, China, and Europe. Immigrants are sometimes welcomed and sometimes turned away. In the 1940s, the U.S. government encouraged Mexicans to come work in the United States as contract laborers (the **Bracero Program**). Several decades later, U.S. authorities were hard at work building a fence along the country's southern border in an effort to stem the inflow of migrants. This shift shows the important influence of government policy and public opinion on migration. Migration is sometimes a choice, but for many people it is a survival strategy. The "Lost Boys of Sudan" fled their homelands between the ages of 7 and 17 in the face of a devastating civil war in the closing decades of the twentieth century. They walked tremendous distances seeking refuge from the conflict. Many lost their lives along the way; others ended up in **refugee camps** in Kenya, Uganda, and the more stable parts of Sudan. More recently, millions of Syrians have sought refuge from the civil war wracking their homeland—settling in camps in Turkey, Lebanon, Jordan, and elsewhere.

It is hard to generalize about migration because it has so many causes and consequences. In some cases people want to leave a troubled place; in other cases they are forced to leave; and in yet others they are enticed by what another place might have to offer. Moreover, migration flows vary along gender, socioeconomic class, age, race, and ethnic lines. The Lost Boys of Sudan principally came from two ethnic groups that were caught up in the fighting. Not infrequently, labor migration is either heavily male or female, depending on particular job requirements and associated assumptions about gender roles. Geographers who study migration seek to understand who migrates, where they come from, when they migrate, and where they go.

In 2007, the number of undocumented migrants in the United States peaked at 12 million. In 2010, the number fell to 11.2 million as a result of the economic recession in the United States, but it is on the rise again with 11.7 undocumented migrants in 2013. The goal of most undocumented migrants is to work in the United States and send money home to their families. Monies migrants send home are called **remittances**. Haitians living in the United States, Canada, and the Caribbean sent home over $1.9 billion in remittances in 2012, a figure equivalent to 30 percent of Haiti's gross domestic product and far outpacing the value of Haitian exports. It is estimated that one in ten Haitians resides abroad, with some 500,000 Haitians in the United State alone. Thirty-six percent of Haiti's population is under 15 and, among the working-age population, the unemployment rate in 2010 was estimated at 40.6 percent. In addition, the country's gross national income per capita is $1240, far lower than the regional average of $10,870. One of five Haitian households receives remittances from abroad.

The economies of many poorer countries in the Caribbean, Africa, Central and South America, and parts of Eurasia depend on remittances sent to their citizens. In 2011, Ghanaian immigrants sent an estimated $119 million home, largely from the United States, the United Kingdom, Italy, and Nigeria. Ghana's government, in an effort to make it easier for remittances to flow into the country, established a Diaspora Support Unit within the Ministry of Foreign Affairs.

The downturn in the U.S. economy after 2007 generated a new flow of money called **reverse remittances**: money flowing from Mexico to the U.S. Mexican immigrants sent nearly $24 billion home in 2007 but only $22 billion in 2013. Remittances to Mexico make up 19 percent of household incomes in urban areas and 27 percent of household incomes in rural areas of Mexico. Unemployed, undocumented migrants in the United States have asked families in Mexico for financial support.

Not all immigrants are undocumented. Of the estimated 41.7 million immigrants in the United States today, 30 million are documented immigrants (Fig. 3.2). Countries recognize the

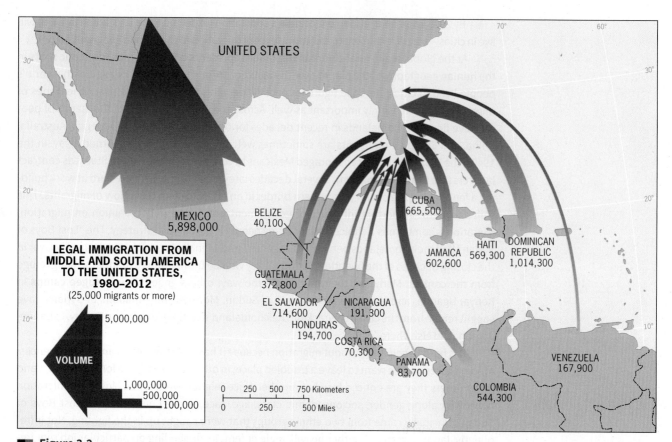

■ Figure 3.2

Documented Immigration from Middle and South America to the United States, 1980–2012. *Data from*: United States Department of Homeland Security, *Yearbook of Immigration Statistics*, 2012.

need for immigrant labor, and many have policies allowing, indeed encouraging, legal immigrants to work under temporary visas to fill a need. Thousands of people who work in the United States and Canada are there on temporary visas to fill seasonal jobs in agriculture and forestry. In the United States, over 45,000 agricultural laborers enter the country each year under a formally sanctioned program that allows unskilled laborers into the country as long as no Americans want the jobs. Canada began to allow agricultural laborers into the country in 1966. In both Canada and the United States, the vast majority of documented agricultural laborers come from Mexico. Canadian companies travel to Mexico to recruit agricultural laborers from rural Mexico and laborers for the hotel industry from urban areas of Mexico.

After September 11, 2001, many countries tightened up border security. In recent years, the United States has earmarked significant sums for building fences along its border with Mexico, hiring additional border patrol agents and installing new technology to intercept undocumented migrants. In the process, the cultural landscape of the border region is changing. The government is erecting specially designed fences that are difficult to climb, though there are openings in the fences where people across the border can speak with one another. The new fences and security south of San Diego, California, are pushing those seeking to cross the border without documentation farther east into the desert. The fences there are marked by empty water bottles and memorials to Mexicans who have died trying to cross the border (Fig. 3.3).

Even though globalization has promoted a freer flow of goods across the world, and the North American Free Trade Agreement (NAFTA) was designed to facilitate trade among Mexico, the United States, and Canada, the free flow of people is far from realized. It is not unusual to wait in line for two or more hours when crossing the border from Canada or Mexico into the United States. The flow of undocumented migrants has slowed in recent years, but that may well have more to do

ASSOCIATED PRESS

■ **Figure 3.3**
Tijuana, Mexico. Tijuana and San Diego, California, are separated by a highly guarded border infrastructure that in this section includes two walls to discourage crossing by those who do not have visas. Human rights activists placed crosses on the wall to memorialize people who died while attempting to cross into the United States.

with changing economic circumstances than with walls and fences. Undocumented immigrants go to great lengths to find their way into the United States; similarly, the U.S. government goes to great lengths to deter the influx of undocumented migrants. In this chapter, we examine various types of migration and ask why migrants choose to leave a particular place and why they go to another. We also examine the barriers governments erect to slow human migration, questioning why government policies shift and how policies affect migration flows. By looking at human migration through a geographic lens, we seek to shed light on the nature and meaning of migration flows and to gain an appreciation for why people migrate, where they migrate, and how people, places, and landscapes change as a result of the movement of people.

Key Questions FOR CHAPTER 3

1. What is migration?
2. Why do people migrate?
3. Where do people migrate?
4. How do governments affect migration?

WHAT IS MIGRATION?

Movement is inherently geographical because it affects the distribution of peoples and alters the character of the places from which migrants come and to which they go. Movement also changes people, as well as the way they see themselves in the world. Human movement speeds the diffusion of ideas and innovations; it intensifies spatial interaction and transforms regions.

The movement of humans takes several forms. Mobility occurs at scales ranging from the local to the global—from the daily to once in a lifetime. **Emigration** refers to the movement of people away from a place; **immigration** is the reverse—the movement of people to a place.

Geographers recognize three basic types of movement. **Cyclic movement** involves shorter, regular trips away from home for defined amounts of time. **Periodic movement** involves longer periods away from home undertaken from time to time. Actual **migration** carries with it a degree of permanence that is not characteristic of the other two forms of movement: The mover may never return "home."

Cyclic Movement

Cyclic movement describes a regular journey that begins at a home base and returns to the exact same place. The great majority of people have a daily routine that takes them through a regular sequence of short moves within a local area. These moves create what geographers call **activity spaces**. The scale of activity space varies across societies. You may go to classes every weekday and perhaps to a job as well, creating a relatively confined and stable activity space, diversified by shopping trips and social activities.

Commuting is also a cyclic movement. Commuting—the journey from home to work and home again—takes from minutes to hours and can involve several modes of transportation. The average North American commuter travels a greater distance each day than the average Chinese villager does in a year. Advances in transportation technology have expanded daily activity spaces. Cars and vast infrastructure enable people to commute over long distances. In Washington, D.C., commuters combine use of their cars, commuter trains, and the metro to travel upwards of 100 miles each way, each day, commuting not only from the surrounding suburbs but also from Delaware, West Virginia, and central Virginia. By airplane, commuters arrive at work in Washington, D.C., from New York City. Others, such as members of Congress, commute from their home State, keeping houses there and apartments in the Washington, D.C., area.

Another form of cyclic movement is seasonal movement. Every autumn, hundreds of thousands of people leave their homes in Canada and the northern parts of the United States and seek the winter sun in Florida and other "Sun Belt" States, returning in the spring. This seasonal transfer has huge economic consequences (and electoral significance) in depopulated northern towns and burgeoning tourist centers in the South.

This kind of seasonal movement is a luxury. Another type of cyclic movement, **nomadism**, is a matter of survival, culture, and tradition. Nomadism is dwindling across the world, but it can still be found in parts of Asia and Africa. Westerners often envision nomadism as an aimless wandering across steppe and desert by small groups of rootless roamers, people who claim no territory. In reality, nomads need to know their territory well in order to find water, food, and shelter in their cyclic movements. Nomadic movement is purposeful and takes place along long-familiar routes, repeated time and again. The nomads move their animals to visit water sources and pastures that have served their ancestors for centuries. Weather conditions may affect the timing of their route, but barring obstacles such as fenced international borders or the privatization of long-used open country, nomads engage in cyclic movement.

Periodic Movement

Periodic movement does not necessarily involve returning to the same places, and sometimes it takes place at irregular intervals. Periodic movement involves *a longer period of time* away from the home base than cyclic movement. Some migrant laborers are involved in periodic movement—for example, millions of workers in the United States and tens of millions worldwide move periodically to take advantage of employment opportunities. The need for migrant labor in the farm fields of California, Florida, and other parts of the United States creates a large flow of cross-border movers, many of whom eventually become immigrants.

A specialized form of periodic movement is **transhumance**, which is a system of pastoral farming in which ranchers move livestock according to the seasonal availability of pastures. This is a periodic form of movement because, unlike classic nomadism, it involves a substantial period of residential relocation in a different place. In Switzerland, for example, farmers drive cattle up mountain slopes to high, fresh pastures during the summer, and farm families follow the herds, taking up residence in cottages that are abandoned during the cold winter. In the "Horn" of Northeast Africa, hundreds of thousands of people follow their livestock from highland to lowland and back in search of pastures renewed by seasonal rainfall.

Periodic movement takes on other forms as well. If you leave home to attend a college far away, you are living away from home for four (or more) years. Although you may retain a home address in your place of origin, you now spend the majority of your time in your new abode (traveling home at irregular times), and your mobility cannot be categorized as cyclic.

Military service is another form of periodic movement. In a given year, several million U.S. citizens, including military personnel and their families, are moved to new locations where they will spend tours of duty that can last several years. Someone in the service moving from military base to military base would be engaged in periodic movement because they are not returning to the same place.

Migration

When movement results in permanent relocation across significant distances, it is classified as *migration*. The process of migration involves the long-term relocation of an individual, a household, or larger group to a new locale outside the community of origin.

International migration, movement across country borders, is also called transnational migration. When a migrant leaves the home country, he or she is classified as an

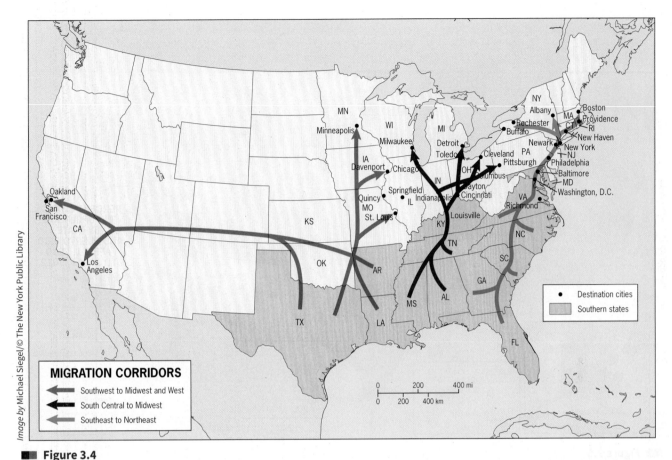

MIGRATION CORRIDORS

← Southwest to Midwest and West

← South Central to Midwest

← Southeast to Northeast

■ **Figure 3.4**

Migration Patterns of African Americans in the United States in the Early Twentieth Century. In a movement now called the Great Migration, African Americans left the South and moved along three migration paths into cities of the North and in California. Migrants had the promise of jobs, as expanding industrial sectors in northern cities, including Detroit, Chicago, and Baltimore needed more laborers.

emigrant (one who migrates out) of the home country. When the same migrant enters a new country, he or she is classified as an immigrant (one who migrates in) to the new country. Emigration subtracts from the total population of a country, and immigration adds to it.

Countries also experience **internal migration**—migration that occurs within a single country's borders. Mapping internal migration routes reveals patterns of well-defined streams of migrants that change over time. Early in the twentieth century, a major migration stream took tens of thousands of African American families from the South of the United States to the industrializing cities of the Northeast and Midwest (Fig. 3.4). The advent and diffusion of mechanical cotton pickers resulted in fewer employment opportunities in the South. Southern States, where slavery was legal before the Civil War, enacted Jim Crow laws separating blacks and whites in schools, hospitals, public spaces, public transportation, and even cemeteries. It is estimated that 5 million to 8 million African Americans migrated from the South to industrialized northern cities between 1900 and 1970. African Americans fled the segregated South and headed north to the growing industrial cities of Chicago, Detroit, and Baltimore.

More recently, economic opportunities in the South have begun to reverse the Great Migration. A growing number of middle-class, college-educated African Americans are moving to southern cities such as Atlanta, Dallas, and Charlotte. Other internal migration trends are significant as well: migrants moving to the economically dynamic regions of the Sun Belt and Far West (Fig. 3.5); people escaping from large cities and rural areas to move to medium-sized cities for retirement or family-friendly lifestyles; and wealthy individuals seeking solace and space moving into environmentally attractive rural areas, trying to keep the area "rural" while pushing out farmers.

Mobility within the United States depends on the country's economy. After decades of increasing levels of mobility, the U.S. population had what William Frey of the Brookings Institute called the "least mobile period in postwar American society" following the downturn in the economy between 2007 and 2008. The mortgage crisis and higher unemployment rates led to a pronounced reduction in the long-distance moves, according to a study by the Brookings Institute. Would-be movers "were unable to find financing to buy a new home, buyers for their existing homes, or a new job in more desirable areas" (Frey 2009).

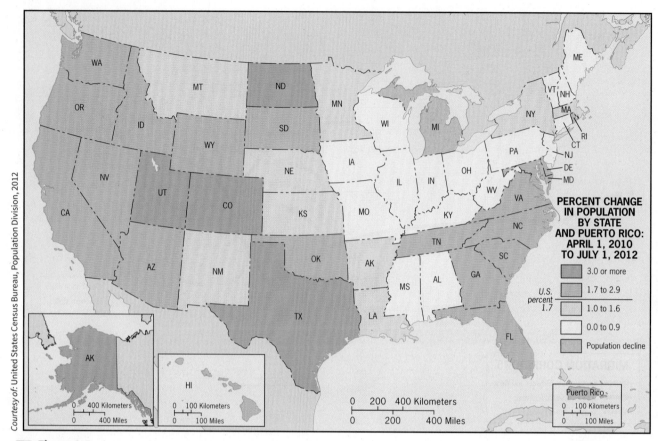

Courtesy of: United States Census Bureau, Population Division, 2012

PERCENT CHANGE IN POPULATION BY STATE AND PUERTO RICO: APRIL 1, 2010 TO JULY 1, 2012

- 3.0 or more
- 1.7 to 2.9
- *U.S. percent 1.7* — 1.0 to 1.6
- 0.0 to 0.9
- Population decline

■ **Figure 3.5**

Population Change 2010–2012 by State. States with growing economies, including North Dakota, which is experiencing an oil boom, grew in population between 2010 and 2012. Midwestern States from Iowa along the Great Lakes to Pennsylvania grew at a much slower rate (with the population of Michigan actually declining), as the manufacturing sector remained weak in the Midwest.

International migrants also frequently move within their destination countries. Since the 1940s, millions of people from Latin America have migrated to the American Southwest and Florida. Most migrants have stayed in these same basic regions, perhaps migrating part of the year to work in agricultural fields. In 1986, the U.S. government passed the Immigration Reform and Control Act (IRCA), legislation that gave amnesty and permanent residence to 2.6 million migrants who had been living in the United States for a long period of time. The newly legal migrants under IRCA could move anywhere, and during the 1990s, many moved to the Great Plains and Midwest as well as to the South (Fig. 3.5). Migrants found the South attractive for the same reasons other Americans did.

In Peru, which has a less mobile society than the United States, the pattern of internal migration is generally from rural to urban. Migrants have left rural areas and moved to Lima, the capital. Global and national investment capital is concentrated in Lima. The capital represents the major focus of economic opportunity for the rural population. Lima receives the vast majority of Peru's migrants, regardless of age, gender, or marital status.

thinking *geographically*

Choose one type of cyclic or periodic movement and then think of a specific example of the kind of movement you chose. Now, determine how this movement changes the home, the destination, and the lives of the migrants.

WHY DO PEOPLE MIGRATE?

Migration can be the result of a voluntary action, a conscious decision to move from one place to the next. It can also be the result of an involuntary action, a forced movement imposed on a group of people. **Forced migration** involves the imposition of authority or power, producing involuntary movements that cannot be understood based on theories of choice. **Voluntary migration** occurs after a migrant weighs options and choices, even if somewhat desperately or not so rationally.

The distinction between forced and voluntary migration is not always clear-cut. The enormous European migration to the United States during the nineteenth and early twentieth centuries is often cited as a prime example of voluntary migration. However, some European migration can be construed as forced. The British treatment of the Irish during their colonial rule over Ireland can be seen as political persecution, which led to forced migration. The British took control of nearly all Irish Catholic lands and discouraged the operation of the Catholic Church in Ireland. Until 1829, the British enforced penal laws preventing Irish Catholics from buying land, voting, or carrying weapons. The mass exodus of migrants from Ireland to North America in the mid-1800s can be seen as forced, both because of the British treatment of the Irish and because of the collapse of the agricultural economy due to the so-called Potato Famine from 1845 to 1852. But it can also be seen as voluntary in that although some Irish had other options, they chose to go to North America.

At the scale of an individual region or country, we can question whether a decision to migrate is forced or voluntary. At the scale of the household, the decision to migrate is all the more complex. For certain members of a migrating household, the move may be under duress; for others the move may be a preferred choice. The neutral title "migrant" veils the complexities of decision making at the household scale. Geographic studies of gender in migration demonstrate that at the household scale, power relationships, divisions of labor, and gender identities all factor into migration flows. At the household scale, decisions are made, in geographer Victoria Lawson's terms, in a "cooperative conflict bargaining process." Who has a say in this process and how much of a say each individual has depend on gendered power relationships and responsibilities in the household.

Studies of gender and migration find that, in many regions, men are more mobile than women and men migrate farther than women. Generally, men have more choices of employment than women, and women earn less than men in the jobs they find at the destination locations. One study of migration in Mexican households found that strongly patriarchal households tend to shield young women from migrating, sending young men out to work instead. Mexican households without a strong patriarchy more commonly send young, unmarried women to the city or another country to gain employment.

Ultimately, the decision or directive to migrate happens to an individual migrant within a household, place, country, region, and world, each of which has its own dynamics. The key difference between voluntary and forced migration, however, is that voluntary migrants have an option—at the very least, where to go or what to do once there; forced migrants do not.

Forced Migration

The largest and most devastating forced migration in the history of humanity was the Atlantic slave trade during the European colonial period, which carried tens of millions of Africans from their homes to South America, the Caribbean, and North America. The number of Africans sold into slavery will never be known, but estimates range from 12 million to 30 million. Many lost their lives in transit to the Western Hemisphere. Figure 3.6 shows an approximation of the numbers who survived the journey, as well as the destinations of the trans-Atlantic African deportees.

Because slavery plays a major role in U.S. history, many students in the United States assume that the vast majority of African slaves were taken to the southeastern United States. However, as the map shows, a considerable majority of Africans were forced across the Atlantic to the Caribbean region, to coastal Central America, and to Brazil.

The Atlantic slave trade began early in the sixteenth century, when Spain and Portugal brought Africans to the Caribbean. In the early decades of the seventeenth century, African slaves arrived in small numbers on plantations in coastal eastern North America. Wealth promised through plantation agriculture from the southeastern United States to Brazil created a demand for slaves by plantation owners, who paid European shippers for slaves. Those shippers, in turn, paid African raiders for slaves.

Of all crops produced on plantations in the Americas and Caribbean during the 1700s, sugar was the most important economically. Figure 3.6 reflects the scramble for sugar islands in the Caribbean, as the map names Spanish, British, Danish, French, and Dutch colonies in the Caribbean as destinations for slaves. Add the coffee, fruit, and sugar plantations in Brazil and the cotton plantations of the southeastern United States, and the destinations of slaves on the map make sense.

The terror and destruction of slave raiding afflicted large areas of Africa. Europeans and African raiders exploited much of West Africa from Liberia to Nigeria and inland to the margins of the Sahara. So many Africans were taken from the area that is now Benin in West Africa to Bahia in Brazil that significant elements of the local culture remained intact in the transition. Today Bahia and Benin have strong ties, and cultural exchanges are growing stronger. The entire Equatorial African coastal region fell victim to the slave trade as well, when Portuguese slave traders raided the Portuguese domains of Angola and Mozambique. Arab slave raiders were active in East Africa and the Horn of Africa (present-day Somalia), penetrating Equatorial Africa and often cooperating with Europeans. Zanzibar, off the coast of mainland Tanzania, long was a major slave market.

We know proportionately where slaves ended up, but we can never gauge the full impact of this horrific period. In *A Colonizer's Model of the World*, geographer James Blaut discussed the sheer loss to African civilizations that occurred when Europeans and African raiders enslaved significant populations. The Atlantic slave trade also changed the Caribbean, where the vast majority of people on many of its islands are of African-Caribbean descent, and few, if any, indigenous peoples remain. In combination, the slave trade inflicted incalculable damage on African societies and communities, and changed the cultural and ethnic geography of both source and destination regions.

Although no forced migration in human history compares in magnitude to the Atlantic slave trade, other forced

Adapted with permission from: Philip D. Curtin, *The Atlantic Slave Trade*. University of Wisconsin Press, 1969, p. 57 and Donald K. Fellows, *Geography*. John Wiley & Sons, Inc., 1967, p. 121

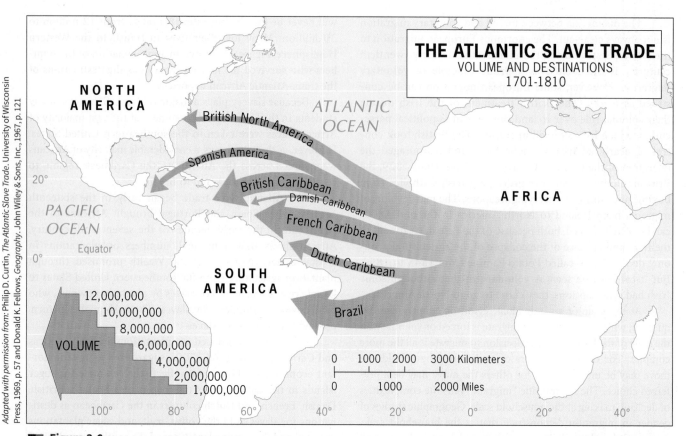

■ **Figure 3.6**

The Atlantic Slave Trade. For every African brought to the United States, eight or more were brought to the Caribbean and Central and South America. Demand for sugar increased between 1701 and 1810, encouraging the intensive production of the crop in the Caribbean. Europeans purchased enslaved people to labor on the sugar plantations. As a result, the majority of enslaved people brought from Africa to the Americas landed in the Caribbean.

migrations have shaped the contemporary demographic map of the world. For 50 years beginning in 1788, Great Britain shipped tens of thousands of convicts from Britain to Australia, where they had a lasting impact on the continent's population geography. In the 1800s, the U.S. government took lands from thousands of Native Americans and forcibly moved tribes to other areas of the country, many far from their traditional homelands. In the Soviet Union during Stalin's ruthless rule between the late 1920s and 1953, the government forcibly moved millions of non-Russians from their homes to remote parts of Central Asia and Siberia for political reasons. During the 1930s in Germany, the Nazis were responsible for a significant forced migration of Jews from portions of western Europe that fell under their control.

Forced migration still happens today. It continues to occur, for example, in the form of countermigration, in which governments detain migrants who enter or attempt to enter their countries illegally and return the migrants to their home countries. It also occurs in the wake of armed conflicts and environmental disasters such as those discussed below.

Human trafficking is another ongoing example of forced migration and an issue of concern in the international community. Sex trafficking, child sex trafficking, forced labor, bonded or debt bondage labor, involuntary domestic servitude, forced child labor, and the recruitment of child soldiers all fall within the broad umbrella of human trafficking. This modern form of slavery likely affects millions worldwide at any given time, though data are notoriously unreliable due to the informal and illegal nature of these practices, the stigma surrounding human trafficking, and the reluctance of some governments to act. The U.S. Department of State's annual Trafficking-in-Persons (TIP) report identified 40,000 victims in 2013, far fewer than many nongovernmental organizations and social scientists believe exist. The Congressionally mandated TIP report has become an important feature of U.S. foreign policy. The report places countries on a series of tiers, depending on how well they have reported on and combatted human trafficking within their borders. If they rate poorly, they are placed on a watch list. If countries are placed on or fall to the lowest tier, they may face economic sanctions or the cessation of aid. The conditions of human trafficking are profoundly unsettling and detail the extent to which forced migration continues to shape human experiences, cultural landscapes, and migration patterns.

Push and Pull Factors in Voluntary Migration

Why do people choose to migrate? Researchers have been intrigued by this question for more than a century. Studies of voluntary migration flows indicate that the intensity of a migration flow varies with factors such as similarities between the source and the destination, the effectiveness of the flow of information from the destination back to the source, and the physical distance between the source and the destination.

Over a century ago, British demographer Ernst Ravenstein sought an answer to the question of why people voluntarily migrate. He studied internal migration in England, and on the basis of his data he proposed several **laws of migration**, many of which are still relevant today, including:

1. Every migration flow generates a return or counter-migration.
2. The majority of migrants move a short distance.
3. Migrants who move longer distances tend to choose big-city destinations.
4. Urban residents are less migratory than inhabitants of rural areas.
5. Families are less likely to make international moves than young adults.

Ravenstein also posited an inverse relationship between the volume of migration and the distance between source and destination; that is, the number of migrants to a destination declines as the distance they must travel increases. Ravenstein's idea is an early observation of the **gravity model**, which predicts interaction between places on the basis of their population size and distance between them. The gravity model assumes that spatial interaction (such as migration) increases as the size and importance of places becomes greater, and decreases as the distance between them grows. The balance between population size and distance predicts the likelihood of migration. In mathematical terms, the model holds that migration potential can be calculated by multiplying the size of the populations of two places, and then dividing the product by the distance between them. That calculation had more meaning in an age before airplane travel and the Internet, when physical distance meant something different from what it means today. But even now more migrants move shorter rather than longer distances, suggesting the model still has some relevance.

Although the gravity model gives us a guide to expected migration, migration is not as simple as a mathematical equation. When an individual, family, or group of people makes a voluntary decision to migrate, push and pull factors come into play. **Push factors** are the conditions and perceptions that help the migrant decide to leave a place. **Pull factors** are the circumstances that effectively attract the migrant to certain locales from other places, the decision of where to go. A migrant's decision to emigrate from the home country and migrate to a new country results from a combination of push

and pull factors, and these factors play out differently depending on the circumstance and scale of the migration. Because a migrant is likely to be more familiar with his or her place of residence (source) than with the locale to which he or she is moving (destination), a migrant will likely perceive push factors more accurately than pull factors. Push factors include individual considerations such as work or retirement conditions, cost of living, personal safety and security, and, for many, environmental catastrophes or even issues such as weather and climate. Pull factors tend to be vaguer and may depend solely on perceptions construed from things heard and read rather than on experiences in the destination place. Often, migrants move on the basis of unrealistically positive images and expectations regarding their destinations.

When considering pull factors, the principle of **distance decay** comes into play (Fig. 3.7). Prospective migrants are likely to have more complete perceptions of nearer places than of farther ones, which confirms the notion that the intensity of human activity, process, or function declines as distance from its source increases. Since interaction with faraway places generally decreases as distance increases, prospective migrants are likely to feel much less certain about distant destinations than about nearer ones. This prompts many migrants to move to a locale closer to home than they originally contemplated.

Migration streams may appear on maps as long, unbroken routes, but in fact they often consist of a series of stages, a phenomenon known as **step migration**. A peasant family in rural Brazil, for example, is likely to move first to a village, then to a nearby town, later to a city, and finally to a metropolis such as São Paulo or Rio de Janeiro. At each stage a new set of pull factors comes into play.

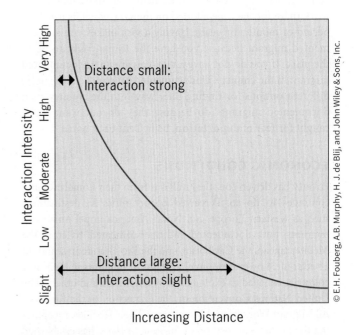

■ **Figure 3.7**

Distance Decay. The farther from the hearth in time and distance, the less likely a trait or innovation will diffuse.

Not all migrants from one place follow the same steps. When 1000 people leave a village and migrate to a town in a given year, most, if not all, of them may dream of making it to, and in, the "big city." But only about 500 may actually move from town to city, and of these, only 200 eventually reach the metropolis that impelled them to move in the first place. Along the way the majority are captured by **intervening opportunity**. This happened during the Great Migration when African Americans by the tens of thousands migrated northward after World War I to seek work in growing cities such as Chicago and Cleveland. Many found employment in St. Louis and Cincinnati; that is, they encountered intervening opportunities along their northbound routes.

Types of Push and Pull Factors

What specific factors impel people to pull up stakes and leave the familiar for the uncertain? What factors help migrants choose a destination? Research has shown that typically a combination of factors, not just one, leads to deciding it is time to move and deciding where to go. Any single factor can be either a push for the migrant to leave the home country or a pull to the new country. Which factor matters most depends on the migrant and the circumstances surrounding the decision to migrate.

LEGAL STATUS

Migrants can arrive in a country with or without the formal consent of the host country. Each country around the world determines who is allowed to enter and under what circumstances. If you apply for and receive a work visa from another country, you are legally allowed to live in the country and work there for the time allotted on the visa, which is usually a period of months or years. Having a visa makes you a documented migrant because you have the formal right to be in the place. If you do not have a visa, you are an undocumented migrant in the country. Undocumented migrants choose quite different options for finding their way into the country than documented migrants do because they do not want to be caught for fear of **deportation**, being sent back home.

ECONOMIC CONDITIONS

Poverty has driven countless millions from their homelands and continues to do so. Perceived opportunities in destinations such as western Europe and North America impel numerous migrants, both documented and undocumented, to cross the Mediterranean, the Caribbean, and the Rio Grande in search of a better life. Lower economic positions of migrants in their host countries can lead to exploitation by employers and others. The United Nations Convention on the Protection of the Rights of All Migrant Workers and Members of Their Families, recognizing the precarious position of migrant workers, has established standards of treatment for migrant workers. Fifty-eight states, most of which are countries that send more migrants than they receive, have ratified or signed the convention. Even though no member of the European Union and only 4 of 19 states in the G-20 states have signed it (the 20 largest economies in the world including the European Union, which primarily receive migrants), the convention's statements on human trafficking and the right of migrant workers to equal wages influence the migration policies of many nonsignatory states.

The global recession of 2008 dramatically altered internal migration patterns in the United States. During economic downturns, populations tend to be less mobile. At the turn of the second decade of the twenty-first century, the lack of economic opportunities for would-be migrants and the inability of Americans to sell their homes slowed internal migration dramatically. Florida, a State that previously received large numbers of internal migrants, recorded a net loss in migration for the first time since the 1940s. Other previously booming States such as Arizona and Nevada recorded similarly low numbers. At the same time, typical sending States—Massachusetts, California, and New York—saw 90 percent fewer migrants leave between 2008 and 2010 than had left earlier in the decade.

POWER RELATIONSHIPS

Gender, ethnicity, race, and money are all factors in the decision to migrate. Power relationships already embedded in society enable the flow of migrants around the world. Employers who hire migrant workers often know what kinds of migrants would work best for them.

Women in the Middle East hire Southeast Asian women to work as domestic servants, housekeepers, and nannies. Geographer Paul Boyle points out that by hiring women from abroad, the female head of household establishes a relationship in which the employee's "ethnicity and citizenship status differentiates them from their female employer and this influences the power relationships that underpin the working arrangements." In their study of placement agencies that help people hire domestic workers, Stiell and England found that in Toronto, Canada, placement agencies portrayed certain ethnicities according to scripted stereotypes. For instance, workers from the Caribbean went from being portrayed as "docile, jolly and good with children" to being depicted as "difficult, aggressive and selfish." Soon after, employers sought to hire women from the Philippines whom, at the time, placement agencies portrayed as "'naturally' docile, subservient, hardworking, good natured, domesticated, and willing to endure long hours of housework and child-care with little complaint."

Race is also a factor in the hiring of migrant workers. For example, carpet companies in Dalton, Georgia, the carpet capital of the world, began hiring Mexican workers after the 1986 passage of IRCA because they saw them as hard workers who were loyal to one company. In the same time frame, North and South Carolina also experienced surges in the Mexican migrant population. Geographer Jamie Winders cites the work of several researchers in the South whose research "raises the issue of displacement of black workers by Mexican migration—a topic hinted at by many studies but addressed by few." Issues of race and migrant status in hiring can spill over into neighborhoods, as they did recently in Raleigh, North Carolina. In the last 10 years conflicts have arisen over affordable housing between the African Americans who lived in Raleigh's neighborhoods and Mexican migrants who moved into the neighborhoods for the same affordable housing.

Geographer Paul Boyle also cites power relationships based on money in the growing migration industry, whereby migration flows are contractually arranged in order to fill labor needs for particular economic sectors throughout the world. Contractors give migrants advances on their earnings, help them migrate to the new country or region within a country, and then take migrants' wages in order to pay for advances and other needs the contractor supplies to the migrants.

Political Circumstances

Throughout history, oppressive regimes have engendered migration streams. Desperate migrants fled Vietnam and Cambodia by the hundreds of thousands as new regimes came to power in the wake of the Vietnam War. In 1972 Uganda's dictator, Idi Amin, expelled 50,000 Asians and Ugandans of Asian descent from his country. The Cuban communist dictatorship expelled more than 125,000 Cubans in 1980 in the "Mariel Boatlift." Politically driven migration flows are marked by both escape and expulsion.

Armed Conflict and Civil War

The dreadful conflict that engulfed the former Yugoslavia during the 1990s drove as many as 3 million people from their homes, mostly into western Europe. Many people became permanent emigrants, unable to return home. During the mid-1990s, a civil war engulfed Rwanda in Equatorial Africa, a conflict that pitted militant Hutu against the minority Tutsi and "moderate" Hutu. The carnage claimed an estimated 800,000 to 1 million lives and produced huge migration flows into neighboring Zaïre (now Congo) and Tanzania. More than 2 million Rwandans fled their homeland.

As we discuss in more detail below, for more than 30 years people from Afghanistan have left the country in search of safety first from a succession of upheavals. Well over 10 million Afghans have been refugees since 1979, fleeing mainly to Pakistan and Iran. More recently, the ongoing civil war in Syria has contributed to a significant percentage of worldwide refugees and internally displaced peoples. Recent and longstanding conflicts in Subsaharan Africa, particularly Sudan, South Sudan, the Democratic People's Republic of the Congo, Somalia, and Mali, represent another large percentage of what the United Nations Refugee Agency calls their "population of concern," an estimated 40 million refugees, internally displaced peoples, asylum seekers, and stateless peoples.

Environmental Conditions

Environmental crises including earthquakes, hurricanes, volcanic eruptions, and tsunamis also stimulate migrations. Because many migrants return, the net outflow generated by such momentary crises is often temporary, but this is not always the case. Between the 2000 and 2010 censuses, the population of New Orleans fell by 11 percent as a result of the devastation of Hurricane Katrina in 2005 and the economic recession since. The proportion of children in New Orleans' population also fell, from 27 percent in 2000 to 23 percent in 2007. Mapping where children live in New Orleans reflects another trend in post-Katrina New Orleans: Families with children in the New Orleans region are moving out of the city center and close-in suburbs and into the farther suburbs and exurbs, including Belle Chasse (Fig. 3.8).

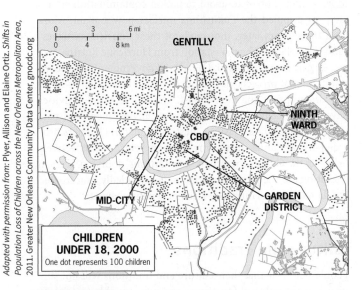

Adapted with permission from: Plyer, Allison and Elaine Ortiz. Shifts in Population Loss of Children across the New Orleans Metropolitan Area, 2011. Greater New Orleans Community Data Center, gnocdc.org

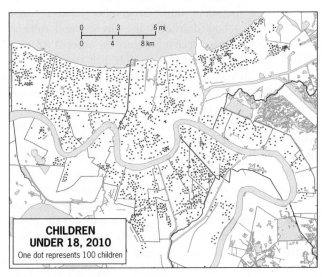

■■ **Figure 3.8**
Population Density of Children Under Age 18 in New Orleans, 2000 and 2010. Families with children were less likely to return to New Orleans to reside after Hurricane Katrina. A dramatic drop in the number of young people in the city, especially in Mid-city, Gentilly, the Garden District, and the Ninth ward, has led to the need for fewer schools and has changed the vibe of neighborhoods.

GUEST FIELD NOTE

Plymouth, Montserrat

This photo shows the damage caused by the 1995 eruption of the Sourfriere Hills volcano on the Caribbean Island of Montserrat. In the foreground you can see the gray volcanic ash clogging the roadbed, and in the background is the abandoned capital city of Plymouth. Many buildings cannot even be entered because the ash has buried their first floors or caved in their ceilings. This scene illustrated for me the complexities of migration in the face of natural disasters. Many Montserratians fled to the United States when Plymouth was destroyed and were given "temporary protected" immigration status. The U.S. government told Montserratian refugees to leave in 2005—not because the volcanic crisis was over or because the housing crisis caused by the volcano was solved. Rather, the U.S. government expected the volcanic crisis to last at least 10 more years; so, the Monsterratians no longer qualified as "temporary" refugees.

Credit: Jason Dittmer, University College London

Jason Dittmer, University College London

■ **Figure 3.9**

Some environmental crises, such as volcanic eruptions, bring long-term environmental changes to the landscape, making return migration difficult, if not impossible. For example, the Caribbean island of Montserrat had a small population of about 10,000 prior to a volcanic eruption that began in 1995. The volcano has been active since then, prompting a migration flow. Geographer Jason Dittmer (2004) studied how drastically the physical and cultural landscapes of Montserrat changed since the onset of volcanic activity. Dittmer explains that roughly half the island has been proclaimed an Exclusion Zone, a region that includes the capital city of Plymouth (Fig. 3.9). People are not allowed in this zone of active volcanic activity. The people who remained must now live in the northern part of the island where the soils are thin, the land is rocky, and making a living is difficult. Over 7000 people migrated off the island, and the remaining 3000 migrated to the northern coast of the island, where the effects of the volcano are less felt.

Not all environmental conditions that lead to migration are the result of natural processes; human activities also play a large role. The effects of human-induced climate change, namely sea-level rise and increasingly erratic weather events, are projected to contribute to future migration strands as "climate refugees" from low-lying areas seek refuge elsewhere. One report suggests that the world will see as many as 150 million climate refugees from 40 countries by 2050. In 2009, the president of the Maldives held a cabinet meeting underwater to draw attention to the plight of his country, where all 400,000 Maldivians are likely to become refugees due to sea-level rise in the near future. Similarly, nuclear accidents and other industrial disasters have contributed to migration flows. In 2011, as many as 83,000 Japanese were forced to leave their homes to avoid radiation contamination after a tsunami crippled the Fukushima nuclear power plant. More than three years later, thousands of these "nuclear refugees" remain displaced. The devastation from Hurricane Katrina, too, was largely human-caused. Decades of government-sponsored flood-control projects and resource extraction activities mark the landscape of the Gulf Coast. Over time these activities have dramatically altered the physical environment and particularly Louisiana's coastline, destroying natural barriers provided by wetlands, increasing erosion rates, and effectively bringing the Gulf of Mexico to New Orleans' doorstep. Human alterations to the physical environment decidedly exacerbated the damage from Hurricane Katrina, a natural event.

Culture and Traditions

People who fear that their culture and traditions will not survive a major political transition, and who are able to migrate to places they perceive as safer, will often do so. When the British partitioned South Asia into a mainly Hindu India and an almost exclusively Muslim Pakistan in 1947, millions of

Muslim residents of India migrated across the border to the new Islamic state, and millions of Hindus migrated from Pakistan to secular India—an estimated 8 million in all. In the 1990s after decades of Soviet obstruction, more than 2 million Jews left the former Soviet Union for Israel and other destinations. The decline in minority white power and uncertain political conditions in South Africa during the mid-1990s impelled many whites to emigrate to Australia, Europe, and North America.

Technological Advances

For some migrants, emigration is no longer the difficult and hazardous journey it used to be. Although most migrants, especially refugees, still move by foot, some use modern forms of transportation and communication, the availability of which can itself encourage migration.

Gone is the time when would-be emigrants waited months, even years, for information about distant places. News today travels faster than ever, including news of job opportunities and ways to reach desired destinations. Television, radio, cellular phone, and telephone stimulate millions of people to migrate by relaying information about relatives, opportunities, and already established communities in destination lands. Advances in communication technology strengthen the role of **kinship links** as push or pull factors. When deciding where to go, a migrant is often pulled to places where family and friends have already found success. Thus, Turks quickly heard about Germany's need for migrant labor after World War II, and Algerians knew where the most favorable destinations were in France in the same time period.

When a migrant chooses a destination and writes, calls, or communicates through others to tell family and friends at home about the new place, the migrant helps create a positive perception of the destination for family and friends, and may promise help with migration by providing housing and assistance obtaining a job. Geographers call flows along and through kinship links **chain migration**. When a migrant reassures family and friends that a new community has been formed, a place where they can feel home, further migration often occurs along the same chain. Chains of migration built upon each other create **immigration waves** or swells in migration from one origin to the same destination.

Think about a migration flow within your family, whether internal, international, voluntary, or forced. The flow can be one you experienced or one you only heard about through family. List the push and pull factors. Then, write a letter in the first person (if you were not involved, pretend you were your grandmother or whoever) to another family member at "home" describing how you came to migrate to the destination and the circumstances you encountered when you arrived.

WHERE DO PEOPLE MIGRATE?

Several major global-scale migration flows have occurred over the past 500 years—flows characterized by the movement of hundreds of thousands of people migrating along the same general path. Important population shifts have taken place at the regional and national scales as well. In this section of the chapter, we focus on the destinations of these major migration flows. Looking at migration flows at the global, regional, and national scales provides only a generalized picture of human movement, however. At the local and household scales, each individual or family migration reflects life-altering decisions, and those decisions collectively foster global change.

Global Migration Flows

Before 1500, long-distance migration occurred haphazardly, typically in pursuit of spices, fame, or exploration. Things changed in the age of European **colonization**. Colonization is a physical process whereby the colonizing entity takes over another place, putting its own government in charge and either moving its own people into the place or bringing in indentured outsiders to gain control of the people and the land. First, Europeans colonized the Americas and the coasts of Africa and parts of Asia from the 1500s to the 1800s. Then, starting in the late 1800s and into the 1900s, Europeans colonized interior Africa and Asia.

The major flows of global migration from 1500 on are shown in Figure 3.10. The migration flows include movements from Europe to North America (1); from southern Europe to South and Central America (2); from Britain and Ireland to Africa and Australia (3); from Africa to the Americas during the period of slavery (4); and from India to eastern Africa, Southeast Asia, and Caribbean America (5).

Among the greatest human migrations in recent centuries was the flow from Europe to the Americas. Emigration from Europe (1 and 2 in Fig. 3.10) began slowly. Before the 1830s, perhaps 2.75 million Europeans left to settle overseas. The British went to North America, Australia, New Zealand, and South Africa (3). From Spain and Portugal, many hundreds of thousands of Europeans emigrated to Middle and South America. Early European colonial settlements grew, even in coastal areas of present-day Angola, Kenya, and Indonesia. The rate of European emigration increased sharply between 1835 and 1935, with perhaps as many as 75 million departing for colonies in Africa and Asia and for economic opportunities in the Americas. Although millions of Europeans eventually returned to their homelands, the net outflow from Europe was enormous, as evidenced by the sheer number of Canadians and Americans who identify themselves as being of European ancestry.

As already discussed, the Americas were the destination of another mass of immigrants: African slaves. African slaves were among the early non-American Indian settlers in this country (4). Although this migration is mapped as just one of the eight major

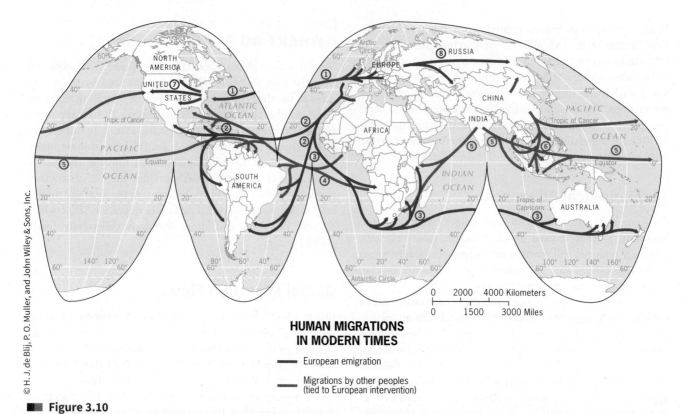

© H. J. de Blij, P. O. Muller, and John Wiley & Sons, Inc.

**HUMAN MIGRATIONS
IN MODERN TIMES**

—— European emigration

—— Migrations by other peoples
(tied to European intervention)

■ **Figure 3.10**

Major Routes of Human Migration Between 1500 and 1950. 1. Europeans moving to North America during and after the colonial period. 2. Movement of southern Europeans to South and Central America during the colonial period. 3. Movement of British and Irish to Africa and Australia during the colonial period. 4. Africans transported to the Western Hemisphere as slaves. 5. Indians brought to other British colonies to serve administrative and commercial roles. 6. Chinese migrants to Southeast Asia and the Americas in the nineteenth and twentieth centuries. 7. Westward migration in the United States. 8. Eastward migration of Russians across Siberia and into Central Asia.

migration streams, its immense and lasting impact on both sides of the Atlantic sets it apart from all the others.

Even as the Atlantic slave trade was in progress, European colonialism generated major migrations in other places in the world. The British, who took control over South Asia, transported tens of thousands of "indentured" workers from present-day India, Pakistan, and Sri Lanka to East and South Africa (see symbol (5) in Fig. 3.10). Today, people of South Asian ancestry are substantial minorities in South Africa, Kenya, and Tanzania. South Asian immigrants in eastern and southern Africa became business leaders in the region. South Asians control a disproportionate share of commerce and hold significant wealth in the region, fueling ethnic friction.

Long before the British arrived in India, Hindu influences radiated into Southeast Asia, reaching the Indonesian islands of Java and Bali. Later, the British renewed the Indian migration stream, bringing South Asians to the Malay Peninsula (including Singapore) and to their Pacific holdings, including Fiji (Fig. 3.10).

The British were also instrumental in relocating Asians, mainly from India, to such Caribbean countries as Trinidad and Tobago and Guyana, the trans-Pacific stream labeled 5 in Fig. 3.10. The Dutch were pivotal in the migration of many Javanese from what is today Indonesia to the former Dutch dependency of Suriname along the same route.

Guest Workers

Significant global migration flows in recent decades have come in response to governmental efforts to promote immigration to fill labor needs. The countries of Europe that were major participants in World War II lost millions of young men in the long conflict. After the war, European countries, rebuilding their economies with the help of the U.S.-sponsored Marshall Plan, found themselves in need of laborers. Two flows of migration into Western European countries began: first within the European region, as workers from poorer European countries and regions migrated to economically growing areas; and second from outside of Europe, as millions of foreign workers immigrated from North Africa (the majority to France) and Turkey (mostly to Germany) as well as from the Caribbean region, India, and Africa (many to the United Kingdom).

Western European governments called the labor migrants **guest workers**—a term that is now used to describe migrant labor in other places as well. The laws allowing guest workers into Europe assumed the workers would fill the void left by those who died during World War II, and then they would return to their home countries. Instead, most guest workers stayed both because they wanted to and because they were needed. Two to three generations of Turks have now been born in Germany, making them far more than "guests." The German government, which had for decades defined German citizens as those of German descent, allowed Turks to become citizens of the country in 2005.

Not only in Germany, but in countries around the world, millions of guest workers live outside of their home country and send remittances from their jobs home. Guest workers often work as agricultural laborers or in service industries, including hotels, restaurants, and tourist attractions. The home states of these workers are fully aware that their citizens have visas and are working abroad. In many instances, the economies of the home countries come to rely on the remittances, and the home governments work with destination countries and with the international labor organization to protect the rights of the guest workers.

Despite the legal status of guest workers and the work of governments and international organizations to protect them, many employers abuse them because guest workers are often unaware of their rights. Long hours and low pay are common, but guest workers continue to work because the money is better than they would ordinarily receive and because they are supporting families at home.

When the need for labor declines, destination governments can squeeze out guest workers. At the same time, the government of the home country can pull out its guest workers, bringing them home when conditions in the destination region become perilous. For example, over 30,000 Indonesians were working in the Middle East before the 2003 Iraq War; the Indonesian government decided to pull its workers home just before the war began.

Guest workers are documented migrants who have work visas, usually short term. Often the destination governments extend the visas if certain sectors of the economy still need laborers. Whether short or long term, the international flow of guest workers changes the ethnic, linguistic, and religious mosaic of the places where they go. In Europe, for example, guest workers from Turkey, North Africa, South Asia, and other former colonial holdings have altered the cultural landscape of the region. New temples, mosques, restaurants, grocery stores, shops, and service industries geared toward migrants have taken root in Europe's cultural landscape.

Regional Migration Flows

The huge flows of migrants mapped in Figure 3.10 were unprecedented and meet few rivals in terms of sheer numbers today. Although some global migration flows already discussed

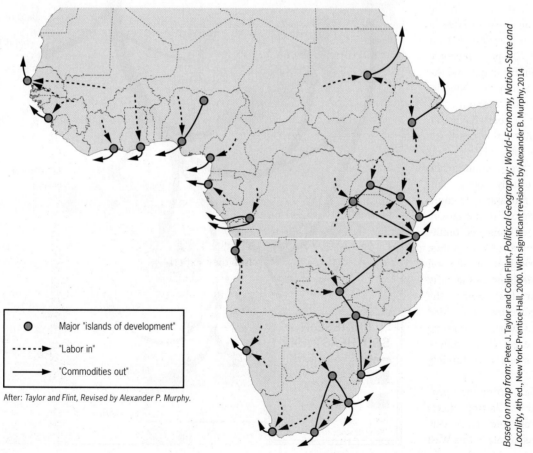

Based on map from: Peter J. Taylor and Colin Flint, Political Geography: World-Economy, Nation-State and Locality, 4th ed., New York: Prentice Hall, 2000. With significant revisions by Alexander B. Murphy, 2014

Legend:
- ● Major "islands of development"
- ----▶ "Labor in"
- ——▶ "Commodities out"

After: Taylor and Flint, Revised by Alexander P. Murphy.

■ Figure 3.11

Islands of Development in Subsaharan Africa.   Islands of development are cities that receive foreign and domestic investment. Migrants from rural areas and neighboring countries are pulled toward these cities to find work. Commodities produced in islands of development are typically exported.

were forced and some were voluntary, each occurred at a global scale and across major world regions. Migration also occurs at a regional scale, with migrants going to a neighboring country to take advantage of short-term economic opportunities, to reconnect with their cultural group across borders, or to flee political conflict or war.

ECONOMIC OPPORTUNITIES

To understand migration flows from one poor country to another, it is not sufficient to analyze the flow at the global scale. We need to understand where the region fits into the global interaction picture and to see how different locations within the region fit into interaction patterns at both global and regional scales. Cities in the developing world are typically where most foreign investment goes, where the vast majority of paying jobs are located, and where infrastructure is concentrated. These port cities become so-called **islands of development** within larger less-developed regions (Fig. 3.11).

Within the region of West Africa, the cities in the oil-producing areas of Nigeria are islands of development. In the mid-1970s, poorer people in Togo, Benin, Ghana, and the northern regions of Nigeria, perceiving that economic life was better in coastal Nigeria, were lured to the coast for short-term jobs while the oil economy was good. The migrants, usually young men, worked as much as they could and sent almost all the money they earned home as remittances to support their families. They worked until the oil economy declined in the early 1980s. At that point, the Nigerian government decided the foreign workers were no longer needed. Two million foreign workers were forcibly pushed out.

Global economic processes and the lasting effects of European colonialism certainly played a role in this West African migration flow. By looking at migration flows at the regional scale, we can see

regional economic influences and the pull of islands of development in places such as Nigeria.

European colonialism also had an impact on regional migration flows in Southeast Asia. Europe's colonial occupation of Southeast Asia presented economic opportunities for the Chinese. During the late 1800s and early 1900s, millions of Chinese laborers fled famine and political strife in southern China to work as contract laborers in Southeast Asia (Fig. 3.12). Many remained, and today their descendants constitute a Chinese minority in Southeast Asian countries that accounts for substantial portions of the population: 14 percent in Thailand, 23 percent in Malaysia, and 74 percent in Singapore. The Chinese minority in Indonesia accounts for only about 3 percent of the total population, but Indonesia has more than 200 million people, so its Chinese minority is one of Southeast Asia's largest clusters. Over time, the

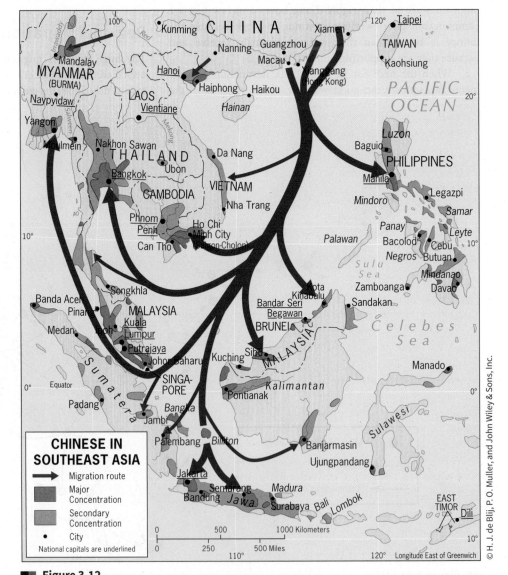

■ **Figure 3.12**
Chinese in Southeast Asia. The great majority of Chinese who live in Southeast Asia migrated from southeastern China.

overseas Chinese in Southeast Asia became leaders in trade, commerce, and finance in the region, taking an economic position much like that of Southern Asians in Eastern and Southern Africa. The presence of overseas Chinese migrants has sometimes led to significant discord in receiving countries. In May 2014, longstanding Sino-Vietnamese tensions erupted into violent protests after China announced plans to build an oil rig in an area in the South China Sea that is also claimed by Vietnam. Rioters attacked Chinese migrants, 21 of whom died, and set fire to Chinese businesses (many of which were actually owned by Taiwanese migrants).

A significant recent example of regional migration is the movement of peoples from Mexico and countries farther south into the United States. That migration rapidly accelerated in the 1970s and 1980s—peaking around the year 2000 with close to 1 million immigrants arriving each year. The number of migrants fell off sharply after the economic downturn of 2008, but the imprint of this decades-long migration is still very much in evidence. Mexican immigrants alone now comprise close to 4 percent of the U.S. population, and they play a fundamentally important economic role in many States and locales.

RECONNECTION OF CULTURAL GROUPS

Regional migration flows also center on reconnecting cultural groups across borders. A migration stream with enormous consequences is the flow of Jewish immigrants to Israel. At the turn of the twentieth century, fewer than 50,000 Jewish residents lived in what was then Palestine. From 1919 to 1948, the United Kingdom of Great Britain and Northern Ireland held control over Palestine, and Britain encouraged Jews, whose ancestors had fled more than a thousand years earlier from the Middle East to Europe, to return to the region. By 1948, as many as 750,000 Jews resided in Palestine, when the United Nations intervened to partition the area and establish the independent state of Israel. The original boundaries of the new state are shown in orange in Figure 3.13. Following the division of the land between the newly created Israeli state and the state of Palestine, another migration stream began when 600,000 Palestinian Arabs fled or were pushed out of Israeli territories. Palestinians sought refuge in neighboring Jordan, Egypt, Syria, and beyond.

Through a series of wars, Israel expanded its area of territorial control (Fig. 3.13) and actively built settlements for new Jewish immigrants in Palestinian territories (Fig. 3.14). Jewish immigrants from the Eurasian region continue to migrate to Israel. Following the collapse of the Soviet Union in the early 1990s, thousands of Jews who had been unable to practice their religion in the Soviet Union migrated to Israel. Today Israel's population of 7.8 million, including almost 2 million Arab Israelis, continues to grow through immigration as well as substantial natural increase.

CONFLICT AND WAR

At the end of World War II, as many as 15 million Germans migrated westward from their homes in Eastern Europe, either voluntarily or because they were forced to leave. Before the East German government built the Berlin Wall and the Iron Curtain divided Western and Eastern Europe, several million Germans fled Soviet-controlled East Germany into what was then West Germany. And millions of migrants left Europe altogether to go to the United States (1.8 million), Canada (1.1 million), Australia (1 million), Israel (750,000), Argentina (750,000), Brazil (500,000), Venezuela (500,000),

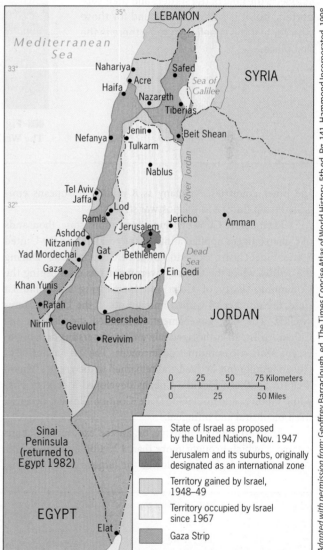

Adapted with permission from: Geoffrey Barraclough, ed. The Times Concise Atlas of World History, 5th ed. Pg. 141. Hammond Incorporated, 1998.

■ Figure 3.13

Changing Boundaries of Israel. The areas in green on the map along with the areas in yellow were the territory of Palestine under the 1947 United Nations plan. After partition, Palestine quickly lost the areas in green to Israel. Israel returned the Gaza Strip to Palestine in 2005. The areas in yellow on the map are the "Occupied Territories," including the West Bank, to the west of the River Jordan and the Golan Heights, west of Syria.

FIELD NOTE

"Just a few miles into the West Bank, not far from Jerusalem, the expanding Israeli presence could not be missed. New settlements dot the landscape, often occupying strategic sites that are also easily defensible. These 'facts on the ground' will certainly complicate the effort to carve out a stable territorial order in this much-contested region. That, of course, is the goal of the settlers and their supporters, but it is salt on the wound for those who contest the Israeli right to be there in the first place."

© Alexander B. Murphy

■ **Figure 3.14**
The West Bank, Outside Jerusalem, Israel.

and other countries. As many as 8 million Europeans emigrated from Europe in the postwar stream.

Even before Cuba became a communist state, thousands of Cuban citizens applied annually for residency in the United States. Fidel Castro came to power in Cuba in 1959. During the 1960s, while the Cuban government was establishing the Communist Party of Cuba and formalizing a communist state, the number of Cuban immigrants in the United States swelled. The U.S. government formalized the flow as the Cuban Airlift, an authorized movement of persons desiring to escape from a communist government. The vast majority of Cuban immigrants arrived and remained in the greater Miami area. In southern Florida, Cubans developed a core of Hispanic culture, and in 1973, Dade County, Florida, declared itself bicultural and bilingual.

In 1980 another massive, organized exodus of Cubans occurred, which brought more than 125,000 Cubans to U.S. shores. Special legislation allowed the large group to become naturalized citizens over time. The Cuban influx persisted throughout the 1980s, and then in 1994 over 30,000 Cubans fled for the United States. By that point, the Soviet Union had collapsed, and its financial support for the Cuban government was cut substantially. The 1994 exodus pushed diplomats in both the United States and Cuba to come to an agreement on Cuban migration. In 1995, the U.S. government established a new policy designed to stem the flow of Cuban migrants to the United States.

National Migration Flows

National migration flows can also be thought of as internal migration flows. Internal migration can be quite significant. In the United States, a massive two-centuries-long migration stream has carried the center of population west and more recently also south, as Figure 3.15 shows. As the American populace migrates westward, it is also shifting from north to

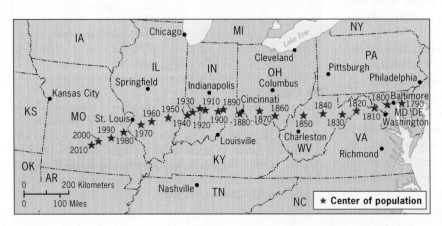

■ **Figure 3.15**
Changing Center of Population.   The steady march west has been unrelenting, with the slight southward trend reflecting increased migration to the Southwest over the past few decades.   *Data from:* United States Census Bureau, *Statistical Abstract*, 2011.

south, to reflect migration flows from south to north and back again. After the American Civil War, and gaining momentum during World War I, millions of African Americans migrated north to work in the industrial Northeast and Midwest. This internal migration flow continued during the 1920s, declined during the depression years of the 1930s, and then resumed its upward climb.

In the 1970s, the trend began to reverse itself: African Americans began leaving the North and returning to the South. The reversal had several causes. Although the civil rights movement in the 1960s did not change conditions in the South overnight, it undoubtedly played a role in the reverse migration. Disillusionment with deteriorating living conditions in the Rustbelt of the urban North and West, coupled with growing economic opportunities in southern cities, also drew African Americans southward. African Americans who lived in northern cities migrated to southern cities, not to rural areas, as the urban economies of the Sun Belt began to grow.

Russia also experienced a major internal migration, but in Russia people migrated east, from the heartland of the Russian state (near Moscow and St. Petersburg) to the shores of the Pacific. This eastward migration significantly altered the cultural mosaic of Eurasia, and understanding this migration flow helps us understand the modern map of Eurasia. During the tsarist (1800s–1910s) and communist (1920s–1980s) periods, Russian and Soviet rulers tried to occupy and consolidate the country's far eastern frontier, moving industries eastward, building railroads and feeder lines, and establishing Vladivostok on the Pacific Coast as one of the world's best equipped naval bases. As Russia and then the Soviet Union expanded outward and to the east, the country incorporated numerous ethnic minorities.

During the communist period, the Soviet government also employed a policy of **Russification**, which sought to assimilate all the people in the Soviet territory into the Russian culture. One way the Soviets pushed for Russification was by encouraging people of Russian heritage to move out of Moscow and St. Petersburg and fill in the country. By 1980, as many as 30 million Russians had moved out toward the borders. After the collapse of the Soviet Union in 1991, some people moved back to their original homelands, but the map will long carry the impact of Russia's eastward expansion.

Mexico offers a more recent example of significant internal migration driven by international migration. Northern Mexico was the most important source-region for the Mexican migration to the United States described above. By 2005, an estimated one out of every two people born in the northern Mexican State of Zacatecas lived in the United States. As a result, the northern areas of Mexico experienced a labor shortage. In response, Mexican workers from areas farther south in the country migrated northward, taking jobs especially in Mexico's agricultural sector. Many such migrants were Huichol Indians, one of Mexico's indigenous populations. Ironically, the Huichol in northern Mexico are experiencing the same kind of substandard living conditions, lack of acceptance by locals, and exploitation by employers that many

Mexicans from the north experienced once they arrived in the United States.

The Special Case of Refugees

You may have seen a story on the televised news showing thousands upon thousands of poor people fleeing a crisis in their home region or country by walking. They put their few earthly possessions and their babies on their backs and walk. They walk to another town. They walk beyond their country's border. They walk to a refugee camp without adequate food, water, or amenities. International agencies try to mount emergency relief efforts while disease spreads, dooming infants and children and emaciating adults. As they walk, they remember all they are leaving behind: the only life they have known. But in the midst of war and persecution, it is too hard to hold onto this life. So, they walk.

The vast majority of refugees do not make it far from home. The Office of the United Nations High Commissioner for Refugees (UNHCR) estimates that 83 percent of refugees flee to a country in the same region as their home country. The world's refugee population has grown steadily since the founding of the Refugee Convention in 1951, which established an international law specifying who is a refugee and what legal rights they have. The main goal of the 1951 Refugee Convention was to help European refugees following the end of World War II. The UNHCR helped to repatriate most of the refugees from World War II.

In 1970, the United Nations reported that 2.9 million persons were refugees; the majority were Palestinian Arabs dislocated by the creation of the state of Israel and the armed conflicts that followed. In 1980, the global refugee total had nearly tripled, to over 8 million. By 2013, the UNHCR reported 11.1 million refugees fleeing from their homes and across country borders (Fig. 3.16).

The United Nations agency that monitors the refugee problem is the key organization supporting refugees. It organizes and funds international relief efforts and negotiates with governments and regimes on behalf of the refugees. But UNHCR is not alone in tracking this global problem; other offices often contradict UNHCR's data, arguing that the situation is even worse than the United Nations suggests.

The 1951 Refugee Convention defines a **refugee** as "a person who has a well-founded fear of being persecuted for reasons of race, religion, nationality, membership of a particular social group, or political opinion." Countries interpret this definition in different ways, especially since the phrase "well founded" leaves much room for judgment.

Perhaps the biggest problem with the UN definition has to do with internally displaced persons (called IDPs, sometimes called internal refugees). **Internally displaced persons** are people who have been displaced within their own countries, such as the victims of Hurricane Katrina, but they do not cross international borders as they flee. IDPs tend to remain undercounted, if not almost invisible. In 2013, UNHCR estimated that 20.8 million people (in addition to the 11.1 million

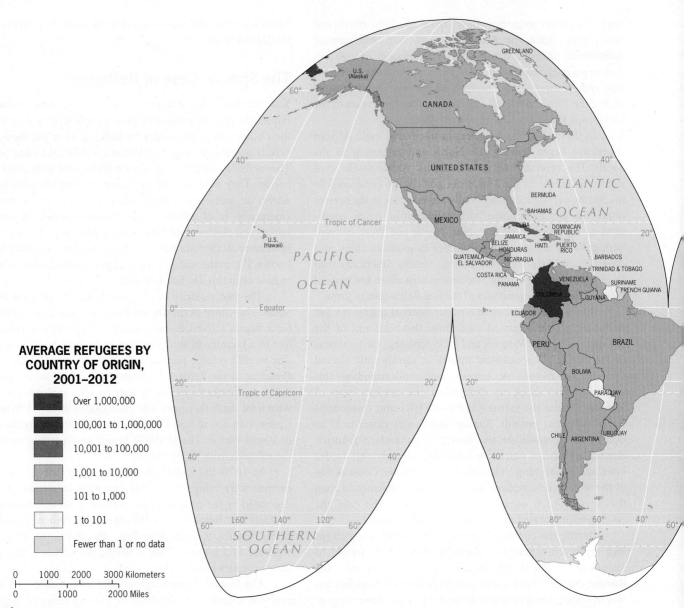

AVERAGE REFUGEES BY COUNTRY OF ORIGIN, 2001–2012

- Over 1,000,000
- 100,001 to 1,000,000
- 10,001 to 100,000
- 1,001 to 10,000
- 101 to 1,000
- 1 to 101
- Fewer than 1 or no data

0   1000   2000   3000 Kilometers
0   1000   2000 Miles

■ **Figure 3.16**

Average Number of Refugees by Country of Origin from 2001 to 2012.   This map highlights the home countries of the world's refugees. Afghanistan and Iraq had the highest average number of refugees between 2001 and 2012. The war in Afghanistan generated more than twice as many refugees as the war in Iraq. Civil war in Sudan and continuing strife in Somalia also caused millions to leave their home countries and be classified as refugees. The data are reported through 2012; so, refugees generated by civil war in Syria are not as evident as the protests against Assad and ensuing full scale civil war began in 2011.   *Data from*: World Bank, 2014.

international refugees) were IDPs—forced to abandon their homes. The United Nations and international law distinguish between *refugees*, who have crossed one or more international borders during their move and encamped in a country other than their own, and *internally displaced persons*, who abandon their homes but remain in their own countries.

Because the status of a refugee is internationally defined and recognized and comes with legal rights, the UN Refugee Agency and the world's states must distinguish between refugees and migrants who may be just as poor or desperate but who do not qualify for refugee status. When a refugee meets the official criteria, he or she becomes eligible for assistance,

including possible **asylum**, which is the right to protection in the first country in which the refugee arrives. Other migrants do not have the right to asylum. Refugee status can extend over decades and become the very basis for a way of life, as has happened in the Middle East. In Jordan, Palestinian refugees have become so integrated into the host country's national life that they are regarded as permanent refugees, but in Lebanon other Palestinians wait in refugee camps for resettlement and still qualify as temporary refugees.

The United Nations helps ensure that refugees and internally displaced persons are not forcibly returned to a homeland where persecution is still continuing. Once the violence subsides

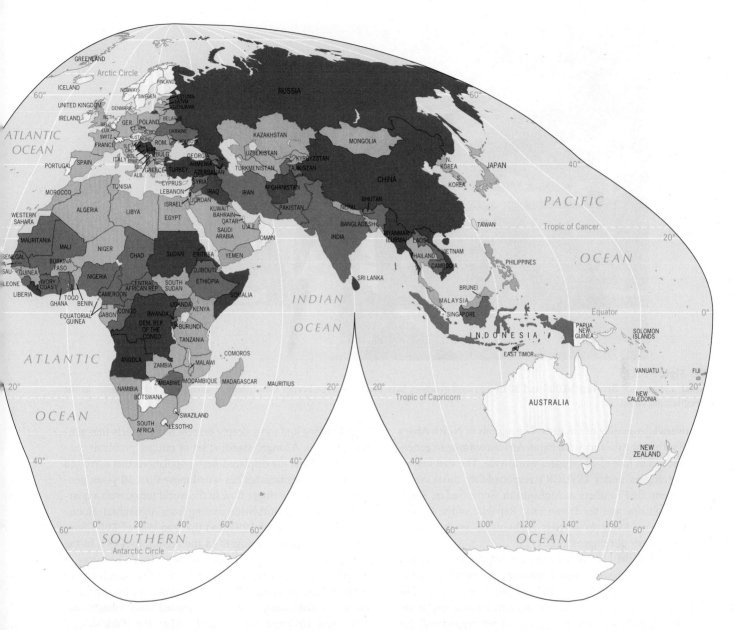

in a place and the conditions improve, the UNHCR helps return refugees to their homelands, a process called **repatriation**.

In the 1990s, hostilities broke out between the Hutu and Tutsi ethnic groups in Rwanda that led to a genocide killing hundreds of thousands and a disastrous exodus of more than one million refugees who fled to neighboring Democratic Republic of the Congo (then called Zaire), Tanzania, and Uganda. The Tutsi–Hutu strife in Rwanda spread to neighboring Burundi and dislocated tens of thousands. After the civil war in Rwanda calmed down in 1996, the UNHCR and the World Health Organization watched and aided as 500,000 Rwandans returned from across the border in the Democratic Republic of Congo.

In addition, some 9 million Syrians have been uprooted since the outbreak of civil war in 2011. Most refugees fled to neighboring Turkey, Lebanon, Jordan, and Iraq, which already had substantial refugee populations from other regional conflicts. In 2012, UNHCR built the temporary Zaatari refugee camp in Jordan near the Syrian border. The camp, only 7.8 square kilometers (3 sq mi), has become a more permanent living space for over 100,000 refugees from the conflict who live in harsh conditions and cramped quarters. Another 50,000 to 80,000 Syrian refugees have fled across the border to the tiny town of Arsal, Lebanon. The refugees now outnumber the local population in Arsal, and the "town's electrical grid, waste management system and water supply are struggling to serve a population almost three times its original size" (Gebeily and Haines-Young 2014) (Fig. 3.17). In addition, 6 million Syrians remain internally displaced, and an estimated 100,000 have been resettled in Europe and elsewhere.

REGIONS OF DISLOCATION

The refugee situation changes frequently as some refugees return home, conditions permitting, and as other new streams suddenly form. Yet we can make certain generalizations about

Ratib Al Safadi/Anadolu Agency/Getty Images

■■ **Figure 3.17**
Arsal, Lebanon.   Between 50,000 and 80,000 Syrians refugees have fled across the border into Lebanon since 2011, taking shelter in the Arsal refugee camp.

the overall geography of refugees. The regions of North Africa and Southwest Asia and Subsaharan Africa continue to generate more than half of all refugees worldwide. The vast majority of refugees under UNHCR's responsibility today, some 60 percent, fled conflicts in Afghanistan, Syria, Sudan, South Sudan, Somalia, and the Democratic Republic of the Congo. Syria appears likely to surpass Afghanistan as the largest source country of refugees in 2014.

In 2010 the United Nations reported that festering war and conflict in the world was diminishing the number of refugees who were repatriated (returned home) each year. The High Commissioner on Refugees stated that a majority of the world's refugees had been refugees (and not repatriated) for more than five years. Most refugees move without any more goods than they can carry with them. When the United States and its allies began their retaliatory bombing in Afghanistan following the terrorist attack on New York and Washington in September 2001, tens of thousands of Afghan refugees climbed across mountain passes to reach the relative safety of Pakistan, able only to bring a few personal belongings. Most refugees make their first "step" on foot, by bicycle, wagon, open boat, or crowded caravan (Fig. 3.18). Refugees are suddenly displaced, limiting their options, and most have few resources to invest in their journey. As a result, the vast majority of the world's refugees come from relatively poor countries and they travel to neighboring countries that are also poor. The impact of refugee flows is certainly felt most in the poorest countries of the world.

North Africa and Southwest Asia
This geographic region extending from Morocco in the west to Afghanistan in the east contains some of the world's

longest-lasting and most deeply entrenched conflicts that generate refugees. A longer-standing set of refugee problems centers on Israel and the displaced Arab populations that surround it. Conflict in Afghanistan has lasted more than 30 years, generating the largest refugee flow in the world today, with a quarter of the refugees worldwide coming from Afghanistan alone.

The Gulf War of 1991 and the Iraq War of 2003 have generated millions of refugees in the region. In 1991, in the aftermath of the Gulf War that followed Iraq's invasion of Kuwait, a significant percentage of the Kurdish population of northern Iraq, threatened by the surviving military apparatus and under Baghdad's control, abandoned their villages and towns and streamed toward and across the Turkish and Iranian borders. The refugee movement of Iraq's Kurds involved as many as 1.85 million people and riveted world attention on the plight of people who are condemned to such status through the actions of others. It led the United States and its allies to create a secure zone for Kurds in northern Iraq in the hope of persuading displaced Kurds in Turkey and Iran to return to their country. But this effort was only partially successful. The events surrounding the Gulf War severely dislocated the Kurdish people of Iraq, as Figure 3.18 shows; many remain refugees in Turkey as well as Iran. The war in Iraq generated over 2 million refugees, most of whom are living in neighboring Syria and Jordan, and 2.8 million IDPs. Following the outbreak of civil war in Syria in 2011, hundreds of thousands of Kurds, some of whom had sought refuge in Syria only a few years earlier, were forced to flee. Some 200,000 Syrian Kurds became refugees in Iraq. In contrast to the tensions that have arisen following the influx of Syrian refugees into Lebanon, Jordan, and Turkey, Iraqis have

ASSOCIATED PRESS

■■ **Figure 3.18**

Pakistan.   Refugees from Afghanistan pour across the border into Pakistan in crowded caravans after the U.S. military action began in Afghanistan in 2001.

been more welcoming, perhaps because many have been displaced themselves. To make matters even more complex, there is still a sizable population of Iranian refugees in Iraq stemming from the Iran–Iraq conflict over three decades ago, including members of the exiled People's Mujahedin of Iran, or MEK, that remain in a camp and are vulnerable to attack.

During the 1980s, Afghanistan was caught in the Soviets' last imperialist campaign and paid an enormous price for it. The Soviet invasion of Afghanistan at the end of 1979, in support of a puppet regime, as well as Afghan resistance, generated a double migration stream that carried millions westward into Iran and eastward into Pakistan. At the height of the exodus, 2.5 million Afghans were estimated to be living in camps in Iran, and some 3.7 million gathered in tent camps in Pakistan's northwestern province and in southern Baluchistan. The Soviet invasion seemed destined to succeed quickly, but the Russian generals underestimated the strength of Afghan opposition. U.S. support for the Muslim forces in the form of weapons supplies helped produce a stalemate and eventual Soviet withdrawal, but this was followed by a power struggle among Afghan factions. As a result, most of the more than 6 million refugees in Iran and Pakistan, about one-quarter of the country's population, stayed where they were.

In 1996, the Taliban, an Islamic fundamentalist movement that began in northwest Pakistan, emerged in Afghanistan and took control of most of the country, imposing strict Islamic rule and suppressing the factional conflicts that had prevailed since the Soviet withdrawal. Although several hundred thousand refugees moved back to Afghanistan from

Pakistan, the harsh Taliban rule created a countermigration and led to further refugee movement into neighboring Iran, where their number reached 2.5 million. Eventually, Afghanistan became a base for anti-Western terrorist operations, which reached a climax in the attack on the United States on September 11, 2001. Even before the inevitable military retaliation began, and despite efforts by both Pakistan and Iran to close their borders, tens of thousands of Afghan refugees flooded across, intensifying a refugee crisis that is now more than a quarter-century old.

Amidst the crises in Israel/Palestine, Iraq, Syria, and Afghanistan, nearly every country in Southwest Asia is currently experiencing the impact of refugees.

Africa

During the last decade of the twentieth century and the first years of the twenty-first, several of the world's largest refugee crises occurred in Subsaharan Africa. In the 1990s and early 2000s, refugee flows in West, Central, and East Africa combined to put Subsaharan Africa at the head of the world's refugee flows. Today, however, there are fewer refugees in Subsaharan Africa than in North Africa and Southwest Asia.

Despite ongoing problems with political instability in the region, the refugee situation has improved in some parts of Subsaharan Africa in recent years. In 1997, civil wars in Liberia and Sierra Leone sent columns of hundreds of thousands of refugees streaming into Guinea and the Ivory Coast. The UNHCR reported more than 1.5 million refugees in West Africa in 1997. In 2013, the number of refugees in West

Africa declined to under 270,000 as a result of improved political stability and repatriation. The largest refugee flows in Subsaharan Africa now come out of Central and East Africa, including the Democratic Republic of the Congo, Sudan, and Somalia.

Sudan, which began a second civil war in 1983, demonstrates the complexities of refugee crises in Subsaharan Africa today. The conflict in Sudan was originally between the north, which is largely Arab and Muslim, and the south, which is majority black African and Christian or animist. Sudan, a country whose borders exist because of European colonialism, was home to traditional religions in the south, Christianity brought by Western missionaries in the south, and Islam brought by North African traders in the north.

The government in Khartoum, located in the largely Muslim north, waged a campaign of genocide aimed at ethnic groups in the Christian and animist south during the north–south civil war, which lasted from 1983 to 2005. The government of Sudan funded the Janjaweed militia, which practiced a scorched-earth campaign, burning villages throughout the south.

The civil war between north and south in Sudan caused immense damage. Over 2.2 million people died in the fighting or starved as a result of the war. More than 5 million people were displaced, with over 1.6 million fleeing to neighboring Uganda alone. Both sides of the Sudanese civil war interfered with the efforts of international agencies to help the refugees.

In 1999, Sudan began exporting oil, which is extracted from southern Sudan. Global attention to the humanitarian crisis of the Sudanese civil war prompted the northern government to agree to a compromise. In 2002, the north and south brokered a temporary peace deal, but shortly thereafter, violence began in the Darfur region in western Sudan. The entire north of Sudan is largely Muslim, but only two-thirds of the northerners speak Arabic as their native language. The other one-third are Muslim but are not ethnically Arab. The non-Arab Muslims are part of at least 30 different ethnic groups in the Darfur region of western Sudan. The Arab Muslim government (located in the north) began a campaign of genocide against the non-Arab Muslims in Darfur. The Janjaweed has waged a genocide campaign against the non-Arab, Muslim, darker-skinned Africans in Darfur—a campaign that includes killing over 400,000 people, raping women and girls, taking lands and homes from Africans, and displacing 2.5 million people (Fig. 3.19).

In 2004, U.S. Secretary of State Colin Powell labeled the Janjaweed's actions in Darfur a **genocide**. The 1948 Convention on Genocide defines genocide as "acts committed with intent to destroy, in whole or in part, a national, ethnical, racial, or religious group." The international community is trying to negotiate an end to the government-backed campaign in Darfur, with mixed success. In the meantime, South Sudan in 2011 voted to secede from Sudan. Ironically, the new border, which was created as a solution to a civil war and refugee crisis, has already generated new refugee flows in the region. Many people living in the borderlands between Sudan and South Sudan are unhappy with the placement of the international boundary. In 2012 the countries fought a six-month-long border war, displacing thousands. Violence in South Sudan has resumed as different groups vie for power. In a country of 12 million, recent violence has displaced 1.3 million people, with over

■ **Figure 3.19**
Bredjing, Chad. Refugees from the Darfur region of Sudan bake bread near their tent in Chad's largest refugee camp.

Scott Nelson/Getty Images

300,000 South Sudanese fleeing across the border. The long-lasting refugee and IDP crisis in Sudan and South Sudan help us understand the complexity of political conflict and migration flows in Subsaharan Africa. The Muslim against Muslim conflict in Darfur demonstrates that political conflict is not just religious; it is also ethnic and political.

Regionally, neighboring countries have not helped create stability for the country. Since 1998, just under 6 million people have died in violence in neighboring Democratic Republic of the Congo. Violence in the Democratic Republic of the Congo was partially spurred by the instability created as a result of refugee flows from the 1994 war in neighboring Rwanda. In 2009, attacks by the rebel group Lord's Resistance Army in the northeastern portion of the Democratic Republic of the Congo generated over 1 million refugees.

South Asia

In terms of refugee numbers, South Asia is the third-ranking geographic realm, mainly because of Pakistan's role in accommodating Afghanistan's refugees. During the Soviet intrusion in the 1980s, the UNHCR counted more than 3 million refugees; during the 1990s, the total averaged between 1.2 and 1.5 million. That number rose when U.S.-led forces began retaliating against terrorist bases in October 2001. Today, Afghanistan has an enormous refugee crisis with more than 2 million refugees living outside of Afghanistan, mostly in Pakistan and Iran.

The other major refugee problem in South Asia stems from a civil war in Sri Lanka. This conflict, which formally ended in 2009, arose from demands by minority Tamils for an independent state on the Sinhalese-dominated and -controlled island. The conflict cost tens of thousands of lives and severely damaged the economy. The United Nations reports that about 200,000 people are internally displaced. The United Nations, the European Union, and the Canadian government are working to repatriate the IDPs, particularly in the northern provinces of Sri Lanka. An estimated 90,000 internally displaced persons are uprooted in Sri Lanka today.

Climate change will likely have a significant impact on the refugee picture in South Asia in the decades to come. While the effects of climate change will be felt worldwide, scientists believe Bangladesh will be "ground zero" for climate refugees. The country's 156.6 million citizens live in a river delta one-fifth the size of France, most of which is no more than 6.1 meters (20 ft) above sea level and through which 230 major rivers and streams flow. The country is thus unusually vulnerable to flooding and typhoons. The situation is made worse by human alterations of the environment; extensive groundwater pumping is causing cities to sink, and mangrove deforestation has increased erosion rates and removed natural barriers against storm surges. By 2050, 17 percent of the country may well be inundated. For years, so-called environmental refugees have been moving from Bangladesh into neighboring India, but India is building a border wall to ward off further migration. In a country already facing significant demographic challenges, climate change puts Bangladesh in an even more precarious position.

Southeast Asia

Southeast Asia is a reminder that refugee problems can change quickly. Indochina was the scene of one of the twentieth century's most desperate refugee crises when a stream of between 1 and 2 million people fled Vietnam in the aftermath of the long war that ended in 1975. In the early 1990s, Cambodia produced an exodus of 300,000 refugees escaping from their country's seemingly endless cycle of violence, ending up in refugee camps on the Thailand side of the border. Today, the largest camps in this realm are for IDPs in Myanmar (formerly Burma). Victims of the 2004 tsunami, the 2008 cyclone, and the repressive rule of generals who are seeking to subjugate the country's minorities seek refuge in the camps.

Europe

In the 1990s, the collapse of Yugoslavia and its associated conflicts created the largest refugee crisis in Europe since the end of World War II. In 1995, the UNHCR reported the staggering total of 6,056,600 refugees, a number that some observers felt was inflated by the Europeans' unusually liberal interpretations of the United Nations' rules for refugee recognition. Nevertheless, even after the cessation of armed conflict and the implementation of a peace agreement known as the Dayton Accords, the UNHCR still reports over 100,000 IDPs in the area.

Other Regions

The number of refugees and internally displaced persons in other geographic realms is much smaller. In the Western Hemisphere, only Colombia has a serious internally displaced person problem, numbering around 5.7 million people, caused by the country's protracted political violence coupled with its struggle against narcotics. Colombia's IDP numbers were the largest in the world until 2013, when Syria's civil war generated two million more IDPs than Colombia. Significant areas of Colombia's countryside are vulnerable to armed attack by "narcoterrorists" and paramilitary units; these rural areas are essentially beyond government control, and thousands of villagers have died in the crossfire. Hundreds of thousands more have left their homes to seek protection. Elsewhere in the Western Hemisphere recent earthquakes have displaced millions. A 2010 earthquake in Chile killed hundreds and displaced 2 million Chileans. Six weeks before the Chilean quake, an earthquake in Haiti killed 200,000 people and displaced 1.5 million. Four years later 280,000 Haitian IDPs are still in camps, according to UNHCR. Another 200,000 of the displaced Haitians are living with host families.

People who abandon their familiar surroundings because conditions have become unlivable perform an ultimate act of desperation. In the process, they often face unimaginable challenges and hardships. Refugee and internally displaced person populations are a barometer of the world's future.

Imagine you are from an extremely poor country, and you earn less than $1 a day. Choose a country to be from, and look for it on a map. Assume you are a potential migrant facing a desperate situation. You look at your access to transportation and the opportunities you have to go elsewhere. Be realistic, and describe how you determine where you will go, how you will get there, and what you will do once you get there.

HOW DO GOVERNMENTS AFFECT MIGRATION?

The control of immigration, legal and illegal, the granting of asylum to asylum-seeking refugees, and the fate of cross-border refugees, permanent and temporary, have become hot issues around the world. In Europe, right-wing political parties whip up anti-immigrant sentiment. In California, the state government demands federal monies to provide services for hundreds of thousands of illegal immigrants; if the federal government cannot control its borders, they argue, states should not have to foot the bill. And in the United States today, the federal government faces reproach both from those who want to stop the flow of migration from Mexico and those who argue for opening the United States' doors for migrants from humanitarian crises, including Haiti. In, or at the western edge of, the West Bank, a security barrier is being built in an effort to control the flow of Palestinians into Israel (Fig. 3.20).

Efforts to restrict migration flows are nothing new. Media coverage, political debates, and political wrangling only make it seem so. In the fourteenth century, China built the Great Wall in part as a defensive measure but also as a barrier to emigration (by Chinese beyond the sphere of their authority) and immigration (mainly by Mongol "barbarians" from the northern plains). The Berlin Wall, the Korean DMZ (demilitarized zone), the fences along the Rio Grande—all are evidence of governments' desire to control the movement of people across their borders.

Legal Restrictions

Typically, the obstacles placed in the way of potential immigrants are legal, not physical. In the United States, restrictive legislation on immigration can be traced to 1882, when Congress approved the Oriental Exclusion Acts (1882–1907). Congress designed **immigration laws** to prevent the immigration of Chinese people to California. In 1901, the Australian government approved the Immigration Restriction Act, which ended all nonwhite immigration into the newly united country. The Australian government was particularly

■■ **Figure 3.20**
Security Barrier Near Jerusalem.   In the wake of decades of conflict, controlling the movement of people has become an increasingly prominent policy response on the part of the Israeli government.

targeting Japanese, Chinese, and South Asian immigrants. The act also prohibited immigration by South Pacific Islanders who worked on Australia's large sugar plantations. The Australian government furthered action against the plantation workers (the Kanakas) by deporting the South Pacific Islanders by the end of 1906. These immigration policies created what is known as the *White Australia Policy*, which remained in effect until the 1970s.

Waves of Immigration in the United States

Changes in a country's migration policies are reflected in the number of people entering the country and the origin of the immigrants (see Fig. 3.21). The United States experienced two major waves of immigration before 1930 and another great wave in recent decades. Major changes in the government's migration policies are reflected in this graph. Push factors are also reflected in Figure 3.21, as people in different regions found reasons to leave their home and migrate to the United States.

During the 1800s, the United States opened its doors to immigration. Most of the immigrants arrived from Europe, especially Northern Europe (Scandinavia) and western Europe (including Ireland, Great Britain, Germany, and France). In the later part of the 1800s, a greater proportion of Europeans who immigrated to the United States came from southern and eastern Europe (including Italy, Spain, Portugal, Russia, and Poland).

Following World War I, political tides in the United States turned toward *isolationism*—a policy that favors staying out of entanglements abroad. In addition, at that time, Congress feared the growing migration from eastern and southern Europe. Many whites in the United States at the time saw migrants from this area of the world as darker skinned and therefore inferior. In this context, Congress passed restrictive legislation in 1921, deterring immigration from southern and eastern Europe. Congress set immigration quotas limiting immigration to the United States to 3 percent of the number of a given European country's nationals living in the United States in 1910. In 1910, the greatest proportion of immigrants in the United States came from Northern and western

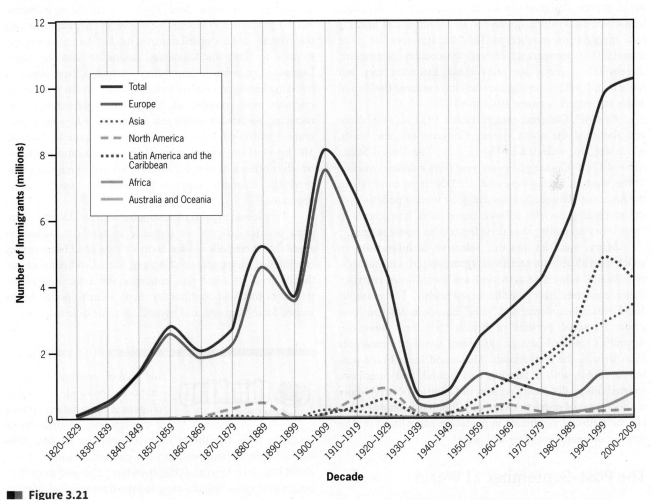

Figure 3.21

Immigration to the United States by Region, 1820 to 2010. During the first wave of migration to the United States, from 1820 to 1930, the vast majority of migrants to the United States came from Europe. During the second wave of migration, from 1930 to the present, a shift occurred and migrants to the United States mainly come from Latin America and Asia. *Data from:* United States Census Bureau, 2012.

Europe; thus the quotas meant that migration from Northern and western Europe greatly outpaced immigration from southern and eastern Europe (Fig. 3.21).

In 1924, Congress altered the Immigration Act by lowering the quota to 2 percent and making 1890 the base year, further reducing the annual total to 150,000 immigrants and further discouraging eastern and southern European migration.

The rapid fall in total immigration to the United States is clearly shown in Figure 3.21. Just prior to the Great Depression, Congress passed the National Origins Law in 1929, which limited immigration to 150,000 persons per year. Congress also tied immigration quotas to the national origins of the U.S. population in 1920. As a result, Congress in effect prevented substantial immigration from Asia. With these laws in effect and the Great Depression in full swing, immigration slowed to a trickle during the 1930s.

After 1940, Congress modified the restrictions on immigration. In 1943, Congress gave China equal status to that of European countries and in 1952 granted Japan a similar status. In 1952, immigration began to rise again (Fig. 3.21) after Congress passed a new Immigration and Nationality Act. Congress designed the act to incorporate all preceding legislation, establishing quotas for all countries and limiting total immigration numbers to 160,000. However, far more than 160,000 immigrants entered the country as refugees, thereby filling quotas for years ahead. Estimates vary, but more than 7 million immigrants may have entered the United States as refugees between 1945 and 1970.

By 1965, Congress recognized the 1952 act as a failure and abolished the quota system. Congress set new limits, which are also reflected in Figure 3.21. The United States allowed 170,000 immigrants per year from countries outside of the Western Hemisphere and 120,000 from countries in the Americas. Refugee policies and guest worker policies over the succeeding decades allowed many more immigrants to come into the country than these limitations would suggest.

Many countries practice **selective immigration**, in which individuals with certain backgrounds (criminal records, poor health, subversive activities) are barred from entering. Other countries have specific requirements. For example, South Africa long demanded "pure" European descent; New Zealand favored persons of British birth and parentage; Australia's assisted-passage program favored immigrants from Britain, the Netherlands, Malta, and Italy; Brazil preferred people with a farming background; and Singapore courted financially secure persons of Chinese ancestry. Many of these types of restrictions are gone, but most countries that are the target of significant immigration place limits on the number of immigrants they will accept.

The Post–September 11 World

Since September 11, 2001, U.S. government immigration policies have incorporated security concerns. Prior to that date, the U.S. border patrol was concerned primarily with drug trafficking and human smuggling. The new government policies affect asylum-seekers and both documented and undocumented immigrants.

After September 11, the U.S. government designated 33 countries as places where al-Qaeda or other terrorist groups operate, and the government automatically detained anyone from one of these 33 countries who entered the United States looking for asylum under a policy called "Operation Liberty Shield." On March 25, 2003, Human Rights Watch criticized the policy, contending that it created "a blanket suspicion of links to terrorism based on nationality alone." On April 17, 2003, the Department of Homeland Security quietly terminated "Operation Liberty Shield." Nonetheless, controls along the U.S. border are much tighter than they were prior to 9-11, with implications not just for the flow of immigrants, but for business and commerce in border regions as well.

In the wake of terrorist attacks in Europe—including major bombings in Madrid in 2004 and London in 2005—European state governments have also focused more attention on immigration matters. Whereas the United States government pursued a "hard" approach, expanding immigration controls after 9-11, the free movement of peoples among the majority of European countries has led state governments to seek to limit undocumented migration into the larger European space while promoting internal policies aimed at fostering immigrant buy-in to the host society. In some cases, migrants must complete an "integration agreement" before receiving permanent status and access to social welfare programs. Austria's integration package, for example, includes 300 hours of language training and a civic education course—which is often a burden for recently arrived immigrants who need the financial support provided by social welfare programs.

People and organizations opposed to the U.S. and European policies adopted in response to terrorist incidences argue that these policies may do more than good because they can intensify misunderstanding and hatred. Whether or not that is true, it seems that concerns about the migration–terrorism link will continue to shape security policy in the United States, Europe, and beyond for some time to come.

One goal of international organizations involved in aiding refugees is repatriation—return of the refugees to their home countries once the threat against them has passed. Take the example of refugees from the conflict in Sudan. Think about how their land and their lives have changed since they became refugees. You are assigned the daunting task of repatriating refugees. What steps would you have to take to rediscover a home for these refugees?

Summary

In the last 500 years, humans have traveled the globe, mapped it, connected it, and migrated across it. In this chapter, we discussed major global, regional, national, and local migration flows. Migration can occur as a result of a conscious decision, resulting in a voluntary migration flow, or migration can occur under duress, resulting in forced migration. Both kinds of migration have left an indelible mark on the world and on its cultural landscapes. Governments attempt to strike a balance among the need for migrant labor, the desire to help people in desperate circumstances, and the desire to stem the tide of migration.

As the world's population mushrooms, the volume of migrants will likely continue to expand. In an increasingly open and interconnected world, neither physical barriers nor politically motivated legislation will hold back tides that are as old as human history. Migrations will also further complicate an already complex global cultural mosaic—raising questions about identity, race, ethnicity, language, and religion, the topics we turn to in the next four chapters.

Geographic Concepts

Bracero Program
refugee camps
remittances
reverse remittances
cyclic movement
periodic movement
migration
activity spaces
nomadism
transhumance
international migration
emigration
immigration
internal migration

forced migration
voluntary migration
human trafficking
laws of migration
gravity model
push factors
pull factors
distance decay
step migration
intervening opportunity
deportation
kinship links
chain migration
immigration wave

colonization
guest workers
regional scale
migration
islands of development
Russification
refugees
internally displaced persons
asylum
repatriation
genocide
immigration laws
selective immigration

Learn More Online

About Immigration to the United States
www.uscis.gov

About Refugees
www.unhcr.org

About Geographic Mobility and Movement in the United States
www.census.gov/hhes/migration/

About the Origin of the World's Migrants Interactive map from Pew Research
http://www.pewglobal.org/2014/09/02/global-migrant-stocks/

Watch It Online

About Migration and Identity
www.learner.org/resources/series85.html#program_descriptions
click on Video On Demand for "A Migrant's Heart"

About the United States–Mexico Border Region
www.learner.org/resources/series180.html#program_descriptions
click on Video On Demand for "Boundaries and Borderlands"

LOCAL CULTURE, POPULAR CULTURE, AND CULTURAL LANDSCAPES

Preserving Culture

This used to be an Italian restaurant. Not anymore, the young man with a thick New York accent said to me, offering a few expletives to describe the Chinese moving into the neighborhood, as well as a prediction: "It's probably gonna be a Chinese restaurant next."

Positano stood, along with dozens of other Italian restaurants on Mulberry Street, at the heart of Little Italy, an ethnic neighborhood in New York City that dates to 1880 (Figure 4.1). By 1900, upwards of 10,000 Italian immigrants clustered in Little Italy, which at its greatest extent covered 50 square blocks of Manhattan.

Young Chinese men left work on the railroads in California and settled in New York, establishing Chinatown south of Little Italy in the late 1800s. In the 1910s, Chinese immigrants established a business association, and in the 1920s a Chinese food industry took root in the neighborhood.

After World War II, second and third generations of Italians were moving to other parts of the city. The *New York Times* reported that in 1950, 50 percent of the residents of Little Italy identified as Italian-American, but that by 2010 only 5 percent identified as Italian-American.

The United States overturned constraints on Chinese immigration in 1965, and after that Chinese immigrants moved into Chinatown in droves. Chinatown expanded into Little Italy, and today only 3 blocks on Mulberry Street constitute the heart of Little Italy. "Of the 8600 residents counted by the census's American Community Survey in the heart of Little Italy in 2009, nearly 4400 were foreign-born. Of those, 89 percent were born in Asia" (Roberts 2011). Many of the Asians in Chinatown today are from Southeast Asia, especially Vietnam and Malaysia.

The closing of Italian restaurants including Positano is not only the result of a declining Italian population in the neighborhood. Little Italy is also pressured from the west by

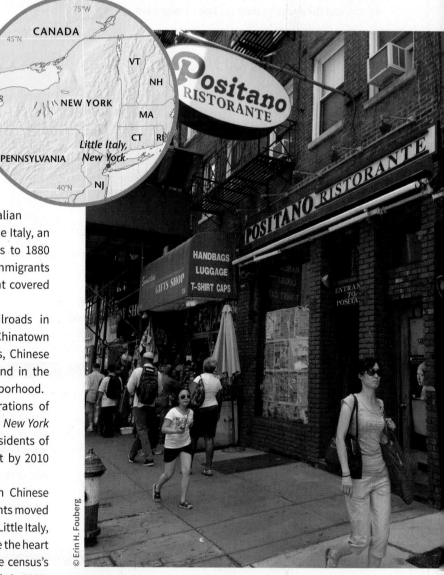

■ Figure 4.1

New York, New York. An Asian woman and child walk past the closed Italian eatery Positano in Little Italy. The restaurant, windows now lined by newspaper, closed in January 2014. The *New York Post* reported eight Italian eateries closed within a year's time, as new landlords have doubled rents. Down the block, a former restaurant now houses a year-round Christmas store, and the owners pay $50,000 a month in rent.

the upscale SoHo neighborhood. New landlords are purchasing buildings and raising the rent on retail spaces in Little Italy. Positano closed after the rent jumped, and the New York Post reported in 2014 that "Eight eateries have shut down in the past year" as rents have doubled.

Immigrant groups establish ethnic neighborhoods in cities, imprinting the place with cultural traits from their homeland, from eateries to specialty shops to churches. Having a place where people with a shared identity belong helps sustain a local culture. In this chapter, we examine what local cultures are and how they make an imprint on the landscape in both cities and rural areas. We consider how innovations in popular culture are created and diffused; and, we study how cultural landscapes are shaped and changed overtime by popular and local cultures.

Key Questions FOR CHAPTER 4

1. What are local and popular cultures?
2. How are local cultures sustained?
3. How is popular culture diffused?
4. How can local and popular cultures be seen in the cultural landscape?

WHAT ARE LOCAL AND POPULAR CULTURES?

A culture is a group of belief systems, norms, and values practiced by a people. Although this definition of culture sounds simple, the concept of culture is actually quite complex. A group of people who share common beliefs can be recognized as a culture in one of two ways: (1) the people may call themselves a culture or (2) other people (including academics) can label a certain group of people as a culture. Traditionally, academics label cultural groups as either folk cultures or as part of popular culture. The idea is that a **folk culture** is small, incorporates a homogeneous population, is typically rural, and is cohesive in cultural traits, whereas **popular culture** is large, incorporates heterogeneous populations, is typically urban, and experiences quickly changing cultural traits. Instead of using this polarity of folk and popular cultures, some academics now see folk and popular cultures as ends of a continuum, defining most cultures as fitting somewhere between folk and popular.

We find folk culture to be a limiting concept because it requires us to create a list of characteristics and look for cultures that meet the list. This methodology of defining folk cultures leaves much to be desired. Once we have our list of characteristics, we must ask ourselves, are the Amish a folk culture? Are the Navajo a folk culture? And it is in this very process that we get frustrated with the concept of folk culture. It is not how we academics define a culture that matters; it is how the people define themselves that counts.

We are interested in questions such as: do the Amish have a group identity, and what cultural practices do they share? How do the Amish navigate through popular culture and defend their local customs? Why do a group of Americans in a small town identify themselves as Swedish Americans and hold festivals to commemorate important Swedish holidays, while other Swedish Americans in other parts of the country function completely unaware of the Swedish holidays? Why do certain ethnic holidays such as St. Patrick's Day transcend ethnicity to be celebrated as a part of popular culture?

In this chapter, we chose to use the concept of local culture rather than folk culture. A **local culture** is a group of people in a particular place who see themselves as a collective or a community, who share experiences, customs, and traits, and who work to preserve those traits and customs in order to claim uniqueness and to distinguish themselves from others.

Local and popular cultures are not ends of a continuum. Both cultures exist in the same places and spaces, manifest in different ways, and are constantly being refined. In an era of globalization, popular culture diffuses around the globe, being embraced by some and rejected by others, all the while infiltrating every corner of the globe. Local cultures persist, and in many places the communities thrive, but they face constant pressure from larger cultural groups and from the enveloping popular culture. The variety of ways people choose to accept, reject, or alter the diffusion of popular cultural practices is remarkable. Some local cultures rely primarily on religion to maintain their belief systems; others rely on community celebrations or on family structures; and still others rely on a lack of interaction with other cultures.

Local cultures are constantly redefining or refining themselves based on interactions with other cultures (local and popular) and diffusion of cultural practices (local and popular). Local cultures also affect places by establishing neighborhoods, building churches or community centers to celebrate important days, and by expressing their material and nonmaterial cultures in certain ways.

The **material culture** of a group of people includes things they construct, such as art, houses, clothing, sports, dance, and foods. **Nonmaterial culture** includes beliefs, practices, aesthetics (what is seen as attractive), and values of a group of people. What members of a local culture produce in their material culture reflects the beliefs and values of their nonmaterial culture.

Unlike local cultures, which are found in relatively small areas, popular culture is ubiquitous and can change in a matter of days or hours. Popular culture is practiced by a heterogeneous group of people: people across identities and across the world. Like local culture, popular culture encompasses music, dance, clothing, food preferences, religious practices, and aesthetic values. The main paths of diffusion of popular culture are the transportation, marketing, and communication networks (including social networks) that interlink vast parts of the world.

Fashions diffuse incredibly quickly today. When Kate Middleton, Duchess of Cambridge, graced Westminster Abbey in a lace wedding gown designed by Sarah Burton for the House of Alexander McQueen at an estimated cost of $65,000, dress designers around the world interpreted or copied the gown within hours (Fig. 4.2). Fewer than ten hours after the wedding aired at 5:30 A.M. Eastern Time, dress designers at Kleinfeld Bridal Salon in New York had replicated Middleton's dress, and they started selling it for $3500 within 48 hours.

In popular culture, fashion trends spread very quickly through the interconnected world; it is a classic case of **hierarchical diffusion**. Hierarchical diffusion can occur through a hierarchy of places. The hierarchy in the fashion world typically begins with the runways of major fashion houses in world cities, including London, Milan, Paris, and New York, which act as the **hearth**, the point of origin. The next tier of places includes flagship stores for the fashion house and editorial headquarters of fashion magazines, also located in global cities. Department store brands interpret the runway fashions for consumption by a larger audience, and the suburban mall receives the innovation. Hierarchical diffusion can also occur through a hierarchy of people. In this case, a designer is the hearth, models are the next tier, celebrities and editors and writers of major magazines follow, and subscribers to fashion magazines follow in close order. Finally, anyone walking through a shopping mall can become a "knower" in the diffusion of a fashion innovation.

We do not see local and popular cultures as being ends of a continuum; rather, we see both operating on the same plane, affecting people and places in different ways across different scales. For example, you may go to a major department

Samir Hussein/WireImage/Getty Images, Inc.

■ **Figure 4.2**
London, United Kingdom. Catherine Middleton, Duchess of Cambridge, enters Westminster Abbey in a wedding gown reminiscent of Grace Kelly's. Sarah Burton of the House of Alexander McQueen, located in London, designed the lace gown. Members of the Royal School of Needlework hand cut and sewed the intricate lace. The Official Royal Wedding website reported that each sewer washed his or her hands every 30 minutes and replaced the needles every three hours to keep the dress pristine and the work exact.

store such as Target or Wal-Mart and see Hutterites or Mennonites dressed in distinctive local clothing in the midst of the ultimate in popular culture: a major international department store. Traditions such as painting henna on one's hands or practicing mystical Kabbalah beliefs are carried from centuries-old customs of local cultures to the global popular culture through a popular culture icon or through the corporations (such as marketing firms) that work to construct popular culture (Fig. 4.3).

Both local cultures and popular cultures are constantly navigating through a barrage of customs diffused from each other and across scales, through a complex of political and economic forces that shape and limit their practices, and through global communications and transportation networks that intricately link certain parts of the world and distance others.

Josiah Kamau/BuzzFoto/FilmMagic

■ **Figure 4.3**
New York. In a truly global fashion, New York City tattoo artist Keith McCurdy flew to the Dominican Republic to ink a design based on traditional Indian henna over an existing tattoo based on a traditional New Zealand design on the hand of Barbados-born singer Rihanna.

In this chapter, we focus on how local cultures are sustained despite the onslaught of popular culture, how popular culture diffuses and is practiced in unique ways in localities of the world, and how local and popular cultures are imprinted on the cultural landscape.

Employing the concept of hierarchical diffusion, describe how you became a "knower" of your favorite kind of music—where is its hearth, and how did it reach you?

HOW ARE LOCAL CULTURES SUSTAINED?

During the 1800s and into the 1900s, the U.S. government had an official policy of **assimilation**. The federal government wanted to assimilate indigenous peoples into the dominant culture in order to make American Indians into "Americans" rather than "Indians." Canadians, Australians, Russians, and other colonial powers adopted similar policies toward indigenous peoples, using schools, churches, and government agents to discourage native practices. In the United States, the federal government forced tribal members to settle in one place and to farm rather than hunt or fish. Public and missionary school teachers punished tribal members for using their native language.

Government agents rewarded the Indians they deemed most "American" with citizenship and paid jobs. The federal government even employed East Coast women from 1888 until 1938 to live on reservations and show the native women how to be "good housewives" by teaching them Victorian ways of cooking, cleaning, and sewing.

Today, several churches and governments have apologized for assimilation policies. In 2008, the governments of Australia and Canada each officially apologized to their indigenous populations: Aboriginals in Australia and First Nations and Inuit in Canada.

The Australian Parliament unanimously passed a motion stating: "We apologize for the laws and policies of successive parliaments and governments that have inflicted profound grief, suffering and loss on these our fellow Australians." Former Australian Prime Minister Kevin Rudd apologized specifically for the government's policy of taking Aboriginal children from their homes and placing them in residential schools—a policy that lasted from the 1800s until the late 1960s.

Canadian Prime Minister Stephen Harper likewise cited the disastrous outcomes of the assimilation policies in his apology to Canada's 1.3 million indigenous people. Prime Minister Harper apologized for the abuse and the lasting negative effects of Canada's residential schools, stating: "We now recognize that it was wrong to separate children from rich and vibrant cultures and traditions, that it created a void in many lives and communities, and we apologize for having done this. We now recognize that, in separating children from their families, we undermined the ability of many to adequately parent their own children and sowed the seeds for generations to follow." Speaking to the indigenous people seated in the House of Commons, he continued, "Not only did you suffer these abuses as children, but as you became parents, you were powerless to protect your own children from suffering the same experience, and for this we are sorry."

The United States government has not formally apologized to American Indians for the policy of assimilation. American Indians in the United States are working to push back assimilation and popular culture by reviving the customs of their local cultures. Many tribes are teaching younger generations their language, reviving their traditional religion, and eating the foods and herbs of their lands, the foods and herbs on which their ancestors depended.

Local cultures are sustained through **customs**. A custom is a practice that a group of people routinely follows. People have customs regarding all parts of their lives, from eating and drinking to dancing and sports. To sustain a local culture, the people must retain their customs. The customs change in small ways over time, but they are maintained despite the onslaught of popular culture.

Researcher Simon Harrison recognizes that local cultural groups purposefully and often fervently define themselves as unique, creating boundaries around their culture and distinguishing themselves from other local cultures. In the age of globalization, where popular culture changes quickly and diffuses rapidly, Harrison finds that local cultures typically have two goals: keeping other cultures out and keeping their own culture in.

For example, a local culture can create a boundary around itself and try to keep other cultures out in order to avoid "contamination and extinction." Harrison uses the example of the Notting Hill carnival in London to describe how Londoners from the West Indies (the Caribbean) claimed the festival as their own, in conjunction with an increasing sense of collective West Indies cultural identity. The festival did not begin as a West Indies celebration. As people from the West Indies shared experiences of "unemployment, police harassment and poor housing conditions" during the 1970s, they began to define themselves as a local culture and redefined the festival as a West Indian celebration.

A local culture can also work to avoid **cultural appropriation**, the process by which other cultures adopt customs and knowledge and use them for their own benefit. Harrison explains that cultural appropriation is a major concern for local cultures because people outside the local culture often privatize the cultural knowledge of a local culture, including natural pharmaceuticals or musical expression, to accumulate wealth or prestige. Local cultures can thus work to keep their customs and knowledge to themselves, to avoid cultural appropriation.

Around the world, local cultures desire to keep popular culture out, keep their culture intact, and maintain control over customs and knowledge. Geographers also recognize that through these actions, places become increasingly important. When defining a place (a town or neighborhood) or a space for a short amount of time (an annual festival) as quintessentially representing the local culture's values, members of a local culture reinforce their culture and their beliefs.

Rural Local Cultures

Members of local cultures in rural areas often have an easier time maintaining their cultures because of their isolation. By living together in a rural area, members of a local culture can more easily keep external influences on the outside. It is no accident that we find Anabaptist groups, such as the Hutterites, the Amish, and the Mennonites, living in rural areas of South Dakota, Pennsylvania, and Virginia, respectively.

For the past five centuries, Anabaptist groups have migrated to rural areas beyond these three states (often fleeing persecution) with the expressed purpose of living apart and staying together. During the Protestant Reformation, Anabaptists broke from both the Catholic Church and the new Protestant churches. Followers of the new religion were called Anabaptists, meaning baptized again, because of their belief in adult baptism, despite having been baptized as infants in the Catholic or Protestant churches.

Anabaptists broke from the state as well as the church; they stressed pacifism and soon suffered persecution. As a consequence, Anabaptists migrated east to Moravia and Austria, and then to Russia and the Ukraine. Continually moving to rural areas to live apart, alone, and avoid persecution, a group of Anabaptists called the Hutterites, named for leader Jacob Hutter, eventually migrated to North America in the second half of the 1800s.

Old Order Anabaptist groups are often shown in stereotypical ways in the popular media, but major differences exist across Old Order Amish, Mennonites, Hutterites, and Brethren. Hutterites are the only Anabaptist group who live communally (Fig. 4.4). Rather than living with immediate family on a farmstead, Hutterites live in colonies of about 100 people, with individuals ranging in ages from infant to elderly. More than 425 colonies are located in Minnesota, South

■ **Figure 4.4**
Stratford, South Dakota. A Hutterite boy who lives in the Hutterville Farm colony near Stratford, South Dakota. Distinctive modes of dress and ways of living help to sustain group identity.

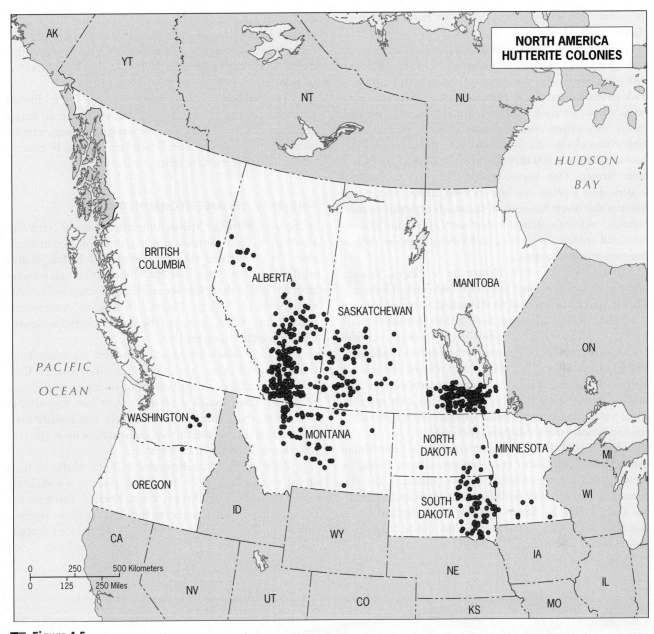

Figure 4.5
Hutterite Colonies in North America. *Data from:* www.hutterites.org, last accessed July 10, 2014.

Dakota, North Dakota, Saskatchewan, Montana, and Alberta (Fig. 4.5). In their book *On the Backroad to Heaven,* Donald Kraybill and Carl Bowman explain that the lynchpin of each colony is the Hutterite religion. Members of the colony join together for a 30-minute service every night as well as on Sundays. The most prominent position in a colony is held by the minister, who speaks in archaic German, reading sermons written in the sixteenth century.

Unlike the Amish, Hutterites readily accept technologies that help them in their agricultural pursuits. Hutterite colonies were generally slow to accept technologies such as cameras and cell phones out of concern that they would encourage individualistic behaviors or undermine the Hutterite religion. Today, it is common for young adult Hutterites to

use cell phones and Internet dating sites to find suitable marriage partners in colonies in other states or countries.

Colonies assign separate jobs and tasks to men and women, which reinforces a patriarchal social structure. Kraybill and Bowman explain that marriages happen across colonies, and women move to their husband's colony after marrying. If a Hutterite woman from Alberta meets a Hutterite man from North Dakota through an Internet dating site, and they eventually decide to marry, the Canadian woman will move to the United States. As a result, a single colony is usually composed of only one or two surnames. Moving to their husband's colony perpetuates women's weaker political position in the colony. Women are expected to rear many children, averaging five or six currently, but the colony as a whole is responsible for raising and disciplining the child.

Hutterite colonies specialize in diversified agriculture, raising feed, food, and livestock on up to 10,000 acres. Hutterite men often barter with neighboring farmers to fix machinery, trade goods, and lend help. The minister and other male leaders in the colony work with lawyers and bankers to keep the colony corporation operating smoothly and profitably. The most economically successful colonies have created products used in agriculture that they produce in their shops and sell to other farmers. One colony produces stainless steel animal feeders, and another markets its own animal feed. Some colonies also invest hundreds of thousands of dollars in computerized milking systems for their dairy operations, in computerized systems for feeding and raising hogs, or even in livestock processing plants.

From 1950 to 1970 Mennonites in Alberta, Canada, migrated to more northern areas of Canada and to Bolivia in Central America in search of rural farmland. Geographer Dawn Bowen traced this migration, finding that Mennonites were willing to move to places as remote as Bolivia or the northern reaches of Alberta, Canada, because of their desire to find a place where they could farm, found their own schools, and practice their religion without pervasive pressures from popular culture. Rurality enables local cultures to define their own space, to create a place, town, or rural landscape that reflects their values, and to practice customs relatively unfettered.

Historically, the economic activities of American Indian tribes, including whale or bison hunting, salmon fishing, or growing wild rice, were the focal point of their daily life, and numerous customs and festivals revolved around them. In the early 1800s in North America, Plains Indians tribes migrated during the year based on the bison; they made tools, shelter, and clothing out of the bison; and they held

dances and ceremonies that surrounded the bison hunt. When a local culture discontinues its major economic activity, it faces the challenge of maintaining the customs that depended on the economic activity and, in turn, sustaining its culture.

When a local culture decides to reengage in a traditional economic activity or other cultural custom, it can no longer decide in isolation. The tribe must navigate through varying opinions among its members, limitations imposed by governments, and perceptions of other cultures.

THE MAKAH AMERICAN INDIANS

In the late 1990s, the Makah American Indians of Neah Bay, Washington, did what environmentalists considered unthinkable: They reinstated the whale hunt. The Makah hunted whales for 1500 years, but the United States government stopped them in the 1920s because the gray whale had become endangered. In 1994, the National Oceanic and Atmospheric Association (NOAA) removed the eastern North Pacific gray whale from the endangered list.

In 1999, when the Makah reinstated the whale hunt, tribal members interviewed by journalists spoke to their traditional culture as their reason for returning to the hunt (Fig. 4.6). They needed to return to their past, they said, to understand their ancestors, to re-create and solidify their local culture. In the midst of a popular culture onslaught, the Makah sought refuge in their history.

Although the Makah wanted to hunt whales as their ancestors did, their 1999 hunts took place in a completely different context from that of a century before. This time, the Makah hunted whales under the watchful eye of the International Whaling Commission; they faced numerous protests by Greenpeace and local environmentalists; and they found

■ **Figure 4.6**
Neah Bay, Washington. The whale hunt is a traditional Makah practice. Support for maintaining it is a way of resisting the forces of assimilation.

themselves in federal court with the George W. Bush administration on their side supporting the reinstatement of the whale hunt.

The Makah wanted to hunt with their traditional canoes and harpoons because they wanted to hunt as the tribe's elders and ancestors did. However, in the context of the twentieth and twenty-first centuries, the choice of tools for the Makah's hunt was not up to them alone. Actors at the regional, national, and global scale influenced not only whether the Makah could hunt whales but also the methods they used in their hunt. The International Whaling Commission dictated that the Makah hunt gray whales with a .50 caliber rifle, arguing the rifle would kill the whale more quickly and humanely than the harpoons their ancestors used. In May 1999 the Makah hunted and killed a gray whale, using a .50 caliber rifle.

The Makah hunt ended up in court in the United States and under consideration by the International Whaling Commission. In July 2012, the International Whaling Commission extended the license for subsistence hunting of gray whale by the Makah until 2018.

American Indians are not the only Americans looking to the customs of their ancestors to reinvigorate their local cultures. Throughout the rural United States, small towns were built by immigrants from Europe, and many local cultures have defined entire small towns as places to maintain their culture and to teach others about their customs and beliefs.

Little Sweden, U.S.A.

The residents of Lindsborg, Kansas, proclaim their town Little Sweden, U.S.A. Geographer Steven Schnell asked why a town of 3300, which a few decades ago had little or no sign of Swedishness on its landscape, transformed itself into a place where Swedish culture is celebrated every day in gift stores on Main Street and in buffets in restaurants (Fig. 4.7).

GUEST FIELD NOTE

Lindsborg, Kansas

Lindsborg, Kansas, founded by Swedish Lutherans in 1869, has remade itself in recent decades as "Little Sweden, U.S.A." Swedish gift shops, restaurants, and ethnic festivals, along with faux-Swedish storefronts, all attract visitors interested in the Swedish American heritage. Here you see a Dala horse, a traditional Swedish folk craft that has been adopted as the town symbol. Note, too, the Swedish and American flags flying in the background. Most visitors to the town assume one of two things: Either the town is an island of nineteenth-century culture passed on unchanged for generations, or it is a crock of Disneyesque fakery cooked up to draw in gullible tourists. The fascination of fieldwork is that it undermines any such simplifications. I found ethnicity here to be complex, quirky, ever-changing, and very much a part of the people's lives. Swedishness in Lindsborg has been invented and reinvented time and time again through the decades, as people constantly look for answers to that most basic of questions: Who am I?

Credit: Steven M. Schnell, Kutztown University of Pennsylvania

Courtesy of Steven Schnell

■ **Figure 4.7**

Cynics would argue the reason is purely economic, but there is more to it than that. Certainly, Lindsborg benefits economically from tourists who flock to buy Swedish trinkets and celebrate Swedish festivals. Nonetheless, as Schnell found, on a daily basis the people of Lindsborg benefit from promoting a sense of a shared history and a common place in this world. In the 1930s, the townspeople shared stories about the roles of Swedes in American history and the importance of their Swedishness to Lindsborg. From that base, the townspeople began to celebrate their Swedish heritage in the 1950s, highlighting the "everyday existence" (the local culture) of the Swedes who immigrated to Lindsborg. During festivals today, the townspeople, whether Swedish or not, dress up in peasant clothes modeled after those worn by Swedish immigrants in the 1800s. Geographer James Shortridge (1996) refers to this as **neolocalism**, seeking out the regional culture and reinvigorating it in response to the uncertainty of the modern world.

The Makah, the Hutterites, and the people of Lindsborg have something in common: Each is inundated with a pulsating popular culture that challenges their place in the world. Each has chosen to maintain or reconnect with its local culture. For the Hutterites, the goal is to maintain what they have, to adopt only those technologies that advance their agricultural pursuits, and to limit those that challenge their religion. Central concerns for the Makah include thinking in their own language, embracing their history, and coming to know who they are despite what others have done to subvert their identity. The people of Lindsborg seek to celebrate the Swedish immigrants who made the place unique and connect with others around them.

Urban Local Cultures

Some local cultures have successfully built a world apart, a place to practice their customs, within a major city by constructing tight-knit **ethnic neighborhoods**. Hasidic Jews in Brooklyn, New York, and Italian Americans in the North End of Boston, Massachusetts, maintain their distinct local cultures in urban environments.

Runners of the New York City Marathon can see the ethnic neighborhoods of New York City's boroughs firsthand. Running through Brooklyn, they pass through a predominantly Mexican neighborhood full of Mexican flags and mariachi bands, followed in sharp contrast by a Hasidic Jewish neighborhood with streets lined with men and boys on one side and women and girls on another, all dressed in clothes modeled after eighteenth-century Russian and Polish fashions (Fig. 4.8).

In the North End of Boston, the Italian community still celebrates the feast days of Italian saints. Twelve religious societies, each focusing on an Italian saint, hold festivals between June and September. Members of the society march through the North End holding a statue of their saint, collecting money and adorning the saint with it. The Romaband, an Italian band that has been in existence since 1919, leads each

society through the streets of the North End. Each march ends with a street celebration, including vendors selling everything from fried calamari to hot dogs.

Having their own ethnic neighborhood enables members of a local culture in an urban area to set themselves apart and practice their customs. Schools, houses of worship, food stores, and clothing stores all support the aesthetics and desires of members of the local culture. The greatest challenge to local cultures in cities is the migration of members of other local cultures or ethnic groups into the neighborhood. Local cultures in Brooklyn and the North End work to maintain their culture and customs as young artists and professionals move into their respective neighborhoods. Rents and housing costs are climbing in each neighborhood, and the cultural landscapes are starting to reflect the neighborhood's new residents. A new arts community is inundating the traditionally Hasidic neighborhood of Brooklyn called Williamsburg. Today, you will find art galleries, artistically painted old warehouses converted into residences, and even a new brewery. In Boston, young professionals are taking advantage of the North End neighborhood's favorable location, choosing apartments there so they can walk to their jobs in the city center. Today, you will find apartments in the North End being renovated to appeal to the area's newest residents.

Local Cultures and Cultural Appropriation

Local cultures, whether rural or urban, often find themselves trying to keep their customs for themselves, to prevent others from appropriating their customs for economic benefit. Anthropologists and geographers have studied how others are using local cultural knowledge, customs, and even names. For example, the estate of Crazy Horse (a Lakota Indian leader) sued a brewery that produced Crazy Horse beer.

The process through which something (a name, a good, an idea, or even a person) that previously was not regarded as an object to be bought or sold becomes an object that can be bought, sold, and traded in the world market is called **commodification**. Commodification affects local cultures in numerous ways. First, their material culture, their jewelry and clothing, their food and games, can be commodified by themselves or by nonmembers. Similarly, their nonmaterial culture, their religion, language, and beliefs, can be commodified, often by nonmembers selling local spiritual and herbal cures for ailments. Local cultures may also be commodified as a whole—think of tourist buses "observing" the Amish culture of Lancaster, Pennsylvania, or travel agencies offering trekking trips with "traditional" Nepalese guides on spiritual journeys through the Himalayas.

When commodification occurs, the question of **authenticity** follows. When local cultures or customs are commodified, usually one image or experience is typecast as the "authentic" image or experience of that culture, and it is that image or

FIELD NOTE

"One of the most amazing aspects of running the New York City marathon is seeing the residents of New York's many ethnic neighborhoods lining the streets of the race. Running through the Hasidic Jewish neighborhood in Williamsburg, Brooklyn was striking: even before noticing the traditional dress of the neighborhood's residents, I noticed the crowd was much quieter—the people were not yelling, they were clapping and quietly cheering."

Spencer Platt/Getty Images

■ **Figure 4.8**
Williamsburg, Brooklyn, New York.

experience that the tourist or buyer desires. However, local cultures are dynamic, and places and people change over time. To gain an "authentic" sense of place, people need to experience the complexity of a place directly rather than the stereotype of a place. An "authentic" local culture does not fit into a single experience or image; rather, an "authentic" local culture is one that is complex and not stereotyped.

The act of stereotyping local culture is quite confusing for the members of the local culture because rarely is there consensus that all things must be done in one traditional way. Tourists in Lancaster County, for example, may be disappointed to see some Amish driving tractors across their fields. European, Canadian, American, or Australian trekkers in

Nepal desire the same "authentic" experience that a travel website promotes in the Himalayas.

Authenticity of Places

During the process of colonization, Europeans tagged the cultures they encountered as either savage or mystic. "Authentic" tourist destinations are often designed to exploit the mystical in local cultures. A South African theme park, The Lost City (built on the site of the resort Sun City), capitalizes on *mystical images of Africa described in a legend*, thereby "freezing" the continent to a time that never existed (Fig. 4.9).

© Lindsay Hebberd/Corbis

Figure 4.9
Sun City, South Africa. The Lost City resort in Sun City evokes the mystical images of Africa described in a legend. Landscapes such as this blur what is "authentic" and what is not.

A local culture need not be "mystical" in order to create an authentic place. The city of Branson, Missouri, is capitalizing on a local culture in the Ozarks, melding a number of people and perceptions in one place for tourists to consume. Geographer Johnathan Bascom studied the processes by which the city of Branson has effectively tapped its local customs, such as food preferences, history, and music, to create an "authentic" identity for Branson that sets it apart from neighboring towns. Branson becomes "authentic," and surrounding towns that try to capitalize on their rural, country heritage become "copies."

GUINNESS AND THE IRISH PUB COMPANY

Theme parks and entertainment venues overtly choose a stereotype and perpetuate it, but a discerning tourist or consumer may be aware of what is occurring. The act of corporations commodifying the mystique of local cultures to drive profits can, however, be less obvious to the consumer. The Guinness Brewing Company of Dublin, Ireland, created a business plan in 1991 aimed at capitalizing on the global mystique of the traditional Irish pub. Guinness saw the sales of its stout beer declining in Ireland and the United Kingdom and decided to go global.

Guinness formed a partnership with the Irish Pub Company, which has offices in Dublin, Atlanta, the United Arab Emirates, and Australia. The Irish Pub Company studied traditional Irish pubs and created five Irish pub prototypes—shop, country, Victorian, Celtic, and brewery. A hotel owner in Naples, Florida, or a businessperson in Dubai, United Arab Emirates (Fig. 4.10), to cite two examples, might work with

the Irish Pub Company to choose a good site and to choose the pub type. The specifications are sent to Ireland, and the pub itself is built in Ireland and shipped abroad. Along with the pub, the Irish Pub Company provides food recommendations, training, music suggestions, and notably, Irish bartenders trained in their Dublin "pub school." The Irish Pub Company also sells bric-a-brac (Irish antiques and reproductions) to give the place the feel of an Irish pub. Of course, every pub has Guinness on tap. All of these components create what the Irish Pub Company refers to as ambience that leads to craic (an Irish term for fun).

Guinness and the Irish Pub Company have built over 1000 pubs in 40 countries around the world (Fig. 4.11).

© LensCapp/Alamy

Figure 4.10
Dubai, United Arab Emirates. An old Irish truck marks the entrance to an Irish Pub Company pub in Dubai.

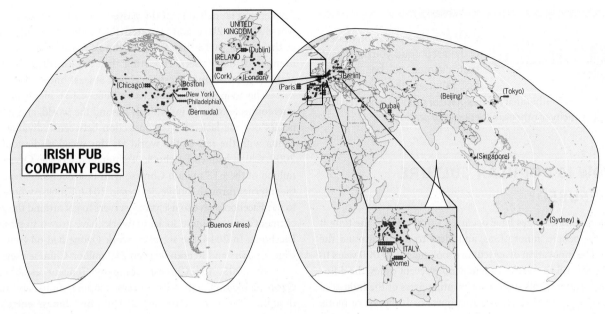

Figure 4.11
Irish Pubs Designed by the Irish Pub Company. The distance decay principle is evident here, with the greatest number of pubs located in Europe and North America, as is the Irish Pub Company. The map also highlights the diffusion of popular culture to world cities, including Buenos Aires and Singapore. *Data from:* Irish Pub Company, by e-mail and http://www.irishpubcompany.com/pubsworldwide.asp, last accessed July 2011.

Remarkably, dozens of the pubs are in Ireland proper. The most enigmatic of the pubs is in Las Vegas, Nevada. The Irish Pub Company designed and built a pub called Nine Fine Irishmen that spans 9000 square feet in the New York-New York Hotel and Casino and spills an additional 20,000 square feet onto Las Vegas Boulevard. The "authentic" Irish pub in "authentic" New York in the "Disneyfied" Las Vegas is one mashup we can chew on for a while.

The commodification of local customs freezes customs in place and time for consumption, with claims of "authenticity" abounding. The search for "authentic" local cultures implies an effort to identify peoples who are seemingly untouched by change or external influence. However, all local cultures (rural and urban) are dynamic, and all have been touched by external influences throughout their existence (Fig. 4.12). The search for an "authentic" local culture merely perpetuates myths about local cultures. Members of local cultures are constantly renegotiating their place in this world and making sense of who they are in the midst of the popular culture onslaught.

FIELD NOTE

"The Dingle Peninsula in Ireland was long one of the more remote parts of the country, and even its largest town, Dingle, was primarily an agricultural village just a few decades ago. As I walked through the streets of town, I noticed the colorful inns and houses of the older town. The 'Little Bridge Pub' on the corner of this intersection in the older town is an 'authentic' pub, the kind that the Irish Pub Company works to replicate."

© Alexander B. Murphy

Figure 4.12
Dingle, Ireland

What is the last place you went to or the last product you purchased that claimed to be "authentic?" What are the challenges of defending the authenticity of this place or product while refuting the authenticity of other similar places or products?

HOW IS POPULAR CULTURE DIFFUSED?

Extraordinary changes have occurred since 1900 in the time it takes for people, innovations, and ideas to diffuse around the globe. The innovation of agriculture took nearly 10,000 years to diffuse around the world. In much more recent times, the diffusion of developments such as the printing press or the Industrial Revolution was measured over the course of 100 years or more.

During the twentieth century, however, the pace of diffusion shrank to months, weeks, days, and in some cases even hours. Simultaneously, the spatial extent of diffusion has expanded, so that more and more parts of Earth's surface are affected by ideas and innovations from faraway places. For example, the social networking site Facebook, which Mark

Zuckerberg launched in 2004, passed 500 million subscribers worldwide in 2010 and reported 1.23 billion monthly users at the end of 2013. In 2013, Facebook released data on the number of daily users, reporting that one-third of the U.S. and UK populations access Facebook at least once a day.

The map of Facebook users (Fig. 4.13) highlights the interconnectedness of individuals around the world, and it also points out the lack of interconnection between individuals in China with the rest of the world via this social media tool. In 2009, China banned Facebook, Twitter, and Google. Over 500 million of the 618 million Chinese with Internet access reached the internet through mobile devices in 2014. Chinese who want to use Facebook have to use proxy servers to get around the government's ban. Chinese social networks have grown in place of Facebook. In 2014, the social network Qzone had 644 million Chinese users and Renren boasted 210 million Chinese users.

In 2005, the Chinese company Tencent established Qzone, a blogging cite where users can post photos and their thoughts. Tencent, established in 1998 by Chinese entrepreneur Huateng Ma, is an internet service provider that also owns QQ, an instant messaging application. As of March 2014, Tencent was the "fifth largest Internet company in the world—currently valued at over $140 bn" (Gittleson 2014).

QQ is more than an instant messaging service. Users link their accounts to bank cards and "use the platform to do

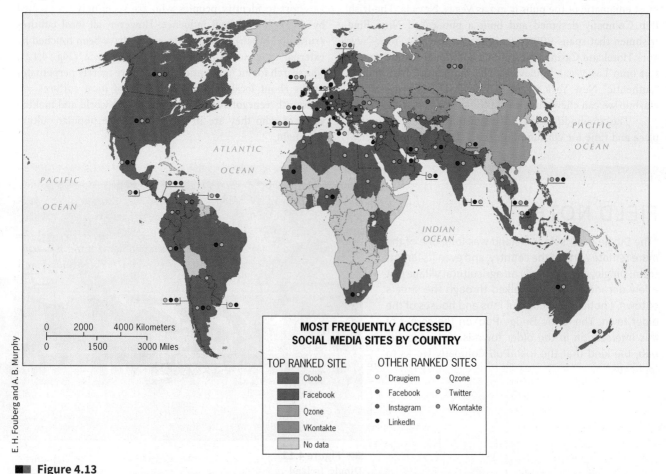

MOST FREQUENTLY ACCESSED SOCIAL MEDIA SITES BY COUNTRY

TOP RANKED SITE
- Cloob
- Facebook
- Qzone
- VKontakte
- No data

OTHER RANKED SITES
- Draugiem
- Facebook
- Instagram
- LinkedIn
- Qzone
- Twitter
- VKontakte

0   2000   4000 Kilometers
0   1500   3000 Miles

E. H. Fouberg and A. B. Murphy

■ **Figure 4.13**
Social Networks Worldwide.   The most popular social networks vary across the world, with Facebook having the largest imprint.   *Data from*: Alexa.com, September 2014.

© NetPhotos/Alamy

■ **Figure 4.14**
Beijing, China. Renren, the Facebook of China, is a popular social network among college students. It now has over 210 million registered users. Wang Xing, who launched and sold Renren, has since launched Chinese versions of Twitter and Groupon.

everything from book a table at a restaurant to order a taxi" (Gittleson 2014). During the Chinese New Year, money is often exchanged as gifts. QQ tapped into that market and offered a service to send gifts of money through its platform during the holiday. According to the BBC, "more than 200 million users signed up for the service in 15 days."

Chinese entrepreneur Wang Xing launched the Chinese social network Xiaonei ("on campus"), which copied Facebook down to its color scheme, in 2005 and 2006. Now known as Renren, which means "everybody" (Fig. 4.14), the site functions as a Chinese Facebook. China allows Renren and its competitor, Kaixin001, to operate because they have agreed to the political censorship mandated by the Chinese government. For example, according to a report in business magazine *Fast Company*, Renren censors "a range of sensitive keywords, including terms related to the Dalai Lama, the 1989 Tiananmen Square massacre, and Chinese dissidents including 2010 Nobel Peace laureate Liu Xiaobo" (Rabkin 2011). Renren users report that they receive a warning message when they update their status or post a comment that is censored by Renren.

Controlling information flow is increasingly difficult in China, and many argue that despite being censored, Renren and its competitors allow for freer flow of ideas than previously was possible in communist China.

Transportation and communication technologies have altered **distance decay**. No longer does a map with a bull's-eye surrounding the hearth of an innovation describe how quickly the innovation will diffuse to areas around it (Fig. 4.15a). Rather, what geographer David Harvey called **time–space compression** explains how quickly innovations diffuse and refers to how interlinked two places are through transportation and communication technologies (Fig. 4.15b).

In the past few decades, major world cities have become much closer to one another as a result of modern technologies, including airplanes, high-speed trains, expressways, wireless connections, fax machines, e-mail, and telephone. Places that lack transportation and communications technologies are now more removed from interconnected places than ever. All of the new technologies create the infrastructure through which innovations diffuse. Because the technologies link some places more closely than others, ideas diffuse through interconnected places rapidly rather than diffusing at constant rates across similar distances.

Hearths of Popular Culture

Popular culture diffuses hierarchically in the context of time–space compression, with diffusion happening most rapidly across the most compressed spaces. As we saw in the last section, even local customs practiced for centuries in one place can be swept up into popular culture. How does a custom, idea, song, or object become part of popular culture? It is relatively easy to follow the communications, transportation, and marketing networks that account for the diffusion of popular culture, but how do we find the hearths of popular culture, and how do certain places establish themselves as the hearths of popular culture?

ESTABLISHING A HEARTH

All aspects of popular culture—music, sports, television, and dance—have a hearth, a place of origin. Typically, a hearth begins with contagious diffusion: Developers of an idea or innovation may find they have followers who dress as they do or listen to the music they play. A multitude of American musical groups (REM, Hootie and the Blowfish, MGMT) began as college bands or in college towns. They play a few sets in a

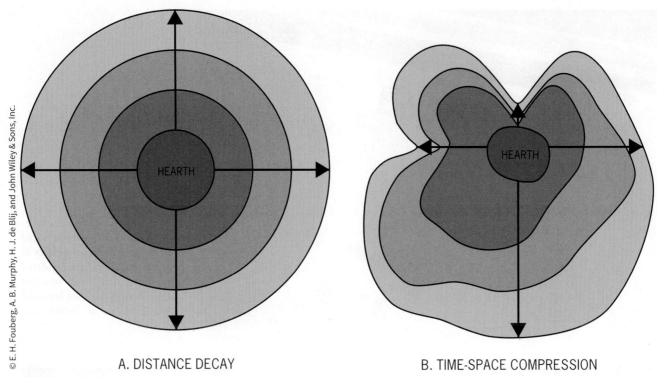

A. DISTANCE DECAY   B. TIME-SPACE COMPRESSION

■■ **Figure 4.15a, b**
Distance Decay and Time–Space Compression.   With distance decay, the likelihood of diffusion decreases as time and distance from the hearth increases. With time–space compression, the likelihood of diffusion depends on the connectedness (in communications and transportation technologies) among places.

campus bar or at a campus party and gain followers. The group starts to play to bars and campuses in nearby college towns, and soon they produce their own music and sell it at their concerts.

Bands that begin on college campuses or in college towns and build from their base typically establish a hearth for their sound's diffusion first through contagious diffusion and then through hierarchical diffusion. College towns including Athens, Georgia; Burlington, Vermont; and Charlottesville, Virginia, are the perfect nesting spaces for new bands. The Dave Matthews Band created and perfected their sound in Charlottesville, Virginia, in the early 1990s. Lead singer and guitarist Dave Matthews was born in South Africa and landed in Charlottesville as a young adult after living in Johannesburg, New York, and London (Fig. 4.16).

Matthews was a bartender in Charlottesville when he met Ross Hoffman, a local songwriter who mentored Matthews in song writing. The Dave Matthews Band was formed when Matthews invited Carter Beuford (drums), LeRoi Moore (saxophone, who died in 2008), Stefan Lessard (bass), and Boyd Tinsley (violin) to join him in creating a demo of some of his songs. The Dave Matthews Band's first live show was in Charlottesville on Earth Day in April 1991. The band played bars throughout the Charlottesville area from 1991 through 1993. Manager Coran Capshaw followed the path of diffusion carved by the Grateful Dead and Phish, through a grassroots campaign of word of mouth (contagious diffusion).

Jacqueline Reede

■■ **Figure 4.16**
Detroit Lakes, Minnesota.   Dave Matthews of the Dave Matthews Band performs at the 10,000 Lakes Music Festival in 2009.

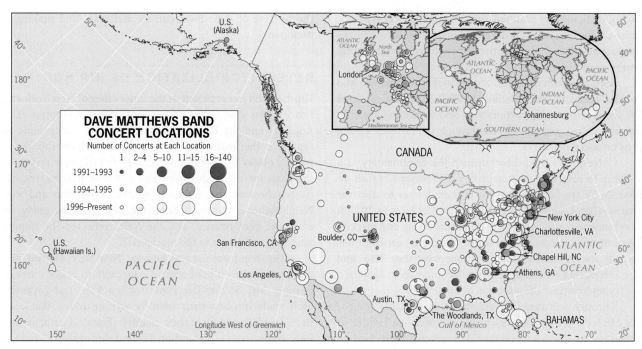

■■ Figure 4.17
World Distribution of Dave Matthews Band concerts.   The earliest Dave Matthews Band concerts, noted by red circles on the map, were in college towns in North America. After 1996, as noted by the light yellow circles on the map, when Dave Matthews Band concerts diffused beyond North America and Europe, the band connected first with the lead singer's home country of South Africa.   *Data from:* http://www. bmbalmanac.com, last accessed June 2014. Compiled by Kim Johnson, Liz Sydnor, and Lennea Mueller.

Hierarchical diffusion of the band soon followed, through the hierarchy of college towns in the United States (Fig. 4.17). The Dave Matthews Band played 200 nights a year in fraternities, sororities, bars, and clubs throughout the American South, following the same circuit as college band Hootie and the Blowfish. The band encouraged fans to record their music and send it to friends; this helped to establish audiences for the band in college towns far removed from Charlottesville.

Their first album, released in 1993, was on the band's independent label. It hit the college charts, and a union with RCA soon followed with their second album, Under the Table and Dreaming, released in 1994. As *Entertainment Weekly* explained in 1995, "By playing nearly 200 gigs a year and releasing their own CDs, they built up such a zealous following that when Under the Table entered the album chart at No. 34, neither MTV nor most of America had even heard of them." The band's first video was not released until three months after their first single, "What Would You Say," hit the Billboard charts.

The Dave Matthews Band became broadly popular after 1995 and began playing large arenas throughout the United States and in Australia. The band continues to rely on its fan base for support. Manager Capshaw and the Dave Matthews Band were early adopters of using the Internet to stay connected with fans. Today, the official Dave Matthews Band fan club has over 80,000 online members, each of whom pays $35 a year to belong.

The music of groups including the Dave Matthews Band, Phish, Grateful Dead, and Jimmy Buffet also diffuses relocationally, as fans follow the musicians along their concert routes, living in their cars and selling tie-dyed shirts and beaded necklaces out of the backs of their vehicles in the parking lots of concert venues.

The action of following the bands for years (an estimated 500 to 1000 fans traveled to every Grateful Dead concert) led fans to create their own customs and culture. As with other acts of pilgrimage (see Chapter 7 on religion), environmental effects can be grave. Prior to their final concert, Phish (breaking up for the second time) used their website to beg their fans to leave their beloved rural Vermont as they found it. Founded in 2004, Reverb, a nonprofit organization, helps bands, including the Dave Matthews Band, create environmentally conscious concerts by having bands purchase carbon offset credits for each of their concerts, supporting recycling, selling eco-friendly merchandise, and setting up Reverb Eco-Villages at concert venues to encourage eco-friendly behaviors among fans.

MANUFACTURING A HEARTH

The question of whether a college band "makes it" depends greatly on the choices and actions of record producers and corporate music media giants. Marketing companies, such as the Audience, founded by Oliver Luckett, Sean Parker, and Ari Emanuel, generate and produce popular culture by waging meticulously planned, though seemingly grassroots, social-media campaigns whereby teens on social networks promote new acts to one another through crossovers among fandoms.

A 2014 documentary produced by Frank Koughan and Douglas Rushkoff for *Frontline* on PBS entitled *Generation Like* looks at the roles corporations and marketing agencies play in creating popular culture through interactions among teens on social networks.

Correspondent Rushkoff created the documentary as a followup to his 2001 documentary *The Merchants of Cool*. In 2001, MTV tracked down teens in their homes to discover what was "cool" and then resell it to a broader base. In 2014 it is no longer necessary for media, entertainment, and marketing companies to track down teens. The digital generation is virtually always online telling everyone what they "like" and why, interacting with others of similar interests or fandoms, and trying to attract the attention of celebrities.

Through software that analyzes "likes," media companies can look at a list of a celebrity's followers on Twitter or Instagram to discern commonalities among their fans in order to carefully plan marketing campaigns for new products, movies, and music. Everyday people like Tyler Oakley—who as of July 2014 had 4 million YouTube subscribers, 2 million followers on Instagram, and more than 2.6 million followers on Twitter—can use their large fan base or fandom to leverage corporate sponsors and advertising opportunities. This "fame" is, according to Rushkoff, an online currency that is used in media campaigns to create what is "cool" in popular culture.

Social networks create opportunities for constant contagious and hierarchical diffusion. Teens become "knowers" of new trends both contagiously—by reading posts from friends (although they may have been fed the information through a celebrity post)—and hierarchically by **opinion leaders** with large fan bases like Tyler Oakley. In 2013, Oakley promoted products from Pepsi and Taco Bell through YouTube videos and social networks. He strategically invites fans to interact with him during his videos and interjects fan comments into his videos and through retweets. While local news and other media companies are trying to mimic Oakley's success in interacting with fans, often in an awkward way, Oakley and other opinion leaders have mastered the art, which has given them social currency to pair up with major corporations and help create and shape popular culture.

With this kind of infrastructure behind the production of popular culture, we might expect popular culture to act as a blanket, evenly covering the globe. But even as popular culture has diffused throughout the world, it has not blanketed it, hiding all existing local cultures underneath it. Rather, one aspect of popular culture (such as music or food) will take on new forms when it encounters a new locality and the people and local culture in that place. Geographers and anthropologists call this the **reterritorialization** of popular culture: a term referring to a process in which people start to produce an aspect of popular culture themselves, doing so in the context of their local culture and place and making it their own.

RETERRITORIALIZATION OF HIP HOP

Hip-hop and rap grew out of the inner cities of New York and Los Angeles during the 1980s and 1990s. Compton (Los Angeles) and the Bronx and Harlem (New York) came to represent the hearths of hip-hop. These neighborhoods, as well as places in Detroit and Atlanta (which later served as the basis for the midwestern and southern hearths, respectively), became the authentic spaces of hip-hop and rap. Neighborhood venues became the best place to enjoy an authentic performance, and the lyrics reflected the importance of local places to the music itself.

Hip-hop from the Los Angeles, New York, Detroit, and Atlanta hearths diffused abroad, especially to major cities in Europe. MC Solaar, Die Fantastischen Vier, and Jovanotti each made hip-hop their own by writing music that connected with the youth of their country (France, Germany, and Italy, respectively). As hip-hop diffused throughout Europe, it mixed with existing local cultures, experiences, and places, reterritorializing the music to each locale.

In Southeast Asia, Indonesia serves as a good example of the process of reterritorialization. Imported hip-hop diffused first to a small group of people in Indonesia; then, Indonesians began to create hip-hop music themselves. Through the creation of their own music, Indonesian hip-hop artists integrated their local culture with the practices of the "foreign" hip-hop hearth to create a hybrid that was no longer foreign.

As hip-hop has diffused and grown, artists have addressed the major concerns of their local cultures in their lyrics. Hip-hop artists in the United States wrote about social issues in the 1980s and 1990s, and some wrote about violence, crime, and surviving urban life in the gangsta rap of the 1990s. Other artists write more about having fun and partying. In France and Germany, American hip-hop music diffused first to immigrants living in major cities. In France, for example, some of the first hip-hop artists were African, Arab, and Spanish immigrants writing about the racism they experienced in France.

The results of reterritorialization are seen in the ways hip-hop artists around the world compose lyrics about the real problems surrounding them and sample music from their local cultures in their music. In 2005, the U.S. State Department launched Rhythm Road, sending hip-hop artists to Muslim countries as part of diplomatic efforts in the "War on Terror." The program is credited both with inspiring revolutionary democracy and inciting radicalization against the U.S. During the Arab Spring in 2011, Tunisian hip-hop artist El Général (Fig. 4.18) helped spur massive political change by posting his song "Mr. President" on Facebook. The words he rapped about government corruption spoke to Tunisians and Egyptians, inspiring revolutionaries in both countries.

FETHI BELAID/AFP/Getty Images

■■ **Figure 4.18**
Tunis, Tunisia. Tunisian hip-hop artist El Général helped spark the Arab Spring with his anthem "Mr. President."

Replacing Old Hearths with New: Beating Out the Big Three in Popular Sports

Baseball, football, and basketball are historically the big three sports in the United States. During the 1800s and 1900s, they all benefited from advances in transportation technology, communication technology, and institutionalization. First, the railroad connected cities across the country, allowing baseball teams to compete and baseball to diffuse. The telegraph enabled newspapers to report baseball scores, which added to the sport's following. In the late 1880s, electric lighting made basketball a nighttime spectator sport, played inside gymnasiums. The founding of the National Football League in 1920 helped institutionalize the sport of football (by creating institutions to support it, formalize it, and regulate it), with rules for the game remaining relatively unchanged since then.

During much of the twentieth century, the big three dominated sports popular culture. Figures including Mark McGwire, Michael Jordan, and Brett Favre found their ways onto Wheaties boxes and reached icon status. In the last decades of the twentieth century, advertising contracts and corporate sponsorship padded and eventually surpassed the salaries of the biggest sports heroes.

While the big three continued to draw millions of fans and huge crowds to their venues, a growing number of alternative sports captured the imagination of young sports fans. Popular films (including *Endless Summer*) of the 1960s immortalized the freedom of surfing. In the 1970s, sidewalk surfing, now known as skateboarding, diffused from its hearth in Southern California. In the 1980s, snowboarding found a following but initially met strong resistance on ski slopes in the United States.

The debut of ESPN's X Games in 1995 and the proliferation of video games involving extreme sports propelled previously alternative sports into popular culture. Snowboarding debuted as a winter Olympic sport in 1998. Video games sparked interest in such sports, even among kids who had never tried them before. Tony Hawk, the famous skateboarder, worked with Activision to create several versions of Tony Hawk's Pro Skater, with average annual sales of $180 million. In 2001, sales relating to video games were higher than the movie industry's box office receipts. That same year, baseball took a back seat to skateboarding, with more children under the age of 18 skateboarding than playing baseball.

Extreme sports greats, like Tony Hawk, gain corporate sponsors, create their own brands, and sign lucrative advertising deals. Hawk, who retired from competitive skate boarding in 1999, reportedly generates more than $200 million a year in revenue through sponsorships, skate tours, and sales of his skateboards, clothing lines, and video games. Hawk combined popular sports with popular music, creating his Boom Boom Huck Jam tour that features famous skateboarders, BMX bike riders, and motorcycle stunt drivers, neatly choreographed and enhanced by alternative live music. Tony Hawk, Inc., employs 24 full-time employees to oversee Hawk's branded products.

■ **Figure 4.19**
Sochi, Russia.   Olympic gold medal winner Sage Kotsenburg celebrates at the end of the Men's Snowboard Slopestyle Final at the Sochi Winter Olympics in 2014.

Advertisers who court the 12–34 age demographic, fans looking for athletes who are outside of major league sports, and fans who desire a sport that is different from their parents' sport drove the expansion of extreme sports into mainstream popular culture. Rising stars in extreme sports look to Tony Hawk and see the business side of professional snowboarding and skating. Sage Kotsenburg, who won a gold medal at the 2014 Sochi Olympics (Figure 4.19), reportedly read "every book he could find about finance and money management" before becoming a professional snowboarder (Kragthorpe 2014).

Like new music or other forms of popular culture, extreme sports have become more popular, mainstream, and commodified. Once that happens, the fan base turns its attention to a new extreme sport, and the corporate sponsors begin to tap into the new popular sport, helping it follow the same path to popular, mainstream, and commodified status.

One of the best known recent examples of this trend is the popularization of ultimate fighting. In the early 1990s, advertising executives and sports promoters drew from a long history of mixed martial arts fights in Brazil to produce a series of fights in the United States among different martial arts and boxing experts to see who was the best fighter. The new fights, called mixed martial arts, grew a fan base through live matches and pay per view on cable television. Early mixed martial arts fights had just a few rules, including no head-butting and no weight classes.

The fan base grew quickly, and by 1993, the Ultimate Fighting Championship (UFC) formed to serve as a professional organization for mixed martial arts (Fig. 4.20). The

■ **Figure 4.20**
Toronto, Canada.   Light Heavyweight Jon "Bones" Jones won his fight with Alexander Gustafsson in September 2013.

sport continued to grow during the 1990s, with the establishment of rules over time allotments for matches, the institutionalization of promotions and marketing, and the growth in popularity of ultimate fighting reality television shows. The rules of the UFC, including seven weight classes and specifications for the fighting arena called "the Octagon" or "the Cage," have been institutionalized as the basis for ultimate fighting worldwide. References to ultimate fighting and ultimate fighters (such as Chuck Liddell's appearance on HBO's *Entourage*) are diffusing into other aspects of popular culture, spreading both the commodification and the popularization of the sport.

Identity and the desire to remain outside of popular culture will continue to spur the creation of extreme sports to rival the big three. In discussing the production of popular culture, geographer Clayton Rosati explained that the foundation of industrial capitalism is not simply "meeting the existing needs of the public." Rather, industrial capitalism demands that corporations continue to produce goods that "become socially desirable." The need for corporations to create the "new" so that they have something to sell that is "socially desirable" applies to all markets, whether music, entertainment, or athletics. Skateboarding and ultimate fighting will be followed by the next extreme sport and the next, as long as corporations can spur the consumption of the new.

Stemming the Tide of Popular Culture—Losing the Local?

Assimilation policies practiced by American, Canadian, Russian, Australian, and New Zealand governments were official policies designed for the express purpose of disrupting and changing indigenous, local cultures. Western, democratic governments no longer have official policies of assimilation. Yet, for people in many local cultures and in regions that are not hearths of popular culture, popular culture itself can feel like a policy of assimilation.

Popular media such as music, television, and film from the United States and the United Kingdom diffuse quickly. American and British products can now be seen and heard around the world. If you turn on the television in Harare, Zimbabwe, you can easily find reruns of a 10-year-old American television show or a contemporary CNN broadcast. If you go to a cinema in Seoul, South Korea, you can choose among several just-released American films shown in English with Korean subtitles.

The influence of Europe, the United States, Japan, and South Korea in global popular culture makes many people feel threatened by cultural homogenization. At the global scale, North America, western Europe, Japan, India, and South Korea exert the greatest influence on popular culture at present. Each region acts as a major hearth for certain aspects of popular culture. North American influences are seen mainly in movies, television, music, sports, and fast food; Japan's influences are primarily in children's television programs, electronic games, and new entertainment technologies; western Europe's in fashion, television, art, and philosophy; South Korea's in television dramas, movies, and popular music; and India's mainly in movies.

South Korea has made a mark on popular culture from television to popular music. In 1995, Chinese television stations began broadcasting South Korean television dramas. The South Korean dramas typically aired late at night, often after midnight, but they quickly gained a large following in China. The Chinese government changed a law that restricted Korean content on television to 15 percent of air time, and in response South Korean popular television dramas took off in China. An entire wave of South Korean popular culture, including television shows, movies, fashions, and music diffused throughout China, Japan, and Southeast Asia. Hallyu (also called Hanryu) are waves of South Korean popular culture that move quickly through Asia and have resulted in significant growth in the South Korean entertainment and tourism industries (Fig. 4.21).

Beginning with television dramas and movies, Hallyu expanded to music in the early part of this century. South Korean popular music, known as K-pop, has followed the same path of diffusion. The Chinese government allowed Korean band H.O.T. to play in a stadium in Beijing in 2002. Today, K-pop bands, including Super Junior (called SuJu) and Girls Generation; K-pop recording artists, including Psy, Rain, and BoA; and Korean movie stars, including Bae Yong Joon, have fans throughout East Asia, Southeast Asia, and increasingly in the Middle East.

Ironically, South Korea was quite protective of its entertainment industry in the post-World War II era, for fear that Japan, which formerly colonized South Korea, would export its entertainment industry to South Korea and overpower South Korea's entertainment industry. But Hallyu has diffused not only to China but also to Japan. In turn, millions of Japanese and Chinese are taking Korean language classes, traveling and studying abroad in South Korea, and adopting South Korean fashions.

A 2009 article in *Tourism Geographies* describes the diffusion and proliferation of Hallyu in Asia:

> *Having first penetrated the Chinese mainland, the Korean cultural phenomenon of Hallyu, in particular Korean television, has spread throughout the East and South-east of Asia, including Japan, Hong Kong, Taiwan, Singapore, Malaysia, Thailand, Vietnam, Philippines and later even to the Middle East and East Europe. The infatuation with Korean popular culture and celebrities has not stopped at popular media consumption but has also led to more general interest in popular music, computer games, Korean language, food, fashion, make-up and appearance, and even plastic surgery (Kim et al. 2009).*

When popular culture displaces or replaces local culture, it will usually be met with resistance. In response to an influx of American and British films, the French government

FIELD NOTE

"Just days before the Japanese tsunami in 2011, I walked out of the enormous Lotte department store in Seoul, South Korea, and asked a local where to find a marketplace with handcrafted goods. She pointed me in the direction of the Insa-dong traditional market street. When I noticed a Starbucks sign written in Korean instead of English, I knew I must be getting close to the traditional market. A block later, I arrived on Insa-dong. I found quaint tea shops and boutiques with handcrafted goods, but the market still sold plenty of bulk-made goods, including souvenirs like Korean drums, chopsticks, and items sporting Hallyu stars. Posters, mugs, and even socks adorned with the faces of members of Super Junior smiled at the shoppers along Insa-dong."

© Erin H. Fouberg

■ **Figure 4.21**
Seoul, South Korea.

heavily subsidizes its domestic film industry. French television stations, for example, must turn over 3 percent of their revenues to the French cinema. The French government also stemmed the tide of American and British music on the radio by setting a policy in the 1990s requiring that 40 percent of on-air time be in French. Of the 40 percent, half must be new artists. These policies directly benefited the French hip-hop industry. By performing in French, the new artists received quite a bit of air time on French radio.

Through policies and funding, the French government has helped maintain its cultural industries, but in countless other cases, governments and cultural institutions lack the means or the will to promote local cultural productions.

Concern over the loss of local distinctiveness and identity is not limited to particular cultural or socioeconomic settings. We find such concern among the dominant societies of wealthier countries, where it is reflected in everything from the rise of religious fundamentalism to the establishment of semiautonomous communes in remote locations. We find this concern among minorities (and their supporters) in wealthier countries, where it can be seen in efforts to promote local languages, religions, and customs by constructing barriers to the influx of cultural influences from the dominant society. We find it among political elites in poorer countries seeking to promote a nationalist

ideology that is explicitly opposed to cultural globalization. And we find it among social and ethnic minorities in poorer countries that seek greater autonomy from regimes promoting acculturation or assimilation to a single national cultural norm.

Geographers realize that local cultures will interpret, choose, and reshape the influx of popular culture. People interpret individual cultural productions in very different ways, depending on the cultural context in which they view them. What people choose to adopt from popular culture, how they reterritorialize it, and what they reject help shape the character and culture of people, places, and landscapes.

Read about the U.S. government effort to use hip-hop in the War on Terror in "America's Hip-Hop Foreign Policy" in the *Atlantic* (theatlantic.com/international/archive/2014/03/americas-hip-hop-foreign-policy/284522/). Determine whether and how the U.S. could use social networks to help make hip-hop diplomacy more successful.

HOW CAN LOCAL AND POPULAR CULTURES BE SEEN IN THE CULTURAL LANDSCAPE?

The tension between globalized popular culture and local culture can be seen in **cultural landscapes**, the visible imprint of human activity on the landscape. Human imprint includes everything from how people have changed and shaped the environment to the buildings, signs, fences, and statues people erect. Cultural landscapes reflect the values, norms, and aesthetics of a culture. On major roadways in North American towns and suburbs, the landscape is a series of big box stores, gas stations, and restaurants that reflect popular culture (Fig. 4.22). As you drive down one of these roadways, one place looks like the next. You drive past TGI Fridays, Applebee's, Wal-Mart, Target, and McDonald's. Then, several miles down the road, you pass another conglomeration (clustering) of the same stores. Geographer Edward Relph coined the word **placelessness** to describe the loss of uniqueness of place in the cultural landscape to the point that one place looks like the next.

Globalization and cultural diffusion have led to the convergence of cultural landscapes worldwide. Three developments are at the heart of this convergence: (1) particular architectural forms and planning ideas have diffused around the world; (2) individual businesses and products have become so widespread that they now leave a distinctive landscape stamp on far-flung places; and (3) the wholesale borrowing of idealized landscape images has promoted a blurring of place distinctiveness, if not actual convergence.

The global diffusion of the skyscraper provides a clear illustration of the first point—particular architectural forms and planning ideas have diffused around the world (Fig. 4.23). In the second half of the 1800s, with advancements in steel production and improved costs and efficiencies of steel use, architects and engineers created the first skyscrapers. The fundamental difference between a skyscraper and another building is that the outside walls of the skyscraper do not bear the major load or weight of the building; rather, the internal steel structure or skeleton of the building bears most of the load. The Home Insurance Building of Chicago is typically credited as the first building to meet these specifications.

From Singapore to Johannesburg and from Caracas to Toronto, the commercial centers of major cities are dominated by tall buildings, many of which were designed by the same architects and engineering firms. With the diffusion of the skyscraper around the world, the cultural landscape of cities has been profoundly impacted. Skyscrapers require substantial land clearing in the vicinity of individual buildings, the construction of wide, straight streets to promote access, and the reworking of transportation systems around a highly centralized model. Skyscrapers are only one example of the globalization of a particular landscape form. The proliferation of skyscrapers in Taiwan, Malaysia, and China in the 1990s marked the integration of these economies into the major players in the world economy (Fig. 4.24). Today, the growth of skyscrapers in Dubai, United Arab Emirates, signals Dubai's world city status.

Reading signs is an easy way to see the second dimension of cultural landscape convergence: the far-flung stamp of global businesses on the landscape. Walking down the streets of Rome, you will see signs for Pizza Hut and Subway. The main tourist shopping street in Prague hosts Dunkin' Donuts and McDonald's. A tourist in Munich, Germany, will wind through streets looking for the city's famed beer garden dating from 1589, the Hofbräuhaus and will happen upon the Hard Rock Café, right

■ **Figure 4.22**
Roseville, Minnesota. A series of signs advertising national chains creates a nondescript landscape on Snelling Avenue in this St. Paul suburb. Across the street from where this photo was taken is the site of T-1, the first Target store ever built, which was recently torn down and replaced with the largest Target store in the world.

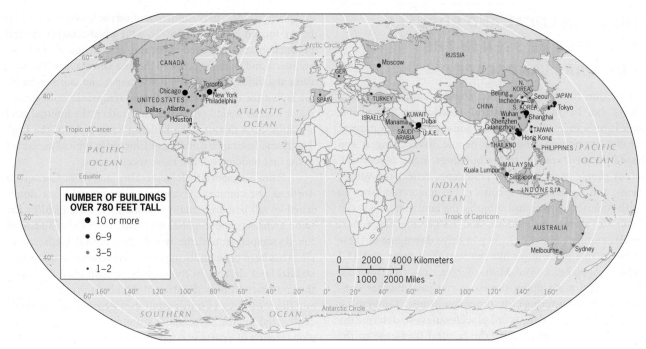

■■ Figure 4.23

World Distribution of Skyscrapers.   The map shows the number of skyscrapers that are taller than 700 feet. The map reflects the growing importance of East Asia as a business center—particularly China. But Dubai stands out as well, a city that has staked its future on its role as an international commercial node.   *Data from*: Emporis, Inc., 2005.

■■ Figure 4.24

Kuala Lampur, Malaysia. The Petronas Towers. When the Pretronas were completed in 1998, they were the tallest buildings in the world. They were overtaken by Taipei 101 in 2004, which in turn was dwarfed by the Burj Khalifa in Dubai in 2010.

next door (Fig. 4.25). If the tourist had recently traveled to Las Vegas, he might have déjà vu. The Hofbräuhaus Las Vegas, built in 2003, stands across the street from the Hard Rock Hotel and Casino. The storefronts in Seoul, South Korea, are filled with Starbucks, Dunkin' Donuts, and Outback Steakhouses. China is home to more than 3,200 KFC restaurants; KFC's parent company, Yum!, controls 40 percent of the fast-food market in China.

Marked landscape similarities like these can be found everywhere from international airports to shopping centers. Global corporations that develop spaces of commerce have wide-reaching impacts on the cultural landscape. Architectural firms often specialize in building one kind of space—performing arts centers, stadiums, medical laboratories, or international airports. Property management companies have worldwide holdings and encourage Gap, The Cheesecake Factory, Barnes and Noble, and other companies to lease space in all of their holdings. Facilities such as airports and college food courts begin to look the same even though they are separated by thousands of miles.

The third dimension of cultural landscape convergence is the wholesale borrowing of idealized landscape images across the world. As you study the cultural landscape, you may notice landscape features transplanted from one place to another—regardless of whether the landscape feature even "fits."

The strip in Las Vegas, Nevada, represents an extreme case of the tendency toward convergence, with various structures designed to evoke different parts of the planet. The popular Venetian Hotel and Casino in Las Vegas replicates the Italian city of Venice, including canals. The Las Vegas Sands

■ **Figure 4.25**
Munich, Germany. In modern-day Munich, the famed Hofbräuhaus shares a street corner with the Hard Rock Café. The juxtaposition of different cultural-commercial traditions is increasingly common.

■ **Figure 4.26a**
Venice, Italy. UNESCO World Heritage Site. Designation as a World Heritage Site is reserved for sites with great cultural-historical significance. But as the two photos below suggest, knockoffs of such sites are not uncommon—eroding the distinctiveness of places.

■ **Figure 4.26b**
The Venetian Hotel and Casino in Las Vegas, Nevada.

■ **Figure 4.26c**
The Venetian Hotel and Casino in Macau, China.

Corporation, a casino developer and owner, built the Venetian Hotel and Casino across the Pacific from Las Vegas in Macao in 2007. The port city of Macao was once a colony of Portugal but reverted to Chinese control in 1999. The Venetian Macao Resort cost $2.4 billion and is three times the size of the largest casino in Las Vegas (Fig. 4.26b). Gambling is illegal in mainland China, but Macao's recent incorporation into China and its special status allow gambling to flourish on the small island.

The borrowing of landscape is not confined to grand-scale projects like the Venetian. A more common borrowed landscape in North America is the town center. Town centers popping up in suburbia in North America have a similar look—one that is familiar if you have walked on Main Street, U.S.A. at Disneyland or Disney World, or if you have visited the centers of any number of "quaint" historic towns on the eastern seaboard. Each town center is designed to make you think of all things American and to feel immediately "home" in the place.

In less obvious ways, cultural borrowing and mixing are happening all around the world. This idea is behind the **global–local continuum** concept. This notion emphasizes that what happens at one scale is not independent of what happens at other scales. Human geography is not simply about documenting the differences between places; it is also about understanding the processes unfolding at different scales that produce those differences. What happens in an individual place is the product of interaction across scales. People in a local place mediate and alter regional, national, and global processes, in a process called **glocalization**. The character of place ultimately comes out of a multitude of dynamic interactions among local distinctiveness and wider-scaled events and influences.

Cultural Landscapes of Local Cultures

What makes travel interesting for most people is the presence of variety in the cultural landscape. Travel beyond the tourist sites and the main roads, and one will easily find landscapes of local cultures, even in wealthy countries such as the United States and Canada. By studying cultural landscapes, you can gain insight into the social structures of local cultures. In everything from the houses to the schools to the churches to the cemeteries, a local cultural landscape reveals its foundation.

Founders and early followers of the Church of Jesus Christ of Latter-day Saints created the Mormon landscape of the American West as they migrated westward under persecution

and in search of a place where they could practice their religion freely. The Mormon Church began in New York, and then Joseph Smith and his followers moved westward to Independence, Missouri. From there, Mormons migrated farther west to present-day Salt Lake City, Utah. The easiest place to see the foundations of the Mormon cultural landscape are in the small towns established by Mormons throughout Utah and stretching into Arizona, Nevada, and Idaho (Fig. 4.27).

Geographers, including Donald Meinig, Richard Francaviglia, and Allen Noble, have studied the Mormon landscape and found the roots of the Mormon culture inscribed in the local landscape. If you drove from Chicago west to Las Vegas and traveled through the rural areas of Nebraska and Utah on your path, you would immediately notice one fundamental difference in the landscape: farmsteads in the plains replaced by farming villages in the west. In the Great Plains, the Homestead Act encouraged farmers to establish single farmsteads where a farm family lived alone on their 160 acres and the nearest neighbor was down the dirt road. In the rural Mormon

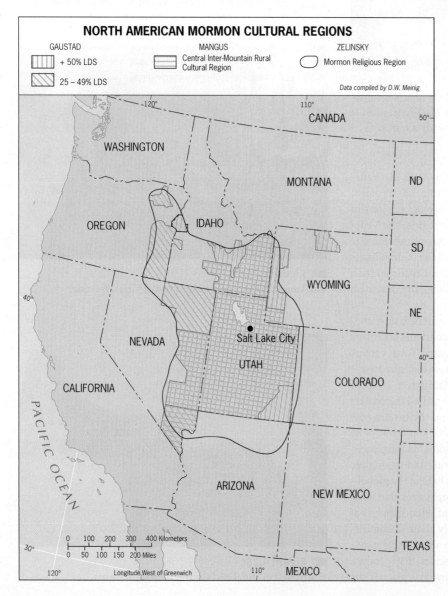

■ Figure 4.27
The Mormon Cultural Region.   The Mormon culture region surrounds Salt Lake City, Utah where Mormon migrants established farms and farming communities. The religion diffused both through migration and missionary work to solidify a Mormon cultural region in North America. From this base, Mormon missionaries have diffused the religion to widespread parts of the world.   *Adapted with permission from:* D.W. Meinig, "The Mormon Culture Region: Strategies and Patterns in the Geography of the American west, 1847–1964," *Annals of the Association of American Geographers,* 55, 2 (1965), p. 196.

GUEST FIELD NOTE

Paragonah, Utah

I took this photograph in the village of Paragonah, Utah, in 1969, and it still reminds me that fieldwork is both an art and a science. People who know the American West well may immediately recognize this as a scene from "Mormon Country," but their recognition is based primarily on their impressions of the place. "It is something about the way the scene looks," they may say, or "it feels like a Mormon village because of the way the barn and the house sit at the base of those arid bluffs." These are general impressions, but how can one prove that it is a Mormon scene? That is where the science of fieldwork comes into play. Much like a detective investigating a crime scene or a journalist writing an accurate story, the geographer looks for proof. In this scene, we can spot several of the ten elements that comprise the Mormon landscape. First, this farmstead is not separate from the village, but part of it—just a block off of Main Street, in fact.

Next we can spot that central-hall home made out of brick; then there is that simple, unpainted gabled-roof barn; and lastly the weedy edge of a very wide street says Mormon Country. Those are just four clues suggesting that pragmatic Mormons created this cultural landscape, and other fieldwork soon confirmed that all ten elements were present here in Paragonah. Like this 40-year-old photo, which shows some

Richard Francaviglia

■ **Figure 4.28**
Paragonah, Utah.   Photo taken in 1969.

signs of age, the scene here did not remain unchanged. In Paragonah and other Mormon villages, many old buildings have been torn down, streets paved, and the landscape "cleaned up"—a reminder that time and place (which is to say history and geography) are inseparable.

Credit: Richard Francaviglia, Geo.Graphic Designs, Salem, Oregon

landscape, early settlers established farming villages where houses clustered together and croplands surrounded the outskirts of the village (Fig. 4.28). Clustering houses together in a farming village allowed Mormons to protect each other, a paramount concern because the religion's followers were experiencing persecution in the East and because the settlers' fears were raised by stories of Indians attacking villages in the West. Equally importantly, through clustering they sought to join together for services in each village's chapel.

Geographer Richard Francaviglia offers several factors that delimit the Mormon landscape in the western United States and Canada, including symmetrical brick houses that look more similar to houses on the East Coast than to other pioneer houses, wide streets that run due north–south and east–west, ditches for irrigation, poplar trees for shade, bishop's storehouses for storing food and necessities for the poor, and unpainted fences. Because the early Mormons were farmers and were clustered together in villages, each block in the town was quite large, allowing for one-acre city lots where a farmer could keep livestock and other farming supplies in town. The streets were wide so that farmers could easily turn a cart and horses on them.

The morphology (that is, the size and shape of a place's buildings, streets, and infrastructure) of a Mormon village tells us a lot, and so too can the shape and size of a local culture's housing. In Malaysia, the Iban, an indigenous people, live along the Sarawak River in the Borneo region of the country in longhouses. Each longhouse is home to an extended family of up to 200 people. The family and the longhouse function as a community, sharing the rice farmed by the family, supporting each other through frequent flooding of the river (the houses are built on stilts), and working together on the porch that stretches the length of the house. The rice paddies surrounding each longhouse are a familiar shape and form throughout Southeast Asia, but the Iban longhouse tells you that you are experiencing a different kind of place—one that reflects a unique local culture.

 Focus on the cultural landscape of your college campus. Think about the concept of placelessness. Determine whether your campus is a "placeless place" or whether the cultural landscape of your college reflects the unique identity of the place. Imagine you are hired to build a new student union on your campus. How could you design the building to reflect the uniqueness of your college?

Summary

Advances in transportation and communications technology help popular culture diffuse at record speeds around the world today. Popular culture changes quickly, offering new music, foods, fashions, and sports. Popular culture envelops and infiltrates local cultures, presenting constant challenges to members of local cultures. Some members of local cultures have accepted popular culture, others have rejected it, and still others have forged a balance between the two.

Customs from local cultures are often commodified, propelling them into popular culture. The search for an "authentic" local culture custom generally ends up promoting a stereotyped local culture or glorifying a single aspect of that local culture. Local culture, like popular culture, is dynamic, and the pursuit of authenticity disregards the complexity and fluidity of cultures.

Geographic Concepts

culture	assimilation	time–space compression
folk culture	custom	opinion leaders
popular culture	cultural appropriation	reterritorialization
local culture	neolocalism	cultural landscape
material culture	ethnic neighborhood	placelessness
nonmaterial culture	commodification	global-local continuum
hierarchical diffusion	authenticity	glocalization
hearth	distance decay	

Learn More Online

About the Irish Pub Company
www.irishpubcompany.com

About the Makah Tribe
www.makah.com

About the City of Lindsborg
www.lindsborgcity.org/

About the Hutterites
www.hutterites.org

Watch It Online

Generation Like
www.pbs.org/wgbh/pages/frontline/generation-like/

Merchants of Cool
www.pbs.org/wgbh/pages/frontline/shows/cool/

The Way the Music Died
www.pbs.org/wgbh/pages/frontline/shows/music/

IDENTITY: RACE, ETHNICITY, GENDER, AND SEXUALITY

Building Walls

Traveling on the Indonesian island of Bali, I saw a brick-making facility and stopped to visit. Boys and women were building bricks by hand, in the hot sun. I watched young boys scoop wet mud from a quarry by a creek into their wheelbarrows. They poured the mud into wooden forms. Once the bricks began to dry and harden in the sun, someone had to turn the bricks repeatedly to prevent them from cracking. The woman in Figure 5.1 worked ten hours a day, six days a week, turning, stacking, and restacking bricks to prevent them from cracking.

More than a century ago, bricks were made this way in the United States. Today, the brick-making industry in the United States makes use of a great deal of technology and robotics to manufacture bricks. Instead of using the sun to bake the bricks, brick-making factories in the United States employ enormous tunnel-shaped kilns. The *Mississippi Business Journal* described how bricks are made in one factory: "Clay and water go in one end of the new 590 foot tunnel kiln and brick pallets will roll out the other end as robots and employees work side by side."

What hit me harder than the difference in technology between the two countries is the difference in labor. In Bali, women and boys make bricks. In the United States, the vast majority of brick-makers are men, aided by machines. One company estimated that 98 percent of its operations' employees in the factory are men. What makes brick-making a job for women and boys in Bali and a job for men and robots in the United States? *Does being a brick-maker mean different things in each of these places?*

Throughout the world, different cultures and societies have different ideas about what jobs are appropriate for men

© H. J. de Blij

■ **Figure 5.1**

Bedugul, Indonesia. A woman turns bricks at a brick-making facility in the village of Bedugul on the Indonesian island of Bali. She works in the formal economy for low wages and long hours.

and for women. Geographers, especially those who study gender, realize that people create divisions of labor that are *gendered*. Geographers Mona Domosh and Joni Seager define **gender** as "a culture's assumptions about the differences between men and women: their 'characters,' the roles they play in society, what they represent." Divisions of labor are one of the clearest ways in which societies are gendered.

In Bali, brick-making is still done by hand by boys and women. The industry is not technologically sophisticated, and bricks are made one by one. Even beyond brick-making facilities, most of the factory jobs in Indonesia and in poorer countries of the world go to women instead of men. Factory managers often hire women over men because they see women as an expendable labor pool. Researcher Peter Hancock (2000) studied gender relations and women's work in factories in Indonesia and reported, "Research in different global contexts suggests that factory managers employ young women because they are more easily exploited, less likely to strike or form membership organizations, are comparatively free from family responsibilities, and more adept at doing repetitive and delicate tasks associated with assembly line work."

In many societies in poorer countries, young women are seen as the financial supporters of their families. Women migrate from rural areas and travel to cities or central industrial locales (such as export production zones—EPZs) to produce and earn a wage that is then sent home to support the schooling of their brothers and younger sisters (until these girls are also old enough to leave home and work).

In Indonesia and in neighboring Malaysia and the Philippines, many women temporarily migrate to the Middle East to work as domestics, cooking, cleaning, and providing childcare in order to send money home to support the family. In the United States, rarely does an oldest daughter migrate to the city to labor in a factory so that she can pay for her younger brothers' schooling.

Although public education in the United States is free and open to boys and girls, American society still has gendered divisions of labor. The few women who work in brick-manufacturing facilities in the United States are typically assigned to tasks that require little lifting—such as gluing pieces of the various types of brick to boards so that salespeople can use them as samples. A long-standing assumption in American society is that work requiring heavy lifting needs to be completed by men and that good-paying, unionized jobs need to go to men because men are the "heads of the household." Times are changing and gendered work is being increasingly challenged, but assumptions about gender still have an impact on the labor market.

Society creates boxes in which we put people and expect them to live. These boxes are in a sense stereotypes embodying assumptions we make about what is *expected from* or *assumed about* women, men, members of certain races or ethnic groups, and people with various sexual preferences. By creating these boxes, society can assign entire professions or tasks to members of certain categories—for example, "women's work"—thereby gendering the division of labor. Places, notably the kitchen of a home or a store in the mall, can also be gendered. People are constantly negotiating their personal identities, finding their ways through all the expectations placed on them by the boxes society puts around them, and modifying and reinforcing the social relations that create the places where they work and live.

Rarely do the social relations that create gendered divisions of labor focus only on gender. The social relations in a place also create boxes for other identities. In this chapter, we focus on gender, race, ethnicity, and sexuality. We examine how people and society construct identities, how place factors into identity, and how geography reflects and shapes power relationships among different groups of people.

Key Questions FOR CHAPTER 5

1. What is identity, and how are identities constructed?
2. How do places affect identity, and how can we see identities in places?
3. How does geography reflect and shape power relationships among groups?

WHAT IS IDENTITY, AND HOW ARE IDENTITIES CONSTRUCTED?

A man gets off the airplane, walks to the baggage carousel to find his suitcase, and is greeted by dozens of black suitcases. He walks to the parking garage to find his car and sees a sea of black cars that all look the same. The narrator intones, "Maintain your identity. Drive a Saab."

Identities are marketed through cars, clothing, club memberships, jewelry, and houses. Advertisements often convey the impression that we can purchase our identity. Yet, identity is much more personal than what we drive, wear, belong to, or where we live. Geographer Gillian Rose (1995) defines **identity** as "how we make sense of ourselves." How do we each define ourselves? We construct our own identities through experiences, emotions, connections, and rejections. We work through derivations and delineations to find an identity that meshes with who and where we are at any given time. An identity is a snapshot, an image of who we are at that moment. Identities are fluid, constantly changing, shifting, and becoming. Place and space are integral to our identities because our experiences in places and our perceptions of places help us make sense of who we are.

In addition to defining ourselves, we define others and others define us. One of the most powerful ways to construct an identity is by **identifying against** other people. To identify against, we first define the "Other," and then we define ourselves in opposing terms. Edward Said wrote thoughtfully about how Europeans, over time, constructed an image of regions that are now commonly called the Middle East and Asia. He described the circumstances that led Europeans to define this area as the "Orient," a place with supposedly mystical characteristics that were depicted and repeated in European art and literature. In a similar vein, geographer James Blaut wrote eloquently about how Europeans came to define Africans and Native Americans as "savage" and "mystical." Through these images of the "Other," which developed during periods of European exploration and colonialism, Europeans defined themselves as "not mystical" or "not savage" and, therefore, as "civilized." These ideas are still part of our vernacular speech even today, as seen in references to "the civilized world" or a time "before civilization." Phrases like these invariably carry with them a sense of superiority in opposition to an "Other."

One of the most powerful foci of identity in the modern world is the state. State nationalism has been such a powerful force that in many contexts people think of themselves first and foremost as French, Japanese, American, or the like. Nationalist identities are a product of the modern state system, so we defer consideration of this form of identity to the chapter that focuses on the rise of the state system (Chapter 8). But nationalist identities coexist with all sorts of other identities that divide humanity—identities that can trump state nationalism in certain contexts and certain scales of interaction. Language and religion can function as foci of identity, and we will turn to these in the next two chapters. This chapter takes up several other important foundations of identity—those based on race, gender, ethnicity, and sexuality. We look at issues of identity construction, place, and scale by way of an analysis of race. We examine ethnicity and sexuality as identities that are shaped by and that in turn shape place. Our concluding discussion in this chapter looks at power relationships through the lenses of gender and ethnicity.

Race

Race provides an excellent example of how a change in geographic context shapes definitions of identity. The various "races" people identify are tied to physical attributes of humans that have developed over time as modern humans spread around the world. Closer to the poles, humans developed lighter skin pigment so that skin could absorb sunlight that bodies could convert into vitamin D during the half of the year when the region received sunlight. Closer to the equator, humans developed darker skin pigment with higher amounts of melanin, which protects the skin from ultraviolet radiation emitted by the sun.

In precolonial Africa, societies had lines of division that sometimes reflected differences in skin tones. In colonial Africa, however, all of the different shades of "black" in Africa came to be viewed as one by European colonizers. The clumping of various societies and peoples into a few racial categories based on skin pigment still occurs in the modern world. Think of how often we are asked to complete applications, census forms, product warranty information, surveys, and medical forms that ask us to check a box identifying ourselves by race,

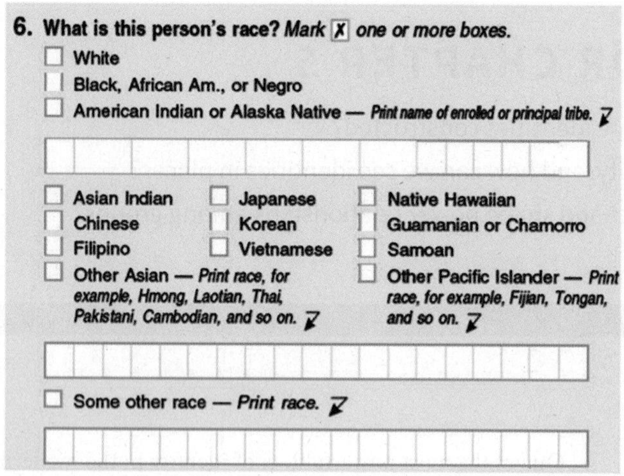

6. What is this person's race? *Mark* X *one or more boxes.*

☐ White
☐ Black, African Am., or Negro
☐ American Indian or Alaska Native — *Print name of enrolled or principal tribe.* ↘

[blank write-in boxes]

☐ Asian Indian   ☐ Japanese   ☐ Native Hawaiian
☐ Chinese   ☐ Korean   ☐ Guamanian or Chamorro
☐ Filipino   ☐ Vietnamese   ☐ Samoan
☐ Other Asian — *Print race, for*   ☐ Other Pacific Islander — *Print*
example, Hmong, Laotian, Thai,   *race, for example, Fijian, Tongan,*
Pakistani, Cambodian, and so on. ↘   *and so on.* ↘

[blank write-in boxes]

☐ Some other race — *Print race.* ↘

[blank write-in boxes]

■ **Figure 5.2**

United States. Although biologically there is only one human race, we are often asked to choose race boxes for ourselves. This page of the 2010 United States Census asks the individual, "What is this person's race?" and directs the individual to "Mark one or more races to indicate what you consider yourself to be." The 2010 Census listed 14 racial categories, as well as a place to write in a specific race not listed on the form. Since 2000, the Census has allowed individuals to choose more than one race as their identity.

for example, "white," "black," "Asian" (Fig. 5.2). Such practices institutionalize and reinforce modern ways of viewing race. With each box we check, we learn to think the categories of race on the census are natural, fixed, mutually exclusive, and comprehensive. The more social scientists study race, the more we recognize racial categories are constructed, fluid, overlapping, and incomplete.

Where did society get the idea that humans fall into different, seemingly unchangeable categories of race? Throughout history, societies in different parts of the world have drawn distinctions among peoples based on their physical characteristics, but many of societies' modern assumptions about race grew out of the period of European exploration and colonialism since 1500. Benedict Anderson notes that even before 1500, before the Age of Exploration and colonialism, wealthy Europeans defined themselves as superior to those living elsewhere, suggesting that socioeconomic differences can fuel the sense of superiority attached to race known as **racism**. With the onset of the colonial era, what changed in Europe is that even poorer Europeans came to define themselves as superior to the people in the colonies. Anderson (1982) explains:

Colonial racism was a major element in that conception of "Empire" which attempted to weld dynastic legitimacy and national community. It did so by generalizing a principle of innate, inherited superiority on which its own domestic position was (however shakily) based to the vastness of the overseas possessions, covertly (or not so covertly) conveying the idea that if, say, English lords were naturally superior to other Englishmen, no matter: these other Englishmen were no less superior to the subjected natives.

The stories the commoners heard about the "mystical" and "savage" "Others" fostered feelings of superiority. One of the easiest ways to define the "Other" is through skin color because it is visible. Differences in the color of skin, then, became the basis for a fundamental social divide.

What society typically calls a "race" is in fact a combination of physical attributes in a population. Differences in skin, eye, and hair color likely result from a long history of adaptation to different environments. Sunlight stimulates the production of melanin, which protects skin from damaging ultraviolet rays; the more melanin that is present, the darker the skin will be. Biologists explain that this helps to explain why, over the millennia, humans living in low latitudes (closer to the equator, from tropical Africa through southern India to Australia) had darker skins. Over the millennia, natural selection in higher latitudes, closer to the North and South Poles, favored those with the least amount of pigmentation. People with less pigmentation could more easily absorb ultraviolet rays, which, in the higher latitudes, are sparse in winter months when the amount of sunlight is lower and less direct. When humans absorb ultraviolet light, their bodies in turn produce vitamin D, which is a necessary nutrient for survival.

Although melanin varies by latitude, skin color is not a reliable indicator of genetic closeness. The indigenous peoples of southern India, New Guinea, and Australia, for example, are about as dark-skinned as native Africans, but native Africans, southern Indians, and Aboriginal Australians are not closely related genetically (Fig. 5.3). No biological basis exists for dividing the human species into four or five groups based on skin color. Instead, those racial categories are the product of how particular cultures have dominantly viewed skin color.

The racial distinctions found in places today are the product of cultural history, power relationships, and local political developments over the past few centuries. Geographer Benjamin Forest (2001) gives us a global overview of racial distinctions:

In Britain, the term "black" refers not only to Afro-Caribbeans and Africans, but also to individuals from the Indian subcontinent. In Russia, the term "black" is used to describe "Caucasians," that is, people such as Chechens from the Caucasus region. In many parts of Latin America, particularly Brazil, "racial" classification is really a kind of class placement, in which members of the wealthy upper class are generally considered as "white," members of the middle class as mixed race or Mestizo, and members of the lower class as "black." Indeed, because racial classifications are based on class standing and physical appearance rather than ancestry, "the designation of one's racial identity need not be the same as that of the parents, and siblings are often classified differently than one another."

In each of these cases, and in countless others, people have constructed racial categories to justify power, economic exploitation, and cultural oppression.

FIELD NOTE

"We were traveling in Darwin, Australia, in 1994 and decided to walk away from the modern downtown for a few hours. Darwin is a multicultural city in the midst of a region of Australia that is largely populated by Aboriginals. At the bus stops on the outskirts of the city, Aboriginals reached Darwin to work in the city or to obtain social services only offered in the city. With a language barrier between us, we used hand gestures to ask the man in the white shirt and his son if we could take their picture. Gesturing back to us, they agreed to the picture. Our continued attempts at sign language soon led to much laughter among the people waiting for the next bus."

© H. J. de Blij

■■ **Figure 5.3**
Darwin, Australia.

Race and Ethnicity in the United States

Unlike a local culture or ethnicity to which we may choose to belong, race is an identity that is more often assigned. In the words of geographer Benjamin Forest (2001): "In many respects, racial identity is not a self-consciously constructed collection of characteristics, but a condition which is imposed by a set of external social and historical constraints." In the United States, racial categories are reinforced through residential segregation, racialized divisions of labor, and the categories of races recorded by the United States Census Bureau and other government and nongovernmental agencies.

Definitions of race in the United States historically focused on dividing the country into "white" and "nonwhite." Our understanding of race has changed over time, but those in the public eye, whether golfer Tiger Woods or President Barack Obama, are still asked to explain their racial identity (Figure 5.4). Governments have also determined racial identities, especially during the 20th century

William Thomas Cain/Getty Images

■■ **Figure 5.4**
President Barack Obama. In March 2008, running for his first term as president, Obama addressed the issue of his racial identity by explaining, "I am the son of a black man from Kenya and a white woman from Kansas.... I am married to a black American who carries within her the blood of slaves and slaveowners—an inheritance we pass on to our two precious daughters." He described his far-flung family as being made of "every hue" and "scattered across three continents."

when several countries limited immigration to those who were "white." In the early 1900s, immigration to the United States shifted from northern and western Europe to southern and eastern Europe and the United States government redefined what constituted "white" so that people with olive-colored skin from the Mediterranean would count as "white."

As a result of immigration and differences in fertility rates, the United States is becoming increasingly racially diverse (Table 5.1). At the same time, how Americans define "race" is changing. Before 2000, the United States Census classified "Hispanic" as a race. This categorization was chosen because people in Latin America, as in North America, represent different races. Before the 2000 census, a white person from Venezuela, a black person from Brazil, and a native person from Bolivia were all classified as "Hispanic." This example demonstrates the arbitrary nature of racial and ethnic classifications. In this example, coming from Latin America "trumped" all other identities, and the person was defined as "Hispanic." In 2000, the Census recognized that Hispanic is not a race and that it is better defined as an ethnicity. However, the word "Hispanic" means coming from a country where Spanish is the pre-

dominant language, including Spain, Mexico, and many countries in Central and South America and the Caribbean. In our example above, the black person from Brazil who was classified as "Hispanic" should not have been under this definition. The predominant language in Brazil is Portuguese, not Spanish.

Because of the redesignation of "Hispanic" as an ethnicity, in the boxes provided by the United States Census Bureau a person can now be "White, non-Hispanic," "White, Hispanic," "Black, non-Hispanic," "Black, Hispanic," and so forth.

In 2010, the United States Census recognized that "Hispanic" excludes people from Latin America who are not native Spanish speakers. The Census also recognized that some people, including United States Supreme Court Justice Sonia Sotomayor, prefer the term *Latina* or *Latino* to *Hispanic*. In 2010, the United States Census Bureau described the Hispanic ethnicity as "Hispanic, Latino, or Spanish origin," and continued to list Hispanic as an ethnicity and not a race.

With the evolution in understanding of race and ethnicity, it is sometimes difficult to choose the right term to describe an individual or group of people. In this chapter and in the rest of the textbook, we use the most precise

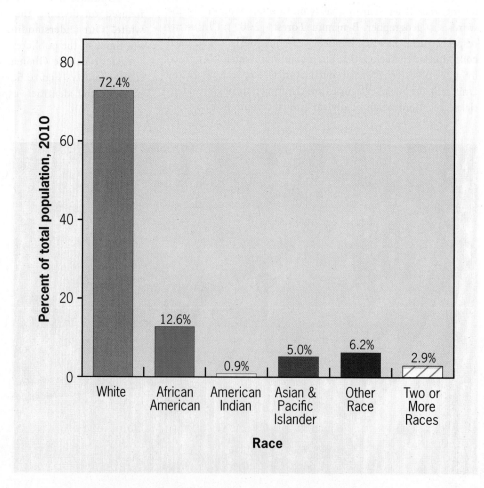

TABLE 5.1
Population of the United States by Race, 2010. In 2000 and in 2010, the United States Census Bureau, for the first time, allowed Americans to categorize themselves as one race or more than one race. The "two or more races" self-designation is projected to grow in the decades ahead. *Data from*: United States Census Bureau, 2010.

description possible. Instead of a generic term like *Hispanic,* if we are talking about a group of immigrants from Bolivia, we call them immigrants from Bolivia. If we discuss a study about Cree Indians in Canada, we describe the Cree tribe, not a generic term such as First Nations. In general references, we use the term *Hispanic* instead of *Latino* or *Latina* in accordance with the results of a 2013 Pew Research survey. This survey of Americans who defined themselves as Hispanic or Latino reported that "half (50%) say they have no preference for either term. But among those who *do* have a preference, 'Hispanic' is preferred over 'Latino' by a ratio of about 2 to 1."

In the United States, 64 percent of the Hispanic population is of Mexican origin, and 9 percent of people who define themselves as Hispanic are of Puerto Rican descent. In the 2000 and 2010 censuses, all persons who defined themselves as Hispanic also defined themselves by a racial category. By combining race and ethnicity boxes, statisticians can still separate the American population into "White, non-Hispanic" and "everyone else." According to the data projections provided after the 2010 Census, the population of "everyone else" will surpass (in numbers) the "White, non-Hispanic" population around 2042 (Table 5.2).

Residential Segregation

Racism has affected the distribution of African Americans, American Indians, and others throughout the history of the United States. During the past century, some of the most dramatic geographic impacts of racism could be found at the neighborhood scale. Historically, states, cities, and towns passed laws that promoted residential segregation by disallowing the migration of certain racial groups into particular neighborhoods. Laws passed during and after the civil rights movement of the 1960s in the United States made it illegal to legislate residential segregation. Despite these changes, many cities in the United States remain strongly segregated along racial lines.

Geographers Douglas Massey and Nancy Denton defined **residential segregation** as the "degree to which two or more groups live separately from one another, in different parts of the urban environment." Massey and Denton defined different kinds of residential segregation in a 1988 article, explaining that residential segregation is complex because:

groups may live apart from one another and be "segregated" in a variety of ways. Minority members may be distributed

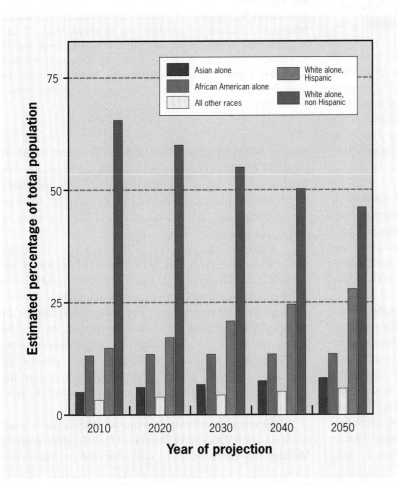

TABLE 5.2

Estimated Percentage of United States Population by Race and Ethnicity Until 2050.   In 2000, the United States Census Bureau began to calculate race and Hispanic origin separately, allowing people to place themselves in one or more race categories plus one of two Hispanic origin categories (Hispanic or Non-Hispanic). According to the race categories provided in the 2010 census estimates, starting in 2042, the "White, non-Hispanic" population will no longer be the majority population in the United States.   *Data from:* United States Census, 2010.

so that they are overrepresented in some areas and under-represented in others, varying on the characteristic of even-ness. They may be distributed so that their exposure to majority members is limited by virtue of rarely sharing a neighborhood with them. They may be spatially concen-trated within a very small area, occupying less physical space than majority members. They may be spatially cen-tralized, congregating around the urban core, and occupy-ing a more central location than the majority. Finally, areas of minority settlement may be tightly clustered to form one large contiguous enclave, or be scattered widely around the urban area.

A special report issued by the United States Census Bureau in 2002 statistically analyzed, charted, and mapped residential segregation in metropolitan areas of the country, using the following five statistical measurements of segrega-tion: evenness, exposure, concentrated, centralized, and clus-tered. These five measurements directly correspond to the five types of segregation outlined by Massey and Denton.

In the 2002 Census Bureau report, the authors reported on the levels of residential segregation in metropolitan areas of the United States between 1980 and 2000. They found that overall residential segregation by race/ethnicity is on the decline. For each of the four identities they researched—American Indians and Alaska Natives; Asians, Native Hawaiians, and Pacific Islanders; Black/African Americans; and Hispanics/Latinos—they calculated five statistical mea-sures of residential segregation.

The researchers reported that all five measures showed a decrease in residential segregation for African Americans between 1980 and 1990 and another such decrease between 1990 and 2000. A report after the 2010 census found that residential segregation for African Americans peaked in the 1960s and 1970s and declined again between 2000 and 2010. In 2010, the most residentially segregated large metro-politan area for African Americans was Milwaukee, Wisconsin (Fig. 5.5).

In 2000, when using an average of all five measures of segregation, the most residentially segregated metropolitan area for American Indians and Alaska Natives was Phoenix-Mesa, Arizona, and the least residentially segregated was Oklahoma City. In 2000, the four least residentially segre-gated metropolitan areas (with at least 3 percent of the popu-lation American Indian) were all in Oklahoma.

Grouping Asians, Native Hawaiians, and Pacific Island-ers, researchers of the 2000 report found 30 metropolitan areas with at least 3 percent of the population fitting one of these identities. Based on calculations for all five statistics of residential segregation, the most residentially segregated metropolitan area for Asians/Pacific Islanders was San Francisco, followed by New York and Los Angeles. The data and maps change depending on how statistics are calculated. A report that appeared after the 2010 census examined Asian segregation using a dissimilarity index with white popula-

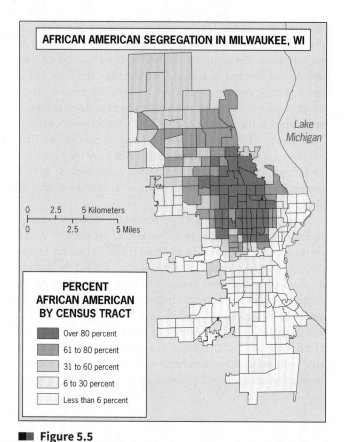

■■ Figure 5.5

Residential Segregation of African Americans in Milwaukee, Wisconsin. Percent African American by census tract. African American neighborhoods are concentrated on the north end of Milwaukee. First settled in the 1800s by Germans, northern Milwaukee became predominantly African American during the Great Migration (see Chapter 3). *Data from*: United States Census Bureau, 2010.

tions in 102 large metropolitan areas. The report, based on the 2010 census data, found Buffalo/Niagara Falls to be the most segregated for Asians (not including Pacific Islanders) based on the dissimilarity index and considering all large metropolitan areas, not just those with at least 3 percent of the population being Asian.

Baltimore, Maryland (Fig. 5.6) is one of the more residentially integrated cites in the United States for Asians as well as for Hispanics/Latinos. The report based on the 2000 census found that the cities with the highest number of Hispanic residents experienced the greatest degree of residential segregation. The analysis focused on the 36 large metropolitan areas with a Hispanic population account-ing for at least 3 percent of the total urban population. The city with the greatest residential segregation for Hispanics was New York, and Baltimore was one of the least segregated.

The numbers and maps produced by the Census Bureau based on 2000 data and by Brookings Institute demographer William Frey based on 2010 data show the outcomes of a

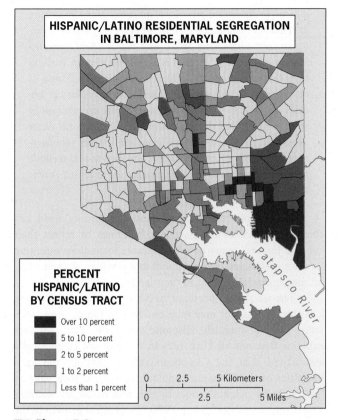
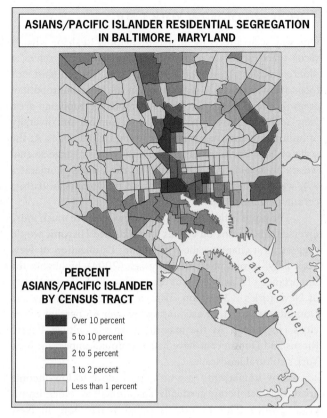

■■ **Figure 5.6**
Residential Segregation of Latinos and Asians/Pacific Islanders in Baltimore, Maryland. Baltimore, Maryland, is one of the least segregated cities for Hispanics and Asians/Pacific Islanders. The Hispanic population is distributed throughout the city with some neighborhoods standing out as strongly Hispanic. The City of Baltimore began encouraging immigrants to settle in the city in 2012 in hopes to grow the population by 10,000 families. If the program is successful, by the 2020 census, the proportion of Hispanics in the city will increase, and the pattern and neighborhood concentration may change. *Data from*: United States Census Bureau, 2010.

variety of stories, but they do not tell us the stories that created these patterns. Why does residential segregation persist in some places and not in others? In some of the most segregated cities, people know where the "Other" lives and will purposely choose to live in neighborhoods with people like themselves. Real estate agents and community leaders may consciously or subconsciously direct people to their "own" neighborhoods (blockbusting and redlining are discussed in Chapter 9). In almost all cities, race is related to class, making it difficult to afford a higher-class neighborhood that is also populated by another race. In other cities, residents may choose to live in a blighted neighborhood because it is their neighborhood, one they have helped create and that reflects their culture.

Identities Across Scales

The way we make sense of ourselves in an increasingly globalized world is complex. We have different identities at different scales: individual, local, regional, national, and global.

At the individual scale, we may see ourselves as a daughter, a sister, a golfer, or a student. At the local scale, we may see ourselves as members of a community, leaders of a campus organization, or residents of a neighborhood. At the regional scale, we may see ourselves as Southerners, as north Georgians, as Atlantans, as Yankees living in the South, or as migrants from another region of the world. At the national scale, we may see ourselves as American, as college students, or as members of a national political party. At the global scale, we may see ourselves as Western, as educated, as relatively wealthy, or as free.

One way to view an individual's various identities is to treat them as nested, one inside of the other; the appropriate identity is revealed at the appropriate scale. In this vein, each larger territorial extent of geographic space has its own corresponding set of identities. Today, more geographers see identities as fluid, intertwined, and context dependent rather than as neatly nested. Identities affect each other in and across scales, and the ways places and peoples interact across scales simultaneously affect identities within and across scales.

The Scale of New York City

One way scale affects identity is by helping to shape what is seen—what identity is apparent to others and to ourselves at different scales. To demonstrate this idea, we can shift our focus from residential segregation in all large metropolitan areas in North America to one enormous metropolitan area, New York City. New York has a greater number and diversity of immigrants than any other city in the United States. At the scale of New York, we can see how identities change so that we are no longer simply Hispanic (as the Census enumerates us); we are Puerto Rican or Mexican or Dominican from a certain neighborhood.

The point is that the people in New York are much more diverse than the box on census forms labeled Hispanic would suggest. In a chapter called "Changing Latinization of New York City," geographer Inés Miyares (2004) highlights the importance of Caribbean culture to New York. The majority of New York's 2.3 million Hispanics are Puerto Ricans and Dominicans (together accounting for over 65 percent of the city's Hispanics). As the majority Hispanic culture, Puerto Ricans and Dominicans have had a profound impact on New York's cultural landscape.

New immigrants to a city often move to low-income areas that are being gradually abandoned by older immigrant groups. This process is called **succession**. In New York, Puerto Ricans moved into the immigrant Jewish neighborhood of East Harlem in the early twentieth century, successively assuming a dominant presence in the neighborhood. With the influx of Puerto Ricans, new names for the neighborhood developed, and today it is frequently called Spanish Harlem or El Barrio (meaning "neighborhood" in Spanish). As the Puerto Rican population grew, new storefronts appeared, catering to the Puerto Rican population, including travel agencies (specializing in flights to Puerto Rico), specialty grocery stores, and dance and music studios.

Similar to the immigrant flow from Puerto Rico, the large-scale immigrant flow from the Dominican Republic that began in 1965 resulted in a distinct neighborhood and cultural landscape. Dominican immigrants landed in the Washington Heights/Inwood neighorhood of upper Manhattan, a neighborhood previously occupied by immigrant Jews, African Americans, Puerto Ricans, and Cubans. Miyares reports that although a Jewish cultural landscape persists, including a Jewish university, synagogues, and Jewish delicatessens, the cultural landscape of Washington Heights is clearly Dominican—from store signs in Spanish to the presence of the colors of the Dominican flag (Fig. 5.7).

New York is unique because of the sheer number and diversity of its immigrant population. The city's cultural landscape reflects its unique population. As Miyares explains:

Since the overwhelming majority of New York City's population lives in apartments as opposed to houses, it is often difficult to discern the presence of an ethnic group by looking at residential housescapes. However every neighborhood has a principal commercial street, and this is often converted into an ethnic main street. It is commonly through business signs that immigrants make their presence known. Names of businesses reflect place names from the home country or key cultural artifacts. Colors of the national flag are common in store awnings, and the flags themselves and national crests abound in store décor. Key religious symbols are also common. Immigrants are so prevalent and diverse that coethnic proprietors use many kinds of visual clues to attract potential customers.

Throughout the process, new immigrants need not change the facades of apartment buildings to reflect their culture. Instead, many new immigrants focus their attention on the streetscapes, offering goods and services for their community and posting signs in their language.

The Caribbean presence in New York City is so strong a visitor or resident may miss the cues in the cultural landscape that distinguish Hispanic neighborhoods. Miyares explains that not all Hispanics in the city are categorically assimilated into the Caribbean culture. Rather, the local identities of the Hispanic populations in New York vary by "borough, by neighborhood, by era, and by source country and entry experience." Since 1990, the greatest growth in the Hispanic population of New York has been Mexican. Mexican migrants have settled in a variety of ethnic neighborhoods, living alongside new Chinese immigrants in Brooklyn and Puerto Ricans in East Harlem. The process of succession continues in New York, with Mexican immigrants moving into and succeeding other Hispanic neighborhoods, sometimes producing tensions between and among the local cultures.

In New York and in specific neighborhoods like East Harlem, the word "Hispanic" does little to explain the diversity of the city. At these scales, different identities are claimed and assigned, identities that reflect local cultures and neighborhoods. The overarching category "Hispanic" tells us even less about diversity when one moves up the scale to the United States, but as long as that category persists in the Census, people will be encouraged to think about it as a meaningful basis for understanding social differences.

Recall the last time you were asked to check a box for your race. Does that box factor into how you make sense of yourself individually, locally, regionally, nationally, and globally? What impact might it have on how other people view you?

GUEST FIELD NOTE

Washington Heights, New York

It is a warm, humid September morning, and the shops along Juan Pablo Duarte Boulevard are already bustling with customers. The Dominican flag waves proudly from each corner's traffic signal. Calypso and salsa music ring through the air, as do the voices of Dominican grandmothers negotiating for the best prices on fresh mangos and papayas. The scents of fresh *empanadas de yuca* and *pastelitos de pollo* waft from street vendor carts. The signage, the music, the language of the street are all in Spanish and call out to this Dominican community. I am not in Santo Domingo but in Washington Heights in upper Manhattan in New York City.

Whenever I exit the "A" train at 181st Street and walk toward St. Nicholas Avenue, renamed here Juan Pablo Duarte Boulevard for the founding father of the Dominican Republic, it is as if I have boarded a plane to the island. Although there are Dominicans living in most neighborhoods of New York's five boroughs, Washington Heights serves as the heart and soul of the community. Dominicans began settling in Washington Heights in 1965, replacing previous Jewish, African American, and Cuban residents through processes of invasion and succession. Over the past 40 years they have established a vibrant social and economic enclave that is replenished daily by transnational connections to the residents' homeland. These transnational links are pervasive on the landscape, and include travel agencies advertising daily flights to Santo Domingo and Puerto Plata and stores handling *cargas, envios,* and *remesas* (material and financial remittances) found on every block, as well as *farmacias* (pharmacies) selling traditional medicines and *botanicas* selling candles, statues, and other elements needed by practitioners of Santería, a syncretistic blending of Catholicism and Yoruba beliefs practiced by many in the Spanish Caribbean.

Courtesy of Inés Miyares, Hunter College of the City University of New York

■ **Figure 5.7**

Credit: Inés Miyares, Hunter College of the City University of New York.

HOW DO PLACES AFFECT IDENTITY, AND HOW CAN WE SEE IDENTITIES IN PLACES?

The processes of constructing identities and identifying against an "Other," just like any other social or cultural process, differ from place to place and are rooted in places. When we construct identities, part of what we do is infuse place with meaning by attaching memories and experiences to it. This process of infusing a place "with meaning and feeling" is what Gillian Rose and countless other geographers refer to as "developing a sense of place." Like identity, our **sense of place** is fluid; it changes as the place changes and as we change.

Of particular interest to geographers is how people define themselves through places. Our sense of place becomes part of our identity, and our identity affects the ways we define and experience place. Rose (1995) explains:

> One way in which identity is connected to a particular place is by a feeling that you belong to that place. It's a place in which you feel comfortable, or at home, because part of how you define yourself is symbolized by certain qualities of that place. The geographer Relph, for example, has even gone so far as to claim that "to be human is to live in a world that is filled with significant places: to be human is to have to know your place."

The uniqueness of a place can become a part of who we are.

■ **Figure 5.8**
New Glarus, Wisconsin. Immigrants from Switzerland established the town of New Glarus in 1845. The Swiss American town takes pride in its history and culture, as the flags at the New Glarus Hotel Restaurant demonstrate.

© Don Smetzer/Alamy

Ethnicity and Place

Ethnicity offers a good example of how identities affect places and how places affect identities. The idea of **ethnicity** as an identity stems from the notion that people are closely bounded, even related, in a certain place over time. The word "ethnic" comes from the ancient Greek word *ethnos*, meaning "people" or "nation." Geographer Stuart Hall (1995) explains, "Where people share not only a culture but an ethnos, their belongingness or binding into group and place, and their sense of cultural identity, are very strongly defined." Hall makes clear that ethnic identity is "historically constructed like all cultural identities" and is often considered natural because it implies ancient relations among a people over time.

This definition may sound simple, but the concept of ethnicity is not. In the United States, for example, a group of people may define their ethnicity as Swiss American. Switzerland is a state in Europe. The people in Switzerland speak four major languages and other minor ones. The strongest identities in Switzerland are most often at the canton level—a small geographically defined area that distinguishes cultural groups within the state. So, which Swiss are Swiss Americans? The way Swiss Americans see Switzerland as part of who they are may not exist in Switzerland proper (Fig. 5.8). Ethnicity sways and shifts across scales, across places, and across time. A map showing all recognizable ethnic areas would look like a three-dimensional jigsaw puzzle with thousands of often-overlapping pieces—some no larger than a neighborhood, others as large as entire countries.

Ethnic identity is greatly affected by scale and place. In 2002, the *Washington Post* reported on the thriving South Asian community in Fairfax County, Virginia, a suburb of Washington, D.C. In South Asia, the countries of Pakistan and India have a history of animosity, and people identify themselves by country within the region of South Asia and by areas within each country. However, in Fairfax County, Virginia, a world apart from India and Pakistan, many South Asians identify with each other. A South Asian video rental store rents both Pakistani and Indian movies. South Asian grocery stores carry foods from both countries and areas within the countries. The geographical context of suburban Washington, D.C., fosters a collective South Asian identity.

Cultural groups often invoke ethnicity when race cannot explain differences and antagonism between groups. Just as "racial conflicts" are rooted in perceptions of distinctiveness based on differences in economics, power, language, religion, lifestyle, or historical experience, so too are "ethnic conflicts." A conflict is often called ethnic when a racial distinction cannot easily be made. For example, using physical appearance and skin color, an observer cannot distinguish the ethnic groups in many of the conflicts around the world. The adversaries in post–World War II conflicts in Northern Ireland, Spain, the former Yugoslavia, Sri Lanka, Ivory Coast, or Rwanda cannot be identified racially; thus "ethnicity" becomes the marker of difference.

In some instances, the term *ethnicity* is reserved for a small, cohesive, culturally linked group of people who stand apart from the surrounding culture (often as a result of migration). Like other aspects of culture, ethnicity is a dynamic phenomenon that must be understood in terms of the geographic context and scales in which it is situated.

CHINATOWN IN MEXICALI

The border region between the United States and Mexico is generally seen as a cultural meeting point between Mexicans and Anglo Americans. Yet the ethnic composition of people in the border region is more varied than Mexican and Anglo.

Through migration, people from Germany, Russia, India, China, Japan, and many other places also live in the cities and rural areas of the United States–Mexico border region. Over time some of the migrants to this region have blended into the larger community, and others have created distinct patterns of settlement and ethnically imprinted cultural landscapes.

The town of Mexicali is the capital of the State of Baja California (located in Mexico, just south of the State of California in the United States). Not far from the central business district of Mexicali lies one of the largest Chinatowns in Mexico. A 1995 study of the Mexicali Chinatown by geographer James R. Curtis showed that it has been the crucible of Chinese ethnicity in the Mexicali Valley throughout much of the twentieth century. Chinese began arriving in 1902, brought there by the Colorado River Land Company, which started growing cotton in Mexicali when diversion of the Colorado River brought water to irrigate fields in the area. Chinese settled the town of Mexicali, and by 1919 more than 11,000 Chinese were either permanent or temporary residents of the valley. They established a thriving Chinatown in the heart of Mexicali that served as the uncontested center of Chinese life in the region for decades (Fig. 5.9).

Mexicans migrated into Mexicali over time, but the Chinese of Mexicali remained prominent players in the social and economic life of the city during the twentieth century. Chinese owned and operated restaurants, bars, retail trade establishments, commercial land developments, currency exchanges, and more. By 1989, Chinese owned nearly 500 commercial or service properties. In an effort to sustain their cultural traditions and add to the cultural life of the city, they established the China Association, which plays an active role in Mexicali's social and civic life.

Mexicali's Chinatown is experiencing a transformation, as Chinese residents have dispersed to the edges of the city and beyond (many because they can afford to move out of town now). Relatively few Chinese continue to live in the city's Chinatown; some have even moved across the border to Calexico (a city of 27,000 on the California side of the border), while retaining business interests in Mexicali. Yet Mexicali's Chinatown continues to play an important symbolic and functional role for individuals of Chinese ancestry in the area, who are still shaping the region's social and economic geography. Even if the ethnic population in a region is small, ethnic-group identity and consciousness can have a lasting effect on the cultural landscape.

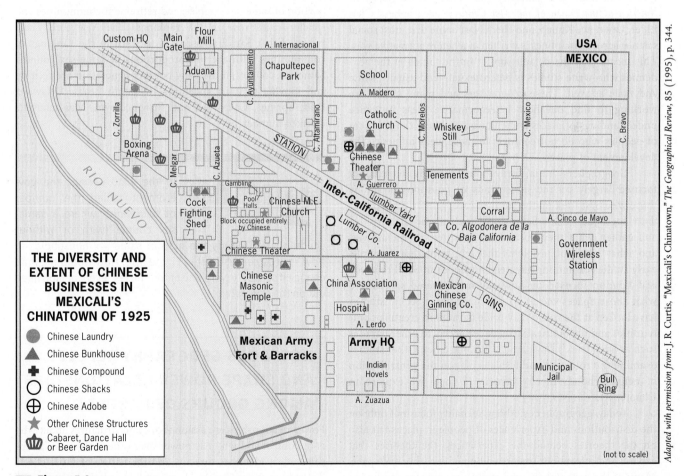

Adapted with permission from: J. R. Curtis, "Mexicali's Chinatown," The Geographical Review, 85 (1995), p. 344.

■ **Figure 5.9**
Chinatown in Mexicali, Mexico. The diversity and extent of Chinese businesses in Mexicali's Chinatown of 1925 is shown in this map. The city still has over 100 Chinese restaurants today.

Identity and Space

One way of thinking about place is to consider it as a cross section of space. Doreen Massey and Pat Jess (1995) define **space** as "social relations stretched out" and **place** as "particular articulations of those social relations as they have come together, over time, in that particular location." Part of the social relations of a place are the embedded assumptions about ethnicity, gender, and sexuality, regarding what certain groups "should" and "should not" do socially, economically, politically, even domestically. Geographers who study identities, gender, ethnicity, race, and sexuality, realize that when people make places, they do so in the context of surrounding social relationships. We can, for example, create places that are **gendered**—places seen as being appropriate for women or for men. A building can be constructed with the goal of creating gendered spaces within it, or a building can become gendered by the way people make use of it.

SEXUALITY AND SPACE

Sexuality is part of humanity. Just as gender roles are culturally constructed, so too do cultures decide sexual norms. In their installment on "Sexuality and Space" in *Geography in America at the Dawn of the 21st Century*, geographers Glen Elder, Lawrence Knopp, and Heidi Nast argue that most social science across disciplines is written in a heteronormative way. This means that the default subject in the minds of the academics who write studies is heterosexual—and usually white and male as well. These geographers and many others are working to find out how heternormative ideas influence understandings of places and cultures, and how the practices of peoples who do not conform to these ideas influence the development of places.

Geographers' initial forays into the study of sexuality focused largely on the same kinds of questions posed by those who first took up the study of race, gender, and ethnicity. Geographers ask where people with shared identity live and gather, what they do to create a space for themselves, and what kinds of problems they confront. For example, early studies examining gay neighborhoods in San Francisco and London focused on how gay men created spaces and what those spaces meant to gay identities. Specific studies have looked at the role of gay pride parades in creating communities and the political struggle for access to other parades such as St. Patrick's Day parades in some cities. Other studies examine the role gays and lesbians play in the gentrification of neighborhoods in city centers (a topic we explore in Chapter 9).

Today, geographers studying sexuality focus not only on the distributions and experiences of people in places but also on the theories behind the experiences, the theories that explain and inform our understanding of sexuality and space. Many of the geographers who study sexuality are employing queer theory in their studies. By using the term **queer theory**, Elder, Knopp, and Nast explain that social scientists (in

geography and other disciplines) are appropriating a commonly used word with negative connotations and turning it in a way that "highlights the contextual nature" of opposition to the heteronormative and focuses on the political engagement of queers with the heteronormative. Geographers also concentrate on extending fieldwork on sexuality and space beyond the Western world of North America and Europe to the rest of the world, exploring and explaining the local contexts of political engagement.

In 2000, the United States Census Bureau began counting the number of same-sex households in the United States. In 2010, the Census added same-sex marriage to their counts. These data, by census tract—a small area in cities and a larger area in rural America—made it possible for Gary Gates and Jason Ost to publish *The Gay and Lesbian Atlas*. Their detailed maps of major cities in the United States show concentrations of same-sex households in certain neighborhoods of cities (Fig. 5.10), such as Adams-Morgan and DuPont Circle in Washington, D.C., and the West Village and Chelsea in Manhattan (Fig. 5.11).

Demographer Gary Gates analyzed the geography of same-sex couples in the United States after the 2010 Census. He found a changing pattern, as cities with well-established gay and lesbian neighborhoods fell in the rankings of the proportion of same-sex couples, and retirement communities and smaller cities rose in the rankings. The *New York Times* reported that San Francisco fell to 28th in the rankings of communities with the top proportions of same-sex couples. Same-sex couples in the baby boomer generation are retiring and moving to cities including Rehoboth Beach, Delaware, Palm Springs, California, and Provincetown, Massachusetts (ranked number 1).

In the 2010 census, the government tallied the number of *households* where a same-sex couple (with or without children) lived. Study the map of same-sex households in New York by census tract in Figure 5.10. How would the map change if sexuality were one of the "boxes" *every* person filled out on the census?

HOW DOES GEOGRAPHY REFLECT AND SHAPE POWER RELATIONSHIPS AMONG GROUPS OF PEOPLE?

Power relationships are assumptions and structures about who is in control and who has power over others. Power relationships affect identities directly, and the nature of those effects depends on the geographical context in which they are situated. Power relationships also affect cultural landscapes by determining what is seen and what is not. Massey and Jess (1995)

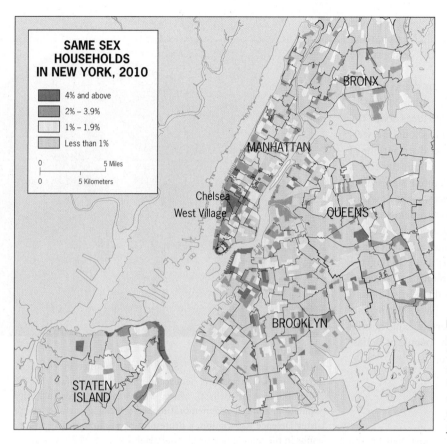

■ **Figure 5.10**

Same-Sex Households in New York, 2010.
The map shows the concentrations of same-sex households in New York, by census tract. Chelsea and West Village, both on the west side of lower Manhattan, stand out as having a large concentration of same sex households. *Data from:* United States Census Bureau, 2010.

FIELD NOTE

"It's July 26, 2011, and I happen to be in New York City the weekend just after the State of New York legalized same-sex marriages. I cut it close getting to the airport so I could catch the first part of the annual Gay Pride parade. The parade, which started on the edge of the Chelsea neighborhood at 36th Street, traveled down 5th Avenue toward where I took this photograph near Union Square, and ended in the West Village. Always a boisterous, celebratory event, the parade has a special feel this year as celebrants cheer what many describe as one of the great civil rights victories of the current era."

© Alexander B. Murphy

■ **Figure 5.11**

New York, New York.

contend that power is central to the study of place, as power controls "the contest over how the place should be seen, what meaning to give it" and power constructs the "imaginative geography, the identities of place and culture."

Power relationships do much more than shape the cultural landscape. Power relationships can also subjugate entire groups of people, enabling society to enforce ideas about the ways people should behave or where people should be welcomed or turned away—thus altering the distribution of peoples. Policies created by governments can limit the access of certain groups. Jim Crow laws in the United States once separated "black" spaces from "white" spaces, right down to public drinking fountains. Even without government support, people create places where they limit the access of other peoples. For example, in Belfast, Northern Ireland, Catholics and Protestants defined certain neighborhoods as excluding the "other" through painting murals, hanging bunting, and painting curbs (Fig. 5.12). In major cities in the United States, local governments do not create or enforce laws defining certain spaces as belonging to members of a certain gang, but the people themselves create these spaces, as the people of Belfast do, through graffiti, murals, and building colors.

Just Who Counts?

The statistics governments collect and report reflect the power relationships involved in defining what is valued and what is not. Think back to the Constitution of the United States prior to the Fourteenth Amendment, when the government enumerated a black person as three-fifths of a white person. Until 1924, the U.S. government did not recognize the right of all American Indians to vote even though the Fifteenth Amendment guaranteed the right to vote regardless of race in 1870. The U.S. government separated American Indians into those who were "civilized" enough to be citizens and those who were not ("Indians not taxed") until 1924, when it recognized the citizenship of all American Indians born in the United States. In 1920, enough states finally ratified the Nineteenth Amendment to the Constitution, which extended voting rights regardless of sex, to allow women to vote. Despite progress in counting people of all races, ethnicities, and sex, some charge that the United States Census Bureau continues to undercount minority populations (see Chapter 2).

Throughout the world, the work of women is often undervalued and uncounted. When the United States and other state governments began to count the value of goods and services produced within state borders, they did so with the assumption that the work of the household is reserved for women and that this work does not contribute to the productivity of the state's economy. The most commonly used statistic on productivity, the gross national income (the monetary worth of what is produced within a country plus income received from investments outside the country), does not include work in the home. The gross national income (GNI) includes neither the unpaid labor of women

© Erin H. Fouberg

■■ **Figure 5.12**

Belfast, Northern Ireland. Signs of the conflict in Northern Ireland mark the cultural landscape throughout Belfast. In the Shankhill area of Belfast, where Protestants are the majority population, a mural commemorating Steve McKeag, member of the Ulster Defence Association, a Protestant paramilitary organization, stands in the middle of a residential neighborhood. McKeag is called "Top Gun" for killing 12 Catholics, most of whom were ordinary citizens, in the 1990s. He died in his home of a drug overdose in 2000 at the age of 30.

in the household nor, usually, the work done by rural women in less wealthy countries. GNI counts only the formal economy (what is reported to and taxed by government), not the informal economy (economic activities not counted or taxed by government).

Scholars estimate that if women's productivity in the household alone were given a dollar value by calculating what it would cost to hire people to perform these tasks, the gross national income (GNI) for all countries of the world combined would grow by about one-third. In poorer countries, women produce more than half of all the food; they also build homes, dig wells, plant and harvest crops, make clothes, and do many other things that are not recorded in official statistics as being economically productive because they are in the informal economy (Fig. 5.13).

Despite these conditions, the number of women in the "official" labor force is rising while the proportion of men in the labor force globally declined between 1990 and 2010. In *The World's Women 2010: Trends and Statistics*, the United Nations reported that "women are predominantly and increasingly employed in the services sector" of the formal economy. Combining paid work with work in the informal economy and unpaid domestic work, "women work longer hours than men do." The proportion of women in the labor force grew in all

© Alexander B. Murphy

■■ **Figure 5.13**
South Korea. The women in this photo sit near one of the ancient temples in southern Korea, selling the modest output from their own market gardens. This activity is one part of the informal economy, the "uncounted" economy in which women play a large role.

regions reported by the United Nations except Asia and eastern Europe. In South America, for example, the percent of women in the labor force rose from 38 in 1990 to 59 in 2010. In North Africa, the participation of women in the labor force increased from 23 percent in 1990 to 29 percent in 2010, while over the same time period in Subsaharan Africa, women accounted for 60 percent of the labor force.

Even though women are in the official labor force in greater proportions than ever before, they continue to be paid less and have less access to food and education than men in nearly all cultures and places around the world. A 2010 report from the United Nations stated that two-thirds of the 774 million illiterate adults in the world are women and that women account for 60 percent of the world's poorest citizens. The United Nations Development Program reports that "75 percent of the world's women cannot get bank loans because they have unpaid or insecure jobs and are not entitled to property ownership." As a result, women worldwide only own "one percent of the world's wealth."

The World's Women 2010 reported regional variations in agriculture employment for women. In Africa, for example, the proportion of women employed in agriculture ranges from a low of 19 percent in countries in southern Africa to a high of 68 percent in countries in eastern, middle, and western Africa. In Northern Africa, 42 percent of women are employed in agriculture and 41 percent of women are employed in services. In Asia, employment of women in agriculture ranges from 11 percent in eastern Asia, where 76 percent of women are employed in the service sector, to South Asia, with 55 percent of women working in agriculture and 28 percent in the service sector.

Although the number of women working in industries globally is small relative to the proportion of men, it is rising.

Employment of women in the industrial sector was slowed by the global economic downturn of the 2008, as well as by mechanization, which leads to job reductions and hence to layoffs of women workers. In the maquiladoras of northern Mexico (see Chapter 10), for example, many women workers lost their jobs when labor markets contracted between 2001 and 2002, and then again between 2008 and 2010.

As the foregoing discussion has highlighted, many women engage in informal economic activity—that is, private, often home-based activities, including tailoring, beer brewing, food preparation, and soap making. Women who seek to move beyond subsistence activities but cannot enter the formal economic sector often turn to such work. In the migrant slums on the fringes of many cities, informal economic activity is the mainstay of communities.

Statistics showing how much women produce and how little their work is valued are undoubtedly interesting. Yet, the work geographers who study gender have done goes far beyond the accumulation of data. Since the 1980s, geographers have asked why society talks about women and their roles in certain ways and how these ideas, heard and represented throughout our lives, affect geographic circumstances and how we understand them. For example, Ann Oberhauser (2003) and her co-authors explained that people in the West tend to think that women are employed in the textile and jewelry-making fields in poorer countries because the women in these regions are "more docile, submissive, and tradition bound" than women in more prosperous parts of the world. A geographer studying gender asks where these ideas about women come from and how they influence women's work possibilities and social positions in different places—key elements in making places what they are.

GUEST FIELD NOTE

One of the leading causes of mortality and morbidity among children under the age of five in developing countries is waterborne disease. My research has focused on building an understanding of the factors that contribute to the vulnerability of young children to this significant public health problem. I have conducted my research in communities located in the relatively remote Karakoram Range of northern Pakistan. Of interest to me is the microenvironment of water-related disease risk, and in particular, the factors at the household and local scale that influence the prevalence and severity of childhood illness. One of the primary methodological strategies that I employ in this research involves household microstudies, which entail in-depth interviews with family members (primarily mothers who are the principal child health providers), child health histories, and structured observations. One of the most important findings of this research in these mountain communities, in my opinion, is that the education, social networks, and empowerment of women are all critical to breaking the cycle of disease impacts and to ensuring long-term child survival.

Credit: Sarah J. Halvorson, University of Montana

Sarah J. Halvorson

■ **Figure 5.14**

Vulnerable Populations

Power relations can have a fundamental impact on which populations or areas are particularly vulnerable to disease, death, injury, or famine. Geographers use mapping and spatial analysis to predict and explain what populations or people will be affected most by natural hazards, including earthquakes, volcanoes, hurricanes, and tsunamis, or by environmental policies. The study of vulnerability requires thinking geographically because social, political, economic, or environmental change does not affect all people and places in the same way. Rather, vulnerability is fundamentally influenced by geographically specific social and environmental circumstances.

Fieldwork is often the best way to understand how power structures in society create vulnerable groups at the local scale and how those vulnerable groups might be affected by particular developments. Through fieldwork and interviews, geographers can see differences in vulnerability within groups of people.

Geographer Sarah Halvorson (2004) studied differences in the vulnerabilities of children in northern Pakistan. She examined the vulnerability of children to diarrheal diseases by paying attention to "constructions of gender, household politics, and gendered relationships that perpetuate inherent inequalities and differences between men and women and within and between social groups."

Halvorson studied 30 families, 15 of whom had a low frequency of diarrhea and dysentery and 15 of whom had a

high frequency of these diseases. Through her fieldwork, Halvorson came to understand that several tangible resources, including income and housing, and several intangible resources, such as social status and position within the family structure, all influenced the vulnerability of children to diarrheal diseases in northern Pakistan. Halvorson found that people with higher incomes generally had lower disease rates, but that income was not the only relevant factor (Fig. 5.14). The least vulnerable children and women were those who had higher incomes and an established social network of support. In cases where income was low, if a woman had a strong social network, her children were more likely to be in the low-disease group.

Geographer Joseph Oppong recognized that the spatial analysis of a disease can reveal what populations are most vulnerable in a country. In North America and Europe, HIV/AIDS is much more prevalent among homosexual and bisexual men than among heterosexual men and women. In Subsaharan Africa, women have much higher rates of HIV/AIDS than men. As Oppong (1998) explains, "AIDS as a global problem has unique local expressions that reflect the spatial distribution and social networks of vulnerable social groups."

According to Oppong, in most of Subsaharan Africa, HIV/AIDS rates are highest for women in urban areas and for women who work as sex workers. However, in Ghana, HIV/AIDS rates were lower for women in the urban area of Accra.

Oppong postulates that women in Accra have lower HIV/AIDS rates because they have greater access to health care than women in rural areas. Women in rural areas who were not treated for malaria had higher incidences of HIV/AIDS, according to his research. Oppong also found that women in polygamous relationships in the Muslim part of northern Ghana had lower HIV/AIDS rates. Oppong offers two theories to explain why Muslim women in polygamous relationships had lower HIV/AIDS rates: First, as a matter of cultural practice, most Muslims tend to avoid sexual promiscuity, and second, Muslims in Ghana practice circumcision, which helps lower the rate of HIV/AIDS transmission in that part of the country.

Fieldwork helps geographers apply vulnerability theory to understand how existing spatial structures, power relationships, and social networks affect the susceptibility of people to diseases and other hazards around the world.

Women in Subsaharan Africa

Migration flows, birth rates, and child mortality rates affect the gender composition of cities, states, and regions. Some regions of the world have become male-dominated, whereas other regions have become female-dominated—at least numerically.

Much of Subsaharan Africa, especially rural areas, is dominated numerically by women. In this region of the world,

most rural-to-urban migrants are men. Domosh and Seager (2001) point out that men leave rural areas to work in heavy industry and mines in the cities, "while women are left behind to tend the farms and manage the household economy. Indeed parts of rural South Africa and Zimbabwe have become feminized zones virtually depopulated of men."

In the large region of Subsaharan Africa, women outnumber men in many rural areas. Women in Subsaharan Africa have heavy responsibilities, coupled in many places with few rights and little say (Fig. 5.15). Women produce an estimated 70 percent of the region's food, almost all of it without the aid of modern technology. Their backbreaking hand cultivation of corn and other staples is an endless task. As water supplies decrease, the exhausting walk to the nearest pump gets longer. Firewood is being cut at ever-greater distances from the village, and the task of hauling it home becomes more difficult every year. As men leave for the towns, sometimes to marry other wives and have other children, the women left in the villages often struggle for survival.

Even though a woman in this position becomes the head of a household, if she goes to a bank for a loan she may well be refused; traditional banks throughout much of Africa do not lend money to rural women. Not having heard from her husband for years and having reared her children, she might wish to apply for title to the land she has occupied and farmed for decades, but in many places land titles are not awarded to women.

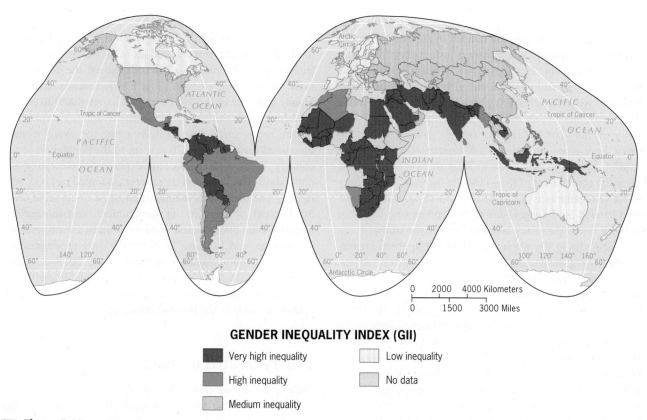

GENDER INEQUALITY INDEX (GII)

- Very high inequality
- High inequality
- Medium inequality
- Low inequality
- No data

■ **Figure 5.15**
Gender Inequality Index (GII) 2013.   The GII measures inequality in labor-market participation, access to reproductive health, and empowerment. The GII measures how much achievement is lost by women as a result of inequalities in these three areas.   *Data from:* United Nations Development Program, Human Development Report 2013.

FIELD NOTE

"I am filled with admiration for the women and girls carrying water on their heads up the bank from the Niger River. Other women are at the water's edge, filling their buckets. These women are performing a daily ritual requiring incredible endurance and strength. Once they carry their buckets to their dwellings, they will likely turn to preparing the evening meal."

© Alexander B. Murphy

Figure 5.16
Along the banks of the Niger River just outside Mopti, Mali.

Young girls soon become trapped in the cycle of female poverty and overwork. Often there is little money for school fees; what is available first goes to pay for the boys. As soon as she can carry anything at all, the girl child goes with her mother to weed the fields, bring back firewood, or fetch water (Fig. 5.16). She will do so for 12 hours a day, 7 days a week, during all the years she remains capable of working. In east Africa, cash crops such as tea are sometimes called "men's crops" because the men trade in what the women produce. When the government of Kenya tried to increase productivity on the tea plantations in the 1970s and 1980s, the government handed out bonuses—not to the women who did all of the work but to the men who owned title to the land!

Since the 1990s, women have lobbied for greater representation in governments in southern and eastern Africa. Uganda was a leader in affirmative action for women by setting up a quota or guarantee that women must hold at least 20 percent of the legislative seats. In South Africa, Apartheid, the systematic oppression of the majority black population by the minority white population, ended in 1994. The South African government established a constitution with universal suffrage (voting rights) in 1997. The constitution does not include an affirmative action policy for women's representation in the parliament. Instead, major political parties, starting with the African National Congress (ANC), reserved a certain percentage of their seats won for women.

Today, the country where women hold the highest proportion of legislative seats is neither Uganda nor South Africa.

Rather, another African country, Rwanda, is the first country in the world where women hold more than 50 percent of the legislative seats. Women in Rwanda passed the 50 percent mark in the 2008 election (Fig, 5.17). Rwanda suffered a bloody civil war in the 1990s in which over 800,000 people died (one-tenth of the population at the time), a majority of whom were men. Immediately after the war, women accounted for more than 70 percent of the population of the country. Today, women make up 55 percent of the voting-age population. The Rwandan constitution, adopted in 2003, recognizes the equality of women and set a quota of at least 30 percent women in all government decision-making bodies. Of the 80 legislative seats in Rwanda, 24 are reserved for women, and in these 24 seats, the only candidates are women and only women can vote. In the 2013 elections, women won 26 seats in the legislature in addition to the 24 seats reserved for women, and now women hold 62.5 percent of the seats in the Rwanda legislature.

Dowry Deaths in India

On a 2004 *Oprah!* show, the talk show hostess interviewed journalist Lisa Ling about her travels through India and her reports on dowry deaths in India. The Chicago audience looked stunned to discover that thousands of girls in India are still betrothed through arranged marriages and that in some extreme cases, disputes over the dowry, which is the price to be paid by the bride's family to the groom's father, have led to the death of the bride. The bride may be brutally punished, often burned, or killed for her father's failure to fulfill a marriage agreement. Only a small fraction of India's girls are involved in **dowry deaths,** but the practice is not declining. According to the Indian government, in 1985, the number was 999; in 1987, 1786 women died at the hands of vengeful husbands or in-laws; in 1989, 2436 perished; in 2001, more than 7000 women died; and in 2012, it was reported that 8233 women died from dowry deaths. These figures report only confirmed dowry deaths; many more are believed to occur but are reported as suicides, kitchen accidents, or other fatal domestic incidents.

The power relationships that place women below men in India cannot simply be legislated away. Government entities in India (federal as well as State) have set up legal aid offices to help women who fear dowry death and seek assistance. In 1984, the national legislature passed the Family Courts Act, creating a network of "family courts" to hear domestic cases, including dowry disputes. But the judges tend to be older males, and their chief objective, according to women's support groups, is to hold the family together—that is, to force the threatened or battered woman back into the household. Hindu culture attaches great importance to the family structure, and the family courts tend to operate on this principle.

Recognizing that movement away from arranged marriages and dowries among the Indian population is slow in coming, Ling and Oprah took the issue of dowry deaths to the global scale—to generate activism in the West and create change at the local scale in India. Ling explained that the place of women in India has changed little. She described women as a financial burden on the bride's family, who must save for a sizable dowry to marry her off. Ling describes the dowry as a financial transaction; through marriage the burden of the woman moves from the bride's family to her husband's family. Yet Oprah and Ling interviewed a woman in India to show that global change can help make local change possible. Nisha Sharma was to marry in front of 1500 guests in a town just outside of the capital of New Delhi. On her wedding day, the groom's family demanded $25,000 in addition to the numerous luxury items they had already received as dowry (including washing machines, a flat-screen TV, and a car). Nisha's father refused to pay, the man's family became violent, and Nisha called the police on her cell phone. She has become a local hero. Her story also serves as an example of how global technology (in this case a cell phone) can help combat the practice of dowry deaths.

India is starting to see the impact on marriage of its booming economy and growing proportion of educated young women and men in well-paid jobs. The number of love marriages is on the rise (Fig. 5.18), and many couples in love marriages in India are meeting online. The number of divorces is also on the rise, with 1 in 1000 marriages ending in divorce in India today. Although this is one of the lowest divorce rates in the world, it is also double the country's divorce rate five years ago. These changes will not necessarily result in fewer dowry deaths in the short run in India. An article in *The Times of India* in 2010 explained that in the city of Chennai, where the information technology boom is in full swing, police reported a rise in dowry deaths. This rise was likely a result of increasing materialism among the middle class and an accompanying feeling of desperation for more goods and cash, coupled with the fact that many men in less powerful positions have begun to act out violently.

Understanding shifting gender relations and power structures in India is very difficult. Just as some statistics point to an improving place of women in Indian society, other statistics confirm that India still gives preference to males overall. India's 2011 census reported a sex ratio of 940 girls for every 1000 boys, which seems to be an improvement over the 2001 sex ratio of 933 girls for every 1000 boys. However, the sex ratio for children 0 to 6 years in India was at a record low of 914 girls for every 1000 boys in 2011. The 2011 census data surprised many because between 2001 and 2011, while India gained unprecedented economic growth, the number of girls ages 0 to 6 dropped from 927 in 2001 to 914 in 2011. Many pregnant women in India, especially in northern states, undergo gender-determining tests (ultrasound and amniocentesis) and elect to have abortions when the fetus is a girl. Girls who make it to birth may suffer female infanticide as many parents fear the cost of dowries and place little social value on girls.

In India and elsewhere, directing the attention of people in far-flung places to social ills—moving the issues up in scale—has the potential to create change. Yet problems cannot really be solved unless power relations shift at the family, local, regional, and national scales. As the number of women and men in the middle class in urban India continues to rise, love marriages will continue to rise as well. The number of dowry deaths, arranged marriages, and divorces in the country will continue to fluctuate as power relations shift across gender and scales.

Shifting Power Relations Among Ethnic Groups

In Chapter 4, we discussed local cultures that define themselves ethnically. The presence of local ethnic cultures can be seen in the cultural landscapes of places we discussed in Chapter 4: "Little Sweden" in Kansas and the Italian North End in Boston. In many places, more than one ethnic group lives in a place, creating unique cultural landscapes and revealing how power relations factor into the ways ethnicities are constructed, revised, and solidified, where ethnic groups live, and who is subjugating whom.

Three urban geographers—John Frazier, Florence Margai, and Eugene Tettey-Fio—tracked the flow of people and shifts in power relations among the multiple ethnic groups that have lived in Alameda County, California, in their book *Race and Place: Equity Issues in Urban America.* Alameda County borders San Francisco and includes the cities of

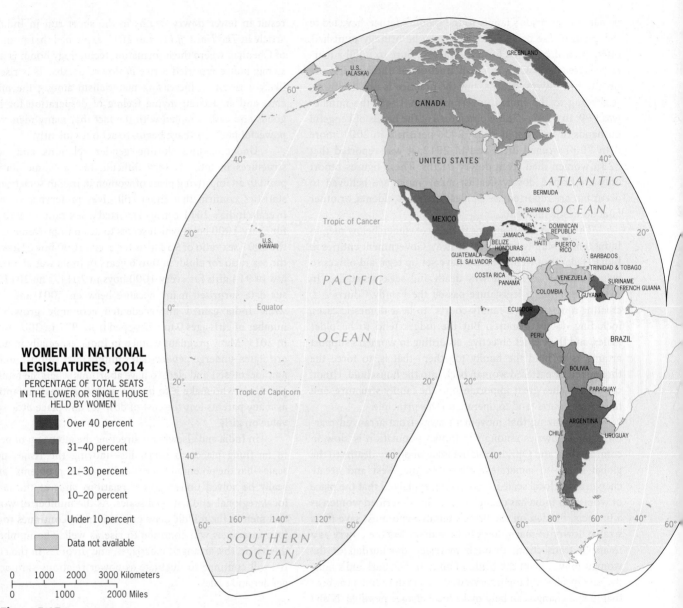

WOMEN IN NATIONAL LEGISLATURES, 2014

PERCENTAGE OF TOTAL SEATS
IN THE LOWER OR SINGLE HOUSE
HELD BY WOMEN

- Over 40 percent
- 31–40 percent
- 21–30 percent
- 10–20 percent
- Under 10 percent
- Data not available

0   1000   2000   3000 Kilometers
0   1000   2000 Miles

■ **Figure 5.17**

Women in National Legislatures, 2014.   Compare and contrast the pattern of the Gender Inequality Index (GII) in Figure 5.15 with this map of Women in National Legislatures. Several countries in Subsaharan Africa are high on the GII but have a large proportion of women in the national legislatures. Countries such as the United States and Australia have low gender inequality, but they do much less well when it comes to female representation in legislative bodies.   *Data from*: www.ipu.org/wmn-e/classif.htm.

Berkeley and Oakland. Latinos populated the region prior to the Gold Rush. After 1850, migrants from China came to the county. The first Asian migrants to the county were widely dispersed, but the first African Americans lived in a segregated section of the county.

Areas with multiple ethnicities often experience an ebb and flow of acceptance over time. When the economy is booming, residents are generally more accepting of each other. When the economy takes a downturn, residents often begin to resent each other and can blame the "Other" for their economic hardship. In Alameda County, much of the population resented Chinese migrants when the economy took a

downturn in the 1870s. The United States government passed the first Chinese Exclusion Act, which prohibited immigration of Chinese in 1882. Chinese exclusion efforts persisted for decades afterward in Alameda County and resulted in the city of Oakland moving Chinatown several times.

During the 1910s, the economy of the region grew again, but the city of Oakland limited the Chinese residents to Chinatown, using ethnic segregation to keep them apart from the rest of the population. Frazier, Margai, and Tettey-Fio (2003) described how the location and homogeneity of Oakland's Chinatown were dictated by law and not matters of choice for the Chinese:

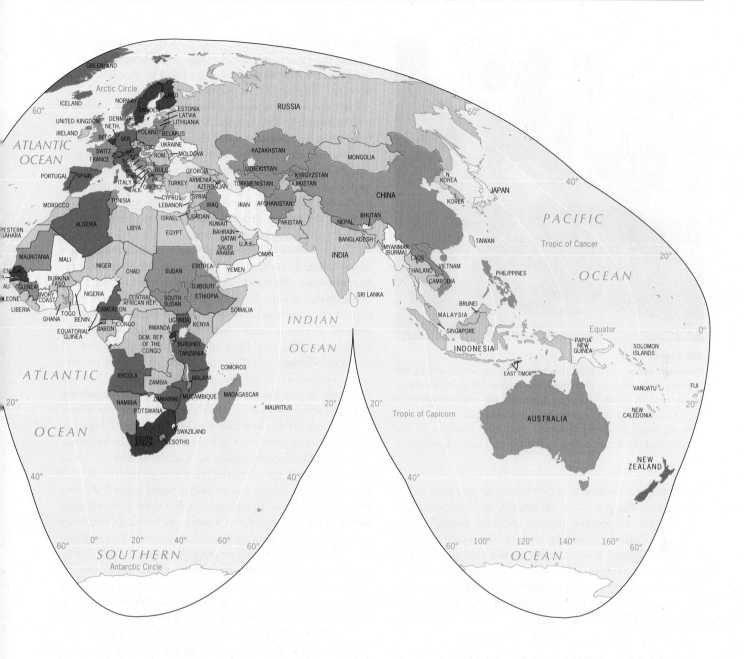

At a time when the Chinese were benefiting from a better economy, the "whites only" specifications of local zoning and neighborhood regulations forced separatism that segregated the Oakland Chinese into the city's Chinatown. What today is sometimes presented as an example of Chinese unity and choice was, in fact, place dictated by law.

Chinese were segregated from the rest of Oakland's population until World War II. When the war began, residents of Alameda County, like much of the rest of the United States, focused on the Japanese population in the county, segregating, blaming, and interning them in relocation centers.

After World War II, the ethnic population of Asians in Alameda County became more complex. The Asian population alone doubled in the decade between 1980 and 1990 and diversified to include not only Chinese and Japanese but also

Koreans, Vietnamese, Cambodians, and Laotians. In Alameda County today, as in much of the rest of the United States, the first wave of immigrants from Asia (mainly from China, India, and Korea), who came to the region already educated, are not residentially segregated from the white population. However, the newer immigrants from Asia (mainly Southeast Asia—during and following the Vietnam War) are segregated from whites residentially, mixing much more with the African American population in inner-city neighborhoods. Here, Asians experience a high rate of poverty, much as the Hispanic and African American populations in the same regions of the county do.

In California and in much of the rest of the United States, the "Asian" box is drawn around a stereotype of what some call the "model minority." Frazier and his colleagues explain the myth of the model minority: The myth "paints

■ Figure 5.18
Mumbai, India.   Arranged marriages were the norm not long ago in India, and the family of the bride was expected to provide a dowry to the groom's family. Arranged marriages are still widespread in parts of rural India, but in urban areas they are rapidly giving way to love marriages following romantic courtships. Evidence of this cultural shift is not hard to find on the streets of India's major cities.

Asians as good, hardworking people who, despite their suffering through discrimination, harassment, and exclusion, have found ways to prosper through peaceful means." Other researchers have debunked the myth by demonstrating statistically the different levels of economic success experienced by various Asian peoples, with most success going to the first wave of migrants and lower-paying jobs going to newer migrants. Both groups are burdened by the myth that stereotypes them as the "model minority."

POWER RELATIONS IN LOS ANGELES

Over the last four decades, the greatest migration flow into California and the southwestern United States has come from Latin America and the Caribbean, especially Mexico. The 2010 census reported a 43 percent increase in the Hispanic or Latino population of the country. The city of Los Angeles had over 3.79 million people, 48.48 percent of whom were Hispanic. The Hispanic population in the city grew from 39.32 percent of the population in 1990 to 48.48 percent by 2010.

The area of southeastern Los Angeles County is today "home to one of the largest and highest concentrations of Latinos in Southern California," according to a study by geographer James Curtis. Four decades ago, this area of Los Angeles was populated by working-class whites who were segregated from the African American and Hispanic populations through discriminatory policies and practices. Until the 1960s, southeastern Los Angeles was home to corporations

such as General Motors, Bethlehem Steel, and Weiser Lock. During the 1970s and 1980s, corporations began to close as the United States went through a period of deindustrialization (see Chapter 11). As plants shut down and white laborers left the neighborhoods, a Hispanic population migrated into southeastern Los Angeles. A housing crunch followed in the 1980s, as more and more Hispanic migrants headed to southeastern Los Angeles. With a cheap labor supply now readily available in the region again, companies returned to southeastern Los Angeles, this time focusing on smaller-scale production of textiles, pharmaceuticals, furniture, and toys. In addition, the region attracted industrial toxic-waste disposal and petrochemical refining facilities.

In his study of the region, Curtis records the changes to the cultural landscape in the process. He uses the term **barrioization** (derived from the Spanish word for neighborhood, *barrio*) to describe a change that saw the Hispanic population of a neighborhood jump from 4 percent in 1960 to over 90 percent in 2000. With the ethnic succession of the neighborhood moving from white to Hispanic, the cultural landscape changed to reflect the culture of the new population. The structure of the streets and the layout of the housing remained largely the same, giving the Hispanic population access to designated parks, schools, libraries, and community centers built by the previous residents and rarely found in other barrios in Southern California. However, the buildings, signage, and landscape changed as "traditional Hispanic houseescape elements, including the placement of fences and yard shrines as well as the use of bright house colors" diffused through the barrios. Curtis explains that these elements were added to existing structures, houses, and buildings originally built by the white working class of southeastern Los Angeles.

The influx of new ethnic groups into a region, the replacement of one ethnic group by another within neighborhoods, changes to the cultural landscape, the persistence of myths such as the "model minority" myth about Asian Americans, and an economic downturn can create a great deal of volatility in a city.

On April 29–30, 1992, Los Angeles became engulfed in one of the worst incidents of civil unrest in United States history. During two days of rioting 43 people died, 2383 were injured, and 16,291 arrested. Property damage was estimated at approximately $1 billion, and over 22,700 law enforcement personnel were deployed to quell the unrest. According to the media, the main catalyst for the mass upheaval was the announcement of a "not guilty verdict in the trial of four white police officers accused of using excessive force in the arrest of Rodney King, a black motorist." (Johnson et al. 1992, 356). To the general public, the Los Angeles riots became yet another symbol for the sorry state of race relations between blacks and whites in the United States. Yet, a geographic perspective on the Los Angeles riots helps us understand that they were not simply the product of localized reactions to police brutality, but reflected sweeping economic, political, and ethnic changes unfolding at regional and even global scales.

The riots took place in South Central Los Angeles. Like the region of southeast Los Angeles described above, the

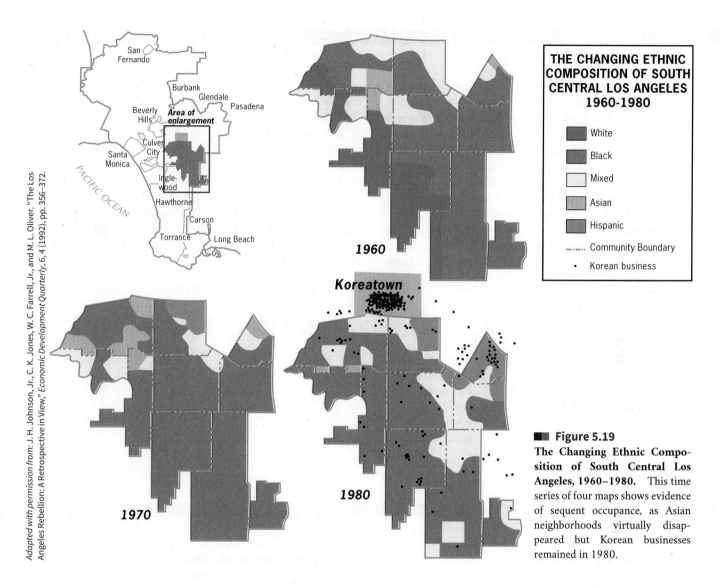

Adapted with permission from: J. H. Johnson, Jr., C. K. Jones, W. C. Farrell, Jr., and M. L. Oliver. "The Los Angeles Rebellion: A Retrospective in View," *Economic Development Quarterly*, 6, 4 (1992), pp. 356–372.

THE CHANGING ETHNIC COMPOSITION OF SOUTH CENTRAL LOS ANGELES 1960-1980

- White
- Black
- Mixed
- Asian
- Hispanic
- – · – Community Boundary
- · Korean business

■ Figure 5.19
The Changing Ethnic Composition of South Central Los Angeles, 1960–1980. This time series of four maps shows evidence of sequent occupance, as Asian neighborhoods virtually disappeared but Korean businesses remained in 1980.

South Central area was once a thriving industrial region with dependable, unionized jobs employing the resident population. By the 1960s, however, the population of South Central Los Angeles was working-class African American, and the population of southeastern Los Angeles was working-class white. After 1970, South Central Los Angeles experienced a substantial decrease in the availability of high-paying, unionized manufacturing jobs when plants closed and relocated outside of the city and even outside the country. The people of South Central Los Angeles lost over 70,000 manufacturing jobs between 1978 and 1982 alone!

Geographer James Johnson and his colleagues explored the impact of economic loss on the ethnic and social geography of South Central Los Angeles. They found that the population of the area was over 90 percent African American in 1970, but by 1990, the population was evenly split between African Americans and Hispanics. This change in population composition was accompanied by a steady influx of Korean residents and small-business owners seeking a niche in the rapidly changing urban area (Fig. 5.19).

Johnson and his colleagues argued that the Los Angeles riots were more than a spontaneous reaction to a verdict. They were rooted in the growing despair and frustration of different ethnic groups competing for a decreasing number of jobs in an environment of declining housing conditions and scarce public resources. At a time when significant unemployment is affecting communities all over the United States, Johnson et al.'s work shows the importance of looking beyond the immediate catalysts of particular news events to the local, national, and global geographical contexts in which they unfold.

Geographers who study race, ethnicity, gender, or sexuality are interested in the power relations embedded in a place from which assumptions about "others" are formed or reinforced. Consider your own place, your campus, or your locality. What power relations are embedded in this place?

Summary

Identity is a powerful concept. The way we make sense of ourselves is a personal journey that is mediated and influenced by the political, social, and cultural contexts in which we live and work. Group identities such as gender, ethnicity, race, and sexuality are constructed, both by self-realization and by identifying against and across scales. When learning about new places and different people, humans are often tempted to put places and people into boxes, into myths or stereotypes that make them easily digestible.

The geographer, especially one who spends time in the field, recognizes that how people shape and create places varies across time and space and that time, space, and place shape people, both individually and in groups. James Curtis ably described the work of a geographer who studies places: "But like the popular images and stereotypical portrayals of all places—whether positive or negative, historical or contemporary—these mask a reality on the ground that is decidedly more complex and dynamic, from both the economic and social perspectives." What Curtis says about places is true about people as well. What we may think to be positive identities, such as the myths of "Orientalism" or of the "model minority," and what we know are negative social ills, such as racism and dowry deaths, are all decidedly more complex and dynamic than they first seem.

Geographic Concepts

gender	residential segregation	place
identity	succession	gendered
identifying against	sense of place	queer theory
race	ethnicity	dowry deaths
racism	space	barrioization

Learn More Online

About the Gay and Lesbian Atlas
www.urban.org/pubs/gayatlas/

About Racial and Ethnic Segregation in the United States, 1980–2000
www.census.gov/hhes/www/housing/resseg/papertoc.html

About the Murals in Northern Ireland
http://cain.ulst.ac.uk/mccormick/intro.htm

About Society Constructing Gender
www.bbc.com/news/world-europe-24767225

About Gender Composition in India
http://censusmp.gov.in/censusmp/All-PDF/5Gender Composition21.pdf

Watch It Online

About Ethnicity and the City
www.learner.org/resources/series180.html#program_descriptions
click on Video On Demand for "Boston: Ethnic Mosaic"

About Ethnic Fragmentation in Canada
www.learner.org/resources/series180.html#program_descriptions

click on Video On Demand for "Vancouver: Hong Kong East" and "Montreal: An Island of French"

About Migration and Identity
www.learner.org/resources/series85.html#program_descriptions
click on Video on Demand for "A Migrant's Heart"

CHAPTER

6

LANGUAGE

FIELD NOTE

What Should I Say?

In stores throughout Brussels, Belgium, you can see the capital city's bilingualism all around you—literally. From McDonald's to health insurance offices (Fig. 6.1) to the metro, signs in Brussels are posted in duplicate, with one in Flemish (a variant of Dutch) and one in French.

Walking into a travel agency in Brussels one afternoon, I immediately noticed the signs in duplicate: Two signs towered over the woman behind the counter; two signs advertised a new budget airline carrier that would be serving the Brussels airport; two signs labeled the restrooms; and two signs announced the travel agency's hours of operation.

I debated for a minute whether to speak to the person behind the counter in French or Flemish. She was speaking Flemish with the person in front of me, but I decided to use French since my knowledge of that language is better. The student from Italy who stood behind me in line apparently had no such debate. She stepped up to the counter, asked her question in English, and received a reply in excellent English.

© Erin H. Fouberg

■ **Figure 6.1**
Brussels, Belgium. A health insurance office in the bilingual capital city of Brussels displays duplicates of each of their posters, one in French and one in Flemish.

Many geographers are initially drawn to the discipline through maps. However, maps, especially at the world or continental scale, generalize so much information that they hide the complexities of everyday life. Once you become a geographer, you begin to question every map you examine. Look at the European map of languages (Fig. 6.2), and zero in on Belgium. The map shows a neat line dividing Flemish speakers (a Germanic language) in the northern region of Flanders from French speakers (a Romance language) in the southern region of Wallonia.

Behind this neat line on the language map is a complicated, at times contentious, linguistic transition zone. To understand language patterns in Belgium, we must also study the issue at the local scale. Although the bilingual capital of Brussels is located in the Flemish-speaking north (Flanders), for upwards of 80 percent of the locals, French is the mother tongue (Fig. 6.3).

LANGUAGES OF EUROPE

0   200   400   600 Kilometers

0   100   200   300 Miles

Major Indo-European Branches

Germanic group

WESTERN GERMANIC   NORTHERN GERMANIC
1 Dutch   5 Danish   8 Icelandic
2 German   6 Swedish   9 Faeroses
3 Frisian   7 Norwegian
4 English

Romance group

10 Portuguese   14 French
11 Spanish   15 Italian
12 Catalan   16 Rhaeto-Romance
13 Provençal   17 Romanian

Slavic group

WEST SLAVONIC   EAST SLAVONIC   SOUTH SLAVONIC
18 Polish   22 Russian   25 Slovene
19 Slovak   23 Ukrainian   26 Serbo-Croatian
20 Czech   24 Belarusian   27 Macedonian
21 Sorbian   28 Bulgarian

Other Indo-European Branches

Celtic group

BRITTANIC   GAULISH
29 Breton   31 Irish Gaelic
30 Welsh   32 Scots Gaelic

Baltic group

33 Latvian   34 Lithuanian

Hellenic

35 Greek

Thracian/Illyrian group

36 Albanian

Thracian/Illyrian group

37 Romani

Uralic Language Family

Finno-Ugric group

38 Ginnish   41 Estonian
39 Karelian   42 Hungarian
40 Saami

Samoyedic group

44 Samoyedic

Altaic Language Family

Turkic group

45 Turkish

Other Languages

Basque

46 Basque

Areas with significant concentrations of other languages (usually adjacent national languages).

Boundary between languages.

Boundary between Indo-European and non-Indo-European languages.

■ **Figure 6.2**

Languages of Europe.   Language families and sub-families are regionally concentrated in Europe. Within the Indo-European language family, Germanic languages are in the north, Romance languages are in the south, and Slavic languages are in the east. Celtic languages are found in the far west, more remote areas of the region.

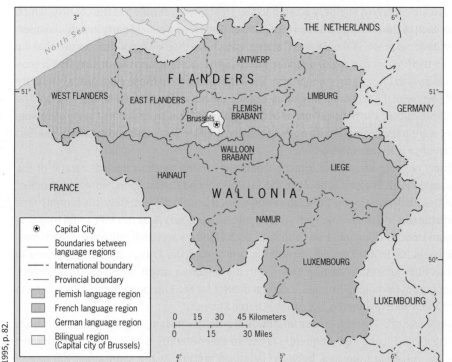

■■ Figure 6.3

Divided Belgium. Flemish, French, and German dominate the different administrative areas in Belgium. Basing administrative units on language means that disagreements among the units, even on noncultural issues, tend to reinforce tensions among the language communities.

In Belgium, economic differences between linguistic groups have been a divisive issue for generations. During the nineteenth century, French speakers controlled the industrial economy and government of the country. The concentration of industry in southern Belgium strengthened their position. The French-speaking elite in Brussels and other Flemish cities began a process of "Frenchification." They promoted French and used it when interacting with their counterparts in other countries. By the twentieth century, a majority of the people in Brussels spoke French, although people in the areas surrounding Brussels continued to speak Flemish.

Many people in northern Belgium (surrounding Brussels) opposed the growing Frenchification of Flanders. The leaders of the Flemish movement initially sought linguistic rights, specifically the right of Flemish speakers to use their language in public affairs, court proceedings, and schools. Yet they were constantly frustrated by the opposition of French speakers to their demands. By the 1920s, the Flemish leadership began calling for the country to be partitioned along linguistic lines so that those living in northern Belgium could control their own affairs.

By the 1960s, a fixed partition scheme was established, which divided the country into Flemish-speaking Flanders in the north and French-speaking Wallonia in the south. The government recognizes Brussels as a distinct region, a bilingual capital, but places strict limits on the use of French in the rest of northern Belgium.

The partitioning process produced upheavals throughout the country. The experience helped strengthen the sense of Flemish identity and fueled a countermovement among the French Walloons. With language-group identity on the rise, conflicts between linguistic "communities" became a central feature of Belgian political life. After the 1960s, Belgian heavy industry became less competitive, and the country's economy shifted to high technology, light industry, and services, with much of the new economy concentrating in Flemish-speaking Flanders. As a result, the economic power in Belgium flipped, with the French-speaking industrial south taking a back seat to the Flemish-speaking north. Today, Wallonia has an unemployment rate of almost 17 percent, and economists consider unemployment in Wallonia to be structural, making it difficult for the economy or job market to bounce back. Flanders, on the other hand, has an unemployment rate below 9 percent, one of the lower unemployment rates in Europe.

The vast majority of power and decision making rests with the individual governments of Flanders and Wallonia rather than with a centralized government in Brussels. With their newfound wealth, many in Flanders wanted to see greater federalization of the country, which would give each of the two regions even more power. Today, no political party in Belgium operates at the national scale. Wallonia and Flanders each have their own political parties that vie for power in their respective regions. Under the circumstances, it is not surprising that it took Belgium 589 days to form a government after the 2010 elections. In those elections, a moderate separatist party won the most parliamentary seats in the more prosperous Flanders region. The *New York Times* quoted the political leader of the separatist Flemish nationalist party as saying, "We do not want a revolution. We do not want to declare Flanders independent overnight. But we do believe in a gradual evolution."

Brussels is going in another direction entirely, serving as the principal capital of the European Union (EU). Brussels is home to the EU Council and Commission. Moreover, much of the committee work done by the European Parliament takes place in Brussels (the formal home of the Parliament is in Strasbourg, France). The role Brussels serves as the EU capital may prevent Belgium from splitting into two countries. Both Flanders and Wallonia have vested interests in Brussels, so neither would abandon it lightly. And the French-speaking majority in Brussels has little interest in casting its lot with the region in which it is situated—Flanders. Some have proposed making Brussels a capital district for the European Union, much like the District of Columbia (Washington, D.C.) in the United States.

The example of Belgium gives us a multitude of insights into language. Language questions are often politicized. Language frequently is tied to other identity issues, and socioeconomic divisions can exacerbate tensions between language groups. At the same time, the role of English continues to expand as the dominant language of global commerce, electronic communication, and popular culture.

In this chapter, we question what languages are and examine the roles they play in cultures. We study the spatial distribution of the world's languages and learn how they diffuse, change, rise to dominance, and even become extinct. Finally, we examine how language contributes to making places unique.

Key Questions FOR CHAPTER 6

1. What are languages, and what role do languages play in cultures?
2. Why are languages distributed the way they are?
3. How did certain languages become dominant?
4. What role does language play in making places?

WHAT ARE LANGUAGES, AND WHAT ROLE DO LANGUAGES PLAY IN CULTURES?

A scene in Quentin Tarantino's cult classic movie *Pulp Fiction* shows Vincent and Jules in the front seat of a car talking about France. Vincent, trying to demonstrate his knowledge of French culture, turns to Jules and says, "You know what they call a....a....a quarter pounder with cheese in Paris?" Jules replies, "They don't call it a quarter pounder with cheese?" Vincent, ever the expert, explains in a few choice words that France uses the metric system and that the French would not know what a quarter pounder is. Then, he explains, "They call it a 'royale' with cheese." Jules, surprised, asks, "What do they call a Big Mac?" Vincent explains, "Well a Big Mac is a Big Mac, but they call it 'Le Big Mac.'"

This humorous exchange shows the juxtaposition of two opposing forces in our globalized world: globalization of culture and preservation of local and national culture. Are the two contradictory, or can we have globalized restaurants, food, music, and culture while preserving local languages?

Language is a fundamental element of local and national culture. The French government has worked diligently, even aggressively, to protect the French language, dating back to 1635 and the creation of the Académie Française, an institution charged with standardizing and protecting the French language. Since the 1970s, diffusion of globalized terms (linguists calls these loanwords or borrowed words) into France has posed an enormous challenge for the Académie Française.

With the support of many French people, the French government passed a law in 1975 banning the use of foreign words in advertisements, television, and radio broadcasts, as well as official documents, unless no French equivalent could be found. In 1992, France amended its constitution to make French the official language. In 1994, the French government passed another law to stop the use of foreign (mainly English) words in France, with a hefty fine imposed for violators. The law mandates French translations for globalized words, requiring the use of official French terms in official communications rather than le meeting, le weekend, le drugstore, or le hamburger. The Internet, where 50 percent of Internet users browse in English or Chinese (Fig. 6.4), has posed another set of challenges for the Académie Française. Many of the translations the Académie requires are somewhat cumbersome. For example, the official translation of e-mail was "courrier electronique," but the Académie shortened it to "courriel."

In addition to demonstrating the conflicting forces of globalized language and local or national language, the example of France reveals that language is much more than a way of communicating. A **language** is a set of sounds and symbols that is used for communication. But language is also an integral part of culture, reflecting and shaping it.

Language and Culture

Language is one of the cornerstones of culture; it shapes our very thoughts. We can use vast vocabularies to describe new experiences, ideas, and feelings, or we can create new words to represent these things. Who we are as a culture, as a people, is reinforced and redefined moment by moment through shared language. Language reflects where a culture has been, what a culture values, even how people in a culture think, describe, and experience events. Perhaps the easiest way to understand the role of language in culture is to examine people who have experienced the loss of language under pressure from others. During the colonial period, both abroad and within countries, colonizers commonly forced the subjugated peoples to speak the language of the colonizer. These language practices continued in many places until recently and were enforced primarily through public (government) and church (mission) schools.

American, Canadian, Australian, Russian, and New Zealand governments each had policies of forced assimilation during the twentieth century, including not allowing indigenous peoples to speak native languages. For example, the United States forced American Indians to learn and speak English. Both mission schools and government schools

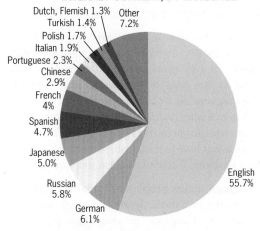

INTERNET CONTENT, BY LANGUAGE

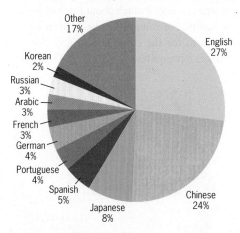

INTERNET USERS, BY LANGUAGE SPOKEN

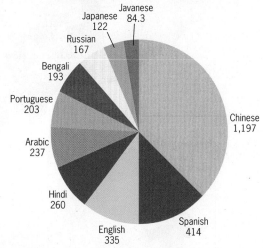

TOP 10 LANGUAGES, BY MILLIONS OF SPEAKERS

Figure 6.4

Languages Used on the Internet.   The disproportionate impact of English is evident.   *Data from*: Red Line, 2014; W3Techs.com, 2014; and Ethnologue, 2014.

enforced English-only policies in hopes of assimilating American Indians into the dominant culture. In an interview with the producers of an educational video, Clare Swan, an elder in the Kenaitze band of the Dena'ina Indians in Alaska, eloquently described the role of language in culture:

> No one was allowed to speak the language—the Dena'ina language. They [the American government] didn't allow it in schools, and a lot of the women had married non-native men, and the men said, "You're American now so you can't speak the language." So, we became invisible in the community. Invisible to each other. And, then, because we couldn't speak the language—what happens when you can't speak your own language is you have to think with someone else's words, and that's a dreadful kind of isolation [emphasis added].

Shared language makes people in a culture visible to each other and to the rest of the world. Language helps cement cultural identity. Language is also quite personal. Our thoughts, expressions, and dreams are articulated in our language; to lose that ability is to lose a lot.

Language can reveal much about the way people and cultures view reality. For example, some African languages have no word or term for the concept of a god. Some Southeast Asian languages have no tenses, reflecting a less sharp cultural distinction between then and now. Given the American culture's preoccupation with dating and timing, it is difficult for many in the United States to understand how speakers of these languages perceive the world.

Language is so closely tied to culture that people use it as a weapon in cultural conflict and political strife. In the United States, where the Spanish-speaking population is growing (Fig. 6.5), some Spanish speakers and their advocates are promoting the use of Spanish in the public arena. In turn, people opposed to the use of Spanish in the United States are leading counter movements to promote "Official English" policies. Of course, Spanish is one of many non-English languages spoken in the United States, but it overshadows all others in terms of number of speakers and is therefore the focus of the official English movement (Table 6.1). During the 1980s, over 30 different States considered passing laws declaring English the State's official language. Some 30 States today have declared English the official language of the State either by statute or by amending the State constitution (one law was subsequently overturned by the courts). A few States have passed English-plus laws,

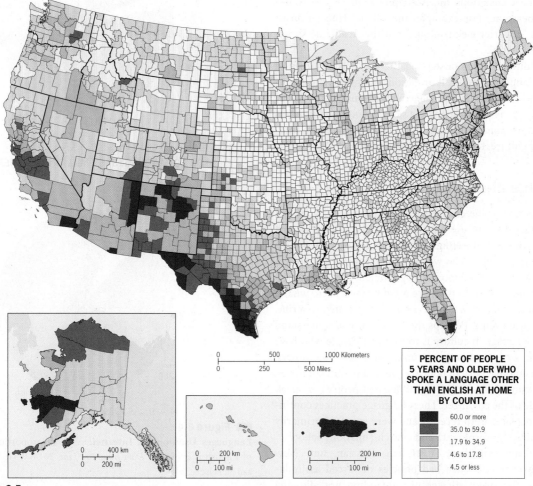

■■ **Figure 6.5**

Percent of People 5 Years and Older Who Speak a Language Other than English at Home in the United States.   The data presented include all non-English languages by county. Latino migration in the Southwest, parts of California, and southern Florida is particularly evident.   *Data from*: United States Census Bureau, 2010.

TABLE 6.1
Top Ten Non-English Languages Spoken at Home by People over the Age of 5 in the United States, 2014.

TOP TEN LANGUAGES SPOKEN AT HOME BY NON-ENGLISH SPEAKERS		
Language	Total	Percent
1. Spanish	35,468,501	12.4
2. Chinese	2,600,150	0.9
3. Tagalog	1,513,734	0.5
4. French	1,305,503	0.5
5. Vietnamese	1,251,468	0.4
6. German	1,109,216	0.4
7. Korean	1,039,021	0.4
8. Russian	881,723	0.3
9. Arabic	845,396	0.3
10. Italian	753,992	0.3

Data from: United States Census Bureau Statistical Abstract, 2014.

encouraging bilingualism for non-English speakers, and a few other States are officially bilingual, including Hawai'i (Hawai'ian and English), or have bilingual education, including New Mexico (Spanish and English).

In Quebec, Canada, the focus is on passing laws that promote the use of the province's distinct version of the French language. Canada is officially bilingual, a reflection of the colonial division of the country between France and Great Britain. Government documents and even scholarly journals are printed in both English and French. Most of the country's French speakers live in the province of Quebec. The majority of people in Quebec speak French at home.

Since the 1970s, the Québécois (the people of Quebec) have periodically called for more independence for their province within Canada, even voting on secession at times. Although a majority has never voted for secession, the provincial government has passed several laws requiring and promoting the use of French in the province. In 1977, the Quebec government compelled all businesses in the province to demonstrate that they functioned in French. Upon passage of this law, many businesses and individuals moved out of the province of Quebec into neighboring Ontario. In 1993, the Quebec government passed a law requiring the use of French in advertising (Fig. 6.6). The Quebec law allows the inclusion of both French and English (or another language) translations on signage, as long as the French letters are twice the size of the other language's letters. In 2013, the province's strict language policies made international news when an Italian restaurant was asked to provide French-language translations for menu items, including pasta. The outrage over Pastagate, as the scandal became known, led the provincial government to promise to respond to language compliance complaints in a

■■ **Figure 6.6**

Quebec Province, Quebec.   The imprint of the French Canadian culture is evident in the cultural landscape of Rue Saint-Louis in Quebec. Here, the architecture and store signs confirm that this region is not simply Canadian; it is French Canadian.

more "balanced" and "measured" manner, recognizing that menus and bank statements cannot be held to the same standard as educational materials and signage.

Not all of Quebec's residents identify with the French language. Within the province, a small proportion of people speak English at home, others speak indigenous languages, and still others speak another language altogether—one associated with their country of origin. When the Quebec Parliament passed several laws promoting French during the 1980s and 1990s, members of Canada's First Nations, including the Cree and Mohawk, who live in Quebec, expressed a desire to remain part of Canada should Quebec secede from the country. During the same period, Quebec has experienced a flow of international migrants, many of whom seek residence in Quebec as a way to enter Canada and North America at large. These new immigrants must learn French under Quebec law.

Quebec, like any other place, is susceptible to change. Calls for independence in Quebec are waning since the separatist political party has captured fewer seats in recent parliamentary elections for the province. Nonetheless, the Québécois still feel a connection to France. The province even has a presence in Paris in the *Maison Quebec* (House of Quebec), an embassy-like entity of the province. As people, ideas, and power flow through the province, change will continue. Yet the province's laws, programs, presence in France, and the desire of the Québécois to remain loyal to their French language will keep the language alive as the province continues to experience change.

What Is a Language?

Many geography textbooks differentiate languages based on a criterion of mutual intelligibility. **Mutual intelligibility** means that two people can understand each other when speaking. The argument goes that if two of us are speaking two different languages, say Spanish and Portuguese, we will not be able to understand each other, but if we are speaking two dialects of one language, we will achieve mutual understanding. Yet linguists have rejected the criterion of mutual intelligibility as strongly as geographers have rejected environmental determinism.

First, mutual intelligibility is almost impossible to measure. Even if we used mutual intelligibility as a criterion, many languages would fail the test. Famous linguist Max Weinreich once said that "a language is a dialect with an army." Think about it. How could we possibly see Mandarin Chinese and Cantonese Chinese as dialects of the same language, when two people speaking the language to each other cannot understand what each other is saying? Both can read the standard form of Chinese that has been built up by a strongly centralized Chinese government. But the spoken dialects are not mutually intelligible. Yet, we see Chinese as one language because of the weight of political and social institutions that lie behind it.

A further complication with the mutual intelligibility test is revealed in Scandinavia, where, for example, a Danish speaker and a Norwegian speaker (at least one from Oslo) will be able to understand what each other is saying. Yet we think of Danish and Norwegian as distinct languages. Having a Norwegian language helps Norwegians identify themselves as Norwegians rather than as Danes or Scandinavians. Other languages that are recognized as separate but are mutually intelligible in many (or nearly all) aspects are Serbian and Croatian, Hindi and Urdu, and Navajo and Apache.

Given the complexities of distinguishing languages from dialects, the actual number of languages in use in the world remains a matter of considerable debate. The most conservative calculation puts the number at about 3000. However, most linguists and linguistic geographers today recognize between 5000 and 7000 languages, including more than 600 in India and over 2000 in Africa.

Standardized Language

Language is dynamic: New discoveries, technologies, and ideas require new words. Technologically advanced societies are likely to have a **standard language**, one that is published, widely distributed, and purposely taught. In some countries, the government sustains the standard language through official state examinations for teachers and civil servants. Ireland promotes the use of the Irish (Celtic) language by requiring all government employees to pass an Irish-language examination before they can be hired. The phrase "the King's English" is a popular reference to the fact that the English spoken by well-educated people in London and its environs is regarded as British Received Pronunciation (BRP) English—that is, the standard.

Who decides what the standard language will be? Not surprisingly, the answer has to do with influence and power. In France, the Académie Française chose the French spoken in and around Paris as the official, standard language during the sixteenth century. In China, the government chose the Northern Mandarin Chinese heard in and around the capital, Beijing, as the official standard language. Although this is China's official standard language, the linguistic term *Chinese* actually incorporates many variants. The distinction between the standard language and variations of it is not unique to China; it is found in all but the smallest societies. The Italian of Sicily is quite different from the Italian spoken north of Venice, and both tongues differ from the standard Italian spoken in Florence and Tuscany, the region where many leaders of the Italian Renaissance wrote and published in what became the standard Italian language.

Dialects

Variants of a standard language along regional or ethnic lines are called **dialects**. Differences in vocabulary, syntax (the way words are put together to form phrases), pronunciation, cadence (the rhythm of speech), and even the pace of speech all mark a speaker's dialect. Even if the written form of a statement adheres to the standard language, an accent can reveal the regional home of a person who reads the statement aloud. In the United States, the words "horse" and "oil" are written the same way in New England and in the South, but to the Southerner, the New Englander may be saying "hahse," and to the New Englander, the Southerner seems to be saying "all."

Linguists think about dialects in terms of **dialect chains** distributed across space. Dialects nearest to each other geographically will be the most similar (greater spatial interaction), but as you travel across the space, the dialects become less intelligible to each other because less interaction occurs. If all of these dialects are part of one language, which one of the dialects is *the language*? This question points to another challenge in defining languages. Is one of the many English dialects in the world the one, true English? Language is actually an umbrella for a collection of dialects, and we tend to see one of these dialects as the "true" language only because it is the one we speak or because it is the one a government claims as the standard.

Frequently, dialects are marked by actual differences in vocabulary. A single word or group of words can reveal the source area of the dialect. Linguistic geographers map the extent of particular words, marking their limits as isoglosses. An **isogloss** is a geographic boundary within which a particular linguistic feature occurs, but such a boundary is rarely a simple line. Usually, outlying areas of usage extend beyond the isogloss. Fuzzy isoglosses may signify that the dialect has expanded or contracted. Linguists who study dialects examine pronunciations, vocabularies, use of colloquial phrases, and syntax to determine isoglosses.

Linguistic geographer Hans Kurath published atlases of dialects in the United States, defining northern, southern, and midland dialect in the eastern part of the country. In the mid-1900s, Kurath drew distinct isoglosses among the three dialects, based on pronunciation of certain sounds and words. A more recent study of American dialects by linguist Bert Vaux used a 122-question online survey to map dialects in the United States. Maps of the soda, pop, and coke question (Fig. 6.7) and the hero, sub, poor-boy question reveal the prominent dialects of New England and the deep South, the fuzzy border between the two regions (Kurath's Midland dialect), the mixture of dialects in much of the rest of the country, and a few scattered areas outside the dialect regions where one or the other dialect dominates.

Linguist Bert Vaux's study of dialects in American English points to the differences in words for common things such as soft drinks and sandwiches. Describe a time when you said something and a speaker of another dialect did not understand the word you used. Where did the person with whom you were speaking come from? Was the word a term for a common thing? Why do you think dialects have different words for common things, things found across dialects, such as soft drinks and sandwiches?

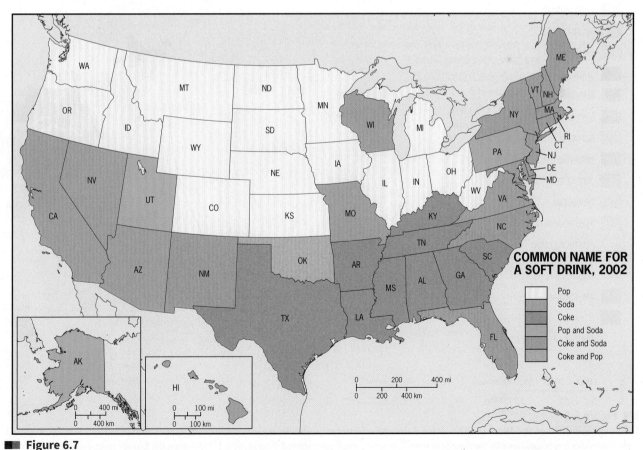

■ **Figure 6.7**
Common Name for a Soft Drink in the United States, by State, 2002. *Data from*: Bert Vaux, Harvard Survey of North American Dialects. http://cfprod01.imt.uwm.edu/Dept/FLL/linguistics/dialect/, accessed September 2005.

WHY ARE LANGUAGES DISTRIBUTED THE WAY THEY ARE?

The first step in mapping the distribution of world languages is to classify languages. Linguists and linguistic geographers classify languages in terms that are also used in biology and for the same reasons: like species, some languages are more closely related to one another than others. At the global scale, we classify languages into **language families**. Each family encompasses multiple languages that have a shared but fairly distant origin. We break language families into **subfamilies** (divisions within a language family), where the commonalities are more definite and their origin is more recent. The

spatial extent of subfamilies is smaller than language families, and every individual language has its dialects, whose territorial extent is smaller still.

Definition and Debate

Although language families and subfamilies seem to be a logical way to classify languages, the classification of languages is subject to intense debate. Defining a language family is a daunting challenge: Some linguists argue that there are not just a few, but many dozens of language families. So when you study Figure 6.8, be aware that this is only one depiction of the world's geography of languages today. This map shows the distribution of some 20 language families, among which

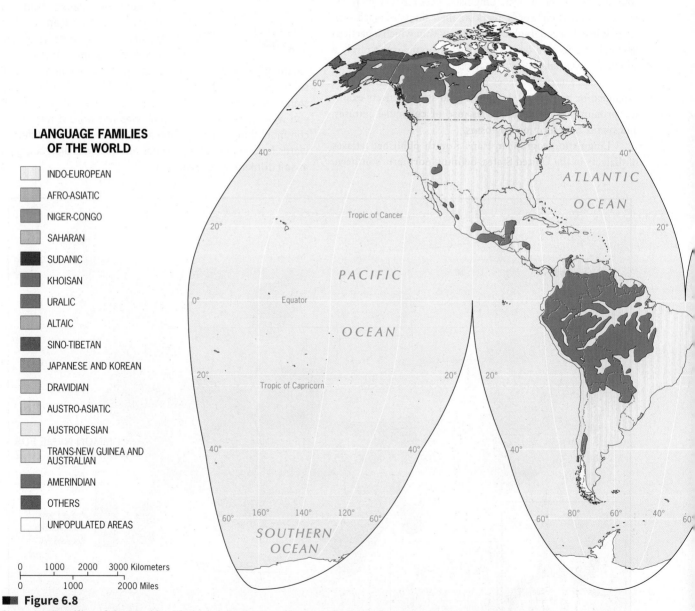

LANGUAGE FAMILIES OF THE WORLD

- INDO-EUROPEAN
- AFRO-ASIATIC
- NIGER-CONGO
- SAHARAN
- SUDANIC
- KHOISAN
- URALIC
- ALTAIC
- SINO-TIBETAN
- JAPANESE AND KOREAN
- DRAVIDIAN
- AUSTRO-ASIATIC
- AUSTRONESIAN
- TRANS-NEW GUINEA AND AUSTRALIAN
- AMERINDIAN
- OTHERS
- UNPOPULATED AREAS

```
0    1000   2000   3000 Kilometers
0        1000        2000 Miles
```

■ **Figure 6.8**

Language Families of the World. The global distribution of language families reflects centuries of spatial interaction and flows of migrants. Indo-European languages came to the Americas from Europe through relocation diffusion after 1500 during the European colonial era. Languages in China and Southeast Asia are connected in the Sino-Tibetan language family as a result of centuries of spatial interaction. *Adapted with permission from*: Hammond, Inc., 1977.

the Indo-European language family has the widest distribution and claims the largest number of speakers. What you see here, of course, results from a combination of contiguous as well as relocation diffusion: Indo-European languages spread from a western source in all directions into Eurasia, but colonialism also transplanted Indo-European languages to the Americas, Africa, and Australia.

Even when it comes to individual languages, complicated issues arise. English is the most widely spoken Indo-European language; its speakers encircle the world with more than 350 million in North America, 60 million in Britain and Ireland, 205 million in Australia and New Zealand, and tens of millions more in South Africa, India, and elsewhere in the postcolonial world. Hundreds of millions of people speak versions of English as a second or third language. Our map does not reflect this complexity, but the Indo-European family has actually diffused even more than Figure 6.8 suggests.

Sometimes you will see Chinese listed as the language with more speakers than any other, but herein lies still another complication. Although Figure 6.8 shows China and neighboring areas to be the heartland of the Sino-Tibetan language family, "Mandarin" Chinese, called *Putonghua* in China, is in common use by less than half of China's population of 1.36 billion. China has more than 1400 dialects, many of them mutually incomprehensible. What unites the "People of Han" is not their ability to understand each other's spoken word, but their ability to read the characters in which Chinese is written. When you watch television in China, you will see

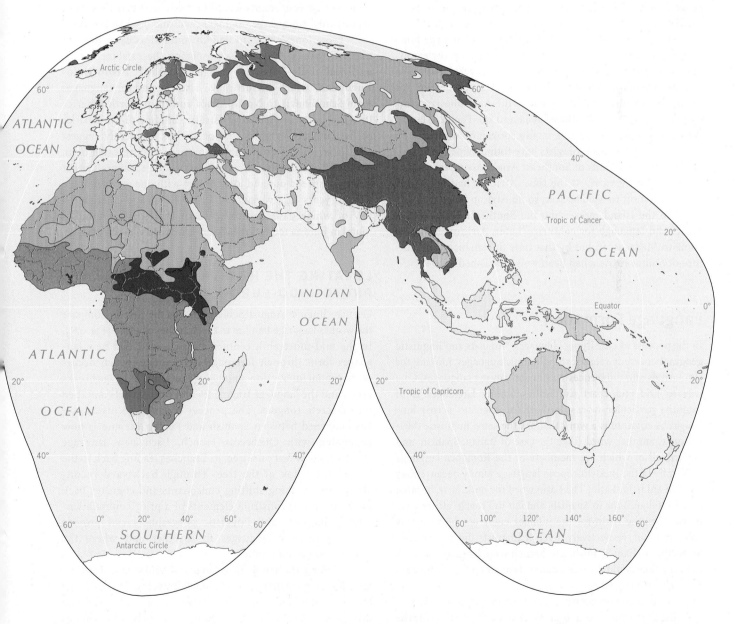

news reports and other programs subtitled by Chinese characters so that speakers of many different dialects can read and understand what is being said. But this does not mean that a billion Chinese speak Mandarin.

At the other end of the scale, the world map of languages shows several language families spoken by dwindling, often marginally located or isolated groups. The Indo-European languages of European colonizers surround the language families of Southeast Asia. Languages in the Austro-Asiatic language family survive in the interior of eastern India and in Cambodia and Laos. Languages in the Austronesian family are numerous and quite diverse, and many of the individual languages are spoken by fewer than 10 million people. Remoteness helps account for the remaining languages in the Amerindian language family. These languages remain strongest in areas of Middle America, the high Andes, and northern Canada.

If we look carefully at the map of world language families, some interesting questions arise. Consider, for example, the island of Madagascar off the East African coast. The primary languages people in Madagascar speak belong not to an African language family but to the Austronesian family, the languages of Southeast Asia and the Pacific Islands. Why is a language from this family spoken on an island so close to Africa? Anthropologists have found evidence of seafarers from the islands of Southeast Asia crossing the Indian Ocean to Madagascar. At the time, Africans had not sailed across the strait to Madagascar, so no African languages diffused to the island, preserving the Southeast Asian settlements and language for centuries. Later, Africans began to come to Madagascar, but by that time the language and culture of Southeast Asia had been well established.

Language Formation

In the process of classifying languages, linguists and linguistic geographers study relationships among languages, looking for similarities and differences within and among languages. One way to find and chart similarities among languages is to examine particular words, looking for cognates across languages. A **cognate** is a word that has the same linguistic derivation as another word. Take the case of Italian, Spanish, and French, all of which are members of the Romance language subfamily of the Indo-European language family because they are derived from Latin. The Latin word for milk, *lacte*, became *latta* in Italian, *leche* in Spanish, and *lait* in French; all are cognates. Also, the Latin for the number eight, *oto*, became *otto*, *ocho*, and *huit*, respectively. Even if linguists did not already know that Italian, Spanish, and French were languages rooted in Latin, they could deduce a connection among the languages through such cognates.

More than two centuries ago William Jones, an Englishman living in South Asia, undertook a study of Sanskrit, the language in which ancient Indian religious and literary texts were written. Jones discovered that the vocabulary and grammatical forms of Sanskrit bore a striking resemblance to the ancient Greek and Latin he learned while in college. "No philologer [student of words] could examine all three," Jones wrote, "without believing them to have sprung from some common source, which, perhaps, no longer exists." His idea was a revolutionary notion in the 1700s.

During the nineteenth century Jakob Grimm, a scholar and a writer of fairy tales, suggested that cognates might prove the relationships between languages in a scientific manner. He explained that related languages have similar, but not identical, consonants. He believed these consonants would change over time in a predictable way. Hard consonants, such as the *v* and *t* in the German word *vater*, softened into *vader* (Dutch) and *father* (English). Using Grimm's theory that consonants became softer as time passed, linguists realized that consonants would become harder as they went "backwards" toward the original hearth and original language.

From Jones's notions and Grimm's ideas came the first major linguistic hypothesis, proposing the existence of an ancestral Indo-European language called **Proto-Indo-European**, which in turn gave rise to modern languages from Scandinavia to North Africa and from North America through parts of Asia to Australia. Studies of similarities across language families that occur less frequently suggest that Proto-Indo-European was, in turn, an outgrowth of an earlier **Proto-Eurasiatic** language. As the speakers of that language spread out and lost contact with one another some 15,000 years ago, variants of Proto-Eurasiatic emerged—a few of which gave rise to seven of the language families found in Eurasia today. Proto-Indo-European was one of these.

LOCATING THE HEARTH OF PROTO-INDO-EUROPEAN

German linguist August Schleicher was the first to compare the world's language families to the branches of a tree (Fig. 6.9). In the mid-nineteenth century, he suggested that new languages form through **language divergence**, which occurs when spatial interaction among speakers of a language breaks down and the language fragments first into dialects and then into discrete tongues. The process of language divergence has happened between Spanish and Portuguese and is now happening with Québécois French. Each new language becomes a new leaf on a tree, its branches leading back to the hearth, the trunk of the tree. Through **backward reconstruction** (tracking shifting consonants and cognates back in an effort to reconstruct elements of a prior common language), linguists and linguistic geographers can provide insight into how languages fit together and where the branches were once joined.

Finding the trunk of a language family is a daunting task, for reconstructing even a small branch of the language tree is complicated. Languages do not change solely through divergence (the splitting of branches); they also change through convergence and extinction. If peoples with different languages have consistent spatial interaction, **language convergence** can take place, collapsing two languages into

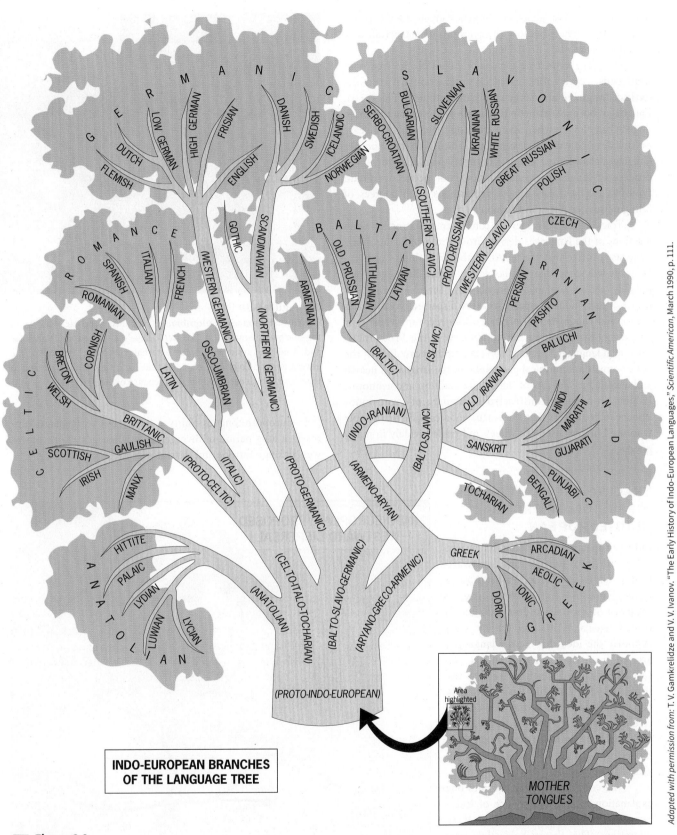

INDO-EUROPEAN BRANCHES
OF THE LANGUAGE TREE

MOTHER TONGUES

Adapted with permission from: T. V. Gamkrelidze and V. V. Ivanov. "The Early History of Indo-European Languages," *Scientific American*, March 1990, p. 111.

■■ Figure 6.9

Indo-European Branches of the Language Tree.   The inset shows all of the languages of the world in a massive tree. The Indo-European language family makes up just one part of that massive tree and is highlighted in this figure. Compare this figure to the map of the Indo-European languages in Europe (Figure 6.2) and notice how the language groups in Europe are related on this tree and where the languages on this tree are geographically located in Europe.

one. Instances of language convergence create special problems for researchers because the rules of reconstruction may not apply or may be unreliable.

Language extinction creates branches on the tree with dead ends, representing a halt in interaction between the **extinct language** and languages that continued (Fig. 6.10). Languages become extinct either when all descendants perish (which can happen when an entire people succumb to disease or invaders) or when descendants choose to use another language, abandoning the language of their ancestors. The process of language extinction does not occur overnight; typically, it takes place across generations, with degrees of bilingualism occurring in the interim.

Tracking the divergence, convergence, extinction, and locations of the languages derived from Proto-Indo-European, linguists theorize that the hearth of the Proto-Indo-European language was somewhere in the vicinity of the Black Sea—very possibly central Anatolia (present-day Turkey). From this hearth, Proto-Indo-European speakers dispersed, vocabularies grew, and linguistic divergence occurred, spurring new languages. By analyzing the vocabulary of the Proto-Indo-European language, linguists and geographers can discern the environment and physical geography of the language's hearth and also deduce aspects of the people's culture and economy. Judging from the reconstructed vocabulary of Proto-Indo-European, it appears that the language dates back to a people who used horses, used the wheel, and traded widely in many goods.

© Eye Ubiquitous/Superstock

█ Figure 6.10

Northwest Amazon, Colombia. The Barasana people, who live in the northwest Amazon in Colombia, have maintained their language and land-use systems despite external pressures. In 1991, the government of Colombia recognized the legal right of the Barasana to their land, which has aided the maintenance of their language.

Indo-European tongues. Shifts in the derivative languages represent a long period of divergence in languages as one moves west through Europe and east into South Asia.

TRACING THE ROUTES OF DIFFUSION OF PROTO-INDO-EUROPEAN

Indo-European spread from its hearth westward into Europe and eastward into what is now Iran, Pakistan, and India (Fig. 6.11). In the former case, the presence of Europe's oldest Indo-European language, Celtic, in the far west supports the idea that newer languages arrived from the east. Migrants to the east likely moved through areas to the south of the Caspian Sea, ultimately penetrating into the Indus and Ganges river basins some 3500 years ago. A second wave of Indo-European speakers moved into present-day Iran some 700 years later.

The **conquest theory** provides one explanation for the dominance of Indo-European tongues in the wake of these migrations. This theory holds that early speakers of Proto-Indo-European spread from east to west on horseback, overpowering earlier inhabitants and beginning the diffusion and differentiation of

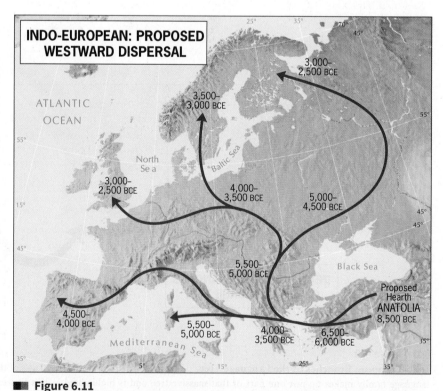

INDO-EUROPEAN: PROPOSED WESTWARD DISPERSAL

ATLANTIC OCEAN

North Sea

Baltic Sea

Black Sea

Mediterranean Sea

3,000–2,500 BCE
3,500–3,000 BCE
3,000–2,500 BCE
4,000–3,500 BCE
5,000–4,500 BCE
5,500–5,000 BCE
Proposed Hearth ANATOLIA 8,500 BCE
4,500–4,000 BCE
5,500–5,000 BCE
4,000–3,500 BCE
6,500–6,000 BCE

█ Figure 6.11

Indo-European Language Family: Proposed Westward Dispersal. Approximate timings and routes for the westward dispersal of the Indo-European languages.

Based on: Bouckaeret et al, 2012.

■■ **Figure 6.12**

Indo-European Language Family: Proposed Hearth and Dispersal Hypothesis. This theory proposes that the Indo-European language family began in Anatolia and dispersed eastward into South Asia and westward into Europe.

An alternative agricultural theory proposes that Proto-Indo-European spread with the diffusion of agriculture. Citing the archaeological record, Luca Cavalli-Sforza and Albert Ammerman proposed that for every generation (25 years) the agricultural frontier moved approximately 18 kilometers (11 mi). This means farmers would have completely penetrated the European frontier over several thousand years, which is what the archaeological record suggests (Fig. 6.12). With established farming providing a more reliable food supply, population could increase. As a result, a slow but steady wave of farmers dispersed into Europe and mixed with nonfarming peoples. But some of the nonfarming societies in their path held out, and their languages persevered. Thus, Etruscan did not become extinct until Roman times, and Euskera (the Basque language) survives to this day as a probable direct link to Europe's pre-farming era.

The Languages of Europe

The map of world languages (Fig. 6.8) demonstrates how widely spread the Indo-European language family is across the globe, dominating not just Europe, but significant parts of Asia (including Russia and India), North and South America, Australia, and portions of Southern Africa. About half the world's people speak Indo-European tongues. The Indo-European language family is broken into subfamilies including Romance, Germanic, and Slavic. And each subfamily is broken into individual languages, such as English, German, Danish, and Norwegian within the Germanic subfamily.

The language map of Europe (Fig. 6.2) shows that the Indo-European language family prevails in this region, with pockets of the Uralic family occurring in Hungary (the Ugric subfamily) and in Finland and adjacent areas (the Finnic subfamily), and a major Altaic language, Turkish, dominating Turkey west of the Sea of Marmara.

Celtic people first brought Indo-European tongues into Europe when they spread across the continent over 3000 years ago. Celtic speech survives in the British Isles and northwestern France, but in most places Celtic tongues fell victim to subsequent migrations and empire building. These historical developments led to the creation of a European linguistic pattern characterized by three major subfamilies: Romance, Germanic, and Slavic.

THE SUBFAMILIES

The **Romance languages** (French, Spanish, Italian, Romanian, and Portuguese) lie in the areas of Europe that were once controlled by the Roman Empire. Over time, local languages mixed with Latin, which the Roman Empire introduced to the region. The Romance languages have much in common because of their Latin connection, but they are not mutually comprehensible. Spanish and Portuguese remain closely related to each other, but even there, reading between the two languages is easier than speaking between them.

The **Germanic languages** (English, German, Danish, Norwegian, and Swedish) reflect the expansion of peoples out of Northern Europe to the west and south. Some Germanic peoples spread into areas dominated by Rome, and at the northern and northeastern edges of the Roman Empire their tongues gained ascendancy. Other Germanic peoples spread into areas that were never part of an ancient empire (present-day Sweden, Norway, Denmark, and the northern part of the Netherlands). The Germanic character of English bears the imprint of a further migration—that of the Normans into England in 1066, bringing a Romance tongue to the British Isles. The essential Germanic character of English remained, but many new words were added that are Romance in origin.

The **Slavic languages** (Russian, Polish, Czech, Slovak, Ukrainian, Slovenian, Serbo-Croatian, and Bulgarian) developed as Slavic people migrated from a base in present-day Ukraine close to 2000 years ago. Slavic tongues came to dominate much of eastern Europe over the succeeding centuries. They, too, overwhelmed Latin-based tongues along much of the eastern part of the old Roman Empire—with the notable exception of an area on the western shores of the Black Sea, where a Latin-based tongue either survived the Slavic invasion or was reintroduced by migrants. That tongue is the ancestor of the modern-day Romance language: Romanian.

RELATIONSHIP TO THE POLITICAL PATTERN

A comparison of Europe's linguistic and political maps shows a high correlation between the languages spoken and the political organization of space (see Fig. 6.2). The Romance languages, of Romanic-Latin origin, dominate in five countries, including Romania. The eastern boundaries of Germany coincide almost exactly with the transition from Germanic to Slavic tongues. Even at the level of individual languages, boundaries can be seen on the political map: between French and Spanish, between Norwegian and Swedish, and between Bulgarian and Greek.

In some places, however, linguistic and political borders are far from coincident. The French linguistic region extends into Belgium, Switzerland, and Italy, but in France, French coexists with Basque in the southwest, a variant of Dutch in the north, and a Celtic tongue in the northwest. The Celtic languages survive in the western region of France called Brittany (Breton), in the northern and western parts of Wales (Welsh), in western Ireland (Irish Gaelic), and in the western Highlands and islands of Scotland (Scots Gaelic). The use of

Romanian extends well into Moldavia, signifying a past loss of national territory. Greek and Albanian are also Indo-European languages, and their regional distribution corresponds significantly (though not exactly) with state territories. Figure 6.2 underscores the complex cultural pattern of eastern Europe: German speakers in Hungary; Hungarian speakers in Slovakia, Romania, and Yugoslavia; Romanian speakers in Greece and Moldavia; Turkish speakers in Bulgaria; and Albanian speakers in Serbia.

Although the overwhelming majority of Europeans and Russians speak Indo-European languages, the Uralic and Altaic language families are also represented. Finnish, Estonian, and Hungarian are major languages of the Uralic family, which, as Figure 6.8 shows, extends across Eurasia to the Pacific Coast. The Altaic family to which Turkish belongs is equally widespread and includes Turkish, Kazakh, Uigur, Kyrgyz, and Uzbek languages.

One language on the map of Europe stands out for two reasons: First, it covers a very small land area, and second, it is *in no way related to* any other language family in Europe. Did you find it? This tantalizing enigma is the Basque language, Euskera. Isolated in the Andorra Mountain region between Spain and France, the Basque people and their Euskera language survived the tumultuous history of Europe for thousands of years—never blending with another language or diffusing from the Andorra region. (Some recent genetic evidence points to a link between Euskera and an extinct language in the Middle East.) The Basques have a strong identity tied to their language and independent history, an identity that was cemented by repression under fascist dictator Francisco Franco, who ruled Spain during and after World War II. In response, a Basque separatist group began demanding autonomy within Spain—periodically resorting to violence in pursuit of the cause. The Spanish government finally recognized Basque autonomy in its 1979 constitution, granting the Basque region its own parliament, giving the Basque language official status, and transferring some taxation and education powers from the capital to the Basque region. A group of Basque separatists continued to demand more, for a time waging a campaign of violence against Spanish targets and even moderate Basque leaders. The situation has calmed down in recent years, but agitation for greater autonomy for the Basques continues (Fig. 6.13).

Languages of Subsaharan Africa

The world map of language families masks the extreme fragmentation of languages in parts of the world such as Subsaharan Africa. In Subsaharan Africa, the map of world language families reflects the dominance of the Niger-Congo language family. By including language subfamilies, we can gain a more meaningful picture of Subsaharan Africa's linguistic diversity (Fig. 6.14).

Figure 6.13
San Sebastián, Spain. Graffiti on the wall of this building uses the English language, "Freedom for the Basque Country," to show support for the Basque separatist movement.

Studying language subfamilies helps us understand migration and settlement patterns in Subsaharan Africa. The oldest languages of Subsaharan Africa are the Khoisan languages, which include "click" sounds. Although they once dominated much of the region, Khoisan languages were marginalized by the invasion of speakers of Bantu languages. Studying the languages in the Bantu subfamily, we can see that the languages are still closely related, with similar prefixes and vocabularies. Similarities among the Bantu languages mean that the languages have been in Subsaharan Africa for a shorter time—typically, the longer a language has been in a place, the more likely sounds will have shifted and languages splintered.

Focusing on the country scale reveals the linguistic diversity of Subsaharan Africa. Nigeria encompasses several subfamilies of the Niger-Congo family, and its population includes speakers of two major Subsaharan African language families. Indeed, Nigeria's 173.6 million people speak more

Figure 6.14
Language Families of Africa. The geographical distribution of African language families and their subfamilies show the history of spatial interaction among Africans. For example, in the Niger-Congo family region, the people in the Bantu subfamily area historically interacted with each other, developing connections among and diffusing languages in the Bantu subfamily. What this maps hides is the role that the language of colonists plays in many parts of Africa—serving as a lingua franca among speakers of different languages and dialects.

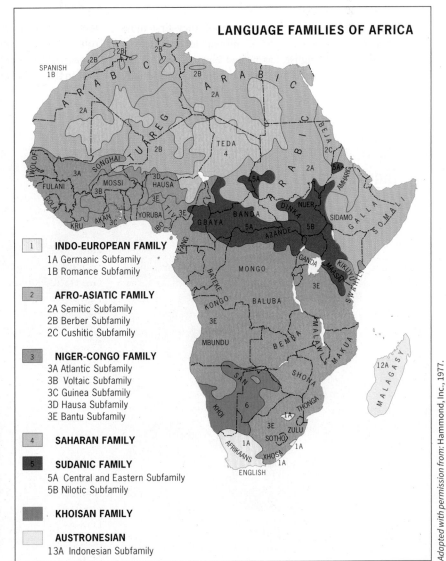

LANGUAGE FAMILIES OF AFRICA

| 1 | **INDO-EUROPEAN FAMILY** |
1A Germanic Subfamily
1B Romance Subfamily

| 2 | **AFRO-ASIATIC FAMILY** |
2A Semitic Subfamily
2B Berber Subfamily
2C Cushitic Subfamily

| 3 | **NIGER-CONGO FAMILY** |
3A Atlantic Subfamily
3B Voltaic Subfamily
3C Guinea Subfamily
3D Hausa Subfamily
3E Bantu Subfamily

| 4 | **SAHARAN FAMILY** |

| 5 | **SUDANIC FAMILY** |
5A Central and Eastern Subfamily
5B Nilotic Subfamily

KHOISAN FAMILY

AUSTRONESIAN
13A Indonesian Subfamily

Adapted with permission from: Hammond, Inc., 1977.

than 500 different languages. The three most prominent languages are distributed regionally: Hausa is in the north and is spoken by some 39 million, Yoruba is in the southwest and is spoken by 22 million, and Ibo is in the southeast and is spoken by more than 24 million people (Fig. 6.15). Of the remaining languages spoken in Nigeria, the vast majority are spoken by fewer than one million people. These minor languages persist because daily survival, community, and culture are tied closely to the local scale in Nigeria. Even people who leave their home towns for work send money back to support the local culture and economy.

Were it not for British colonialism, the country of Nigeria would never have existed. The diverse people of this place have been amalgamated into the Nigerian borders for less than 150 years. As we will see in Chapter 8, European colonists are responsible for the arbitrary borders of most of Africa—borders that ignore cultural divides. When Nigeria gained its independence in 1962, the government decided to adopt English as the "official" language, as the three major regional languages are too politically charged and thus unsuitable as national languages.

When Nigeria's children go to school, they first must learn English, which is used for all subsequent instruction. Certainly, the use of English has helped Nigeria avoid some conflicts based on language, but Nigerian educators, especially in the north, are having second thoughts about the policy. Upon entering school, children who have grown up speaking a local language are suddenly confronted with a new, unfamiliar tongue. The time and energy spent learning English take away from learning other subjects. Moreover, for many students, knowledge of English is irrelevant when they emerge from school (as many do after only six years). Some argue against deference to a language brought by colonists who arbitrarily established their multilinguistic and multiethnic country in the first place. Yet from a communication perspective, English is a common denominator for the country that cannot easily be abandoned.

Education affects the distribution of languages across the globe and within regions and countries. Thinking about different regions of the world, consider how education plays a role in the distribution of English speakers. Who learns English in each of these regions and why? What role does education play in the global distribution of English speakers?

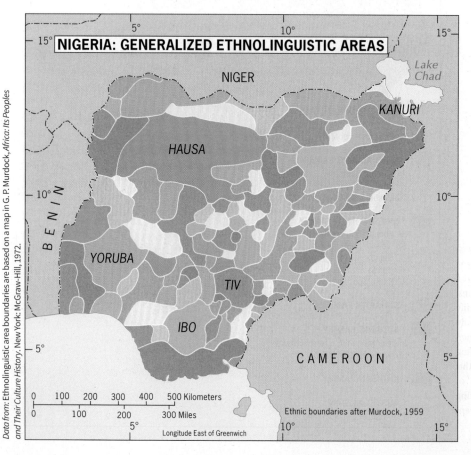

Data from: Ethnolinguistic area boundaries are based on a map in G. P. Murdock, Africa: Its Peoples and Their Culture History. New York: McGraw-Hill, 1972.

NIGERIA: GENERALIZED ETHNOLINGUISTIC AREAS

NIGER

Lake Chad

KANURI

HAUSA

BENIN

YORUBA

TIV

IBO

CAMEROON

0   100   200   300   400   500 Kilometers
0   100   200   300 Miles

Ethnic boundaries after Murdock, 1959

Longitude East of Greenwich

■ **Figure 6.15**
Nigeria: Generalized Ethnolinguistic Areas. This map demonstrates the mosaic of languages in Nigeria by shading each of the country's ethnolinguistic areas. The colors represent diversity; they do not show associations among ethnolinguistic areas.

HOW DID CERTAIN LANGUAGES BECOME DOMINANT?

Just a few thousand years ago most habitable parts of Earth were characterized by a tremendous diversity of languages. With the rise of empires, of more technologically sophisticated literate societies, some languages began to spread over larger areas. By 2000 years ago, languages such as Chinese and Latin had successfully diffused over large regions. The Han Empire in China and the Roman Empire in Europe and North Africa knit together large swaths of territory, encouraging the diffusion of one language over substantial chunks of territory. The most powerful and wealthiest people were the first to learn Chinese and Latin in these empires, as they had the most to lose by not learning these languages. Local languages and illiteracy continued among the poor in the empires, and some blending of local with regional languages occurred. When the Roman Empire disintegrated, places within the former empire became much more isolated from one another, prompting a round of linguistic divergence.

In the late Middle Ages, the invention of the Gutenberg printing press and the rise of nation-states worked to spread literacy and stabilize certain languages through widely distributed written forms. Johann Gutenberg perfected the printing press, inventing the movable-type printing press, the Gutenberg press, in Germany in 1440. In 1452, Gutenberg printed the first Gutenberg Bible (the sacred text for Christians), which brought the scriptures out of churches and monasteries. The printing press diffused quickly in the century following—throughout Europe and beyond. It allowed for an unprecedented production of written texts in languages besides Latin. The printing press made it possible to print the Bible in vernacular languages, such as French or German, rather than Latin, which in turn gave rise to standardized variants of those languages. The Luther Bible played this role for German, as did the King James Bible for English.

The rise of relatively large independent states was equally important (see Chapter 8), for these political entities had a strong interest in promoting a common culture, often through promotion of a common language (such as French or Dutch). Political elites who were literate and had access to written texts brought peoples together and played a key role in distributing printed texts. Moreover, as the leaders of countries such as England and Spain sought to expand their influence overseas through mercantilism and colonialism, they established networks of communication and interaction, helping to diffuse certain languages over vast portions of Earth's surface.

Since 1500, the world has experienced several waves of globalization ranging from European colonialism to American-led globalization, resulting in widespread cultural, linguistic, political, and economic interaction. Trade and commerce stimulated the formation of new, hybrid languages to facilitate such interaction, but other local languages collapsed under the onslaught of change. Although new languages are created through trade and interaction over time, local languages with few native speakers have increasingly become extinct. Globalization is shrinking the world's linguistic heritage. National Geographic Explorer in Residence Wade Davis estimates that half of "the world's 7000 languages are endangered." Davis argues that most languages are lost because one group dominates another and the dominant language is privileged.

Lingua Franca

Even before the expansion of trade encouraged the global diffusion of languages such as English and Spanish, regional trade encouraged people speaking different tongues to find ways to communicate with one another. A **lingua franca** is a language used among speakers of different languages for the purposes of trade and commerce. A lingua franca can be a single language, or it can be a mixture of two or more languages. When people speaking two or more languages are in contact and they combine parts of their languages in a simplified structure and vocabulary, we call it a **pidgin language**.

The first widely known lingua franca was a pidgin language. During the 1200s, seaborne commerce in the Mediterranean Sea expanded, and traders from the ports of southern France (the Franks) revitalized the ports of the eastern Mediterranean. But the local traders did not speak the seafarers' language. Thus began a process of convergence in which the tongue of the Franks was mixed with Italian, Greek, Spanish, and Arabic. The mixture came to be known as the Frankish language, or lingua franca, and it served for centuries as the common tongue of Mediterranean commerce.

The term *lingua franca* is still used to denote a common language used for trade and commerce that is spoken by peoples with different native tongues. Arabic became a lingua franca during the expansion of Islam, and English did so in many areas during the colonial era. English is the only linguistic common denominator that binds together multilingual India—both in India itself and among those from the subcontinent who have migrated to other areas (Fig. 6.16).

A different sort of a lingua franca in wide use today is Swahili, the lingua franca of East Africa. Through centuries of trade and interaction, Swahili developed from an African Bantu language mixed with Arabic and Persian, encompassing 100 million speakers from southern Somalia to northern Mozambique and from coastal Kenya and Tanzania to Uganda and the East African Great Lakes region. Swahili has a complex vocabulary and structure, and while millions of East Africans communicate in the language, most still learn and speak a local language as their first or primary language. Swahili has gained prominence since 2000 because of its status as the most widely used African language on the Internet. The British Broadcasting Corporation (BBC) has a

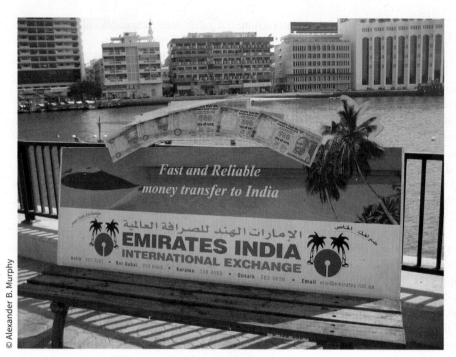

© Alexander B. Murphy

■ **Figure 6.16**
Dubai, United Arab Emirates. The message on this bench is aimed at Indian migrants living in the United Arab Emirates and is written in English, the lingua franca of virtually all Indian migrants on the Arabian Peninsula.

Swahili language website, and Wikipedia offers pages of its free encyclopedia in Swahili.

Over time a pidgin language may gain native speakers, becoming the first language children learn in the home. When this happens, we call it a creolized or Creole language. A **Creole language** is a pidgin language that has developed a more complex structure and vocabulary and has become the native language of a group of people. The word *Creole* stems from a pidgin language formed in the Caribbean from English, French, and Portuguese languages mixed with the languages of African slaves. The language became more complex and became the first language of people in the region, replacing the African languages.

Pidgin and Creole languages are important unifying forces in a linguistically divided world. They tend to be simple and accessible, and therefore disseminate rapidly. In Southeast Asia a trade language called Bazaar Malay is heard from Myanmar (Burma) to Indonesia and from the Philippines to Malaysia; it has become a lingua franca in the region. A simplified form of Chinese also serves as a language of commerce even beyond the borders of China.

Multilingualism

In a world of some 200 political entities and several thousand languages, most countries are characterized, to varying degrees, by *multilingualism*—the use of more than one language by sectors of the population. In the United States, the current issue of Spanish as a second language is only the most recent manifestation of a debate that is as old as the country itself. Canada is

officially a bilingual state, but quite a few Canadians speak a language other than English or French at home.

To be sure, a few virtually **monolingual states**—countries where almost everyone speaks the same language—do exist. These include Japan in Asia; Uruguay in South America; Iceland, Denmark, Portugal, and Poland in Europe; and Lesotho in Africa. Even these countries, however, have small numbers of people who speak other languages; for example, more than a half-million Koreans live in Japan. In fact, as a result of migration and diffusion, no country is truly monolingual today. English-speaking Australia has more than 180,000 speakers of Aboriginal languages. Predominantly Portuguese-speaking Brazil has some 1.5 million speakers of Amerindian languages.

Countries in which more than one language is in use are called **multilingual states**. In some of these countries, linguistic fragmentation reflects strong cultural pluralism as well as divisive forces. This is true in former colonial areas where colonizers threw together peoples speaking different languages, as happened in Africa and Asia.

Multilingualism takes several forms. In Canada and Belgium, the two major languages each dominate particular areas of the country. In multilingual India, the country's official languages generally correspond with the country's States (Fig. 6.17). In Peru, centuries of acculturation have not erased the regional identities of the American Indian tongues spoken in the Andean Mountains and the Amazonian interior, and of Spanish, spoken on the coast. In Gabon, 42 recognized languages coexist as part of a complex linguistic mosaic.

Official Languages

Countries with linguistic fragmentation often adopt an **official language** (or languages) to tie the people together. In former colonies, the official language is often one that ties them to their colonizer, as the colonizer's language invariably is one already used by the educated and politically powerful elite. For Gabon, that language is French, for Angola it is Portuguese, and for Ghana it is English. States adopt an official language in an effort to promote communication and interaction among peoples who speak different local and regional languages.

Designating an official language is not without risks. As we noted earlier in this chapter in the case of Nigeria, the long-term results of using a foreign language may not be positive. In some countries, citizens object to using a language that they associate with colonial repression. Some former colonies have chosen not just one but two official languages: the European colonial language plus one of the country's own major languages. English and Hindi, for example, are official languages of India. Similarly, English and Swahili are official languages of Tanzania. In Mauritania, French and Arabic are official languages. South Africa has perhaps the largest number of official tongues. In a nod to its complex colonial and postcolonial history, South Africa's constitution mandates 11 official languages. But this solution is not always enough. When India gave Hindi official status, riots and disorder broke out in non-Hindi areas of the country. Kenya, which at first made English and Swahili its official languages, decided to drop English in the face of public opposition to rules requiring candidates for public office to pass a test of their ability to use English.

The European Union is not a country, but it recognizes 24 official languages, and the United Nations has 6 official languages: Arabic, Chinese, English, French, Russian, and Spanish. In each of these cases, the international organization offers simultaneous translation among the official languages to any member of the parliament (European Union) or the general assembly (United Nations) who requests it. Each international organization also maintains its website in all official languages. The European Union only produces legislation and policy documents of "major public importance" in all of its official languages; other documents are translated only into the languages relevant to each document. All United Nations documents must be translated into all the official languages (and sometimes German as well) prior to being published.

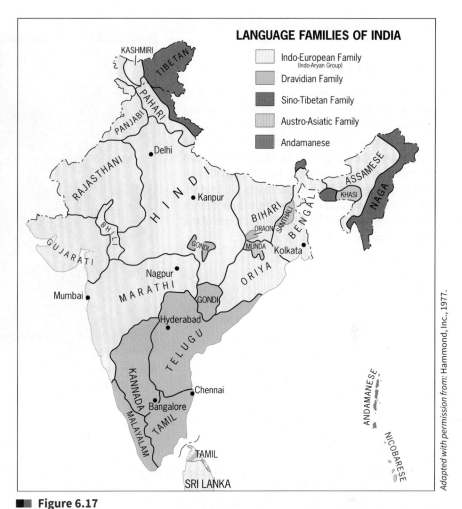

LANGUAGE FAMILIES OF INDIA

- Indo-European Family (Indo-Aryan Group)
- Dravidian Family
- Sino-Tibetan Family
- Austro-Asiatic Family
- Andamanese

Adapted with permission from: Hammond, Inc., 1977.

■■ **Figure 6.17**

Language Families of India.   The language map of India reflects the history of spatial interaction in the region. Southern India, where Dravidian languages are spoken, was not incorporated in every empire that ruled northern India over the last 2,500 years. The presence of Indo-European languages in northern India demonstrates the region's historical connectedness to areas to the west, including Central Asia, where Indo-European languages are also found.

The Prospect of a Global Language

What will the global language map look like 50 years from now? More and more people are using English in a variety of contexts. English is now the standard language of international business and travel (the lingua franca), much of contemporary popular culture bears the imprint of English, and the computer and telecommunications revolution relies heavily on the use of English terminology. Does this mean that English is on its way to becoming a global language?

FIELD NOTE

"English is an important part of the curriculum even at a small school for deaf children in remote Bhutan. The children and I began communicating by writing questions to each other on the blackboard. Their English is quite good, and I am reminded once again of the incredible global reach of English, despite its idiosyncrasies. In English, light is pronounced as if it were lite, the past tense of the verb to read is read, but the past tense of the word to lead is led."

© Alexander B. Murphy

Figure 6.18
Paro, Bhutan.

If global language means the principal language people use around the world in their day-to-day activities, the geographical processes we have examined so far do not point to the emergence of English as a global tongue. Population growth rates are generally lower in English-speaking areas than they are in other areas, and little evidence shows people in non-English speaking areas willing to abandon their local language in favor of English. Indeed, since language embodies deeply held cultural views and is a basic feature of cultural identity, many people actively resist switching to English.

Yet if **global language** means a common language of trade and commerce used around the world, the picture looks rather different. Although not always welcomed, the trend throughout much of the world is to use English as a language of cross-cultural communication—especially in the areas of science, technology, travel, business, and education (Fig. 6.18). Korean scholars are likely to communicate with their Russian counterparts in English; Japanese scientific journals are increasingly published in English; Danish tourists visiting Italy commonly use English to get around; and the meetings of most international financial and governmental institutions are dominated by English. Under these circumstances, the role of English as an international language of commerce will likely grow.

We must be careful in this conclusion, however. Anyone looking at the world 200 years ago would have predicted French as the principal language of cross-cultural communication in the future. Times are different now, of course. The role of English in the computer revolution alone makes it hard to imagine a fundamental shift away from the dominance of English in international affairs. Yet, economic and political influences on language use are always in flux, and nothing is inevitable.

thinking *geographically*   Choose a country in the world. Imagine you become a strong leader of a centralized government in the country. Pick a language used in the country other than the tongue spoken by the majority. Determine what policies you could put in place to make the minority language an official language of the country. What reactions would your initiative generate? Who would support it and who would not?

WHAT ROLE DOES LANGUAGE PLAY IN MAKING PLACES?

The cultural geographer Yi-Fu Tuan has studied the role and function of language in the shaping of places. He researched the way people use language as a tool to give perceptual meaning to areas on Earth's surface, large and small. Each

place has a unique location and constitutes a reflection of human activities, ideas, and tangible, durable creations. Tuan argued that by simply naming a place, people in effect call that place into being, and thereby impart a certain character to it.

Geographers call place-names **toponyms**. Such names often refer to the social processes going on in a particular area, and these may determine whether a toponym is passed down or changed, how the people will interpret the history of a place, and how the people will see a place. Tuan contrasts the examples of "Mount Prospect" and "Mount Misery" to help us understand that a name alone can color the character of a place and even the experiences of people in a place. If you planned to travel to "Mount Prospect," your expectations and even your experiences might well be quite different than they would be if you took a trip to "Mount Misery."

The Ten Toponyms

A toponym can give us a quick glimpse into the history of a place. Simply by knowing who named the place and how the name was chosen helps us understand the uniqueness of that place. In his book, *Names on the Land: A Historical Account of Place-Naming in the United States* (1982), English professor George Stewart recognized that certain themes dominate American toponyms. Stewart developed a classification scheme focused on ten basic types of place-names, including: *descriptive* (Rocky Mountains), *commendatory* (Paradise Valley, Arizona), and *possession* (Johnson City, Texas) (Table 6.2). Stewart explains that some of the most interesting toponyms are *manufactured*, such as Truth or Consequences, New Mexico, which voted to change its name in response to an incentive offered by a 1950s-era radio game show. Stewart's final category of toponyms is *shift names*. Shift names include relocated names, examples of relocation diffusion and typically found in migrant communities (Lancaster, England to Lancaster, Pennsylvania).

Knowing Stewart's ten categories of toponyms at the very least helps us understand that a story lies behind every

TABLE 6.2
Toponym Classification Scheme Designed by George Stewart.

Type of Toponym	Example
Descriptive	Rocky Mountains
Associative	Mill Valley, California
Commemorative	San Francisco, California
Commendatory	Paradise Valley, Arizona
Incidents	Battle Creek, Michigan
Possession	Johnson City, Texas
Folk	Plains, Georgia
Manufactured	Truth or Consequences, New Mexico
Mistakes	Lasker, North Carolina
Shift	Lancaster, Pennsylvania

toponym. The stories of toponyms quite often have their roots in migration, movement, and interaction among people. When languages diffuse through migration, so too do toponyms. Studying the toponyms in a place can tell us much about the historical migration of peoples. George Stewart's classic book on toponyms reveals many clusters of migrants and corresponding toponyms. Often the toponyms remain long after the migrants moved on. Clusters of Welsh toponyms in Pennsylvania, French toponyms in Louisiana, and Dutch toponyms in Michigan reveal migration flows and can also provide insight into language change and the evolution of dialects.

Toponyms and Globalization

Brazil provides an interesting case study of migration flows and toponyms. Most Brazilian toponyms are Portuguese, reflecting the Portuguese colonization of the land. Amid the Portuguese toponyms sits a cluster of German toponyms in the southern state of Santa Catarina. The map of the state is marked by the place-naming activities of German immigrants. For example, the German word for flower is "Blume," and several last names in German begin with "Blum." The German immigrants had a fondness for the tropical flowers they saw in Brazil: southern Brazil is therefore dotted with towns named Blumenau, Blumberg, Blumenhof, Blumenort, Blumenthal, and Blumenstein. Brazilian toponyms also reveal the enormous flow of forced migration from West Africa to Brazil during the slave trade. The Brazilian State of Bahia has a number of toponyms that originated in West Africa, especially Benin and Nigeria.

The toponyms we see on a map depend in large part on who produced the map. Some embattled locales have more than one name at the same time. Argentineans refer to a small cluster (archipelago) of islands off the southeast coast of South America as the Malvinas, but the British call the same cluster of islands the Falkland Islands. In 1982, Argentina invaded the Malvinas, but the British forces fought back, and the islands remain under British control. British, American, and other allies call and map the islands as the Falklands, but Argentineans continue to call and map the islands as the Malvinas. The war ended in a matter of weeks, but the underlying dispute lingers, and so do both names.

Changing Toponyms

Tuan explained that when people *change the toponym* of a place, they have the power to "wipe out the past and call forth the new." For example, people in a small town in Wales feared the loss of the Welsh language and despised the role the English had played in diminishing the use of the Welsh language. They also wanted to boost their local economy by attracting tourists to their town. A century ago, the people renamed their town with a Welsh word unpronounceable by others: Llanfairpwllgwyngyllgogerychwyrndrobwllllantysiliogogogoch (Fig. 6.19).

© Alexander B. Murphy

■■ **Figure 6.19**
Llanfairpwllgwyngyllgogerychwyrndrobwllllantysiliogogogoch, Wales.   The town with the self-proclaimed longest name in the world attracts hordes of tourists each year to a place whose claim to fame is largely its name.

The name accurately describes the geographical context within which the town in northern Wales is situated: "The Church of St. Mary in the hollow of white hazel near the rapid whirlpool by the church of St. Tysilio of the red cave." Since 1988, Wales has had an official policy of teaching both Welsh and English in the schools in order to preserve and boost usage of the Welsh language. Saying the name of this town correctly is now a benchmark for students learning Welsh, and the residents of the town take pride in their ability to pronounce it.

Toponyms are part of the cultural landscape. Changes in place-names give us an idea of the layers of history, the layers of cultural landscape in a place. For example, on the Kenai Peninsula in Alaska, where Clare Swan (whom we cited earlier in this chapter) is from, the changing place-names give us insight into identity questions in the place. Natives in one town on the Kenai Peninsula called their home Nanwalek in the early 1800s; when the Russians came in and took over the peninsula, they changed the name to Alexandrof. Americans mapped Alaska and then made it a State, and in the process, they changed the name to English Bay. In 1991, the townspeople changed the name of their home back to Nanwalek. When you arrive in Nanwalek, you will see native people, see signs of the Russian Orthodox religion, hear them speak English, and then talk with the native people who are reviving their native language and culture. The changes in the place-name provide insight into the cultural landscape.

POSTCOLONIAL TOPONYMS

The question of changing toponyms often arises when power changes hands in a place. When African colonies became independent countries, many of the new governments immediately changed the toponyms of places named after colonial figures. The new governments renamed several countries: Upper Volta to Burkina Faso, Gold Coast to Ghana, Nyasaland to Malawi, and Northern and Southern Rhodesia to Zambia and Zimbabwe, respectively. Countries in Asia also chose new toponyms to mark their independence and separate themselves from their past: East Pakistan became Bangladesh, and the Netherlands East Indies became Indonesia.

Newly independent countries also changed the names of cities, towns, and geographic features to reflect their independence. Thus, Leopoldville (named after a Belgian king) became Kinshasa, capital of the Congo; Salisbury, Zimbabwe, named after a British leader, became Harare; and Lourenço Marques, Mozambique, commemorating a Portuguese naval hero, became Maputo. However, newly independent countries did not wipe all colonial names and references from their maps. Etoile (the Congo), Colleen Bawn (Zimbabwe), and Cabo Delgado (Mozambique) remain on the postcolonial map.

Sometimes the push to rename a toponym from one that reflects a colonial heritage occurs long after independence. In India, the large port city of Bombay was renamed Mumbai in 1995, despite the fact that India became independent from Britain some 50 years earlier. In this case, a nationalist party won local elections and implemented a long sought-after name change. The party renamed the city Mumbai, a toponym that both reinforces the city's Marathi identity and celebrates its patron Hindu goddess, Mumbadevi. Not everyone embraced the change, however; many locals continue to use Bombay—particularly those who are not Marathis.

Similarly, in 1996 the southern Indian city of Madras officially changed its name to Chennai. This change reflects the efforts of local leaders to honor the influence of Tamil language and culture in the southern State of Tamil Nadu. In another example, a Canadian bay named after British explorer Frobisher is now called Iqaluit Bay, reverting back to its indigenous Inuit name. But efforts to rename colonial-era cities have faced resistance as well. Often the local non-indigenous community is most resistant, arguing that the name change would erase their history. By and large, however, the push to change colonial-era names has been successful. These shifts have also led to confusion in the global arena, illustrated by embarrassing public gaffes when former colonial-era names have been used erroneously by political leaders in speeches and policy documents. In 2005 the United Nations published two manuals to standardize and keep up with changing toponyms in an increasingly globalized world.

POSTREVOLUTION TOPONYMS

Independence prompts name changes, and so too do changes in power through coups and revolutions. During his reign, authoritarian dictator General Mobutu Sese Seko changed the name of the Belgian Congo in Subsaharan Africa to Zaïre. At first, other governments and international agencies did not take this move seriously, but eventually they recognized Mobutu's Zaïre. Governments and companies changed their maps and atlases to reflect Mobutu's decision. The government of Zaïre changed the name of their money from the franc to the zaïre, and they even changed the name of the Congo River to the Zaïre.

In 1997, the revolutionary leader Laurent Kabila ousted Mobutu and established his regime in the capital, Kinshasa. Almost immediately, he renamed the country. Zaïre became the Democratic Republic of the Congo (reflecting the colonial name). Again, governments and companies reacted, changing their maps and atlases to reflect Kabila's decision.

Recent revolutions in power in Russia and South Africa have led to many changes in toponyms in these countries. When the Soviet Union began, the communist government changed many places named for tsars who were in power before them, replacing them (of course) with Soviet names. Once the Soviet Union collapsed, a new round of name changes occurred, often going back to Tsarist-era names. In the new Russia, Leningrad reverted to St. Petersburg, Sverdlovsk went back to Yekaterinburg (its name under the tsars), and Stalingrad was renamed Volgograd (for the river). These changes reverberated across the entire former Soviet sphere, with many cities in Central Asia abandoning Russified toponyms. Reformers, nationalists, and lingering communists argued bitterly over the toponym changes, and many people continued to address their mail according to their city's former name.

In the same time frame, South Africa experienced a major revolution that also resulted in a fundamental change in governance. The government of South Africa wrestled with pressures for and against toponym changes. The government restructured the country's administrative framework, creating nine provinces out of four and giving some of the new provinces African names (Mpumalanga for the new Eastern Transvaal, Gauteng for a new central province). One of the old provinces, Natal, has become Kwazulu-Natal. The government also changed some names of towns and villages, but South Africa's map still includes many names from the Boer-British and Apartheid periods. A push to change the name of the capital from Pretoria to the more indigenous Tshwane has been challenged by white South Africans who say the city was named Pretoria when it was founded and that the current name is therefore uniquely South African. Name changes can evoke strong reactions from people, and the South African government is trying to move slowly and carefully to avoid arousing emotions in their still-divided country.

MEMORIAL TOPONYMS

People can choose to change a toponym to memorialize an important person or event. Hundreds of parks in the United States are named Memorial Park to commemorate a person or event. Towns or government agencies can vote to change the name of a school, a library, or a public building to memorialize people who have played a role in shaping the place or who have had an enormous influence on people in the place.

Certain events such as decolonization or a political revolution can spur changes in toponyms, and so too can revolutions in thought and behavior. The civil rights movement of the 1960s in the United States left many lasting impressions of people and events, especially in the South, where many protests, sit-ins, and marches occurred. Geographer Derek Alderman explains that, in recent decades, African Americans in the South have "taken a particularly active role in reconstructing commemorative landscapes—from calling for the removal of Confederate symbols from public places to the building of memorials and museums honoring the civil rights movement." Streets are often the focal point of commemoration in the cultural landscape because so many people travel along them daily, serving as a constant reminder of the person or event being memorialized.

Alderman studied the practice of changing street names to memorialize Martin Luther King Jr. (MLK), the major African American leader of the civil rights movement.

Although streets named after MLK are found throughout the United States, the greatest concentration of memorial streets are in the South, especially in Georgia (King's home state) and Mississippi (Fig. 6.20). Alderman studied the distribution of MLK streets in the South, comparing their locations with census data on race and socioeconomics. He found that although MLK streets are found in both cities and rural areas, "MLK streets are located—whether by choice or by force—in census areas that are generally poorer and with more African Americans than citywide averages" (Fig. 6.21). Alderman tempers this finding with a caution that not all MLK streets are located in poorer areas of cities. Even when MLK streets are located in depressed areas, the African American population may have purposely chosen a street because it runs through an African American neighborhood. Alderman's subsequent studies explore the scale of the city and the contested views of what kinds of streets should be named for MLK—be they residential, commercial, major thoroughfares (perhaps those that connect white and African American neighborhoods), or residential streets in largely African American neighborhoods.

The presence of streets named for civil rights leaders in the cultural landscapes of the American South creates a

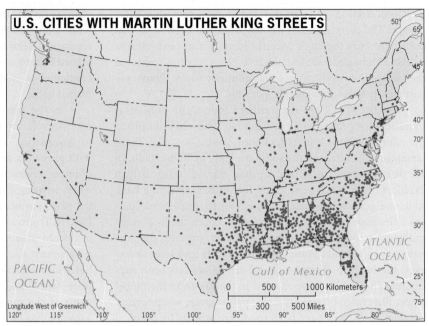

Figure 6.20

Cities in the United States with a Street Named for Martin Luther King Jr.   Commemorating Martin Luther King through street naming displays a strong concentration in the southeastern United States (almost 70% of all MLK-named roads) even as it is a national trend. King hailed from Georgia and the South was an early battleground in the Civil Rights Movement. Moreover, African Americans still make up a significant proportion of the southern population across varying sizes of cities involved in the naming process.   Data drawn from several sources by Derek Alderman, Janna Caspersen, Matthew Mitchelson, and Chris McPhilamy, 2014.

significant counterbalance to the numerous places of commemoration named for leaders of the Confederacy during the Civil War (see Chapter 1).

GUEST FIELD NOTE

Greenville, North Carolina

Greenville, North Carolina, changed West Fifth Street to Martin Luther King Jr. Drive in 1999. Originally, African American leaders wanted all of Fifth Street renamed—not just part of it—but residents and business owners on the eastern end strongly opposed the proposal. After driving and walking down the street, I quickly realized that King Drive marked an area that was predominantly black with limited commercial development, whereas East Fifth was mostly white and more upscale. When I interviewed members of Greenville's African American community, they expressed deep frustration over the marginalization of the civil rights leader. In the words of one elected official, "The accomplishments of Dr. King were important to all Americans. A whole man deserves a whole street!" Naming streets for King is a controversial process for many cities, often exposing continued racial tensions and the

Figure 6.21

potential for toponyms to function as contested social boundaries within places.

Credit: Derek Alderman, University of Tennessee

COMMODIFICATION OF TOPONYMS

The practice of commodifying (buying, selling, and trading) toponyms is growing. International media corporations that reach across the globe bring known names to new places, drawing consumers to the place based on what they have heard or experienced elsewhere. For example, the Disney Corporation opened Tokyo Disneyland in 1983 and Disneyland Paris in 1990, both places that capitalize on the success of Disneyland and Disneyworld in the United States. As corporations spread their names and logos to other places, they seek to "brand" places, creating or re-creating places that consumers associate with places of the same brand.

In recent years, the activities of corporations with a global reach have been stamped on the landscape. Stadiums are especially susceptible to this form of commodification: FedEx Field, Verizon Center, TD Bank Garden, CenturyLink Field, and Coors Field are perfect examples. In 2004, the cash-strapped Metropolitan Transit Authority (MTA) in New York City proposed renaming the metro stops, bridges, and tunnels after corporate sponsors. The plan was approved in 2013, and metro riders have been assured the name changes will not elicit confusion. Corporate sponsors are only eligible to buy naming rights provided they have "a unique or iconic geographic, historic or other connection" to a particular MTA facility "that would readily be apparent to typical MTA customers."

This place was first named by Gabrielino Indians. In 1769, Spanish Franciscan priests renamed the place. In 1850, English speakers renamed the place. Do not use the Internet to help you. Use only maps in this book or in atlases to help you deduce what this place is. Maps of European exploration and colonialism will help you the most. Look at the end of the chapter summary for the answer.

Summary

The global mosaic of languages reflects centuries of divergence, convergence, extinction, and diffusion. Linguists and linguistic geographers have the interesting work of uncovering, through deep reconstruction, the hearths of the world's language families. Some languages, such as Basque, are not easily explained. Other languages are the foci of countless studies, many of which come to differing conclusions about their ancient origins.

As certain languages, such as English and Chinese, gain speakers and become global languages, other languages become extinct. Some languages come to serve as the lingua franca of a region or place. Governments choose official languages, and through public schools, educators entrench an official language in a place. Some countries, faced with the global diffusion of the English language, defend and promote their national language. Whether mandating that signs be written a certain way or requiring a television station to broadcast some proportion of programming in the national language, governments can preserve language, choose a certain dialect as the standard, or repel the diffusion of other languages.

Regardless of the place, people, or language used, language continues to define, shape, and maintain culture. How a person thinks about the world is reflected in the words used to describe and define it.

Answer to Final Thinking Geographically Question: Los Angeles, California.

Geographic Concepts

language
mutual intelligibility
standard language
dialects
dialect chains
isogloss
language families
subfamilies
cognate
Proto-Indo-European

Proto-Eurasiatic
language divergence
backward reconstruction
language convergence
extinct language
conquest theory
Romance languages
Germanic languages
Slavic languages
lingua franca

pidgin language
Creole language
monolingual states
multilingual states
official language
global language
place
toponym

Learn More Online

About Learning Foreign Languages Online:
www.bbc.co.uk/languages

About Maps of Dialect Differences in
the United States
www4.uwm.edu/FLL/linguistics/dialect/maps.html

About the most recent Pop vs. Soda Map
www.tekstlab.uio.no/cambridge_survey/

About Careers as a Language Professional:
careers.un.org/lbw/home.aspx?viewtype=LE
ec.europa.eu/dgs/translation/translating/index_en.htm

Watch It Online

About the Loss of Native Languages in Alaska
www.learner.org/resources/series85.html#program_descriptions
click on Video On Demand for "Alaska: The Last Frontier?"

About the Impact of Technology on Language Development:
www.pbs.org/wgbh/pages/frontline/digitalnation/learning/literacy/hey-prof-i-just-txtd-u-my-paper.html

RELIGION

Peace Walls

I felt uneasy as I stood in the Clonnard Martyrs Memorial Garden. Built to honor Catholics who had fallen during the Troubles between Catholics and Protestants, the gardens were more of a brick patio with brick walls than a garden. A 40-foot-tall peace wall towered behind the gardens, and next to the garden stretching along the wall was a row of houses settled by Catholics. On the other side of the peace wall was the Protestant Shankhill neighborhood, where I had been 10 minutes earlier. My sense of unease came from a sound that I typically find comforting, children laughing.

I looked over the brick wall of the memorial garden to see the children. It was a scene I could see in my backyard on a summer evening, kids jumping on a trampoline (Fig. 7.1), but I did not see trees, grass, swing sets, barbeques, or the other familiarities of backyards in my neighborhood. The peace wall loomed behind the trampoline, and on the other side was the child's home. The back side of his house was shielded by a rather large cage. I looked up at the wall again and realized the cage was there to protect the back door and windows from anything being flung over the wall from the Protestant Shankhill neighborhood into the Catholic Falls neighborhood.

© Erin H. Fouberg

■ **Figure 7.1**

Belfast, Northern Ireland. A child jumps on a trampoline in a backyard in the Catholic Falls neighborhood. A 40-foot-tall peace wall stands to the left of the trampoline, dividing this Catholic neighborhood from the Protestant Shankhill neighborhood on the other side.

Built beginning in the 1960s to separate Catholics and Protestants in hopes of suppressing violence, the Belfast peace walls have now stood 20 years longer than the Berlin Wall (1961–1989). This wall, which runs more than 3 miles (5 km) through the city, is the largest of the city's

99 peace walls. The peace wall between Shankhill and Falls has five gates that are open between about 7 A.M. and 7 P.M., Monday through Friday. Otherwise, you have to go all of the way around the wall to get from one neighborhood to the next.

The peace walls are quite visible, but the residents of this area of Belfast also carry invisible lines in their minds of routes that are safe and paths that are not. Geographer Frederick Boal established through extensive field research in 1969 that Protestants and Catholics in Belfast chose to separate themselves in their rounds of daily activity, their **activity spaces**. Boal found that members of each group traveled longer distances to shop in grocery stores tagged as their respective religion, walked further to catch a bus in a neighborhood belonging to their own religion, gave their neighborhood different toponyms, read different newspapers, and cheered for different football (soccer) teams.

In the journal *Children's Geographies*, Madeleine Leonard (2006) studied how teens in Belfast negotiate living in **interface areas** where Catholic and Protestant neighborhoods meet and where violence and trauma occurred. She found that teens identify with the Protestant football team (the Rangers) or the Catholic football team (the Celtics), but they consciously choose not to wear their team's gear when they go into shared spaces such as leisure areas in the city. Likewise, teens who go into a park or shared public space report that they do not call each other by name if their names are commonly Catholic (like Paddy) or Protestant (like Billy).

Children growing up in religious interface areas around the world experience childhood in distinct ways, learning to choose when to share identities, what routes are safe, which door to use to enter a movie theater, which grocery store to shop, and which football team to support. Particularly violent religious interface areas like Palestine/Israel, Iraq, and Sudan appear on the news, but thousands of religious interface areas around the world, like Belfast, receive less global media attention while being a very real part of everyday life for the children, teens, and adults who live there.

In this chapter we study the origins, diffusions, and transformations of the world's great religions, their regional patterns, and their cultural landscapes. As we will find, religion can unite and divide, flourish and stagnate, surge and fade. Understanding the changing map of world religions and the role of religion in culture is essential to appreciating human geography.

Key Questions FOR CHAPTER 7

1. What is religion, and what role does it play in culture?
2. Where did the world's major religions originate, and how do religions diffuse?
3. How is religion seen in the cultural landscape?
4. What role does religion play in political conflicts?

WHAT IS RELIGION, AND WHAT ROLE DOES IT PLAY IN CULTURE?

Religion and language lie at the foundation of culture: Both confer and reflect identity. Like languages, religions are constantly changing. Although religious leaders and bureaucracies sometimes attempt to slow the pace of change, religions nevertheless change over time.

Religions diffuse through both contagious and hierarchical forms of expansion diffusion, as well as through relocation diffusion. In any of these cases, leaders or followers of a religion interact with people who do not espouse the religion, and the interactions sometimes lead to conversion. Spatial interaction occurs through migration, missionary efforts, and even conquest. Along these paths, major religions of the world have diffused.

FIELD NOTE

"Each religion approaches the disposition of the deceased in its own way, and cultural landscapes reflect religious traditions. In largely Christian, Western regions, the deceased are buried in cemeteries. The Hindu faith, which is predominantly found in India, requires cremation of the deceased. When the British colonized both India and Kenya in the late nineteenth and early twentieth centuries, they brought Indians to Kenya as 'bonded laborers' to lay the Kenya-Uganda railroad (Bhowmick 2008). The number of Indians in Kenya peaked at 175,000 in 1962 and is approximately 100,000 today, large enough to need a crematorium, the equivalent of a Hindu funeral home."

© H. J. de Blij

■ **Figure 7.2**
Mombasa, Kenya.

The cultural landscape is marked by religion—most obviously by church, synagogues, temples, and mosques, cemeteries and shrines, statues and symbols (Fig. 7.2). Other more subtle markers of religion dot the landscape as well. The presence or absence of stores selling alcohol or of signs depicting the human form in particular ways reflects prevailing religious views. Religion is also proclaimed in modes of dress (veils, turbans) and personal habits (beards, ritual scars). The outward display of religious beliefs often reveals the inward structure of a religion. For example, in the Islamic Republic of Pakistan, in 1991, the government proclaimed that possessing a beard would be a condition for the appointment of judges. The beard requirement was an outward display of religion, and it also shows the inward structure of Islam in Pakistan, where women have not been in a place of judicial power.

Religion is an extraordinarily difficult concept to define. Geographers Robert Stoddard and Carolyn Prorak define religion as "a system of beliefs and practices that attempts to order life in terms of culturally perceived ultimate priorities" (2004). They explain that the idea of "perceived ultimate priorities" is often expressed in terms of *should*: People explain and justify how they and others should behave based on their religious beliefs. From eating habits to dress codes, religions set standards for how adherents should behave (Fig. 7.3). "Shouldness" goes beyond religion to other belief systems, but in this chapter we focus on formal religions, their distribution, and their role in making and shaping places and cultures. The idea that a "good" life has rewards and that "bad" behavior risks punishment has an enormous influence on cultures, on how people behave, and on how people perceive and evaluate the behavior of others.

Religion is also seen in places and practices that do not involve large buildings or expansive cemeteries. We can see religion in the worship of the souls of ancestors who are thought to inhabit natural objects such as mountains, animals, or trees; in the belief that a certain living person possesses special abilities granted by a supernatural power; and in the belief in a deity or deities, as in the great world religions. In some places, societies are so infused with religion that religious tradition strongly influences behaviors during waking hours through ritual and practice and even during periods of sleep in prescribing what direction a person should face when sleeping.

Across the multitude of religions, some practices such as ritual and prayer are common. Rituals may mark important events in people's lives: birth and death, attainment of adulthood, or marriage. Rituals are typically expressed at regular intervals in a routine manner, as is done on certain days in the Christian and Jewish worlds, certain times of the day in the Muslim world, or according to certain astronomical events in the Jewish, Hindu, Muslim, and Christian worlds. A common ritual is prayer, whether at mealtime, at sunrise and sundown, at night upon retiring, or in the morning when arising (Fig. 7.4).

Although religious beliefs and prescriptions influence many societies, in other places, religion, at least in its organized form, has become less significant in the lives of people. **Secularism** is the indifference to or rejection of formal religion. The most secular countries in the world today are in Europe. A 2009 Pew survey asked people in 56 countries how important religion is in their lives. Among the wealthiest countries surveyed, the United States stood out as the highest, with 55 percent of Americans surveyed saying religion is very important in

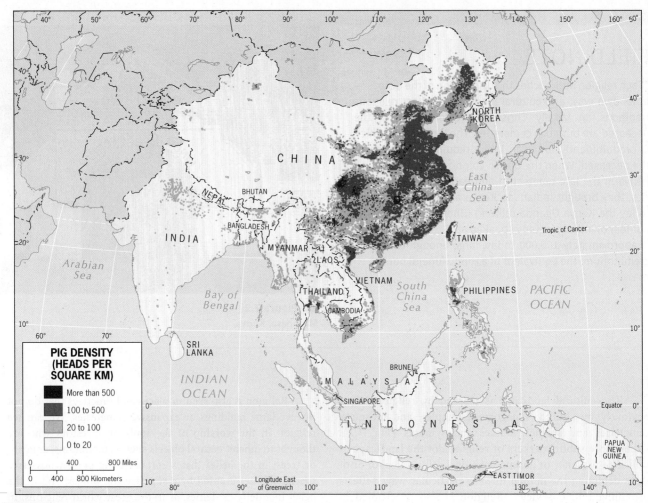

Figure 7.3

Pork Production and Religious Prohibitions.   Pork is the most common meat source in China, but pork production is slim to none in predominantly Muslim countries, including Bangladesh and Indonesia and in the predominantly Hindu country of India, where pork consumption is prohibited for religious reasons.   *Source: Geographical Trends in Livestock Densities and Nutrient Balances, 2011. http://pigtrop.cirad.fr*

their lives. Only 13 percent of people surveyed in France, 19 percent in Great Britain, and 7 percent in the Czech Republic agreed that religion is very important in their lives. Regionally, survey respondents in Subsaharan Africa, South Asia, Southwest Asia, and South America more strongly agreed that religion is very important in their lives: 98 percent in Senegal, 97 percent in Bangladesh, 95 percent in Indonesia, and 78 percent in Brazil.

Regardless of Europe's present-day secularism, religion certainly has had a critical role in the history of Europe. During the Middle Ages and into the colonial period, the Christian church was a dominant force politically, economically and culturally in Europe. Because Christianity was a major part of life in Europe for

Figure 7.4

New York, United States.   A Muslim man takes a break from serving food off a vendor cart to pray on a busy Manhattan street.

centuries, much of the region's art, architecture, history, customs, and cultural norms derive from Christian beliefs and teachings. Even in a secular society, and regardless of your religious beliefs, what you eat, when you work, when you shop, and what you are allowed to do are influenced by religion.

Organized religions have had a powerful effect on human societies. Religion has been a major force in combating social ills, sustaining the poor, promoting the arts, educating the deprived, and advancing medical knowledge. However, religion has also blocked scientific study, encouraged the oppression of dissidents, supported colonialism and exploitation, and condemned women to an inferior status in many societies. Religion is, if nothing else, one of the most complex and often controversial aspects of the human condition.

Compare and contrast the maps of world religions and world language families (Chapter 6). Then consider the map of major global immigration movements (Chapter 3) and how migration has helped religions and languages diffuse through relocation diffusion. Describe how migration, religion, and language affect and change one another to shape cultures.

WHERE DID THE MAJOR RELIGIONS OF THE WORLD ORIGINATE, AND HOW DO RELIGIONS DIFFUSE?

Despite the wide variety of religions found around the world, they are commonly classified into three categories based on their approaches to the concept of divinity.

Adherents of **monotheistic religions** worship a single deity, a God ('Allah' in Arabic). Believers in **polytheistic religions** worship more than one deity, even thousands. **Animistic religions** are centered on the belief that inanimate objects, such as mountains, boulders, rivers, and trees, possess spirits and should therefore be revered. Throughout much of human history, virtually all religions were either animistic, polytheistic, or both. Somewhere around 3500 years ago, however, a monotheistic religion developed in Southwest Asia called Zoroastrianism. Some believe that the monotheism of late Judaism, Christianity, and Islam can be traced to Zoroastrian influences. Others believe that Judaism itself was the first monotheistic religion. Whichever the case, the eventual diffusion of Christianity and Islam spread monotheistic ideas throughout much of the world and marked a major theological shift away from the long dominance of polytheistic and animist beliefs in most places. The transformation from polytheistic to monotheistic religions happened quite rapidly in Subsaharan Africa. In 1900, neither Islam nor Christianity had many followers in Subsaharan Africa. By 2012, the number of Muslims in Subsaharan Africa had grown from 11 million to 248 million, and the number of Christians had grown from 7 million to 517 million.

By 500 BCE, four major hearths of religion and philosophy had developed in the world (Fig. 7.5). From a hearth in South Asia, along the Indus River Valley, came Hinduism; from a hearth on the eastern Mediterranean came Judaism; from a hearth on the Huang He (Yellow River) Valley in China came Chinese philosophies; and from the northern shores of the Mediterranean Sea came Greek philosophy. These early-established religions and philosophies profoundly impacted other religions, as the arrows in Figure 7.5 demonstrate. Philosophies and religions diffused from their hearths, affecting one another and influencing the ways founders established newer religions. The two religions with the greatest number of

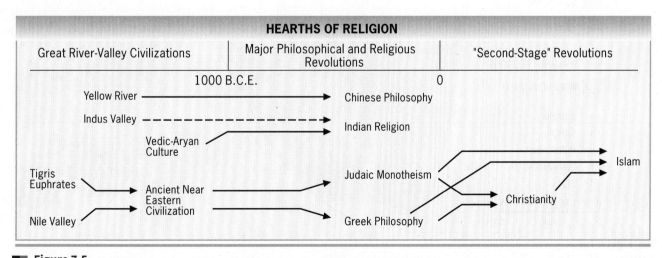

■ Figure 7.5
Hearths of Major World Religions. © *Adapted with permission from:* Albert M. Craig, William M. Graham, Donald Kagan, Stephen Ozment, and Frank M. Turner. *The Heritage of World Civilizations*, 7th ed., New York: Prentice Hall, 2006.

adherents in the world today, Christianity and Islam, were both influenced by Judaism and Greek philosophy.

The World Map of Religions Today

The map in Figure 7.6 provides a global overview of the distribution of the world's major religions. Any map of world religions is a generalization, and caution must be used when making observations from the map. First, the shadings on the map show the major religion in an area, thereby masking minority religions, many of which have a significant number of followers. India, for example, is depicted as a Hindu region (except in the northwest), but other religions, including Islam and Sikhism, attract millions of adherents in India. Of the 1.2 billion people in India, 161 million are Muslims,

which makes India the third largest Muslim country in the world behind Indonesia and Pakistan.

Second, some of the regions shown as belonging to a particular religion are places where faiths have penetrated relatively recently and where traditional religious ideas influence the practice of the dominant faith. Many Christian and Muslim Africans, for example, continue to believe in traditional spirits even as they profess a belief in a universalizing religion. A 2010 Pew Research survey of 25,000 people in 19 African countries found that "Large numbers of Africans actively participate in Christianity or Islam yet also believe in witchcraft, evil spirits, sacrifices to ancestors, traditional religious healers, reincarnation and other elements of traditional African religions." The survey found that 25 percent of Christian Africans and 30 percent of Muslim Africans they interviewed believed in the protective

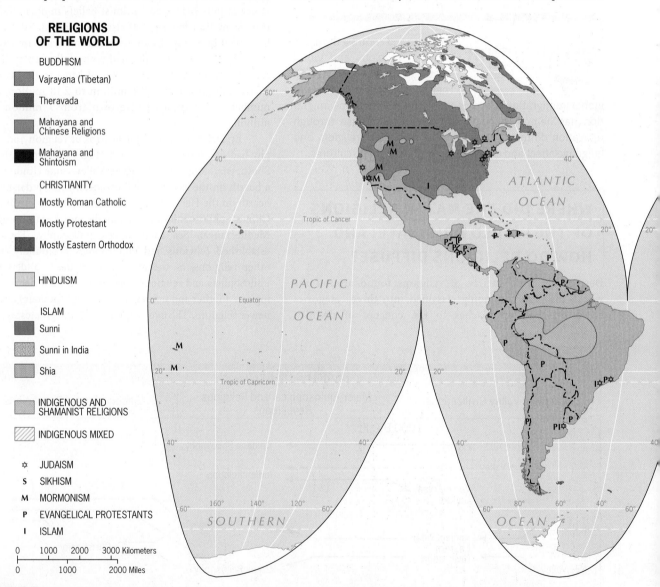

■ **Figure 7.6**

Religions of the World. *Data from*: Several sources, including Hammond, Inc., 1977; H. J. de Blij, P. O. Muller, and A. Winkler Prins, *The World Today*, 4e, 2008; State Department Religious Freedom Report, CIA World Factbook, Pew Forum on Religion and Public Life, and author observations.   © E. H. Fouberg, A. B. Murphy, H. J. de Blij, and John Wiley & Sons, Inc.

power of sacrifices to spirits or ancestors. The country with the highest percentage of respondents who held this belief was Tanzania with 60 percent, and the lowest was Rwanda with 5 percent.

In Cameroon, 42 percent of those surveyed believed in the protective power of sacrifices to spirits or ancestors. For example, the Bamileke tribe in Cameroon lives in an area colonized by the French, who brought Catholicism to the region. The Bamileke are largely Christian today, but they also continue to practice aspects of their traditional animist religion. Ancestors are still very important in the lives of the Bamileke; many believe ancestors decide everything for them. It is common practice to take the skull of a deceased male member of the tribe and place it in the basement of the home of the family's oldest living male. Birth practices also reflect traditional religious practices. The Bamileke bury the

umbilical cord in the ground outside their home so that the baby remembers where he or she came from. Members of the Bamileke tribe also commonly have two weddings: one in the church and one traditional.

A final limitation of Figure 7.6 is that it does not reflect the rise in secularism in the world, especially in Europe. In a number of areas, many people have moved away from organized religion entirely. Thus, France appears on the map as a Roman Catholic country, yet a large proportion of people in France profess adherence to no particular faith.

Despite the limitations of the map of world religions, it illustrates how far Christian religions have diffused (2.2 billion adherents worldwide), the extent of the diffusion of Islam (1.6 billion), the connection between Hinduism (950 million adherents) and one of the world's major population concentrations, and the continued importance of Buddhism

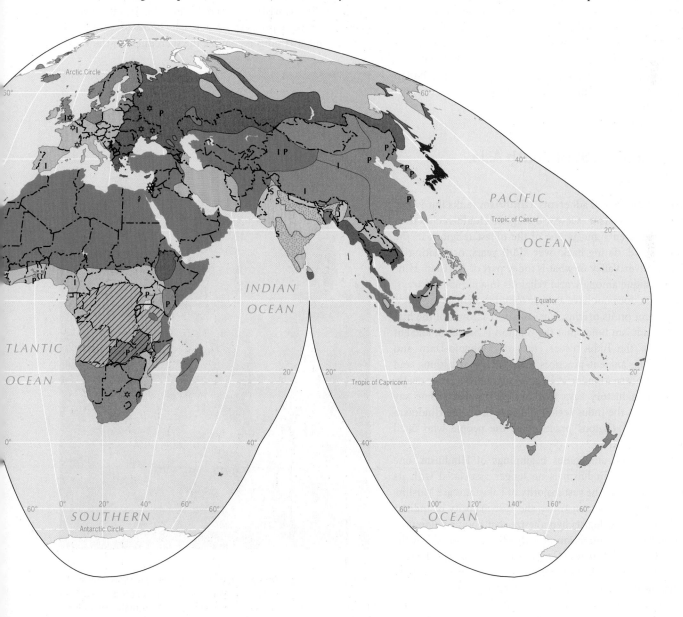

(347 million followers) in parts of Asia. Many factors help explain the distributions shown on the map, but each of the widespread religions shares one characteristic in common: They are all universalizing religions. **Universalizing religions** actively seek converts because they view themselves as offering belief systems of universal appropriateness and appeal. Christianity, Islam, and Buddhism all fall within this category, and their universalizing character helps explain their widespread distribution.

Universalizing religions are relatively few in number and of recent origin. Throughout human history, a greater number of religions have not actively sought converts. Rather, a given religion has been practiced by one particular culture or ethnic group. In an **ethnic religion**, adherents are born into the faith and converts are not actively sought. Ethnic religions (405 million followers) tend to be spatially concentrated—as is the case with traditional religions, which are found primarily in small areas of Asia, the Pacific, Africa, and South America. The principal exception is Judaism (14 million adherents), an ethnic religion whose adherents are widely scattered through Southwest Asia, Europe, North America, and South America as a result of forced and voluntary migrations.

From the Hearth of South Asia

HINDUISM

In terms of number of adherents, **Hinduism** ranks third after Christianity and Islam as a world religion. Hinduism has over 1 billion adherents and is one of the oldest religions in the modern world, dating back over 4000 years, originating in the Indus River Valley of what is today part of Pakistan. Hinduism is unique among world religions in a number of ways. The religion does not have a single founder, a single theology, or agreement on its origins. The common account of the history of Hinduism holds that the religion is based on ancient practices in the Indus River cities of Mohenjo-Daro and Harappa. The ancient practices included ritual bathing and belief in reincarnation, or at least a long journey after death. The common history says that Aryans invaded (some say migrated into) the Indus region and gave the name Hinduism to the diverse religious practices of the people who lived along the Indus River.

Despite the ambiguous beginnings of Hinduism, one thing is certain: Hinduism is no longer associated with its hearth in Pakistan. The vast majority of Pakistanis are Muslim, and as Figure 7.6 demonstrates, the vast majority of Indians are Hindu. Archaeologists hypothesize that flooding along the Indus spurred the migration of early Hindus eastward to the Ganges River. The Ganges (*Ganga*, as Indians call it) is Hinduism's sacred river. Hindus regard its ceaseless flow and spiritual healing power as earthly manifestations of the Almighty.

Just as there is no consensus on Hinduism's origins, there is a lack of agreement on defining Hinduism relative to other major world religions. Some define Hinduism as a polytheistic religion because of the presence of many gods. However, many Hindus define their religion as monotheistic. The one god is Brahman (the universal soul), and the other gods in the religion are various expressions of Brahman. Western academics define Hinduism today as an ethnic religion because Hindus do not actively seek converts. At the same time, historical evidence shows Hindus migrating into Southeast Asia and diffusing their religion, as a universalizing religion would, before the diffusion of Buddhism and Islam into Southeast Asia (Fig. 7.7). Although Hinduism is now more of an ethnic religion, the religion has millions of adherents in the populous region of South Asia, extending beyond India to Bangladesh, Myanmar, Sri Lanka, and Nepal.

The Hindu religion is not centrally organized. The religion does not have an administrative or bureaucratic structure like Christianity and Islam. The Hindu religion does not have a prophet or a single book of scriptures, although most Hindus recognize the sacredness of the *Vedas*,

© Alexander B. Murphy

■ **Figure 7.7**

Angkor Wat, Cambodia. The extensive walled structure at the temple complex in Angkor Wat marks the earliest period of Hinduism's diffusion into Southeast Asia. Eventually, Buddhism replaced Hinduism in Cambodia, and many Hindu temples such as this one were abandoned.

four ancient collections of texts that have particular sacred status.

Hinduism is a conglomeration of beliefs characterized by a great diversity of institutional forms and practices. The fundamental doctrine is *karma*, which has to do with the transferability of the soul. According to Hindu doctrine, all beings have souls and are arranged in a hierarchy. The ideal is to move upward in the hierarchy and then escape from the eternal cycle of *reincarnation* through union with Brahman (the universal soul). A soul moves upward or downward according to the individual's behavior in the present life. Good deeds and adherence to the faith lead to a higher level in the next life, whereas bad behavior leads to demotion to a lower level. All souls, those of animals as well as humans, participate in this process. The principle of reincarnation is a cornerstone of Hinduism.

Hinduism's doctrines are closely bound to Indian society's caste system, for castes themselves are steps on the universal ladder. The **caste system** locks people into particular social classes and imposes many restrictions, especially in the lowest of the castes and in those considered beneath the caste system, Dalits. Until a generation ago, Dalits could not enter temples, were excluded from certain schools, and were restricted to performing the most unpleasant tasks. The coming of other religions to India, the effects of modernization during the colonial period, the work of Mahatma Gandhi, and affirmative action policies helped loosen the social barriers of the caste system. Today the Indian government's affirmative action policies reserve seats in universities and jobs in government for scheduled castes, scheduled tribes, and Dalits.

DIFFUSION OF HINDUISM

Hinduism evolved in what is today Pakistan. From there, Hinduism migrated to the Ganges River and diffused throughout South Asia and into Southeast Asia before the advent of Christianity. Hinduism first attached itself to traditional faiths and then slowly replaced them. Later, when Islam and Christianity appeared and were actively spread in Hindu areas, Hindu thinkers attempted to integrate certain new teachings into their own religion. For example, elements of the Sermon on the Mount (Jesus' sermon in which he described God's love for the poor and the peacemakers) now form part of Hindu preaching, and Christian beliefs contributed to the weakening of caste barriers. In other instances, the confrontation between Hinduism and other faiths led to the emergence of a **syncretic** or compromise religion. Islam stimulated the rise of Sikhism, whose followers disapproved of the worship of idols and disliked the caste system but retained the concepts of reincarnation and karma. Given its current character as an ethnic religion, it is not surprising that Hinduism's geographical extent is relatively small. Throughout most of Southeast Asia, Buddhism and Islam overtook the places where Hinduism had diffused during its universalizing period. In overwhelmingly Muslim Indonesia,

the island of Bali remains a Hindu outpost. Bali became a refuge for Hindu holy men, nobles, and intellectuals during the sixteenth century (Fig. 7.8), when Islam engulfed neighboring Java, which now retains only architectural remnants of its Hindu age. Since then, the Balinese have developed a unique faith, still based on Hindu principles but mixed with elements of Buddhism, animism, and ancestor worship. Religion plays an extremely important role in Bali. Temples and shrines dominate the cultural landscape, and participation in worship, festivals, and other ceremonies of the island's unique religion is almost universal. Religion is so much at the heart of Balinese culture that it is sometimes described as a celebration of life.

Outside South Asia and Bali, Hinduism's presence is relatively minor. Over the last two centuries, Hinduism has diffused to small parts of the world through migration. During the British colonial era, the British transported hundreds

© Alexander B. Murphy

■ **Figure 7.8**
Bali, Indonesia.   The town of Ubud in central Bali is dotted with Hindu temples. Hinduism arrived in Southeast Asia some 2000 years ago. It was gradually replaced by Buddhism, and then Islam came to the southern parts of the region. Bali became a refuge for believers in Hinduism; it is the one place in Indonesia where Hinduism continues to dominate today.

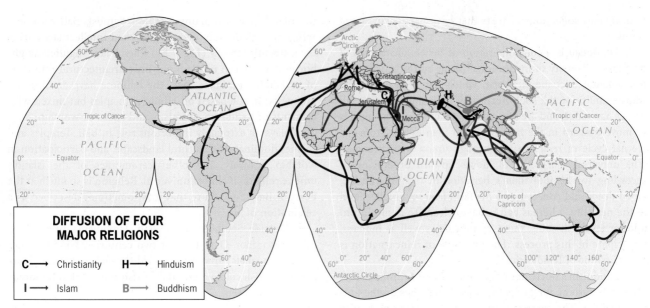

■ Figure 7.9

Diffusion of Four Major World Religions.   The hearths and major routes of diffusion are shown on this map. It does not show smaller diffusion streams: Islam and Buddhism, for example, are gaining strength in North America, although their numbers are still comparatively small.   © E. H. Fouberg, A. B. Murphy, and H. J. de Blij, John Wiley & Sons, Inc.

of thousands of Hindu adherents as bonded laborers from India to their other colonies in East and South Africa, the Caribbean, northern South America, and the Pacific Islands (see Fig. 7.2). Because Hinduism is not a universalizing religion today, the relocation diffusion produced pockets rather than regions of Hinduism.

BUDDHISM

Buddhism splintered from Hinduism over 2500 years ago. Buddhism and several other religions appeared in India as a reaction to questions about Hinduism's teachings at the time. Reformers questioned Hinduism's strict social hierarchy that protected the privileged and kept millions in poverty. Prince Siddhartha, who was heir to a wealthy kingdom in what is now Nepal, founded Buddhism. Siddhartha was profoundly shaken by the misery he saw around him, which contrasted sharply with the splendor and wealth in which he had been raised. Siddhartha came to be known as Buddha, the enlightened one. He may have been the first prominent Indian religious leader to speak out against Hinduism's caste system. Salvation, he preached, could be attained by anyone, no matter what his or her caste. Enlightenment would come through knowledge, especially self-knowledge; elimination of greed, craving, and desire; complete honesty; and never hurting another person or animal.

After Buddha's death in the fifth century BCE at the age of 80, the faith grew rather slowly until the middle of the third century BCE, when the Emperor Asoka became a convert. Asoka was the leader of a large and powerful Indian empire that extended from the Punjab to Bengal and from the Himalayan foothills to Mysore. He not only set out to

rule his country in accordance with the teachings of Buddha; but also sent missionaries to carry Buddha's teachings to distant peoples (Fig. 7.9). Buddhism spread as far south as Sri Lanka and later advanced westward toward the Mediterranean, north into Tibet, and east into China, Korea, Japan, Vietnam, and Indonesia, over a span of about ten centuries (Fig. 7.8). Although Buddhism diffused to distant lands, it began to decline in its region of origin. During Asoka's rule there may have been more Buddhists than Hindu adherents in India, but after that period Hinduism gained followers in India. Today Buddhism is practiced by relatively few in India, but it thrives in Sri Lanka, Southeast Asia, Nepal, Tibet, and Korea. Along with other faiths, Buddhism is part of Japanese culture.

Like Christianity and Islam, Buddhism changed as it grew and diffused, and now the religion is strongly regional with three major forms. Buddhism's various branches have an estimated 488 million adherents, with Mahayana, Theravada, and Vajrayana (Tibetan) Buddhism claiming the most adherents. Theravada Buddhism translates as "the way of the elders." The hearth of Theravada Buddhism was established first, and it was the first branch of Buddhism to diffuse, spreading to Sri Lanka, Myanmar (Burma), Thailand, Laos, and Cambodia. Theravada Buddhism holds that salvation is a personal matter, achieved through good behavior and religious activities, including periods of service as a monk or nun. Theravada Buddhists tie their teachings back to the historical Buddha and contend that their beliefs are the "true Buddhism."

Mahayana Buddhism was the second form of Buddhism established in northern India, and it diffused into China, Vietnam, Korea, and Japan. Mahayana Buddhism translates as

■ Figure 7.10

Kyoto, Japan. In Japan, both Buddhism and Shintoism make their marks on the cultural landscape. This Shinto shrine, with its orange trim and olive-green glazed tiles, is visible after passing under a torii—a gateway usually formed by two wooden posts topped by two horizontal beams turned up at their ends—which signals that you have left the secular and entered the sacred world.

"the greater vehicle," and the idea is that more people can achieve enlightenment through its teachings than through the strict teachings of Theravada Buddhism. The Buddha is regarded as a divine savior, and other great Buddhists are regarded as bodhisattvas (those who have reached enlightenment) and are worshipped along with the Buddha. Mahayana Buddhists do not serve as monks, but they spend much time in personal meditation and worship, believing that achieving enlightenment helps all beings on Earth. Mahayana Buddhism was influenced by Chinese and Japanese religions, including Taoism and Shintoism.

The third largest branch of Buddhism is Vajrayana (Tibetan), which emphasizes the role of the guru or lama as religious and political leader. Vajrayana Buddhism was the last branch to be established, diffusing north from India into Tibet and Mongolia. Gurus in Vajrayana Buddhism use mantras, tantras, and meditation to help followers achieve enlightenment faster than the bodhisattva approach in Mahayana Buddhism, which can take several lifetimes.

Buddhism has become a global religion over the last two centuries, diffusing to many areas of the world, but not without conflict in its wake. Militant regimes have attacked the religion in Cambodia, Laos, and Vietnam. In Thailand, Buddhism has been under pressure owing to rising political tensions. At the same time, Buddhism has gained adherents in the Western world.

SHINTOISM

Buddhism is mixed with a local religion in Japan, where **Shintoism** is found. This ethnic religion, which is related to

Buddhism, focuses particularly on nature and ancestor worship (Fig. 7.10). The Japanese emperor made Shintoism the state religion of Japan in the nineteenth century, giving himself the status of divine-right monarch. At the end of World War II, Japan separated Shintoism from the emperor, taking away the state sanctioning of the religion. At the same time, the role of the emperor in Japan was diminished and given a ceremonial status. The number of Shinto adherents in Japan is somewhere between 105 and 118 million, depending on the source. The majority of Japanese observe both Buddhism and Shintoism.

From the Hearth of the Huang He River Valley

TAOISM

While the Buddha's teachings were gaining converts in India, a religious revolution of another kind was taking place in China. Two major schools of Chinese philosophy, Taoism and Confucianism, were forming. The beginnings of **Taoism** are unclear, but scholars trace the religion to an older contemporary of Confucius, Lao-Tsu, who published a volume titled *Tao-te-ching*, or "Book of the Way." In his teachings, Lao-Tsu focused on the proper form of political rule and on the oneness of humanity and nature: People, he said, should learn to live in harmony with nature. This idea gave rise to the concept of **Feng Shui**—the art and science of organizing living spaces in order to channel the life forces that exist in nature in favorable ways. According to tradition, nothing should be done to nature without consulting *geomancers*, people who know the desires of the powerful spirits of ancestors, dragons, tigers, and other beings that occupy the natural world and can give advice on how to order things according to Feng Shui.

Among the Taoist virtues are simplicity and spontaneity, tenderness, and tranquility. Competition, possession, and even the pursuit of knowledge are to be avoided. War, punishment, taxation, and ceremonial ostentation are viewed as evils. The best government, according to Lao-Tsu, is the least government. Thousands of people began to follow Taoism. Taoist temples include statues of deities who teach specific lessons, along with the yin-yang symbol to remind followers of the duality of life, and swords to remind adherents that struggle is part of life.

CONFUCIANISM

Confucius lived from 551 to 479 BCE, and his followers constructed a blueprint for Chinese civilization in almost every field, including philosophy, government, and education. In religion, Confucius addressed the traditional Chinese tenets that included belief in heaven and the existence of the soul, ancestor worship, sacrificial rites, and shamanism. He held that the real meaning of life lay in the present, not in some future abstract existence, and that service to one's fellow humans should supersede service to spirits.

Confucianism is mainly a philosophy of life, and like Taoism, it had great and lasting impacts on Chinese life. Appalled at the suffering of ordinary people at the hands of feudal lords, Confucius urged the poor to assert themselves. He was not a prophet who dealt in promises of heaven and threats of hell. He denied the divine ancestry of China's aristocratic rulers, educated the landless and the weak, disliked supernatural mysticism, and argued that human virtues and abilities, not heritage, should determine a person's position and responsibilities in society.

After his death in 479 BCE, Confucius came to be revered as a spiritual leader, and his teachings diffused widely throughout East and Southeast Asia. Followers built temples in his honor all over China. From his writings and sayings emerged the Confucian Classics, a set of 13 texts that were the focus of education in China for 2000 years. Over the centuries, Confucianism (with its Taoist and Buddhist ingredients) became China's state ethic, although the Chinese emperor modified Confucian ideals over time. For example, one emperor made worship of and obedience to the emperor part of Confucianism. In government, law, literature, religion, morality, and many other ways, the Confucian Classics have been the guide for Chinese civilization.

DIFFUSION OF CHINESE RELIGIONS

Confucianism diffused early into the Korean Peninsula, Japan, and Southeast Asia, where it has long influenced the practice of Buddhism. More recently, Chinese immigrants expanded the influence of the Chinese religions in parts of Southeast Asia and helped to introduce their principles into societies ranging from Europe to North America.

The diffusion of Chinese religions even within China has been tempered by the Chinese government's efforts to suppress religion in the country. The communist government that took control of China in 1949 attempted to ban religion, in this case Confucianism, from public practice. But after guiding all aspects of Chinese education, culture, and society for 2000 years, Confucianism did not fade easily from the Chinese consciousness.

Geomancy is still a powerful force in China today, even in urban areas with large populations. Geographer Elizabeth Teather (1999) studied the rise of cremation and columbaria (resting places for ashes) in Hong Kong, investigating the impact Feng Shui has had on the structures and the continued influence of Chinese religious beliefs on burial practices in the densely populated city of Hong Kong. Traditional Chinese beliefs favor a coffin and burial plot aligned with Feng Shui teachings. However, with the growth of China's population, the government has strongly encouraged cremation over the past few decades. The availability of burial plots in cities like Hong Kong is quite low, and the costs of burial plots have risen in turn.

Teather explains that although cremation is on the rise in Hong Kong, traditional Chinese beliefs are dictating the final resting places of ashes. Most Chinese people, she states, have a "cultural need to keep ancestral remains appropriately stored and in a single place." In North America and Europe, a family often chooses to scatter the ashes of a cremated loved one, but a Chinese family is more likely to keep the ashes together in a single identifiable space so that they can return to visit the ancestor during Gravesweeping Festivals—annual commemorations of ancestors during which people visit and tend the graves of their ancestors. Teather describes how Feng Shui masters are consulted in the building of columbaria and how Feng Shui helps dictate the price placed on the niches for sale in the columbaria, with the lowest prices for the niches near the "grime of the floor."

From the Hearth of the Eastern Mediterranean

JUDAISM

Judaism grew out of the belief system of the Jews, one of several nomadic Semitic tribes living in Southwest Asia about 4000 years ago. The roots of Jewish religious tradition lie in the teachings of Abraham (from Ur), who is credited with uniting his people to worship only one God. According to Jewish teaching, Abraham and God have a covenant in which the Jews agree to worship only one God, and God agrees to protect his chosen people, the Jews.

The history of the Jews is filled with upheaval. Moses led them from Egypt, where they had been enslaved, to Canaan, where an internal conflict developed and the nation split into two branches, Israel and Judah. Israel was subsequently wiped out by enemies, but Judah survived longer, only to be conquered by the Babylonians and the Assyrians. The Jews regrouped to rebuild their headquarters, Jerusalem,

FIELD NOTE

"The Orthodox Jewish community in Long Beach, New York, is large enough that the Dunkin Donuts on Beech Street is kosher. Supervised by a Rabbi, kosher-prepared foods follow strict requirements of what foods can be eaten, what can be eaten together, how animals are slaughtered, and how foods are prepared. In addition to the kosher Dunkin Donuts, another sign of the large Orthodox Jewish community in Long Beach is the Eruv, a line encircling the town that distinguishes private space from public space. The Eruv is not noticeable, as it generally follows utility lines and the boardwalk. But the Eruv creates a private space that allows Orthodox Jews to carry keys, foods, and even babies on the Sabbath."

© Erin H. Fouberg

■ **Figure 7.11**
Long Beach, New York.

but then fell victim to a series of foreign powers. The Romans destroyed their holy city in 70 CE and drove the Jews away, scattering adherents to the faith to Europe and North Africa. Jews retained only a small presence on the eastern shores of the Mediterranean until the late nineteenth century.

Our map shows that, unlike most other ethnic religions, Judaism is not limited to contiguous territories. Rather, Judaism is distributed throughout parts of Southwest Asia and North Africa, Russia, Ukraine, Europe, and parts of North and South America (Fig. 7.6). According to *The Atlas of Religion*, of all the world's 14 million Jews, 40.5 percent live in the United States, 40.2 percent live in Israel, and then in rank order, less than 5 percent live in France, Canada, the United Kingdom, Russia, and Argentina. Judaism is one of the world's most influential religions, although it claims few adherents compared to Christianity, Islam, and Hinduism.

During the nineteenth century, a Reform movement developed with the objective of adjusting Judaism and its practices to current times. However, many feared that this reform would cause a loss of identity and cohesion, and the Orthodox movement sought to retain the old precepts. Orthodox Jews typically are the strictest followers of Jewish dietary laws requiring the consumption of kosher foods (Fig. 7.11). Between the Reform and Orthodox extremes is a sector that is less strictly orthodox but not as liberal as that of the reformers; it is known as the Conservative movement.

These three branches differ significantly in ideas and practices, but Judaism is united by a strong sense of ethnic distinctiveness.

DIFFUSION OF JUDAISM

The scattering of Jews after the Roman destruction of Jerusalem is known as the **diaspora**—a term that now signifies the spatial dispersion of members of any ethnic group. The Jews who went north into Central Europe came to be known as *Ashkenazim*, and the Jews who scattered across North Africa and into the Iberian Peninsula (Spain and Portugal) are called *Sephardim*. For centuries, both the Ashkenazim and the Sephardim were persecuted, denied citizenship, driven into ghettos, and massacred.

In the face of constant threats to their existence, Jews were sustained by extraordinary efforts to maintain a sense of community and faith. The idea of a homeland for the Jewish people, which became popular during the nineteenth century, developed into the ideology of **Zionism**. Zionist ideals are rooted in the belief that Jews should not be absorbed into other societies. The horrors of the Nazi campaign against Jews from the 1930s through World War II, when the Nazis established concentration camps and killed some six million Jews, persuaded many Jews to adopt Zionism. Jews from all over the world concluded that their only hope of survival was to establish a strongly defended homeland on the shores of the eastern Mediterranean. Aided by sympathetic members of the international community, the Zionist goal of a Jewish state became a reality in 1948, when a United Nations resolution carved two states, Israel and Palestine, out of the territory of the eastern Mediterranean.

While adherents to Judaism live across the world, many Jews have moved to Israel since its establishment in 1948. The Israeli government passed the Law of Return in 1950, which recognizes the rights of every Jew to immigrate to Israel. In 2012, over 7000 Jews left the former Soviet Union for Israel, along with over 2000 Jews from the United States and Canada and over 2000 from France and the United Kingdom. Since the fall of communism in the former Soviet Union in 1989, more than one million people have migrated from the former Soviet Union to Israel.

CHRISTIANITY

Christianity can be traced back to the same hearth in the Mediterranean as Judaism, and like Judaism, Christianity stems from a single founder—in this case Jesus. Christian teachings hold that Jesus is the son of God, placed on Earth to forgive people of their sins and to teach people how to live according to God's plan. Christianity split from Judaism, and it, too, is a monotheistic religion. Jesus of Nazareth was born in Bethlehem, and during his lifetime, he traveled through the eastern Mediterranean region preaching, performing miracles, and gaining followers. Christians celebrate Easter as the day Jesus rose from the dead after being crucified three days prior (Good Friday). According to Christian teaching, the crucifixion of Jesus fulfilled an ancient prophecy and changed the fate of Jesus' followers by giving them eternal life.

The first split in Christianity, between Roman Catholicism and the **Eastern Orthodox Church**, developed over a number of centuries. At the end of the third century, the Roman Emperor Diocletian attempted to keep the empire together by dividing it for purposes of government. His divisions left a lasting legacy. When the Roman Empire fell and broke apart, the western region, centered on Rome, disintegrated. The eastern region, with Constantinople (now Istanbul in Turkey) at its heart, continued on, and later became known as the Byzantine Empire (Fig. 7.12). Christianity thrived there and radiated into other areas, including the Balkan Peninsula. This split into west and east at the end of the Roman Empire became a cultural fault line over time. It was formally recognized in 1054 CE when the Roman Catholic Church (centered in Rome) and the Eastern Orthodox Christian Church (centered in Constantinople) separated.

The Eastern Orthodox Church suffered blows when the Ottoman Turks defeated the Serbs in Kosovo in 1389, the Turks took Constantinople in 1453, and the Soviet Union suppressed Eastern Orthodox churches in the twentieth century (Fig. 7.13).

The **Roman Catholic Church** claims the most adherents of all Christian denominations (more than 1 billion). Centered in Rome, Catholic theology teaches the infallibility of the pope in interpreting Jesus' teachings and in formulating ways to navigate through the modern world. The power of the Roman Catholic Church peaked in the Middle Ages, when the Church controlled sources of knowledge and worked in conjunction with monarchs to rule much of western Europe.

During the Middle Ages, Roman Catholic authorities often wielded their power in an autocratic manner and distanced themselves from the masses. The widespread diffusion of the Black Death during the 1300s and the deaths that resulted caused many Europeans to question the role of religion in their lives. The Roman Catholic Church itself also experienced divisions within its hierarchy, as evidenced by the Western Schism during the early 1300s, which at one point resulted in three people claiming to be the pope. Reformers to the Church soon followed. During the fifteenth and sixteenth centuries, John Huss, Martin Luther, John Calvin, and others challenged fundamental teachings of Roman Catholicism and opposed the practices of Church leaders—leading to the Protestant Reformation. The Protestant sects of Christianity compose the third major branch of Christianity. Like Buddhism's challenge to Hinduism, the Protestant Reformation affected Roman Catholicism, which answered some of the challenges to its theology in the Counter-Reformation.

Christianity is the largest and globally the most widely dispersed religion. Christian churches claim more than

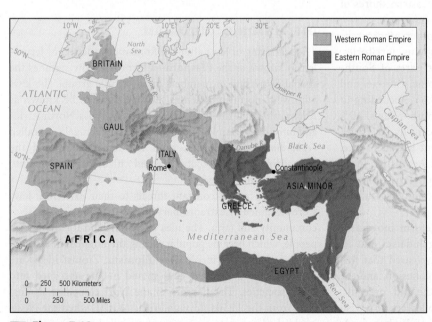

■ Figure 7.12

The Roman Empire, Divided into West and East. This map reflects the split in the empire, with the western empire focusing on Rome and the eastern empire focusing on Constantinople.   © H. J. de Blij, A. B. Murphy, and E. H. Fouberg, and John Wiley & Sons, Inc.

■ Figure 7.13

Religions in the Former Yugoslavia. The split in the Christian Church between Catholic and Eastern Orthodox and the expansion of the Ottoman Turks into southeastern Europe are reflected in the map of ethnic and religious groups in the former Yugoslavia. During much of the twentieth century, seven now independent countries were part of one country, Yugoslavia. After a civil war in the 1990s, they split. Slovenia and Croatia are predominantly Catholic. Serbia, Montenegro, and Macedonia are Eastern Orthodox. Bosnia and Herzegovina is split among Croats, Serbs, and Muslims. Kosovo is Muslim and Eastern Orthodox. Although never physically part of Yugoslavia, Albania, with a predominantly Muslim population, is part of the same religious fault line that cuts through the Balkan Peninsula.

2.2 billion adherents, including some 558 million in Europe and the former Soviet Union; approximately 266 million in North America; about 531 million in Latin America; perhaps 517 million in Africa; and an estimated 286 million in Asia. Christians thus account for 31 percent of the members of the world's major religions. Roman Catholicism, as noted earlier, is the largest segment of Christianity. Figure 7.6 reveals the strength of Roman Catholicism in parts of Europe and North America, and throughout much of Central and South America. Among religious adherents in parts of North America, Australia, New Zealand, and South Africa, Protestant churches prevail. Eastern Orthodox churches have as many as 200 million followers in Europe, Russia and its neighboring states, Africa (where a major cluster exists in Ethiopia), and North America.

DIFFUSION OF CHRISTIANITY

The dissemination of Christianity occurred as a result of expansion combined with relocation diffusion. In western Europe, Christianity declined during the centuries immediately after the fall of the Roman Empire. Then a form of contagious diffusion took place as the religious ideas that had been kept alive in remote places such as coastal Ireland and Scotland spread throughout western Europe. In the case of the Eastern Orthodox faith, contagious diffusion took place from the religion's hearth in Constantinople to the north and northeast. **Protestantism** began in several parts of western Europe and expanded to some degree through contagious diffusion. Much of its spread in Northern and Central Europe, however, was through hierarchical diffusion, as political leaders would convert—sometimes to escape control from

Rome—and then the population would gradually accept the new state religion.

The worldwide diffusion of Christianity occurred during the era of European colonialism beginning in the sixteenth century. Spain invaded and colonized Central and South America, bringing the Catholic faith to those areas. Protestant refugees who were tired of conflict and oppression in Europe came to North America in large numbers. Western European colonists, aided by missionaries, brought Catholicism to Congo, Angola, Mozambique, and the Philippines. The Christian faith today has over 33,000 denominations. Hundreds of these denominations engage in proselytizing (purposeful spreading of religious teachings) around the world, creating an incredibly complex geographical distribution of Christians within the spaces of the world map that are shaded in "Christian" (Fig. 7.6).

The Christian faith has always been characterized by aggressive and persistent proselytism, and Christian missionaries created an almost worldwide network of conversion during the colonial period that endures and continues to expand today (Fig. 7.14).

ISLAM

Like Christianity, **Islam**, the youngest of the major religions, can be traced back to a single founder, in this case, Muhammad, who was born in Mecca in 570 CE. According to Muslim belief, Muhammad received the truth directly from Allah in a series of revelations that began in 612 when the Prophet was about 42 years old. During these revelations, Muhammad spoke the verses of the Qu'ran (Koran), the Islamic holy book. Muhammad admired the monotheism of

SAM PANTHAKY/AFP/Getty Images

■■ **Figure 7.14**
Ahmedabad, India. Catholic nuns from the order of the Missionaries of Charity distribute free rations to impoverished women on the anniversary of the funeral of Mother Teresa, the founder of the religious order. The building in the background is the Shishu Bhavan, an orphanage for discarded babies operated by the same nuns.

Judaism and Christianity; he believed Allah had already revealed himself through other prophets, including Judaism's Abraham and Christianity's Jesus. Muhammad came to be viewed as the one true prophet among Muslims.

After his visions, Muhammad had doubts that he could have been chosen to be a prophet but was convinced by further revelations. He subsequently devoted his life to the fulfillment of the divine commands. In those days the eastern Mediterranean and the Arabian Peninsula were in religious and social disarray, with Christianity and Judaism coexisting with polytheistic religions. Muhammad's opponents began to combat his efforts. The Prophet was forced to flee Mecca, where he had been raised, for Medina, and he continued his work from this new base.

In many ways, the precepts of Islam revised Judaic and Christian beliefs and traditions. The central precept of Islam is that there is but one god, who occasionally reveals himself through the prophets—first and foremost Muhammad, but Abraham and Jesus are regarded as non-divine prophets. Another key precept is that Earthly matters are profane; only Allah is pure. Allah's will is absolute; he is omnipotent and omniscient. Muslims believe that all humans live in a world that was created for their use but only until the final judgment day.

Adherents to Islam are required to observe the "five pillars" of Islam (repeated expressions of the basic creed, frequent prayer, a month of daytime fasting, almsgiving, and, if possible, at least one pilgrimage to Mecca in one's lifetime). The faith dictates behavior in other spheres of life as well. Islam forbids alcohol, smoking, and gambling. In Islamic settlements, the people build mosques to observe the Friday prayer and to serve as social gathering places (Fig. 7.15).

Islam, like all other major religions, is divided—principally between **Sunni** Muslims (the great majority) and the **Shi'ite** or Shiah Muslims (concentrated in Iran). Smaller sects of Islam include Wahhabis, Sufis, Salafists, Alawites, Alevis, and Yazeedis. The religion's main division between Sunni and Shi'ite occurred almost immediately after Muhammad's death, and was caused by a conflict over his succession. Muhammad died in 632 CE, and to some, the rightful heir to the Prophet's caliphate (area of influence) was Muhammad's son-in-law, Ali. Others preferred different

© Alexander B. Murphy

■■ **Figure 7.15**
Kuala Lampur, Malaysia. The sprawling National Mosque serves as a landscape reminder of Islam's dominant religious role in the country.

candidates who were not necessarily related to Muhammad. The ensuing conflict was marked by murder, warfare, and lasting doctrinal disagreements. The Sunni Muslims eventually prevailed, but the Shi'ite Muslims, the followers of Ali, survived in some areas. Then, early in the sixteenth century, an Iranian (Persian) ruling dynasty made Shi'ite Islam the only legitimate faith of that empire—which extended into what is now southern Azerbaijan, southeastern Iraq, and western Afghanistan and Pakistan. This gave the Shi'ite branch unprecedented strength and created the foundations of its modern-day culture region centered on the state of Iran.

Descendants of Muhammad through his daughter Fatimah and his son-in-law Ali are recognized through titles that honor them, including sayyids, syeds or sharifs. They generate respect from both Sunni and Shi'ites. However, Shi'ites place much more emphasis on lineage. Shi'ite veneration of the descendants of Muhammad has contributed to a much more centralized and hierarchical clergy than that in the Sunni world.

In the Shi'ite branch, imams are religious leaders. Shi'ites treated the early Imams as the sole source of true knowledge, and

their successors continue to have great social and political authority. Sunni Islam is less centralized; an imam is simply a religious leader or scholar. Nonetheless, the Sunni branch has given rise to more doctrinaire offshoots of the religion over the centuries.

DIFFUSION OF ISLAM

At the time of his death in 632 CE, Muhammad and his followers had converted kings on the Arabian Peninsula to Islam. The kings then used their armies to spread the faith across the Arabian Peninsula through invasion and conquest. Moving west, in waves of invasion and conquest, Islam diffused throughout North Africa. By the early ninth century, the Muslim world included emirates extending from Egypt to Morocco, a caliphate occupying most of Spain and Portugal, and a unified realm encompassing Arabia, the Middle East, Iran, and most of what is today Pakistan. Ultimately, the Arab Empire extended from Morocco to India and from Turkey to Ethiopia. Through trade, Muslims later spread their faith across the Indian Ocean into Southeast Asia (Fig. 7.16). As Muslim traders settled trading ports in Southeast Asia, they

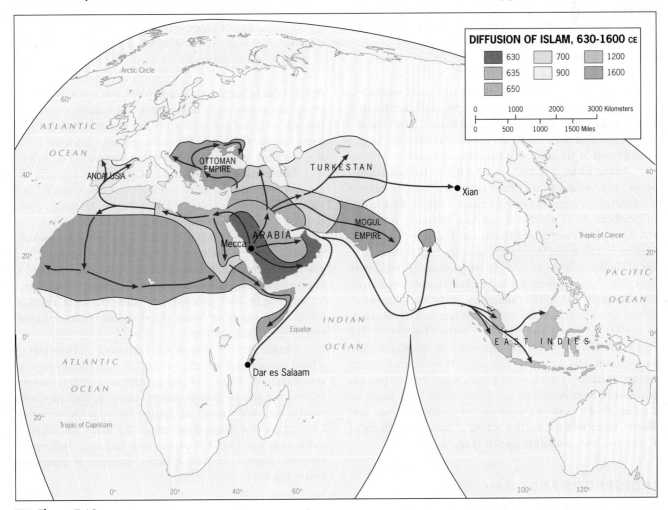

■ **Figure 7.16**
Diffusion of Islam. The map shows the diffusion of Islam from 600 CE to 1600 CE. The hearth of Islam is the dark brown area on the map where Islam was established by 630. By 650, Islam diffused through the areas in tan and in orange. As of 700, Islam diffuses through the pink region of the map. By 900, Islam reached the area in light green in Spain, North Africa, and Central Asia. By 1200, Islam reached Indonesia through trade. Islam diffused into Southeast Europe, South Asia, and North Africa by 1600. © H. J. de Blij, P. O. Muller, and John Wiley & Sons, Inc.

© Alexander B. Murphy

■ **Figure 7.17**
London, England.   This mosque in East London serves the United Kingdom's largest Muslim community. It attests to the scale of Islamic migration to the United Kingdom since World War II. Global religions are not grouped into neat geographical spaces; they are now found side by side all over the world.

established new secondary hearths of Islam and worked to diffuse the religion contagiously from the secondary hearths. Recent diffusion of Islam into Europe (beyond Spain and the Balkan Peninsula), South Africa, and the Americas has largely been a result of migration—of relocation diffusion.

Today, Islam, with more than 1.6 billion followers, ranks second to Christianity in global number of adherents. Islam is the fastest growing of the world's major religions, dominating in Northern Africa and Southwest Asia, extending into Central Asia, the former Soviet Union and China, and including clusters in Indonesia, Bangladesh, and southern Mindanao in the Philippines. Islam is strongly represented in India, with over 161 million adherents, and in Subsaharan Africa, with approximately 248 million adherents. Islam has followers in Bosnia and Albania and has substantial numbers of adherents in the United States and western Europe (Fig. 7.17). The largest Muslim country is actually outside of the Middle East, in Southeast Asia. Indonesia has over 209 million adherents. In fact, of Islam's 1.6 billion followers, more than 80 percent live outside Southwest Asia and North Africa (Pew Research Center 2012). And not everyone in Southwest Asia and North Africa is Muslim. The region is home to millions of Christians, Jews, and other smaller religious sects.

INDIGENOUS AND SHAMANIST

Finally, Figure 7.6 identifies large areas in Africa and several other parts of the world as "Indigenous and Shamanist." **Indigenous religions** are local in scope, usually have a reverence for nature, and are passed down through family units and groups (tribes) of indigenous peoples. No central tenet or belief can be ascribed to all indigenous religions. We do not group indigenous religions because they share a common theology or belief system. Instead, we group indigenous religions because they share the same pressures from the diffusion of global religions—and they have survived (Fig. 7.18).

Shamanism is a community faith in which people follow their shaman—a religious leader, teacher, healer, and visionary. Various peoples in Africa, Native America, Southeast Asia, and East Asia have embraced shamans from time to time, and they had similar effects on the cultures of widely scattered peoples. Perhaps if these shamanist religions had developed elaborate bureaucracies and sent representatives to international congresses, they would have become more similar and might have evolved into another world religion. Unlike Christianity or Islam, the shamanist faiths are small and comparatively isolated.

Shamanism is a indigenous religion, an intimate part of a local culture and society, but not all indigenous religions are shamanist. Many indigenous African religions involve beliefs in a god as creator and provider, in divinities both superhuman and human, in spirits, and in a life hereafter. Christianity and Islam have converted many followers of indigenous religions, but as the map indicates, indigenous religions continue to have a strong presence in significant areas (Fig. 7.6).

THE RISE OF SECULARISM

The world map of religion might mislead us into assuming that all or even most of the people in areas portrayed as Christian or Buddhist do in fact adhere to these faiths. This is not

FIELD NOTE

"Arriving at the foot of erosion-carved Uluru just before sunrise, I do not find it surprising that this giant monolith, towering over the Australian desert, is a sacred place to local Aboriginal peoples. Throughout the day, the changing sun angle alters its colors until, toward sunset, it turns a fiery red that yields to a bright orange. At night it looms against the moonlit, starry sky, silent sentinel of the gods. Just two years before this, my first visit in 1987, the Australian government had returned Ayers Rock (named by European settlers after a South Australian political leader) to Aboriginal ownership, and reclaimed its original name, Uluru. Visitors continued to be allowed to climb the 1100 feet (335 m) to the top, from where the view over the desert is awesome.

My day had begun eventfully when a three-foot lizard emerged from under my motel-room bed, but the chain-assisted climb was no minor challenge either. At the base you are warned to be 'in good shape' and some would-be climbers don't make it, but the rewards of persisting are dramatic. Uluru's iron-rich sandstone strata have been sculpted into gullies and caves, the latter containing Aboriginal carvings and paintings, and on the broad summit there are plenty of places where you can sit quietly to contemplate the historic, religious, and cultural significance of a place that mattered thousands of years before globalization reached Australia."

Figure 7.18
Uluru, Australia.

the case. Even the most careful analysis of worldwide church and religious membership produces a total of about 5.8 billion adherents—in a population of over 6.9 billion (Pew Research Center 2012). The figure 5.8 billion adherents is inflated when we start to analyze the difference between those who say they are members of a religion and those who are active followers of a religion. When polled about their church-going activities, fewer than 3 percent of the people in Scandinavia reported frequent attendance, and in France and Great Britain, less than 10 percent reported attending church at least once a month. The lack of members active or otherwise underscores the rise of **secularism**—indifference to or rejection of organized religious affiliations and ideas.

The level of secularism throughout much of the Christian and Buddhist worlds varies from country to country and regionally within countries. A 2009 Pew Research poll asked whether people felt religion was very important to them. Only 24 percent of Italians agreed with this statement, whereas 55 percent of Americans felt religion was very important to them. In France, the government recently banned the wearing of overt religious symbols in public schools. The French government wanted to remove the "disruption" of Muslim girls wearing hijab (head scarves), Jewish boys wearing yarmulke (skullcaps), and Christian students wearing large crosses to school. The French government took the position that banning all religious symbols was the only egalitarian approach.

Looking at polls that ask about the importance of religion for people in a country does not give us the complete picture, however. The 30 percent of Canadians who agreed religion is very important to them would be much, much lower if we removed recent or second-generation immigrants from the tally. Immigrants often hold onto their religion more fervently in part to help them ease into a new place and to link into a community in their new home. Buddhists and Hindus on Canada's west coast and Muslims in the eastern part of Canada have a higher rate of adherence to their religion than many long-term residents of the country.

In some countries, antireligious ideologies are contributing to the decline of organized religion. Church membership in Russia, which dropped drastically during the twentieth century under communist rule, rebounded after the collapse of the Soviet system but to much lower numbers. Maoist China's drive against Confucianism was, in part, an antireligious effort, and China continues to suppress some organized religious practices, as reports of religious persecution continue to emanate from China.

In many areas labeled Christian on the world map of religions, from Canada to Australia and from the United States to western Europe, the decline of organized religion as a cultural force is evident. In the strongly Catholic regions of southern Europe and Latin America, many people are dissatisfied with the papal teachings on birth control, as the desire for larger families wanes in these regions of the world. In Latin America, the Catholic Church is being challenged by rapid social change, the diffusion of Evangelical Protestant denominations into the region, and sexual abuse scandals similar to those that have occurred in the United States and Canada.

Secularism has become more widespread during the past century. People have abandoned organized religion in growing numbers. Even if they continue to be members of a church, their participation in church activities has declined. Traditions have also weakened. For example, there was a time when almost all shops and businesses were closed on Sundays, preserving the day for sermons, rest, and introspection. Today, shopping centers are mostly open as usual, and Sunday is increasingly devoted to business and personal affairs, not to church. To witness the rise of secularism among Christians in America first-hand, explore your town, city, or suburb on a Sunday morning: How many people are wearing casual clothes and hanging out at the coffee shop reading newspapers, and how many people are attending church services?

At the same time that secularism is on the rise in the United States, many people who do follow their religion seem to be doing so more fervently. Religious traditions are stronger in some cultural regions of the United States than in others, and Sunday observance continues at a high level in, for example, the Mormon culture area of the United States. Even though Catholic dioceses are closing churches and declaring bankruptcy in some parts of the Northeast, other Catholic dioceses are building new churches and enormous activity halls in other parts of the country. Moreover, Evangelical and other alternative churches are growing rapidly in some parts of the United States and western Europe. Entire industries, including Christian music and Christian publications, depend on the growing commitment of many Americans and Europeans to their religion.

The division between secularism and fervent adherence is not confined to the Christian world. Secularism is growing in South Korea, where half of the population does not profess adherence to any particular religion. Although major faiths are experiencing an overall decline in adherence, several smaller religions are growing in importance: Baha'i, Cao Dai, Jainism, and the Spiritual Church of Brazil, for example.

Migration plays a large role in the diffusion of religions, both universalizing and ethnic. As Europe becomes more secular, migrants from outside of Europe continue to settle in the region. Imagine Europe 30 years from now. Predict where in Europe secularism will be the most prominent and where religious adherence will strengthen.

HOW IS RELIGION SEEN IN THE CULTURAL LANDSCAPE?

Religion marks cultural landscapes with houses of worship such as churches, mosques, synagogues, and temples; cemeteries dotted with religious symbols and icons; stores designated for sales of religious goods; and even services provided to religious adherents who travel to sacred sites. When adherents voluntarily travel to a religious site to pay respects or participate in a ritual at the site, the act of travel is called a **pilgrimage**. Geographers who study religion are interested in the act of pilgrimage and its impacts on place, people, religion, culture, and environment.

Sacred sites are places or spaces people infuse with religious meaning. Members of a religious group may define a space or place as sacred out of either reverence or fear. If a sacred site is held with reverence, adherents may be encouraged to make a pilgrimage to the sacred site for rejuvenation, reflection, healing, or fulfillment of a religious commitment.

In ancient human history, sacred spaces were typically features in the physical geographic landscape, such as buttes, mountain peaks, or rivers. In more recent history, as universalizing religions diffused across the world, sacred sites were abandoned, usurped, or altered. Geographer Mary Lee Nolan studied Irish sacred sites and observed that many of the remote physical geographic features of the Irish landscape were sacred to the Celtic people (Fig. 7.19). When Roman Catholicism diffused to Ireland, the Catholic Church usurped many of these features, infusing them with Christian meaning. Nolan described the marriage of Celtic sacred sites and Christian meaning:

> The early Celtic Church was a unique institution, more open to syncretism of old and new religious traditions than was the case in many other parts of Europe. Old holy places, often in remote areas, were "baptized" in the new religion or given new meaning through their historical, or more often legendary, association with Celtic saints. Such places were characterized by sacred site features such as heights, insularity, or the presence of holy water sources, trees, or stones.

Nolan contrasted Irish sacred sites with those in continental Europe, where sacred sites were typically built in urban, accessible areas. In continental Europe, Nolan found that the "sacred" (bones of saints or images) was typically brought to a place in order to infuse the place with meaning.

In many societies, certain features in the physical geographic landscape remain sacred to religious groups. Access to and use of physical geographic features are constrained by private ownership, environmental concerns, and the act of designating certain sacred spaces as public recreational or tourist areas. Geographer Kari Forbes-Boyte (1999) studied Bear Butte, a site sacred to members of the Lakota and Cheyenne people in the northern Great Plains of the United States and a site that became a state park in the 1960s. Bear Butte is used today by both Lakota and Cheyenne people in religious

GUEST FIELD NOTE

At St. Declan's Holy Well in Ireland, I found a barbed wire fence substituting for the more traditional thorn tree as a place to hang scraps of clothing as offerings. This tradition, which died out long ago in most parts of Continental Europe, was one of many aspects of Irish pilgrimage that led me to speculate on 'Galway-to-the-Ganges' survival of very old religious customs on the extreme margins of an ancient Indo-European culture realm. My subsequent fieldwork focused on contemporary European pilgrimage, but my curiosity about the geographical extent of certain ancient pilgrimage themes lingered. While traveling in Asia, I found many similarities among sacred sites across religions. Each religion has formation stories, explanations of how particular sites, whether Buddhist monasteries or Irish wells, were recognized as sacred. Many of these stories have similar elements. And, in 1998, I traveled across Russia from the remote Kamchatka Peninsula to St. Petersburg. Imagine my surprise to find the tradition of hanging rag offerings on trees alive and well all the way across the Russian Far East and Siberia, at least as far as Olkon Island in Lake Baikal.

Figure 7.19
Ardmore, Ireland.

Credit: Mary Lee Nolan, Oregon State University.

ceremonies and by tourists who seek access to the recreational site. Nearby Devils Tower, which is a national monument, experiences the same pull between religious use by American Indians and recreational use by tourists.

Places such as Bear Butte and Devils Tower experience contention when one group sees the sites as sacred and another group does not. In many parts of the world, sacred sites are claimed as holy or significant to adherents of more than one religious faith. In India, for example, several sites are considered sacred by Hindus, Buddhists, and Jains. Specifically, Volture Peak in Rajgir in northeastern India is holy to Buddhists because it is the site where Buddha first proclaimed the Heart Sutra, a very important canon of Buddhism. Hindus and Jains also consider the site holy because they hold Buddha to be a god or prophet. The site has created little discord among religious groups. Pilgrims of all faiths peacefully congregate in the place year after year. Other sacred sites are not so fortunate: Some of the most contentious sites are in Jerusalem, a city that three major world religions regard as holy.

Sacred Sites of Jerusalem

The ancient city of Jerusalem is sacred to Jews, Christians, and Muslims. Jews saw Jerusalem as sacred before the birth of Jesus, but most Jews fled from the city and surrounding area during the diaspora. For Jews, Jerusalem remained sacred even though they did not control it, and when the Zionist movement gained strength, Jews set their sights on controlling the sacred city once again. The most important sacred site for Jews is the Western Wall (also called the Wailing Wall), at the edge of the Temple Mount in Jerusalem (Fig. 7.20). The Temple Mount occupies the top of a modest hill where, according to the Torah (the sacred book of Judaism that is also part of the Old Testament of Christianity's sacred book, the Bible), Abraham almost sacrificed his son Isaac. On this hill, Jews built two temples, each of which was destroyed by invaders. The Western Wall is all that remains of the second temple, and Jews gather in the place to remember the story of Abraham and the destruction of the temples and to offer prayers. The name "Wailing Wall" evokes the sounds of mourning over the temple's demise made by Jewish pilgrims and recognizes the suffering of Jews over time.

For Christians, Jerusalem is sacred both because of the sacrifice Abraham was willing to make of his son at the Temple Mount and because Jesus' crucifixion took place just outside of the city's walls. Jesus was then buried in a tomb that Roman Emperor Constantine later marked with a basilica that is now the Church of the Holy Sepulchre (Fig. 7.21). Christians believe that from that tomb Jesus rose from the dead on Easter. For centuries the Roman, and then the Byzantine, Empire controlled the city and protected the sacred site.

© Alexander B. Murphy

■ **Figure 7.20**
Jerusalem, Israel. The Western Wall (foreground, right), which is sacred to Jews, stands right next to the Dome of the Rock (background, left), which is sacred to Muslims.

In the seventh century, Muslim armies took control over the city from the Byzantine Empire. Muslims constructed a mosque called the Dome of the Rock adjacent to the Western Wall to mark the site where Muslims believe Muhammad arrived from Mecca and then ascended into heaven (Fig. 7.20). The site Jews call Temple Mount is called al-Haram al-Sharif (the Noble Sanctuary) by Muslims.

Christians and Muslims fought the Crusades of the Middle Ages over the question of who should control the sacred land of Jerusalem. Between 1095 and 1199, European political and religious leaders organized a series of Crusades to retake the so-called Holy Land. The first Christian crusaders captured Jerusalem in 1099, ruling the city for almost 100 years. As the first crusaders made their way across what is modern-day Turkey on their way to Jerusalem, they also left a series of conquests in their wake—laying claim to the city of Antioch and a number of other strategically important sites. Some of the crusaders returned to western Europe, but many settled, mingled, and intermarried with the local people.

Muslims ultimately retook Jerusalem in 1187, and later Christian crusaders were unable to conquer it again. The Crusades helped cement a commitment by Christians to protect the Church of the Holy Sepulchre. Similarly, the Crusades cemented a commitment by Muslims to protect the Dome of the Rock and later Zionism cemented a commitment by Jews to protect the Western Wall. The commitment by three major

Reuters/© Corbis

■ **Figure 7.21**
Jerusalem, Israel. The Church of the Holy Sepulchre is sacred to Christians who believe it is the site where Jesus Christ rose from the dead. Inside the church, a Christian worshipper lights a candle at Jesus' tomb.

religions to protect and control their sacred sites has led to political turmoil that echoes far beyond Jerusalem, as we will see in the next section of this chapter.

Landscapes of Hinduism and Buddhism

Traditional Hinduism is more than a faith; it is a way of life. Pilgrimages follow prescribed routes, and rituals are attended by millions of people. Festivals and feasts are frequent, colorful, and noisy. Hindus believe that the erection of a temple, whether modest or elaborate, bestows merit on the builder and will be rewarded. As a result, the Hindu cultural landscape—urban as well as rural—is dotted with countless shrines, ranging from small village temples to structures so large and elaborate that they are virtually holy cities. The location of shrines is important because Hindus prescribe that such holy places should minimally disrupt the natural landscape. Whenever possible, a Hindu temple is located in a "comfortable" position, for example, under a large, shady tree. Hindus also want their temples to be near water because many gods will not venture far from water and because water has a holy function, ritual bathing, in Hinduism (Fig. 7.22). A village temple should face the village from a prominent position, and followers must make offerings frequently. Small offerings of fruit and flowers lie before the sanctuary of the deity honored by the shrine.

The cultural landscape of Hinduism is the cultural landscape of India, its main culture region. As one travels through India, the Hindu faith is a visual as well as an emotional experience. Temples and shrines, holy animals by the tens of millions, distinctively garbed holy men, and the sights and sounds of long processions and rituals all contribute to a unique atmosphere (Fig. 7.23).

When Buddha received enlightenment, he sat under a large tree, the Bodhi (enlightenment) tree at Bodh Gaya in India. The Bodhi tree now growing on the site is believed to be a descendant of the original tree. The Bodhi tree has a thick, banyan-like trunk and a wide canopy of leafy branches. Because of its association with the Buddha, the tree is revered and protected. Buddhists make pilgrimages to Bodh Gaya and other places where Buddha may have taught beneath Bodhi branches. With Buddhism, the Bodhi tree diffused as far as China and Japan, its purposeful planting marking the cultural landscape of numerous villages and towns.

Buddhism's architecture includes some magnificent achievements, especially the famed structures at Borobudur in central Java (Indonesia). Buddhist shrines include stupas, bell-shaped structures that protect burial mounds. Buddhists also construct temples that enshrine an image of Buddha in his familiar cross-legged pose, as well as large monasteries that tower over the local landscape. The pagoda is perhaps Buddhism's most familiar structure. Its shape is derived from the relic (often funeral) mounds of old. Every fragment of its construction is a meaningful representation of Buddhist philosophy (Fig. 7.24).

■■ **Figure 7.22**
Varanasi, India. Hindus perform morning rituals in the Ganges River at one of Hinduism's most sacred places, the city of Varanasi, known as the city of Lord Shiva. For Hindus, the river itself is a sacred site.

FIELD NOTE

"In the summer of 2007, the newer, Hi-Tec city area of Hyderabad, India, was under construction. Migrant workers built new roads, apartment houses, and office buildings throughout the city. Beautiful homes reflected the wealth accrued by many. In front of the new homes, I saw Hinduism in the cultural landscape where owners built temples for their favorite Hindu god. In the older part of the city, I visited Golconda Fort, built more than 1500 years ago. On the day I was there, Hindu women participated in the Bonalu Festival as an act of honoring Mother Goddess. The women climbed nearly 400 steps to the top of the fort, carrying with them offerings of food. At the top, I was welcomed into the temple. I took off my shoes and took part in a festival that began in the mid-1800s, when Hindu women began the festival to ward off the anger of the gods, as the city stood under the siege of the bubonic plague."

© Erin H. Fouberg

■ **Figure 7.23**
Hyderabad, India.

FIELD NOTE

"To reach the city of Yangon, Myanmar (Burma), we had to transfer to a ferry and sail up the Rangoon River for several hours. One of Southeast Asia's most spectacular Buddhist shrines is the golden Shwedogon Pagoda in the heart of Yangon. The golden dome (or *chedi*) is one of the finest in Southeast Asia, and its religious importance is striking: eight hairs of the Buddha are preserved here. Vast amounts of gold have gone into the creation and preservation of the Shwedogon Pagoda; local rulers often gave the monks their weight in gold—or more. Today, the pagoda is a cornerstone of Buddhism, drawing millions of faithful to the site."

© H. J. de Blij

■ **Figure 7.24**
Yangon, Myanmar.

Along with the religious structures such as temples, we can see evidence of religion in the cultural landscapes of the dead. Traditionally, Hindus, and more recently Buddhists, and Shintoists cremate their dead. Thus, wherever a large pocket of Hindus, Buddhists, or Shintoists live, a crematorium will be nearby. The Hindu crematorium in Kenya stands in stark contrast to much of the rest of the cultural landscape and signals the presence of a large Hindu population (see Fig. 7.2).

The cultural landscapes of South Asian religions extend into Southeast Asia, where several religions that began in the South Asian hearth (including Hinduism and Buddhism) diffused into the region. Later, Islam replaced the South Asian religions in many of these places, and even later Christian missionaries gained adherents in Southeast Asia when Christian governments encouraged the migration of their people and their religion to their colonies in these areas. Today, we can stand in Singapore, study the cultural landscape, and see the influences of Christianity, Buddhism, Hinduism, and Islam.

Landscapes of Christianity

The cultural landscapes of Christianity's branches reflect the changes the faith has undergone over the centuries. In medieval Europe the cathedral, church, or monastery was the focus of life. Other buildings clustered around the tower, steeple, and spire of the church that could be seen (and whose bells could be heard) for miles in the surrounding countryside (Fig. 7.25). In the square or plaza in front of the church, crowds gathered for ceremonies and festivals, and the church was always present—even if the event was not primarily religious. Good harvests, military victories, public announcements, and much else took place in the shadow of the symbol of religious authority. As a result of mercantilism and colonialism, Europeans exported the ornate architecture of European Christian churches wherever they settled (Fig. 7.26).

The Reformation, the rise of secularism, and the decline of organized religion are reflected in the cultural landscape as well. Many of the ornate churches in the town squares of medieval cities now function as museums instead of serving active congregations. Other churches in secular regions are closing their doors or

© Alexander B. Murphy

■ **Figure 7.25**
Antwerp, Belgium.   The cathedral in Antwerp was built beginning in 1352 and still dominates the central part of town.

■ **Figure 7.26**
Mombasa, Kenya.   Built at the end of the nineteenth century, the neo-gothic Holy Ghost Cathedral reflects the European colonial imprint on the city. The sign in the street next to the cathedral serves as a reminder of a more recent external cultural influence—this time from China. The number of Chinese in the city is not large, but Chinese immigrants have found niches in the restaurant business and as purveyors of Chinese traditional medicine.

© Alexander B. Murphy

© Franco Origlia/Getty Images

■■ **Figure 7.27**
Vatican City.   Pope Francis waves to pilgrims as he arrives in the Popemobile at St. Peter's Square for his weekly audience. Thousands gather each week to see the pope and hear him greet visitors in multiple languages.

significantly reducing the number of religious services offered. Yet, not all of Europe's sacred sites have become secularized. Famous cathedrals continue to hold services while tourists peruse the interior of the vast churches. And other sacred sites of Christianity, such as churches for specific saints, places where significant events occurred, and Vatican City in Rome, are still major pilgrimage sites in Europe. When in Rome, the leader of the Catholic Church, the pope, holds an outdoor service for pilgrims to Vatican City, attracting thousands of followers to St. Peter's Square each week (Fig. 7.27).

Cities in Europe are also home to centuries-old Christian cemeteries. Traditionally, Christians bury, rather than cremate, their dead, and in cities, the cemeteries are often crowded with tombstones. Outside of European cities and in North America, Christian cemeteries can resemble large parks. These cemeteries often reflect class differences: Some graves are marked by simple tombstones, whereas others are elaborate structures. With rising land-use pressures and the associated costs of burial, however, cremation is becoming increasingly common among Christians—particularly in North America and western Europe.

RELIGIOUS LANDSCAPES IN THE UNITED STATES

The United States, a predominantly Christian country, demonstrates considerable diversity in its religious cultural landscapes. In *The Cultural Geography* of the United States, geographer Wilbur Zelinsky constructed a map identifying religious regions in the country. Figure 7.28 presents a modified version of Zelinsky's map.

The New England region is strongly Catholic; the South's leading denomination is Baptist; the Upper Midwest has large numbers of Lutherans; and the Southwest is predominantly Spanish Catholic. The broad midland region extending from the Middle Atlantic to the Mormon region (in the western United States) has a mixture of denominations in which no single church dominates; this is also true of the West. As Figure 7.28 shows, some regions represent local clustering, such as the French Catholic area centered in New Orleans and the mixed denominations of Peninsular Florida, where a large Spanish Catholic cluster has emerged in metropolitan Miami.

In a 2008 study, geographers Barney Warf and Mort Winsberg used data on religious adherents by county in the United States to discern what counties and regions of the country have the most and the least religious diversity. Warf and Winsberg defined religious diversity as having a variety of religions within a small spatial unit, in this case a county. One way the authors mapped religious diversity is presented in Figure 7.29, a map showing counties with the least religious diversity in the darkest colors. In counties with the darkest shading, one religion accounts for 64 percent or more of all religious adherents in the county. In comparing Figure 7.29 to Figure 7.28, we can see that the Mormon region in Utah and southern Idaho, the Southern Baptist region in the South, and the Catholic region of the Northeast are some of the least diverse regions in the country. In these regions, you can expect to see the imprint of one major religion throughout the cultural landscape. By contrast, religious regions characterized by many lightly colored counties have a rich religious mix.

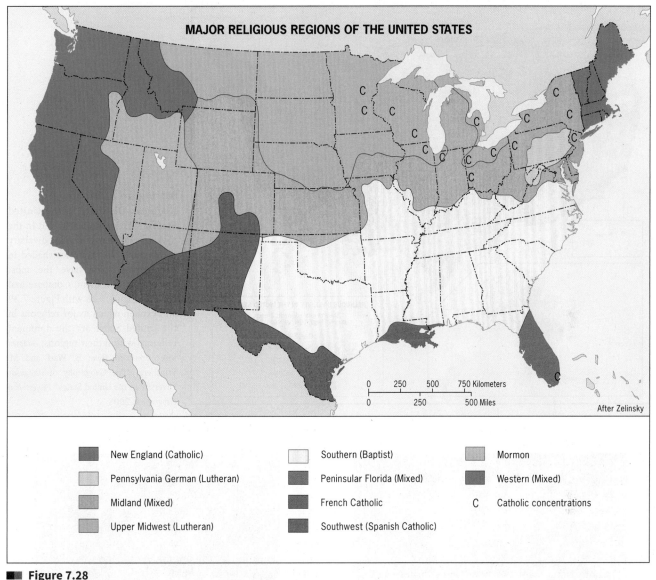

MAJOR RELIGIOUS REGIONS OF THE UNITED STATES

0   250   500   750 Kilometers
0   250   500 Miles

After Zelinsky

■ New England (Catholic)
□ Southern (Baptist)
■ Mormon

■ Pennsylvania German (Lutheran)
■ Peninsular Florida (Mixed)
■ Western (Mixed)

■ Midland (Mixed)
■ French Catholic
C   Catholic concentrations

■ Upper Midwest (Lutheran)
■ Southwest (Spanish Catholic)

■ **Figure 7.28**
Major Religious Regions of the United States.   A generalized map of the religious regions of the United States shows concentrations of the major religions.   *Adapted with permission from*: W. Zelinsky, *The Cultural Geography of the United States*, rev. ed., Englewood Cliffs, NJ: Prentice Hall, 1992, p. 96.

The plain white churches of the South and Lutheran Upper Midwest coincide with the Protestant Church's pragmatic spending of church money—not on art and architecture as the Catholic Church historically did (Fig. 7.30). Conversely, many Catholic churches in the United States, both in the Northeast and in Chicago, as well as in other immigrant-magnet cities, were built by immigrants who lived in ethnic neighborhoods. Immigrants spent their own money and used their building skills to construct ornate churches and dozens of cathedrals that tied them back to their country of origin and demonstrated their commitment to their faith (Fig. 7.31).

Landscapes of Islam

Elaborate, sometimes magnificently designed mosques whose balconied **minarets** rise above the townscape dominate Islamic cities, towns, and villages. Often the mosque is the town's most imposing and most carefully maintained building. Five times every day, from the towering minarets, the faithful are called to prayer. The sounds emanating from the minarets fill the streets as the faithful converge on the holy place to pray facing Mecca.

At the height of Islam's expansion into eastern North Africa and southern Europe, Muslim architects incorporated earlier Roman models into their designs. The results included some of the world's greatest architectural master-pieces, such as the Alhambra Palace in Granada and the Great Mosque of Cordoba in Spain. Islam's prohibition against depicting the human form led to the wide use of geometric designs and calligraphy—the intricacy of which is truly astounding (Fig. 7.32). During the eleventh century, Muslim builders began glazing the tiles of domes and roofs.

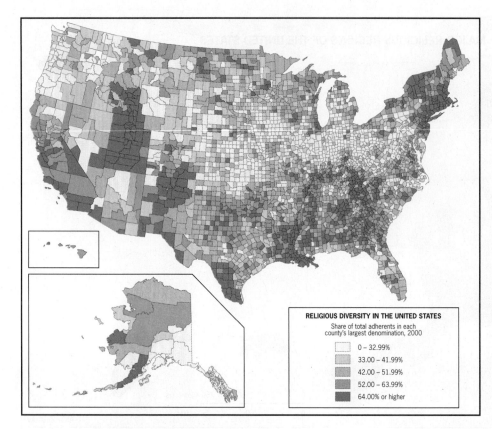

RELIGIOUS DIVERSITY IN THE UNITED STATES
Share of total adherents in each
county's largest denomination, 2000

- 0 – 32.99%
- 33.00 – 41.99%
- 42.00 – 51.99%
- 52.00 – 63.99%
- 64.00% or higher

■ **Figure 7.29**
Religious Diversity in the United States. The counties shaded in the darkest color have the least diversity in religions. The counties shaded in the lightest color have the most diversity within them. Compare and contrast Figure 7.28 with Figure 7.29 and explain which major religions in the United States are the dominant religions within their region. *Adapted with permission from*: B. Warf and M. Winsberg, "The Geography of Religious Diversity in the United States," *Professional Geographer*, 2008.

■ **Figure 7.30**
Brown County, South Dakota. The Scandinavian Lutheran Church was founded by immigrants from northern Europe. The simple architecture of the church is commonly found in Protestant churches in the Great Plains.

■ **Figure 7.31**
Zell, South Dakota. St. Mary's Catholic Church was built by nuns in 1875 to serve Catholic immigrants and American Indians. The more ornate architecture and stained glass of St. Mary's Church is commonly found in Catholic churches in the Great Plains.

■■ **Figure 7.32**

Isfahan, Iran. The dome of this mosque demonstrates the geometric art evident in Muslim architecture. The towers to the right of the dome are minarets from which the call to prayer is broadcast.

To the beautiful arcades and arched courtyards, they added the exquisite beauty of glass-like, perfectly symmetrical cupolas. Muslim architecture represents the unifying concept of Islamic monotheism: the perfection and vastness of the spirit of Allah.

Islam achieved its greatest artistic expression, its most distinctive visible element, in architecture. Even in the smallest town, the community helps build and maintain its mosque. The mosque symbolizes the power of the faith and its role in the community. Its primacy in the cultural landscape confirms the degree to which, in much of the Muslim world, religion and culture are one.

One of the best-known pilgrimages in the modern world is the Muslim pilgrimage to Mecca, the **hajj**. The hajj is one of the five pillars of Islam. Religious doctrine implores all Muslims (if financially and physically able) to make the pilgrimage to Mecca at least once during their lifetime. Each year, over 1.3 million Muslims from outside of Saudi Arabia and over 1 million from inside the country make the hajj (Fig. 7.33). The pilgrimage requires the faithful to follow certain steps of reverence in a certain order and within a certain time frame. As a result, the pilgrims move from Mecca through the steps of the hajj en masse. In 2004, over 250 pilgrims were trampled to death as hordes of people followed the steps of the pilgrimage, and in 1990 over 1400 pilgrims suffered the same fate. The Saudi government now restricts the number of visas granted each year to Muslims

from outside of the country. Yet, the number of pilgrims continues to climb, and the services needed for Muslim pilgrims during the hajj and during the rest of the year now employ four times as many people in Saudi Arabia as the oil industry does. The landscape around Mecca reflects the growing number of pilgrims year round, as towers of apartment buildings and hotels encircle the sacred city.

Geographer Surinder Bhardwaj has studied non-hajj pilgrimages in Islam, which include "visits to sacred shrines of holy men, the graves of saints and Imams, and the tombs of martyrs of the faith" (1998). Although some sects of Islam see non-hajj pilgrimage as non-Islamic, the ziarats (non-hajj pilgrimages) are important to a growing number of Muslims. Bhardwaj points out that the hajj is obligatory but the ziarat is voluntary. He explains that study of the ziarat helps geographers understand the many variations and regional forms of Islam in the world today. For example, Bhardwaj describes how the ziarat in Indonesia (the country with the largest number of Muslims) reflects the continued influence of pre-Islamic ways. Especially in the interior of Indonesia, Islam has mixed with Buddhism and Hinduism, both of which stress the importance of pilgrimage. Similar to Ireland, where the Catholic Church usurped Celtic sacred sites, Bhardwaj found that many sites in Indonesia that were sacred under Hinduism and Buddhism were usurped by Islam, which changed the object of pilgrimage from non-Muslim to Muslim.

©AP/Wide World Photos

■ **Figure 7.33**
Mecca, Saudi Arabia.   Pilgrims circle the holy Kaaba in the Grand Mosque in Mecca during the hajj.

 Choose a pilgrimage site, such as Mecca, Vatican City, or the Western Wall, and describe how the act of pilgrimage (in some cases by millions) alters this place's cultural landscape and environment.

WHAT ROLE DOES RELIGION PLAY IN POLITICAL CONFLICTS?

Religious beliefs and histories can bitterly divide peoples who speak the same language, have the same ethnic background, and make their living in similar ways. Such divisions arise not only between people adhering to different major religions (as with Muslims and Christians in the former Yugoslavia) but also among adherents of the same religion. Some of the most destructive conflicts have pitted Christian against Christian and Muslim against Muslim.

Religious conflicts usually involve more than differences in spiritual practices and beliefs. Religion often functions as a symbol of a wider set of cultural and political differences. The "religious" conflict in Northern Ireland is not just about different

views of Christianity, and the conflict between Hindus and Muslims in India has a strong political as well as religious dimension. Nevertheless, in these and other cases religion serves as the principal symbol around which conflict is organized.

Conflicts Along Religious Borders

A comparison between Figure 7.6 and a political map of the world (see Fig. 8.3) reveals that some countries lie entirely within the realms of individual world religions, whereas other countries straddle **interfaith boundaries**, the boundaries between the world's major faiths. Many countries that lie astride interfaith boundaries are subject to potentially divisive cultural forces—particularly when the people see their religious differences as a source of social division within their country. This is the case in several countries in Africa that straddle the Christian–Muslim interfaith boundary (Fig. 7.34). Other countries with major religious disputes straddle **intrafaith boundaries**, the boundaries within a single major faith. Intra-faith boundaries include divisions between Christian Protestants and Catholics (Northern Ireland), divisions between Muslim Sunni and Shi'ite (Iraq), and the like.

Interface areas, where interfaith and intrafaith boundaries occur, may be peaceful, or they can spur enormously violent political conflict. Israel/Palestine and Nigeria provide

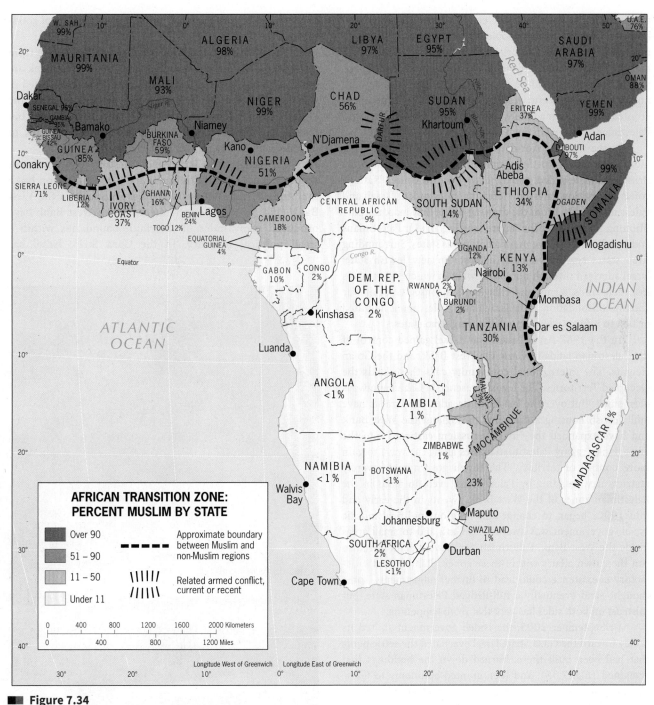

■ Figure 7.34

African Transition Zone. Percent Muslim by Country. The divide shown on the map marks interfaith boundaries between religions. Considerable conflict has occurred in the transition zone.   © H. J. de Blij, P. O. Muller, and John Wiley & Sons, Inc.

examples of interfaith conflicts, and Northern Ireland is an example of an intrafaith conflict. In each case, religious difference is not the only factor, but it certainly plays an important symbolic and perceptual role.

Israel and Palestine

Earlier in this chapter, we discussed the history of the conflict over the sacred space of Jerusalem. The region of Israel and

Palestine is home to one of the most contentious religious conflicts in the world today. In the aftermath of World War I, European colonialism came to a region that had previously been controlled and fought over by Jews, Romans, Christians, Muslims, and Ottomans. A newly formed League of Nations (a precursor to the United Nations) recognized British control of the land, calling the territorial mandate Palestine. At that point, the vast majority of people living in the land were Muslim Palestinians. The goal of the British government was to meet Zionist goals and to create, in Palestine, a national homeland for the Jewish people (who had already begun to migrate to the area). The British explicitly assured the world that the religious and civil rights of existing non-Jewish peoples in Palestine would be protected. The British policy did not produce a peaceful result, however. Civil disturbances erupted almost immediately, and, by 1947–1948, Jews and Palestinians engaged in open warfare.

In the wake of World War II and the Holocaust, many more Jews moved to the region. Shortly after the war, the British mandate ended, and the newly formed United Nations voted to partition Palestine—creating independent Israeli and Palestinian states. From the drawing of the first map, the partitioning plan was set for failure (see Fig. 3.11). Palestinians and Israelis were to live in noncontiguous states. Surrounding Arab states reacted violently against the new Jewish state. Israel survived through numerous wars in which Palestinians lost their lands, farms, and villages. As a consequence of war and the consolidation of the Israeli state, Palestinians migrated or fled to refugee camps in neighboring Arab states.

In the 1967 Arab–Israeli War, Israel gained control of the Palestinian lands in Gaza, the West Bank, and the Golan Heights. The international community calls these lands the Occupied Territories. The Jewish presence in Gaza has always been small. But over the last three decades, the Israelis have built Jewish housing settlements throughout the West Bank and have expanded the city of Jerusalem eastward into the West Bank (razing Palestinian houses along the way) to gain more control of territory. The Israeli government severely restricts new building by Palestinians, even on lands in the Palestinian zones of the West Bank. Events in the early and mid-1990s began to change this religious-political mosaic as self-government was awarded to Gaza and to small areas inside the West Bank. Palestinian Arabs were empowered to run their own affairs within these zones. Stability and satisfactory coexistence could lead to further adjustments, some thought—and eventually a full-fledged Palestinian state, but mistrust on both sides has kept that from happening.

In September 2005, the Israeli government shifted its policy toward the Gaza Strip. Israel evacuated the settlements that had been built there, burned down the buildings that remained (Fig. 7.35), and then granted autonomy to Gaza. The Palestinians living in the Gaza Strip rejoiced—visiting the beaches that were previously open only to Israeli settlers and traveling across the border into Egypt to purchase goods. Although Palestinians now have a degree of autonomy within the Gaza Strip, they are economically isolated, the standard of living has dropped, and continued conflict with Israel has taken a major toll.

The Israeli government tightly controls the flow of Palestinians and goods into and out of the Gaza Strip. Gaza is surrounded by fences, and in some places a wall—with land mines in certain areas and dust roads to show footprints. Dozens of tunnels between Egypt and Gaza have been used to supply arms, fuel, and goods to the Hamas government in Gaza. In 2014, Egypt agreed with Israel to recognize Hamas as a terrorist organization and to shut down the flow of goods through the tunnels.

The situation in the West Bank is slightly different from that in the Gaza Strip. Palestinian lands in the West Bank are not contiguous, and the Palestinian government is located in Gaza, not the West Bank. Israel is also building fences in the West Bank, not following the 1947 West Bank border but instead carving out Israeli settlements in the West Bank to include them on Israel's side of the fence.

The situation in Israel and Palestine today does not reflect a simple interfaith boundary. The tiny region has a multitude of interfaith boundaries, especially in the West Bank (Fig. 7.36). The settlements in the West Bank have produced many miles of interfaith boundaries within a small political territory. In the Gaza Strip, Israel has

© AP/Wide World Photos

■ **Figure 7.35**

Erez Crossing, Gaza Strip. The Israeli Army withdrew from the Gaza Strip in 2005, after occupying the territory for 38 years. Israeli troops demolished the Israeli Army liaison offices on September 9, 2005, in preparation for completing the Israeli retreat from the Gaza Strip on September 11, 2005.

The West Bank

- Israeli settlements inside Occupied Territory protected by Security Barrier
- Palestinian areas
- Israeli-controlled areas in the West Bank
- Syrian territory occupied by Israel
- Israeli settlements as of 2011
- Road
- Security Barrier, completed and planned

Source: Israeli Ministry of Defence

■ Figure 7.36

The West Bank.   Palestinian territories in the West Bank are punctuated by Israeli settlements. The security fence surrounds the West Bank, and in several places it juts into the West Bank to separate Israeli settlements from Palestinian areas.   *Adapted with permission from*: C. B. Williams and C. T. Elsworth, *The New York Times*, November 17, 1995, p. A6. © The New York Times.

worked to secure the interfaith boundary by building a wall around Gaza to keep Palestinians in the territory and out of Israel. Tensions have mounted, and both sides took to air attacks across the walled boundary in the summer of 2014. The prospects for peace between Israelis and Palestinians are greatly complicated by the fact that each side feels it has a historic (in the minds of some, even a divine) right to the land and by the violence inflicted on each side by the other.

Nigeria

Like other countries in West Africa, Nigeria is predominantly Muslim in the north, and Christian and animist in the south. With over 168 million people, Nigeria is Africa's most populous country. Since 1999, when the country emerged from years of military rule, Nigeria has witnessed persistent violence along the interfaith boundary between these communities, which has cost tens of thousands of lives.

As with many such conflicts, the causes of north–south violence in Nigeria cannot be attributed solely to different religious beliefs. Due to differences in climates, in northern Nigeria, many people engage in cattle herding, whereas in the south of the country, most rural peoples are farmers. As land has become scarcer, the fertile grasslands of central Nigeria have become coveted by both cattle herders and farmers. In addition to forms of agriculture, the north and south of Nigeria differ on several fronts (Fig. 7.37). Nigeria has a rich oil economy, and the oil economy and jobs tied to it are concentrated in the south. Southern Nigeria has higher per capita GDP and greater concentration of wealth than northern Nigeria. Northern Nigeria is dominated by the Hausa-Fulani ethnic group while the south is more diverse. Western-style education is more accepted in the south than in the north, and the south has higher female literacy rates than the north. Finally, access to health care, as reflected in the percentage of 1-year-olds who have received all the basic vaccinations, is higher in the south than the north.

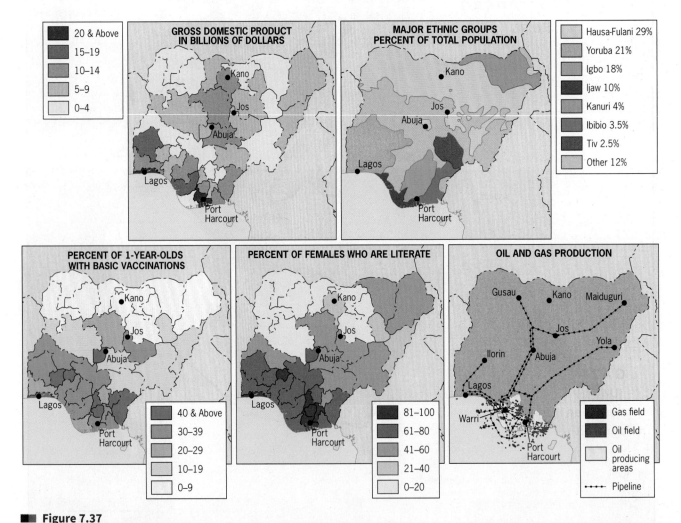

■◀ Figure 7.37
The North and South of Nigeria. Nigeria's oil resources are concentrated in the south. Northern Nigeria has lower GPD per capita rates, lower levels of female literacy, and less access to health care than southern Nigeria. Northern Nigeria is dominated by two ethnic groups, the Hausa-Fulani and Kanuri, both predominantly Muslim, and southern Nigeria has more diverse ethnic groups, whose members are predominantly Christian or animist. *Data from*: Nigeria Demographic and Health Survey 2008; platts.com; wikipedia.org; africacenter.org; and bbc.com.

Since 2009, the worst violence in Nigeria has taken place in the northern half of the country, along the interfaith boundary and in the northeast where the extremist Muslim group, Boko Haram, operates. Mohammed Yusuf began the organization in 2002 in Maiduguri, Nigeria, with the goal of pushing Western-style education out of northern Nigeria. The words "Boko Haram" roughly translate to "Western education is forbidden" in the Hausa language. Yusuf built an Islamic school, which drew mainly students from the Kanuri ethnic group. Yusuf then used the school to recruit members to Boko Haram. The U.S. State Department reported that Boko Haram "receives the bulk of its funding from bank robberies and related criminal activities, including extortion and kidnapping for ransom" and has received some funds and training from al-Qaeda in the Islamic Maghreb (2014).

In 2009, Nigerian police killed the founder of Boko Haram. In response, members armed themselves, found a new leader, and began issuing attacks in 2011. At first, the group focused attacks on police and military as vengeance for the killing of their leader. In 2012, Boko Haram turned their attention to attacking schools (*New York Times* 2014). In 2014, northern Nigeria made global news when members of the terrorist organization kidnapped 250 teenage girls from their school in Chibok (Fig. 7.38).

The violence may have its roots in the struggle for access to land, political power, and resources, but religion has served as a key marker of difference in the region. Violence along the interfaith Christian–Muslim boundary reinforces the perceptual importance of the boundary and promotes a sense—whether right or wrong—that religious differences represent the most important obstacle to social cohesion in Nigeria.

Northern Ireland

A number of western European countries, as well as Canada and the United States, have large Catholic communities and large Protestant communities, and often these are reflected in the regional distribution of the population. In most places, the split between these two sects of Christianity along intrafaith lines creates little if any rift today. The most notable exception is Northern Ireland.

Northern Ireland and Great Britain (which includes England, Scotland, and Wales) form the United Kingdom of Great Britain and Northern Ireland (the UK). This was not always the case. For centuries, the island of Ireland was its own entity, marked by a mixture of Celtic religious practices and Roman Catholicism. As early as the 1200s, the English began to infiltrate the island of Ireland, taking control of its agricultural economy. Colonization began in the sixteenth century, and by 1700, Britain controlled the entire island. During the 1800s, the Irish colony produced industrial wealth for Britain in the shipyards of the north. Protestants from the island of Great Britain (primarily Scotland) migrated to Ireland during the 1700s to Northern Ireland to take advantage of the political and economic power granted to them in the colony. During the 1800s, migrants were drawn to northeastern Ireland where industrial jobs and opportunities were greatest. During the colonial period, the British treated the Irish Catholics harshly, taking away their lands, depriving them of their legal right to own property or participate in government, and regarding them as second-class citizens.

In the late 1800s, the Irish began reinvigorating their Celtic and Irish traditions; this strengthening of their identity fortified their resolve against the British. In the early 1900s,

■■ **Figure 7.38**
Abuja, Nigeria. Malala Yousafzai, a Pakistani who was attacked by the Taliban while on a school bus in her home country at the age of 15 in 2012, holds a picture of kidnapped schoolgirl Sarah Samuel with her mother Rebecca Samuel, during a visit to Abuja, Nigeria, Sunday July 13, 2014. Malala Yousafzai traveled to Abuja in Nigeria to meet the relatives of 250 schoolgirls who were kidnapped by Boko Haram in northern Nigeria. The hashtag #BringBackOurGirls was used in a social media campaign in spring 2014 in response to the kidnapping of the Nigerian girls.

the Irish rebelled against British colonialism. The rebellion was successful throughout most of the island, which was Catholic dominated, leading to the creation of the Republic of Ireland. But in the 1922 settlement ending the conflict, Britain retained control of six counties in the northeast, which had Protestant majorities. These counties constituted Northern Ireland, which became part of the United Kingdom. The substantial Catholic minority in Northern Ireland, however, did not want to be part of the United Kingdom (Fig. 7.39)—particularly since the Protestant majority, constituting about two-thirds of the total population (about 1.6 million) of Northern Ireland, possessed most of the economic and political advantages.

As time went on, economic stagnation for both populations worsened the situation, and the Catholics in particular felt they were being repressed. Terrorist acts by the Irish Republican Army (IRA), an organization dedicated to ending British control over all of Ireland by violent means if necessary, brought British troops into the area in 1968. Although the Republic of Ireland was sensitive to the plight of Catholics in the North, no official help was extended to those who were engaging in violence.

In the face of worsening conflict, Catholics and Protestants in Northern Ireland increasingly distanced their lives and homes from one another. The cultural landscape marks the religious conflict, as each group clusters in its own neighborhoods and celebrates either important Catholic or Protestant dates (see Fig. 6.11). Irish geographer Frederick Boal wrote a seminal work in 1969 on the Northern Irish in one area of Belfast. Boal used fieldwork to mark Catholic and Protestant neighborhoods on a map, and he interviewed over 400 Protestants and Catholics in their homes. Boal used the concept of **activity space** to demonstrate how Protestants and Catholics had each chosen to separate themselves in their rounds of daily activity.

Although religion is the tag-line by which we refer to "The Troubles" in Northern Ireland, the conflict is much more about nationalism, economics, oppression, access to opportunities, terror, civil rights, and political influence. But religion and religious history are the banners beneath which the opposing sides march, and church and cathedral have become symbols of strife rather than peace.

Belfast now has 99 peace lines, or peace walls, separating Catholic and Protestant neighborhoods. In the 1990s,

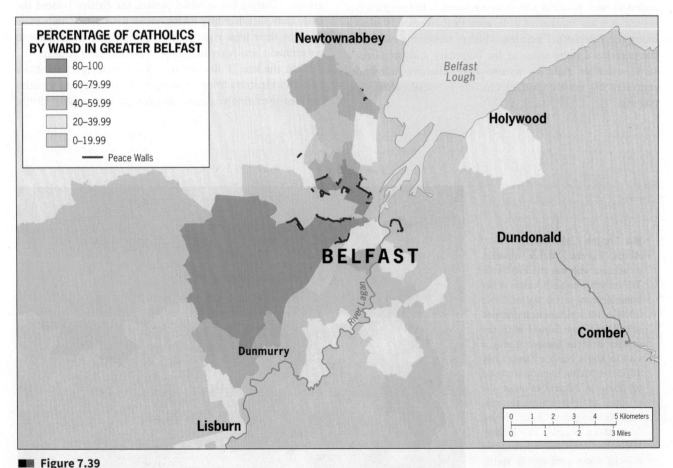

■ Figure 7.39

Religious Affiliation and Peace Lines in Belfast, Northern Ireland. Catholic neighborhoods are clustered west of the Central Business District and west of the River Lagan. Protestant neighborhoods are separated from Catholic neighborhoods by Peace Walls in West Belfast.

Boal updated his study of Northern Ireland and found hope for a resolution. Boal found that religious identities were actually becoming less intense among the younger generation and among the more educated. He found Catholics and Protestants intermixing in spaces such as downtown clubs, shopping centers, and college campuses.

In April 1998, the parties involved in The Troubles adopted the Anglo-Irish peace agreement known as the Belfast Agreement and Good Friday Agreement, which raised hopes of a new period of peace in Northern Ireland.

In her 2006 study, Leonard found teens that grew up in Catholic or Protestant neighborhoods rarely interacted with the "Other" and that "some children restricted their movements" to local neighborhoods and demonstrated little mobility beyond their respective neighborhood. Belfast, and Northern Ireland more broadly, have made major strides toward reconciliation in recent years. Mixing across Christian faiths is more common among the educated and less common among those living in distinctly Catholic or Protestant neighborhoods. The two sides have made major strides toward reconciliation in recent years, but the conflict has not gone away.

Religious Fundamentalism and Extremism

The drive toward **religious fundamentalism** is often born out of frustration over the perceived breakdown of society's morals and values, lack of religious authority, failure to achieve economic goals, loss of a sense of local control, failure of a government to protect a religion, or a sense of violation of a religion's core territory. Regardless of the religion, a fundamentalist group holds its religious beliefs as nonnegotiable and uncompromising.

People in one society often fear fundamentalism in other societies without recognizing it in their own. What many call fundamentalism is sometimes better defined as extremism. **Religious extremism** is fundamentalism carried to the point of violence. The attacks on the United States in September 2001 reinforced the tendency of many Americans to equate extremism with Islam. Yet Christian extremism is also a potent force, as witnessed in the United States when religious zealots kill physicians who perform legal abortions. Fundamentalists can be extremists, but by no means are all fundamentalists, whether Christian, Muslim, Jewish, or any other religion, extremists.

Today the forces of globalization affect religions. Education, radio, television, and travel have diffused notions of individual liberties, sexual equality, and freedom of choice—but also consumerism and secularism. In the process, the extent of cultural diffusion and innovation has accelerated. Some churches have managed to change with the times, allowing women to serve as priests and homosexuals to marry, and generally liberalizing their doctrines. Others have gone in the opposite direction, reaffirming fundamental or literalist interpretations of religious texts and trying to block modern influences and external cultural interference.

CHRISTIANITY

The Roman Catholic Church has long resisted innovations deemed incompatible with the fundamentals of the faith. Among the issues giving rise to disputes are birth control, family planning, and the role of women in the religious bureaucracy. The major religions tend to be male-dominated, and few women have managed to enter the hierarchy. This is true in the Roman Catholic Church, where women are not allowed to serve as priests. The Roman Catholic Church has over 1 billion adherents and has a global diplomatic and political presence, affecting policies in numerous places and on many topics. For example, the Roman Catholic Church preaches against the use of artificial means of birth control as well as abortion. During the September 1994 United Nations Conference on Population and Development, the Roman Catholic Church allied itself with Islamic countries against advocates of population control.

In the United States, certain sects of the Catholic Church continue to hold Mass in Latin and are much more fundamentalist than the rest of the Church. Some of these sects are part of the Catholic Church and continue to operate within the purview of the Church. Others stand apart from the Catholic Church and do not recognize the pope, nor does the Vatican sanction them. For example, actor/director Mel Gibson belongs to the Holy Family Church, which does not recognize the pope, and the Vatican does not recognize that church as part of the Catholic Church. Gibson's church is most associated with the Traditionalist Catholic Movement, a fundamentalist movement that believes the Mass should still be conducted in Latin and that modern popes and clergy are not following the traditional theology and practices of the Church.

In the United States, Christian fundamentalism is also associated with Protestant faiths. Preaching a doctrine of strict adherence to the literal precepts of the Bible, many Protestant Christian fundamentalists believe that the entire character of contemporary society needs to be brought into alignment with biblical principles. Fundamentalist Protestant churches range from tiny churches to enormous warehouse-style churches with thousands of members. Regardless of the size of the congregation, fundamentalist Protestant churches have become increasingly active in political and social arenas—arguing for prayer in public schools, the teaching of creationism in science courses, a strict ban on abortion, and the adoption of laws outlawing gay marriage (Fig. 7.40). In the process, they have gained considerable influence, especially in local politics (school boards and city councils).

JUDAISM

Like all other major religions, Judaism has fundamentalist sects. The most conservative of the three major sects of Judaism is Orthodox. Yet, the Orthodox sect itself is divided into

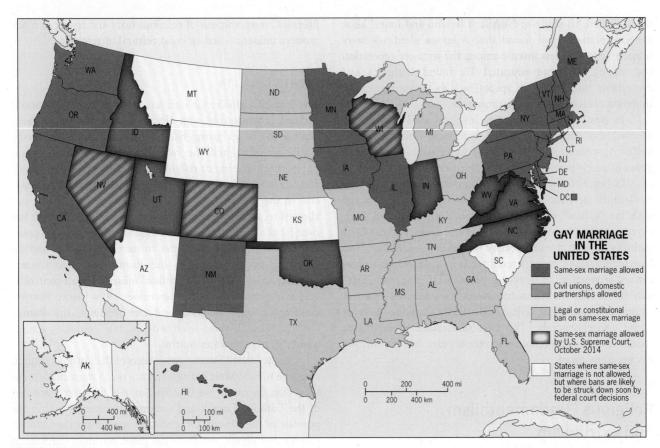

■ Figure 7.40

Gay Marriage in the United States. The map looks much different from what it did just a few years ago—a reflection of a remarkably rapid embrace of gay marriage across the United States. The map will continue to change, as recognition of same-sex marriage is in the courts in Virginia, Colorado, and other states. *Data from: National Journal,* 25 June 2014. http://www.nationaljournal.com/domesticpolicy/same-sex-marriage-decision-in-utah-could-go-all-the-way-to-the-supreme-court-this-fall-20140625.

several different schools of thought, teachings, and synagogues. Much diversity exists among Orthodox Jews, with varying views on Israel, education, and interaction with non-Orthodox Jews. Fundamentalist Jews who have migrated to Israel tend to vote for more conservative candidates in Israeli elections, affecting election outcomes. Similarly, some fundamentalist Jews who remain in Europe or North America send money to certain politicians in Israel in support of policies such as Israeli settlements on the West Bank.

Judaism also has its extremist element—people whom the majority of Jews denounce and whom the government of Israel has even banned from the country. Among the Jewish extremist groups is the Kach and Kahane Chai—followers of the late American-born, Israeli Rabbi Meir Kahane. Rabbi Kahane espoused anti-Arabism in his teachings, and his followers (Kahane Chai) continue to do so. Members of Kach or Kahane Chai are suspected in several terrorist acts in Israel.

ISLAM

Other major faiths must also confront the pressures of change. Not all Muslim communities, for example, adhere precisely to the rules of the Qu'ran prohibiting the use of alcohol. The laws of Islam, which (like some other religions) are very strict

when interpreted literally, are not applied with equal force throughout the Muslim world.

Prior to September 11, the growth of a fundamentalist movement, the Taliban in Afghanistan, provided a particularly striking example of how quickly a fundamentalist government can use extremism to change a place. The Taliban regime seized control of much of the country during the 1990s and asserted the strictest fundamentalist regime in the contemporary world. The leadership imposed a wide range of religious restrictions, sought to destroy all statues depicting human forms, required followers of Hinduism to wear identifying markers, and forbade women to appear in public with their head exposed.

The Taliban in Afghanistan also provided a haven for the activities of Islamic extremists who sought to promote an Islamic holy war, or **jihad**, against the West in general and the United States in particular. One of the key figures in the Islamic extremist movement of the past decade, Osama bin Laden, helped finance and mastermind a variety of terrorist activities conducted against the United States, including the destruction of the World Trade Towers, the attack on the Pentagon, and the downing of Flight 93 on September 11, 2001. Bin Laden is now dead, but those following in his footsteps are a product of a revolutionary Islamic movement that views the West as a great enemy and that opposes both the westernization and liberalization of the traditionally Islamic realms. These beliefs are certainly not representative of Islam as a whole, but they are religious beliefs. Indeed, they can be traced to a form of Islam, known as Wahhabi Islam, which developed in the eighteenth century in opposition to what was seen as sacrilegious practices on the part of Ottoman rulers. The champions of the opposition movement called for a return to a purportedly pure variant of Islam from centuries earlier. The Saudi Arabian state is the hearth of Wahhabi Islam today, as the Saudi Royal family has championed Wahhabi Islam since the 1800s. Saudis fund Wahhabi Islamic schools, called madrassas, around the world.

A variety of forces have fueled the violent path on which the Wahhabi extremist movement has embarked, but some of these forces are unambiguously geographic. Perhaps the most important is the widely held view among movement followers that "infidels" have invaded the Islamic holy land over the past 80 years. Of particular concern to Islamic extremists are the presence of American military and business interests in the Arabian peninsula, the establishment of the state of Israel, and the support European and American governments have given Israel. A principal goal of the movement is to bring an end to what are seen as improper territorial incursions. A second geographically related concern of Wahhabi extremists is the diffusion of modern culture and technology and its impact on traditional lifestyles and spiritual practices. Ridding the Islamic world of such influences is also a major goal.

Islamic fundamentalists who have resorted to violence in pursuit of their cause (thereby becoming extremists) are relatively small in number. The majority of Muslims in the Middle East do not support Islamic extremism. Pew Research (2014) reported a rise in concerns about Islamic extremism throughout the Middle East. Nigerians were increasingly concerned about Boko Haram; those surveyed in 14 Islamic countries had a majority negative opinion about Al-Qaeda; the majority of people surveyed in Pakistan opposed the Taliban; and Palestinians had majority unfavorable views of Hezbollah and Hamas.

Summary

Religion is a major force in shaping and changing culture. The major world religions today all stem from an area of Eurasia stretching from the eastern Mediterranean to China. Major world religions are distributed regionally, with Hinduism in India; Buddhism, Taoism, Shintoism, and Chinese philosophies in East and Southeast Asia; Islam reaching across North Africa, through the Middle East and into Southeast Asia; Shamanist religions mainly in Subsaharan Africa; and Christianity in Europe, Western Asia, the Americas, Australia, and New Zealand. Judaism, another major world religion, is not as concentrated. Today, Judaism has a base in Israel and has adherents scattered throughout Europe and the Americas.

As the 2014 Boko Haram kidnapping of 250 teenage girls in Nigeria made clear, religious beliefs can drive people to extremist behaviors. On a day-to-day basis, however, religion more typically drives cultures—shaping how people behave, how people perceive the behaviors of others, and how people across place, scale, and time interact with each other.

Geographic Concepts

activity spaces
interface areas
religion
secularism
monotheistic religion
polytheistic religion
animistic religion
universalizing religion
ethnic religion
Hinduism
caste system
syncretic
Buddhism
Shintoism
Taoism

Feng Shui
Confucianism
Judaism
diaspora
Zionism
secularism
interfaith
intrafaith
extremism
Christianity
Eastern Orthodox Church
Roman Catholic Church
Protestant
Islam
Sunni

Shi'ite
indigenous religions
Shamanism
pilgrimage
sacred sites
minarets
hajj
interfaith boundaries
intrafaith boundaries
activity space
religious fundamentalism
religious extremism
jihad

Learn More Online

About Devils Tower
www.nps.gov/deto

About Religions of the World
www.bbc.co.uk/religion/religions

About the Sacred Sites in Jerusalem
http://news.bbc.co.uk/hi/english/static/in_depth/middle_east/2000/holy_places/default.stm

Watch It Online

Christianity in European History
Choose among several programs. Click on Video on Demand.
www.learner.org/resources/series58.html#program_descriptions

The Confucian Tradition
http://www.learner.org/courses/worldhistory/unit_video_12-2.html

Sacred Sites in Jerusalem
Choose program 17 "Jerusalem, Capital of Two States."
Click Video on Demand.
www.learner.org/resources/series180.html#program_descriptions

POLITICAL GEOGRAPHY

Challenging the Political-Territorial Order

I n the summer of 2012 I found myself at the European Central Bank, looking up at a large sign out front displaying the symbol of the euro, the common currency adopted by many European Union countries (Fig. 8.1). For more than a decade, Europe's common currency has been a visible representation of a project that has reshaped the political map of the continent. The states of the EU have pooled key aspects of their sovereignty, creating a new political-territorial unit that has become an increasingly significant actor in local and global affairs.

A building and a sign representing the European integration project were not all that was on display the day of my visit. In the shadow of both was an encampment of a group of people from the "Occupy Frankfurt" movement. Occupy Frankfurt was one of many "occupy" movements around the world that sprang up to contest growing socioeconomic inequalities and the concentration of economic power in relatively few hands. Their goals were economic, but also political; the occupy protests sought to draw attention to the ways in which political institutions and practices sustain what they regard as unfair economic arrangements.

© Alexander B. Murphy

■ **Figure 8.1**
The European Central Bank in Frankfurt, Germany. The bank has played an important role in Europe's ongoing experiment with integration, but that role is increasingly being challenged.

The juxtaposition of elements that greeted me that day showed how dynamic the world's political geography is. Since the seventeenth century, sovereign states have been the bedrock of the international political order. In 1648, at the end of the Hundred Years' War, western European governments defined the territory of their country and exerted substantial control over their populations. States claimed to represent the people within their borders and organized militaries against external incursions. Europeans diffused the system of sovereign states throughout the world through colonialism and trade. As European states assumed positions of global

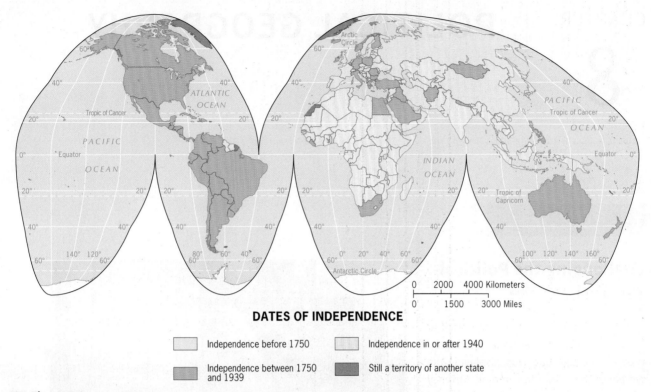

DATES OF INDEPENDENCE

- Independence before 1750
- Independence between 1750 and 1939
- Independence in or after 1940
- Still a territory of another state

■■ **Figure 8.2**
Dates of Independence for States. The first major wave of independence movements between 1750 and 1939 occurred mainly in the Americas. The second major wave of independence movements after 1940 occurred mainly in Africa and Asia. South Sudan became the most recently recognized independent state in July, 2011, bringing the total number of member states in the United Nations to 193. *Data from: United Nations, 2014.*

dominance, breaking empires in other regions of the world into colonies, which eventually became independent states through decolonization of the Americas in the early nineteenth century and Africa in the mid-twentieth century (Fig. 8.2).

Decolonization was fueled by the desire for political and economic independence. Former colonies became states, gaining political independence under international law; and each new country was theoretically sovereign, legally having the ultimate say over what happened within its borders. But the legacies of colonialism were inescapable, ranging from entrenched internal inequalities to external economic dependencies that made it difficult to obtain political and economic stability. Moreover, each new country was comprised of a mixture of peoples, cultures, languages, and religions that had been grouped together during the colonial period.

With globalization in the twentieth century, being economically independent is virtually impossible not only for former colonies but also for the European powers that colonized them. The rise of the EU and the adoption of a common currency represent efforts to create a political and economic unit at a different scale—one that its proponents hope can be a more influential global actor than any individual country could be and that can produce economic and social advantages within its borders. There have clearly been many successes, but that unit finds itself increasingly under attack from a variety of directions. Facilitated by new technologies and heightened global interconnections, movements such as Occupy Frankfurt are representative of a new type of challenge to the way politics is organized geographically.

Political activity is as basic to human culture as language or religion. All individuals, groups, communities, nations, governments, and supranational organizations engage in political activity. Each desires power and influence to achieve personal and public goals. Whether or not we like politics, each of us is caught up in these processes, with effects ranging from the composition of school boards to the conduct of war.

In this chapter, we examine how geographers study politics. Political geographers study the spatial assumptions and structures underlying politics, the ways people organize space, the role territory plays in politics, and the problems that result from changing political and territorial circumstances. The state continues to be an influential political actor, and we thus devote considerable attention to the geographical foundations of the modern state system. We also consider a few of the key large-scale changes that are shaping life in the early twenty-first century.

Key Questions FOR CHAPTER 8

1. How is space politically organized into states and nations?
2. How do states spatially organize their governments?
3. How are boundaries established, and why do boundary disputes occur?
4. How does the study of geopolitics help us understand the world?
5. What are supranational organizations, and what is the future of the state?

HOW IS SPACE POLITICALLY ORGANIZED INTO STATES AND NATIONS?

Political geography is the study of the political organization of the world. Political geographers study the spatial manifestations of political processes at various scales: how politically meaningful spaces came into being and how these spaces influence outcomes. At the global scale, the most influential political-territorial are individual countries, which are commonly called states. A **state** is a politically organized territory with a permanent population, a defined territory, and a government. To be a state, an entity must be recognized as such by other states.

The present-day division of the world political map into states is a product of endless accommodations and adjustments within and between human societies. The political map of the world is the world map most of us learn first. We study the names of the countries and perhaps each country's capital. It hangs in the front of our classrooms, it is used to organize maps in our textbooks, and it becomes so natural looking to us that *we begin to think it is natural.*

The world map of states is anything but natural. The mosaic of states on the map represents a way of politically organizing space that is less than 400 years old. Just as people create places, imparting character to the landscape and shaping culture, people make states. States and state boundaries are made, shaped, and refined by people, their actions and their interactions. The very idea of dividing the world into discrete territorially defined units of governance is one created and exported by people.

Central to the state are the concepts of **territory** and territoriality. As geographer Stuart Elden has pointed out, the modern concept of territory arose in early modern Europe as a system of political units came into being with fixed, distinct boundaries and at least quasi-independent governments. **Territoriality** is the process by which such units come into being. Territoriality, however, can take place at different scales. In a book published in 1986, geographer Robert Sack defined territoriality as "the attempt by an individual or group to affect, influence, or control people, phenomena, and relationships, by delimiting and asserting control over a geographic area." Sack sees human territoriality as a key ingredient in the construction of social and political spaces. He calls for a better understanding of the human organization of the planet through a consideration of how and why certain territorial strategies are pursued at different times and in different places.

Today, territoriality is tied to the concept of **sovereignty**. As Sack explained, territorial behavior implies an expression of control over a territory. In international law, the concept of sovereignty is territorially defined. Sovereignty refers to a government's right to control its own territory, both politically and militarily. The state governments of the world have the last say, at least legally, over their respective territories. When the international community recognizes an entity as a state, it also recognizes the entity as being sovereign within its borders. Under international law, states are sovereign, and they have the right to defend their **territorial integrity** against incursion from other states.

The Modern State Idea

In the 1600s, Europeans were not the only ones who behaved territorially, organized themselves into distinct political units, or claimed sovereignty. Because territoriality manifests itself in different ways, ideas about the relationship between political arrangements and geographical space varied from place to place.

In North America, American Indian tribes behaved territorially but not necessarily exclusively. Plains tribes shared hunting grounds with neighboring tribes that were friendly, and they fought over hunting grounds with neighboring tribes that were unfriendly. Territorial boundaries were usually not delineated on the ground. Plains tribes also held territory communally, so that individual tribal members did not "own" land. Similarly, in Southeast Asia and in Africa, state-like political entities also existed. In all of these places, and in Europe before the mid-1600s, rulers held sway over a people, but there was no collective agreement among them about how territory would be organized or what rulers could do within their respective domains.

The European state idea deserves particular attention because it most influenced the development of the modern state system. We can see traces of this state idea more than two millennia ago near the southeastern shores of the Mediterranean Sea, where distinct kingdoms emerged within discrete territories. The works of Greek philosophers on governance and aspects of ancient Greece and Rome play parts in the modern state idea. The emergence of larger-scale political-territorial units in the western portions of Late Medieval Europe developed as the feudal system broke down. In the case of what are now England and France, a single ruler was able to gradually wrest power and territory from weak feudal arrangements. At the same time, increasingly autonomous cities emerged in northern Italy and northwestern Europe where urban elites sought some degree of independence from the structures of power that dominated elsewhere. Following these developments, Early Modern European scholars advanced new ways of thinking about political space. Aiming to promote peace, great thinkers of the time drew on the concept of property rights as developed in ancient Greece and Rome to presuppose a territorial order whereby entities were free from outside control and rulers had absolute power over their realm.

By the early seventeenth century, a few larger-scale political-territorial units in western Europe (notably England, France, and Spain) coexisted with a complicated patchwork of state-like entities, including the Republic of Venice, Brandenburg, the Papal States of central Italy, the Kingdom of Hungary, and a large number of minor German states—many with poorly defined borders (Fig. 8.3). The emerging political map was accompanied by the development of **mercantilism**,

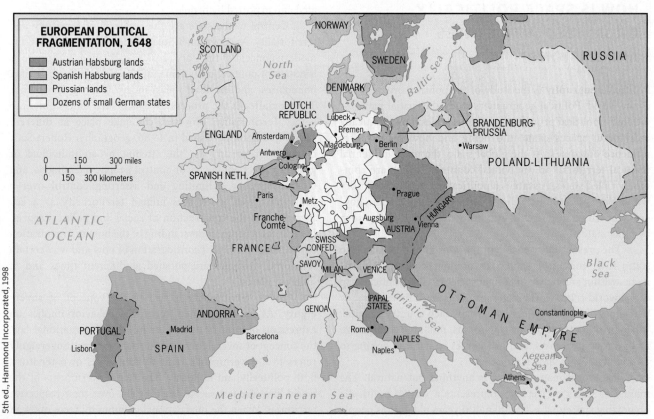

Adapted with permission from: Geoffrey Barraclough, ed., *The Times Concise Atlas of World History*, 5th ed., Hammond Incorporated, 1998

■ **Figure 8.3**
European Political Fragmentation in 1648. At the time the treaty known as the Peace of Westphalia was agreed to in 1648, Europe was divided into a few larger territories and dozens of small principalities. With the treaty, each territory and principality became a sovereign state, with the legal right to have the last say.

which led to the accumulation of wealth through plunder, colonization, and the protection of home industries and foreign markets. Rivalry and competition intensified in Europe as well as abroad. Powerful royal families struggled for dominance in eastern and southern Europe. Instability was the rule, strife occurred frequently, and repressive governments prevailed.

The event in European history that marks the formal beginning of the modern state system is the **Peace of Westphalia**, negotiated in 1648 among the princes of the states making up the Holy Roman Empire, as well as a few neighboring states. The various treaties that constituted this peace put an end to Europe's most destructive internal struggle over religion during the Thirty Years' War. They contained new language recognizing the rights of rulers within defined, demarcated territories. The language of the treaties laid the foundations for a Europe made up of mutually recognized territorial states.

The rise of the Westphalian state system marked a fundamental change in the relationship between people and territory. In previous eras, *where* a society lived constituted its territory; in the Westphalian system it became the *territory* that defined the *society*. Territory is treated as a fixed element of political identification, and states define exclusive, nonoverlapping territories.

Even well after the Peace of Westphalia, absolutist rulers controlled most European states. During the later seventeenth and eighteenth centuries, however, the development of an increasingly wealthy middle class and monarchial regimes that were increasingly out of touch with the lives of their subjects proved to be the undoing of absolutism in parts of western Europe. City-based merchants gained money, influence, and prestige, while the power of the nobility was increasingly challenged. The traditional measure of power—land—became less important. The merchants and businessmen demanded political recognition. In the 1780s, a series of upheavals began that changed the sociopolitical face of the continent, most notably the French Revolution of 1789. The revolution, conducted in the name of the French people, ushered in an era in which the foundations for political authority came to be seen as resting with a state's citizenry, not with a hereditary monarch.

Nations

The popular media and press often use the words *nation, state,* and *country* interchangeably. Political geographers use *state* and *country* interchangeably (often preferring *state*), but the word *nation* is distinct. State is a legal term in international law, and the international political community has some agreement about what this term means. *Nation,* on the other hand, is a culturally defined term, and few people agree on exactly what it means. Some argue that a nation is simply the people within a state's borders, for example, all people who live in Germany. Yet the term is also used to describe peoples who do not have a state (the Kurds, indigenous groups, and the like).

The aforementioned ambiguity reflects the fact that a **nation** was traditionally understood to be a group of people who think of themselves as one based on a sense of shared culture and history, and who seek some degree of political-territorial autonomy. This idea encompasses different kinds of culturally defined nations. Nations variously see themselves as sharing a religion, a language, an ethnicity, or a history. How a nation is defined depends on the people who see themselves as part of the nation. One of the most widely read scholars on nationalism today, Benedict Anderson, defines the nation as an "imagined community": It is imagined because one will never meet all of the people in the nation, and it is a community because individuals nonetheless see themselves as part of the larger national group.

All nations are ultimately mixtures of different peoples. The French are often considered to be the classic example of a nation, but the most French-feeling person in France today is the product of a melding together of a wide variety of cultural groups over time, including Celts, Ancient Romans, Franks, Goths, and many more. If the majority of inhabitants of modern France belong to the French nation, it is because, during the formation of the French territorial state, the people came to think of themselves as French—not because the French nation existed as a primordial group that has always been distinct.

People in a nation tend to look to their past and think, "we have been through much together," and when they look to their future they often think, "whatever happens, we will go through it together." A nation is identified by its own membership; therefore, we cannot simply define a nation as the people within a territory. Indeed, rarely does a nation's extent correspond precisely with a state's borders. Many countries have multiple nations within their borders. For example, in the country of Belgium, two nations, the Flemish and the Walloons, exist within the state's borders.

Nation-State

Over time the European idea that the map of *states* should look like the map of *nations* became the aspiration of governing elites around the world. A **nation-state** is a politically organized area in which nation and state occupy the same space. Since few (if any) states are nation-states, the importance of the concept of the nation-state lies primarily in the idea behind it. In the effort to form nation-states, some states have chosen to privilege one ethnic group at the expense of others, and other states have outlined a common history and culture. Either way, the state works to temper identities that might challenge the state's territorial integrity.

The goal of creating nation-states dates to the French Revolution, which sought to replace control by a monarchy or colonizer with an imagined cultural-historical community of French people. The Revolution initially promoted **democracy**, the idea that the people are the ultimate sovereign—that is, the people, the *nation,* have the ultimate say over what happens within the state. Each nation, it was argued, should have its own sovereign territory, and only when that is achieved can true democracy and stability exist.

People began to see the idea of the nation-state as the ultimate form of political-territorial organization, the appropriate unit entitled to sovereignty, and the best route to stability. The key problem associated with the idea of the nation-state is that it assumes the presence of reasonably well-defined, stable nations living contiguously within discrete territories. Very few places in the world come close to satisfying this requirement. Nonetheless, in the Europe of the late-eighteenth and nineteenth centuries, many believed the assumption could be met.

The quest to form nation-states in the Europe of the 1800s gave rise to the age of nationalism. We can view nationalism from two vantage points: that of the people and that of the state. When *people* have a strong sense of nationalism, they have a loyalty to and a belief in the nation itself. This loyalty does not necessarily coincide with the borders of the state. A *state*, in contrast, seeks to promote a sense of nationhood that coincides with its own borders. In the name of nationalism, a state with more than one nation within its borders may attempt to build a single national identity out of the divergent people within its borders. In the name of nationalism, a state may also promote conflict with another state that it sees as threatening to its territorial integrity.

Even though the roots of nationalism lie in earlier centuries, the nineteenth century was the true age of nationalism in Europe. In some cases the pursuit of nationalist ambitions produced greater cohesion within long-established states, such as in France or Spain; in other cases nationalism became a rallying cry for bringing together people with some shared historical or cultural elements into a single state, such as in the cases of Italy or Germany. Similarly, people who saw themselves as separate nations within other states or empires launched successful separatist movements. Ireland, Norway, and Poland all serve as examples of this phenomenon.

European state leaders used the tool of nationalism to strengthen the state. The modern map of Europe is still fragmented, but much less so than in the 1600s (Fig. 8.3). In the process of creating nation-states in Europe, states absorbed smaller entities into their borders, resolved conflicts by force as well as by negotiation, and defined their borders more precisely.

To help people within the borders relate to the dominant national ideal, state governments seek to provide security, infrastructure, and goods and services for their citizens. States support education, health care, and a military to preserve the state and to create a connection between the people and the state—to build a nation-state. European states even used the colonization of Africa and Asia in the late 1800s and early 1900s as a way to promote nationalism. People could take pride in their nation's vast colonial empire. People could identify themselves with their nation, be it French, Dutch, or British, by contrasting themselves with the people in the colonies whom they defined as mystical or savage. By defining themselves in relation to an "Other," the state and the people

helped identify the supposed "traits" of their nation; in so doing, they began to build a nation-state.

Multistate Nations, Multinational States, and Stateless Nations

People with a sense of belonging to a particular nation rarely all reside within a single state's borders. The lack of fit between nation and state therefore creates complications. Such complications might include states containing more than one nation, nations residing in more than one state, and even nations without a state at all.

Nearly every state in the world is a **multinational state**, a state with more than one nation inside its borders. The people living in the former state of Yugoslavia never achieved a strong sense of Yugoslav nationhood. Millions of people who were citizens of Yugoslavia never had a Yugoslav nationality. They identified themselves as Slovenes, Croats, Serbs, or members of other nations or ethnic groups. Yugoslavia was a state that was comprised of more than one nation, and it eventually collapsed.

When a nation stretches across borders and across states, the nation is called a **multistate nation**. Political geographer George White studied the states of Romania and Hungary and their overlapping nations (Fig. 8.4). As he has noted, the territory of Transylvania is currently in the middle of the state of Romania, but it has not always been that way. For two centuries, Hungary's borders stretched far enough east to encompass Transylvania. The Transylvanian region today is populated by Romanians and by Hungarians, and places within Transylvania are seen as pivotal to the histories of both Hungary and Romania. In keeping with the nation-state ideal, it is not surprising that both Romania and Hungary have interests in Transylvania, and some Hungarians continue to look upon the region as a territory that has been illegitimately lost. White explains how important territory is to a nation: "The control and maintenance of territory is as crucial as the control and maintenance of a national language, religion, or a particular way of life. Indeed, a language, religion or way of life is difficult to maintain without control over territory." In the case of Romania and Hungary, as in other similar situations, territory is as important as "language, religion, or way of life." When multiple nations or states claim attachments to the same piece of territory, the potential for conflict is significant.

Another complication that arises from the lack of fit between nations and states is that some nations do not have a state; they are **stateless nations**. The Palestinians are an example of a stateless nation. The Palestinian Arabs have gained control over the Gaza Strip and fragments of the Occupied Territories of the West Bank and Golan Heights. These territories may provide the foundations of a future state. The United Nations agency for Palestinian refugees records 5 million registered Palestinian refugees. Well over half of these refugees continue to live in Jordan,

GUEST FIELD NOTE

Cluj-Napoca, Romania

To Hungarians, Transylvania is significant because it was an important part of the Hungarian Kingdom for a thousand years. Many of their great leaders were born and buried there, and many of their great churches, colleges, and architectural achievements are located there too. For example, in the city of Cluj-Napoca (Kolozsvár in Hungarian) is St. Michael's Cathedral, and next to it is the statue of King Matthias, one of Hungary's greatest kings. Romanians have long lived in the territory too, tracing their roots back to the Roman Empire. To Romanian nationalists, the existence of Roman ruins in Transylvania is proof of their Roman ancestry and their right to govern Transylvania because their ancestors lived in Transylvania before those of the Hungarians. When archaeologists found Roman ruins around St. Michael's Cathedral and King Matthias's statue, they immediately began excavating them, which in turn aggravated the ethnic Hungarians. Traveling in

Courtesy of Steven Schnell

■ **Figure 8.4**

Transylvania made me very aware of how important places are to peoples and how contested they can be.

Credit: © George White, Frostburg State University.

Lebanon, Syria, and other Arab states. Over 2 million Palestinians live in the Gaza Strip and West Bank; however, the international community does not universally recognize the Palestinian lands as a state.

A much larger stateless nation is the Kurds, a group comprised of between 25 and 30 million people living in an area called Kurdistan that covers parts of six states (Fig. 8.5). In the aftermath of the 1991 Gulf War, the United Nations established a Kurdish Security Zone north of the 36th parallel in Iraq, and that area continues to have significant autonomy in present-day Iraq. The no-fly zone in the Kurdish region of northern Iraq has created a relatively peaceful place compared to continued violence in southern Iraq. Violent acts still mar the Kurdish north, but prosperity has also come to the region through petrodollars. A recent travel article in the *New York Times* described new theme parks and gated communities that reflect the affluence in the city of Erbil, which is the Kurdish capital city in Iraq. The article also described Erbil's 6000-year-old citadel as a reminder that the city is "one of the oldest continuously inhabited cities in the world."

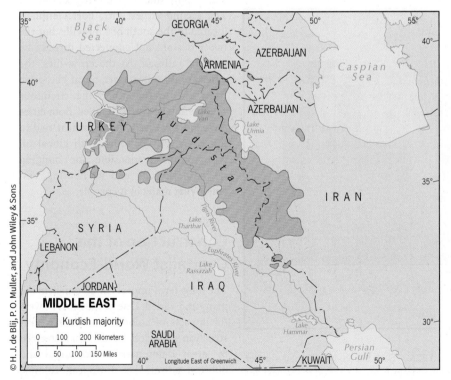

© H. J. de Blij, P. O. Muller, and John Wiley & Sons

MIDDLE EAST

Kurdish majority

0   100   200 Kilometers
0   50   100   150 Miles

■ **Figure 8.5**
Kurdish Region of the Middle East.

An independent Kurdish state seems unlikely, at least in the near future. In addition to northern Iraq, the Kurds form the largest minority in Turkey, where the city of Diyarbakir is the unofficial Kurdish capital of Turkey. Relations between the 10 million Kurds in Turkey and the Turkish government in Ankara have been volatile, and Turkey regards the Kurdish region as part of the state's core territory. Without the consent of Turkey, establishing a truly independent Kurdish state will be difficult.

European Colonialism and the Diffusion of the Nation-State Model

Europe exported its concepts of state, sovereignty, and the desire for nation-states to much of the rest of the world through two waves of colonialism (Fig. 8.6). In the sixteenth century, Spain and Portugal took advantage of an increasingly well-consolidated internal political order and newfound wealth to expand their influence to increasingly far-flung realms during the first wave of colonialism. Later joined by Britain, France, the Netherlands, and Belgium, the first wave of colonialism established a far-reaching political and economic system. After independence movements in the Americas during the late 1700s and 1800s, a second wave of colonialism began in the late 1800s. The major colonizers were Britain, France, the Netherlands, Belgium, Germany, and Italy. The colonizing parties met for the Berlin Conference in 1884–1885 and arbitrarily laid out the colonial map of Africa without reference to indigenous cultural or political

arrangements. Driven by motives ranging from economic profit to national pride to the desire to bring Christianity to the rest of the world, colonialism projected European power and a European approach to organizing political space into the non-European world (Fig. 8.7).

With Europe in control of so much of the world, Europeans laid the ground rules for the emerging international state system, and the modern European concept of the nation-state became the model adopted around the world. Europe also established and defined the ground rules of the capitalist world-economy, creating a system of economic interdependence that persists today.

During the heyday of **colonialism**, the imperial powers exercised ruthless control over their domains and organized them for maximum economic exploitation. The capacity to install the infrastructure necessary for such efficient profiteering is itself evidence of the power relationships involved: Entire populations were regimented in the service of the colonial ruler. Colonizers organized the flows of raw materials for their own benefit. The tangible evidence of that organization (plantations, ports, mines, and railroads) are prominent features of the cultural landscape to this day.

The colonial era is now largely behind us, but the political organization of space and associated economic arrangements are still very much with us. Most of the former colonies are now independent states, but their economies are anything but independent. In many cases, raw material flows are as great as they were before the colonial era came to an end. For example, today in Gabon, Africa, the railroad goes from the interior forest, which is logged for plywood, to the major port and capital city, Libreville. The second largest city, Port Gentil, is located to the south of Libreville, but the two cities are not connected directly by road or railroad. As the crow flies, the cities are 90 miles apart, but if you drive from one to the other, the circuitous route will take you 435 miles. Both cities are export focused. Port Gentil is tied to the global oil economy, with global oil corporations responsible for building much of the city and its housing, and employing many of its people.

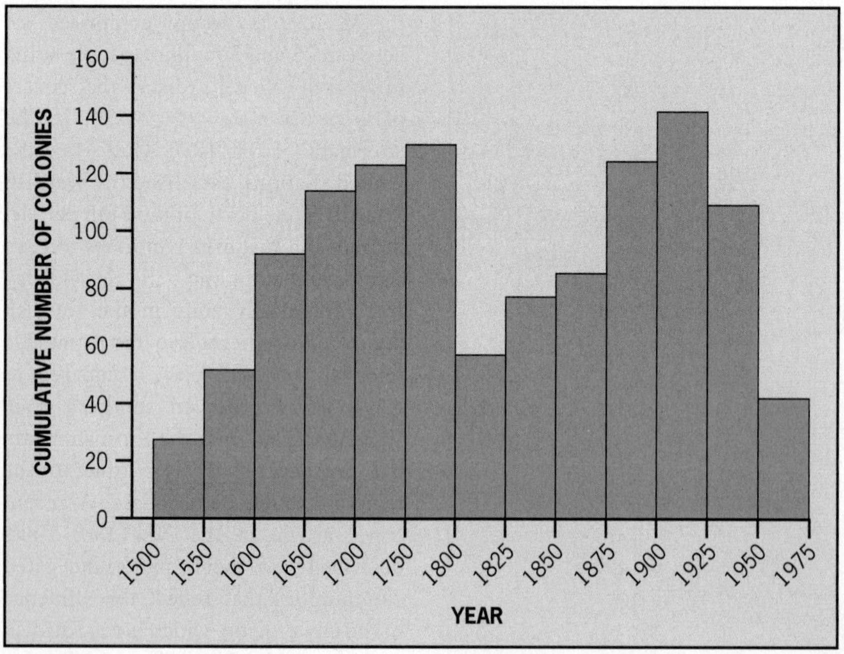

Adapted with permission from: Peter J. Taylor and Colin Flint, *Political Geography: World-Economy, Nation-State and Locality*, 4th edition., New York: Taylor & Francis, 2000.

■ Figure 8.6

Two Waves of Colonialism Between 1500 and 1975. Each bar shows the total number of colonies around the world. When the total number drops from one period to the next, for example from 1950 to 1975, the drop reflects the number of colonies that became independent between those two dates.

Construction of the Capitalist World-Economy

The long-term impacts of colonialism are many and varied. One of the most powerful impacts of colonialism was the construction of a global order characterized by great differences in economic and political power. The European colonial enterprise gave birth to a globalized economic order in which the European

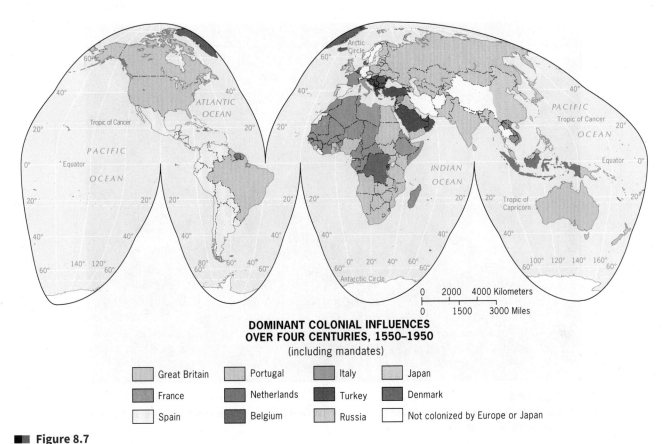

**DOMINANT COLONIAL INFLUENCES
OVER FOUR CENTURIES, 1550–1950**
(including mandates)

Great Britain	Portugal	Italy	Japan
France	Netherlands	Turkey	Denmark
Spain	Belgium	Russia	Not colonized by Europe or Japan

■■ **Figure 8.7**

Dominant Colonial Influences, 1550–1950. The map shows the *dominant* European or Japanese colonial influence in each country over the four centuries.   © H. J. de Blij, John Wiley & Sons.

states and areas dominated by European migrants emerged as the major centers of economic and political activity. Through colonialism, Europeans extracted wealth from colonies and put colonized peoples in a subservient position.

Of course, not all Europeans profited equally from colonialism. Enormous poverty persisted within even the most powerful European states. Moreover, sustaining control over colonies was costly. In the late seventeenth century, the high cost of maintaining the large Spanish colonial empire was beginning to take a toll on the Spanish economy. Western Europeans were not the only people to profit from colonialism. During the period of European colonialism (1500–1950), Russia and the United States expanded over land instead of overseas, profiting from the taking of territory and the subjugation of indigenous peoples. Japan was a regional colonial power, controlling Korea and other parts of East and Southeast Asia as well as Pacific Islands. But the concentration of wealth that colonialism brought to Europe, and to parts of the world dominated by European settlers, including the United States, Canada, and Australia, is at the heart of the highly uneven global distribution of power that continues today.

The forces of colonialism played a key role in knitting together the economies of widely separated areas, which gave birth to a global economic order—a world-economy. Wealth is unevenly distributed in the world-economy, as can be seen in

statistics on per capita gross national income (GNI): Bangladesh's GNI is only $2070, whereas Norway's GNI is $64,030. But to truly understand why wealth is distributed unevenly, we cannot simply study each country, its resources, and its production of goods. Rather, we need to understand where countries fit in the world-economy. That is, we need to see the big picture.

Think of a pointillist painting. Specifically, envision the magnificent work of nineteenth-century French painter Georges Pierre Seurat, *Sunday Afternoon on the Island of La Grande Jatte* (Fig. 8.8). The painting hangs in the Art Institute of Chicago. If you have the opportunity to see the painting and if you stand close enough, you will see Seurat's post-Impressionist method of painting millions of points or dots—single, tiny brush strokes, each a single color. When you step back again, you can gain a sense of how each dot fits into the picture as a whole.[1] In the last few decades, social scientists have sought to understand how each dot, how each country and each locality, fit into the picture of the world as a whole. If you focus on a single dot or even each dot one at a time, you miss the whole. Even if you study every single dot and add them together, you still miss the whole. You need to step back

---

[1]We give credit to former student Kelsey Lynd, who came up with this metaphor for world-systems theory in a political geography class at the University of Mary Washington in 1999.

■ **Figure 8.8**
Chicago, Illinois.   Sunday Afternoon on the Island of La Grande Jatte, by Georges Pierre Seurat, hangs in the Art Institute of Chicago.

and see the whole, as well as the individual dots, studying how one affects the other. By now, this should sound familiar: It is one of the ways geographers think about **scale**.

Political geographers took note of one sociologist's theory of the world-economy and added much to it. Building on the work of Immanuel Wallerstein, proponents of **world-systems theory** view the world as much more than the sum total of the world's states. Much like a pointillist painting, world-systems theorists hold that to understand any state, we must also understand its spatial and functional relationships within the world-economy.

Wallerstein's publications number in the hundreds, and the political and economic geography publications tied to world-systems theory number in the thousands. To simplify the research, we can study the three basic tenets of world-systems theory, as Wallerstein defines them:

1. The world-economy has one market and a global division of labor.

2. Although the world has multiple states, almost everything takes place within the context of the world-economy.

3. The world-economy has a three-tier structure.

According to Wallerstein, the development of a world-economy began with capitalist exchange around 1450 and encompassed the globe by 1900. **Capitalism** means that in the world-economy, individuals, corporations, and states own land and produce goods and services that are exchanged for profit. To generate a profit, producers seek the cheapest production and costs. For example, when labor (including salaries and benefits) became the most expensive component of production costs, corporations sought to move production from North Carolina to Mexico and then to China, simply to take advantage of cheaper labor. In addition to the world labor supply, producers gain profit by commodifying whatever they can. **Commodification** is the process of placing a price on a good, service, or idea and then buying, selling, and trading that item. Companies create new products, generate new twists on old products, and create demand for the products through marketing. As children, none of the authors of this book could have imagined buying a bottle of water. Now, the sale of water in bottles is commonplace.

Second, despite the existence of approximately 200 states, most economic interactions take place within the context of the world-economy (and have since 1900). Colonialism played a major role in establishing this system by exporting the European state idea and facilitating the construction of an interdependent global economy. When colonies became independent, gaining the legal status of sovereign states was relatively easy for most colonies. The United Nations Charter even set up a committee to help colonies do so after World War II. But gaining true economic independence is all but impossible. The economies of the world are tied together, generating intended and unintended consequences that fundamentally change places.

Lastly, world-systems theorists see the world-economy as a three-tiered structure comprised of a core, a periphery, and a semiperiphery (an intermediary or transitional

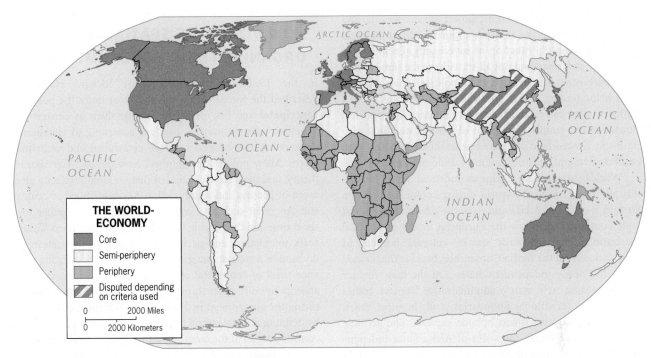

■■ **Figure 8.9**

The World-Economy.   One representation of core, periphery, and semiperiphery based on a calculation called World-Economy Centrality, derived by sociologist Paul Prew. The authors took into consideration factors not quantified in Prew's data, including membership in the European Union, in moving some countries from the categories Prew's data recommended to other categories.   *Data from*: Paul Prew, *World-Economy Centrality and Carbon Dioxide Emissions: A New Look at the Position in the Capitalist World-System and Environmental Pollution, American Sociological Association, 12*, 2 (2010): 162–191.

category). The **core** and the periphery are not just places but the sites where particular processes take place. The core is where one is most likely to find higher levels of education, higher salaries, and more technology—core processes that generate more wealth in the world-economy. The **periphery** more commonly has lower levels of education, lower salaries, and less sophisticated technology—peripheral processes associated with a more marginal position in the world-economy.

Figure 8.9 presents one way of dividing up the world in world-systems terms. The map designates some states as part of the **semiperiphery**—places where core and periphery processes are both occurring—places that are exploited by the core but in turn exploit the periphery. The semiperiphery acts as a buffer between the core and periphery, preventing the polarization of the world into two extremes.

Political geographers, economic geographers, and other academics continue to debate world-systems theory. Detractors argue that it overemphasizes economic factors in political development, that it is very state-centric, and that it does not fully account for how places move from one category to another. Nonetheless, Wallerstein's work has encouraged many to see the world political map as a system of interlinking parts that need to be understood in relation to one another and as a whole. As such, the impact of world-systems theory has been considerable in political geography, and it is increasingly commonplace for geographers to refer to the

kinds of core–periphery distinctions suggested by world-systems theory.

World-systems theory helps explain how colonial powers were able to amass and sustain great concentrations of wealth. During the first wave of colonialism, colonizers extracted goods from the Americas and the Caribbean and exploited Africa for slave labor, amassing wealth through sugar, coffee, fruit, and cotton production. During the second wave of colonialism, which happened after the Industrial Revolution, colonizers set their sights on cheap industrial labor, cheap raw materials, and large-scale agricultural plantations.

Not all core countries in the world today were colonial powers, however. Countries including Switzerland, Singapore, and Australia have significant global clout even though they were never classic colonial powers, and that clout is tied in significant part to their positions in the global economy. The countries gained their core positions through access to the networks of production, consumption, and exchange in the wealthiest parts of the world and through their ability to take advantage of that access.

World-Systems and Political Power

Are economic power and political power one and the same? No, but certainly economic power can bring political power.

In the current system, economic power means wealth, and political power means the ability to influence others. Political power is not simply a function of sovereignty. Each state is theoretically sovereign, but not all states have the same ability to influence others or achieve their political goals. Having wealth helps leaders amass political power. For instance, a wealthy country can establish a mighty military. But political influence is not simply a function of hard power; it is also diplomatic. Switzerland's declared neutrality, combined with its economic might, aids the country's diplomatic efforts.

World-systems theory helps us understand how Europe politically reorganized the world during colonialism. When colonialism ended in Africa and Asia, the newly independent people continued to follow the European model of political organization. The arbitrarily drawn colonial borders of Africa, dating from the Berlin Conference, became the boundaries of the newly independent states. On the map, former colonies became new states; administrative borders transformed into international boundaries; and, in most cases, colonial administrative towns became capitals. The greatest political challenge facing the states of Africa since independence has been building nation-states out of incredibly divergent (sometimes antagonistic) peoples. The leaders of the newly independent states continually work to build nation-states in the hope of quelling division among the people, securing their territory, and developing their economic (as well as other) systems of organization.

The Enduring Impact of the Nation-State Idea

Major players in international relations still seek solutions to complex political conflicts by trying to redraw the political map in an effort to bring political and national borders into closer correspondence. Faced with the disintegration of the former Yugoslavia or the complex problems of Israel/Palestine, for example, the tendency is often to propose new state boundaries around nations, with the goal of making the nation and state fit. Drawing neat boundaries of this sort is usually impossible, and the creation of new territories can lead to different ethnonational problems. Regardless of the multitude of problems and lack of simple solutions to nation and state conflicts, the European territorial state idea became the world model, and that idea is still shaping how the world is thought about and governed today.

Imagine you are the leader of a newly independent state in Africa or Asia. Determine what your government can do to build a nation that corresponds with the borders of your state. Consider the roles of education, government, military, and culture in your exercise in nation-building.

HOW DO STATES SPATIALLY ORGANIZE THEIR GOVERNMENTS?

In the 1950s, political geographer Richard Hartshorne described the forces within the state that unify the people as **centripetal** and the forces that divide them as **centrifugal**. Whether a state continues to exist, according to Hartshorne, depends on the balance between centripetal and centrifugal forces. Many political geographers have debated Hartshorne's theory, and most have concluded that we cannot select a given event or process and simply define it as centrifugal or centripetal. An event such as a war can pull the state together for a short time and then divide the state over the long term. Timing, scale, interaction, and perspective factor into unification and division in a state at any given point. Instead of creating a balance sheet of centripetal and centrifugal forces, governments attempt to unify states through nation-building, through structuring the government in a way that melds the nations within, by defining and defending boundaries, and through expressing control over all of the territory within those boundaries.

By looking at how different governments have attempted to unify the peoples and territories within their domains, we are reminded how important geography is. Governance does not take place in a vacuum. The unique characteristics of places shape whether any possible governmental "solution" solves or exacerbates matters.

Form of Government

The internal political geographic organization of states can have an impact on state unity. Most states in the world are either unitary or federal states.

Until the end of World War II, many European states, including multinational states, were highly centralized, with the capital city serving as the focus of power. Few states sought to accommodate minorities (such as Bretons in France or Basques in Spain) or outlying regions where identification with the state was weaker. Political geographers call these highly centralized states **unitary** governments. The administrative framework of a unitary government is designed to ensure the central government's authority over all parts of the state. The French government divided the state into more than 90 *départements*, but their representatives came to Paris not just to express regional concerns but to implement central-government decisions back home.

One way of governing a multinational state is to construct a *federal* system, organizing state territory into regions, substates (which we refer to as States), provinces, or cantons. In a strong **federal** system, the regions have much control over government policies and funds, whereas in a weak federal system, the central government retains a significant measure of power. Most federal systems are somewhere in between, with governments at the state scale and at the substate scale each having control over certain revenues and particular policy areas. Giving control over certain policies (especially culturally relative policies) to smaller-scale governments is one strategy for keeping the state as a whole together.

Federalism functions differently depending on the context. In Nigeria, the 36 constituent States choose their own judicial system. In the Muslim north, 12 States have Shari'a laws (legal systems based on traditional Islamic laws), and in the Christian and animist south, the States do not (Fig. 8.10). Shari'a law in the northern states of Nigeria is only applied to Muslims, not to Christians and Animists. The move to Shari'a law in the north came at the same time as democracy swept Nigeria in 2000. Nigerians in the north hoped stricter laws would help root out corruption among politicians, although it has failed to do so. Supporters of the Shari'a tradition also cite the need to curb rampant crime, prostitution, and gambling. Some northerners seek to expand Shari'a law to other States. That idea is a motivating force for the Islamic fundamentalist group Boko Haram, which has resorted to violence in an effort to overthrow the existing government and bring into being an Islamic state. The movement has used bombings, assassinations, and abductions to advance its agenda. The Nigerian government has declared a state of emergency in the country's northeast and has put significant resources toward fighting the militant group, but Nigeria's security forces have been largely unsuccessful in rooting out the organization's leaders and supply networks. Many Nigerians, in the north as well as the south, oppose Boko Haram's tactics, but chronic poverty, widespread corruption, and north–south tensions play into the organization's hands.

In the United States, States take different approaches to matters such as the death penalty, access to alcohol (Fig. 8.11), and the right to carry concealed weapons, but many of the fundamentals of the legal system do not differ among States.

Federalism accommodates regional interests by vesting primary power in provinces, States, or other regional units over all matters except those explicitly given to the central government. The Australian geographer K. W. Robinson described a federation as "the most geographically expressive of all political systems, based as it is on the existence and accommodation of regional differences... federation does not create unity out of diversity; rather, it enables the two to coexist."

Choosing a federal system does not always quell nationalist sentiment. After all, the multinational states of the Soviet Union, Yugoslavia, and Czechoslovakia fell apart, despite their federalist systems, and the future of Belgium and Iraq as single states is in some doubt.

Devolution

Devolution is the movement of power "downwards" from the central government to regional governments within the

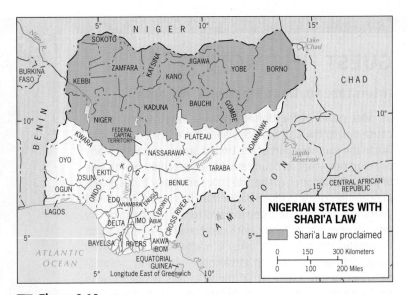

■ **Figure 8.10**
States in Nigeria with Shari'a Law. *Data from:* BBC, http://news.bbc.co.uk/2/hi/africa/1962827.stm#map.

state. Sometimes devolution is achieved by reworking a constitution to establish a federal system that recognizes the status of the regional governments, as Spain has done. In other places, governments devolve power without altering constitutions, almost as an experiment. In the United Kingdom, the Northern Ireland Assembly, a parliamentary body, resulted from devolution, but the British government suspended its activities in 2002 and then reinstated the assembly in 2007. Devolutionary forces can emerge in all kinds of states, old and young, large and small. These forces arise from several sources of internal division: ethnocultural, economic, and territorial.

ETHNOCULTURAL DEVOLUTIONARY MOVEMENTS

Many of Europe's devolutionary movements came from nations within a state that define themselves as being ethnically, linguistically, or religiously distinct.

The capacity of ethnocultural forces to stimulate devolutionary processes has been evident, for example, in eastern Europe. Parts of the eastern European map have changed quite drastically over the past two decades, and two countries, Czechoslovakia and Yugoslavia, succumbed to devolutionary pressures. In the case of Czechoslovakia, the process was peaceful: Czechs and Slovaks divided their country, creating a new international border in 1992. As Fig. 8.12 shows, however, one of the two new states, Slovakia, is not homogeneous. About 11 percent of Slovakians are Hungarian, and that minority is concentrated along the border between Slovakia and Hungary. The Hungarian minority, concerned about linguistic and cultural discrimination, has at times demanded greater autonomy or self-governance to protect its heritage in the new state of Slovakia.

GUEST FIELD NOTE

Interstate 40, Near Blackwell, Arkansas

In most states in the United States, a "dry county" might cause one to think of a place where there is very little rain. But in the southern part of the United States, there are many dry counties—that is, counties with laws forbidding the sale of packaged alcohol. In the late 1800s and early 1900s, keeping counties dry was much easier than it is today. A hundred years ago, it took up to a day to travel to the next town or city on very poor roads. Today, with cars traveling 70 mph on an interstate, the same trip takes a matter of minutes. Why would counties continue to ban alcohol sales today? Many of the reasons are cultural. Of the Arkansas residents who attend church, most are Baptists (see Fig. 7.28) or other Protestant denominations. Many of these churches prohibit consumption of alcoholic beverages. The Arkansas legislature supports dry counties by requiring counties that want to sell packaged liquor to get 38 percent of the voters in the last election to sign a petition. It only takes 10 percent of that voter pool to get any other issue on the ballot. Today, however, many dry counties in Arkansas are known as "damp." Damp counties are those where restaurants, country clubs, and social organizations can apply and receive a license to serve alcohol by the drink. This arrangement seems counterintuitive to the idea of a dry county. But

■ **Figure 8.11**

business and economic development authorities want damp counties to encourage investment and growth in the local economy.

Credit: Paul T. Gray, Jr., Russellville High School.

Compared to the constituent units of the former Yugoslavia (discussed in detail in Chapter 7), other countries shown in Figure 8.13 have dealt with devolutionary pressures more peacefully. Elsewhere in the world, however, ethnocultural fragmentation has produced costly wars. For example, ethnocultural differences were at the heart of the civil war that wracked Sri Lanka (South Asia) between the 1980s and 2009, with the Sinhalese (Buddhist) majority ultimately suppressing the drive by the Tamil (Hindu) minority for an independent state.

Devolutionary forces based on ethnocultural claims are gaining momentum in places that have long looked stable from the outside. The communist government of China has pragmatically, and in many cases relatively successfully, integrated 56 ethnic nations into the state of China. China has acknowledged the precarious place of the minority nations within the larger Han-dominated state by extending rights to minorities, including the right to have two children under the government's one-child policy. Some nations within China continue to challenge the state, however. In China's far west, Tibetan and Uyghur separatist movements have become more visible, but the Chinese government's firm hold and control of the media and Internet makes it difficult, if not impossible, for separatist groups to hold Egyptian-style protests in China. Hence, some resort to terrorist attacks.

Devolution does not *necessarily* fuel greater calls for independence; it can, in fact, help to calm tensions by giving constituent groups within a state a sense of control over their own affairs. That hope led the United Kingdom, in 1997, to allow Scotland to establish its own parliament, which had last met in 1707. The 129 members of the Scottish Parliament swear allegiance to the Queen of England, but they are in a position to dictate how a variety of issues in Scotland will be handled, including education, health, housing, and police. Those concessions were not enough to head off a referendum on independence in September 2014 (ultimately unsuccessful), but they make it more difficult for the champions of independence to paint Scotland as subservient to London. Parliaments were also established in Wales and Northern Ireland in the late 1990s, but their powers were more limited.

ECONOMIC DEVOLUTIONARY FORCES

Devolutionary pressures often arise from a combination of sources. In Catalonia, ethnocultural differences play a significant role, but economics plays a role as well; with some 8 percent of Spain's territory and just 16 percent of its population, Catalonia produces some 35 percent of all Spanish exports by value and 54 percent of its high-tech exports.

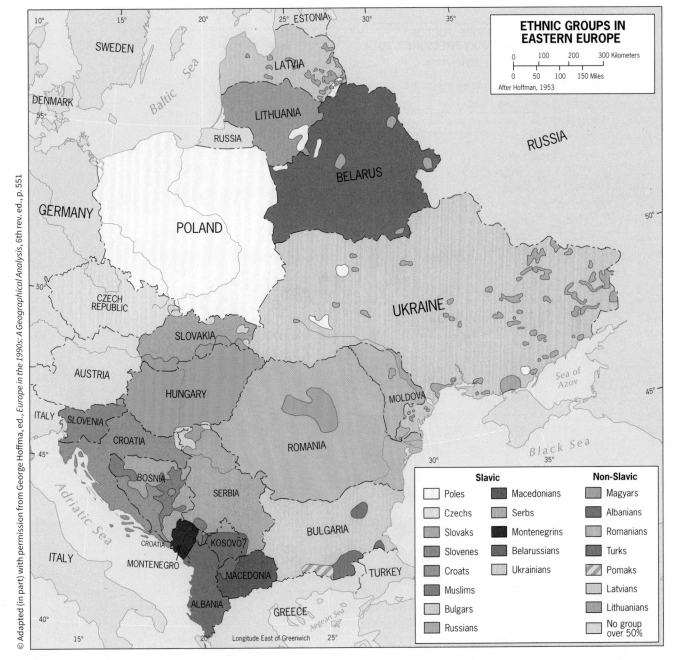

© Adapted (in part) with permission from George Hoffma, ed., *Europe in the 1990s: A Geographical Analysis*, 6th rev. ed., p. 551

■ Figure 8.12

Ethnic Mosaic of Eastern Europe.   The ethnic groups in this map are largely based on language. The presence of Russians in Ukraine, Belarus, and Latvia is a result of the Soviet policy of Russification, where Russians were moved throughout the Soviet Union to help spread the Russian culture and establish a Soviet national identity based on Russian culture. The central part of Romania, where there is a concentration of Magyars, is Transylvania, a land important to both Hungarians and Romanians.

What is more, nearly 70 percent of all Spanish exports pass through the region (Fig. 8.14). Pro-independence groups in Catalonia held a referendum in April 2011 seeking a vote for independence. The vote failed, but devolutionary forces continue to argue that Catalonia's economy pays more into the Spanish government than it receives from the state of Spain. In 2013, pro-independence groups announced plans to hold another referendum, prompting the Spanish government to reply that it would block the poll.

Economic forces have also fostered devolutionary pressures in Italy. Demands for autonomy for Sardinia are deeply rooted in the island's economic circumstances, with accusations of neglect by the government in Rome high on the list of grievances. Italy also faces serious devolutionary pressures on its mainland peninsula because of north–south differences. The Mezzogiorno region lies to the south, below the Ancona Line (an imaginary border extending from Rome to the Adriatic coast at Ancona). The wealthier north stands in sharp

Figure 8.13

Europe: Foci of Devolutionary Pressures, 2014.   Devolutionary movements in Europe are found where a nation with a shared history has the political goal of greater autonomy, unification with the rest of their nation, or independence. In 2014 Scotland voted on whether to secede from the United Kingdom, with 55 percent of the people voting against independence.

contrast to the poorer south. Despite the large subsidies granted to the Mezzogiorno, the development gap between the north, very much a part of the European core, and the south, part of the European periphery, has been widening. Some Italian politicians have exploited widespread impatience with the situation by forming organizations to promote northern interests, including devolution. One of these organizations, the Northern League, has raised the prospect of an independent state called Padania in the northern part of Italy centered on

the Po River. After a surge of enthusiasm, the Padania campaign faltered, but it pushed the Italian government to focus more attention on regional inequalities within the country.

Brazil provides another example of the interconnections between devolutionary movements and economics. As in northern Italy, a separatist movement emerged in the 1990s in a better-off region in the south that includes the three southernmost States of Rio Grande do Sul, Santa Catarina, and Parana. Southerners complained that the

■ **Figure 8.14**

Barcelona, Spain. Barcelona's long-standing economic and political significance is indelibly imprinted in the urban landscape. Once the heart of a far-flung Mediterranean empire, Barcelona went on to become a center of commerce and banking as the Iberian Peninsula industrialized. In the process, the city became a center of architectural innovation where major streets are lined with impressive buildings—many with intricate stone façades.

government was misspending their tax money on assistance to Amazonia in northern and interior Brazil. The southerners found a leader, manufactured a flag, and demanded independence for their Republic of the Pampas. The Brazilian government responded by outlawing the separatists' political party, but the economic differences between north and south continue, and devolution pressures will certainly arise again.

TERRITORIAL INFLUENCES ON DEVOLUTION

We have seen how political decisions and cultural and economic forces can generate devolutionary processes in states. Devolutionary events have at least one feature in common: they most often occur on the margins of states. Note that every one of the devolution-affected areas shown in Figure 8.13 lie on a coast or on a border. Distance, remoteness, and marginal location frequently strengthen devolutionary tendencies (see

Box 8.1). The regions most likely to seek devolution are those far from the national capital. Many are separated by water, desert, or mountains from the center of power and adjoin neighbors that may support separatist objectives.

Note also that many islands are subject to devolutionary processes: Corsica (France), Sardinia (Italy), Taiwan (China), Singapore (Malaysia), Zanzibar (Tanzania), Jolo (Philippines), Puerto Rico (United States), Mayotte (Comoros), and East Timor (Indonesia) are notable examples. As this list indicates, some of these islands became independent states, while others were divided during devolution. Insularity clearly has advantages for separatist movements.

Not surprisingly, the United States faces its most serious devolutionary pressures on the islands of Hawai'i (Fig. 8.15). The year 1993 marked the hundred-year anniversary of the United States' annexation of Hawai'i. In that year, a vocal minority of native Hawai'ians and their sympathizers demanded the return of rights lost during the "occupation." These demands included the right to reestablish an independent state called Hawai'i (before its annexation Hawai'i was a Polynesian kingdom) on several of the smaller islands. Their hope is that ultimately the island of Kauai, or at least a significant part of that island, which is considered ancestral land, will become a component of the independent Hawai'ian state.

At present, the native Hawai'ian separatists do not have the numbers, resources, or influence to achieve their aims. The potential for some form of separation between Hawai'i and the mainland United States does exist, however. The political geographer Saul Cohen has argued that political entities situated in border zones between geopolitical powers may become gateway states, absorbing and assimilating diverse cultures and traditions and emerging as new entities, no longer dominated by one or the other. Hawai'i, he suggests, is a candidate for this status.

Territorial characteristics can play a significant role in starting and sustaining devolutionary processes. Distance can be compounded by differences in physical geography—a feeling of remoteness can be fueled by being isolated in a valley or separated by mountains or a river. Basic physical-geographic and locational factors can thus be key ingredients in the devolutionary process.

Electoral Geography

The partitioning of state territory into electoral districts represents another key component of a state's internal political geography. Electoral geographers examine how the spatial configuration of electoral districts and the voting patterns that emerge in particular elections reflect and influence social and political affairs. Various countries use different voting systems to elect their governments. For example, in the 1994 South African election, government leaders introduced a system of majority rule while awarding some power to each of nine newly formed regions. The overall effect was to protect, to an extent, the rights of minorities in those regions.

BOX 8.1

The Territorial Configuration of States

Classical political geography devoted considerable attention to the ways in which different territorial configurations might influence state stability. The focus of attention was on the potential centrifugal or centripetal impacts of differently shaped states (see figure). Particularly before the advent of modern transportation and communication, it was easier for a central government to knit together the territory of a compact state—one in which the distance from the geometric center to any point on the boundary did not vary greatly—than it was for states lacking this characteristic. Some states are fragmented, consisting of two or more separate pieces; examples include the Philippines and Indonesia. This fragmentation makes certain kinds of interactions more difficult. Other states are elongated (Chile, Vietnam), making integration more difficult. Still others have a protruded or prorupted area—one that extends out from a more compact core; this area sometimes has developed in different ways from the core (e.g., the southern portion of Thailand). Finally, a few states are perforated by another country (e.g., South Africa by Lesotho).

The shape of states no longer receives a great deal of attention because it is increasingly clear that other factors have more influence on the viability and integrity of states. The Côte d'Ivoire (Ivory Coast) is relatively compact, but the country struggles with ethnoregional differences. Norway is elongated and the United States is fragmented, but these are

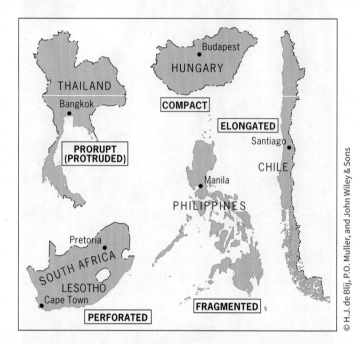

comparatively well-integrated states. The point is that the legitimacy and effectiveness of governmental and social institutions, and the position of states in the global economy, tend to be far more significant than shape. But shape is not entirely irrelevant. There is a long-standing north–south divide in Vietnam, and Thailand has struggled to integrate its prorupted south. The key is to view shape as a matter that varies in influence depending on the political, economic, and historical circumstances at play.

FIELD NOTE

"As I drove along a main road through a Honolulu suburb I noticed that numerous houses had the Hawai'i State flag flying upside down. I knocked on the door of this house and asked the homeowner why he was treating the State flag this way. He invited me in and we talked for more than an hour. 'This is 1993,' he said, 'and we native Hawai'ians are letting the State government and the country know that we haven't forgotten the annexation by the United States of our kingdom. I don't accept it, and we want our territory to plant our flag and keep the traditions alive. Why don't you drive past the royal palace, and you'll see that we mean it.' He was right. The Iolani Palace, where the Hawai'ians' last monarch, Queen Liliuokalani, reigned until she was deposed by a group of American businessmen in 1893, was draped in black for all of Honolulu to see. Here was devolutionary stress on American soil."

■ **Figure 8.15**
Honolulu, Hawai'i.

In the 1994 election in South Africa, the leading political party, the African National Congress, designated at least 35 percent of its slate of candidates to women, helping South Africa become one of the world leaders in the percent of women who hold seats in a national legislative body (see Fig. 5.17).

The geographic study of voting behavior is especially interesting because it helps us assess whether people's voting tendencies are influenced by their geographic situation. Maps of voting patterns often produce surprises that can be explained by other maps, and geographic information systems have raised this kind of analysis to new levels. Political geographers study church affiliation, income level, ethnic background, education attainment, and numerous other social and economic factors to gain an understanding of why voters in a certain region might vote the way they do.

The domain in which electoral geographers can have the most concrete influence is in the drawing of electoral districts. In a democracy with representatives elected by district, the spatial organization of the districts determines whose voice is heard in a given place—with impacts on who is elected. A voter's most direct contact with government is at the local level. The United States Constitution establishes a system of **territorial representation**. In the Senate, each major territorial unit (State) gets two representatives, and the 435 members of the House of Representatives are elected from territorially defined districts that have similar-sized populations.

The Constitution requires a census every ten years in order to enumerate the population and reapportion the representatives accordingly. **Reapportionment** is the process by which districts are moved according to population shifts, so that each district encompasses approximately the same number of people. For example, after the 2010 census, several States in the so-called Rust Belt, including Pennsylvania, Ohio, and Michigan, lost representatives, whereas the Sun Belt States of Georgia, South Carolina, and Florida, along with the southwestern States of Arizona, Nevada, and Utah gained representatives.

In the United States, once reapportionment is complete, individual States go through the process of redistricting, each following its own system. The criteria involved in redistricting are numerous, but the most important is equal representation, achieved by ensuring that districts have approximately the same populations. In addition, the Supreme Court prefers compact and contiguous districts that keep political units (such as counties) intact. Finally, the courts have repeatedly called for representational equality of racial and linguistic minorities.

Even after the civil rights movement of the 1950s and 1960s in the United States, minorities were refused voting rights in a multitude of districts and States around the country. County registrars would close their doors when African Americans came to register to vote, and intimidation kept many away from voting at the polls. Even in places where minorities were allowed to register and vote, the parties drawing the voting districts or choosing the electoral system would make it nearly impossible for the election of a minority to occur. For example, if a government has to draw ten districts in a State that is 60 percent white, 30 percent African American, and 10 percent Hispanic, it can easily dilute the minority voters by **splitting** them among multiple districts, ensuring that the white population holds the majority in each district.

In 1982, the United States Congress amended the 1965 Voting Rights Act by outlawing districts that have the effect of weakening minority-voting power. In a series of decisions, the courts interpreted this amendment to mean States needed to redistrict in a way that would ensure minority representation. Using this criterion in the redistricting that followed the 1990 census, States increased the number of majority–minority districts in the House of Representatives from 27 to 52. **Majority–minority districts** are packed districts in which a majority of the population is from the minority. In the hypothetical State described above, a redistricting following this criterion could have the goal of creating at least three majority-minority districts and a fourth where minorities had a sizable enough population to influence the outcome of the election.

Ideally, majority–minority districts would be compact and contiguous and follow existing political units. Political geographers Jonathan Leib and Gerald Webster have researched the court cases that have resulted from trying to balance these often-conflicting criteria. To pack minorities who do not live compactly and contiguously, States have drawn bizarrely shaped districts, connecting minority populations with meandering corridors and following Interstates to connect urban areas that have large minority populations (Fig. 8.16).

Strange-looking districts constructed to attain certain political ends are nothing new in American politics. In 1812, Governor Elbridge Gerry of Massachusetts signed into law a district designed to give an advantage to his party—a district that looked so odd to artist Gilbert Stuart that he drew it with a head, wings, and claws. Stuart called it the "salamander district," but a colleague immortalized it by naming it a gerrymander (after the governor). Ever since, the term **gerrymandering** has been used to describe "redistricting for advantage." Certainly, many of the districts now on the United States electoral map may be seen as gerrymanders, but for an important purpose: to provide representation to minorities who, without it, would not be represented as effectively in the House of Representatives. Despite this well-intentioned goal, others argue that the packing of minorities into majority–minority districts simply concentrates minority votes, creating a countrywide government that is less responsive to minority concerns.

The larger point is that the spatial organization of voting districts is a fundamentally geographical phenomenon, and it can have profound impacts on who is represented and who is not—as well as peoples' notions of fairness. And that is only the beginning people's. The voting patterns that emerge from particular elections can help reinforce a sense of regionalism and can shape a government's response to issues in the future. Small wonder, then, that many individuals who have little general understanding of geography at least appreciate the importance of its electoral geography component.

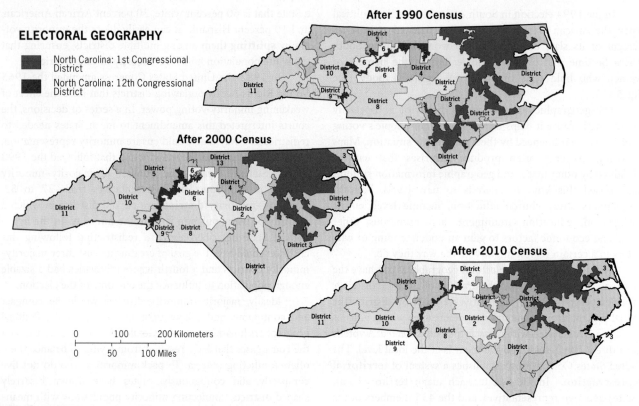

ELECTORAL GEOGRAPHY

North Carolina: 1st Congressional District

North Carolina: 12th Congressional District

After 1990 Census

After 2000 Census

After 2010 Census

0   100   200 Kilometers

0   50   100 Miles

■■ **Figure 8.16**

Electoral Geography.   North Carolina's congressional districts in 1992, 2002, and 2012. In 1992, North Carolina concentrated minorities into majority–minority districts. In 2002, North Carolina made its districts more compact and explained they were based on criteria other than race, in accordance with Supreme Court decisions during the 1990s. Using the same criteria, North Carolina redistricted again after the 2010 census, shaping districts that once again prioritized concentrating minorities while trying to achieve compactness and contiguity.   *Data from*: United States Census, 2012.

Choose an example of a devolutionary movement and consider which geographic factors favor, or work against, greater autonomy (self-governance) for the region. Would granting the region autonomy strengthen or weaken the state in which the region is currently located?

HOW ARE BOUNDARIES ESTABLISHED, AND WHY DO BOUNDARY DISPUTES OCCUR?

The territories of individual states are separated by international boundaries, often referred to as borders. Boundaries may appear on maps as straight lines or may twist and turn to conform to the bends of rivers and the curves of hills and valleys. But a boundary is more than a line, far more than a fence or wall on the ground. A **boundary** between states is actually a vertical plane that cuts through the rocks below (called the

subsoil) and the airspace above, dividing one state from another (Fig. 8.17). Only where the vertical plane intersects Earth's surface (on land or at sea) does it form the line we see on the ground.

Many borders were established on the world map before the extent or significance of subsoil resources was known. As a result, coal seams and aquifers cross boundaries, and oil and gas reserves are split between states. Europe's coal reserves, for example, extend from Belgium underneath the Netherlands and on into the Ruhr area of Germany. Soon after mining began in the mid-nineteenth century, these three neighbors began to accuse each other of mining coal that did not lie directly below their own national territories. The underground surveys available at the time were too inaccurate to pinpoint the ownership of each coal seam.

During the 1950s–1960s, Germany and the Netherlands argued over a gas reserve that lies in the subsoil across their boundary. The Germans claimed that the Dutch were withdrawing so much natural gas that the gas was flowing from beneath German land to the Dutch side of the boundary. The Germans wanted compensation for the gas they felt they lost. A major issue between Iraq and Kuwait, which in part led to Iraq's invasion of Kuwait in 1990, was the oil in the Rumaylah reserve

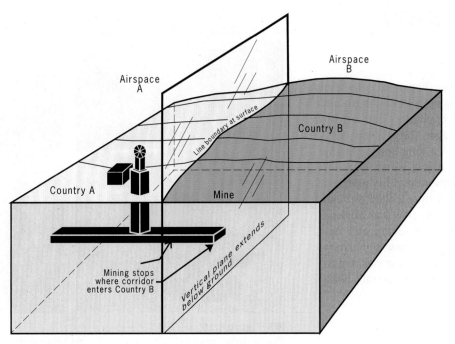

■■ Figure 8.17
The Vertical Plane of a Political Boundary. © E. H. Fouberg, A. B. Murphy, H. J. de Blij, and John Wiley & Sons, Inc.

that lies underneath the desert and crosses the border between the two states. The Iraqis asserted that the Kuwaitis were drilling too many wells and draining the reserve too quickly; they also alleged that the Kuwaitis were drilling oblique boreholes to penetrate the vertical plane extending downward along the boundary. At the time the Iraq–Kuwait boundary was established, however, no one knew that this giant oil reserve lay in the subsoil or that it would contribute to an international crisis (Fig. 8.18).

Above the ground, too, the interpretation of boundaries as vertical planes has serious implications. A state's "airspace" is defined by the atmosphere above its land area as marked by its boundaries, as well as by what lies beyond, at higher altitudes.

■■ Figure 8.18
The International Boundary Between Iraq and Kuwait. Kuwait's northern boundary was redefined and delimited by a United Nations boundary commission; it was demarcated by a series of concrete pillars 1.24 miles (2 km) apart.

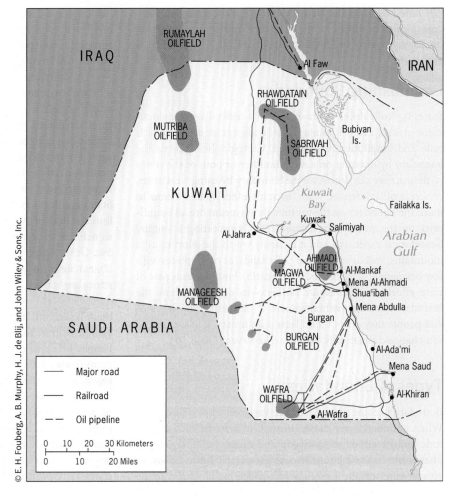

© E. H. Fouberg, A. B. Murphy, H. J. de Blij, and John Wiley & Sons, Inc.

FIELD NOTE

"Seeing the border between Italy and Slovenia marked by a plaque on the ground reminded me of crossing this border with my family as a teenager. The year was 1973, and after waiting in a long line we finally reached the place where we showed our passports to the authorities. They asked us many questions and they looked through the luggage in our trunk. Now that Slovenia is part of the European Union and has signed the Schengen Agreement eliminating border controls between countries, crossing that same border today is literally like a walk in the park."

© Alexander B. Murphy

■ **Figure 8.19**

Piazza della Transalpina.   A square divided between the towns of Gorizia, Italy and Nova Gorica, Slovenia.

But how high does the airspace extend? Most states insist on controlling the airline traffic over their territories, but states do not yet control the paths of satellite orbits.

Establishing Boundaries

States typically *define* the boundary in a treaty-like legal document in which actual points in the landscape or points of latitude and longitude are described. Cartographers *delimit* the boundary by drawing on a map. If either or both of the states so desire, they can *demarcate* the boundary by using steel posts, concrete pillars, fences, walls, or some other visible means to mark the boundary on the ground. By no means are all boundaries on the world map demarcated. Demarcating a lengthy boundary is expensive, and it is hardly worth the effort in high mountains, vast deserts, frigid polar lands, or other places with few permanent settlements. Demarcating boundaries is part of state efforts to *administrate* borders—to determine how the boundaries will be maintained and to determine which goods and people may cross them. How a boundary is administered can change dramatically over time, however (Fig. 8.19).

Types of Boundaries

Boundaries come into being in variable ways (Box 8.2). When boundaries are drawn using grid systems such as latitude and longitude or township and range, political geographers refer to these boundaries as **geometric boundaries**. In North America, the United States and Canada used a single line of latitude west of the Great Lakes to define their boundary. During the Berlin Conference, colonial powers used arbitrary reference points and drew straight lines to establish the boundaries in much of Africa.

At different times, political geographers and other academics have advocated "natural" boundaries over geometric boundaries because they are visible on the landscape as physical geographic features. **Physical-political boundaries** (also called natural-political boundaries) are boundaries that follow an agreed-upon feature in the natural landscape, such as the center point of a river or the crest of a mountain range. The Rio Grande is an important physical-political boundary between the United States and Mexico. Another physical-political boundary follows the crest lines of the Pyrenees separating Spain and France. Lakes sometimes serve as boundaries as well; for example, four of the five Great Lakes of North America are borders between the United States and Canada, and several of the Great Lakes of East Africa are borders between Congo and its eastern neighbors.

Physical features sometimes make convenient political boundaries, but topographic features are not static. Rivers change course, volcanoes erupt, and slowly, mountains erode. People perceive physical-political boundaries as stable, but many states have entered territorial conflicts over borders based on physical features (notably Chile and Argentina). Similarly, physical boundaries do not necessarily stop the flow of people or goods across boundaries, leading some states to reinforce physical boundaries with human-built obstacles (the United States on the Rio Grande). The stability of boundaries has more to do with local historical and geographical circumstances than with the character of the boundary itself.

BOX 8.2

Genetic Political Boundary Types

Leading mid-twentieth-century political geographer Richard Hartshorne (1899–1992) reasoned that how boundaries function is affected by how they came into being. Hartshorne proposed a fourfold genetic classification of boundaries (see figure). An *antecedent boundary* is one that predates the development of large-scale politically organized communities (e.g., the boundary between Malaysia and Indonesia, which passes through sparsely inhabited tropical rainforest). A second category of boundaries evolves as the cultural landscape takes shape. These *subsequent boundaries* are relatively common (e.g., the border between China and Vietnam, which reflects a long-term process of adjustment and modification).

Some boundaries are forcibly drawn by outsiders without reference to cultural patterns. Such *superimposed boundaries* are often contested by groups that straddle the boundary (e.g., the boundary separating Indonesia's West Irian from the country of Papua New Guinea). The fourth, more minor, genetic boundary type is the *relict boundary*—a border that has ceased to function but whose imprints are still evident on the cultural landscape. The boundary between former North Vietnam and South Vietnam is a classic example.

How a boundary came into being does not determine its degree of stability, but it can affect how the boundary is viewed and how it functions. It is one of many ingredients, then, that shapes the landscape of conflict and cooperation in the contemporary world.

GENETIC POLITICAL BOUNDARY TYPES

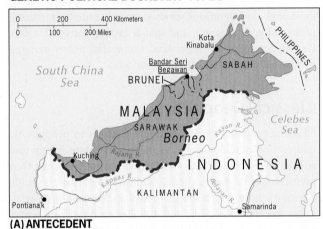

(A) ANTECEDENT

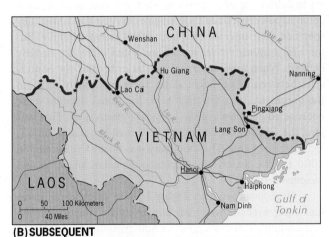

(B) SUBSEQUENT

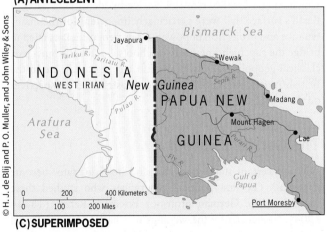

(C) SUPERIMPOSED

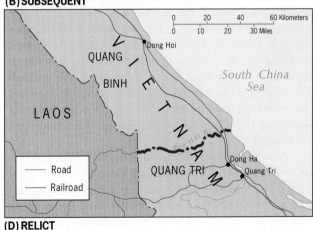

(D) RELICT

© H. J. de Blij and P. O. Muller, and John Wiley & Sons

Boundary Disputes

The boundary we see as a line on a map is the product of a complex series of legal steps that begins with a written description of the boundary. Sometimes that legal description is old and imprecise. Sometimes it was dictated by a stronger power that is now less dominant, giving the weaker neighbor a reason to argue for change. At other times the geography of the borderland has actually changed; the river that marked the boundary may have changed course, or a portion of it has been cut off. Resources lying across a boundary can lead to conflict. In short, states often argue about their boundaries. Boundary disputes take four principal forms: definitional, locational, operational, and allocational.

Definitional boundary disputes focus on the legal language of the boundary agreement. For example, a boundary definition may stipulate that the median line of a river will mark the boundary. That would seem clear enough, but the water levels of rivers vary. If the valley is asymmetrical, the median line will move back and forth between low-water and high-water stages of the stream. This may involve hundreds of meters of movement—not very much, it would seem, but enough to cause serious argument, especially if there are resources in the river. The solution is to refine the definition to suit both parties.

Locational boundary disputes center on the delimitation and possibly the demarcation of the boundary. The definition is not in dispute, but its interpretation is. Sometimes the language of boundary treaties is vague enough to allow mapmakers to delimit the line in various ways. For example, when the colonial powers defined their empires in Africa and Asia, they specified their international boundaries rather carefully. But internal administrative boundaries often were not strictly defined. When those internal boundaries became the boundaries between independent states, there was plenty of room for argument. In a few instances, locational disputes arise because no definition of the boundary exists at all. That was long the case for the Saudi Arabia–Yemen boundary—an oil-rich boundary area. That boundary was finally demarcated in 2000, but the demarcation was not accepted by all parties and violence persists.

Operational boundary disputes involve neighboring states that differ over the way their border should function. When two adjoining countries agree on how cross-border migration should be controlled, the border functions satisfactorily. However, if one state wants to limit migration while the other does not, a dispute may arise. Similarly, efforts to prevent smuggling across borders sometimes lead to operational disputes—especially when one state's efforts are not matched (or are possibly even sabotaged) by its neighbor. And in areas where nomadic ways of life still prevail, the movement of people and their livestock across international borders can lead to conflict.

Allocational boundary disputes of the kind described earlier, involving the Netherlands and Germany over natural gas and Iraq and Kuwait over oil, are becoming more common as the search for resources intensifies. Today many such disputes involve international boundaries at sea. Oil reserves under the seafloor below coastal waters sometimes lie in areas where exact boundary delimitation may be difficult or subject to debate. Another growing area of allocational dispute has to do with water supplies: The Tigris, Nile, Colorado, and other rivers are subject to such disputes. When a river crosses an international boundary, the rights of the upstream and downstream users of the river often come into conflict.

 People used to think physical-political boundaries were always more stable than geometric boundaries. Through studies of many places, political geographers have confirmed that this idea is false. Using the concepts of nation and state, explain why physical-political boundaries can create just as much instability as geometric boundaries.

HOW DOES THE STUDY OF GEOPOLITICS HELP US UNDERSTAND THE WORLD?

Geopolitics is the interplay among geography, power, politics, and international relations on Earth's surface. Political science and international relations tend to focus on governmental institutions, systems, and interactions. Geopolitics brings locational considerations, environmental contexts, territorial ideas and arrangements, and spatial assumptions to the fore. Geopolitics helps us understand the spatial power arrangements that shape international relations.

Classical Geopolitics

Classical geopolitics was born out of efforts to promote the interests of individual states as the modern state system took root in the late nineteenth and early twentieth centuries. Geopoliticians of the time generally fit into one of two camps: the German school, which sought to explain why and how certain states became powerful, and the British/American school, which sought to offer strategic advice by identifying parts of Earth's surface that were particularly important for the maintenance and projection of power. A few geopoliticians tried to bridge the gap, blending the two schools, but for the most part classical geopoliticians who are still writing today are in the British/American school, offering geostrategic perspectives on the world.

The German School

Why are certain states powerful, and how do states become powerful? The first political geographer who studied these issues was the German professor Friedrich Ratzel (1844–1904). Influenced by the writings of Charles Darwin, Ratzel postulated that the state resembles a biological organism whose life cycle extends from birth through maturity and, ultimately, decline and death. To prolong its existence, the state requires nourishment, just as an organism needs food. Such nourishment is provided by the acquisition of territories that provide adequate space for the members of the state's dominant nation to thrive, which is what Ratzel called *Lebensraum*. If a state is confined within permanent and static boundaries and deprived of overseas domains, Ratzel argued, it can atrophy. Territory is thus seen as the state's essential, life-giving force.

Ratzel's theory was based on his observations of states in the nineteenth century, including the United States. It was so speculative that it might have been forgotten if some of Ratzel's German followers in the 1930s had not translated his abstract writings into policy recommendations that ultimately were used to justify Nazi expansionism.

The British/American School

Not long after the publication of Ratzel's initial ideas, other geographers began looking at the overall organization of power in the world, studying the physical geographic map, with a view toward determining the locations of the most strategic places on Earth. Prominent among them was the Oxford University geographer Sir Halford J. Mackinder (1861–1947). In 1904, he published an article titled "The Geographical Pivot of History" in the Royal Geographical Society's *Geographical Journal*. That article became one of the most intensely debated geographic publications of all time.

Mackinder was concerned with power relationships at a time when Britain had acquired a global empire through its strong navy. To many of his contemporaries, the oceans—the paths to colonies and trade—were the key to world domination, but Mackinder disagreed. He concluded that a land-based power, not a sea power, would ultimately rule the world. His famous article contained a lengthy appraisal of the largest and most populous landmass on Earth—Eurasia (Europe and Asia together). At the heart of Eurasia, he argued, lay an impregnable, resource-rich "pivot area" extending from eastern Europe to eastern Siberia (Fig. 8.20). Mackinder issued a warning: If this pivot area became unified, a great empire could be formed.

Mackinder later renamed his pivot area the heartland, and his warning became known as the heartland theory. In his book *Democratic Ideals and Reality* (1919), Mackinder (calling

Eurasia "the World Island") issued a stronger warning to the winners of World War I, stating:

Who rules East Europe commands the Heartland
Who rules the Heartland commands the World Island
Who rules the World Island commands the World

When Mackinder proposed his **heartland theory**, there was little to foretell the rise of a superpower in the heartland. Russia was in disarray, having recently lost a war against Japan (1905), and was facing revolution. Eastern Europe was fractured. Germany, not Russia, was gaining power. But when the Soviet Union emerged and Moscow controlled over much of Eastern Europe at the end of World War II, the heartland theory attracted renewed attention.

In 1943, Mackinder wrote a final paper expressing concern that the Soviet Union, under Stalin, would seek to exert control over the states of Eastern Europe. He offered strategies for keeping the Soviets in check, including avoiding the expansion of the Heartland into the Inner Crescent (Fig. 8.20) and creating an alliance around the North Atlantic to join the forces of land and sea powers against the Heartland. His ideas were not embraced by many at the time, but within ten years of publication, the United States began its containment policy to stop the expansion of the Soviet Union, and the United States, Canada, and Western Europe formed an alliance called the North Atlantic Treaty Organization (NATO). Further proof of the importance of Mackinder's legacy can be seen in the fact that, even after the collapse of the Soviet Union, his theories enjoy widespread currency in Russian foreign policy circles.

Influence of Geopoliticians on Politics

Ratzel and Mackinder are only two of many geopoliticians who influenced international relations. Their writings, grounded in history, current events, and physical geography, sounded logical and influenced many politicians, and in some ways still do. NATO still exists and has not invited Russia to join the military alliance, but it has extended membership to 28 states since the end of the Cold War, including eastern European states. NATO has a working partnership with former republics of the Soviet Union, though the war between Russia and Georgia in 2008 and Russia's 2014 seizure of Crimea (formerly part of Ukraine), produced a chilling effect on NATO's eastward expansion.

Despite the staying power of geopolitical theories, geopolitics declined as a formal area of study after World War II. Because of the influence Ratzel's theory had on Hitler—as championed by another geopolitician, Karl Haushofer—the term *geopolitics* acquired a negative connotation. For some decades after World War II, the term was in such disrepute that few political geographers, even those studying power relationships, would identify themselves as students of geopolitics. Time, along with more balanced perspectives, has

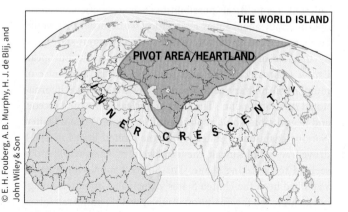

© E.H. Fouberg, A. B. Murphy, H. J. de Blij, and John Wiley & Son

■ **Figure 8.20**

The Heartland Theory. The Pivot Area/Heartland, the Inner Crescent/Rimland, and the World Island, following the descriptions of Halford Mackinder.

reinstated geopolitics as a significant field of study, encompassing efforts to understand the spatial and territorial dimensions of power relationships past, present, and future.

Critical Geopolitics

Rather than focusing on prediction and prescription, many current students of geopolitics focus on revealing and explaining the underlying geographical assumptions and territorial perspectives of international actors. Political geographers Gearoid O'Tuathail and John Agnew refer to those actors in the most powerful states, the core states, as "intellectuals of statecraft." The basic concept behind **critical geopolitics** is that intellectuals of statecraft construct ideas about geographical circumstances and places, these ideas influence and reinforce their political behaviors and policy choices, and those behaviors and choices then affect what happens and how most people interpret what happens.

O'Tuathail has focused particular attention on American geopolitical reasoning—examining speeches and statements by U.S. intellectuals of statecraft. He has drawn attention to how several American leaders often spatialize politics into a world of "us" and "them." Political leaders can shape how their constituents see places and organize international space in their minds. By drawing on American cultural logic and certain representations of America, O'Tuathail argues that presidents have repeatedly defined an "us" that is pro-democracy, independent, self-sufficient, and free and a "them" that is in some way against all of these things.

During the Cold War, President Ronald Reagan coined the term *Evil Empire* for the Soviet Union and represented the United States as "the shining city on a hill." During ensuing presidencies, terrorism replaced the Soviet Union as the "they." Sounding remarkably similar, Democratic President William J. Clinton and Republican President George W. Bush justified military actions against terrorists. In 1998, President Clinton justified American military action in Sudan and Afghanistan as a response to terrorist plans by Osama bin Laden by noting that the terrorists "come from diverse places but share a hatred for democracy, a fanatical glorification of violence, and a horrible distortion of their religion, to justify the murder of innocents. They have made the United States their adversary precisely because of what we stand for and what we stand against." Immediately after September 11, President George W. Bush made a similar claim, arguing that "They [the terrorists] stand against us because we stand in their way." In 2002, President Bush again explained, "I've said in the past that nations are either with us or against us in the war on terror."

Statements such as these are rooted in a particular geopolitical perspective on the world—one that divides the globe into opposing camps. That much may seem obvious, as there are clear ideological fault lines between an organization such as al-Qaeda and a state such as the United States. But critical geopolitics seeks to move beyond such differences to explore the spatial ideas and understandings that undergird particular political perspectives and that shape policy approaches.

One of the most powerful geopolitical ideas since the end of the Cold War in 1989 came from Samuel Huntington (1996), who argued that the world is entering a period when conflicts will increasingly reflect major religious-civilization divides. His emphasis on the importance of the "Islamic World" helped to shape responses to the September 11, 2001 attacks on the United States. The U.S. government, concerned about al-Qaeda's influence, justified military involvement in Iraq and Afghanistan based on the threat of a volatile "Islamic World." That idea was picked up and amplified by countless policy analysts, news commentators, and bloggers.

The critical geopolitics literature does not simply aim to identify geopolitical ideas; it also often critiques them. It is not surprising, then, that commentators began to point out that the "Islamic World" is tremendously diverse, culturally and religiously, and that some of the most intractable conflicts of recent times have been fought within the Islamic World, not between Muslims and others. Belief in the geopolitical significance of a unified "Islamic World" is not any more rational than belief in a geopolitically unified "Judeo-Christian World"—hardly an easy belief to sustain given recent conflicts between Russia and Ukraine. Regardless, if geopolitical ideas are believed, they shape the policies that are pursued and they become the narratives through which we perceive what happens on the ground. An important task for geographers, then, is to understand the ideological roots and implications of geopolitical reasoning by intellectuals of statecraft.

Geopolitical World Order

Geopolitical world orders are the temporary periods of stability in the way international politics is conducted. For example, during the Cold War, the geopolitical world order was bipolar—the Soviet Union and its Warsaw Pact satellites versus the United States and its close allies in Western Europe.

After the Soviet Union collapsed in 1991, the world entered a transition period, again opening up a variety of different geopolitical possibilities. Some politicians spoke optimistically about a new geopolitical world order that would be characterized by the forces that connect nations and states; by the rise of supranational entities such as the European Union (discussed in the next section); and by a promise of multilateral military action should any state violate international rules of conduct. The risks of nuclear war would recede, and negotiation would replace confrontation. When a United Nations coalition of states led by the United States in 1991 drove Iraq out of Kuwait, the framework of a new world order seemed to be taking shape. The Soviet Union, which a few years had been the United States' principal geopolitical antagonist, endorsed the operation. Arab as well as non-Arab forces helped repel the invaders.

Soon, however, doubts and uncertainties began to cloud hopes for a mutually cooperative geopolitical world order. Despite deepening interconnections crossing state lines, national self-interest still acted as a powerful force. Nations wanted to become states, and many did, as the number of United Nations members increased from 159 in 1990 to 184 by 1993 and 193 as of 2011, when South Sudan seceded from Sudan. At the same time, a variety of organizations not tied to specific territories posed a new challenge to the territorially defined state. The number and power of economic and social networks that extend across state borders increased, and nonstate organizations with political agendas that are not channeled through states came to assume a greater role.

Moreover, not everyone embraced the new geopolitical complexity. Some U.S.-based commentators championed a geopolitical world order based on **unilateralism**, with the United States assuming a position of hard-power dominance—believing that any other course of action would risk global instability. The fact that the U.S. military budget is almost as large as all the military budgets of all other states in the world combined puts it in a position to play a significant international role, but recent events have brought into question whether military dominance can achieve the ends unilateralists hope to achieve. The United States' controversial invasion of Iraq significantly undermined its influence in many parts of the globe. A rift developed across the Atlantic between the United States and some European countries, and anti-Americanism surged around the world. The processes of globalization, the diffusion of nuclear weapons, the emergence of China and India as increasingly significant powers, and the growth of networked groups and organizations, including terrorist groups, also represent challenges to American unilateralism and complicate the geopolitical picture.

Nuclear weapons, for example, give even small states the ability to inflict massive damage on larger and distant adversaries. Combined with missile technology, this may be one of the most serious dangers the world faces, which is why the United Nations insisted on dismantling Iraq's nuclear capacity after the 1991 Gulf War and why concerns over Iran's nuclear program are so great. Some states publicize their nuclear weapons programs, whereas other nuclear states have never formally acknowledged that they possess nuclear weapons. Reports of nuclear proliferation have led to military actions in the last few decades. In 1981, when reports of Iraq's nuclear program reached Israel, the Israelis attacked Iraq. As nuclear weapons have become smaller and "tactical" nuclear arms have been developed, the threat of nuclear weapons sales is of growing concern. It is now possible for a hostile state or group to purchase the power with which to threaten the world.

Russia's new assertiveness, first in Georgia in 2008, and then in Ukraine in 2014, raises the specter of a return to Cold War geopolitical realities. But Russia is no longer widely seen as the champion of a political-economic system with broad appeal, and it is a much less formidable military power than was the Soviet Union at its height. Hence, many believe that a Russian rift with its neighbors to the west will simply be one dimension of a rapidly evolving geopolitical order characterized by several influential powers (such as the United States, Germany, China, India, Brazil, and Russia) seeking to exert political and economic influence over regional or global affairs in an increasingly disaggregated world.

When geopolitical strategists and intellectuals of statecraft predict future geopolitical orders, they often assume that individual states will continue to be the dominant actors in the international arena. Yet as we discuss in the next section, many of the same forces that worked against American unilateralism have undermined some of the traditional powers of the state. The rise of regional blocs could alter the system, with key clusters of states functioning as major geopolitical nodes. Alternatively or simultaneously, as we will discuss in Chapter 9, global cities may gain increasing power over issues typically addressed by states.

 Read a major newspaper (in print or online) and look for a recent statement by a world political leader regarding international politics. Adopting a critical geopolitics perspective, what generalizations can you make about the geopolitical views and priorities of the world leader? How does he or she view and divide up the world spatially?

WHAT ARE SUPRANATIONAL ORGANIZATIONS, AND WHAT IS THE FUTURE OF THE STATE?

Ours is a world of contradictions. Over the past couple of decades some French Canadians, Québécois, have demanded independence from Canada even as Canada joined the United States and Mexico in NAFTA (the North American Free Trade Agreement). Flemings in northern Belgium have called for autonomy or even independence despite the fact that Brussels, the capital of Belgium (and Flanders), has served as the de facto capital of the European Union. At every turn we are reminded of the interconnectedness of nations, states, and regions; yet, separatism and calls for autonomy are rampant. In the early decades of the twenty-first century, we appear to be caught between the forces of division and unity.

Despite conflicts arising from these contradictory forces, today hardly a country exists that is not involved in some supranational organization. A **supranational organization** is an entity composed of three or more states that forges an association and forms an administrative structure for mutual benefit and in pursuit of shared goals. The twentieth century witnessed the establishment of numerous supranational associations in political, economic, cultural, and military spheres.

Today, states have formed over 60 major supranational organizations (such as NATO and NAFTA), many of which have subsidiaries that bring the total to more than 100 (Fig. 8.21). The more states participate in such multilateral associations, the less likely they are to act alone in pursuit of a

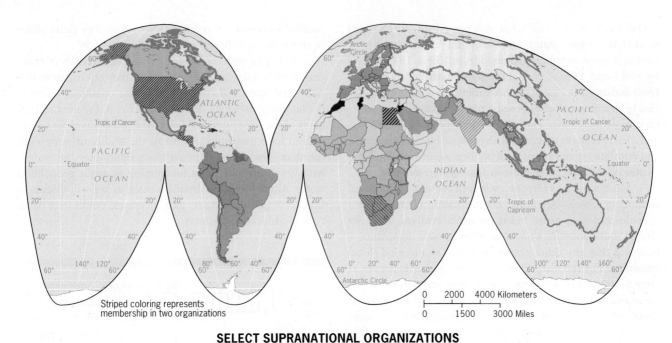

Striped coloring represents
membership in two organizations

0   2000   4000 Kilometers

0   1500   3000 Miles

SELECT SUPRANATIONAL ORGANIZATIONS

■ Agadir Agreement

■ Andean Community

□ Asia-Pacific Economic
Cooperation

■ Asia-Pacific Trade Agreement

■ Association of South East Asian
Nations

■ Caribbean Community and
Common Market

■ Central American
Common Market

■ Central American-Dominican
Free Trade Agreement

■ Common Market for Eastern
and Southern Africa

■ Commonwealth of Independent
States

□ East African Community

■ Economic and Monetary
Community of Central Africa

■ Economic Community of
West African States

■ European Community

■ European Customs Union
(Andorra, Monaco, San Marino,
and Turkey)

■ European Free Trade
Association

■ Gulf Cooperation Council

■ North American Free Trade
Agreement

■ South Africa Customs Union

■ South Africa Development
Community

■ South Asian Preferential Trade
Arrangement

■ Southern Common Market

■ **Figure 8.21**

Select Supranational Organizations. *Data from*: Crawford, Jo-Ann and Roberto V. Fiorentino, "Changing Landscape of Regional Trade Agreements,"
World Trade Organization. http://www.wto.org/english/res_e/booksp_e/discussion_papers8_e.pdf.

self-interest that might put them at odds with other association members. And in most cases participation in a supranational entity is advantageous to the partners, while being left out can have serious negative implications.

From League of Nations to United Nations

The modern beginnings of the supranational movement can be traced to conferences following World War I. Woodrow Wilson, president of the United States, proposed an international organization that would include all the states of the world (fewer than 75 states existed at that point). That idea took on concrete form with the founding of the League of Nations in 1919. Even though it was the idea of an American president, the United States was among the countries that did not join the organization because isolationists in the U.S. Senate opposed membership. In all, 63 states participated in the League, although the total membership at any single time never reached that number. Costa Rica and Brazil left the League before 1930; Germany departed in 1933,

shortly before the Soviet Union joined in 1934. The League later expelled the Soviet Union in 1939 for invading Finland.

The League was born of a worldwide desire to prevent future aggression, but the failure of the United States to join dealt the organization a severe blow. In the mid-1930s, the League had a major opportunity to play a significant international role when Ethiopia's Haile Selassie made a dramatic appeal for help in the face of an invasion by Italy, a member state until 1937. The League failed to take action, and in the chaos of the beginning of World War II the organization collapsed.

Even though the League of Nations ceased functioning, it spawned other supranational organizations. Between World War I and World War II, many states came together to create the Permanent Court of International Justice, which was charged with adjudicating legal issues between states, such as boundary disputes and fishing rights. The League of Nations also initiated international negotiations on maritime boundaries and related aspects of the law of the sea. The conferences organized by the League laid the groundwork for the final resolution of the size of territorial seas decades later.

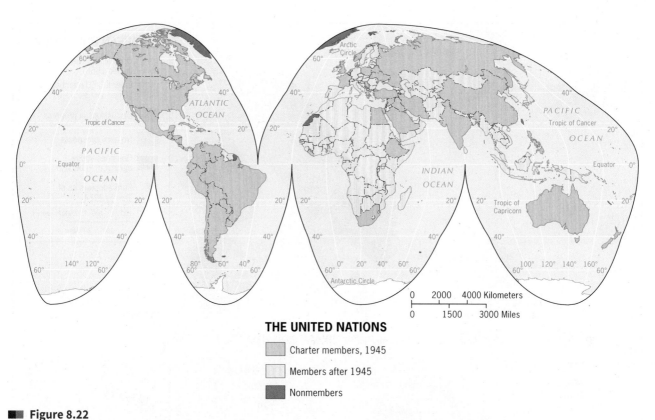

THE UNITED NATIONS

Charter members, 1945

Members after 1945

Nonmembers

■■ **Figure 8.22**
Member States of the United Nations. This map shows charter members, members after 1945 (with dates of entry), and nonmembers of the United Nations. *Data from*: The United Nations.

After World War II, a new organization was founded in an effort to promote international security and cooperation: the United Nations (UN). Membership in the UN has grown significantly since its inception in 1947 (Fig. 8.22). A handful of states still do not belong to the organization, but with the most recent additions in 2011, it now has 193 member states. Additionally, the organization allows permanent observers, including nonmember states Palestine and the Holy See and several supranational and nongovernmental organizations, to participate in the work of the UN General Assembly. The United Nations organization includes numerous less visible but nonetheless significant subsidiaries, including the FAO (Food and Agriculture Organization), UNESCO (United Nations Educational, Scientific and Cultural Organization), and WHO (World Health Organization). Not all United Nations members participate in every United Nations subsidiary, but many people around the world have benefited from their work.

We can find evidence of the United Nations' work in the "world" section of any major newspaper. UN peacekeeping troops have helped maintain stability in some of the most contentious regions of the world. The United Nations High Commissioner on Refugees is called upon to aid refugees in crises in far-flung places. UN documents on human rights standards, such as the Universal Declaration on Human Rights, the Covenant on Civil and Political Rights, and the Covenant on Economic and Social Rights, set a precedent and

laid the groundwork for countless human rights groups working in the world today.

By participating in the United Nations, states commit to internationally approved standards of behavior. Many states still violate the standards embodied in the United Nations Charter, but such violations can lead to collective action, such as economic sanctions or Security Council-supported military action. The United Nations' aid, refugee, and peacekeeping efforts as well as actions in South Africa (Apartheid) and Iraq (the Gulf War) are examples of UN successes, but the organization has its critics as well. Some argue that the composition of its Security Council reflects the world of 1950 more than the world of today. All five permanent members of the Council—the victors of World War II: the United States, United Kingdom, France, China, and Russia (formerly the Soviet Union)—wield veto power over Council resolutions and use the veto regularly, often making the UN ineffective during times of crisis. The ongoing Syrian civil war has showcased Security Council tensions as Russia and China have forcefully vetoed resolutions aimed at greater UN involvement to curb violence directed at civilians. Those who seek UN reform say the Permanent Five and their veto power destroys UN credibility and reinforces outdated power arrangements. Other UN critics express concern about power being vested in an organization that is not directly responsible to voters and that provides little room for nonstate interests. Still others criticize the fact that states such as

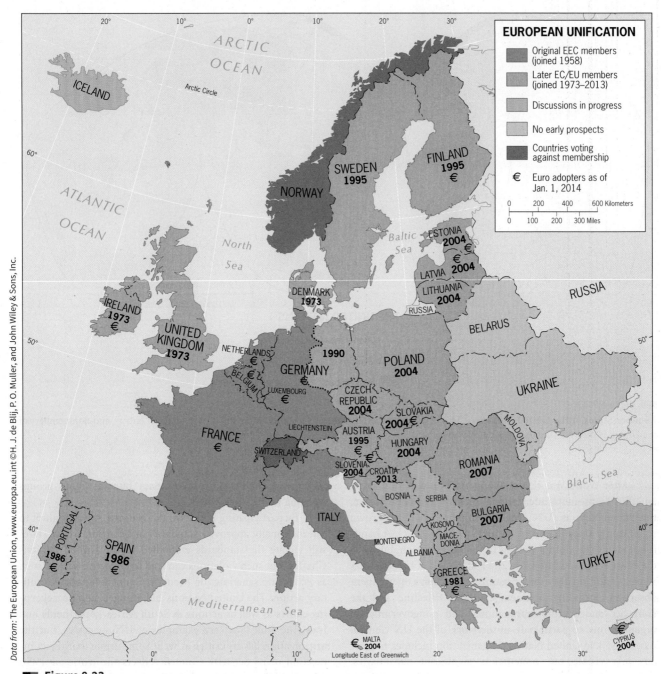

Data from: The European Union, www.europa.eu.int ©H. J. de Blij, P. O. Muller, and John Wiley & Sons, Inc.

EUROPEAN UNIFICATION

- Original EEC members (joined 1958)
- Later EC/EU members (joined 1973–2013)
- Discussions in progress
- No early prospects
- Countries voting against membership

€   Euro adopters as of Jan. 1, 2014

■ **Figure 8.23**

European Supranationalism.   Members of the European Union and their dates of entry.

China and Cuba currently sit on the organization's Human Rights Council. For all its weaknesses, however, the United Nations represents the only truly international forum for addressing many significant problems confronting the globe.

Regional Supranational Organizations

The League of Nations and the United Nations are global manifestations of a phenomenon that is expressed even more strongly at the regional level. States organize supranational organizations at the regional scale to position themselves more strongly economically, politically, and even militarily.

Belgium, the Netherlands, and Luxembourg undertook the first major modern experiment in regional economic cooperation. The three countries have much in common culturally and economically. Dutch farm products are sold on Belgian markets, and Belgian industrial goods go to the Netherlands and Luxembourg. During World War II, representatives of the three countries decided to remove tariffs between them and eliminate import licenses and quotas. In 1944, even before the end of the war, the governments of the three states met in London to sign an agreement of cooperation, creating the *Benelux* (*Be*lgium, the *Ne*therlands, and *Lux*embourg) region.

Following World War II, U.S. Secretary of State George Marshall proposed that the United States finance a European recovery program. A committee representing 16 West European states plus (then) West Germany presented the United States Congress with a joint program for economic rehabilitation, and Congress approved it. From 1948 to 1952, the United States gave Europe some $12 billion under the Marshall Plan, the largest foreign aid program in history. This investment revived European national economies and spurred a movement toward cooperation among European states. That movement was also driven by the rise of an increasingly integrated and potentially threatening Soviet bloc to the east and the desire to create a framework that could help break the pattern of European conflict that had characterized the first half of the twentieth century.

The European Union

From the European states' involvement in the Marshall Plan came the Organization for European Economic Cooperation (OEEC), a body that in turn gave rise to other cooperative organizations. Soon after Europe established the OEEC, France proposed the creation of a European Coal and Steel Community (ECSC), with the goal of lifting the restrictions and obstacles that impeded the flow of coal, iron ore, and steel among the mainland's six primary producers: France, West Germany, Italy, and the three Benelux countries. The six states entered the ECSC and gradually, through negotiations and agreement, enlarged their sphere of cooperation to include reductions and even eliminations of certain tariffs and a freer flow of labor, capital, and commodities beyond steel. This led, in 1958, to the creation of the European Economic Community (EEC).

The success of the EEC induced other countries to apply for membership. Denmark, Ireland, and the United Kingdom joined in 1973, Greece in 1981, and Spain and Portugal in 1986. The organization became known as the European Community (EC) because it began to address issues beyond economics. By the late 1980s, the EC had 12 members: the three giants (Germany, France, and the United Kingdom); the four southern countries (Italy, Spain, Portugal, and Greece); and five smaller states (the Netherlands, Belgium, Luxembourg, Denmark, and Ireland). These 12 members initiated a program of cooperation and unification that led to the formal establishment of a European Union (EU) in 1992. In the mid-1990s, Austria, Sweden, and Finland joined the EU, bringing the total number of members to 15 (Fig. 8.23).

In the late 1990s, the EU began preparing for the establishment of a single currency—the euro (Fig. 8.24). First, all electronic financial transactions were denominated in euros, and on January 1, 2002, the EU introduced euro coins and notes. Not all EU member states are currently a part of the euro zone, but the euro has emerged as a significant global currency.

The integration of ten eastern European and Mediterranean island states into the European Union in 2004, two

© Alexander B. Murphy

■ **Figure 8.24**
Cortina, Italy.   A market in northern Italy advertises the price of fruit in euros.

more in 2007, and one more in 2014 represents a significant development. Integration is a difficult process and often requires painful adjustments because of the diversity of the states involved. Take the case of agricultural practices and policies. These have long varied widely, but some general policy must govern agriculture throughout the European Union. Individual states have found these adjustments difficult at times, and the EU has had to devise policies to accommodate regional contrasts and delays in implementation. In addition, integration requires significant expenditures. Under the rules of the EU, the richer countries must subsidize (provide financial support to) the poorer ones; therefore, the entry of eastern European states adds to the financial burden on the wealthier western and northern European members. A major economic downturn at the end of the first decade of the twenty-first century, and associated financial crises in Greece, Ireland, Spain, and Portugal, put the union under unprecedented pressure. The citizens of wealthier countries such as Germany began to question why they should foot the bill for countries that have not (at least in German eyes) managed their finances responsibly.

The Union is a patchwork of states with many different ethnic traditions and histories of conflict and competition, and some in Europe express concern over losing local control over economic, social, and political matters. Economic success and growing well-being tend to submerge hesitancy and differences, but in the face of difficult economic or social times, divisive forces can, and have, reasserted themselves. Moreover, as the EU gets bigger, it becomes increasingly difficult for individual states (even powerful ones) to shape the direction of the union. And some citizens in smaller states such as Denmark and Sweden worry about getting lost in the mix. As a result, there are growing challenges to the legitimacy of an increasingly powerful EU.

Another difficult problem involves Turkey. Some western Europeans would like to see Turkey join the EU, thereby widening the organization's reach. The government of Turkey has long sought to join, but many Greeks are hesitant to support Turkish membership because of the long-standing dispute between Greece and Turkey over Cyprus and a number of islands off the Turkish coast. Other EU members have expressed concern over Turkey's human rights record and are worried about adding such a large, yet in some ways different, country to the mix. Behind these claims lies an often-unspoken sense among many Europeans that Turkey is not "European" enough to warrant membership, perhaps rooted in a historical and cultural tendency to define Muslims as the "Other." The debate within the EU about Turkey has alienated many

Turkish people, causing them to question their support for EU membership.

How Does Supranationalism Affect the State?

Supranationalism is a worldwide phenomenon. Other economic associations, such as the North American Free Trade Agreement (NAFTA), the Association of Caribbean States (ACS), the Central American Common Market, the Andean Group, the Southern Cone Community Market (MERCOSUR), the Economic Community of West African States (ECOWAS), the Asia-Pacific Economic Council (APEC), and the Commonwealth of Independent States (CIS), have drawn up treaties to reduce tariffs and import restrictions in order to ease the flow of commerce in their regions. Not all of these alliances are successful, but economic supranationalism is a sign of the times, a grand experiment still in progress.

Yet, when we turn back to the European Union, we see a supranational organization that is unlike any other. It is not a state, nor is it simply an organization of states. The European Union is remarkable in that it has taken on a life of its own—with a multifaceted government structure, three capital cities, and billions of euros flowing through its coffers. The European Union is extending into foreign relations, domestic policies, and military policies, with sovereignty over a variety of issues having been transferred "upward" from states to the European Union. One of the authors of this book has studied the degree to which Europeans in some regions are feeling a greater attachment to their region and to the European Union than to their own state (Fig. 8.25). Identifying with the European Union (over the state) is strong in the Benelux countries (the first members) and in regions where people have been disempowered by their state governments. Even though the EU represents the world's boldest attempt to move beyond a political order dominated by states, the challenges it is facing remind us of the continuing power of the state as an international actor and focus of identity.

Other types of movements, however, are also posing major challenges to the state as we know it, raising questions as to whether the division of the world into territorial states is logical, effective, or even necessary. Among these challenges are the demand of nations within states for independence, economic globalization, and the rise of increasingly powerful

■ **Figure 8.25**
Brussels, Belgium.   A woman with a European Union umbrella shops in the flower market in the Grande Place of Brussels. On their website, the European Union states that the number of stars on the flag has no official meaning and that the circle of stars represents "unity, solidarity and harmony among the peoples of Europe."

nonstate or extrastate groups and actors. These latter developments raise the question of whether we are embarking on an era of **deterritorialization** characterized by a geometry of political power less rooted in the power of the territorial state. There is no denying that states continue to provide the territorial foundation from which producers and consumers still operate, and they continue to exert considerable regulatory powers, but economic globalization makes it ever more difficult for states to control economic relations. States are responding to this situation in a variety of ways, with some giving up traditional regulatory powers and others seeking to insulate themselves from the international economy. Still others are working to build supranational economic blocs that they hope will help them cope with an increasingly globalized world. The impacts of many of these developments are as yet uncertain, but it is increasingly clear that states now compete with a variety of other forces in the international arena.

The state's traditional position is being further eroded by the globalization of social and cultural relations. Networks of interaction are being constructed in ways that do not correspond to the map of states. In 2011, when unrest broke out in Egypt, for example, activists used Facebook to garner support. Scholars and researchers in different countries work together in teams. Increased mobility has brought individuals from far-flung places into much closer contact than before. Paralleling all this change is the spread of popular culture in ways that make national borders virtually meaningless. Pharrell Williams is listened to from Iceland to Australia; fashions developed in northern Italy are hot items among Japanese tourists visiting South Korea; Thai restaurants are found in towns and cities across the United States; Russians hurry home to watch the next episode of soap operas made in Mexico; and movies produced in Hollywood are seen on screens from Mumbai to Santiago.

The rise of fundamentalist religious movements with geopolitical goals represents another global phenomenon with potentially significant implications for a future world order. In Chapter 6, we noted that fundamental religious movements sometimes become extremist by inciting violent acts in the name of their faith. Violence by extremists challenges the state—whether undertaken by individuals at the local scale or by widely diffused groups spread across major world realms. The state's mission to combat religious violence can produce support for

the state in the short term, but its inability to defeat extremist attacks may weaken the state in the long term. Terrorist attacks have been threatened or carried out by religious extremists from a variety of different faiths, but the wave of international terrorism that began in the 1980s in the name of Islam has dominated the international scene over the past several decades. The attacks of September 11, 2001, and the invasions of Iraq and Afghanistan that followed, moved terrorism to the geopolitical center stage. Other high-profile terrorist attacks in Madrid, Moscow, Mombasa, and Mumbai have helped to keep it there. Almost daily, newspapers report on terrorist incidents in cities around the world; the University of Maryland's Global Terrorism Database has tracked some 113,000 terrorist-related bombings, assassinations, and kidnappings from 1970 to 2012.

All of the foregoing processes are suggestive of deterritorialization, but the state is far from disappearing, and nationalism continues to be a fundamental social force in the world today. Indeed, in many instances. the state is moving to solidify control over its territory through a process known as **reterritorialization**. For example, in response to concerns over undocumented immigration, some state borders are becoming more heavily fortified, and moving across those borders is becoming more difficult. However one views the balance between deterritorialization and reterritorialization, the state of the geopolitical order is clearly in flux. We appear to be headed toward a world in which the spatial distribution of power is more complex than the traditional map of states would suggest. Describing that spatial distribution will be a challenge for geographers for generations to come.

 Consider how nation, state, and supranational organization are related. Are nations like Scotland more likely to remain within their states and not vote for independence because they are also part of a supranational organization (in the case of Scotland, the European Union)? Will the growth of supranational organizations lead to a decline in nations calling for statehood or will shifting more decision making from the state to the supranational organization actually increase the call for independence of nations within states?

Summary

We tend to take the state for granted, but the modern state idea is less than 400 years old. Politically organizing the world into states diffused around the globe through colonialism and trade. Globalization has brought about other ways of politically organizing space, including supranational organizations like the United Nations and the European Union. These new political entities challenge the sovereignty of the state and may help transition the world to a new political organization. In addition to understanding

political organization of space, political geographers look at how key international decision makers, intellectuals of statecraft, identify the world and construct narratives about how the world works. Geopolitician Halford Mackinder's Heartland Theory influenced perceptions of politics, place and power during the Cold War, and Samuel Huntington's warning of an "Islamic World" continues to shape the narratives of the post-Cold War world.

Geographic Concepts

political geography	colonialism	reapportionment
state	scale	splitting
territory	world-systems theory	majority-minority districts
territoriality	capitalism	gerrymandering
sovereignty	commodification	boundary
territorial integrity	core	geometric boundary
mercantilism	periphery	physical-political boundary
Peace of Westphalia	semiperiphery	heartland theory
nation	centripetal	critical geopolitics
nation-state	centrifugal	unilateralism
democracy	unitary	supranational organization
multinational state	federal	deterritorialization
multistate nation	devolution	reterritorialization
stateless nation	territorial representation	

Learn More Online

About Each State in the World
http://news.bbc.co.uk/2/hi/country_profiles/default.stm

About the United Nations
www.un.org/en/

About the European Union
http://europa.eu/index_en.htmAbout Nationalism
www.nationalismproject.org

About Political Geography
www.politicalgeography.org

About the Electoral Geography of the United States
www.washingtonpost.com/blogs/wonkblog/wp/2014/05/15/americas-most-gerrymandered-congressional-districts/

Watch It Online

Devolution

Slovakia: New Sovereignty. Click on Video on Demand
www.learner.org/resources/series180.html#program_descriptions

International Boundaries

Boundaries and Borderlands. Click on Video on Demand
www.learner.org/resources/series180.html#program_descriptions

Supranationalism and the European Union

Strasbourg: Symbol of a United Europe. Click on Video on Demand
www.learner.org/resources/series180.html#program_descriptions

URBAN GEOGRAPHY

Ghosts of Detroit?

The semicircular-shaped Grand Circus Park in Detroit, Michigan, is divided by several streets, making it look like the hub and spokes of a bicycle wheel from above. The grouping of buildings along Grand Circus Park (Fig. 9.1) reflects the rise, fall, and revitalization of the **central business district (CBD)** in Detroit. The central business district is a concentration of business and commerce in the city's downtown.

The Kales Building is the tall structure on the far left of the photograph. It was once the headquarters of the Kresge Corporation, which became K-Mart. Abandoned in 1986 and left to deteriorate, the Kales Building was renovated at a cost of $15 million in 2005. It now houses over 100 luxury apartments, and in 2011, it was 100 percent occupied.

The short building to the right of the Kales Building, tucked behind the trees, was the Adams Theater. Closed in 1988, the Adams Theater fell into such a severe state of disrepair that it could no longer be saved. The Downtown Detroit Development Authority required investors to save the façade of the building and allowed them to demolish the rest of it. A new building is slated to go up behind the façade.

■ **Figure 9.1**
Detroit, Michigan. The buildings along West Adams Street face Grand Park Circus in Detroit, Michigan. From left to right, the Kales Building, Adams Theater, Grand Park Centre, and Fyfe Apartments have experienced the rise, decline, and revitalization of the neighborhood, which is located in the CBD.

To the right of that building is the Grand Park Centre, which underwent a $7 million renovation in 2000. Grand Park Centre is an office building, but downtown Detroit has an abundance of office space. The occupancy rate was at 65 percent when the property was sold in 2013. The 20-storey building and its 9-story annex fetched between $4 and $5.5 million, prompting local commentator Daniel Burnham to write, "Buildings in downtown Detroit continue to be the real estate equivalent of a $19.95 DVD player on Black Friday: Everyone wants at least one of them, even if they don't exactly know why."

The building on the far right houses the Fyfe Apartments, named for Richard H. Fyfe, who built a fortune in the shoe trade in Detroit. The building was converted to apartments in 1960 and has functioned as apartments since that time. By 2011 the Fyfe Apartments were 97 percent occupied.

Buildings in the Grand Circus Park neighborhood have attracted millions in renovation funds because of the neighborhood's close proximity to the revitalized entertainment district in downtown Detroit. Just around the corner from Grand Circus Park are Comerica Park, Fox Theater, and Ford Field. The property manager of the Kales Building indicated that the central business district of Detroit is bouncing back because of the entertainment district. He said it's now tough to find an apartment there, speculating that people are drawn to living downtown because of high gas prices and low crime rates in the CBD. Another real estate developer contended that the main reason rental units are full in Detroit is because so many people lost their houses in the recent mortgage crisis that they are renting now. Across Grand Circus Park, the Broderick Towers are now almost fully leased after a massive renovation, which will bring a new shopping complex and more apartments to this revitalized neighborhood.

Other neighborhoods of the city are not bouncing back as well. Abandoned high-rise buildings called the ghosts of Detroit (Fig. 9.2) are joined by empty single-family homes. The population of Detroit rose and fell with the automobile industry. The population peaked at 1.8 million in 1950, but a 2014 U.S. Census Bureau report estimates the city's population falling to below 700,000.

Empty high-rise office buildings, apartments, government buildings, hotels, and train depots stand throughout the city like dead trees in a forest. The Lafayette Building (Fig. 9.2) stood across the street from the Book Cadillac Hotel for nearly a century. Once home to the offices of the Michigan Supreme Court, the Lafayette closed due to financial woes and lack of tenants in 1997. In the first decade of the 2000s, the Book Cadillac Hotel benefited from a $200 million renovation, but the Lafayette fell into a greater state of disrepair after that. I took this photograph in October 2008, the same month that a portion of the Lafayette fell off the building to the street below. In 2009, the Detroit City Council voted to demolish the Lafayette, and in 2010, the city tore down the building.

The Lafayette is not the only Detroit building to face such a prospect. The mayor of Detroit announced a plan in 2010 to demolish 10,000 abandoned buildings and houses in Detroit by 2014. As of 2013, Mayor Bing reported that 8966 structures had been demolished. In 2014, however, a task force convened by the Obama administration on urban blight in Detroit issued the most comprehensive study to date and recommended 40,000 additional dilapidated structures and trash-filled lots for demolition or restoration. The study labeled 30 percent of Detroit's properties as dilapidated or heading that way.

© Alexander B. Murphy

■ **Figure 9.2**

Detroit, Michigan.   The Lafayette Building once housed the offices of the Michigan Supreme Court. This photo from 2008 shows the boarded-up first and second floors and broken windows on the third floor. Urban explorers broke into and photographed abandoned buildings in Detroit (several websites are devoted to their photographs and videos), and vandals painted graffiti on the windows of Lafayette and other so-called ghosts of Detroit.

Geographers are leading the study of cities today, focusing on the impacts of developments at different scales on cities, including the ways in which globalization and political-economic shifts are affecting the organization and character of urban areas. Urban geographer Edward Soja urges scholars to think of cities, including Detroit, as integral to the development of societies, not simply as discrete stages on which the human drama plays out. Soja uses the term **synekism** to refer to the "conditions that derive from dwelling together in a particular home place or space" (2003, 273). As a result of people dwelling together in close-knit cities, a set of conditions occur that make change possible. To Soja, cities do not simply reflect changing economies and politics. Rather, cities create the conditions necessary for contemporary economic and political change.

Viewed through the concept of synekism, Grand Circus Park and the Lafayette Building in Detroit are not merely reflections of the changing political economy of Detroit. This block of buildings and the larger city of Detroit created the conditions necessary for industrial production to expand to the global scale and are creating the conditions necessary for portions of Detroit to rebound.

In our study of urban geography in this chapter, we look at the city spatially, examining the forms of cities around the world, the role of people in building and shaping cities, and the changes that cities have undergone over space and time.

Key Questions FOR CHAPTER 9

1. When and why did people start living in cities?
2. Where are cities located and why?
3. How are cities organized, and how do they function?
4. How do people shape cities?
5. What role do cities play in globalization?

WHEN AND WHY DID PEOPLE START LIVING IN CITIES?

Worldwide, more people live in urban areas than in rural areas today. China, a traditionally rural country, reached the point where more than 50 percent of its population lived in urban areas in 2010. According to China's census, the country was 36.1 percent urban in 2000. The rapid urbanization of China is due to the migration of millions of people from rural to urban areas since economic liberalization began in 1979.

Urban refers to the built-up space of the central city and suburbs. Urban areas include the city and surrounding environment connected to the city. An urban place is distinctively nonrural and nonagricultural. Cities are characterized by occupational specialization, where people work in a wide variety of fields. Cities have governments, and their citizens pay taxes to support public services.

For the vast majority of human history, the world was largely rural. From the beginnings of human society to about 3000 BCE, less than 1 percent of people lived in urban areas. With cities established in Mesopotamia, the Nile River, Mesoamerica, and Asia, the proportion of the world's population living in cities rose only slightly.

After the start of the Industrial Revolution in the mid-1700s in Great Britain, urbanization exploded when the number of urban dwellers in states such as Great Britain and the Netherlands outnumbered their rural counterparts. In western Europe, the United States, Canada, and Japan, four out of five people now live in cities or towns (Fig. 9.3). In China, the figure is five out of ten, and in India, the country's 2011 census reported nearly seven out of ten living in rural areas.

The agglomeration of people, services, and goods in cities affords people the luxury of time to innovate. Cities are centers of political power and industrial might, higher education and technological innovation, artistic achievement, and medical

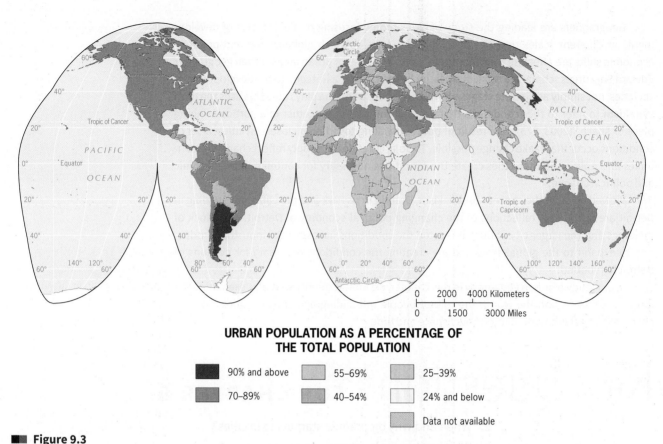

**URBAN POPULATION AS A PERCENTAGE OF
THE TOTAL POPULATION**

■ 90% and above   55–69%   25–39%

■ 70–89%   40–54%   24% and below

Data not available

■ **Figure 9.3**
Urban Population as a Percentage of the Total Population, by Country, 2013.   The regions of Europe, North America, Latin America, Russia, and Southwest Asia and North Africa are the most urbanized.   *Data from*: Population Reference Bureau 2013.

advances. They are the great markets, centers of specialization and interaction, sources of news and information, suppliers of services, and providers of sports and entertainment. Cities are the anchors and instigators of modern culture. A **city** is an agglomeration of people and buildings clustered together to serve as a center of politics, culture, and economics.

In the modern world, urbanization can happen quite quickly. A rural area or a small town can be transformed into a major metropolitan area. During the latter part of the twentieth century, the Chinese government announced a major economic development project in Guangdong, a province in southern China. The Chinese government established a special economic zone (SEZ) in Guangdong Province, and business and industry mushroomed. The small fishing village of Shenzhen in Guangdong Province is adjacent to Hong Kong. Hundreds of industries moved from Hong Kong to Shenzhen to take advantage of lower labor costs. The small fishing village of Shenzhen experienced extraordinary growth as its population, rushing to the area to find work, swelled from 20,000 to 8 million in just three decades. Shenzhen was quickly transformed: Skyscrapers now tower where thatch houses, rice paddies, and duck ponds once stood (Fig. 9.4).

Urbanization that can happen so quickly today took thousands of years to develop originally. The rise of the city is a very recent phenomenon in human history. Human communities have existed for over 100,000 years, but more than 90,000 years passed before people began to cluster in towns. Archaeological evidence indicates that people established the first cities about 8000 years ago. However, only in the last 200 years did cities begin to resemble their modern size and structure.

The Hearths of Urbanization

The switch from hunting and gathering to agriculture occurred prior to urbanization. Archaeologists have found evidence of early agriculture between 10,000 and 12,000 years ago. Most contend that the first cities came "several millennia" after the origins of agriculture (Smith 2009). Geographers Edward Soja and Peter Taylor, in contrast, argue that the first cities came before agriculture, and as evidence, they cite the 12,000-year-old settlement of Catal Huyuk (Fig. 9.5). Archaeologists usually view Catal Huyuk as an agricultural village, not a city.

Agricultural villages were relatively small in size and in population. Everyone living in an **agricultural village** was involved in agriculture, and the people lived at near-subsistence levels, producing just enough to get by. The dwellings in ancient agricultural villages were about the same size and contained about the same number of possessions, reflecting the egalitarian nature (sharing of goods in common among the people) of the societies living in these early villages. The populations were permanent, reflected in the

© H. J. de Blij

■ **Figure 9.4**
Shenzhen, China. Shenzhen changed from a fishing village to a major metropolitan area in just 25 years. Everything you see in this photograph is less than 30 years old; all of this stands where duck ponds and paddies lay less than three decades ago.

dwelling units where people built permanent structures. Egalitarian societies persisted long after agriculture began.

Scholars are fairly certain that these descriptors accurately depict the agricultural villages in the first agricultural hearth, the area of Southwest Asia called the Fertile Crescent. Additional archaeological evidence portrays agricultural villages in the later hearths of agricultural innovation, the Indus River Valley and Mesoamerica, as also fitting these descriptors. When people establish cities, however, these descriptors become inaccurate. In cities, people generate personal material wealth, trade over long distances, live in stratified classes that are usually reflected in the housing stock, and engage in a diversity of economic activities—not just agriculture.

■ **Figure 9.5**
Catal Huyuk. Dated to 12,000 years ago, the early city of Catal Huyuk was in a western extension of the Fertile Crescent, in present-day Turkey. This image is a reproduction of cave art found in Catal Huyuk. Archaeologists believe the cone structure in the background is a volcano, and the squares in the front are houses. *Altered from*: Meece S (2006) A Bird's Eye View–of a Leopard's Spots: The Çatalhöyük 'Map' and the Development of Cartographic Representation in Prehistory. Anatolian Studies: 1–16.

Two components enabled cities to stabilize and grow: **agricultural surplus** and **social stratification.** Archaeologists, anthropologists, and geographers have studied the remains and records of the first cities, creating numerous theories as to how cities came about. Most agree that some series of events led to the formation of an agricultural surplus and a leadership class; which came first varies by theory. The series of events spurring these two components also varies by theory. One theory maintains that advances in technology such as irrigation generated an agricultural surplus, and a leadership class formed to control the surplus and the technology that produced it. Another theory holds that a king or priest-king centralized political power and then demanded more labor to generate an agricultural surplus, which would help the ruler retain political power.

Regardless of how the leadership class was established, we know that once established, it helped generate the surplus and controlled the distribution of that surplus. The link between the surplus and the leadership class is clear in early cities, where the home of the leaders was often positioned close to the grain storage. The **leadership class**, or urban elite, consisted of a group of decision makers and organizers who controlled the resources, and often the lives, of others. The urban elite controlled the food supply, including its production, storage, and distribution. Generating an agricultural surplus enabled some people to devote their efforts to pursuits other than agriculture. The urban elite, for instance, did not work the fields. Rather, they devoted time to other pursuits such as religion and philosophy. Out of such pursuits came the concepts of writing and record keeping. Writing made possible the codification of laws and the preservation of traditions. Urban elites defended themselves by constructing walls on the outskirts of the city. However, the leadership class collected taxes and tribute from people within their control beyond the city walls.

Some cities grew out of agricultural villages, and others grew in places previously unoccupied by sedentary people. The innovation of the city is called the **first urban revolution**, and it occurred independently in six separate hearths, a case of independent invention[1] (Fig. 9.6). In each of the urban hearths, people became engaged in economic activities

---

[1]Some scholars argue that there are fewer than six hearths and attribute some early centers of urbanization to diffusion.

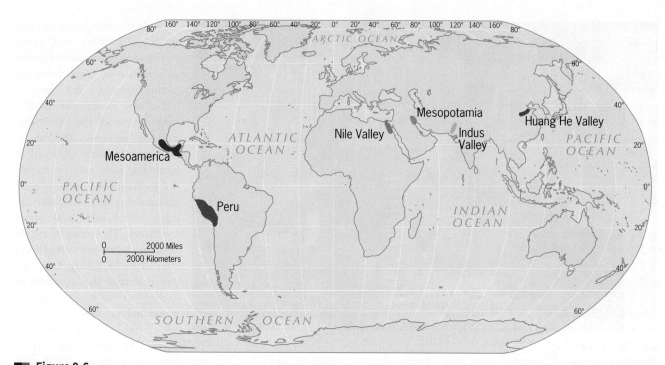

■ Figure 9.6
Six Hearths of Urbanization.   From these hearths, urbanization spread around the world.   © E. H. Fouberg, A. B. Murphy, H. J. de Blij, and John Wiley & Sons, Inc.

beyond agriculture, including specialty crafts, the military, trade, and government.

The six urban hearths are tied closely to the hearths of agriculture. The first hearth of agriculture, the Fertile Crescent, is the first place archaeologists find evidence of cities, dating to about 3500 BCE. This urban hearth is called **Mesopotamia**, referring to the region of great cities (such as Ur and Babylon) located between the Tigris and Euphrates rivers. Studies of the cultural landscape and urban morphology of Mesopotamian cities have found signs of social inequality in the varying sizes and ornamentation of houses. An urban elite erected palaces, protected themselves with walls, and employed countless artisans to beautify their spaces. They also established a priest-king class and developed a religious-political ideology to support the priest-kings. Rulers in the cities were both priests and kings, and they levied taxes and demanded tribute from the harvest brought by the agricultural laborers.

Archaeologists, often teaming up with anthropologists and geographers, have learned much about the ways ancient Mesopotamian cities functioned by studying their organization and form (urban morphology). The ancient Mesopotamian city was usually protected by a mud wall surrounding the entire community, or sometimes a cluster of temples and shrines at its center. Temples dominated the urban landscape, not only because they were the largest structures in town but also because they were built on artificial mounds, often over 100 feet (30 m) high.

In Mesopotamia, priests and other authorities resided in substantial buildings, many of which might be called palaces. Ordinary citizens lived in mud-walled houses packed closely

together and separated only by narrow lanes. Craftspeople set up their workshops lining the narrow lanes. The informal urban housing of Mesopotamia surrounded well-planned central cities.

The second hearth of urbanization, in the **Nile River Valley**, dates back to 3200 BCE. The interrelationship between urbanization and irrigation in this region distinguishes it from other urban hearths. The might of the rulers of the Nile River Valley is reflected in the great pyramids, tombs, and statues they created. Traditional theories hold that slaves built these feats of engineering, but more recent excavations suggest that ordinary citizens built ancient monuments as part of their tax payment.

The third urban hearth, dating to 2200 BCE, is the **Indus River Valley**, another place where agriculture likely diffused from the Fertile Crescent. Unable to decipher ancient Indus writing, scholars are puzzled by Harappa and Mohenjo-Daro, the first cities of the Indus River Valley (Fig. 9.7). The intricate planning of the cities points to the existence of a leadership class, but the houses continued to be equal in size, with no palaces or monuments appearing in the cities. In addition, all the dwellings in the cities had access to the same infrastructure, including wastewater drains and carefully maintained stone-lined wells. The cities had thick walls, and the discovery of coins from as far away as the Mediterranean points to significant trade over long distances.

The fourth urban hearth arose around the confluence of the **Huang He** (Yellow) and **Wei Valleys** of present-day China, dating to 1500 BCE. The Chinese purposely planned their ancient cities to center on a vertical structure in the middle of the city and then built an inner wall around it. Within the inner wall, the people of this hearth typically placed temples and palaces for the leadership class. The urban elite of the Huang He and Wei region demonstrated their power by building enormous, elaborate structures. Around 200 BCE, the Emperor Qin Xi Huang directed the building of the Great Wall of China. Like the Egyptians, he also had an elaborate mausoleum built for himself. An estimated 700,000 laborers worked for over 40 years to craft the intricate faces and weapons, horses, and chariots of an army of over 7000 terracotta warriors who stand guard over his burial place (Fig. 9.8).

Chronologically, the fifth urban hearth, found in **Mesoamerica**, dates to 1100 BCE. The ancient cities of Mesoamerica were religious centers. The Olmec built cities, including San Lorenzo, on the Gulf Coast of Mexico. The Olmec carved stone monuments, and archaeologists believe they moved the volcanic stones 50 miles from the interior of Mexico to the coast. The Olmec civilization died out, but based on cultural teachings of the Olmec, the Maya built cities in the same region that were also centered on religious temples (including Tikal, Chichén-Itzá, Uxmal, and Copán in Fig. 9.9).

The most recent archaeological evidence establishes **Peru** as the sixth urban

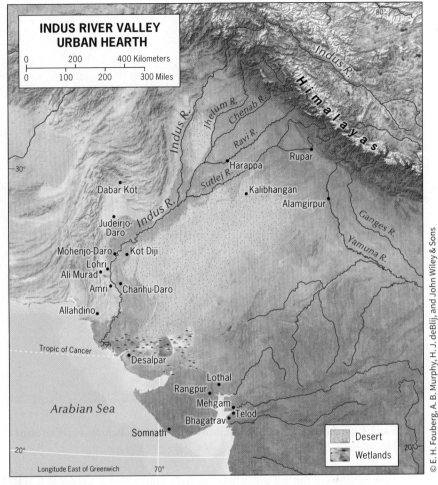

Figure 9.7
Indus River Valley Urban Hearth.   Most cities were sited along rivers and coasts.

© E. H. Fouberg, A. B. Murphy, H. J. deBlij, and John Wiley & Sons

Figure 9.8
Terracotta Warriors Guarding the Tomb of the Chinese Emperor Qin Xi Huang.   An estimated 700,000 laborers worked for over 40 years, around 200 BCE, to craft more than 7000 terracotta warriors who stand guard over the emperor's tomb.

© O. Louis Mazzatenta/National Geographic/Getty Images

hearth chronologically. The Chavín built cities in Peru dating to 900 BCE. The largest settlement, Chavín, was sited at an elevation of 10,530 feet in the Andean highlands.

The Role of the Ancient City in Society

Ancient cities not only were centers of religion and power, but also served as economic nodes. Cities were the chief marketplaces and bases from which wealthy merchants, land and livestock owners, and traders operated. As educational centers, the cities included teachers and philosophers as residents. The cities also had handicraft industries that attracted the best craftspeople and inventors. In all of these roles, ancient cities were the anchors of culture and society, the focal points of power, authority, and change.

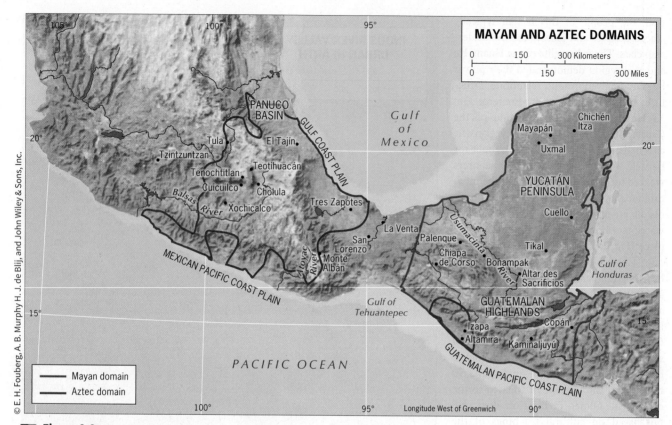

■ **Figure 9.9**

Mayan and Aztec Domains.   Unlike the urban hearths of the eastern hemisphere, many of the earliest cities in the Americas were founded in the highlands.

How large were the ancient cities? We have only estimates because it is difficult to judge from excavated ruins the dimensions of a city at its height or the number of people who might have occupied each residential unit. By modern standards, the ancient cities were not large. The cities of Mesopotamia and the Nile Valley may have had between 10,000 and 15,000 inhabitants after nearly 2000 years of growth and development. That, scholars conclude, is about the maximum sustainable size based on existing systems of food production, gathering, distribution, and social organization, These urban places were geographical exceptions in an overwhelmingly rural world. The modern city we know today did not emerge until several thousand years later.

Diffusion of Urbanization

Urbanization diffused from Mesopotamia in several directions. Populations in Mesopotamia grew as the food supply became more secure and steady. People migrated out from the hearth, diffusing their knowledge of agriculture and urbanization. Diffusion from Mesopotamia happened early, even before agriculture developed independently in some other hearths. In fact, urbanization diffused to the Mediterranean from Mesopotamia (and perhaps the Nile River Valley) more than 3500 years ago, at about the same time cities were developing in the hearth of the Huang He and long before cities originated in Mesoamerica.

Greek Cities

Greece is not an urban hearth because agriculture and urbanization diffused to Greece from Mesopotamia, rather than being independently innovated in Greece. Greece is more accurately described as a **secondary hearth** of urbanization because the Greek city influenced urban developments in Europe and beyond, as European ideas diffused around the world during the colonial era. Greek cities began more than 3500 years ago, when the city of Knossos on the island of Crete became the cornerstone of a system of towns in the Minoan civilization.

By 500 BCE, Greece had become one of the most urbanized areas on Earth. The urbanization of Ancient Greece ushered in a new stage in the evolution of cities. At its height, Ancient Greece encompassed a network of more than 500 cities and towns, not only on the mainland but also on the many Greek islands. Seafarers connected these urban places with trade routes and carried the notion of urban life throughout the Mediterranean region. Athens and Sparta, often vying with each other for power, soon became Greece's leading cities. Athens may have been the largest city in the world at the time, with an estimated 250,000 inhabitants.

With the hilly topography of Greece, the people had no need to build earthen mounds on which to perch temples; these were provided by nature. Every city had its **acropolis** (acro meaning high point; polis meaning city), on which the

© H. J. de Blij

◼ Figure 9.10

Athens, Greece. The rocky hilltop of Athens is home to the Acropolis (acro means high point). The Athens Acropolis is still crowned by the great Parthenon, standing after nearly 25 centuries.

people built the most impressive structures—usually religious buildings. The Parthenon of Athens remains the most famous of all, surviving to this day despite nearly 2500 years of wars, earth tremors, vandalism, and environmental impact (Fig. 9.10). Building this magnificent columned structure, designed by the Athenian architect-engineer Phidias, began in 447 BCE, and its rows of tapering columns have inspired architects ever since.

© H. J. de Blij

◼ Figure 9.11

Athens, Greece. Looking down from the Acropolis, you can see the agora, the ancient trade and market area, which is surrounded by new urban buildings.

Like the older Southwest Asian cities, Greece's cities also had public places. In the Southwest Asian towns, these seem to have been rather cramped, crowded, and bustling with activity, but in Ancient Greece they were open, spacious squares, often in a low part of town with steps leading down to them (Fig. 9.11). On these steps the Greeks debated, lectured, judged each other, planned military campaigns, and socialized. As time went on, this public space, called the **agora** (meaning market), also became the focus of commercial activity.

Greece's cities had excellent theaters. The aristocracy attended plays and listened to philosophical discourses, but for many people life in a Greek city was miserable. Housing was no better than it had been in the Mesopotamian cities thousands of years earlier. Sanitation and health conditions were poor. And much of the grandeur designed by Greece's urban planners was the work of hundreds of thousands of slaves.

Urbanization diffused from Greece to the Roman Empire. Roman urbanization and urban culture diffused throughout western Europe. The city declined in Europe for a time after the fall of the Roman Empire, but Europeans eventually carried Western concepts of city life (drawn from Greece and Rome) around the world through colonialism and capitalism. From Washington, D.C., to Canberra, Australia, the urban landscape shows the imprints of Greco-Roman urban culture.

Roman Cities

The great majority of Greece's cities and towns were located near the Mediterranean Sea on peninsulas and islands, and were linked by sea routes. When the Romans succeeded the Greeks (and Etruscans) as rulers of the region, their empire incorporated not only the Mediterranean shores but also a large part of interior Europe and North Africa (Fig. 9.12). The Roman urban system was the largest yet—much larger than Greece's domain. The capital, Rome, served as the apex of a hierarchy of settlements ranging from small villages to large cities. The Romans linked these places with an extensive transportation network that included hundreds of miles of roads, well-established sea routes, and trading ports along the roads, sea, and rivers. Roman regional planners displayed a remarkable capacity for choosing favorable sites of cities and for identifying suitable locales for settlements. The **site** of a city is its absolute location, often chosen for its advantages in trade or defense, or as a center for religious practice.

The **situation** of a city refers to its position in relation to the surrounding context.

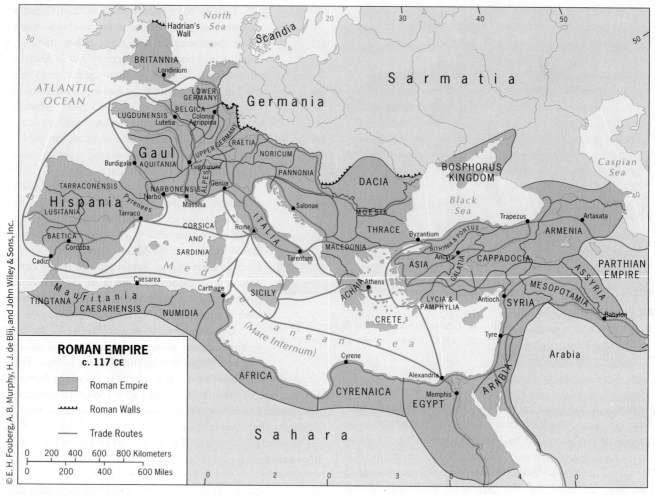

■ **Figure 9.12**

Roman Empire c. 117 CE. The Romans established a system of cities linked by a network of land and sea routes. Many of the Roman cities have grown into modern metropolises.

The site of a city is a function of its absolute location: its precise position on the globe. The situation of a city is its relative location, its place in the region and the world around it. The situation of a city changes over time. For example, Rome was the center of the Roman Empire, but when the Roman Empire dissolved, the situation of Rome changed as well. It developed into the center of the Roman Catholic Church, a role it still plays today. But during the Renaissance when Florence flourished and during the Industrial Revolution when Naples and points north of Rome grew economically, the situation of Rome within Italy as a whole shifted. It no longer was the scientific and economic focal point of the country.

The Romans were greatly influenced by the Greeks, as is evident in Roman mythology and visible in the cultural landscape and **urban morphology** of Roman cities. The urban morphology of a city is the layout of the city, its physical form and structure. Greeks planned their colonial cities in a rectangular grid pattern, and Romans adopted this plan wherever surface conditions made it possible. The Romans took the Greek acropolis (zone of religion and center of power) and agora (zone of public space and the marketplace) and

combined them into one zone: the **Forum**, which served as the focal point of Roman public life (Fig. 9.13).

Throughout the Roman Empire, cities were places of cultural contrast. What still stands in ruins in many places around the Mediterranean are monumental buildings, impressive villas, spacious avenues, ingenious aqueducts and baths, and sewage systems built of stone and pipe (Fig. 9.14). What we can no longer see in the ruins of the empire are the thousands of slaves who built these structures (estimates are that between one-third and two-thirds of the population of the empire was enslaved) and the wretchedly poor who were crammed into overcrowded tenements and lived in filth. The city of the Roman Empire, like the city of today, was home to both rich and poor and reflected both the greatest achievements and the worst failings of civilization.

Urban Growth After Greece and Rome

After the Roman Empire fell in 476 CE, Europe entered an era historians called the Middle Ages, which spanned from about

FIELD NOTE

"There can be few spaces of greater significance to the development of Western civilization than the Roman Forum. This was the nerve center of a vast empire that transformed the face of western Europe, Southwest Asia, and North Africa. It was also the place where the decisions were made that carried forward Greek ideas about governance, art, urban design, and technology. The very organization of space found in the Roman Forum is still with us: rectilinear street patterns; distinct buildings for legislative, executive, and judicial functions; and public spaces adorned with statues and fountains."

Figure 9.13
Rome, Italy.

500 to 1300 (or later in parts of Europe). During the first two-thirds of this period, little urban growth occurred in Europe; in some parts of the continent, urbanism went into sharp decline. The urban growth that did take place during this time occurred on sites of oases and resting places along the Silk Route between Europe and Asia. Many of these places grew into towns, and some, such as Bukhara and Samarqand, became major cities. In Asia, Chinese styles of city-building diffused into Korea and Japan, with Seoul becoming a full-fledged city by 1200 and Kyoto, Japan's historic capital, growing rapidly after the turn of the ninth century.

During Europe's Middle Ages, urbanization continued vigorously outside of Europe. In West Africa, trading cities developed along the southern margin of the Sahara. By 1350, Timbuktu (part of Mali today) was a major city: a seat of government, a university town, a market, and a religious center. The Americas also experienced significant urban growth during Europe's Middle Ages, especially within the Mayan and Aztec empires (Fig. 9.15). The largest pre-Columbian

Figure 9.14
Nimes, France.   Aqueducts outside of Nimes, France, were built during the Roman Empire, about 2000 years ago. Aqueducts made it possible to bring fresh water to relatively large cities at the time.

Figure 9.15
Altun Ha, Belize.   Between 300 and 900 CE, Altun Ha served as a thriving trade and distribution center for the Caribbean merchant canoe traffic. Some of the trails in Altun Ha led all the way to Teotihuacán.

city in the Americas was in the Aztec Empire on the Mexican Plateau. The Aztec capital of Tenochtitlán had nearly 100,000 inhabitants at a time many European cities lay in ruins.

Site and Situation During European Exploration

Early Eurasian urban areas extended in a crescent-shaped zone across Eurasia from England in the west to Japan in the east, including the cities of London, Paris, Venice, Constantinople (Istanbul today), and Tabriz, Samarqand, Kabul, Lahore, Amra, Jaunpur, Xian, Anyang, Kyoto and Osaka. Before European exploration, most cities in the world were sited on trade routes in the interiors of continents, not just in Eurasia, but also in West Africa and indigenous America. Interior trade routes such as the Silk Route and the caravan routes of West Africa sustained these inland cities and, in many cases, helped them prosper.

The relative importance of the interior trade routes changed, however, when European maritime exploration and overseas colonization ushered in an era of oceanic, worldwide trade. With this shift, the situation of cities like Basle (Switzerland) and Xian (China) changed from being crucial nodes on interior trading routes to being peripheral to ocean-oriented trade.

After European exploration took off during the 1400s, the dominance of interior cities declined. Other cities, sited on coasts, gained prominence as their situations changed. In Asia, coastal cities such as Bombay (now Mumbai, India), Madras (Chennai, India), Malacca (Malaysia), Batavia (Jakarta, Indonesia), and Tokyo (Japan) came to the fore. Exploration and oceanic trade altered the situations of cities in West Africa as well. Before 1500, urbanization in West Africa was concentrated in a belt extending along the southern margin of the Sahara, including such cities as Timbuktu (Mali), Niani (Guinea), Gao (Mali), Zaria (Nigeria), Kano (Nigeria), and Maiduguri (Nigeria). Here, cross-desert caravan traffic met boat traffic on the River Niger (where "camel met canoe"), and people exchanged goods from northern deserts for goods from coastal forests. Maritime trade disrupted this pattern of trade. Coastal ports became the leading markets and centers of power, and the African cities of the interior began a long decline.

Coastal cities remained crucial after exploration led to colonialism. During the colonial period, key cities in international trade networks included the coastal cities of Cape Town (South Africa), Lima-Callao (Peru), and New York City.

The trade networks European powers commanded (including the slave trade) brought unprecedented riches to Europe's burgeoning medieval cities, such as Amsterdam (the Netherlands), London (England), Lisbon (Portugal), Liverpool (England), and Seville (Spain). Successful merchants built ornate mansions, patronized the arts, participated in city governance, and supported the reconstruction of city centers. As a result, cities such as Antwerp (Belgium), Copenhagen (Denmark), Lisbon (Portugal), and Genoa (Italy) thrived. A central square became the focus of the city, fronted by royal, religious, public, and private buildings evincing wealth and prosperity, power and influence (Fig. 9.16). Streets leading

FIELD NOTE

"The contemporary landscape of Genoa stands as a reminder of the city's historic importance. Long before Europe became divided up into states, a number of cities in northern Italy freed themselves from the strictures of feudalism and began to function autonomously. Genoa and Venice were two of these, and they became the foci of significant Mediterranean maritime trading empires. In the process, they also became magnificent, wealthy cities. Although most buildings in Genoa's urban core date from a more recent era, the layout of streets and public squares harks back to the city's imperial days. Is it a surprise that the city gave birth to one of the most famous explorers of all time: Christopher Columbus?"

© Alexander B. Murphy

■ **Figure 9.16**
Genoa, Italy.

to these central squares formed arteries of commerce, and the beginnings of "downtowns" emerged.

During the sixteenth and seventeenth centuries, European mercantile cities became the nodes of a widening network of national, regional, and global commerce. So wealthy and powerful were the urban merchants that, supported by their rulers, they were able to found and expand settlements in distant lands. Cities such as Dakar (Senegal), Lourenco Marques (now Maputo, Moçambique), and Saigon (now Ho Chi Minh City, Vietnam) were endowed with the ornate trappings of the mercantile cities of Europe, including elaborately inlaid sidewalks, tree-lined avenues, and neo-Gothic architecture.

The Second Urban Revolution

During the last decades of the eighteenth century, the Industrial Revolution was in full swing in Great Britain. None of Europe's cities was prepared for what lay ahead: an avalanche of changes that ripped the fabric of urban life. Around 1800, western Europe was still overwhelmingly rural. As thousands migrated to the cities with industrialization, cities had to adapt to the mushrooming population, the proliferation of factories and supply facilities, the expansion of transport systems, and the construction of tenements for the growing labor force.

A Second Agricultural Revolution

Before the second urban revolution could take place, a second revolution in agriculture was necessary. During the late seventeenth century and into the eighteenth century, Europeans made a series of important improvements in agriculture, including invention of the seed drill, hybrid seeds, and improved breeding practices for livestock. The second agricultural revolution also improved organization of production, market collaboration, and storage capacities. Agricultural laborers migrated to cities in hopes of obtaining jobs in the formal economy, which included wages usable in the growing cash-based economies of Europe. Manufacturers tapped into the new labor force and expanded industrial production (for a further discussion of industrialization, see Chapter 12).

Not all mercantile cities turned into industrial cities. Many industrial cities grew from small villages or along canal and river routes. The primary determinant in the location of early industrial cities was proximity to a power source. For textile manufacturing, industrial cities had to be sited near fresh water sources to power the water loom. In Great Britain, industrial cities involved in textile manufacturing were located in the Pennines, where fresh water flowed down the hillsides. Industrial cities involved in iron manufacturing were located around Birmingham and Coalbrookdale, which were easily accessible to Britain's coal and iron ore fields.

When industrialization diffused from Great Britain to the European mainland, the places most ready for industrialization had undergone their own second agricultural revolution, had surplus capital from mercantilism and colonialism, and were located near coal fields (Fig. 9.17).

The Chaotic Industrial City

With industrialization, cities became unregulated jumbles of activity. Factories engulfed private homes. Open spaces became garbage dumps. Urban dwellers converted elegant housing into overcrowded slums. Sanitation systems failed, and water supplies were inadequate and often polluted. By the late 1800s, the Industrial Revolution had changed transportation significantly. The steam engine, powered by coal, not only pumped water from mines for coal mining but also powered railroads and steamships. The diffusion of the railroad gave cities that were not near coal fields the chance to industrialize. The central parts of cities such as London, Paris, and Amsterdam retained their preindustrial shape. But with the diffusion of the railroad, railroad tracks knifed through long-stable neighborhoods.

Living conditions were dreadful for workers in cities, and working conditions were shocking. Children worked 12-hour shifts in textile mills, typically six days a week. In industrial cities, health conditions were worse than they had been in medieval times; the air was polluted and the water contaminated. The grimy, soot-covered cities of the British Midlands were appropriately deemed the "black towns." Few if any safety mechanisms protected the laborers, and injuries were common.

In the mid-1800s, as Karl Marx and Frederick Engels (writing in Germany, Belgium, and England) encouraged "workers of the world" to unite, conditions in European manufacturing cities gradually improved. Industrialists were forced to recognize workers' rights, and governments intervened by legislating workers' rights and introducing city planning and zoning. Many manufacturing cities in North America never suffered as much as their European predecessors, although living and working conditions for factory workers (and "blue-collar" workers generally) were far from satisfactory. American manufacturing cities did not altogether escape the problems of the European industrial cities. During the late nineteenth and early twentieth centuries, the American manufacturing city grew rapidly, often with inadequate planning and rapid immigration leading to the development of slums and ghettos.

During the second half of the twentieth century, the nature of manufacturing changed, as did its location: cities repositioned many factories away from congested, overcrowded, expensive urban areas. Companies simply abandoned large manufacturing plants, making "rust belts" out of once-thriving industrial districts. Many of these plants still stand today, overgrown by weeds, with broken windows and cracking walls, while others have been turned into parks and green spaces that showcase industrial relics (Fig. 9.18).

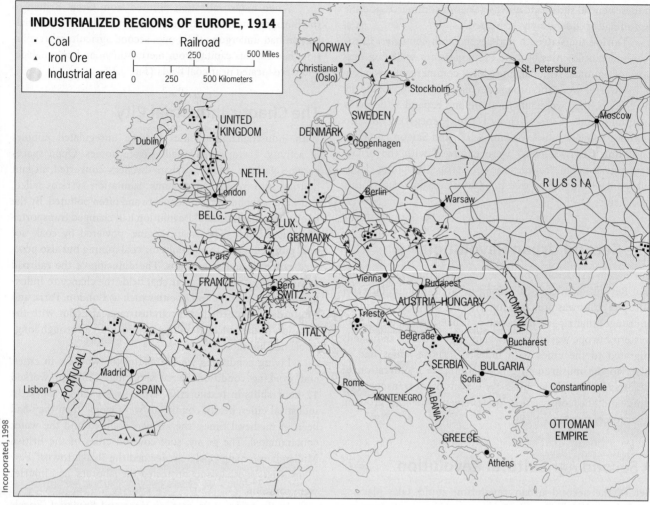

INDUSTRIALIZED REGIONS OF EUROPE, 1914

- Coal
- ▲ Iron Ore
- Industrial area
- —— Railroad

0 250 500 Miles
0 250 500 Kilometers

■■ **Figure 9.17**
Industrialized Regions of Europe, 1914. Industrial centers were close to coal or iron ore deposits and near water transportation, whether coasts or rivers.

FIELD NOTE

"The Ruhr Valley long functioned as the incubator of Germany's industrial economy. Largely destroyed during World War II, the Ruhr rose again to help Germany back to recovery. But as declining transportation costs and rising labor costs prompted heavy industries to move their operations to other parts of the world, factories such as this iron and steel mill on the edge of Duisburg fell silent. Unemployment soared, and the area became depressed. In an effort to rebound, local authorities are now trying to turn a few of these relics into tourist destinations. They are unlikely to compete with the great churches or medieval palaces found elsewhere in Germany, but for the geographer they provide fascinating insights into the urban and economic arrangements that made modern Europe what it is today."

© Alexander B. Murphy

■■ **Figure 9.18**
Duisburg, Germany.

Although factories and factory jobs are not permanent, the urbanization that went along with industrialization is still apparent. Depending on the sometimes variable definition of "urban," western Europe today is more than 75 percent urbanized and urbanization has become a global phenomenon. Worldwide, more people now live in cities than in rural areas.

Archaeologists have found that the houses in Indus River cities, such as Mohenjo-Daro and Harappa, were a uniform size: each house had access to a sewer system, and palaces were absent from the cultural landscape. Derive a theory as to why these conditions were present in these cities that had both a leadership class and a surplus of agricultural goods.

WHERE ARE CITIES LOCATED AND WHY?

When you look at a map in an atlas of the United States or Canada, or at a road map of a State or province, you see an array of places of different sizes, with varying distances between them. The map looks like a jumble, yet each place is where it is because of some decision, some perception of the site or its situation. Site and situation help explain why certain cities were planned and why cities thrive or fail. To understand why a conglomeration of cities is distributed across space the way it is and why cities are different sizes, it is necessary to examine more than one city at a time and see how those cities fit together, into the region, into the state, and into the globe as a whole.

Urban geographers studied the distribution of cities in Europe and the Americas during the 1900s, using quantitative techniques to determine how many cities and what size cities are needed within a certain space. In studying the size of cities and distances between them, urban geographers explored the **trade areas** of different-size cities. Every city and town has a trade area, an adjacent region within which its influence is dominant. Customers from smaller towns and villages come to the city to shop and to conduct other business. An online survey of approximately 50,000 people helped one armchair geographer create a map of trade areas for the contiguous United States (Fig. 9.19). The city's newspapers are read, and its television stations are watched in the surrounding region (Fig. 9.20).

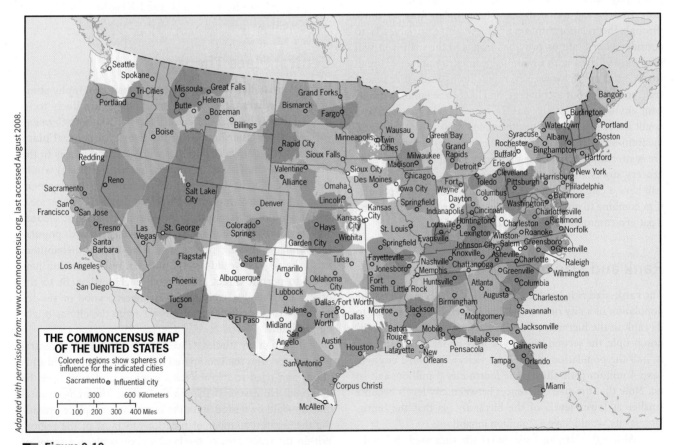

Figure 9.19

Regions of Influence for Cities in the Contiguous United States. This map is based on survey data from over 45,000 voters on commoncensus.org who answered the question, "On the level of North America as a whole, what major city do you feel has the most cultural and economic influence on your area overall?"

Richard Cummins / Getty Images, Inc.

■ **Figure 9.20**

Monterey, California. Business names often reflect the trade area where they are located. Many trade areas have a toponym in the local vernacular that those in the region use. When you travel to a new trade area, you may see the toponymn, such as "Bay Area," "Northern Virginia" or "South Florida," on service vehicles, billboards, and business names. Around Santa Cruz, Elkhorn, and Monterey, California, may businesses use the toponym "Monterey Bay" to describe the trade area.

Across the multitude of quantitative studies in urban geography, three key components arise frequently: population, trade area, and distance. The simplest way to think through the relationship among these three variables is to consider your State or province map. On the map, you will see many villages with unfamiliar names, a number of small towns sited on highways, several medium-sized cities where transportation routes converge, and likely one familiar, dominant city. The largest city has the largest trade area, and as a result fewer places rival it as the major trade area: the several medium-sized cities trade in smaller areas of commerce and are scattered apart from the major city, small towns house the grocery stores and other necessities, and finally villages may still have a café or a gas station. The trade areas and population combine to give us a hierarchy of urban places, following a pattern commonly called the rank-size rule.

Rank and Size in the Urban Matrix

The **rank-size rule** holds that in a model urban hierarchy, the population of a city or town will be inversely proportional to its rank in the hierarchy. Thus, if the largest city has 12 million people, the second largest will have about 6 million (that is, half the population of the largest city); the third city will have 4 million (one-third); the fourth city 3 million; and so on. Note that the size differences between city levels become smaller at lower levels of the hierarchy, so that the tenth-largest city would have 1.2 million inhabitants.

Although German Felix Auerbach suggested the rank-size rule in 1913, linguist George Zipf is credited with establishing the mathematical equation for the rank-size rule in 1941. Since then, scholars across disciplines have tested the rule and questioned when the rule applies and when it does not. Studies in 1966, 1980, and again in 2002 found that the majority of countries had populations with more even distributions than the rank-size rule would predict. Other recent studies have questioned why the rank-size rule fits the countries where it does fit, and these studies have offered answers including a combination of random growth (chance) and economies of scale (efficiency).

The rank-size rule does not apply in all countries, especially countries with one dominant city. States often focus development in one particular city, such as the capital city, thereby bolstering that city and its population above the rest of the cities in the state. In 1939, geographer Mark Jefferson defined a **primate city** as "a country's leading city, always disproportionately large and exceptionally expressive of national capacity and feeling." He saw the primate city as the largest and most economically influential within the state, with the next largest city in the state being much smaller and much less influential.

Many former colonies have primate cities, as the colonial powers often ruled from a single dominant city, where economic and political activities were concentrated. Examples of primate cities in former colonies include Mexico City, Mexico, and Manila, the Philippines. In the noncolonial context, London and Paris each serve as examples of primate cities in the United Kingdom and France, respectively.

Central Place Theory

Walter Christaller wrote the classic urban geography study to explain where cities, towns, and villages are likely to be located. In his book *The Central Places in Southern Germany* (1933), Christaller laid the groundwork for **central place theory**. His goal was to predict where central places in the urban hierarchy (hamlets, villages, towns, and cities) would be located. Christaller began his theory of development with a set of assumptions: First, the surface of the ideal region would be flat and have no physical barriers; second, soil fertility would be the same everywhere; third, population and purchasing power would be evenly distributed; next, the region would have a uniform transportation network to permit direct travel from each settlement to the other; and, finally, from any given place, a good or service could be sold in all directions as far from the city as might be profitable.

Through his studies, Christaller posited an ideal central place system and then compared his model to real-world situations and tried to explain the variations and exceptions he observed. He assumed that in the urban hierarchy, central places would be nested, with the largest central place providing the greatest number of functions to most of the region. Within the trade area of the largest central place, a series of substantial towns would provide functions to several smaller places. The smaller places would then provide fewer central functions to a smaller-yet service area.

To determine the locations of each central place, Christaller needed to define the goods and services provided and calculate the distance people would willingly travel to acquire them. Cities, he postulated, would be regularly spaced, with central places where the same product was sold at the same price located a standard distance apart. He reasoned that a person would not be expected to travel 11 miles to one place to buy an item if it were possible to go only 9 miles to purchase it at another place. Central place theory maintains that each central place has a surrounding complementary region, an exclusive trade area within which the town has a monopoly on the sale of certain goods, because it alone can provide such goods at a given price and within a certain range of travel.

Hexagonal Hinterlands

From the foregoing description of Christaller's theory, you would expect the shape of each central place's trade area to be circular (a bull's-eye shape surrounding each place). But circles either have to overlap or leave certain areas unserved. Hence, Christaller chose perfectly fitted hexagonal regions as the shape of each trade area (Fig. 9.21).

Urban geographers were divided on the relevance of his model. Some saw hexagonal systems everywhere; others saw none at all. Christaller received support from geographers, who applied his ideas to regions in Europe, North America, and elsewhere. In China, both the North China Plain and the Sichuan Basin display the seemingly uninterrupted flatness assumed by Christaller's model. When G. William Skinner examined the distribution of villages, towns, and cities there in 1964, he found a spatial pattern closely resembling the one predicted by Christaller's model. Studies in the U.S. Midwest suggested that while the square layout of the township-and-range system imposed a different kind of regularity on the landscape, the economic forces at work there tended to confirm Christaller's theory.

Christaller recognized that not all his assumptions would be met in reality; physical barriers, uneven resource distributions, and other factors all modify Christaller's hexagons. Nonetheless, his model yielded a number of practical insights. His studies pointed to a hierarchy of urban places that are spatially balanced and also established that larger cities would be spaced farther from each other than smaller towns or villages. Although Christaller's model of perfectly fit hexagons is not often realized, his studies confirm that the distribution of cities, towns, and villages in a region is not an accident but is tied to trade areas, population size, and distance.

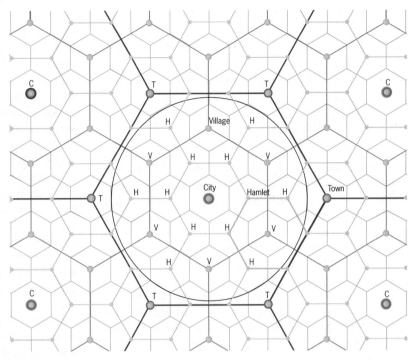

Figure 9.21

Christaller's Hierarchy of Settlements and Their Service Areas.   In this model: C = city, T = town, V = village, H = hamlet.   © E. H. Fouberg, A. B. Murphy, H. J. deBlij, and John Wiley & Sons.

Sketch a map of your city or town and the cities or towns nearby. Make a list of the kinds of goods and services available in each of these towns. Do the ideas about central places presented in this section of the chapter apply to your region?

HOW ARE CITIES ORGANIZED, AND HOW DO THEY FUNCTION?

We all know that cities have certain features in common, and we use geographic terms to identify these features, including downtowns, suburbs, industrial districts, and shopping malls. Cities in various regions of the world also have their own, distinct characteristics. Mumbai, India, looks vastly different from Chicago, Illinois. Tokyo, Japan, is distinct from Lagos, Nigeria. Cities in South America tend to be graced by magnificent plazas not commonly seen in Australia or Subsaharan Africa.

One way to conceptualize the layout of cities is through models that illustrate the structures of cities. Since the 1920s, urban geographers have studied, charted, and mapped cities to create models that describe the urban morphology, functional zonation, and overall layout of cities in world regions.

City models reveal how cities are purposely structured to perform the roles they have as centers of commerce, education, transportation, industry, and governance. The form of cities also reflects the historic, spatial, economic, cultural, and political processes that shaped cities in each world region.

Models of the City

Each model of the city, regardless of the region, is a study in **functional zonation**—the division of the city into certain regions (zones) for certain purposes (functions). Every city in the world is an assemblage of functional zones, orderly designed in some places and jumbled chaos in others. Zones of the city exist and play certain roles in the city's life, whether to house residents, produce goods, educate students, or accommodate government. Each zone or region is part of the larger city.

Globalization has created common cultural landscapes in the financial districts of many world cities. Until little more than 30 years ago, Shanghai, China, was a vast, low-rise Chinese city centered on a colonial-era riverfront with British and French architectural imprints that had endured for more than a century. Today, you might mistake the financial districts in downtown Shanghai for New York City, with its forest of skyscrapers housing international corporations, banks, hotels, and hundreds of thousands of apartment dwellers. You will also see the names of the same corporations and hotels on high-rise buildings in central Mumbai (India), Bangkok (Thailand), Dubai (United Arab Emirates) and Singapore.

With globalization reflected in cultural landscapes around the world, are regional models of cities no longer useful? Quite the opposite: They help us understand the processes that forged cities in the first place and the impact of modern linkages that are now changing cities. In Shanghai, China, for example, the government chose to preserve the unique colonial riverfront architecture and develop around the colonial neighborhood and across the Huangpu River. In South America, cities are protecting historic plazas against modernization through regulations that limit high-rise development to areas outside of the plazas. The city of Paris protects the old city by outlawing high rises. Instead, Paris concentrates skyscraper development in the technology cluster called La Défense, which is located just outside the city proper, a little over 3 miles west of the Arc de Triomphe.

Models of cities give us context for understanding the history and geography of regions and major cities within them. Studying the location and interplay of zones within cities and the changing cultural landscape of cities helps us grasp the interplay of local and global forces that shape urban development.

Functional Zones

Before examining specific models of urban space, we must define some terms commonly used in referring to parts of the city. The term **zone** is typically preceded by a descriptor that conveys the purpose of that area of the city. Urban models treat zones as areas with a relatively uniform land use, for example, an industrial zone or a residential zone. Most models define the key economic zone of the city (if there is such) as the central business district. The American CBD typically has high land values, tall buildings, busy traffic, converging highways, and mass transit systems.

The term **central city** describes the urban area that is not suburban. In effect, the central city refers to the older city as opposed to the newer suburbs. A **suburb** is an outlying, functionally uniform part of an urban area, and is often (but not always) adjacent to the central city. Most suburbs are residential, but some have other land uses, including schools, shopping malls, and office parks.

Suburbanization is the process by which lands that were previously outside of the urban environment become urbanized, as people and businesses from the city move to these spaces. The process of suburbanization holds special interest for human geographers because it involves the transformation of large areas of land from rural to urban uses and affects large numbers of people who can afford to move to larger and more expensive suburban homes. The aesthetic of the suburb reveals the occupants' idealized living patterns because their layout can be planned in response to choice and demand.

In *Contemporary Suburban America* (1981), urban geographer P. O. Muller noted that suburbia "evolved into a self-sufficient urban entity, containing its own major economic and cultural activities, that is no longer an appendage to the central city." Muller found suburban cities ready to compete with the central city for leading urban economic activities such as telecommunications, high-technology industries, and corporate headquarters. In addition to expanding residential zones, the process of suburbanization rapidly creates distinct urban regions complete with industrial, commercial, and educational components.

The overall importance of suburban life in the United States is underscored by the results of the 2000 census, which indicated that no less than 50 percent of the country's population resided in the suburbs (up from 37 percent in 1970); the remaining 50 percent were divided between the central cities (30.3 percent) and nonmetropolitan or rural areas (19.7 percent). Of the population living in metropolitan areas, 62.2 percent resided in the suburbs, which in 2000 had 141 million residents. Thus, the suburbs have become the essence of the modern American city.

Just by using such terms as *residential area* and *central business district*, people acknowledge the existence of a regional structure within cities. When you refer to downtown, or to the airport, or to the city zoo, you are in fact referring to urban regions where certain functions prevail (business activity, transportation, and recreation, in the three just mentioned). All of these urban regions or zones lie near or adjacent to each other and together make up the city. But how are they arranged?

The Spatial Organization of the Typical European City

In the previous section of this chapter we paid considerable attention to the development of the European city. That history is reflected in the geographical structure of the older cities of Europe. The center of those cities are typically characterized by a dense conglomeration of residential, retail, civic, and religious structures. The low degree of functional zonation in the preindustrial urban core is similar to the medieval city. Since many of these cities developed gradually over time, with no overall planning, there is no particular order to the street pattern. Streets are narrow and winding, but some of the neighborhoods are quite well off—a reflection of the advantages in prior eras of living close to the cultural and civic center.

Surrounding these cores is a preindustrial periphery that, in earlier times, housed more of the poorer people. This part of the city was significantly affected by the coming of railroads and larger manufacturing establishments during the industrial era. Functional zonation is somewhat greater there than in the preindustrial core, but it is still comparatively low because their roots can still be traced to an era before large-scale urban planning. Some parts of the preindustrial periphery became wealthy as nineteenth-century urban redevelopment plans paved the way for the emergence of up-scale retail and residential districts.

Beyond the preindustrial core lies a ring of industrial and postindustrial suburbs. These did not grow substantially until well into the twentieth century, and they often are the product of urban planning. As a result, functional zonation is higher in these suburbs. Some developed as commercial centers with high-rise buildings. Others housed millions of migrants streaming into the cities to take industrial jobs, and some of these are now the poorest sections of European cities. Yet others, usually those farther from the center, became bedroom communities for wealthier people with the time and resources to commute to the city for work.

Many of the ethnic neighborhoods in European cities are the product of migrations from former colonies. Algeria was a colony of France, and now Paris and other French cities have distinct Algerian neighborhoods. Similarly, London (the United Kingdom) has a Jamaican neighborhood, and Madrid (Spain) has a distinct Moroccan neighborhood, reflecting colonial ties with these now sovereign countries. Other European countries cultivated relationships with countries outside of Europe after the colonial era. For example, after World War II, Germany invited young men from Turkey to migrate to Germany as guest workers (see Chapter 3). Cities in Germany, such as Frankfurt, have distinct Turkish neighborhoods. The vast majority of migrants currently coming to Europe end up in cities. And most of the migrants to European cities come from the global periphery or from poorer areas in eastern and southern Europe.

Modeling the North American City

Recognition of regularities in the organization of cities has prompted urban geographers to construct spatial models of cities in various world regions. Early models of North American cities emphasized the functional organization of activities within cities (Box 9.1). As modern cities became increasingly complex, the construction of explanatory models became almost impossible. Today's larger cities are regions in themselves, and cities-within-cities make earlier models seem simplistic. Earlier models continue to shed light on some of the spatial characteristics of the urban centers, but contemporary urban geographers recognize these centers as only one part of the expansive urban area that functions somewhat autonomously from the central city around which it is located.

Following World War II, the availability of personal automobiles and the construction of ring roads and other arteries around cities led to rapid suburbanization, especially around new transportation corridors. The outer edges of many urban areas grew quickly and became more functionally independent of the central city. Suburban downtowns emerged to serve their new local economies. Often located near key freeway intersections, these suburban downtowns developed mainly around big regional shopping centers and attracted industrial parks, office complexes, hotels, restaurants, entertainment facilities, and even sports stadiums. Tysons Corner, Virginia (outside Washington, D.C.) and Irvine, California (outside Los Angeles) flourished as **edge cities**. They attracted tens of thousands of nearby suburbanites—offering workplaces, shopping, leisure activities, and all the other elements of a complete urban environment—thereby loosening remaining ties not only to the central city but to other suburban areas as well (Fig. 9.22).

As early as 1973, American suburbs surpassed the central cities in total employment. By the mid-1980s, in some metropolises in the Sun Belt, the majority of jobs in the metropolitan area were located outside the urban core. Rapid population dispersal to outer suburbs not only created distant nuclei but also reduced the volume and level of interaction between the central city and these emerging suburban cities. This situation made the new outer cities of the suburban ring more self-sufficient as locational advantages produced an ever-greater range of retailing and employment activity. Regional shopping centers in the suburban zone became the CBDs of the outer nuclei, and new business and industrial parks sprang up outside the central city. In short, a new decentered urban metropolitan area came into being.

Present-day Los Angeles and Toronto are cited as prime examples of what is sometimes called a **galactic city**—a complex urban area in which centrality of functions is no longer significant. Instead, the old downtown plays the role of a festival or recreational area, and widely dispersed industrial parks, shopping centers, high-tech industrial spaces, edge-city downtowns, and industrial suburbs are the new centers of economic activity.

BOX 9.1

Efforts to model the North American city capture some of the changing characteristics of such cities during the early to mid-twentieth century. The first such model to receive wide attention, the **concentric zone model** (see accompanying figure), resulted from sociologist Ernest Burgess's study of Chicago in the 1920s. Burgess's model divides the city into five concentric zones, defined by their function. As the city grew, land was converted into zones around the outside margins of the city, and the concentric zone model emerged. At the center is the CBD (1), itself subdivided into several subdistricts (financial, retail, theater).

The zone of transition (2) is characterized by residential deterioration and encroachment by business and light manufacturing. Zone 3 is a ring of closely spaced, modest homes occupied by the blue-collar labor force. Zone 4 consists of middle-class residences, and Zone 5 is the suburban ring. Burgess described his model as dynamic: As the city grew, inner zones encroached on outer ones, so that CBD functions

invaded Zone 2 and the problems of Zone 2 affected the inner margins of Zone 3.

In the late 1930s, Homer Hoyt published his **sector model**, partly as an answer to the limitations of the Burgess model. Hoyt focused on residential patterns, explaining where the wealthy in a city chose to live. Hoyt argued that the city grows outward from the center, so a low-rent area could extend all the way from the CBD to the city's outer edge, creating zones that are shaped like a piece of pie. Hoyt found that the pie-shaped pieces describe the high-rent residential, intermediate rent residential, low-rent residential, education and recreation, transportation, and industrial sectors.

Researchers studied both theories, and Chauncy Harris and Edward Ullman argued that neither the concentric rings nor the sector model adequately reflected city structure by the mid-twentieth century. In the 1940s, they proposed the **multiple nuclei model**. Their model recognizes that the CBD was losing its dominant position as the single nucleus of the urban area. Several of the urban regions shown in the figure have their own nuclei.

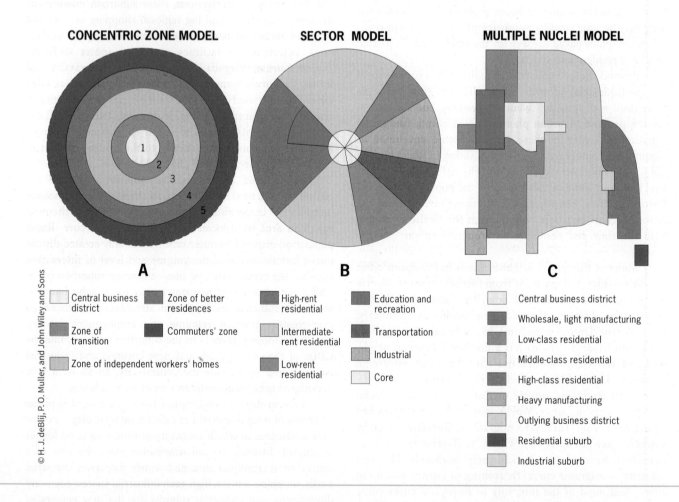

CONCENTRIC ZONE MODEL **SECTOR MODEL** **MULTIPLE NUCLEI MODEL**

A B C

Central business district

Zone of transition

Zone of independent workers' homes

Zone of better residences

Commuters' zone

High-rent residential

Intermediate-rent residential

Low-rent residential

Education and recreation

Transportation

Industrial

Core

Central business district

Wholesale, light manufacturing

Low-class residential

Middle-class residential

High-class residential

Heavy manufacturing

Outlying business district

Residential suburb

Industrial suburb

■■ **Figure 9.22**
Tysons Corner, Virginia.   In the suburbs of Washington, D.C., on Interstate 495 (the Beltway), Tysons Corner has developed as a major edge city, with offices, retail, and commercial services.

© Rob Crandall/The Image Works

Modeling Cities in World Regions

As the number of cities in the world with millions of inhabitants can now be counted in the hundreds, it has become increasingly difficult to model, classify, or typify urban centers. In the 1960s, researchers classified "colonial" cities as urban areas where European transplants dominated the form of the city, laying it out with Western styles. Researchers also drew models of "indigenous" cities that remained remote from globalizing influences and various Western urban forms.

The rapid growth in the population and territorial footprint of **megacities** in the developing world has made it difficult to model many urban areas. Such cities have large populations, a vast territorial extent, and frequently a strained, inadequate infrastructure. For example, Mumbai, India, has more people than the country of Australia. São Paulo, Brazil, covers more land than the country of Belgium. Kinshasa, Democratic Republic of the Congo, is the fastest growing city in Africa. Jakarta, Indonesia, is the largest city in the world without a subway or metro system.

In Middle and South America, Mexico City (Mexico) and São Paulo (Brazil) are now the kinds of megacities that make analysis difficult. Nonetheless, some cities located in South American countries once colonized by Spain have retained a common social-spatial geography. Also, some former colonial cities in Subsaharan Africa have maintained the spatial components lost in megacities such as Lagos (Nigeria) and Kinshasa (Democratic Republic of the Congo).

The South American City

In 1980, geographers Ernst Griffin and Larry Ford studied South American cities and derived a model of the South

American city referred to as the **Griffin–Ford model**. Griffin and Ford found that South American cities blend traditional elements of South American culture with the forces of globalization that are reshaping the urban scene, combining radial sectors and concentric zones.

Anchoring the model is the thriving CBD, which remains the city's primary business, employment, and entertainment focus. The CBD is divided into a traditional market sector and a more modern high-rise sector. Adequate public transit systems and nearby affluent residential areas assure the dominance of the CBD. Emanating outward from the urban core along the city's most prestigious axis is the commercial spine, which is surrounded by the elite residential sector. This widening corridor is essentially an extension of the CBD. It features offices, shopping, high-quality housing for the upper and upper-middle classes, restaurants, theaters, and such amenities as parks, zoos, and golf courses. At the end of the elite spine sector lies an incipient edge city shown as "mall" on the model and flanked by high-priced residences. This development reflects the emergence of suburban nodes from the North American model in South America's cities.

In the Griffin–Ford model, the remaining concentric zones are home to less-well-off residents, who compose the great majority of the urban population. Socioeconomic levels and housing quality decrease markedly with greater distance from the city center (Fig. 9.23). The zone of maturity in the inner city contains the best housing outside the spine sector, attracting middle-class residents who invest sufficiently to keep their solidly built but aging dwellings from deteriorating. The adjacent zone is one of much more modest housing. Interspersed with the more modest areas are densely populated unkempt areas that represent a transition from inner-ring affluence to outer-ring poverty. The outermost zone of peripheral squatter settlements is home to the impoverished and recent migrants who live in shantytowns. **Shantytowns** are unplanned developments of crude dwellings and shelters made mostly of scrap wood, iron, and pieces of cardboard that develop around cities. Although the ring of peripheral squatter settlements consists mainly of teeming, high-density shantytowns, many residents here are surprisingly optimistic about finding work and improving their living conditions.

A structural element common to many South American cities is the **disamenity sector**, the very poorest parts of cities that in extreme cases are not connected to regular city services and are controlled by gangs and drug lords. The

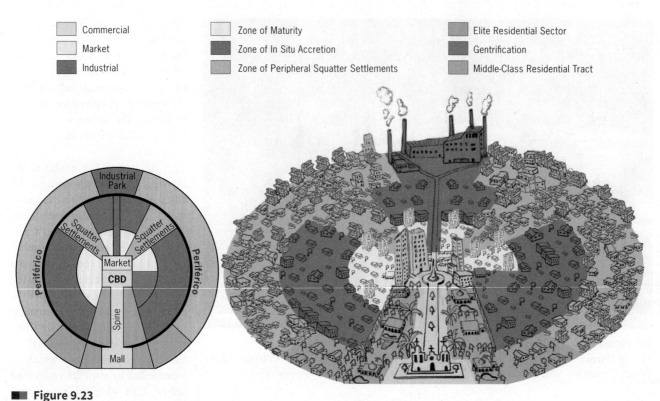

Commercial
Market
Industrial

Zone of Maturity
Zone of In Situ Accretion
Zone of Peripheral Squatter Settlements

Elite Residential Sector
Gentrification
Middle-Class Residential Tract

■■ **Figure 9.23**
Latin American City Model.   This model includes both the zones created in the original Griffin–Ford model and the new Ford model of the South American city.   *Adapted with permission from*: L. Ford, "A New and Improved Model of Latin American City Structure," *The Geographical Review* 86 (1996), p. 438.

disamenity sectors in South American cities contain relatively unchanging slums known as *barrios* or *favelas*. The worst of these poverty-stricken areas often include large numbers of people who are so poor that they are forced to live in the streets (Fig. 9.24). There is little in the way of regular law enforcement within such communities, and drug lords often run the show—or battle with other drug lords for dominance. Such conditions also prevail in places beyond the ring highway or *periférico*, which is now a feature of most South American cities.

Finally, the Griffin–Ford model displays two smaller sectors: an industrial park, reflecting the ongoing concentration of industrial activity in the city, and a gentrification zone, where historic buildings are preserved. Gentrification remains much less common in South American cities than in North America, but it is an emerging phenomenon.

To what extent is the Griffin–Ford model a realistic portrayal of the South American city? The model reflects the enormous differences between the spaces of privilege and the spaces of abject poverty within the South American city. The model also describes elements of sector development evident in many large South American cities, but the concentricity suggested by the model seems to be breaking down. Figure 9.24 incorporates both the original zones of the Griffin–Ford model and the updates Larry Ford added in a 1996 article.

Larry Ford's updated Griffin–Ford model adds a ring highway (*periférico*) around the outskirts of the city, divides the downtown business district into a CBD and a market, adds a mall near the elite space, and leaves space for suburban industrial parks.

The African City

At the beginning of this century, Subsaharan Africa included countries with some of the world's lowest levels of urbanization. In the tropical region of Africa, the majority of the people are farmers, and most countries in the tropics remain under 40 percent urbanized. Outside the tropics, the region is about 57 percent urban. Despite the region's comparatively low overall level of urbanization, Africa now has the world's fastest growing cities, followed by those in South Asia and mainland East Asia and South and Middle America. In contrast, the cities of North America, southern South America, and Australia are growing more slowly, and those of western Europe are barely growing at all.

The imprint of European colonialism can still be seen in many African cities. During the colonial period, Europeans laid out prominent urban centers such as Kinshasa (Democratic Republic of the Congo), Nairobi (Kenya), and Harare

FIELD NOTE

"February 1, 2003. A long-held hope came true today: Thanks to a Brazilian intermediary I was allowed to enter and spend a day in two of Rio de Janeiro's hill-slope *favelas*, an eight-hour walk through one into the other. Here live millions of the city's poor, in areas often ruled by drug lords and their gangs, with minimal or no public services, amid squalor and stench, in discomfort and danger. And yet life in the older *favelas* has become more comfortable as shacks are replaced by more permanent structures, electricity is sometimes available, water supply, however haphazard, is improved, and an informal economy brings goods and services to the residents. I stood in the doorway of a resident's single-room dwelling for this overview of an urban landscape in transition: satellite-television disks symbolize the change going on here. The often blue cisterns catch rainwater; walls are made of rough brick and roofs of corrugated iron or asbestos sheeting. There are no roads or automobile access, so people walk to the nearest road at the bottom of the hill. Locals told me of their hope that they will someday have legal rights to the space they occupy. During his campaign for president of Brazil, former president Lula de Silva suggested that long-term inhabitants should be awarded title, and in 2003 his government approved the notion. It will be complicated: As the photo shows, people live quite literally on top of one another, and mapping the chaos will not be simple (but will be made possible with geographic information systems). This would allow the government to tax

© H. J. de Blij

■ **Figure 9.24**
Rio de Janeiro, Brazil.

residents, but it would also allow residents to obtain loans based on the value of their *favela* properties, and bring millions of Brazilians into the formal economy. The hardships I saw on this excursion were often dreadful, but you could sense the hope for and anticipation of a better future. In preparation for the 2014 World Cup, the city of Rio and government of Brazil demolished several favelas and spent millions of dollars working to provide services to remaining favelas in the path of the public eye."

(Zimbabwe) in the interior, and Dakar (Senegal), Abidjan (Côte d'Ivoire), Luanda (Angola), Maputo (Mozambique), and other ports along the coast. Africa even has cities that are neither traditional nor colonial. The centers of South Africa's major cities (Johannesburg, Cape Town, and Durban) remain essentially Western, with elements of European as well as American models and a veneer of globalization, including high-rise CBDs and sprawling upper-income suburbs.

As a result of this diversity, it is difficult to formulate a model of the African city. Studies of African cities indicate that the central city often consists of not one but three CBDs (Fig. 9.25): a remnant of the colonial CBD, an informal and sometimes periodic market zone, and a transitional business center where commerce is conducted from curbside, stalls, or storefronts. Vertical development occurs mainly in the former colonial CBD; the traditional business center is usually a zone of single-story buildings with some traditional architecture; and the market zone tends to be open-air, informal, yet still important. Sector development marks the encircling zone of

ethnic and mixed neighborhoods (often characterized by strong ethnic identities as people of ethnic kin tend to cluster together). Since many African cities began as mining towns, such operations still occur in conjunction with this zone in some instances. Manufacturing companies still function here—taking advantage of the proximity to a nearby labor force. Invariably, fast-growing African cities are encircled by vast shantytowns rapidly growing as a result of significant in-migration.

The Southeast Asian City

Some of the most populated cities in the world are in Southeast Asia. The city of Kuala Lumpur, Malaysia, is a complex of high-rise development, including the 1483-foot-tall Petronas Towers, which until recently was the world's tallest building. The city of Jakarta, Indonesia, called Jabotabek by the locals, is an enormous conurbation of Bogor, Tangerang, and Bekasi.

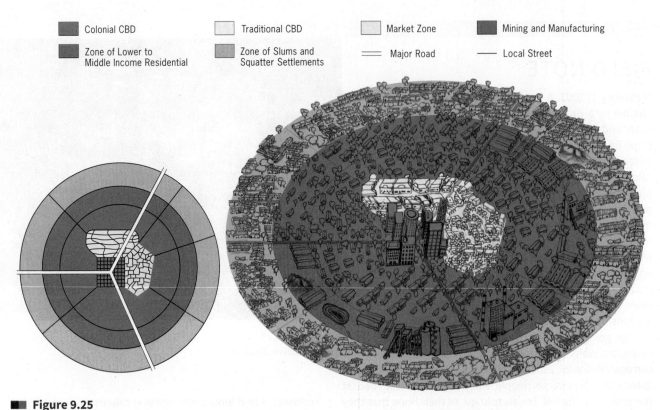

Colonial CBD Traditional CBD Market Zone Mining and Manufacturing

Zone of Lower to Middle Income Residential Zone of Slums and Squatter Settlements Major Road Local Street

■■■ **Figure 9.25**
Subsaharn Africa City Model. One model of the African city includes a colonial CBD, a traditional CBD, and a market zone.
© E. H. Fouberg, A. B. Murphy, H. J. de Blij, and John Wiley & Sons, Inc.

In 1967, urban geographer T. G. McGee studied the medium-sized cities of Southeast Asia and found that they exhibit similar land-use patterns, creating a model referred to as the **McGee model** (Fig. 9.26). The focal point of the city is the old colonial port zone combined with the largely commercial district that surrounds it. McGee found no formal CBD; rather, he found the elements of the CBD present as separate clusters surrounding the old colonial port zone: the government zone; the Western commercial zone (practically a CBD by itself); the alien commercial zone, dominated by Chinese merchants whose residences are attached to their places of business; and the mixed land-use zone that contains miscellaneous economic activities, including light industry. The other nonresidential areas are the market-gardening zone at the outskirts of the urban area and, still farther from the city, a recently built industrial park or "estate."

The residential zones in McGee's model are similar to those in the Griffin–Ford model of the South American city. Other similarities between the McGee and Griffin–Ford model are the hybrid structure of sectors and zones, an elite residential sector that includes new suburbs, an inner-city zone of middle-income housing, and peripheral low-income

squatter settlements. One main difference is that the McGee model includes middle-income housing in a suburban zone, reflecting the larger middle class in these cities of the global semiperiphery and the small middle class in South American cities.

Regardless of the region or city, we recognize that models do not explain how or why cities are organized the way they are. A model of a city shows us an end product, whether planned or not, and suggests the forces that created that end product.

Employing the concepts defined in this section of the chapter, compare and contrast the Latin American city model with either the African city or Southeast Asian city model. What is similar—can you see influences of colonialism in each model; are the poorest residential areas located on the outskirts of the city; where are the wealthiest residential areas located relative to manufacturing zones?

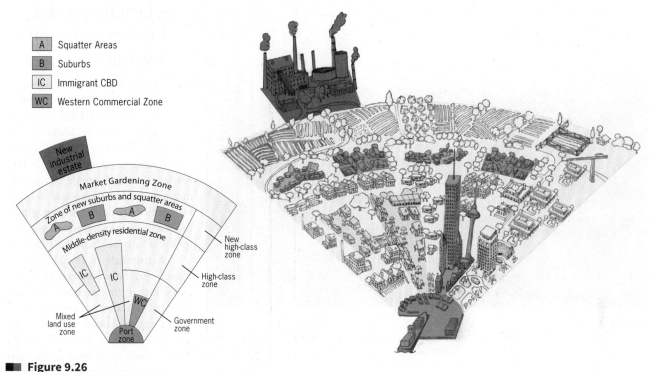

Legend:
- A Squatter Areas
- B Suburbs
- IC Immigrant CBD
- WC Western Commercial Zone

New industrial estate

Market Gardening Zone

Zone of new suburbs and squatter areas

Middle-density residential zone

New high-class zone

High-class zone

Mixed land use zone

Government zone

Port zone

■ Figure 9.26

Southeast Asian City Model.   A model of land use in the Southeast Asian city includes sectors and zones within each sector.   *Adapted with permission from*: T. G. McGee, *The Southeast Asian City*, London: Bell, 1967, p. 128.

HOW DO PEOPLE SHAPE CITIES?

People and institutions make places, including cities. The roles individual people, governments, corporations, developers, financial lenders, and realtors play in shaping cities vary across the world. Government planning agencies can directly affect the layout of cities by restricting the kinds of development allowed in certain regions or zones of cities.

Through **zoning laws**, cities divide up the city and designate the kinds of development allowed in each zone. Portland, Oregon, is often described as the best planned city in North America because it is built around free transportation in the central city to discourage the use of cars. Portland is a compact city with office buildings and residential zones in close proximity to encourage walking, biking, and public transportation. On the other hand, Houston, Texas, is the only large city that does not have zoning laws on the books. Houstonites voted against the creation of zoning laws three different times (most recently in 1993).

In addition to government planning and zoning laws, people shape cities by choosing to live in certain neighborhoods and by opening stores, houses of worship, and even sporting fields that reflect the values of their culture. If you wander through the neighborhoods of any city and pay close attention, you can see differences in the existence of single-family or multifamily homes, in particular styles of construction and building materials, in the distance between houses, in the nature and style of vegetation around houses, in the distance between the houses and the streets, and even in the amount of space devoted to automobile movement and storage.

Comparing and contrasting the urban cultural landscapes of two cities helps us understand the different social and cultural forces at play. Compare Figure 9.27 with Figure 9.28. Analyze each picture and guess which city is located in a wealthy country in the world and which is located in a poor country. What factors can you consider? You may look at the presence or absence of high-rise buildings, the aesthetics of the buildings, the road, and the distance between houses. After doing so, you might guess that Figure 9.27 is in the wealthy country. Look again. This time, look for whether there are telephone and electrical wires, and note what building materials were used. Figure 9.27 is actually in a poorer country; it is the city of Lomé, Togo, in Subsaharan Africa. Figure 9.28 is part of a suburb of Tokyo, Japan. Japanese houses in this middle-class neighborhood are almost on top of each other because the city is so densely populated that land is at a premium. In Lomé, the high rises are part of the CBD, and some of the houses immediately surrounding them are where the wealthy live. The houses in the foreground are where the poor live. Here the roofs are tin or cardboard, the

© Alexander B. Murphy

■■ **Figure 9.27**
Lomé, Togo.   The city's landscape reflects a clear dichotomy between the "haves" and "have-nots."

Shaping Cities in the Global Periphery and Semiperiphery

Many of the world's most populous cities are located in the less prosperous parts of the world, including São Paulo (Brazil), Mexico City (Mexico), Mumbai (India), Dhaka (Bangladesh), and Delhi (India). Across the world, people continue to migrate to cities in response to "pull" factors that are often more imaginary than real; their expectations of a better life mostly fail to materialize.

Particularly in the global economic periphery, new arrivals (and many long-term residents, too) are crowded together in overpopulated apartment buildings, dismal tenements, and teeming slums (Fig. 9.29). New arrivals come from other cities and towns and from the rural coun-

houses are makeshift, and utility lines are lacking. Notice that in this picture of Lomé, we see no evidence of a middle class; this is common in cities of the periphery, where there are "haves" and "have-nots," but little in between.

tryside, often as large families; they add to the cities' rate of natural growth. Housing cannot keep up with this massive inflow. Almost overnight huge shantytowns develop around these cities. The overcrowding and dismal conditions do not

© sack/iStockphoto

■■ **Figure 9.28**
Tokyo, Japan.   The city's landscape reflects the presence of a large middle class in a densely populated city.

GUEST FIELD NOTE

Manila, the Philippines

I passed through cargo shipping piers in Manila, the Philippines, and encountered row after row of hand-built squatter houses. I was struck by the scale of the settlements and the sheer number of people who inhabit them. I was shocked at the level of squalor in people's living conditions. The garbage scavengers in this picture wore cotton gloves and held prods to dig through the trash for items they can use, trade, or sell. The poor and destitute live throughout the city because housing stocks are inadequate, underlying poverty persists, and thousands flock to Manila daily recognizing that petty services and even trash picking often offer more opportunity than life in the rural provinces.

Credit: Johnathan Walker, James Madison University

Figure 9.29

deter additional urban migration; as a result, millions of people spend their entire lives in urban housing of wretched quality.

Cities in poorer parts of the world generally lack enforceable zoning laws. Without zoning laws, cities in the periphery have mixed land use throughout the city. For example, in cities such as Madras, India (and in other cities in India), open space between high-rise buildings is often occupied by squatter settlements (Fig. 9.30). In Bangkok, Thailand, elementary schools and noisy, polluting factories stand side by side. In Nairobi, Kenya, hillside villas overlook some of Africa's worst slums. Over time, such incongruities may disappear, as is happening in many cities in East Asia. Rising land values and greater demand for enforced zoning regulations are transforming the central cities of East Asia. But in South Asia, Subsaharan Africa, Southwest Asia, North Africa, and Middle and South America, unregulated, helter-skelter growth continues.

Across the global periphery, the one trait all major cities display is the stark contrast between the wealthy and the poor. Sharp contrasts between wealthy and poor areas can be found in major cities all over the world—for example, homeless people sleep on heating grates half a block from the White House in Washington, D.C. Yet the intensity and scale of the contrast are greater in cities of the periphery. If you stand in the central area of Cairo, Egypt, you see what appears to be a relatively modern, Mediterranean metropolis (Fig. 9.31). But if you get on a bus and ride it toward the city's outskirts, that impression fades almost immediately as paved streets give way to dusty alleys, apartment buildings to harsh tenements, and sidewalk coffee shops to broken doors and

© Erin H. Fouberg

Figure 9.30

Hyderabad, India. Temporary shelters, built to withstand the summer monsoon, protect the migrants who work to build the new construction in the background.

FIELD NOTE

"Central Cairo is full of the multistory buildings, transportation arteries, and commercial signs that characterize most contemporary big cities. Outside of a number of mosques, few remnants of the old medieval city remain. The first blow came in the nineteenth century, when a French-educated ruler was determined to recast Cairo as a world-class city. Paris's Baron von Hausman transformed the urban core into a zone of broad, straight streets. In more recent years the forces of modern international capitalism have had the upper hand. There is little sense of an overall vision for central Cairo. Instead, it seems to be a hodge-podge of buildings and streets devoted to commerce, administration, and a variety of producer and consumer services."

Figure 9.31
Cairo, Egypt City Center.

windows (Fig. 9.32). Traffic-choked, garbage-strewn, polluted Cairo is home to an estimated 9.1 million people, more than one-fifth of Egypt's population; the city is bursting at the seams. And still people continue to arrive, seeking the better life that pulls countless migrants from the countryside year after year.

Shaping Cities in the Global Core

The goals people have in establishing cities have changed over time. People constantly remake the cities where they live, reinventing neighborhoods or changing layouts to reflect changing goals and aesthetics. During the segregation era in the United States, realtors, financial lenders, and city

FIELD NOTE

"Moving out from central Cairo, evidence of the city's rapid growth is all around you. These hastily built housing units are part of the (often losing) effort to keep up with the city's exploding growth. From a city of just one million people in 1930, Cairo's population expanded to six million by 1986. And then high growth rates really kicked in. Although no one knows the exact size of the contemporary city, most estimates suggest that Cairo's population has doubled in the last 20 years. This growth has placed a tremendous strain on city services. Housing has been a particularly critical problem—leading to a landscape outside the urban core dominated by hastily built, minimally functional, and aesthetically nondescript housing projects."

Figure 9.32
Cairo, Egypt Residential Area.

governments defined and segregated spaces in urban environments. For example, before the civil rights movement of the 1960s, financial institutions in the business of lending money could engage in a practice known as **redlining**. They would identify what they considered to be risky neighborhoods in cities—often predominantly black neighborhoods—and refuse to offer loans to anyone purchasing a house in the neighborhood encircled by red lines on their maps. This practice, which is now illegal, worked against those living in poorer neighborhoods and helped to precipitate a downward spiral in which poor neighborhoods became increasingly rundown because funds were not available for upkeep or to purchase homes for sale.

Before the civil rights movement, realtors could purposely sell a house in a white neighborhood at a very low price to a black buyer. In a practice called **blockbusting**, realtors would solicit white residents of the neighborhood to sell their homes under the guise that the neighborhood was going downhill because a black person or family had moved in. This produced what urban geographers and sociologists call *white flight*—movement of whites from the city and adjacent neighborhoods to the outlying suburbs. Blockbusting led to significant turnover in housing, which of course benefited real estate agents through the commissions they earned as representatives of buyers and sellers. Blockbusting also prompted landowners to sell their properties at low prices to get out of the neighborhood quickly, which in turn allowed developers to subdivide lots and build tenements. Typically, developers did not maintain tenements well, dropping the property values even further.

Developers and governments are also important actors in shaping cities. In cities of the global core that have experienced high levels of suburbanization, people left the city proper for the suburbs in search of single-family homes, yards, better schools, and safety. With suburbanization, city governments lose tax revenue, as middle- and upper-class taxpayers leave the city and pay taxes in the suburbs instead. In order to counter the suburbanization trend, city governments are encouraging commercialization of the CBD and gentrification of neighborhoods in and around that district.

The plans that city governments develop to revive central cities usually involve cleaning streets, sidewalks, and buildings; tearing down old, abandoned buildings; and building up commercial offerings and residences. City governments have often created programs to encourage **commercialization** of CBDs, which entails transforming the central business district into an area attractive to residents and tourists alike. Several cities, including Miami, New York, and Baltimore, have created waterfront "theme" areas to attract visitors. These areas include festival marketplaces, parks with exotic sculptures and play areas, and amusement zones occupying former industrial sites. Cities including Detroit and Minneapolis commercialize their CBDs by building or using tax incentives to attract professional sports stadiums to the central areas in the city. Ventures have been successful in attracting tourists and in generating business,

but they alone cannot revive downtowns because they cannot attract what the core of the city needs most: permanent residents with a stake in its future. The newly commercialized downtowns often stand apart from the rest of the central city.

Beginning in the 1960s, poor central-city neighborhoods located conveniently close to CBDs began to attract buyers who were willing to move back into the city to rehabilitate rundown houses and live in central-city neighborhoods. A process called **gentrification**—the rehabilitation of deteriorated houses in low-income neighborhoods—took hold in areas near the centers of many cities.

In the United States, gentrification began in cities with a tight housing market and defined central-city neighborhoods, including San Francisco, Portland, and Chicago. Gentrification slowed in the 1990s, but it is growing again as city governments encourage gentrification through beautification programs and significant tax breaks to people who buy up abandoned or dilapidated housing. The growing interest in central-city housing has resulted in part from the changing character of American society: the proportion of childless couples (heterosexual and homosexual) is growing, as is the number of single people in the population. Childless couples and singles often choose to live in cities because the suburbs do not look as attractive to them as they typically do to families with young children. Gentrified central-city neighborhoods attract residents who want to live within walking distance of their workplace and close to cultural, entertainment, and recreational amenities, nightlife, and restaurants (Fig. 9.33).

One consequence of gentrification is increased housing prices in central-city neighborhoods. Gentrification usually displaces lower income residents because property taxes rise as land values rise, and the cost of goods and services in the neighborhood, from parking to restaurants, rises as well. For urbanites displaced by gentrification, the consequences can be serious. Rising housing costs associated with gentrification have played a key role in the growing homelessness problem facing American cities.

The suburb is not immune to gentrification. In suburbs that are close to the city or directly connected by commuter rail, people purchase smaller or older homes with the intention of tearing the house down and building a much larger home. The homes intended for suburban demolition are called **teardowns**. In their place, suburbanites build newer homes that often are supersized and stretch to the outer limits of the lot. New supersized mansions are sometimes called **McMansions** (Fig. 9.34).

Like gentrification in the city, the teardown phenomenon changes the landscape and increases average housing values, tax revenue for the city, and the average household income of the neighborhood. Unlike inner-city gentrification, with teardowns the original houses are destroyed instead of preserved. Also unlike inner-city gentrification, teardowns often occur in middle-class and wealthy suburbs such as Greenwich, Connecticut, and Hinsdale, Illinois.

FIELD NOTE

"In 2008, downtown Fort Worth, Texas, looked quite different than it did when I first visited in 1997. In that 11-year period, business leaders in the city of Fort Worth gentrified the downtown. The Bass family, who has a great deal of wealth from oil holdings and who now owns about 40 blocks of downtown Fort Worth, was instrumental in the city's gentrification. In the 1970s and 1980s, members of the Bass family looked at empty, stark, downtown Fort Worth and sought a way to revitalize the downtown. They worked with the Tandy family to build and revitalize the spaces of the city, which took off in the late 1990s and into the present century. The crown jewel in the gentrified Fort Worth is the beautiful cultural center called the Bass Performance Hall, named for Nancy Lee and Perry R. Bass, which opened in 1998."

■ Figure 9.33
Fort Worth, Texas.

■ Figure 9.34
Hinsdale, Illinois. In this upscale suburb of Chicago, a new McMansion stands in the place where a smaller house (similar in size to the one still standing in the right of the photo) used to stand. In the last 20 years, about 25 percent of Hinsdale's houses have been torn down to make room for much larger houses.

Greenwich, a high-end neighborhood in Fairfield County, Connecticut, just outside of New York City, issued 138 permits for teardowns in 2004 (56 more than it did the year before). The collapse of the housing market brought a decline in the number of teardowns in Fairfield County starting in 2007, but in May 2010 the *Wall Street Journal* reported that teardown permits had begun rising again in Fairfield County. Permits in Greenwich, however, did not rise. As noted in the *Wall Street Journal*, "The most expensive corners of Fairfield County, including Greenwich, haven't seen much of a pickup in teardowns, local brokers say. A surplus of homes priced at more than $2 million, and difficulties in getting financing for these purchases, has kept that activity to a minimum."

In Hinsdale (just outside Chicago), one-third of the suburb's houses have been torn down since 1986. Those in favor of teardowns argue that the phenomenon slows urban sprawl by replacing existing homes with new homes, rather than converting farmland to residential lots. Those opposed to teardowns see the houses as too large for their lots, dwarfing the neighboring houses, and destroying the character of the street by demolishing the older homes on it.

Urban Sprawl and New Urbanism

As populations have grown in certain areas of the United States, such as the Sun Belt and the West, urban areas have experienced **urban sprawl**—unrestricted growth of housing, commercial developments, and roads over large expanses of land, with little concern for urban planning. Urban sprawl is easy to spot as you drive down major roadways in any urbanized part of the country. You will see strip malls, big box stores, chain restaurants, huge intersections, and numerous housing developments, all spread out over many acres (Fig. 9.35). Sprawl is a phenomenon of the automobile era. Cities that expanded before the automobile typically grew "up" instead of "out." For instance, Boston grew around the marketplace and port, but it grew before the automobile, resulting in development over smaller areas. When you go through the central city of Boston today, you can walk where you need to go or take the T (metro). Places are built up vertically, and curving, narrow streets and commercial developments with a flavor of the old city (Quincy Market) give the city a cozy, intimate feel.

Does population growth explain which cities experience the most urban sprawl? In a study of sprawl from 1960 through the 1990s, Leon Kolankiewicz and Roy Beck (two anti-sprawl writers) used United States Census data on urbanized areas and found that urban sprawl happened even in urban areas without significant population growth. In the

TABLE 9.1

Most Sprawling Metro Areas with a Population Over 1 Million in the United States. Smart Growth America created an index to measure urban sprawl based on development density, land use mix, activity centering, and street accessibility. These then major metro areas have the lowest density over a wide space, creating urban sprawl. *Data from*: Ewing, R., Rolf Pendall and Don Chen. Measuring Sprawl and Its Impact. Volume 1. Smart Growth America. http://www.smartgrowthamerica.org/documents/MeasuringSprawlTechnical.pdf.

MOST SPRAWLING LARGE METRO AREAS, 2014

Cities with a population of more than one million	State
1. Atlanta-Sandy Springs/Marietta	GA
2. Nashville/Davidson/Murfreesboro/Franklin	TN
3. Riverside-San Bernardino/Ontario	CA
4. Warren/Troy/Farmington Hills	MI
5. Charlotte/Gastonia-Rock Hill	NC/SC
6. Memphis	TN/MS/AR
7. Birmingham-Hoover	AL
8. Rochester	NY
9. Richmond	VA
10. Houston/Sugar Land/Baytown	TX

United States, urban sprawl is more common in the Sun Belt of the South (Atlanta) and in the West (Houston) in urban areas whose population is rapidly growing (Table 9.1). Yet, even in cities such as Detroit and Pittsburgh, where urban populations fell between 1960 and 1990—by 7 percent in Detroit and 9 percent in Pittsburgh—urban sprawl increased the urbanized areas of the cities by 28 percent and 30 percent, respectively. When urban sprawl happens, farmlands and old industrial sites are razed, roads are built or widened, strip malls are erected, and housing developments come to monopolize the horizon.

To counter urban sprawl, a group of architects, urban planners, and developers (now numbering over 2000 in more than 20 countries) proposed an urban design vision they call new urbanism. Forming the Congress for the New Urbanism in 1993, the group defines **new urbanism** as development, urban revitalization, and suburban reforms that create walkable neighborhoods with a diversity of housing and jobs. On their website, the Congress for the New Urbanism explains that "New Urbanists support regional planning for open space, appropriate architecture and planning, and the balanced development of jobs and housing. They believe these strategies are the best way to reduce how

Figure 9.35

Henderson, Nevada. Henderson is the largest suburb of Las Vegas, and it was also the fastest-growing urban settlement in the United States between 1990 and 2000. Many of the houses in this photograph are empty today, as Las Vegas had ranked first or second in the number of home and rental vacancies in United States cities in 2009 and 2010.

Ethan Miller/Getty Images

FIELD NOTE

"When I visited Celebration, Florida, in 1997, one year after residents moved into the first houses in the community, I felt like I was walking onto a movie or television set. The architecture in the Walt Disney-designed new urbanist development looked like a quintessential American town. Each house has a porch, but on the day I was there, the porches sat empty—waiting to welcome the arrival of their owners at the end of the work day. We walked through town, past the 50s'-style movie marquee, and ate lunch at a 50s'-style diner. At that point, Celebration was still growing. Across the street from the 'Bank of Celebration' stood a sign marking the future home of the 'Church in Celebration.'

In 2013, I returned to Celebration, and I spent the day walking the same streets. The 'Church in Celebration,' a Presbyterian community church, was built, and the main street through the town square was hosting an arts festival focused on dogs. The city had grown to 11,000 residents, suffered its first murder, and was experiencing a higher rate of foreclosures than the rest of Florida. The movie theater still stood but no longer showed movies. A Starbucks took up a main corner in town, standing next door to a Morgan Stanley office and an Irish pub. Disney no longer owns the town, but the influence of the Disney vision still stands, with architectural covenants allowing only certain house styles, a few pastel house colors, and hiding the trash and cars in alleys."

■■ **Figure 9.36**
Celebration, Florida.

long people spend in traffic, to increase the supply of affordable housing, and to rein in urban sprawl." New urbanists want to create neighborhoods that promote a sense of community and a sense of place.

The most famous new urbanist projects are cities that new urbanists designed from the ground up, including Seaside, Florida (featured in the movie *The Truman Show*), West Laguna, California, and Kentlands, Maryland. When new urbanists build a town, the design is reminiscent of Christaller over a much smaller area. The planners choose the central shopping areas and open spaces and develop the neighborhoods around them, with housing clustered around the central space so that people can walk to the shopping area within five minutes. One goal of new urbanist designs is to build housing more densely, taking up less space. Along with that, making shopping and other amenities walkable decreases

dependency on the automobile, which in the process helps the environment.

Although some see new urbanist designs as manufactured communities and feel disconnected in a new urbanist space, others see these designs as an important antidote to sprawl. Celebration, Florida, is a remarkable new urbanist space: It is adjacent to Walt Disney's theme parks, was envisioned by Walt Disney himself, and was owned by the Disney Company (Fig. 9.36). Built in 1994, Celebration is centered on Market Street, a shopping district with restaurants (including a 1950s-style diner and a pizza place), a town hall, banks, a post office, and a movie theater with a nostalgic marquee (Fig. 9.37). The town includes schools, a health center, a fitness center, and churches. The Disney Company chose certain architectural styles for the houses in Celebration, and builders initially offered homes and townhouses in

■ **Figure 9.37**
Celebration, Florida. Opened in 1996 with two screens and operated by AMC, the Celebration Cinema closed in 2010. The spires remain landmarks in the town.

a price range from $300,000 to over $1 million. To meet the new urbanist goal of incorporating diverse people in a community, Celebration includes apartments for rent and condominiums for sale.

For geographers new urbanism marks a redefinition of space in the city. Public spaces, they say, become privatized for the enjoyment of the few (the residents of the neighborhood). Geographers Stuart Aitken, Don Mitchell, and Lynn Staeheli note that as new urbanism strives to turn neighborhoods back in time, "spaces and social functions historically deemed public (such as parks, neighborhood centers, shopping districts)" are privatized. The houses with porches that encourage neighbors to talk and the parks that are within walking distance for the residents create "mythic landscapes that are ingratiating for those who can afford them and exclusionary for those who cannot."

Noted geographer David Harvey offers one of the strongest critiques of new urbanism, explaining first that most new urbanist designs are "greenfield" projects designed for the affluent to make suburban areas more livable. This fact is

evidence, Harvey argues, that the new urbanism movement is a kind of "spatial determinism" that does not recognize that "the fundamental difficulty with modernism was its persistent habit of privileging spatial forms over social processes." Harvey, and others who critique new urbanism, claim that new urbanism does nothing to break down the social conditions that privilege some while disadvantaging others; that new urbanist projects take away much of the grittiness and character of the city; and that the "communities" that new urbanists form through their projects are exclusionary communities that deepen the racial segregation of cities.

Despite the critiques against new urbanism, developments in the new urbanist tradition are attracting a growing number of people, and when they are situated within cities, they can work against urban sprawl.

Gated Communities

As you drive through urban spaces in the United States, suburban and central city alike, you will note more and more neighborhoods being developed or redesigned to align with new urbanist principles. In your inventory of landscapes, even more overwhelming will be the proliferation of gated communities. **Gated communities** are fenced-in neighborhoods with controlled access gates for people and automobiles. Often, gated communities have security cameras and security forces (privatized police) keeping watch over the community, as the main objective of a gated community is to create a space of safety within the uncertain urban world. A secondary objective is to maintain or increase housing values in the neighborhood through enforcement of the neighborhood association's bylaws that control everything from the color of a house to the character and size of additions.

During the late 1980s and early 1990s, developers in the United States began building gated communities in urban areas around the country. In a 2001 census of housing, the United States government reported that 16 million people, or about 6 percent of Americans, live in gated communities. The urban design of gating communities has diffused around the globe at record speed, with gated communities now found in Europe, Asia, Africa, and Latin America.

In poorer countries, where cities are divided between wealthy and poor, gated communities provide another layer of comfort for the city's wealthy. In the large cities of Latin America and Africa, you commonly see walls around individual houses belonging to wealthy and middle-class families, walling in yards and pools and keeping out crime. These walls often include barbed wire or shards of glass fixed to the top to discourage intruders from scaling the walls. During the last ten years, many neighborhoods in these cities have added gates around the neighborhoods in addition to the walls. Walled houses and gated communities in the wealthy northern suburbs of Johannesburg, South Africa, are threatening the desegregation of the post-Apartheid city. White, wealthy residents fear crime in the city which, along with neighboring

© Alexander B. Murphy

■ **Figure 9.38**
Guangzhou, China.   This gated housing community just outside the city is much more serene than the teeming metropolis next door.

Pretoria, has a murder rate of 5000 per year (in an area with about 5 million people). In response to their fear of crime, by 2004 people in the suburbs of Johannesburg had blocked off over 2500 streets and posted guards to control access to these streets. Many view the gated communities as a new form of segregation. Since the vast majority of the crimes in the city occur in poor black townships or in the central city, the concern is that these developments only worsen the plight of less well-off segments of society.

Gated communities have taken off in China as well, with communities now crossing socioeconomic classes and assuming a prominent place in the urban landscape (Fig. 9.38). Like the gated communities in Europe and North America, the gated communities of China privatize spaces and exclude outsiders with gates, security cameras, and restricted access. However, China's gated communities are five to ten times more densely populated than Europe's and North America's. Geographer Youqin Huang has found other differences between gated communities in China and those in North America and Europe. China has a long history of gated communities, dating back to the first Chinese cities and persisting since. Huang argues that the "collectivism-oriented culture and tight political control" in China explain why the Chinese government built gated communities during the socialist period and why a proliferation of privately developed gated communities has occurred since China's housing reform in 1998 promoted individual home ownership.

In Europe and North America, gated communities are not only for the wealthy and privileged; the middle and lower classes also have a growing desire to feel safe at home. Some urban planners have encouraged governments to recast low-income housing as small communities, gated from each other, in order to reduce the flowthrough traffic and associated crime. Cities have sometimes torn down enormous high rises, typically ridden with crime and referred to as "the projects," including Cabrini Green in Chicago and Pruitt-Igoe in St. Louis, in an effort to remake the spaces of the poor into "defensible," and more livable, spaces.

Champions of middle-income and low-income neighborhoods seek to create a sense of community and make the spaces "defensible" from undesired activities such as drug dealing and prostitution. One of the best-documented cases of gating a middle-income community is the Five Oaks district of Dayton, Ohio, a neighborhood that is about 50 percent African American and 50 percent white and has a high rate of rentals. Urban planner Oscar Newman encouraged planners in Dayton to divide the 2000 households in the Five Oaks district into ten smaller, gated communities with restricted access. The city turned most of the residential streets in each of these mini-neighborhoods into cul-de-sacs. They have experienced a serious reduction in crime, along with an increase in housing sales and housing values.

Urban Geopolitics

Geographer Stephen Graham coined the term *urban geopolitics* to draw attention to the impact of global-scale geopolitical developments on the character of cities. Urban areas play a central role in twenty-first-century geopolitics. The existence of globe-circling surveillance networks and advanced weaponry has transformed how war is conducted and planned—prompting militant groups to retreat to urban areas where they can hide and take advantage of the urban infrastructure. The door-to-door urban combat that marked the recent United States campaign in Iraq illustrates these changes. A key theme geographers have identified in their studies of contemporary warscapes is **urbicide**, which Graham defines as the deliberate killing of the city. Urbicide was used to describe the conflict in the Balkans in the 1990s. The Yugoslav National Army intentionally destroyed Bosnia's famous Mostar Bridge in 1992 in a move that has since been interpreted not as strategic, but as rooted in the desire to destroy cultural property (Fig. 9.39). Geographer Sara Fregonese has traced the concept of urbicide to Beirut in the 1970s, where local militias used barricades to take control over parts of the city and restrict movement.

■■ Figure 9.39
Mostar, Bosnia and Herzegovina.   Stari Most means Old Bridge, but this photo, taken in 2009, depicts the new bridge that was built in 2004 to replace the one destroyed in 1993. Long considered to be a triumph of Islamic architecture, the new bridge looks exactly like the old one, which long served to connect Islamic and non-Islamic parts of the city.

Terrorism has affected cities in profound ways. In the wake of large-scale terrorist attacks in Beirut, New York, Madrid, London, and Mumbai, geographers and other urban scholars have highlighted changes in everyday urban life, notions of security, and urban technology and defensive infrastructure. Following the attacks, highly visible security apparatuses appeared almost overnight in many cities around the world. In post–9/11 Washington, D.C., concrete barricades, jersey barriers, and bollards now surround government facilities as well as embassies and other high-profile buildings. In some cases, these fixtures close off entire blocks of sidewalks and bike lanes in the name of safety and security. In other cities, local governments have redirected the flow of traffic in the urban core, even closing some streets off to vehicular traffic altogether. London's "ring of steel" was erected as a physical defensive cordon following a spate of small bombings in the 1970s to root out terrorist activities. Surveillance systems, too, have shaped contemporary urban landscapes. Nowhere is this phenomenon more apparent than in London, where highly controversial closed-circuit television (CCTV) cameras are seemingly everywhere, tracking people's movement across public spaces in the name of public safety.

You don't have to look any further than Hollywood to see the ways in which urban violence, security infrastructure, and surveillance technology have transformed urban systems and popular culture. Think about recent espionage and action films, the Jason Bourne, James Bond, and Jack Ryan franchises. Note the extent to which cities are often characters in the plots, providing venues upon which global wars, militant insurgencies, cyber-attacks, bombings, and even entertaining car chases take place. These films often make extensive use of urban surveillance technology as a mechanism to track characters' movements, monitor space, and govern from a distance.

Immigration and the Changing Ethnic Geography of Cities

Immigration is changing the spatial-cultural geography of cities around the world. As immigrants settle in large numbers in transitional areas, locals frequently move out. Walking from the city center of Paris out through immigrant neighborhoods, one can see the cultural landscape change to reflect the significant number of immigrants from the "Maghreb" of Africa, the region of North Africa around Algeria and Morocco. Maghrebis are by far the most numerous inhabitants in the tough, hardscrabble immigrant neighborhoods around Paris, where unemployment is high, crime is widespread, and resentment festers.

Whether a public housing zone is divided into ethnic neighborhoods depends in large part on government policy. Urban geographers Christian Kesteloot and Cees Cortie studied housing policies and zones in Brussels, Belgium, and Amsterdam, the Netherlands. They found that Brussels has very little public housing and that immigrants live in privately owned rentals throughout the city. Kesteloot and Cortie also found that immigrant groups in Brussels who came from a distinct region of their home country (especially rural regions), such as the Turks in Brussels, tend to cluster in ethnic neighborhoods. In contrast, the researchers reported that immigrants who came from cities, such as the Moroccans in Brussels, chose rental units scattered throughout the city and therefore did not establish ethnic neighborhoods in Brussels.

Amsterdam is quite different from Brussels: Amsterdam has a great deal of public housing and few ethnic neighborhoods within the public housing units. When immigration to Amsterdam from former colonies (Indonesia, Surinam) and noncolonies (Morocco and Turkey) increased in the 1960s, Amsterdammers moved from the transition zone of public housing to neighboring towns such as Almere. The Dutch government then implemented a policy in the public housing zone that slowed the creation of ethnic neighborhoods. The Dutch government allots public housing to legal immigrants by assigning homes on a sequential basis in the city's zone of transition, where some 80 percent of the housing stock is public housing. As a result of government assignment of housing, if you walk through the public housing zone of Amsterdam, you will find a family from Suriname living next to an Indonesian family and a Moroccan family, not just other Surinamese. The housing and neighborhoods are multicultural. The ethnic groups maintain their local cultures through religious and cultural organizations rather than through residential segregation. In Amsterdam, the call to Friday prayer for Muslims rings out all over the immigrant areas, as Muslims from various countries are spread throughout the city.

In many cities in the global economic periphery and semiperiphery, a sea of slum development begins where the permanent buildings end, in some cases engulfing and dwarfing the central city. If you stand on a hill outside Lima (Peru) or overlooking the Cape Flats near Cape Town (South Africa), you see an unchanging panorama of makeshift shacks built of every conceivable material, vying for every foot of space, extending to the horizon. You will notice few, if any, trees, and you will see narrow footpaths leading to a few unpaved streets that go into the central city.

Millions of migrants travel to such environments every year. The total number of people living in these types of slum developments is uncertain because government control is impossible and enumeration impractical. In Rio de Janeiro (Brazil), the migrants build their dwellings on dangerous, landslide-prone slopes; in Port Moresby (Papua New Guinea), the migrants sink stilts in the mud and build out over the water, risking wind and waves. In Kolkata (India), thousands of migrants do not even try to erect shelters: There and in many other cities they live in the streets, under bridges,

even in storm drains. City governments do not have the resources to adequately educate, medicate, or police the burgeoning populations, let alone to provide even minimal housing for most.

The people living in most shanty settlements are not really squatters—they pay rent. When the settlements expand outward from the central city, they occupy land owned by previous residents, families who farmed what were once the rural areas beyond the city's edge. Some of the farming families were favored by the former colonial administration; they moved into the cities but continued to own the lands their farms were on. As shanty developments encroached on their lands, the landowners began to charge people rent for living on the dilapidated housing the new residents built on the land. After establishing an owner–tenant relationship, the landowners steadily raise rents, threatening to destroy the flimsy shacks if residents fail to pay. In this way, powerful long-term inhabitants of the city exploit the weaker, more recent arrivals.

The vast slums of cities in poorer parts of the world are typically ethnically delineated, with new arrivals precariously accommodated. For example, Nairobi, Kenya, has a large slum area, one of the worst in Subsaharan Africa in terms of amenities, called Kibera. This settlement houses one million individuals, almost half of Nairobi's approximately 2.5 million slum dwellers, which account for 60 percent of the city's total population. Much of the land where Kibera is located is owned by Nubians, who are of Sudanese descent. The Sudanese Nubians settled in the area of Kibera during the colonial era. Many of the Nubians have become businesspeople in the city of Nairobi. The modern tenants of the shanty settlements in Kibera are largely Luo from western Kenya and Luhya from northwestern Kenya. During the fall of 2001, some of the Kiberian tenants were unable to pay the latest increase in rents. The Nubian landowners came to evict them, and in the fighting that followed, a number of people were killed. Groups of Luo, Luhya, and others even took to fighting among themselves. The government intervened to stabilize the situation. The rent increases were withdrawn, but the fundamental problems—crowding, unemployment, unsanitary conditions, little access to electricity, hunger, and lack of education—remain, and the ethnic groups living in the neighborhoods of Kibera will likely experience fighting again.

The Enduring Impact of Colonialism

The settlement patterns of cities developed during the colonial period often persist long after independence—with enduring impacts on ethnic relations. In a study of the city of Mombasa, Kenya, during the 1960s, H. J. de Blij found that the central city, in effect the island on which Mombasa was built, was informally partitioned among major ethnic groups. Apart from the Swahili who occupied the Old Town and adjacent historic portions of the built-up area, the spatial pattern of occupancy by ethnic groups in the city of

© Alexander B. Murphy

■■ **Figure 9.40**
Mumbai, India.   The millions of people who live in shanties in Mumbai assemble their homes with a variety of materials and tap into electricity to power their satellites.

Mombasa mirrored the status of the ethnic groups in the country of Kenya as a whole. The port of Mombasa, the country's largest, was the city's major employer. The Kikuyu, whose historic homeland lies far away from Mombasa to the north of Nairobi, were privileged by the British during colonial times. Because of their important position during the colonial era, Kikuyu workers and their families living in Mombasa resided closest to the port and to the center of economic power. Although the most powerful workers lived closest to the central commercial district, the Asians (often from India and thus referred to as Indians in Mombasa) who controlled the city's commerce were concentrated on the opposite side of the island, away from the port. Another powerful ethnic group, the Kamba, occupied a zone farther outward from the port. The Mijikenda, a less powerful African ethnic group, migrated from off-island villages to work in Mombasa and lived farther from the commercial center.

Today, as the city's population has grown seven times larger than it was in the 1960s, the spatial pattern of Mombasa still reflects the power of ethnic groups. The most recent immigrants, desperate for jobs, crowd the outer zone of the city, off of the island, and in the shanty settlements.

How do the many millions of urban immigrants living in the slum-ridden rings and pockets of the cities of the global periphery and semiperiphery survive? Extended families share and stretch whatever meager sums they can earn; when one member of the family has a salaried job, his or her income saves the day for a dozen or more relatives. When a member of the family (or several members of a larger community) manages to emigrate to a core country or an island of development and makes good money there, part of that income is sent back home and becomes the mainstay for those left behind. Hundreds of millions of dollars are transferred this way every year; *remittances* make a critical difference in the poorer countries of the world (see Chapter 3).

The Informal Economy

In the vast slums, barrios, and favelas, those who are jobless or unsalaried are not idle. Everywhere you look people are at work, inside or in front of their modest habitats, fixing things, repairing broken items for sale, sorting through small piles of waste for salvageable items, trading and selling goods from makeshift stands (Fig. 9.40). What prevails here is referred to as the **informal economy**—the economy that is not taxed and is not counted toward a country's gross national income. What is generated in the informal economy can add up to a huge total in unrecorded monetary value. The informal economy worries governments because it is essentially a recordless economy and no taxes are paid. Remittances are usually delivered in cash, not via Western Union or a bank. Typically, a trusted community member (who might pay a comparatively small bribe at the airport when passing through immigration) carries remittances to family members.

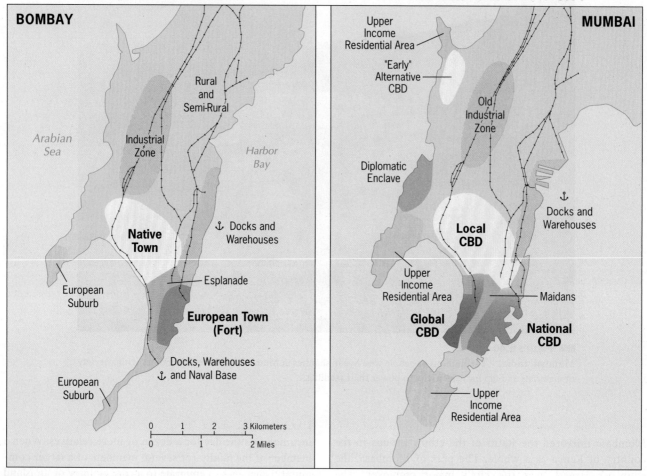

A. THE COLONIAL CITY

BOMBAY

Arabian
Sea

Rural
and
Semi-Rural

Industrial
Zone

⚓ Docks and
Warehouses

**Native
Town**

European
Suburb

Esplanade

**European Town
(Fort)**

Docks, Warehouses
⚓ and Naval Base

European
Suburb

| 0 | 1 | 2 | 3 Kilometers |
| 0 | 1 | | 2 Miles |

B. THE CONTEMPORARY CITY

MUMBAI

Upper
Income
Residential Area

"Early"
Alternative
CBD

Old
Industrial
Zone

Diplomatic
Enclave

⚓ Docks and
Warehouses

**Local
CBD**

Upper
Income
Residential Area

Maidans

**Global
CBD**

**National
CBD**

Upper
Income
Residential Area

■ **Figure 9.41**
The Changing Character of Mumbai, India.   The desire to live near the global business district has made neighborhoods around the coast more attractive in contemporary Mumbai. Developers have expanded the upper income residential areas by filling in land around the two southern peninsulas.   *Adapted with permission from:* Richard Grant and Jan Nijman, "Globalization and the Corporate Geography of Cities in the Less-Developed World," *Annals of the Association of American Geographers,* 92, 2 (2002).

From Colonial to Global CBD

Even as the informal economy thrives among the millions in the shantytowns, the new era of globalization is making a major impact in the larger cities founded or fostered by the colonial powers. In 2002, geographers Richard Grant and Jan Nijman documented this transformation in former colonial port cities, including Mumbai, India. In this city, colonial rule produced an urban landscape marked by strong segregation of foreign and local activities, commercial as well as residential (Fig. 9.41), and high levels of functional specialization and concentration. Adjacent to the port area was a well-demarcated European business district containing foreign (mostly British) companies. Most economic activities in this European commercial area involved trade, transport, bank-

ing, distribution, and insurance. Zoning and building codes were strictly enforced. Physically separated from this European district were the traditional markets and bazaars of the so-called Native Town, a densely populated mix of commercial and residential land uses.

In this era of globalization, a new spatially demarcated foreign presence has arisen. The city now has a global CBD at the heart of the original colonial city, housing mostly foreign corporations and multinational companies and linked mainly to the global economy. The former European Town has a large presence of big domestic companies and a pronounced orientation toward the national (Indian) economy. And the Native Town now has a high concentration of small domestic company headquarters.

 Using the city you sketched in the last "Thinking Geographically" question, consider the concepts and processes introduced in this section of the chapter and explain how people and institutions created this city and the model you sketched.

WHAT ROLE DO CITIES PLAY IN GLOBALIZATION?

Globalization, as we defined the term in the first chapter, is a set of processes and outcomes that occur on the global scale, circumventing and leaping over state boundaries to affect the world. In the processes of globalization, cities are taking over in ways we barely understand. Most statistics about economic activity at the global scale are gathered and disseminated by states. Nonetheless, many of the most important processes occur among and between cities, not states as a whole, masking the integral role world cities play in globalization. **World cities** function at the global scale, beyond the reach of the state borders, functioning as the service centers of the world economy.

Contending that models of cities and hierarchies of cities within states (such as Christaller's) no longer represent what is happening with the city, Taylor and Lang (2004) maintain that the city has become "something else" than a simple CBD tied into a hierarchy of other cities within the state. The world city is a node in globalization, reflecting processes that have "redrawn the limits on spatial interaction," according to Felsenstein, Schamp, and Shachar (2002). A node is a place through which action and interaction occur. As a node, a world city is connected to other cities, and the forces shaping globalization pulse across these connections and through the cities.

Most lists of world cities provide a hierarchy of the most important nodes, the most important world cities, then the next most important, and so forth. Virtually all agree that New York, London, and Tokyo are the most important world cities, but beyond these three, the definition of what makes a world city and the list of world cities changes depending on the perspective of the researcher. Geographers Jon Beaverstock and Peter J. Taylor and their Globalization and World Cities Study Group and Network have produced over 400 research papers, chapters, and books on the geography of world cities over the past few years. By studying which cities provide producer services (integral to the processes of globalization) in the areas of banking, law, advertising, and accounting, these geographers have produced an inventory of world cities mapped in Figure 9.42. They delineate 10 Alpha, 10 Beta, and 35 Gamma world

cities. The Alpha cities (London, Paris, New York, Tokyo, Chicago, Frankfurt, Hong Kong, Los Angeles, Milan, and Singapore) have a global capacity to provide services in the world-economy.

World cities do not exist merely to service players in the global economy. Major world cities such as London and Paris are also capital cities. States concentrate development and encourage interconnectedness between certain cities and the rest of the world. Even though London and Paris are a short distance apart, both function as world cities in part because of the role they play within their respective states: Each became a magnet for economic and political activity within its state, and then the globe.

Some countries such as the United States and Germany have two or more world cities within their borders. They thus do not have a single, distinct primate city. To understand the role of cities in globalization, the services cities provide to places and peoples around the world and the interconnectedness among cities must also be considered. Geographers are now working to uncover the globalized flows and processes occurring across world cities, bringing them closer together.

Cities as Spaces of Consumption

In addition to being nodes in globalization, cities are also products of globalization. Major changes in cities, such as the redevelopment of New York's Times Square and the remaking of Berlin's Potsdamer Platz, are the result of global processes. Frank Roost has found that "the global media industry is becoming the driving force in the reshaping of cities" such as New York and Berlin, turning city centers into **spaces of consumption**. Global media giants such as Time Warner, Viacom, and Walt Disney use cross promotion to encourage the consumption of their products. It is no accident that characters on television sitcoms produced and aired on ABC (a television channel owned by the Walt Disney Company) visit Disney theme parks or host Disney Princess-themed birthday parties on a given episode. These same media companies are investing heavily in urban centers in order to create entertainment spaces, places where tourists can go to consume their products. Media corporations are helping to transform urban centers into major entertainment districts ("variations on a theme park") where items are *consumed*.

For example, in New York City, government entities began to try to redevelop Times Square in the early 1980s. At that time, this area of the city was known for its neon lights, movie houses showing pornographic films, prostitution, and other illicit economic activities. The city sought to push these businesses out of Times Square and return the business district to a conglomeration of restaurants, hotels, bars, and entertainment spaces (as it had been before World War II). Over the decade of the 1980s, the city closed hundreds of small businesses in Times Square. In 1995, Mayor Rudolph

Giuliani reached a deal with Michael Eisner, CEO of Walt Disney. The mayor promised to remove the remaining sex shops, and Eisner committed to renovating the New Amsterdam Theater, a focal point in Times Square (Fig. 9.43). Secured with a $26 million low-interest loan from the State of New York, Disney set the new course for a family-friendly entertainment district in New York. The restored New Amsterdam Theater hosts Disney musicals such as *The Lion King* and *Aladdin* (both based on Disney movies). The Times Square area is assuredly a space of consumption and a variation on a theme park, including themed restaurants (Hard Rock Café, ESPN Zone), cross-promoting themed stores (Warner Brothers Store, Disney Store), and retail stores that cater to families (an enormous Toys R Us with a Ferris wheel inside).

In 2009, then-New York Mayor Michael Bloomberg closed portions of Broadway in Times Square to traffic and created an urban esplanade with lawn chairs and seating to advance his goal of making the city more livable. New Yorkers and tourists took to the new seating and moved in with laptops in hand. Times Square and the Hi-Line Walkway in New York now have bleacher-style seating as well as chairs to encourage New Yorkers to sit a spell and enjoy the city.

Potsdamer Platz in Berlin is also becoming a new space of consumption in the city center. Prior to the bombing of Berlin during World War II, Potsdamer Platz was a center of entertainment for Berlin's middle class. After the war, little was left of the area. Soon, a 500-yard border zone and the Berlin Wall occupied the formerly vibrant area of the city. After reunification, the city divided Potsdamer Platz and sold the land. The two largest owners are the German company Daimler-Benz and the Japanese company Sony. Sony built a huge entertainment structure called the Sony Center for cross promotion. According to Roost, much of the Daimler-Benz structure, Daimler City, is a space of consumption, with entertainment venues, restaurants, bars, and hotels.

Although the tourist focuses on the theme park atmosphere of these spaces of consumption, the renovations of the districts in both of these cities have also brought spaces of media production to the cities. Sony has placed its European headquarters in Berlin, Warner Brothers moved its offices to Times Square, and new office towers around Times Square house many other media companies.

Think through the challenges to the state presented in Chapter 8 and predict whether and under what circumstances world cities might replace states as the basic and most powerful form of political organization in the world. What arguments can be made for and against this proposition?

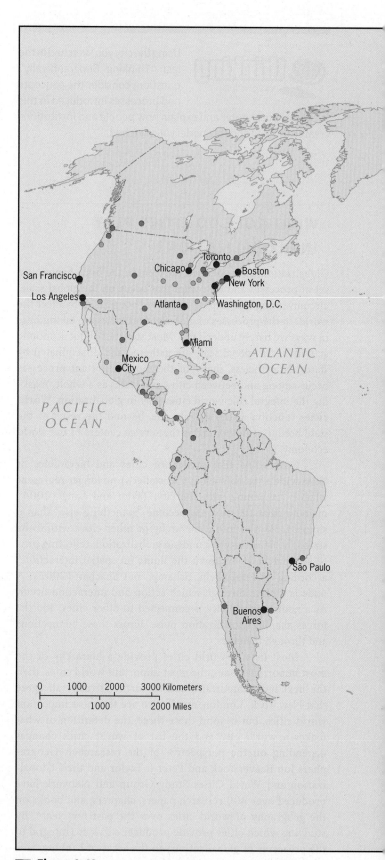

■ **Figure 9.42**
World Cities: Alpha, Beta, and Gamma. *Data from:* "The World According to GaWC 2012," posted 13 January 2014. Globalization and World Cities Research Network, http://www.lboro.ac.uk/gawc/world2012t.html.

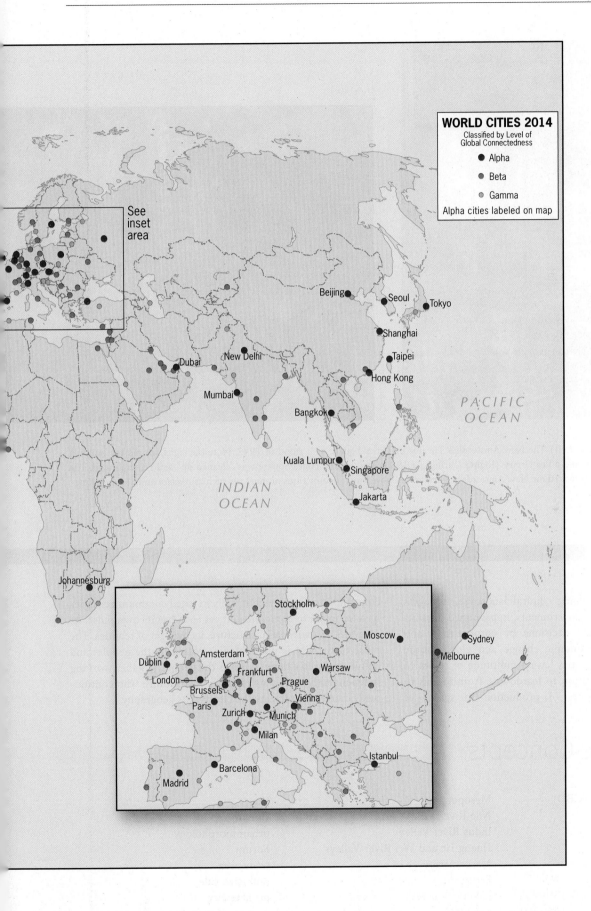

WORLD CITIES 2014
Classified by Level of
Global Connectedness

- Alpha
- Beta
- Gamma

Alpha cities labeled on map

See inset area

Beijing
Seoul
Tokyo
Shanghai
Taipei
Dubai
New Delhi
Hong Kong
Mumbai
Bangkok
PACIFIC OCEAN
Kuala Lumpur
Singapore
Jakarta
INDIAN OCEAN

Johannesburg

Stockholm
Moscow
Sydney
Melbourne

Amsterdam
Dublin
Frankfurt
Warsaw
London
Prague
Brussels
Vienna
Paris
Zurich
Munich
Milan
Istanbul
Barcelona
Madrid

Richard Levine/Alamy Images

© Corbis.Bettmann

■ **Figure 9.43**
New York, New York. (Left) The New Amsterdam Theater in Times Square as it stood in 1947. Note the signs around the building advertising arcade games and a flea circus. (Right) During the 1980s and 1990s, Times Square was "cleaned up" and reinvigorated. The Walt Disney Company renovated the New Amsterdam Theater and now shows productions of musicals such as *Aladdin* and *The Lion King*.

Summary

The city is an ever-changing cultural landscape, its layers reflecting grand plans by governments, impassioned pursuits by individuals, economic decisions by corporations, and processes of political-economic change and globalization. Geographers who study cities have a multitude of topics to examine. From gentrification to teardowns, from favelas to McMansions, from spaces of production to spaces of consumption, from ancient walls to gated communities, cities have so much in common, and yet each has its own pulse, its own feel, its own spatial structure, its own set of realities. The pulse of the city is undoubtedly created by the peoples and cultures who live there. For it is the people, whether working independently or as part of global institutions, who continuously create and recreate the city and its geography.

Geographic Concepts

central business district (CBD)
synekism
urban
city
agricultural village
agricultural surplus
social stratification
leadership class
first urban revolution

Mesopotamia
Nile River Valley
Indus River Valley
Huang He and Wei River Valleys
Mesoamerica
Peru
secondary hearth
acropolis
agora

site
situation
urban morphology
Forum
trade area
rank-size rule
primate city
central place theory
functional zonation

zone
central city
suburb
suburbanization
edge cities
galactic city
megacities
Griffin–Ford model
shantytowns
disamenity sector

McGee model
zoning laws
redlining
blockbusting
commercialization
gentrification
teardowns
McMansions
urban sprawl
new urbanism

gated communities
urbicide
informal economy
world city
spaces of consumption
concentric zone model
sector model
multiple nuclei model

Learn More Online

About Celebration, Florida
www.celebration.fl.us

About the Congress for the New Urbanism
www.cnu.org

About the Decline of Detroit
www.nytimes.com/interactive/2014/05/27/us/Defining-Blight-in-Detroit.html?_r=0

About Globalization and World Cities
www.lboro.com/gawc/

About Urban Sprawl
http://environment.nationalgeographic.com/environment/habitats/urban-sprawl/

About Opposition to Urban Sprawl
www.sierraclub.org/sprawl

About Seaside, Florida
www.seasidefl.com

Watch It Online

About Berlin
www.learner.org/resources/series180.html#program_descriptions

Click on Video On Demand for "Berlin: United We Stand"
www.learner.org/resources/series85.html#program_descriptions

Click on Video On Demand for "Berlin: Changing Center of a Changing Europe"

About Sprawl in Chicago
www.learner.org/resources/series180.html

Click on Video On Demand for "Chicago: Farming on the Edge" *Source*: Smart Growth.org

DEVELOPMENT

Geography, Trade, and Development

Walking down one of the major streets of Timbuktu, Mali (Fig. 10.1), I could hardly believe I was in the renowned intellectual, spiritual, and economic center of the thirteenth to sixteenth centuries. At that time, the place had a great reputation for wealth, which spurred the first European explorations along the African coast. What survives is a relatively impoverished town of some 35,000 people providing central place functions for the surrounding area and seeking to attract some tourist business based on its legendary name.

What happened to Timbuktu? The city's wealth many centuries ago derived from its ability to control the trans-Sahara trade in gold, salt, ivory, kola nuts, and slaves. But when trade patterns shifted with the development of sea trade routes along the west coast of Africa, Timbuktu lost its strategic position and a long period of decline set in.

Timbuktu's story serves as a reminder that where a place is situated in relation to patterns of economic development and exchange can be as important as, or even more important than, the commodities found in that place. Indeed, there are many examples of places where the presence of a valuable commodity does not translate into

© Alexander B. Murphy

■ **Figure 10.1**
Central Square, Timbuktu, Mali. Sited along the Niger River on the edge of the Sahara Desert, Timbuktu was once a major trade center. Goods from the north, carried on camels, were traded with goods from the south brought in on boats. The development of sea trade routes on the west coast of Africa in the sixteenth century allowed traders to circumvent Timbuktu. In turn, the city's central trade role declined.

improved economic lives for those living nearby. The people working on the oil booms in Gabon or Nigeria or workers chopping down rare hardwood trees in Thailand or Malaysia, for example, are not the ones who benefit from most of the wealth associated with demand for the goods they help produce. Instead, international corporations or the wealthiest families in a place, those who own the industry, are the principal beneficiaries.

To understand how the production of a good creates wealth for some and not for others, we must understand the concept of a commodity chain and the role of places in the chain of production. A **commodity chain** is a series of links connecting the many places of production and distribution and resulting in a final product that is then bought and sold on the market. The generation of wealth differs along the commodity chain. Each link along the chain adds a certain value to the commodity, producing differing levels of wealth for the place and the people where the steps of production occur.

What Timbuktu had to offer was the ability to coordinate and facilitate trade based on its geographic site where the Niger River turned north at the edge of the Sahara Desert. The river was the last major water source for those crossing the Sahara from south to north across what is now Mali and Algeria. Timbuktu was a **break-of-bulk location**, where goods traded on one mode of transport, camel, were transported to another mode of transport, boat. The points along the chain where materials and goods are traded change over time, directly impacting the situation of places.

Places along a commodity chain do not all benefit equally from the production of a good. The generation of wealth depends on how production occurs at each step. In Chapter 8 we introduced the concepts of core and periphery. Sophisticated technology, high skill levels, extensive research and development, and high salaries tend to be associated with the segment of global commodity chains located in the core. The segments located in the periphery, by contrast, tend to be associated with low technology, less education, little research and development, and lower wages.

Countries pursue development by becoming nodes along commodity chains, transforming peripheral processes into core ones, and redirecting the profit generated through core processes to improve the periphery. As the twenty-first century unfolds, governments, academics, nongovernmental organizations, and international financial institutions offer ideas about how to lift up the poorer parts of the world. The theories, methods, and recommendations vary, but they all focus on the elusive goals of development.

In this chapter, we review how development is defined and measured and some of the theories of development. We also examine how geography affects development, considering the structures of the world economy. We look at the geographical barriers to and costs of development within countries, and we ask why uneven development occurs not just across the globe but within states.

Key Questions FOR CHAPTER 10

1. How is development defined and measured?
2. How does geographical context affect development?
3. What are the barriers to and the costs of development?
4. How do political and economic institutions influence uneven development within states?

HOW IS DEVELOPMENT DEFINED AND MEASURED?

The economic and social geography of the contemporary world is a patchwork of almost inconceivable contrasts. On the fields in equatorial American and African forests, farmers practice shifting cultivation to grow root crops using ancient methods and rudimentary tools. On the Great Plains of North America, in Ukraine, and in eastern Australia, farmers use expensive, modern machines to plow the land, plant seeds, and harvest grains. Toolmakers in the villages of Papua New Guinea still fashion their implements by hand, as they did many centuries ago; whereas factory workers in Japan or South Korea work with robots to produce automobiles by the shipload for distribution to markets thousands of miles away. Our perception is that Japan and South Korea are more developed than Papua

New Guinea and shifting cultivators in equatorial America and Africa. Our modern notion of development is related to the Industrial Revolution and the idea that technology can improve the lot of humans. Through advances in technology, people can produce more food, create new products, and accrue material wealth. But these things do not necessarily bring happiness (see Chapter 14), social stability, or environmental sustainability, which makes development a narrow, and sometimes controversial, indicator of the human condition.

In the first section of this chapter, we examine methods of measuring development and assess the advantages and disadvantages of each measurement. We also look at models of development that academics have created to try to help countries develop. Both the measurements and models of development assume that development implies progress, and they generally look at development in terms of improvements in technology, production, and socioeconomic well-being. In the second section of this chapter, we look at the geographic context of development to see why development is uneven globally and within countries. We then consider approaches and barriers to development.

Gross National Income

Three common ways of measuring development are development in economic welfare, development in technology and production, and development in social welfare. Beginning in the 1960s, the most common way of comparing development in economic welfare was to use the index economists created to compare countries, the gross national product. **Gross national product (GNP)** is a measure of the total value of the officially recorded goods and services produced by the citizens and corporations of a country in a given year. It includes goods and services made both inside and outside the country's territory, and it is therefore broader than **gross domestic product (GDP)**, which encompasses only goods and services produced within a country during a given year.

In recent years, economists have increasingly turned to **gross national income (GNI)**, which calculates the monetary worth of what is produced within a country plus income received from investments outside the country minus income payments to other countries around the world. GNI is seen as a more accurate way of measuring a country's wealth in the context of a global economy because it accounts for wealth generated by investments outside a country's borders.

In order to compare GNI across countries, economists must standardize the data. The most common way to standardize GNI data is to divide it by the population of the country, yielding the **per capita GNI**. In Japan the per capita gross national income in U.S. dollars in 2013 was $46,140. In the United States it was $53,670. In Norway it was $102,610. But in India it was $1570, in Nigeria it was $2760, and in Indonesia, the world's fourth most populous country, it was $3580. This enormous range across the globe in per capita GNI reflects the often-searing contrasts between rich and poor.

Although the map of per capita GNI clearly shows the startling contrasts between rich and poor in the world, the statistic has several shortcomings. GNI is a limited measure because it includes only transactions in the **formal economy**, the legal economy that governments tax and monitor. Quite a few countries have per capita GNI of less than $1000 per year—a figure so low it seems impossible that people could survive. A key component of survival in these countries is the **informal economy**, the uncounted or illegal economy that governments do not tax and keep track of, including everything from a garden plot in a yard to the black market to the illegal drug trade. The informal economy is a significant element in the economies of many countries, but GNI statistics omit the informal economy entirely (Fig. 10.2).

GNI per capita also masks extremes in the distribution of wealth within a country. The Middle Eastern oil countries of Kuwait and the United Arab Emirates (UAE) have per capita GNIs of $44,940 and $34,320, respectively, both ahead of Spain, Israel, and New Zealand In 2011. These figures give us no hint of what proportion of the population participates in the country's economy, the average citizen's material standard of living, or gaps between genders or among regions. Economic production and the wealth it generates are not distributed evenly across the seven emirates that make up the United Arab Emirates. In 2013, the UBS Billionaire Census reported "40 percent of the Middle East's wealth is held by the region's 157 wealthiest billionaires, known by the term ultra-high net worth (UHNW), compared to 28 percent in Europe, 22 percent in North America and 18 percent in Asia" (Kapur 2013). Billionaires in the UAE own a quarter of the economy and number 4.5 billionaires per million people. Abu Dhabi, the emirate that dominates the banking and financial sector and the petroleum industry, generated over half of the country's GDP in 2010. Dubai, the next largest emirate, generated about 30 percent of the GDP, The Sharjah emirate accounted for 5 percent of the GPD, and the Qaywayn emirate generated less than 1 percent of the country's gross GDP.

Another limitation of GNI per capita is that it measures only outputs (i.e., production). It does not take into account the nonmonetary costs of production, which take a toll on the environment through resource depletion and pollution of air and water. Per capita GNI may even treat such externalities as a plus. For example, the sale of cigarettes augments GNI. If cigarette use causes sickness and hospitalization is required, the GNI figure is boosted further. Conversely, quitting smoking improves health and saves lives but reduces money spent on cigarettes and health care, thus reducing the total production and the GNI in a country.

The limitations of GNI have prompted analysts to look for alternative measures of economic development, ways of measuring the roles technology, production, transportation, and communications play in an economy.

To gauge the use of technology, we can look at the number of workers relative to the production in a certain sector. For example, the United States produces twice the amount of corn as China. At the same time, the United States employed

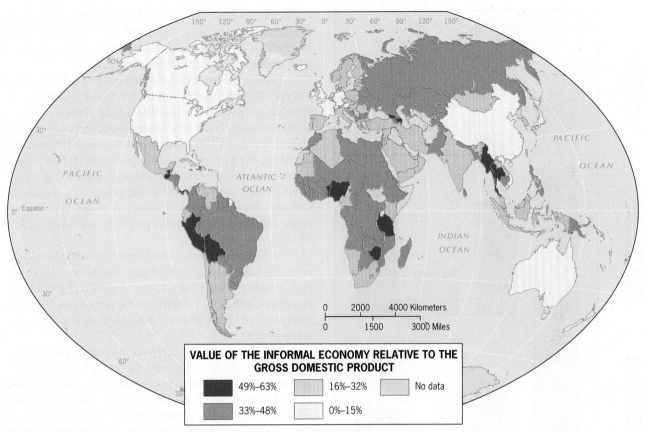

Figure 10.2
Percent of Informal Economy Relative to GDP. The World Bank estimates the contribution of the informal economy to each country's overall economy. Panama and Bolivia have the largest informal economies as a proportion of their GDP at 63.5 percent. Of the countries with data, Switzerland and the United States have the two smallest informal economies relative to their GDP at 8.1 and 8.4 percent, respectively. *Data from*: World Bank, 2013.

about 2 percent of its labor force in the agriculture sector, and China employed about 35 percent of its labor force in agriculture. The large proportion of the labor force employed in agriculture demonstrates that China is still producing agriculture in labor-intensive instead of technologically intensive ways. China can move more of its labor force into other sectors of the economy by adopting more technologically intensive agricultural methods.

A high percentage of laborers engaged in the production of agriculture signals a low overall level of development, as conventionally defined, and a high percentage of workers involved in high-tech industries and services signals a high level of development. Productivity per worker is examined by summing production over the course of a year and dividing it by the total number of persons in the labor force. The World Bank reported that agricultural productivity per worker in the United States was $49,817 in 2011, while China's agricultural productivity per worker was $713 the same year. A more productive workforce also suggests a higher level of mechanization in production.

One good measure of access to technology is access to railway, road, airline connections, telephone, radio, television, and so forth on a per capita basis—a statistic that reflects the amount of infrastructure that exists to facilitate economic activity.

Figure 10.3 highlights some of the extraordinary disparities in communications access, including access to the Internet, mobile cellular subscriptions, and telephone landlines around the world. The world average for Internet and mobile access is increasing, while the world average for landline access is declining. Nonprofit and nongovernmental development agencies, including one called the Living Cities, have called the mobile phone "the great equalizer," connecting hopes of giving the poor better access to education and services to diffusing technologies in cities. In a 2014 study, analysts at Pew Research Center surveyed residents of 24 emerging countries, including Turkey, Venezuela, Kenya, Brazil, and Nigeria. They found that while cell phones "are almost omnipresent in many nations," most people "in the 24 nations surveyed are still offline" (Pew 2014). A high correlation between wealth and Internet access (Fig. 10.4) means that instead of mobile phones equalizing Internet access for rich and poor countries, the technology can either reinforce or exacerbate the **digital divide** between rich and poor. The Pew survey data also confirmed that people with college educations are more likely to have smartphones and thus mobile access to the Internet.

Another way to measure development is to compare the size of the working-age population to the number of older or younger people in the society who are not contributing to the

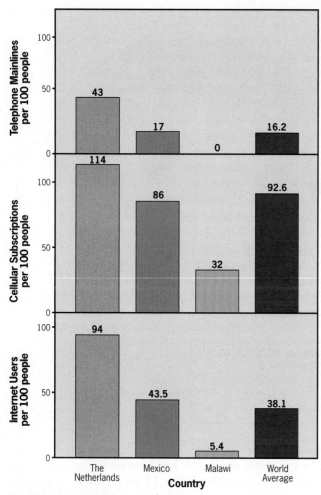

Figure 10.3

Differences in Communications Connectivity, 2013. *Data from:* World Bank, 2013.

of older adults in society can be a financial strain on the country. Aging populations in Japan and Europe require greater investments in health care, elderly housing, and retirement welfare (similar to Social Security in the U.S.).

Another way to look at dependency is to measure the percent of young people, ages birth to 14, relative to the working-age population. The World Bank reports these data as the younger person dependency ratio, and Niger has the highest ratio, with 106 young people for every 100 working-age adults. Eight of the ten countries with the highest younger person dependency ratio are in Subsaharan Africa (Fig. 10.5b). Having a large proportion of young people in a country can also be a financial strain, if countries invest in child care, public education, immunization programs, and health care for children.

In addition to access to technology and dependency ratios, we can use many other statistics to measure social welfare, including literacy rates, infant mortality (Fig. 2.18), life expectancy (Fig. 2.21), caloric intake per person (Fig. 1.2), percentage of family income spent on food, and amount of savings per capita.

The United Nations calculates the Human Development Index (Fig. 10.6) to incorporate the "three basic dimensions of human development: a long and healthy life, knowledge and a decent standard of living." Several statistics, including per capita GDP, literacy rates, school enrollment rates, and life expectancy at birth, factor into the calculation of the Human Development Index.

In 2000, the United Nations held a high-profile summit, during which 189 world leaders adopted the United Nations Millennium Declaration, with the goal of improving the condition of the people in the countries with the lowest standards of human development. At the summit, world leaders recognized the principal barriers to economic development and

country's economy. The *dependency ratio* measures the proportion of dependents in the population relative to every 100 people of working age.

The overall dependency ratio of young and old relative to the working age population can be divided into an older person dependency ratio, population over the age of 64 relative to the working age population, and a younger person dependency ratio, population ages birth to 14 relative to the working age population. The older person dependency ratio (proportion of the population over age 64) in Japan is 41, meaning that every group of 100 working-age adults (ages 15 to 64) is paying taxes to support 41 people over the age of 64 (Fig. 10.5a). Just behind Japan in the older person dependency ratio are European countries including Italy, Germany, and Sweden. The countries with high older person dependency ratios generally have high per capita GNIs, but the larger proportion

Correlation Between Internet Users and GDP Per Capita

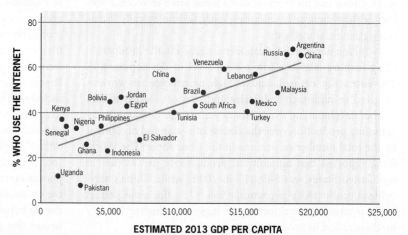

Figure 10.4

Correlation Between Wealth and Internet Access, 2014. The correlation between wealth and Internet access is positive and relatively high, with wealthier countries having greater access to the Internet. *Courtesy of:* Pew Research Global Attitudes Project, 2014.

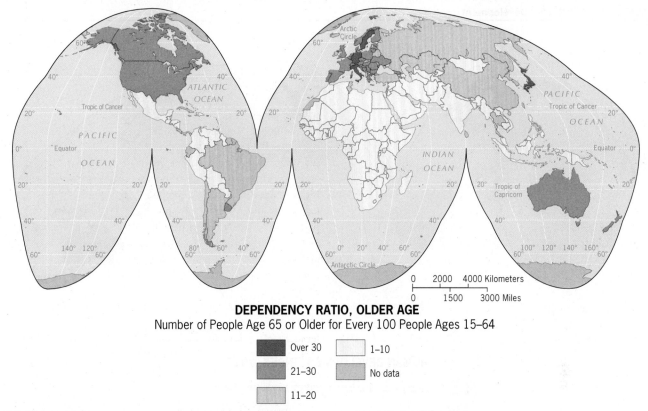

DEPENDENCY RATIO, OLDER AGE
Number of People Age 65 or Older for Every 100 People Ages 15–64

Over 30   1–10

21–30   No data

11–20

■■ **Figure 10.5a**

Older Person Dependency Ratio.   The older person dependency ratio is a measure of the number of people 65 and older relative to 100 working-age adults, between 15 and 64. The working-age adults in the formal economy contribute to a country's tax base, thereby supporting the older population of a country.   *Data from*: World Bank, 2014.

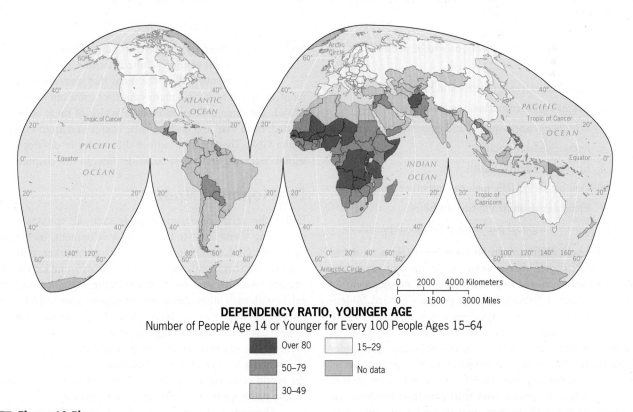

DEPENDENCY RATIO, YOUNGER AGE
Number of People Age 14 or Younger for Every 100 People Ages 15–64

Over 80   15–29

50–79   No data

30–49

■■ **Figure 10.5b**

Younger Person Dependency Ratio.   The younger person dependency ratio is a measure of the number of people birth to age 14 relative to 100 working-age adults, between 15 and 64. The working-age adults in the formal economy contribute to a country's tax base, thereby supporting the younger population of a country.   *Data from*: World Bank, 2014.

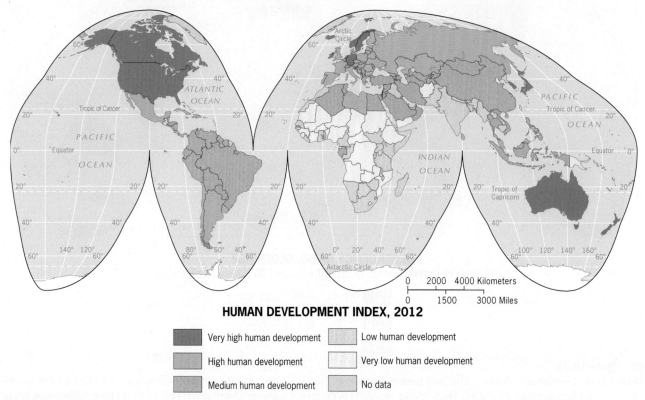

HUMAN DEVELOPMENT INDEX, 2012

Very high human development

High human development

Medium human development

Low human development

Very low human development

No data

■■ **Figure 10.6**

Human Development Index, 2012. The Human Development Index measures development beyond GNI or GDP by taking into account literacy, school enrollment, and other factors that contribute toward quality of life in a country. *Data from*: http://hdr.undp.org/en/media/HDR_2010_EN_Table1_reprint.pdf.

identified eight key development goals to be achieved by the year 2015. They were:

1. Eradicate extreme poverty and hunger.
2. Achieve universal primary education.
3. Promote gender equality and empower women.
4. Reduce child mortality.
5. Improve maternal health.
6. Combat HIV/AIDS, malaria, and other diseases.
7. Ensure environmental sustainability.
8. Develop a global partnership for development.

The eight **Millennium Development Goals** represent a fairly high degree of consensus about the key conditions that need to be changed to achieve economic development. In 2014, the United Nations assessed progress toward Millennium Development Goals. Progress has been made toward reducing undernourishment, but the amount of progress varies by world region (Fig. 10.7). Toward the goal of gender equality, the UN reported progress in the proportion of women in legislatures (see Fig. 5.17) but a lack of progress in the proportion of women who hold part-time employment. Women are more likely than men to hold part-time work, which reflects "gender inequality in family roles, the absence of adequate and affordable childcare and elderly-care facilities," as well as gendered stereotypes regarding the kinds of

occupations women should have and disparities in the labor market for men and women (United Nations 2014).

Looking through all of the maps that measure development, we gain a sense that many countries come out in approximately the same position no matter which of these measures is used. Each map and each statistic shares one limit with per capita GNI: They do not capture differences in development *within* countries, an issue we consider later in this chapter.

Development Models

Using the term *developing* implies that all countries are improving along each indicator of development, increasing per capita GNI, increasing productivity per worker, improving access to communications and technology, and improving literacy rates. Because so many development indicators correlate with each other, development experts question whether improving one—for instance education levels—leads to improving conditions among the other markers of development. Other analysts are concerned whether it is possible for all countries to develop at the same time or if the structures of the world economy require some countries to be on the bottom in order for other countries to be on the top.

Theorists have created development models as guides for governments, nongovernmental organizations, and international financial institutions (including the World Bank, the World Trade Organization, and the International Monetary

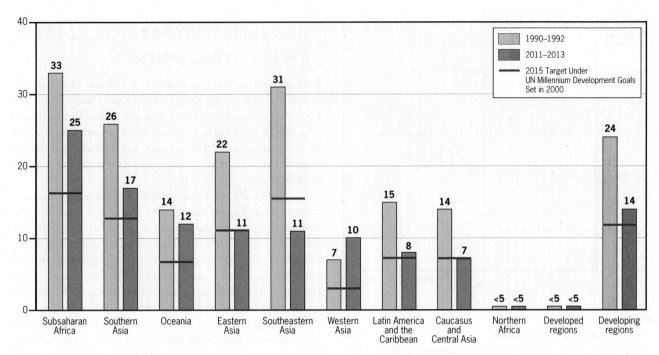

Percent of People Who Are Undernourished by World Region, 1990–1992 and 2011–2013

■■ **Figure 10.7**

Progress in Reducing Undernourishment by Region. The United Nations Millennium Development Goals sought to reduce undernourishment in each world region. According to these data, these goals were achieved in every region except Western Asia, where undernourishment actually rose between 1991–1992 and 2011–2013. *Courtesy of*: United Nations Millennial Development Goals, 2014.

Fund) to help countries develop. The fundamental problem with development models is that each suggests a single trajectory through which all countries move. The underlying message of most development models is that countries can develop if they just behave like a country that is already considered developed.

Development models, then, do not take geographical differences very seriously. Just because Japan moved from a rural, agrarian state to an urbanized, industrial one does not mean that Mali will or that it will do so in the same way. Another criticism of development models is that the very idea of development has a Western bias. Critics argue that some of the measures taken in poorer countries that the West views as progress, such as attracting industry and mechanizing agriculture, can lead to worsened social and environmental conditions for many people in the poorer countries. Still others criticize development models because they do not consider the ability of some countries to influence what happens in other countries, or the different positions countries occupy in the world economy. Instead, development models treat countries as autonomous units moving through a process of development at different speeds.

The classic development model, one that is subject to each of these criticisms, is economist Walt Rostow's **modernization model**. Many theories of development grew out of the major decolonization movements of the 1960s. Concerned with how the dozens of newly independent countries in Africa and Asia would survive economically, Rostow looked

to how the countries that were already economically powerful in the 1960s had gotten where they were.

Rostow's model assumes that all countries follow a similar path to development or modernization, advancing through five stages of development. In the first stage, the society is *traditional*, and the dominant activity is subsistence farming. The social structure is rigid, and technology is slow to change. The second stage brings the *preconditions of takeoff*. New leadership moves the country toward greater flexibility, openness, and diversification. These changes, in turn, will lead to the third stage, *takeoff*. Now the country experiences something akin to an industrial revolution, and sustained growth takes hold. Urbanization increases, industrialization proceeds, and technological and mass-production breakthroughs occur. Next, the economy enters the fourth stage, the *drive to maturity*. Technologies diffuse, industrial specialization occurs, and international trade expands. Modernization is evident in key areas of the country, and population growth slows. Finally, some countries reach the final stage in Rostow's model, *high mass consumption*, which is marked by high incomes and widespread production of many goods and services. During this stage, a majority of workers enter the service sector of the economy.

Another name for Rostow's model (and other models derived from it) is the *ladder of development*. Visually, we can see his five stages of development as rungs on a ladder (Fig. 10.8), with each country climbing the ladder one rung at a time. In addition to the general criticisms of development models, the major problem with Rostow's model is that it

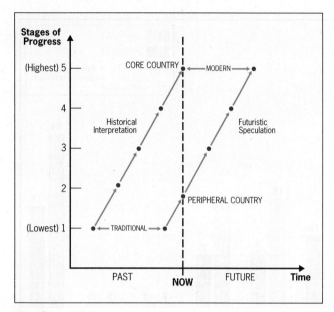

Figure 10.8

Rostow's Ladder of Development. This ladder assumes that all countries can reach the same level of development and that all will follow a similar path. *Adapted with permission from*: P. J. Taylor. "Understanding Global Inequalities: A World-Systems Approach," *Geography*, 77 (1992): 10–21.

provides no larger context to development. Is a climb up the ladder truly dependent on what happens within one country? Or do we need to take into account all of the other countries, their places on the ladder, and how their actions and global forces affect an individual country's movement on the ladder? The theory also misses the particular conditions that can influence development decisions within an individual country, leaving us to wonder where cultural and political differences fit into the picture.

Rostow's model is still influential, despite all of these criticisms. Even the notion of calling wealthy countries "industrialized" and saying poor countries need to "industrialize" implies that economic development can be achieved only by climbing the same ladder of development wealthier countries have already climbed. Yet if a poor country quickly industrialized today through foreign investment, it might not reap much economic benefit, but it could experience severe environmental consequences. The wealthier countries we call "industrial" today are really "postindustrial," as post-Fordist production has moved the manufacturing of goods around the world and many of the wealthiest countries have economies built on the service sector, not the industrial sector (see Chapter 12).

Is the idea of economic development inherently Western? If the West (North America and Europe) were not encouraging the "developing world" to "develop," how would people in the regions of the "developing world" think about their own economies?

HOW DOES GEOGRAPHICAL CONTEXT AFFECT DEVELOPMENT?

Development happens in **context**: It reflects what has happened and what is happening in a place as a result of processes operating at the same time at multiple scales. To understand why some countries are poor and others are wealthy, we need to consider geographical context: the spatial organization, character, and history of a place, and its interactions with the broader world.

Historically, ideas about government and economics diffused from Europe through the world as a result of colonialism, global trade, and the rise of capitalism. The Industrial Revolution and colonialism made colonies dependent on the colonizers and brought wealth to the colonizers. Even after colonialism ended, the economic, political, and social networks created through colonialism persisted. Goods and capital continued to flow from colonies to their former colonizers. The continuation of colonial relationships after formal colonialism ends is called **neo-colonialism**, whereby major world powers continue to control the economies of the poorer countries, even though the poorer countries are now politically independent states.

Development scholars have produced a number of theories to explain the barriers to development under neo-colonialism; these theories are called structuralist theories. A **structuralist theory** holds that difficult-to-change, large-scale economic arrangements shape what is possible for a country's development in fundamental ways. The world economy has a set of structural circumstances, such as the concentration of wealth in certain areas and unequal relations among places, which make it very difficult for poorer countries to improve their economic situation. Structuralists argue that developing countries face a very different set of development circumstances, a different context, than those faced by the countries of western Europe that Rostow looked to as models when constructing his modernization model.

Dependency Theory

Structuralists have developed a major body of development theory called **dependency theory**, which holds that the political and economic relationships between countries and regions of the world control and limit the economic development possibilities of poorer areas. Dependency theorists note, for example, that colonialism created political and economic structures that caused the colonies to become dependent on the colonial powers. They further argue that such dependency helps sustain wealth in developed regions and poverty in other areas, even after decolonization occurs.

Dependency theory contends that economic prosperity is extremely difficult to achieve in regions and countries that have traditionally been dominated by external powers because that dependency continues after independence. For example, 14 countries in Central and West Africa have used the CFA franc as their currency since 1945.[1] They tie the value of their currency to the value of the French franc, and now to the value of the European Monetary Union's euro (France changed to the euro in 2000). The economies of these 14 African countries are tied to the economy of the European Union—they rise and fall together. The CFA franc was set up before African countries gained independence starting in the 1950s and 60s, and the former colonies (12 of the 14 were colonies of France) continue to use the CFA franc because their economies are based on the currency and changing is quite difficult. At the same time, the countries are dependent on France because the French treasury and French parliament set policies that directly affect the economies of 14 African countries.

The countries with the CFA franc had their currency set up by their colonizer during colonialism. Although the United States did not colonize Latin America (except in the Caribbean), several countries in Latin America now recognize that their economy is dependent on the United States and explicitly link their economy to the U.S. dollar. *The Economist* reported that in 2011, 66 countries have currencies (including China, Saudi Arabia, and Bangladesh) tied to the U.S. dollar: More than 40 countries peg the value of their currency to the U.S dollar, and 8 countries have abandoned their currency and have completely adopted the U.S. dollar. The process of adopting the U.S. dollar as a country's currency is called **dollarization**.

For the people of El Salvador, dollarization made sense because the economy of El Salvador depends on the economy of the United States (Fig. 10.9). Over 2 million Salvadorians live in the United States, and in 2010, they sent $3.5 billion in remittances to El Salvador. With this flow of American dollars to El Salvador, many transactions occurred in dollars long before the official switch. The United Nations Development Program estimates that 22.3 percent of families in El Salvador receive remittances. In addition, over two-thirds of El Salvador's exports go to the United States. When the Federal Reserve Board in the United States controls the supply of dollars by altering the interest rates or when the U.S. economy enters a recession, the ramifications are felt directly in El Salvador. The greatest disadvantage of dollarization is surrendering the last say over policies that affect your economy to the United States, and the biggest advantage of dollarization is stabilization of the country's currency because the U.S. dollar is a relatively stable currency.

Like modernization theory, dependency theory is based on generalizations about economic change that pay relatively little attention to geographical differences in culture, politics, and society. Not every country is in the same situation at the same time, so they cannot all follow the same path of development, as modernization theory would have it. Likewise, not every country will be affected by a dependent relationship in

AFP/NewsCom

■ Figure 10.9

San Salvador, El Salvador.   A woman and young boy use dollars to pay for groceries in El Salvador, a country that underwent dollarization in 2001.

the same way. Pegging a currency to or adopting the currency of a wealthier country may be beneficial for one developing country but not for another. Although both models provide some insights, neither is greatly concerned with the spatial and cultural context of particular places—central elements of geographical analysis.

Geography and Context

As geographers, economists, and other social scientists came to realize that studying economic development divorced from geographical, historical, and political context did not reflect reality, geographers began to search for a development theory that encompassed geography, scale, place, and culture. Immanuel Wallerstein's **world-systems theory** is attractive to geographers because it incorporates space (geography) and time (history) as well as power relationships (politics) that shape the context in which development takes place. We discussed world-systems theory in Chapter 8, focusing on how the theory provides insights into the political organization

---

[1]The CFA franc is actually two currencies, one in West Africa and one in Central Africa, but they are closely tied, and so we consider them together as encompassing 14 countries.

of space. In this chapter, we focus on how world-systems theory helps us understand the geography of development.

Wallerstein's division of the world into a **three-tier structure**—the core, periphery, and semiperiphery—helps explain the interconnections among places in the global economy. As discussed in more detail in Chapter 8, core processes generate wealth in a place because they require higher levels of education, more sophisticated technologies, and higher wages and benefits. When core processes are embedded in a place (such as the Telecom corridor in Richardson-Plano, Texas), wealth is generated for the people in that place. Peripheral processes, on the other hand, require little education, lower technologies, and lower wages and benefits. Producing agriculture by hand using little technology may generate a stable food supply in a place, but it does not produce capital, as few formal wages, low education, and little research and technology were required to produce the crop in that place.

Core regions are those where core processes are clustered. Core regions have achieved high levels of economic prosperity and are dominant players in the world economy. When peripheral processes are embedded in a place, the processes often generate little wealth for the people in that place. Periphery regions are areas where peripheral processes are concentrated. They are poor regions that are dependent in significant ways on the core and do not have as much control over their own affairs, economically or politically. The semiperiphery exhibits both core and peripheral processes, and semiperipheral places serve as a buffer between the core and periphery in the world-economy. Countries of the semiperiphery exert more power than peripheral regions but remain heavily influenced by core regions.

Dividing the world into cores, semiperipheries, and peripheries might seem to do little more than replace developed, developing, and underdeveloped with a new set of terms. But the core–periphery model is fundamentally different from the modernization model because it holds that not all places can be equally wealthy in the capitalist world-economy. World-systems theory also makes the power relations among places explicit and does not assume that socioeconomic change will occur in the same way in all places. It is thus sensitive to geographical context, at least in economic terms.

Geographer Peter J. Taylor uses the analogy of a school of tadpoles to demonstrate these ideas. He envisions different places in the world as tadpoles and explains that not all tadpoles can survive to develop into toads. Rather, those who dominate survive, and the others perish. World-systems theorists see domination (exploitation) as a function of the capitalist drive for profit in the global economy. Thus, capitalists can move production quickly from one place to another around the globe to enhance profits, but places that lose a production facility can suffer. Moreover, their coping capacity can be small if, as is often the case, they earlier abandoned traditional ways and shifted to an export economy when external investment first arrived.

Another benefit of Wallerstein's three-tier structure is that he focuses on how a good is produced instead of what is produced. Rostow looked at what is produced, arguing that in order to develop a country needed to move from agricultural production to industrial manufacturing. Wallerstein disagreed and recognized that a country can produce agriculture using core processes and gain wealth while another country can produce the very same agricultural product with peripheral processes and gain almost no wealth. Generating wealth along a commodity chain is not determined by *what is produced*; it depends on *how it is produced*. Farmers can grow cotton with rudimentary tools or with $700,000 combines. Using the $700,000 combine produces more wealth because of all that went into the combine: Educated engineers designed it, laborers manufactured it, marketing professionals and salespeople sold it, the John Deere dealership received $700,000 for it, and the educated farmer employs the combine to markedly increase productivity per worker (Fig. 10.2).

Another reason geographers are drawn to world-systems theory is its applicability at multiple scales. For example, Los Angeles can be described as the core of the Southern California region; the Johannesburg area can be described as the core of the South African state; or the central business district can be studied as the core of São Paulo, Brazil.

Compare and contrast Rostow's ladder of development with Wallerstein's three-tier structure of the world-economy as models for understanding development. Choose a product and break down its commodity chain. Which theory, Rostow's or Wallerstein's, better helps you understand where wealth is accumulated along the commodity chain and where it is not?

WHAT ARE THE BARRIERS TO AND THE COSTS OF DEVELOPMENT?

Regardless of which development theory you find the most persuasive, all the theories agree that structures are built into the world-economy, including the concentration of power in core states and entrenched poverty in peripheral states, that inhibit economic development in the periphery.

Conditions within the periphery, such as high population growth rates (see Chapter 2), lack of education, foreign debt, autocratic (and often corrupt) leadership, political instability, and widespread disease (see Chapter 2) hamper development. It is possible to get into the chicken-or-the-egg debate here: Did the structures of the world-economy create these conditions, or do these conditions help to create the structures of the world-economy? Many think that neither argument can stand alone, but understanding both structures and conditions is important for you to form your own opinion.

Social Conditions

Across the global periphery, as much as half the population is 15 years old or younger (see Fig. 10.5b), making the supply of adult, taxpaying laborers low relative to the number of dependents. Low life expectancies and high infant and child mortality rates stem from inadequate nutrition. Despite the UN's efforts to achieve the Millennium Development Goals, one in four children worldwide had stunted growth in 2012—that is, they do not receive enough calories to grow as tall as they should be for their age. Underweight and stunted children are at risk for "diminished cognitive and physical development" from undernourishment (UN 2014).

Access to public sewage systems, clean drinking water, and health care are low in peripheral countries, making economic development all the more difficult. According to the United Nations, 748 million people still rely on unsafe drinking water from rivers, ponds, and unprotected wells and springs, and 1 billion people still used "open defecation" in 2012. Open defecation spreads disease and is found most often in South Asia, Oceania, and Subsaharan African (UN 2014).

Lack of access to education is also a major problem in the periphery. The number of children in the periphery enrolled in primary school, both boys and girls, has increased since 2000, thanks to governmental efforts to extend education. The government of Rwanda eliminated fees for primary education in 2003, guaranteeing 6 years of primary and 3 years of secondary school for all children in Rwanda, and two years later started distributing funds to schools based on the number of students they were educating. Rwanda successfully increased the proportion of students attending school through grade 6, reporting a 95 percent enrollment rate (Republic of Rwanda 2014). Growing education so quickly makes it difficult to establish quality education, and the government reported in 2011 that the quality of education in Rwanda is lagging, as only 5 percent of "pupils met or exceeded curricular expectations in reading and that a majority do not meet expectation in numeracy" (UNDP 2014).

Governments have used innovative policies, including cash transfer policies such as Brazil's Bolsa Familia and South Africa's Child Support Grant, to create a financial incentive for families to enroll and send their children to school. Historically, children would drop out of primary school or have low attendance in order to help their family by earning wages or by working on the farm or providing child or elderly care at home. Children in peripheral countries typically have to pay a fee for attending school, and it was common for a girl to drop out of school to earn wages to pay school fees for her brother. Cash transfer policies seek to undermine the financial incentive to drop out by providing a financial incentive to enroll in school and attend regularly. Girls who live in rural areas and are from poor families remain the least likely to attend primary school (United Nations 2014).

Brazil's Bolsa Familia conditional cash transfer program began in the 1990s, and former President Lula da Silva expanded the scope of the program in 2003. Bolsa Familia pays families in cash under the condition that their children enroll and attend school (children cannot miss more than 15 percent of classes) and that they receive medical check-ups. One-fourth of the country, about 50 million people, is enrolled in the program, and Brazil credits the program with bringing "36 million Brazilians out of extreme poverty" (Barnes 2013). Bolsa Familia is held up as a model for economic development, as it gives the poor the ability to choose how to spend their financial assistance instead of living within the constraints of separate programs designed to address different aspects of poverty. Conditional cash transfer programs have the added benefit of increasing school attendance for girls and boys alike.

South Africa's conditional cash transfer program has led to an increase in the number of children receiving primary education. However, the schools are in poor condition, and the quality of education is below par. Data from South Africa's national literacy and numeracy tests reveal that "only 15% of 12 year olds (sixth graders) scored at or above the minimum proficiency on the language test" and in math, only 12% were proficient (*The Economist*, South Africa 2012).On the whole, the country of South Africa needs 25,000 new, qualified teachers each year but only 10,000 teachers meet standards (*The Economist* 2012). The South African economy suffers from having a poor education system because the schools do not produce enough graduates to fill jobs in the South African economy that require an educated workforce.

Lack of education for girls is founded on and compounded by the assumption held not just in the periphery but in most of the world that girls will leave their homes (and communities) when they marry and contribute to their husband's family and not their own. The views that girls are less important than boys and that girls cost a family money and provide little financial support are at the root of human trafficking. Mike Dottridge, a modern antislavery activist, explains that **trafficking** happens when "adults and children fleeing poverty or seeking better prospects are manipulated, deceived, and bullied into working in conditions that they would not choose."

Trafficking is not usually considered slavery because the family does not sell a child; instead, the family sends the child away with a recruiter in the hopes that the child will earn money to send home. Trafficked children are often taken to neighboring or nearby countries that are wealthier and in demand of domestic servants. Others are trafficked across the world, again typically to work as domestic servants. Dottridge explains that the majority of trafficked children are girls and that the majority of girls are "employed as domestic servants or street vendors," although some girls are "trafficked into prostitution" (see Chapter 3).

Foreign Debt

Shortly after the decolonization wave of the 1960s, international financial institutions (IFIs), including banks, the World Bank, and the International Monetary Fund, began lending large sums of money to the newly independent states in the periphery and semiperiphery—money earmarked for development projects, especially large infrastructure projects like building highways and dams and building government-owned utility companies to provide electricity and telephone service.

Developing countries were generally able to repay their loans until the world economy shifted in the 1970s. The price of oil rose in the late 1970s, and in the early 1980s commodity prices dropped. Rising oil prices make the production of goods more expensive, and falling commodity prices make it difficult to repay loans as the value of exports declines. The Third World Debt Crisis began as export revenue declined, the cost of oil increased, and state-run companies created in the 1960s and 1970s were found to be both inefficient and draining on government funds.

The World Bank and the International Monetary Fund stepped in to lend more money to developing countries to help them out of the Third World Debt Crisis. The IFIs determined that peripheral and semiperipheral countries needed to restructure their governments and economies in order to develop. To secure the loans, countries had to agree to implement economic or governmental reforms, including privatizing government entities, opening the country to foreign trade, reducing tariffs, and encouraging foreign direct investment. These loans are known as **structural adjustment loans**, and the set of policies surrounding them came to be known as the **Washington Consensus** in the 1980s.

Opponents of to the Washington Consensus argue that the policies support and protect core country economies at the expense of peripheral and semiperipheral economies. Countries had limited options to reject structural adjustment loans because the hefty cost of servicing debts (cost of repayments plus interest) often exceeded revenues from the export of goods and services (Fig. 10.10). Developing countries also needed to demonstrate they were repaying their debts and restructuring their economies to attract multinational corporations that could offer employment to their people and investment in their economies.

Structural adjustment loans were part of a larger trend toward **neoliberalism** in the late twentieth century. Neoliberalism derives from the neo-classical economic idea that government intervention into markets is inefficient and undesirable, and should be resisted wherever possible. These ideas were at the heart of the structural adjustment conditions that were attached to loans and refinancing programs. Neoliberal ideas spurred a trend toward transferring economic control from states to the private sector. As a result, the size of the public sector in a number of countries shrunk. Corporate control expanded, and state and regional governments had less control over their economic destinies. High debt obligations and related neoliberal reforms arguably contributed to the economic and political crisis in Argentina at the end of 2001 and beginning of 2002. Argentina privatized government sectors in the 1990s and took out loans,

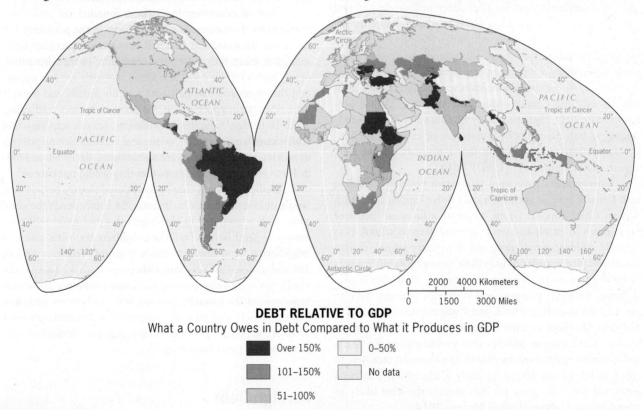

DEBT RELATIVE TO GDP
What a Country Owes in Debt Compared to What it Produces in GDP

- Over 150%
- 101–150%
- 51–100%
- 0–50%
- No data

■■ **Figure 10.10**
External Debt Service as a Percentage of Exports of Goods and Services for Low- and Middle-Income Economies, 2012.   Repaying back loans, let alone paying the interest on the loans, is more difficult for countries with debt much higher than their GDP.   *Data from*: World Bank, 2013. http://data.worldbank.org/indicator/DT.DOD.DECT.EX.ZS.

FIELD NOTE

"Arriving in Argentina during the political and economic upheavals that had begun in 2001, I saw signs of dislocation and trouble everywhere. Beggars pursued pedestrians on the once-fashionable Avenida Florida. Banks had installed protective shutters against angry crowds demanding return of their frozen and devalued deposits. A bus trip on the Patagonian Highway turned into an adventure when masked protesters carrying rocks and burning rags stopped vehicles and threatened their occupants. Newspapers carried reports of starvation in Tucumán Province—in a country capable of producing seven times the food its population needs."

■ **Figure 10.11**
Buenos Aires, Argentina.

© H. J. de Blij

leading to short-term economic growth in the 1990s. In 1999, a recession hit Argentina, and by 2000, the country had a debt equal to 50 percent of its GDP (Blustein 2003) (Fig. 10.11). The IMF extended emergency loans in 2000 and again in 2001. Coupled with unchecked government spending and corruption, Argentina's economy experienced a meltdown, and the country defaulted on its debt in 2002. More than half the population of 38 million ended up in poverty (McCarthy 2007).

By 2005, internal economic growth and aid from Venezuela put Argentina in a position to work out a complex debt restructuring plan that has pulled the country back from the brink. Argentina's agricultural economy bounced back in 2010 with the rise of corn and soy prices. Argentina's economy is stabilizing, but in cases where countries are facing imminent economic, political, and social meltdown, the only alternative may be to default on loans. Defaulting countries then find themselves in a severely disadvantaged position when it comes to attracting future external investment. And if a substantial number of countries were to default at the same time, a global economic crisis could ensue that would work to the disadvantage of almost everyone.

Political Corruption and Instability

Political corruption and instability can greatly impede economic development. In peripheral countries, a wide divide often exists between the very wealthy and the poorest of the poor. In Kenya, for example, the wealthiest 10 percent of the population controls nearly 50 percent of the country's wealth, and the poorest 10 percent control less than 1 percent. The

disenfranchisement of the poor and the competition among the rich for control of the government (and the potential spoils that go along with that) can lead to extreme political instability within a state—as Kenya experienced in 2007–2008. Add to these factors involvement from outside the country, especially by powerful countries, and the political instability can easily escalate, yielding horrid conditions in which military dictators, selfish megalomaniacs, and corrupt governments can come to power.

Countries of the core have established democracies for themselves; since World War II, they have held regularly scheduled democratic elections. But countries in the periphery and semiperiphery have had a much harder time establishing and maintaining democracies. In the process of decolonization, the colonizing countries typically left governments that reflected political and social hierarchies of the colonial period. Some failed, some were overthrown by military coups, and some saw the consolidation of power around a dictatorial strongman. Many countries in the periphery and semiperiphery have alternated repeatedly between quasidemocratic and military governments. Some argue that without considerable wealth, maintaining a liberal democracy is all but impossible.

Opening the homepage of any major newspaper on any given day will reveal a story somewhere in the world that demonstrates the link between economic stability and political stability. In Afghanistan, economic woes represent one of the greatest threats to the stability of the U.S.-supported government in Kabul. More than half of the population is impoverished, and the government lacks the funds to invest in development. Foreign aid—much of it from the United States—has provided some help, but the flow of aid has been variable and its amount insufficient to address the country's searing economic problems. Many analysts see this as a key impediment to achieving stability in Afghanistan. As *The Economist* put it in 2006, "poverty helps the Taliban."

In places where poverty is rampant, politicians often become corrupt, misusing aid and exacerbating the plight of the poor. In Zimbabwe, the year 2002 left many people starving, as poor weather conditions created a meager harvest. The country's ruling party, ZANU-PF, headed by Robert Mugabe, demanded cards from Zimbabweans who registered for the "food for work" program—cards demonstrating membership in the ZANU-PF political party. As conditions worsened in subsequent years, the Mugabe government faced increasing resistance. A potential challenger, Morgan Tsvangirai, emerged in 2008. Members of his opposition party were killed and the challenger was harassed, but after a contested election that many believe Tsvangirai won, a power-sharing agreement came into effect that kept Mugabe as president and made Tsvangirai the prime minister. Some stability returned to the country, but continuing tensions make it difficult to address Zimbabwe's enormous economic problems.

The Zimbabwe case shows that in low-income countries, corrupt leaders can stay in power for decades because the people are afraid to rise up against the leader's extreme power or because those who have risen up have been killed or harmed by the leader's followers. Circumstances and timing need to work together to allow a new government to come to power. When governments become excessively corrupt, other countries and nongovernmental organizations sometimes withdraw development aid to the country. Yet when this happens, everyday people often bear the brunt of hardship. Even when the global community cuts off the corrupt government's aid, core countries and nongovernmental organizations often try to provide food aid to the people. All too frequently, when this type of aid reaches its intended beneficiaries, it is rarely sufficient to meet basic needs or reverse the trajectory of hardship in the country.

Costs of Economic Development

Economic development changes a place. To increase productivity, whether industrial or agricultural, people transform the environment. When a country goes through intensification of industrial production, air and surface water are often polluted. Pollution is not confined to industry. With intensification of *agricultural production*, the introduction of pesticides and herbicides can have deleterious impacts on the soil and groundwater. Tourism can be just as difficult on the environment—taxing the existing infrastructure beyond its capacities. The costs of tourism often stretch far beyond the environment, affecting ways of life and fundamentally altering the cultural landscape.

INDUSTRIALIZATION

In their efforts to attract new industries, the governments of many countries in the global periphery and semiperiphery have set up special manufacturing export zones called **export processing zones (EPZs),** which offer favorable tax, regulatory, and trade arrangements to foreign firms. By 2006, 130 countries had established 3500 EPZs, and many of these had become major manufacturing centers (Engman et al. 2007) (Fig. 10.12). Two of the best known of these zones are the Mexican **maquiladoras** and the **special economic zones** of China (discussed in Chapter 9). Governments locate such zones in places with easy access to export markets. Maquiladora zones in Mexico

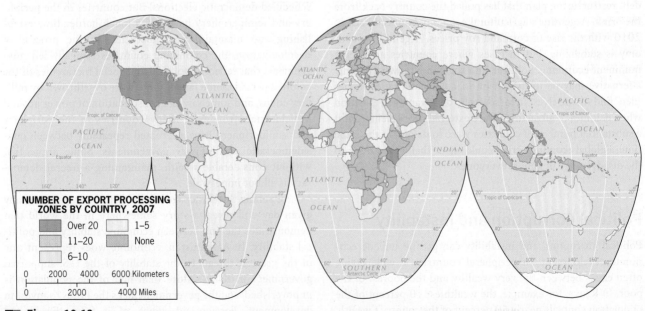

■ **Figure 10.12**

Export Processing Zones. Number of export processing zones by country, 2007. *Data from*: International Labor Organization.

are mainly sited directly across the border from the United States, and the special economic zones of China are located near major ports. These zones typically attract a mix of manufacturing operations, depending on the skill levels of the labor force and the available infrastructure.

The maquiladora program started in 1965 when the Mexican government designated the region of northern Mexico as a maquiladora district, making it a place where raw materials could be shipped into Mexico, manufactured into goods, and then sent back to the United States free of import tariffs. U.S. corporations relocated manufacturing plants to Mexico to take advantage of the program.

Although the maquiladora phenomenon started in 1965, it did not really take off until the 1980s. During the 1980s, American companies recognized the expanding wage and benefit differences between the U.S. and Mexican worker and began relocating to the maquiladora district in northern Mexico. Competition from other parts of the world has since led to the closing of some plants, but some 3000 maquiladoras continue to function, employing 1 million workers and accounting for 50 percent of Mexico's exports. The maquiladora plants produce goods such as electronic equipment, electrical appliances, automobiles, textiles, plastics, and furniture. The plants are controversial both in Mexico and the United States, as corporations that have relocated there avoid the employment and environmental regulations that are in force just a few miles to the north. Many maquiladora factories hire young women and men for low pay and few if any benefits, putting them to work in repetitive jobs, often in environmentally questionable conditions.

In 1992, the United States, Mexico, and Canada established the **North American Free Trade Agreement (NAFTA)**, which prompted further industrialization of the border region. NAFTA took effect January 1, 1994. In addition to manufacturing plants, NAFTA has facilitated the movement of service industries from the United States to Mexico, including data processing operations. Most of the new plants are located in two districts: Tijuana on the Pacific Coast—linked to San Diego across the border—and Ciudad Juarez on the Rio Grande across from El Paso, Texas. In recent years the socioeconomic and environmental contrasts between cities on either side of the U.S.–Mexico border have become increasingly stark. Violent crime has become a particularly serious problem in Juarez, even as El Paso remains comparatively safe, and the slums of Tijuana are a world apart from much of San Diego. Although NAFTA was designed to foster increased interaction in North America, cross-border disparities have worked together with growing U.S. concerns over illegal immigration and the infiltration of foreign terrorists to make the U.S.–Mexico border more tightly controlled and more difficult to cross than in prior decades.

AGRICULTURE

In peripheral countries, agriculture typically focuses on personal consumption or on production for a large agricultural conglomerate. Where zones of larger-scale, modernized agriculture have developed in the periphery, foodstuffs are produced for the foreign market and often have minimal impact on the impoverished conditions of the surrounding lands. Little is produced for the local marketplace because distribution systems are poorly organized and because the local population is typically unable to pay for foodstuffs. If the local population owns land, their landholdings are usually fragmented, creating small plots of land that are difficult to farm in a manner that produces much income. Even on larger plots of land, most farmers are equipped with outdated, inefficient tools and equipment. The main crops tend to be grains and roots; farmers produce little protein because high-protein crops typically have lower yields than grain crops. On the farms in the periphery, yields per unit area are low, subsistence modes of life prevail, and many families are constantly in debt.

Impoverished farmers can ill afford such luxuries as fertilizers, and educational levels are typically too low to achieve widespread soil conservation. As a result, soil erosion is commonplace in most peripheral areas. Severe soil erosion in areas with dry or semiarid climates around deserts results in extreme degradation of the land and the spread of the desert into these lands. Although the expansion and contraction of deserts can occur naturally and cyclically, the process of **desertification** is more often exacerbated by humans destroying vegetation and eroding soils through the overuse of lands for livestock grazing or crop production.

Desertification has hit Africa harder than any of the other continents (Fig. 10.13). More than half of Africa is arid or semiarid, and many people farm the marginal, dry lands of the continent. Land ownership patterns, the need for crops and protein sources (both for local consumption and for export), and power differences among groups of people lead some farmers and ranchers to turn marginal, semiarid lands into farm and ranch lands. Lands that are available for farming or ranching may be used more intensively in order to increase agricultural production (see Chapter 13). In semiarid regions, the decision to farm more intensively and increase agricultural production has the unintended consequence of eroding the land, encouraging outmigration, and creating conflict.

In Subsaharan Africa over the last 50 years, more than 270,000 square miles (700,000 km^2) of farming and grazing land have become desert, extending the Sahara Desert to the south. Some of the African desertification may be caused by climatic fluctuations, but overgrazing, woodcutting, soil exhaustion, and misuse have undoubtedly accelerated the process.

TOURISM

All development strategies have pros and cons, as is well illustrated by the case of tourism. Peripheral island countries in the Caribbean region and in Oceania have become leading destinations for millions of tourists from richer states.

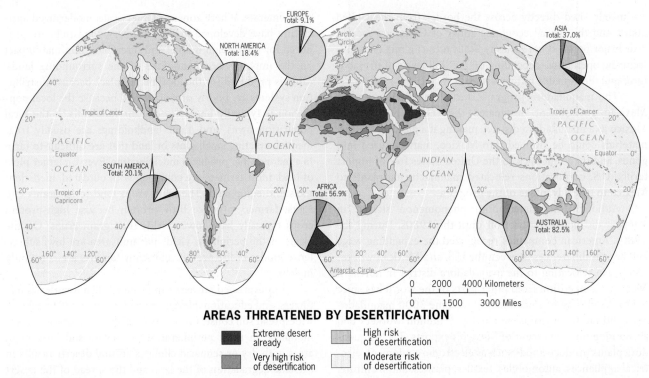

AREAS THREATENED BY DESERTIFICATION

- Extreme desert already
- Very high risk of desertification
- High risk of desertification
- Moderate risk of desertification

■ **Figure 10.13**

Areas Threatened by Desertification. Deserts expand and contract cyclically, but nature's cycles can be distorted by human intervention. This map shows areas threatened or affected by desertification. *Data from*: Several sources, including J. Turk et al., *Environmental Science*, Philadelphia: Saunders, 1984, p. 305.

Tourism is now one of the major industries in the world and has surpassed oil in its overall economic value (see Chapter 12). While tourism can bring employment to peripheral countries, tourism may also have serious negative effects on cultures and environments.

To develop tourism, the "host" country must make substantial investments in infrastructure, including airports, cruise ports, roads, and communication systems. Beautiful hotels, swimming pools, and man-made waterfalls are typically owned by large multinational corporations, not locals. The multinational corporations earn enormous profits, most of which are sent back to owners, shareholders, and executives outside of the country. Tourism can create local jobs, but they are often low-paying and have little job security. In tourist zones, many employees work two or three jobs in order to break even.

Tourism frequently strains the fabric of local communities as well. The invasion of poor communities by wealthier visitors can foster antipathy and resentment. Tourism can also have the effect of altering, and even debasing, local culture (see Chapter 4), which is adapted to suit the visitors' taste. In many instances tourism fosters a "demonstration effect" among locals that encourages them to behave in ways that may please or interest the visitors but that is disdained by the larger local community. Some tourism workers consider employment in the tourist industry dehumanizing because it demands displays of friendliness and servitude that locals find insulting.

A flood of affluent tourists may be appealing to the government of a poor country whose elite may have a financial stake in the hotels where they can share the pleasures of the wealthy. Local entrepreneurs have difficulty tapping into tourist revenues because powerful multinational corporations and national governments often intervene to limit the opportunities of local, small-scale operators in favor of mass, prearranged tourist destinations that isolate the tourist from local society.

Overreliance on tourism can also leave an economy vulnerable if shifting economic circumstances cause a sharp decline in the number of tourists or if natural disasters hit. Because many tourist destinations in poorer countries are beach attractions, natural hazards such as the 2004 tsunami in Southeast Asia can destroy the lynchpin of a country's economy (we discuss the tsunami and other natural hazards in greater detail in Chapter 13). Suffering the loss of thousands of people; dealing with the after-effects of sewage, homelessness, orphans, and the destitute; and coping with rebuilding the tourist destinations must occur while the flow of tourist-related income has stopped.

The cultural landscape of tourism is frequently a study in harsh contrasts: gleaming hotels tower over modest, often poor housing; luxury liners glide past poverty-stricken villages; opulent meals are served in hotels while, down the street, children suffer from malnutrition. If the tourist industry offered real prospects for economic progress in low-income countries, such circumstances might be viewed as temporary, unfortunate by-products. However, the evidence too often points in the other direction.

Think of a trip you have made to a poorer area of the country or a poorer region of the world. Hypothesize how your experience in the place as a tourist was fundamentally different from the everyday lives of the people who live in the place.

HOW DO POLITICAL AND ECONOMIC INSTITUTIONS INFLUENCE UNEVEN DEVELOPMENT WITHIN STATES?

Poverty is not confined to the periphery. Core countries have regions and peoples that are markedly poorer than others. On the Pine Ridge Indian Reservation in the northern Great Plains of the United States, unemployment hovers at 80 percent, and more than 60 percent of the people live in poverty with a per capita income of just over $6000. Other countries of the core have similar regions where peoples' economic lives do not improve when the country's economy grows. In Europe, areas of isolation and stagnation persist—particularly in the east. At the same time, areas within peripheral countries are experiencing rapid economic growth. In each of these cases, the local conditions in these places differ sharply from those prevailing in surrounding areas. Regional contrasts in wealth are a reminder that per capita GNI does not accurately represent the economic development of an individual country. Any statistic that is derived for an entire country hides the variety of economic situations within. Peripheral countries are notoriously marked by severe regional disparities. In Chapter 9 we discussed the stark contrasts between wealthy and poor within Latin American and African cities. When viewed at the scale of the State, major cities (particularly capitals) and their surroundings often look like islands of prosperity, with modern buildings, factories on the outskirts, and modern farms nearby. In some cases roads and rails lead to a bustling port, where luxury automobiles are unloaded for use by the privileged elite and raw materials or agricultural products from the country are exported to points around the world. In these core areas of countries, the rush of "progress" may be evident. If you travel a few miles into the countryside or into a different neighborhood in the city, however, you will likely see a very different picture. The contrasts between rich and poor areas are not simply the result of differences in the economic endowments of places. Government policy frequently affects development patterns as well. Hence, in this section of the chapter we turn to how governments collaborate with corporations to create islands of development, and consider how people try to generate growth in the periphery of the periphery (the poorest regions of peripheral countries).

The Role of Governments

The actions of governments influence whether, how, and where wealth is produced. This is because the distribution of wealth is affected by tariffs, trade agreements, taxation structures, land ownership rules, environmental regulations, and many other manifestations of governmental authority. Government policies shape patterns of development within States—between urban and rural areas and also among sectors of the economy. Governments alone do not determine patterns of wealth and poverty, but they are almost always part of the picture. Consider the case of the Ninth Ward in New Orleans, which was devastated by Hurricane Katrina in 2005. On its surface, what happened to the Ninth Ward was the result of a natural disaster. But the flooding of that part of New Orleans was also the result of government decisions decades ago to build levies and settle flood-prone areas. The concentration of people living there was also the product of innumerable policies affecting housing, the construction of businesses, and the like. Once the hurricane hit, many looked to government to rebuild the devastated section of the city. The shortcomings of governmental response are evident in the landscape today (Fig. 10.14).

Every government policy has a geographical expression, meaning that some regions are favored whereas others are disadvantaged as a result of the implementation of that policy. When policies come together to favor some regions over others, uneven development is the result. And uneven development can easily be exacerbated over time as the wealthy grow wealthier.

Consider the contrasting outcomes of U.S. agricultural policy in parts of rural Wisconsin and rural Appalachia. In rural Wisconsin, farmers typically hold college degrees, usually from land-grant universities, in plant and animal sciences and in agribusiness. A farmer may run a highly mechanized dairy farm where he equips each cow with a barcode and keeps a range of data about that particular cow. The data include any medical attention the cow has needed, how much milk the cow is producing, and when the cow last calved. The farmer feeds the cow a diet geared toward improving or maintaining milk production. When the cow ambles over to the trough to feed, a sensor reads the cow's barcode and automatically mixes the correct balance of proteins, carbohydrates, and nutrients for the cow, dispensing them into the trough for the cow to eat. If the cow has already eaten that day, the computer dispenses nothing into the trough, and the cow is left to amble away.

In parts of rural Appalachia, by contrast, hardscrabble farming is the norm. Farmers have limited education, and there is little mechanization. In short, life in some of the poorest parts of rural Appalachia is a world apart from life on a modern Wisconsin dairy farm. Some of those differences can be attributed to geographic situation and economic swings. But others are the product of government policies that influence educational opportunities, provide subsidies for particular agricultural pursuits, and promote the development of

FIELD NOTE

"As I walked through New Orleans' Lower Ninth Ward more than two years after Hurricane Katrina, it seemed as if the natural disaster had just happened. Street after street of devastated, vacant buildings was all the eye could behold—many still bearing the markings of the emergency crews that had moved through the neighborhood in the wake of the hurricane, showing whether anyone had died inside. It struck me that reconstruction would require a public commitment on the order of what occurred in Europe after World War II, when cities reduced to rubble by bombing were rebuilt almost from scratch. No such commitment ever materialized, but some progress has been made in recent years. Recent census data shows a city that is slightly smaller and slightly richer than the pre-Katrina city, with a somewhat reduced black population, and a modestly expanding number of Hispanics."

© Alexander B. Murphy

■ **Figure 10.14**
Destroyed House in the Lower Ninth Ward, New Orleans.

particular technologies within certain places. The State of Wisconsin supports its $26 billion dairy industry, and the University of Wisconsin receives huge grants and corporate funding to constantly improve dairy farming. Government policy can also help alleviate uneven development. In the case of Appalachia, the U.S. Congress created an Appalachian Regional Commission in 1965 to address poverty in the region. The Commission has orchestrated a program of government investment in roads, schools, health care facilities, and water and sewer systems that has fostered development in parts of the region. Significant parts of Appalachia have benefited from these policies, although pockets of deep poverty remain.

Looking at commodity chains can also help us understand the role of governments in uneven development both within and between states. In her 2005 book *The Travels of a T-Shirt in the Global Economy*, economist Pietra Rivoli described the significant influences governments have on the distribution of wealth between and within states. Rivoli grabs a T-shirt out of a bin at a Walgreens in Florida, buys it, and then traces its production back through the commodity chain to see how it ends up in her hands. The cotton for her T-shirt was grown in West Texas, where the cotton lobby (the political arm of America's cotton producers) has effectively politicked for governmental labor programs and price supports that help the industry grow cotton and sell it at predictable prices.

From West Texas, the cotton bale reaches China by ship. There it is spun into thread and woven into fabric. Women from rural China work in state-owned factories set up in regions that are slated for economic development—cutting

and sewing T-shirts and keeping the textile machines in good repair. The women are considered cheap labor at the global scale, earning about $100 per month. Rivoli reports that over 40,000 garment factories operate in China alone.

The T-shirts are then shipped to the United States for sale. In an attempt to protect T-shirts produced in America with higher labor costs from those produced in China, the U.S. government has established quotas on how many items from various clothing categories can be imported into the United States from China and other countries. An unintended consequence of the quota system has been a "quota market" that allows countries to buy and sell their U.S. quota numbers to producers in other countries (an illegal but rampant practice). Instead of trading in quotas, some production facilities have moved to places where quotas and cheap labor are available—places such as Sri Lanka, Poland, and Lesotho. Rivoli describes how one producer of cotton shirts has moved around the world:

The Esquel Corporation, today the world's largest producer of cotton shirts, started in Hong Kong in the late 1970s, but, unable to obtain quota to sell to the United States, shifted production to mainland China. When the United States tightened Chinese shirt quotas in the early 1980s, Esquel moved production to Malaysia. When Malaysian quota also became difficult to obtain, Esquel moved yet again, this time to Sri Lanka. The globe hopping continued, with the Chinese shirt producer setting up operations in Mauritius and Maldives.

The point is that quota laws, like other policies made by governments, regional trade organizations, and international political regimes (such as the World Trade Organization and the International Labor Organization), affect whether and how regions can produce and exchange goods on the world market.

Islands of Development

In both periphery and core, governments often invest in growing the economy of the capital city so that it can act as a showcase for the country. Capital cities are home to government buildings and jobs; they often house universities, museums, heritage centers, convention centers, and the headquarters of large corporations. After gaining independence, many former colonial states spent lavishly on their capitals, not because such spending was essential to political or economic success but because the states wanted to showcase their independence and their futures, and create a national treasure. European colonizers who focused their wealth and treasures on their capital cities, including the United Kingdom's London, France's Paris, and the Netherlands' Amsterdam, served as models for the newly independent states.

In many countries of the global economic periphery and semiperiphery, the capital cities are by far the largest and most economically influential cities in the state (i.e., primate cities, discussed in Chapter 9). Some newly independent states have built new capital cities, away from the colonial headquarters. Their goals in doing so are to separate themselves from their colonizers, to bring together diverse groups into one state with a city built to reflect their common culture, to extend economic development into the interior of the state, or to help establish control over a region with a population whose loyalties might not be to the state.

Nigeria moved its capital from Yoruba-dominated Lagos along the coast to an ethnically neutral territory in the center of the state: Abuja. Malawi moved its capital from Zomba, deep in the south, to more central Lilongwe. Pakistan moved the capital from the colonial headquarters of Karachi to Islamabad in the far north to symbolize the country's reorientation toward its historically important interior and north. Brazil moved its capital from coastal Rio de Janeiro to centrally located Brasília in order to direct attention to the huge, sparsely populated, yet poorly integrated interior. More recently, Kazakhstan moved its capital from Almaty in the south to Astana in the north, partly to be closer to Russia and the center of the possibly restless Russian population. Malaysia has also recently moved its capital from the colonial capital of Kuala Lumpur to a completely new center called Putrajaya, about 25 miles (40 km) to the south. The Malaysian government decided to build a new, ultramodern seat of government to symbolize the country's rapid economic growth (Fig. 10.15).

Corporations can also make cities focal points of development by concentrating corporate activities in a particular place. Often, corporations build up the cities near the resources they are extracting or near manufacturing centers they have built. Multinational oil companies create subsidiaries in countries of the periphery and semiperiphery, creating or expanding cities near oil reserves. For example, in Gabon, Elf and Shell, two oil companies based in Europe, run ElfGabon and ShellGabon in the Central African country. The oil companies took the small colonial town of Port Gentil in Gabon and turned it into a city that the locals call "oil city." The oil companies built housing, roads, and stores, and provide much of the employment in the town (Fig. 10.16).

When a government or corporation builds up and concentrates economic development in a certain city or small region, geographers call that place an **island of development**. In Chapter 3, we identified islands of development in the periphery and semiperiphery and discussed why people migrate to these cities from rural areas and other poorer cities. The hope for a job drives many migrants to move to these islands of comparative prosperity.

Bazuki Muhammad/Reuters/© Corbis

■■ Figure 10.15
Putrajaya, Malaysia. Putrajaya is the newly built capital of Malaysia, replacing Kuala Lumpur.

FIELD NOTE

"Before the 1970s, Gabon's principal exports were manganese, hardwoods, and uranium ores. The discovery of oil off the Gabonese coast changed all that. This oil storage tank at the edge of Port Gentile is but one reminder of a development that has transformed Gabon's major port city—and the economy of the country as a whole. Oil now accounts for 80 percent of Gabon's export earnings, and that figure is climbing as oil prices rise and new discoveries are made. But how much the average citizen of Gabon is benefiting from the oil economy remains an open question. Even as health care and infrastructure needs remain unmet, the French publication *L'Autre Afrique* listed Gabon's recently deceased ruler as the African leader with the largest real estate holdings in Paris."

© Alexander B. Murphy

■ **Figure 10.16**
Port Gentil, Gabon.

Creating Growth in the Periphery of the Periphery

One of the greatest challenges to development is creating development opportunities outside of islands of development. In the most rural, impoverished regions of less prosperous countries, some nongovernmental organizations try to improve the plight of people. **Nongovernmental organizations (NGOs)** are not run by state or local governments. Rather, NGOs operate independently, and the term is usually reserved for entities that operate as nonprofits. Thousands of NGOs operate in the world today, from churches to charities such as Heifer International. Each NGO has its own set of goals, depending on the primary concerns outlined by its founders and financiers (Fig. 10.17).

Some countries have so many NGOs operating within them that they serve as what *The Economist* (1998) calls "a parallel state, financed by foreigners and accountable to nobody." For example, more than 20,000 NGOs operate within the country of Bangladesh at any time, focusing mainly on the rural areas and villages of the state. But the NGO phenomenon can be a bit of a mirage, masking the depth of problems some places face. In the wake of the 2010 earthquake in Haiti, one respected British newspaper, the *Guardian*, reported that there was approximately one NGO per 1000 people in Haiti, but that much of the money funneled through these NGOs was misappropriated.

One particular kind of program by NGOs that has found success in South Asia and South America is the microcredit program. The idea behind a **microcredit program** is simple: Give loans to poor people, particularly women, to encourage development of small businesses. Programs either have women in the village guarantee each other's credit, or they make future lending to others contingent on repayment by the first borrowers. With repayment rates hovering at 98 percent, microcredit programs can finance themselves, and many NGOs offer the programs (Fig. 10.18).

By providing microcredit to women, NGOs can alter the gender balance in a region, giving more fiscal power to women. Some microcredit programs are credited with lowering birth rates in parts of developing countries and altering the social fabric of cultures by diminishing men's positions of power. Successful microcredit programs also help alleviate malnourishment, as women with incomes can feed themselves and their children.

Microcredit programs have been less successful in places with high mortality rates from diseases such as AIDS. If the borrower is unable to work or if the family has medical and funeral bills, the borrower is much more likely to default on the microcredit loan. When people in the periphery of the periphery experience a multitude of challenges, such as disease, corrupt governments, high mortality rates, high fertility rates, and disruptions from natural hazards, the goal of economic development takes a backseat to daily survival.

thinking
geographically

Find something in your house (an item of clothing, an electronic device, etc.) and, using the Internet, try to trace the commodity chain of production. What steps did the item and its components go through before reaching you? Consider the types of economic processes that were operating at each step and think of the roles governments and international political regimes played along the way.

GUEST FIELD NOTE

Sukabumi, West Java

My own research is based on fieldwork in Indonesia as well as ongoing engagement with students in the United States. The women pictured here collaborated with me on a research/activism project for migrant women workers in Indonesia. The woman on the left ("Rina") had returned from working in Saudi Arabia as a domestic worker for two years. She wanted to return to Saudi Arabia for another contract to earn more money for herself and her family, but she was concerned about her rights and her safety. She had been employed by a person she considered fair and reasonable, but she had heard from friends and neighbors that many migrants had experienced serious abuses while abroad. The woman pictured on the right ("Sorani") is an Indonesian activist who works in support of migrant rights. She discussed with Rina and me her strategies for mobilizing political change, and she helped us to see possibilities for building transnational alliances among American and Indonesian workers, students, and activists. Based on these interviews, as well as many years of working with migrant women working in factories in Indonesia, my own research has increasingly sought to understand the ways in which we in the United States, as scholars, students, workers, and consumers, can better serve global justice.

Credit: Rachel Silvey, University of Toronto.

Rachel Silvey, University of Toronto

■ **Figure 10.17**

© Alexander B. Murphy

■ **Figure 10.18**
Bwindi, Uganda. Women walk by a microcredit agency that works to facilitate economic development in the town.

Summary

The idea of economic development is relatively new; it implies a sense of progressively improving a country's economic situation. The idea took hold in the wake of the Industrial Revolution. Geographers focus on the spatial structure of the economy, assessing how that structure influences the ability of states and regions to reach greater levels of economic development. Geographers also recognize that economic development in a single place is based on a multitude of factors, including the situation within the global economy, the link the place plays in commodity chains, the efficacy of government, the presence of disease, the health and well-being of the population, the presence and amount of foreign debt, the success or failure of government policies, and the influence of nongovernmental programs. Geographers also realize that all of these processes are operating concurrently across scales, making a country's journey toward economic development much more complicated than climbing a ladder.

Geographic Concepts

commodity chain
break-of-bulk location
gross national product (GNP)
gross domestic product (GDP)
gross national income (GNI)
per capita GNI
formal economy
informal economy
digital divide
Millennium Development Goals
modernization model

context
neo-colonialism
structuralist theory
dependency theory
dollarization
world-systems theory
three-tier structure
trafficking
structural adjustment loans
Washington Consensus
neoliberalism

export processing zones (EPZs)
maquiladoras
special economic zones
North American Free Trade
    Agreement (NAFTA)
desertification
island of development
nongovernmental organizations
    (NGOs)
microcredit program

Learn More Online

About Brazil's Bolsa Familia
www.worldbank.org/en/news/opinion/2013/11/04/bolsa-familia-Brazil-quiet-revolution

About Global Poverty
www.worldbank.org/poverty

About Global Economic Development
www.brookings.edu/global.aspx

About United Nations Millennium Goals
www.un.org/millenniumgoals/

Watch It Online

About Gabon
www.learner.org/resources/series180.html#program_descriptions

Click on Video On Demand for "Gabon: Sustainable Resources?"

AGRICULTURE AND THE RURAL LANDSCAPE

Changing Greens

Driving across the semiarid ranchlands of western South Dakota, I noticed the presence of a crop in the landscape that was recently found only in the eastern, moister region of the state: soybeans (Fig. 11.1).

I called a colleague who works in agriculture at South Dakota State University to ask, "When did the cattle ranchers of western South Dakota start growing soybeans?" He replied, "When the soy biodiesel plants started popping up in Nebraska and Kansas and when genetically modified soybeans made it possible to grow the crop here." He explained the development of Roundup Ready soybeans, a particular genetically modified soybean that can grow in more arid regions of the country. First, you plant the soybean; then you use an airplane to spray Roundup, a common weed killer that is manufactured by the company that produces the Roundup Ready soybeans, over the field. The application of Roundup over the entire field

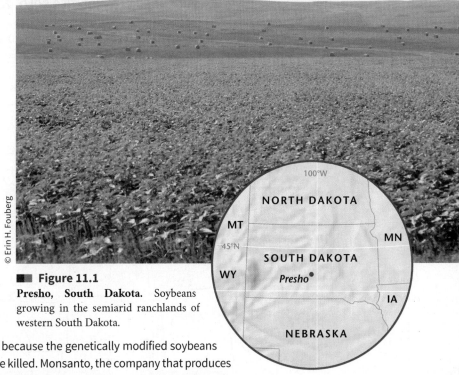

■ **Figure 11.1**
Presho, South Dakota. Soybeans growing in the semiarid ranchlands of western South Dakota.

© Erin H. Fouberg

saves a lot of time and energy for the farmers because the genetically modified soybeans are resistant to the Roundup, but the weeds are killed. Monsanto, the company that produces Roundup, has developed soybeans, corn, cotton, and other crops that are resistant to Roundup.

Counter to the genetically modified Roundup Ready crops, **organic agriculture**—the production of crops without the use of synthetic or industrially produced pesticides and fertilizers—is also on the rise in North America. In wealthier parts of the world, the demand for organic products has risen exponentially in recent years. Sales of organic food in the United States, for example, went from under $200 million in 1980 to $1.5 billion by the early 1990s to over $10 billion by 2003 and $31.5 billion in 2013. Organic foods are now just over 4 percent of all food sales in the country. The growth rate is so strong that some predict organic sales will approach 10 percent of total U.S. food sales within a decade. Parts of western Europe are already approaching that figure—notably Denmark, Sweden, Finland, and parts of Germany.

Agricultural fields are devoted to organic agriculture in the core, semiperiphery, and periphery. Fields devoted to organic agriculture produce all kinds of foodstuffs, including fruits, vegetables, coffee, tea, grains, nuts, and spices. Compared to all agricultural land, the organic segment is still quite small and relatively scattered, but a farmer who can gain organic certification from a government or an internationally recognized third party is increasingly at a competitive advantage (Fig. 11.2).

Although organic crops are grown everywhere, most organic foods are sold in the global economic core: in the United States, Canada, Japan, Europe, and Australia. The best-selling organic crops in the United States are fruits and vegetables, accounting for 43 percent of organic food sales, followed by dairy at 15 percent and packaged food and nondairy beverages at 15 percent and dairy between 9 and 11 percent. Organic products typically cost more than conventional products in the grocery store. Nonetheless, a 2002 report issued by the United States Department of Agriculture explains that in 2000 organic foods crossed a threshold, moving out of health food stores and into supermarkets: "for the first time, more organic food was purchased in conventional supermarkets than in any other venue." Organic foods are sold in well over half of the conventional grocery stores in the United States, with increasing demands for organic animal products such as meats and dairy.

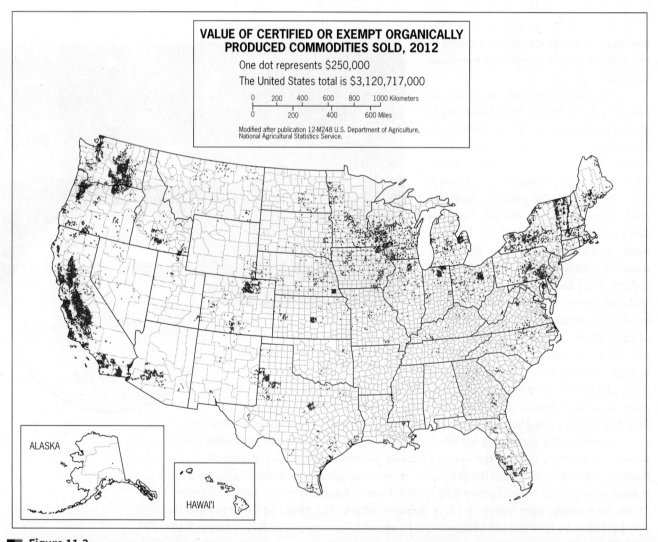

VALUE OF CERTIFIED OR EXEMPT ORGANICALLY PRODUCED COMMODITIES SOLD, 2012

One dot represents $250,000

The United States total is $3,120,717,000

Modified after publication 12-M248 U.S. Department of Agriculture, National Agricultural Statistics Service.

ALASKA

HAWAI'I

■■ **Figure 11.2**

Value of Certified Organically Produced Commodities Sold, 2012.   Farms on the west coast, the Midwest, and the northeast produce the greatest amount of organic commodities based on sales. Northeastern Colorado also has a relatively large area of organic production for sale. This map does not show organically produced crops sold in farmers markets or for self-consumption.

Organic farming has helped some farmers in the core extract themselves to a degree from the control of large, external corporate interests. The role of organic agriculture in the periphery and semiperiphery is similar to that of other major cash crops: Production is almost entirely for export to the global economic core. When organic agriculture bears a fair trade certification, some producers in the periphery and semiperiphery benefit substantially, though they also have to abide by rules established in the core (see the discussion of fair trade coffee in the last section of this chapter).

The organic movement has some clear environmental benefits, particularly in reducing levels of synthetic chemicals in soil and water. The putative health and taste advantages of organic produce help ensure the continued growth of the organic movement. The continually increasing demand for organic products has led the United States Department of Agriculture to certify organic products in the country, giving some degree of standardization to organic agriculture.

In this chapter, we examine the origins of agriculture and trace the geography of changes in the production of food and the raising of livestock from the earliest domestication of plants to such contemporary developments as genetic modification and the turn toward large-scale agribusiness. In the process, we describe the early hearths of agriculture, the geography of technological changes in agriculture, the global pattern of agricultural production, and the imprint of agriculture on the cultural landscape.

Key Questions FOR CHAPTER 11

1. What is agriculture, and where did agriculture begin?
2. How did agriculture change with industrialization?
3. What imprint does agriculture make on the cultural landscape?
4. How is agriculture currently organized geographically, and how has agribusiness influenced the contemporary geography of agriculture?

WHAT IS AGRICULTURE, AND WHERE DID AGRICULTURE BEGIN?

Agriculture is the deliberate tending of crops and livestock to produce food, feed, fiber, and fuel. When we think about agriculture, we tend to think about the production of foodstuffs for humans. Grain is also used for *feed*, grains fed directly to livestock. Raising livestock for milk, eggs, or meat makes up a large segment of U.S. agriculture. Feed also comes from the remnants of biofuel production; in 2012, around 40 percent of all grain produced in the United States was used to produce fuel for cars, not for human or animal consumption.

A common way of classifying economic activities is to focus on what is being produced. Economic activities that involve the extraction of economically valuable products from the earth, including agriculture, ranching, hunting and gathering, fishing, forestry, mining, and quarrying, are called **primary economic activities**. Both the growing of food or feed and the raising of livestock are considered primary economic activities. Activities that take a primary product and change it into something else such as toys, ships, processed foods, chemicals, and buildings are **secondary economic activities**. Manufacturing is the principal secondary economic activity. **Tertiary economic activities** are those service industries that connect producers to consumers and facilitate commerce and trade or help people meet their needs. People who work as bankers, lawyers, doctors, teachers, nurses, salespeople, clerks, and secretaries belong to the tertiary sector. Some analysts separate specialized services into **quaternary** and **quinary economic activities**, distinguishing between those services concerned with information or the exchange of money or goods (quaternary) and those tied to research or higher education (quinary). In this chapter, however, for simplicity's sake we limit ourselves to three categories: primary, secondary, and a broadly conceived tertiary or service sector.

By classifying economic activities into sectors and analyzing the percentage of the population employed in each sector, we can gain insight into how the production of goods is organized, as well as the employment structures of different societies. As we explained in our discussions of world-systems theory in Chapters 8 and 10, the story of any product (such as wheat or rice) can be better illuminated by focusing on how the good is produced (the kinds of technology, research, wages, and education that go into its production), rather than concentrating simply on what is produced. Examining the proportion of people employed in a given economic sector gives us a basic idea of how the good is produced. For example, in Guatemala the agriculture sector accounts for 26 percent of the country's gross domestic product (GDP), and over 50 percent of the labor force is employed in agriculture. Contrast that with Canada, where the agriculture sector accounts for 2.3 percent of GDP and only 2 percent of the labor force is employed in agriculture. The tertiary sector in Canada accounts for 75 percent of the labor force and over 71 percent of GDP, and the tertiary sector in Guatemala accounts for 35 percent of the labor force and 65 percent of the country's GDP.

These data do not tell us exactly how goods are produced, but they are revealing. The high proportion of the labor force involved in agriculture in Guatemala (relative to the role of agriculture in the GDP) tells us that agriculture is still quite labor dependent in Guatemala, implying a lack of mechanization. In Canada, the United States, and much of the rest of the global economic core, agriculture is produced on a large scale for commercial consumption. When agricultural goods are produced in these ways, the number of people working directly in the field is quite small. In the United States, less than 2 percent of the workforce is involved in agricultural production. Thousands of others participate in supporting agricultural production by working in the tertiary sector as research scientists for universities, seed companies, or chemical (antibiotics, pesticides, and herbicides) producers; as lobbyists for industry groups such as wheat producers or cattle ranchers; as engineers who design farm implements; as the people who sell and repair the implements; and as owners and clerks at retail establishments where farmers buy other farm and nonfarm goods.

In the United States, total agricultural production is at an all-time high, but the proportion of the labor force in agriculture is at an all-time low. Mechanization and efficiencies created by new technologies have led to a significant decrease in the number of workers needed in agricultural production. In 1950, one farmer in the United States produced enough to feed 27 people; today, one farmer in the United States produces enough to feed 144 people. The mechanization of agriculture goes beyond machinery such as combines and harvesters. New technologies include hybrid seeds and genetically engineered crops, pesticides, and herbicides, all of which are designed to increase yields. The drive toward economic efficiency has meant that the average size of farms (acres in production) in the United States has been growing, regardless of the kind of agricultural good produced. The U.S. Department of Agriculture keeps data showing the dollar value of agricultural production. The farms with the highest total production have at least $500,000 in annual production. These high-producing farms accounted for 53.7 percent of agricultural goods produced in 2007 (compared with 28.9 percent in 1989). The number of these high-producing farms increased by 33 percent between 2007 and 2012, while the number of smaller farms fell, resulting in a loss of 95,500 farms. Now the largest 4 percent of U.S. farms produce 66 percent of the country's agricultural sales.

Clearly, agriculture in the United States has changed enormously in the last decade. A recent study by the National Research Council of the U.S. National Academy of Sciences identifies four major issues that affect food security worldwide: "1) varying abilities to balance production and consumption across regions and countries, 2) accelerating conversions of agricultural land to urban uses, 3) increasingly energy-intensive food production methods in a world of shrinking fossil fuel resources, and 4) expanding use of food crops for biofuel production." Agricultural production changes rapidly as farmers worldwide react to price fluctuations in fossil fuels, seeds, fertilizers, crops, and land.

To set the stage for understanding the contemporary agriculture picture, in the next section of the chapter, we discuss how people lived before the origins of agriculture and the circumstances that gave rise to the domestication of plants and animals many millennia ago.

Hunting, Gathering, and Fishing

Before the advent of agriculture, hunting, gathering, and fishing were the most common means of subsistence throughout the world. Of course, what people hunted or gathered depended on where they lived. North America provides a good example of the diversity of regional specializations among hunter-gatherers. The oak forests of parts of North America provided an abundant harvest of nuts, sometimes enough to last more than a full year; American Indian communities living in and around these forests therefore collected and stored this food source. Other American Indians living near the Pacific Ocean became adept at salmon fishing. The bison herds of the Great Plains provided sustenance, and so bison served as a focal point for many plains cultures. In the colder climates of North America, people followed the migrations of the caribou herds. In the north, in the coastal zone stretching from present-day Alaska to Russia, the Aleut developed specialized techniques for fishing and for sea mammal hunting.

The size of hunting and gathering clans varied according to climate and resource availability. Hunting and gathering communities in areas of abundance could support larger populations. People living on the margins of forests could gather food in the forest when hunting yielded poor results and then return to hunting when circumstances improved.

Terrain and Tools

Before developing agriculture, hunter-gatherers worked on perfecting tools, controlling fires, and adapting environments to their needs. The first tools used in hunting were simple clubs—tree limbs that were thin at one end and thick and heavy at the other. The use of bone and stone and the development of spears made hunting far more effective. The fashioning of stone into hand axes and, later, handle axes was a crucial innovation that enabled hunters to skin their prey and cut the meat; it also made it possible to cut down trees and build better shelters and tools.

The controlled use of fire was another important early achievement of human communities. The first opportunities to control fire were offered by natural conditions (lightning, spontaneous combustion of surface-heated coal). Archaeological digs of ancient settlement sites suggest that people would capture a fire caused accidentally and would work to keep the fire burning continuously. Later, people learned that fire could be generated by rapid hand rotation of a wooden stick in a small hole surrounded by dry tinder. Fire became the focal point of settlements, and the campfire took on symbolic and functional importance. It was a means of making foods digestible, and it was used to drive animals into traps or over cliffs.

In addition to hunting game on land, humans harvested shellfish, trapped fish by cutting small patches of standing water off from the open sea, and invented tools to catch fish, including harpoons, hooks, and baskets.

Using tools and fire, human communities altered their environments, which helped to establish more reliable food supplies. Along with hunting and gathering, early humans were adept at keeping track of the migration cycles of fish and other animals. American Indians along the Pacific Coast and on Arctic shores, the Ainu of Japan and coastal East Asia, and communities in coastal western Europe caught salmon as they swam up rivers and negotiated rapids and falls. Archaeologists have found huge accumulations of fish bones at prehistoric sites near salmon runs.

Hunter-gatherers migrated to take advantage of cyclical movements of animals and to avoid exhausting the supply of edible plants in any one area. After the summer salmon runs, people hunted deer during the fall and again in the spring, taking advantage of seasonal movements to trap deer where they crossed rivers or in narrow valleys. During the winter, people lived off dried meat and other stored foods.

The First Agricultural Revolution

Out of areas of plenty came agriculture, the deliberate tending of crops and livestock to produce food, feed, fiber, and fuel. Geographer Carl Sauer believed the experiments necessary to establish agriculture and settle in one place would occur in lands of plenty. Only in such places could people afford to experiment with raising plants or take the time to capture animals and breed them for domestication. Sauer studied the geography of the First Agricultural Revolution, focusing on the location of agriculture hearths and what kinds of agricultural innovations took place in those hearths.

Where did **plant domestication** begin? Sauer, who spent a lifetime studying cultural origins and diffusion, suggested that Southeast and South Asia may have been the scene, more than 14,000 years ago, of the first domestication of tropical plants. There, he believed, the combination of human settlements, forest margins, and fresh water streams may have given rise to the earliest planned cultivation of **root crops**—crops that are reproduced by cultivating either the roots or cuttings from the plants (such as tubers, including manioc or cassava, yams, and sweet potatoes in the tropics). A similar but later development may have taken place in northwestern South America.

The planned cultivation of **seed crops**, plants that are reproduced by cultivating seeds, is a more complex process, involving seed selection, sowing, watering, and well-timed harvesting. Again, the practice seems to have developed in more than one area and at different times. Some scholars believe that the first domestication of seed plants occurred in the Nile River Valley in North Africa, but the majority view is that this crucial development took place in a region of Southwest Asia (also called the Fertile Crescent), through which flow the two major rivers of present-day Iraq: the Tigris and the Euphrates (Fig. 11.3). The cultivation of seed crops marked the beginning of what has been called the **First Agricultural Revolution**.

Archaeologists note that a number of changes occurred in Southwest Asia along with plant domestication. First, the plants themselves changed because people would choose seeds from the largest, hardiest plants to save for planting, yielding domesticated plants that grew larger over time than their counterparts in the wild. Archaeologists in Southwest Asia have found preserved seeds, which tell them which plants were being domesticated and when. The grain crops wheat and barley grew well in the warm Southwest Asian climate. Soon, people found that the river-inundated plains of Mesopotamia provided irrigable fields for farming. Agriculture provided a reliable food source, and grain surpluses enabled people to store grain for long-term distribution and use and to settle permanently in one place. In the process, the population of settlements began to increase.

Figure 11.4 depicts the global distribution of plant domestication hearths. In Southeast Asia (Region 1), taro, yams, and bananas were the leading food plants. In Southwest Asia (Region 4), plant domestication centered on wheat, barley, and other grains. In the Mesoamerican region (Region 6), the basic plants were maize (corn), squashes, and several kinds of beans.

Archaeologists continually find new sites to excavate, and as places are analyzed further, academics revise their

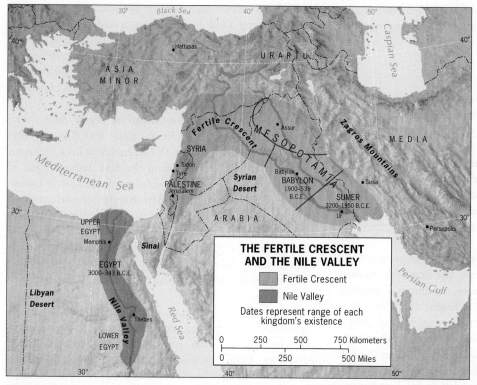

Figure 11.3

The Fertile Crescent and Nile River Valley. The Fertile Crescent and Nile River Valley were two hearths of the First Agricultural Revolution. Modern political boundaries are shown for reference. © E. H. Fouberg, A. B. Murphy, H. J. de Blij, and John Wiley & Sons, Inc.

among the world's first. Another agricultural source region lies in West Africa (Region 9). Archaeological research on agriculture in this area is relatively recent, and analysts are not certain whether agriculture developed independently there.

Table 11.1 may be overwhelming at first glance, but it is worth careful attention. It reveals the enormous range of crops that were cultivated around the world, as well as how, at various times and in different locales, particular groups of crops became the mainstays of life. Soon the knowledge needed to farm such crops diffused outward from these agricultural hearths. For example, both millet and sorghum diffused from the West African region—millet to India and sorghum to China.

In many cases, what we now think of as centers of production of particular crops are not the places where those crops were originally domesticated. The corn (maize) we associate with the American Corn Belt diffused from Mesoamerica (Region 6) into North America. Later, the Portuguese brought it across the Atlantic and into Africa, where it became a staple in some regions. The white potato we associate with Ireland

assumptions about the timing of the emergence of agricultural hearths. The Central China hearth (Region 7) has recently attracted greater attention because new evidence supports a much earlier development of agriculture in this region—so early, in fact, that Chinese farmers may have been

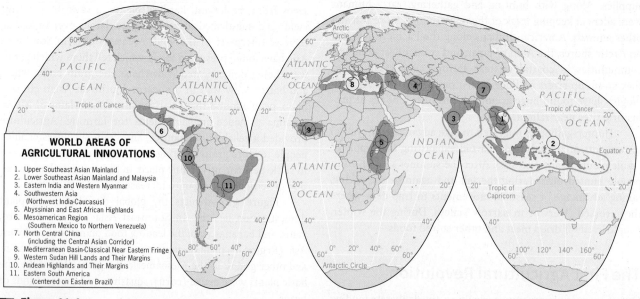

Figure 11.4

Agricultural Hearths. Cultural geographer Carl Sauer identified 11 areas where agricultural innovations occurred. *Adapted with permission from*: C. O. Sauer, *Agricultural Origins and Dispersals*. New York: American Geographical Society, 1952, p. 24.

TABLE 11.1

Chief Source Regions of Important Crop Plant Domestications.   *Adapted with permission from:* J. E. Spencer and W. L. Thomas, *Introducing Cultural Geography*, 1978, John Wiley & Sons, Inc.

A. Primary Regions of Domestications

1. The Upper Southeast Asian Mainlands

Citrus fruits*	Bamboos*	Yams*	Rices*	Eugenias*	Lichi	Teas	Ramie
Bananas*	Taros*	Cabbages*	Beans*	Job's tears	Longan	Tung oils	Water chestnut

2. Lower Southeast Asian Mainland and Malaysia (including New Guinea)

Citrus fruits*	Taros*	Pandanuses	Breadfruits	Lanzones	Vine peppers*	Nutmeg	Areca
Bananas*	Yams*	Cucumbers*	Jackfruits	Durian	Gingers*	Clove	Abaca
Bamboos*	Almonds*	Sugarcanes	Coconuts	Rambutan	Brinjals*	Cardamom	

3. Eastern India and Western Burma

Bananas*	Beans*	Millets*	Grams	Vine peppers*	Mangoes	Safflower	Lotus
Yams*	Rices*	Sorghums*	Eggplants	Gingers*	Kapok*	Jute	Turmeric
Taros*	Amaranths*	Peas*	Brinjals*	Palms*	Indigo	Sunn	Hemp

4. Southwestern Asia (Northwest India-Caucasus)

Soft wheats*	Peas*	Rye*	Beets*	Hemp	Soft Pears*	Pomegranates	Walnuts
Barleys*	Oil seeds*	Onions	Spinach	Apples	Cherries*	Grapes*	Melons
Lentils*	Poppies	Carrots*	Sesames	Almonds*	Plums*	Jujubes*	Tamarind
Beans*	Oats*	Turnips	Flax	Peaches*	Figs	Pistachio	Alfalfa

5. Ethiopian and East African Highlands

Hard wheats*	Sorghums*	Barleys	Beans*	Oil seeds*	Melons*	Coffees	Okras
Millets*	Rices*	Peas*	Vetches	Cucumbers*	Gourds*	Castor beans	Cottons*

6. Meso-American Region (Southern Mexico to Northern Venezuela)

Maizes	Taros*	Tomatoes*	Avocados	Muskmelons	Cottons*
Amaranths*	Sweet potatoes	Chili peppers	Sapotes	Palms*	Agaves
Beans*	Squashes	Custard apples	Plums*	Manioc	Kapok

B. Secondary Regions of Domestications

7. North-Central China (including the Central Asian corridor)

Millets*	Soybeans	Naked oat*	Mulberries	Bush cherries*	Peaches*
Barleys*	Cabbages*	Mustards	Persimmons	Hard pears*	Jujubes*
Buckwheats	Radishes*	Rhubarb	Plums*	Apricots	

8. Mediterranean Basin—Classical Near Eastern Fringe

Barleys*	Lentils*	Grapes*	Dates	Parsnips	Lettuces	Carrots*	Sugar beet
Oats*	Peas*	Olives	Carobs	Asparagus	Celeries	Garlic	Leek

9. Western Sudan Hill Lands and Their Margins

Sorghums*	Rices*	Yams*	Peas*	Melons*	Oil palms	Kola nut
Millets*	Fonio	Beans*	Oil seeds*	Gourds*	Tamarind*	

10. Andean Highlands and Their Margins

White potatoes	Tomatoes*	Beans*	Quinoa	Cubio	Ulluco
Pumpkins	Strawberries	Papayas	Oca	Arrocacha	

11. Eastern South America (centered on eastern Brazil)

Taros*	Peanuts	Cashew nut	Cacao	Cottons*
Beans*	Pineapples	Brazil nut	Passion fruits	Tobaccos

Source: J. E. Spencer and W. L. Thomas, *Introducing Cultural Geography*: 1978. Reproduced by permission from John Wiley & Sons.

*The asterisk indicates domestication of related species or hybridized development of new species during domestication in some other region or regions. Some of these secondary domestications were later than in the original region, but evidence of chronologic priority seldom is clear-cut.

The plural rendering of the crop name indicates that several different varieties/species either were involved in initial domestication or followed thereafter.

The term *oil seeds* indicates several varieties or species of small-seeded crop plants grown for the production of edible oils, without further breakdown.

In regions 2 and 3 the brinjals refer to the spicy members of the eggplant group used in curries, whereas in region 3 the eggplants refer to the sweet vegetable members.

None of the regional lists attempts as complete listing of all crop plants/species domesticated within the region.

The table has been compiled from a wide variety of sources.

and Idaho came originally from the Andean highlands, but was brought to Europe in the 1600s where it became a staple from Ireland to the eastern expanses of the North European Plain. The banana we associate with Mesoamerica came from Southeast Asia, as did a variety of yams. Diffusion of crops and seeds was greatly accelerated by worldwide trade and communications networks established with the development of mercantilism and European colonialism.

Domestication of Animals

Some scholars believe that animal domestication began earlier than plant cultivation, but others argue that animal domestication began as recently as 8000 years ago—well after crop agriculture. Whichever is the case, goats, pigs, and sheep became part of a rapidly growing array of domesticated animals, and in captivity they changed considerably from their wild state. As with the growing of root crops, the notion of **animal domestication** must have emerged over time, in stages.

The process of animal domestication began as people became more sedentary. People kept animals for ceremonial purposes as well as for pets or for other reasons. Quite possibly, animals attached themselves to human settlements as scavengers (foraging through garbage near human settlements) and even for protection against predators, thus reinforcing the idea that they might be tamed and kept. Orphaned young probably were adopted as pets; some wild animals were docile and easily penned up. Goats were domesticated in the Zagros Mountains (in the Fertile Crescent) as long as 10,000 years ago; sheep some 9500 years ago in Anatolia (Turkey); and pigs and cattle shortly thereafter. The advantages of animal domestication—their use as beasts of burden, as a source of meat, and as providers of milk—stimulated the rapid diffusion of this idea among interlinked places and gave the sedentary farmers of Southwest Asia and elsewhere a new measure of security.

Archaeological research indicates that when animals such as wild cattle are penned in a corral, they undergo physical changes over time. In a pen, animals are protected from predators, allowing the survival of animals that would have been killed in the wild. Our domestic versions of the goat, the pig, the cow, and the horse differ considerably from those first kept by our ancestors. In early animal domestication, people chose the more docile, often smaller animals to breed. Archaeologists discern the beginnings of animal domestication in a region by inspecting the bones of excavated animals. They look for places where bones get smaller over time, as this usually indicates early domestication.

As with plant domestication, archaeologists can use the combination of bone fragments and tools to identify general areas where the domestication of particular animals occurred. In Southwest Asia and adjacent parts of the Mediterranean Basin, people domesticated the goat, sheep, and camel. Southeast Asians domesticated several kinds of pigs, the water buffalo, chickens, and some water fowl (ducks, geese). In East India and West Burma (South Asia), people domesticated

cattle, which came to occupy an important place in the regional culture. In Central Asia, people domesticated the yak, horse, some species of goats, and sheep. In the Mesoamerica and the Andean Highlands, early Americans domesticated the llama and alpaca, along with a species of pig and the turkey.

Some species of animals may have been domesticated almost simultaneously in different places. The water buffalo, for example, was probably domesticated in both Southeast and South Asia during the same period. Camels were domesticated in both western and eastern ends of Southwest Asia. The pig was domesticated in numerous areas. Different species of cattle were domesticated in regions other than South Asia. Dogs and cats attached themselves to human settlements very early (they may have been the first animals to be domesticated) and in widely separated regions. Single, specific hearths can be pinpointed for only a few animals, including the llama and the alpaca, the yak, the turkey, and the reindeer.

Efforts to domesticate animals continue today. In East Africa, people are attempting to domesticate the eland, to serve as a source of meat in a region where a stable protein source is greatly needed. Several experimental stations in the savanna are trying to find ways to domesticate Africa's wildlife. They have had some success with a species of eland, but less so with various species of gazelles; they have been unable to domesticate the buffalo (Fig. 11.5). In fact, throughout the world only some 40 species of higher animals have ever been domesticated—and most of these were domesticated long ago. Jared Diamond, author of *Guns, Germs, and Steel*, explains that only five domesticated mammals are important throughout the world: the cow, sheep, goat, pig, and horse. According to Diamond, if we select only the big (over 100 pounds), herbivorous, terrestrial animals, we have 148 species that meet these criteria in the "wild." Only 14 of those 148 have been domesticated successfully, and each of these 14 was domesticated at least 4500 years ago. Modern attempts at animal domestication, even those driven by knowledgeable geneticists, have failed because of problems with the animal's diet, growth rate, breeding, disposition, or social structure.

Thus, the process of animal domestication, set in motion more than 8000 (and perhaps as long as 14,000) years ago, continues. The integrated use of domesticated plants and domesticated animals eased the work burden for early farmers. Animal waste fertilized crops, animals pulled plows, and crops fed animals. The first place where domesticated plants and animals were successfully integrated was Southwest Asia (the Fertile Crescent).

Subsistence Agriculture

Subsistence agriculture—growing only enough food to survive—was the norm throughout most of human history. Subsistence farmers often hold land in common. Surpluses are shared by all the members of the community, accumulation of personal wealth is restricted, and individual advancement at the cost of the group as a whole is limited. Subsistence agriculture declined during the 1900s with the diffusion of

FIELD NOTE

"Attempts to tame wildlife started in ancient times, and still continue. At Hunter's Lodge on the Nairobi-Mombasa road, we met an agricultural officer who reported that an animal domestication experiment station was located not far into the bush, about 10 miles south. On his invitation, we spent the next day observing this work. In some herds, domestic animals (goats) were combined with wild gazelles, all penned together in a large enclosure. This was not working well; all day the gazelles sought to escape. By comparison, these eland were docile, manageable, and in good health. Importantly, they also were reproducing in captivity. Here, our host describes the program."

© H. J. de Blij

■ Figure 11.5
Nairobi, Kenya.

industrialized agriculture and the goal of constantly increasing production both to feed growing populations and to sell more agricultural goods. The United States and other industrialized countries sought to move farmers "beyond" subsistence into industrialized production as part of development programs begun in the 1960s (see Chapter 10).

A return to subsistence agriculture has taken hold in parts of the world where farmers feel production for the global market has not benefited them either financially or culturally. For example, indigenous people in the southern Mexican states of Oaxaca, Chiapas, and Guerrero have largely returned to subsistence agriculture. *The Nation* reported in 2010 that Zapatista farmers have "in effect chosen to withdraw from the national economy, some weaning themselves off expensive chemical fertilizers and subsisting on corn they can grow, harvest, and barter."

Some subsistence farmers are sedentary, living in one place throughout the year, but many others move from place to place in search of better land. The latter engage in a form of agriculture known as **shifting cultivation**. This type of agriculture is found primarily in tropical and subtropical zones, where traditional farmers had to abandon plots of land after the soil became infertile. Once stripped of their natural vegetative cover and deprived of the constant input of nutrients from decaying vegetative matter on the forest floor, soils in these regions can quickly lose their nutrients as rainwater leaches out organic matter. Faced with these circumstances, farmers move to another parcel of land, clear the vegetation, turn the soil, and try again. Shifting cultivation gave ancient farmers opportunities to experiment with various plants, to learn the effects of weeding and crop care, to cope with environmental vagaries, and to discern the decreased fertility of soil after sustained farming.

With shifting cultivation, parcels of land are worked successively. The farmers first clear vegetation from a parcel of land. Next they plant crops that are native to the region: tubers in the humid, warm tropical areas; grains in the more humid subtropics; and vegetables and fruits in cooler zones. When the village grows too large and the distance to usable land becomes too great, part of the village's population may establish a new settlement some distance away. Population densities in areas of shifting agriculture cannot be very high; therefore, shifting cultivation continues only in areas where population densities are low.

One specific kind of shifting cultivation is **slash-and-burn agriculture** (also called swidden, milpa, or patch agriculture), reflecting the central role of the controlled use of fire in places where this technique is used. Trees are cut down and all existing vegetation is burned off. In slash-and-burn, farmers use tools (machetes and knives) to slash down trees and tall vegetation, and then burn the vegetation on the ground. A layer of ash from the fire settles on the ground and contributes to the soil's fertility.

As we discuss in the next section, agriculture has fundamentally changed since shifting cultivation was the global norm, but hundreds of millions of farmers continue to practice some form of subsistence agriculture.

thinking
geographically

Settling down in one place, a growing population, and the switch to agriculture are interrelated occurrences in human history. Hypothesize which of these three happened first, second, and third, and explain why.

HOW DID AGRICULTURE CHANGE WITH INDUSTRIALIZATION?

For the Industrial Revolution (see Chapter 12) to take root, a **Second Agricultural Revolution** had to take place—one that would move agriculture beyond subsistence to generate the kinds of surpluses needed to feed thousands of people working in factories instead of in agricultural fields. Like the Industrial Revolution, the Second Agricultural Revolution was composed of a series of innovations, improvements, and techniques, in this case initially in Great Britain, the Netherlands, Denmark, and other neighboring countries.

By the seventeenth and eighteenth centuries, European farming underwent significant changes. New crops came into Europe from trade with the Americas, including corn and potatoes. Many of the new crops were well suited for the climate and soils of western Europe, bringing new lands (previously defined as marginal) into cultivation.

The governments of Europe helped create the conditions necessary for the Second Agricultural Revolution by passing laws such as Great Britain's Enclosure Act, which encouraged consolidation of fields into large, single-owner holdings. Farmers increased the size of their farms, pieced together more contiguous parcels of land, fenced in their land, and instituted field rotation. Methods of soil preparation, fertilization, crop care, and harvesting improved.

New technologies improved production as well. The seed drill enabled farmers to avoid wasting seeds and to plant in rows, making it simpler to distinguish weeds from crops.

By the 1830s, farmers were using new fertilizers on crops and feeding artificial feeds to livestock. Increased agricultural output made it possible to feed much larger urban populations, enabling the growth of a secondary (industrial) economy. In 1831, Cyrus McCormick, a farmer in Lexington, Virginia, perfected his father's design for a mechanical reaper (Fig. 11.6). At the time, farmers were limited in their production not by what they could sow (plant), but what they could reap (harvest) because harvesting required much more time and labor than planting. Harvesting involved laborers cutting grain with a scythe followed by more laborers who bundled the grain into bales. McCormick's mechanical reaper, which was pulled by horses, both cut and bundled grain. His invention diffused quickly during the 1840s, reportedly increasing yields of individual farmers by at least ten times. McCormick's company eventually became International Harvester and now Case IH, one of the largest agriculture implement companies in the world today.

Advances in breeding livestock enabled farmers to develop new breeds that were either strong milk producers or good for beef. The most common breeds of dairy cattle found in North America today trace their lineage back to the Second Agricultural Revolution in Europe. In the 1700s and 1800s, European farmers bred dairy cattle to adapt to different climates and topography. For example, the black and white Holstein dairy cow came from the Netherlands and is well suited to graze on grass and produce high quantities of milk. Scottish farmers bred the red and white Ayrshire breed of dairy cattle to produce milk well suited for butter and cheese and to forage for food in rough, rocky topography.

Innovations in machinery that occurred with the Industrial Revolution in the late 1800s and early 1900s helped sustain the Second Agricultural Revolution. The railroad helped move agriculture into new regions, such as the United States' Great Plains. Geographer John Hudson traced the major role railroads and agriculture played in changing the landscape of that region from open prairie to individual farmsteads. The railroad companies advertised in Europe to attract immigrants to the Great Plains region, and the railroads took the new migrants to their new towns, where they transformed lands from prairie grass to agricultural fields. Later, the internal combustible engine made possible the invention of tractors, combines, and a multitude of large farm equipment. New

■ **Figure 11.6**
Midwest, United States. Pioneers in 1870 used the mechanical reaper designed by Cyrus McCormick to cut and bundle grain on the prairie. Pulled by horses, the mechanical reaper sped up harvesting and diffused around the world.

banking and lending practices helped farmers afford the new equipment.

Understanding the Spatial Layout of Agriculture

When commercial agriculture is geared to producing food for people who live in a nearby town or city, a geographical pattern of land use based on the "perishability" of products and cost of transportation often emerges. In the 1800s, Johann Heinrich von Thünen (1783–1850) experienced the Second Agricultural Revolution firsthand: He farmed an estate not far from the town of Rostock, in northeast Germany. Studying the spatial patterns of land use around towns such as Rostock, von Thünen noted that as one moved away from the town, one commodity or crop gave way to another. He also noted that this process occurred without any visible change in soil, climate, or terrain. When he mapped this pattern, he found that each town or market center was surrounded by a set of more-or-less concentric rings within which particular commodities or crops dominated.

Nearest the town, farmers generally produced commodities that were perishable and commanded high prices, such as dairy products and strawberries. In this zone, much effort would go into production in part because of the value of the land closer to the city. In von Thünen's time, the town was still surrounded by a belt of forest that provided wood for fuel and building; but immediately beyond the forest the ring-like pattern of agriculture continued. In the next ring, crops were less perishable and bulkier, including wheat and other grains. Still farther out, livestock raising began to replace field crops.

Von Thünen used these observations to build a model of the spatial distribution of agricultural activities around settlements (Fig. 11.7). As with all models, he had to make certain assumptions. For example, he assumed that the terrain was flat, that soils and other environmental conditions were the same everywhere, and that there were no barriers to transportation to market. Under such circumstances, he reasoned, transport costs would govern the use of land. He reasoned that as distance to market increased, the higher transport costs had to be added to the cost of producing a crop or commodity.

The **Von Thünen model** (including the ring of forest) is often described as the first effort to analyze the spatial character of economic activity. The Thünian patterns discerned in many parts of the world are not solely the result of the forces modeled by von Thünen. Differences in climate type and soil quality weigh heavily in the kinds of goods produced in a place. Yet if you drive east out of Denver, heading for Nebraska, you cannot miss a certain zonation that puts dairying and market gardening nearest the city, cash grains such as corn (plus soybeans) in the next zone, more extensive grain farming and livestock raising beyond, and cattle ranching in the outermost zone.

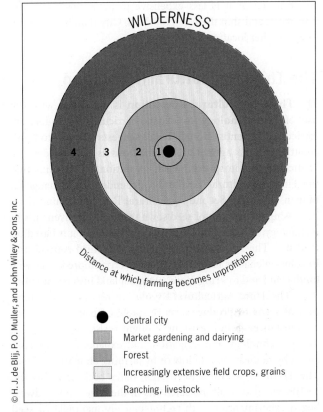

© H. J. de Blij, P. O. Muller, and John Wiley & Sons, Inc.

■■ **Figure 11.7**
Von Thünen's Model. The key influence on land use in the Von Thünen model is the cost of transporting goods to market.

Geographer Lee Liu studied the spatial pattern of agricultural production in one province of China, giving careful consideration to the intensity of the production methods and the amount of land degradation. Liu found that the farmers living in a village would farm lands close to the village as well as lands far away from the village with high levels of intensity. However, the methods used varied spatially, resulting in land improvements close to the village and land degradation farther from the village. In lands close to the village, farmers improved lands through "decades of intensive care," in particular putting organic material onto the fields, which made the grasslands close to the village "fertile and productive." In lands more remote from the village, farmers tended to use more "chemical fertilizer, pesticides, and herbicides" and fewer conservation tactics, resulting in land degradation whereby "the originally fertile remote land became degraded." Liu argued that this pattern in modern China occurs in large part because farmers live in the village, not in the remote fields, and therefore put most of their time and energy into the fields closest to their places of residence.

Even when agricultural production does not conform to the concentric rings of von Thünen's model, his underlying concern with the interplay of land use and transportation costs still explains many agricultural patterns. The fresh flowers grown in the Caribbean for sale in New York City could be viewed as the application of the von Thünen model on a larger scale, for it is less expensive to grow flowers in the Caribbean and ship them to New York City than it is to grow them in other locations.

The Third Agricultural Revolution

The **Third Agricultural Revolution** is associated with the use of **biotechnology** to expand agricultural production. Agricultural scientist Donald Baker suggests one way to think about the three agricultural revolutions is to consider the "critical factor" in spurring each revolution. He explains that the First Agricultural Revolution depended on a change in human effort, the Second Agricultural Revolution hinged on increasing the amount of seed sown through improvements in technology, and the Third Agricultural Revolution is based on land use. The science that went into the Third Agricultural Revolution enables farmers to produce crops more intensively on the land and to bring more, marginal land into production.

The Third Agricultural Revolution relies on hybridization of seeds to produce a more stable crop in a variety of circumstances (wind resistant, drought resistant), intensified use of technology and irrigation, and expanded use of land either by not leaving it fallow or by farming on marginal land. The Third Agricultural Revolution dates back as far as the 1930s, when agricultural scientists in the American Midwest began experimenting with technologically manipulated seed varieties to increase crop yields. In the 1940s, American philanthropists funded research on maize (corn) production in Mexico, trying to find a hybrid seed that would grow better. They did, and by 1960 Mexico was no longer importing corn because production within the country was high enough to meet demand. In the 1960s, the focal point of the Third Agricultural Revolution shifted to India, when scientists at a research institution in the Philippines crossed a dwarf Chinese variety of rice with an Indonesian variety and produced IR8. This new rice plant had a number of desirable properties: It developed a bigger head of grain, and it had a stronger stem that did not collapse under the added weight of the bigger head. IR8 produced much better yields than either of its parents—giving rise to the **Green Revolution**.

The term *Green Revolution* refers the use of biotechnology to create disease-resistant, fast growing hybrid seeds—particularly of staple crops such as rice and wheat. The impact of the Green Revolution in India and other developing countries was so great that the term is often used as a synonym for the Third Agricultural Revolution. Building on the success of IR8, in 1982 scientists produced IR36, bred from 13 parents to achieve genetic resistance against 15 pests and a growing cycle of 110 days under warm conditions, thus making possible three crops per year in some places. By 1992, IR36 was the most widely grown crop on Earth, and in September 1994, scientists developed a strain of rice that was even more productive than IR36. The Green Revolution also brought new high-yield varieties of wheat and corn from the United States to other parts of the world, particularly South and Southeast Asia.

The increased yields of the Green Revolution came at a time of increased concern about global hunger and thus attracted enormous attention. In subsequent decades, most famines resulted from political instability rather than failure in production. India became self-sufficient in grain production by the 1980s, and Asia as a whole saw a two-thirds increase in rice production between 1970 and 1995. These drastic increases in production stemmed not only from new seed varieties but also from the use of fertilizers, pesticides, irrigation, and significant capital improvements.

The geographical impact of the Green Revolution is highly variable, however. Its traditional focus on rice, wheat, and corn means that it has had only limited impact throughout much of Africa, where agriculture is based on different crops and where lower soil fertility makes agriculture less attractive to foreign investment. But innovations are continually being developed. Research has already led to methods for producing high-yield cassava and sorghum—both of which are grown in Africa. Beyond Africa, research on fattening livestock faster and improving the appearance of fruits is having an impact in North and South America.

The promise of increasing food production in a world in which almost a billion people are malnourished has led many people to view the Green Revolution in distinctly positive terms. Others, however, worry about associated social changes, health risks, and environmental hazards. The large-scale monocropping that is often part of Green Revolution agriculture can make farms vulnerable to changes in climate or the infestation of particular pests. Higher inputs of chemical fertilizers, herbicides, and pesticides that go along with Green Revolution agriculture can lead to reduced organic matter in the soil and to groundwater pollution. Moreover, the Green Revolution has worked against the interest of many small-scale farmers who lack the resources to acquire genetically enhanced seeds and the necessary chemical inputs to grow them. One particularly vocal opponent of the Green Revolution in India, Vandana Shiva, argues that

> [T]he Green Revolution has been a failure. It has led to reduced genetic diversity, increased vulnerability to pests, soil erosion, water shortages, reduced soil fertility, micronutrient deficiencies, soil contamination, reduced availability of nutritious food crops for the local population, the displacement of vast numbers of small farmers from their land, rural impoverishment and increased tensions and conflicts. The beneficiaries have been the agrochemical industry, large petrochemical companies, manufacturers of agricultural machinery, dam builders and large landowners.

It is no easy matter to weigh the enormous increases in food production that have occurred in places that have adopted Green Revolution approaches against the types of social and environmental issues highlighted by Shiva.

A 2005 report in *Scientific American* contends that many small farmers have not benefited from the Green Revolution: "The supply-driven strategies of the Green Revolution, however, may not help subsistence farmers, who must play to their strengths to compete in the global marketplace. The average size of a family farm is less than four acres in India, 1.8 acres in Bangladesh and about half an acre in China." Smaller farmers are in a poor competitive position, and their position is further undermined by the fact that a few large corporations with the seed patents for biotechnologically altered grains and a virtual monopoly of the needed chemical inputs can have tremendous power over the agricultural production process. In addition, the need for capital from the West to implement Green Revolution technologies has led to a shift away from production for local consumers toward export agriculture. In the process, local places become subject to the vicissitudes of the global economy, where a downward fluctuation in the price of a given crop can create enormous problems for places dependent on the sale of that crop.

Researchers at the International Rice Research Institute, with help from an $18 billion grant from the Bill and Melinda Gates Foundation, bred a genetically modified "Green Super Rice" that will not have to be transplanted as seedlings but can be seeded directly in the paddy soil. It may yield nearly twice as much rice per acre than the average for strains in current use. The charting of the genome of rice (the 12 chromosomes that carry all of the plant's characteristics) may make it possible to transform rice genetically so that it will continuously acquire more new properties that could make it resistant to a wider spectrum of diseases and pests. The variety is going through its last testing phases and will be available to African and Asian farmers in 2015.

New Genetically Modified Foods

Social scientists are now trying to differentiate the Green Revolution, which is largely based on hybridization of cereal crops, from the biotechnology revolution now underway. Agricultural scientists are now altering the chemical makeup of crops and modifying the genes of plants (genetically modified organisms, GMOs) to create new crops through biotechnology. A few researchers are calling the agricultural revolution in biotechnology a fourth revolution. Agricultural scientist Donald Baker suggests the critical factor in this revolution may be yield per dollar—as farms work directly with giant agribusinesses to produce as much food as possible for each dollar spent.

An entire field of biotechnology has sprung up in the wake of the Third Agricultural Revolution, and the development of genetically engineered crops (GE) or **genetically modified organisms (GMOs)** is its principal target. Since the origin of agriculture, people have experimented with hybrid crops and cross-breeding of animals. What is different today is that genetic modification involves splicing together genes from different species (e.g., tomatoes and salmon) to achieve a particular end. Genetically modified corn has been grown in substantial quantities in the United States for decades. The turn toward other types of GMOs has accelerated over the past 20 years. According to the Grocery

Manufacturers of America, GMOs are now found in 60 to 70 percent of all processed foods in the United States. The United States leads the world in the production of genetically engineered crops, with 88 percent of all acres in corn (up from 25 percent in 2000) and 93 percent of all acres in soybeans (up from 54 percent in 2000) sown with genetically engineered seeds.

A major debate has developed around GMOs. Proponents argue that GMOs can help feed an expanding world population and that hard evidence of negative consequences to their use is lacking. Opponents contend that GMO companies are releasing organisms into the environment without adequate understanding of their environmental, health, or socioeconomic consequences. A particular concern is the impact of pollen dispersal from GMOs on other organisms and the potential for disease-resistant plants to spur the evolution of super-pests.

Some regions have embraced genetically engineered crops, whereas others have banned them. The United States has largely been in the former camp, though there is a growing movement to require labeling of products containing GMOs. In contrast, ideological resistance to genetically engineered foods is strong in western Europe. Agricultural officials in most west European countries have declared GMOs to be safe, but labeling is required and there is strong public reaction against GMOs based on combined concerns about health and taste. Such concerns have spread to less affluent parts of the world as well. In many poorer regions, seeds are a cultural commodity, reflecting agricultural lessons learned over generations. In these regions, many resist the invasion of foreign, genetically engineered crops. But in their search for new markets, major GMO companies are promoting their products in the global periphery and semiperiphery. Many regions there do not have access to the necessary capital and technology to move forward, but the stage is set for growing conflict over GMOs.

Regional and Local Change

Recent shifts from subsistence agriculture to commercial agriculture have had dramatic impacts on rural life. Land-use patterns, land ownership arrangements, and agricultural labor conditions have all changed as rural residents cope with shifting economic, political, and environmental conditions. In Latin America, dramatic increases in the production of export crops (or *cash crops* such as fruits and coffee) have occurred at the expense of crop production for local consumption. In the process, subsistence farming has been pushed to ever more marginal lands. In Asia, where the Green Revolution has had the greatest impact, the production of cereal crops (grains such as rice and wheat) has increased for both foreign and domestic markets. In Subsaharan Africa, total commercialized agriculture has increased, but African farms have remained relatively small and dependent on intensified manual labor.

GUEST FIELD NOTE

Gambia

I am interested in women and rural development in Subsaharan Africa. In 1983, I went to Gambia to study an irrigated rice project that was being implemented to improve the availability of rice, the dietary staple. What grabbed my attention? The donors' assurance that the project would benefit women, the country's traditional rice growers. Imagine my surprise a few months after project implementation when I encountered hundreds of angry women refusing to work because they received nothing for their labor from the first harvest.

In registering women's traditional rice plots as "family" land, project officials effectively sabotaged the equity objectives of the donors. Control now was concentrated under male heads of household who reaped the income produced by female labor. Contemporary economic strategies for Africa depend increasingly upon labor intensification. But whose labor? Human geography provides a way of seeing the significance of gender in the power relations

■ **Figure 11.8**
Gambia.

that mediate culture, environment, and economic development.

Credit: Judith Carney, University of California, Los Angeles.

What this regional-scale analysis does not tell us is how these changes have affected rural communities. These changes can be environmental, economic, and social. A recent study in the small country of Gambia (West Africa) by Judith Carney has shown how changing agricultural practices have altered not only the rural environment and economy, but also relations between men and women (Fig. 11.8). Over the last 30 years, international developmental assistance to Gambia has led to ambitious projects designed to convert wetlands to irrigated agricultural lands, making possible production of rice year-round. By the late 1980s, virtually all of the country's suitable wetlands had been converted to year-round rice production. This transformation created tensions within rural households by converting lands women traditionally used for family subsistence into commercialized farming plots. In addition, when rice production was turned into a year-round occupation, women found themselves with less time for other activities crucial for household maintenance.

This situation underscores the fact that in Africa, as in much of the rest of the less industrialized world, agricultural work is overwhelmingly carried out by women. In Subsaharan Africa and South Asia, 60 percent of all employed females work in the agriculture sector. A geographical perspective helps to shed light on how changes in agricultural practices throughout the world not only alter rural landscapes but also affect family and community relationships.

The Impacts of Agricultural Modernization on Earlier Practices

In the modern world, hunter-gatherers live in the context of a globalized economy and experience pressures to change their livelihoods. In many cases, the state places pressures on hunter-gatherers to settle in one place and farm. Cyclical migration by hunter-gatherers does not mesh well with bounded, territorial states. Some nongovernmental organizations encourage settlement by digging wells or building medical buildings, permanent houses, or schools for hunter-gatherers. Even hunter-gatherers who continue to use their knowledge of seeds, roots, fruits, berries, insects, and animals to gather and trap the goods they need for survival do so in the context of a highly interconnected economic world.

Unlike hunting and gathering, subsistence farming continues to be a relatively common practice in Africa, Middle America, tropical South America, and parts of Southeast Asia (Fig. 11.9). The system of cultivation has changed little over thousands of years. The term *subsistence* can be used in the strictest sense of the word—to refer to farmers who grow food only to sustain themselves and their families, who find building materials and firewood in the natural environment, and who do not enter into the cash economy at all. This definition fits farmers in remote areas of South and Middle America, Africa, and South and Southeast Asia. Yet many farm

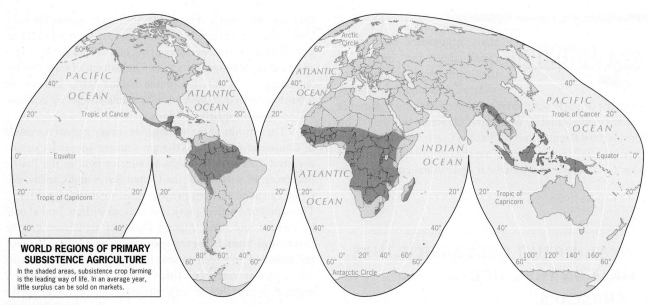

WORLD REGIONS OF PRIMARY SUBSISTENCE AGRICULTURE

In the shaded areas, subsistence crop farming is the leading way of life. In an average year, little surplus can be sold on markets.

■ **Figure 11.9**

World Regions of Primarily Subsistence Agriculture.   Definitions of subsistence farming vary. On this map, India and China are not shaded because farmers sell some produce at markets; in Equatorial Africa and South America, subsistence farming allows little excess, and thus little produce is sold at markets.   © E. H. Fouberg, A. B. Murphy, H. J. de Blij, and John Wiley & Sons, Inc.

families living at the subsistence level periodically sell a small quantity of produce (perhaps to pay taxes). They are not subsistence farmers in the strict sense, but the term *subsistence* is surely applicable to societies where farmers with small plots sometimes sell a few pounds of grain on the market but where poverty, indebtedness, and tenancy are ways of life. For the indigenous peoples of the Amazon Basin, the sedentary farmers of Africa's savanna areas, villagers in much of India, and peasants in Indonesia, subsistence is not only a way of life but a state of mind. Experience has taught farmers and their families that subsistence farming is often precarious and that times of comparative plenty will be followed by times of scarcity.

Subsistence farming has been in retreat for centuries. From 1500 to 1950, European powers sought to "modernize" the economies of their colonies by ending subsistence farming and integrating farmers into colonial systems of production and exchange. Sometimes their methods were harsh: By demanding that farmers pay some taxes, they forced subsistence farmers to begin selling some of their produce to raise the necessary cash. They also compelled many subsistence farmers to devote some land to a crop to be sold on the world market such as cotton, thus bringing them into the commercial economy. The colonial powers encouraged commercial farming by conducting soil surveys, building irrigation systems, and establishing lending agencies that provided loans to farmers. The colonial powers sought to make profits, yet it was difficult to squeeze very much from subsistence-farming areas. Forced cropping schemes were designed to solve this problem. If farmers in a subsistence area cultivated a certain acreage of, say, corn, they were required to grow a

specified acreage of a cash crop as well. Whether this crop would be grown on old land that was formerly used for grain or on newly cleared land was the farmers' decision. If no new lands were available, the farmers would have to give up food crops for the compulsory cash crops. In many areas, severe famines resulted and local economies were disrupted.

Subsistence land use continues to give way to more intensive farming and cash cropping—even to mechanized farming in which equipment does much of the actual work. In the process, societies from South America to Southeast Asia are being profoundly affected. Land that was once held communally is being parceled out to individuals for cash cropping. In the process, small landowners are often squeezed out, leaving the land in the hands of wealthier farmers and the owners of commercialized farming operations.

For too long, the question has been how "to tempt [subsistence farmers] into wanting cash by the availability of suitable consumer goods," as A. N. Duckham and G. B. Masefield wrote in *Farming Systems of the World* in 1970. In the interests of "progress" and "modernization," subsistence farmers were pushed away from their traditional modes of livelihood even though many aspects of subsistence farming may be worth preserving. Regions with shifting cultivation do not have neat rows of plants, carefully turned soil, or precisely laid-out fields. Yet shifting cultivation conserves both forest and soil; its harvests are often substantial given environmental limitations; and it requires better organization than one might assume. It also requires substantially less energy than more modern techniques of farming. It is no surprise, then, that shifting cultivation and specifically slash-and-burn agriculture have been a sustained method of farming for thousands of years.

Many arguments have been raised about the impacts of the Green Revolution, both pro and con. How might the scale at which the Green Revolution is examined affect the arguments that are made about it? What types of factors are likely to be considered if the question is, "has the Green Revolution been good for Asia?" as opposed to "has the Green Revolution been good for a village or a particular agricultural community in India?"

WHAT IMPRINT DOES AGRICULTURE MAKE ON THE CULTURAL LANDSCAPE?

Flying from the West Coast of the United States to the East Coast, if you have a window seat you will see the major imprint agriculture makes on the cultural landscape. The green circles standing out in the grain belts of the country are places where center-pivot irrigation systems circle around a pivot, providing irrigation to a circle of crops. The checkerboard pattern on the landscape reflects the pattern of land survey system and land ownership in much of the country.

The pattern of land ownership seen in the landscape reflects the cadastral system—the method of land survey through which land ownership and property lines are defined. Cadastral systems were adopted in places where settlement could be regulated by law, and land surveys were crucial to their implementation. The prevailing survey system throughout much of the United States, the one that appears as checkerboards across agricultural fields, is the **rectangular survey system**. The U.S. government adopted the rectangular survey system after the American Revolution as part of a cadastral system known as the **township-and-range system**. Designed to facilitate the settlement of non-Indians in the farmlands of the interior of the United States, the system imposed a rigid grid-like pattern on the land (Fig. 11.10). The basic unit was the 1 square mile *section*—and land was bought and sold in whole, half, or quarter sections. The section's lines were drawn without reference to the terrain, and

they thus imposed a remarkable uniformity across the land. Under the Homestead Act, a homesteader received one section of land (160 acres) after living on the land for five years and making improvements to it. The pattern of farms on the landscape in the interior of the United States reflects the township-and-range system, with farms spaced by sections, half sections, or quarter sections.

The imprint of the rectangular survey system is evident in Canada as well, where the government adopted a similar cadastral system as it sought to allocate land in the Prairie Provinces. In portions of the United States and Canada, different cadastral patterns predominate, however (Fig. 11.11). These patterns reflect particular notions of how land should be divided and used. Among the most significant are the **metes-and-bounds survey** approach adopted along the eastern seaboard, in which natural features were used to demarcate irregular parcels of land. One of the most distinctive regional approaches to land division can be found in the Canadian Maritimes and in parts of Quebec, Louisiana, and Texas, where a **long-lot survey system** was implemented. This system divided land into narrow parcels stretching back from rivers, roads, or canals. It reflects a particular approach to surveying that was common in French America.

Many parts of the world do not have cadastral systems, so field patterns are irregular. But whether regular or irregular, societies with property ownership have parcels of land divided into neat, clearly demarcated segments. The size and order of those parcels are heavily influenced not just by land partition schemes, but also by rules about property inheritance. In systems where one child inherits all of the land—such as those associated with the traditional Germanic

■ Figure 11.10

Willamette Valley, Oregon.   The township-and-range system has left its imprint on the landscape near Eugene, Oregon, where the grid pattern of six-mile-by-six-mile townships and the sections of one square mile each are marked by property lines and roads.

© Alexander B. Murphy

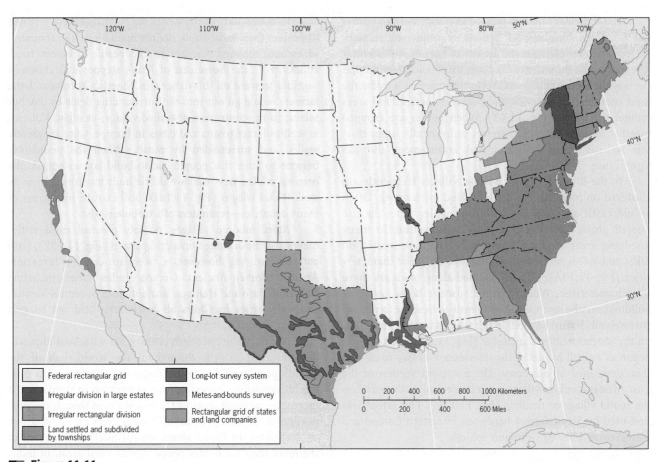

◼ Figure 11.11
Dominant Land Survey Patterns in the United States.   *Data from*: Edward Price, Dividing the Land: *Early American Beginnings of Our Private Property Mosaic. Chicago*: University of Chicago Press, 1995, p. 8 and several other sources.

practice of **primogeniture**, in which all land passes to the eldest son—parcels tend to be larger and farmers work a single plot of land. This is the norm in Northern Europe and in the principal areas of Northern European colonization— the Americas, South Africa, Australia, and New Zealand.

In areas where land is divided among heirs, however, considerable fragmentation can occur over time. The latter is the norm throughout much of Asia, Africa, and Southern Europe, as well as most of the allotted Indian reservations in the United States. Therefore, farmers living in villages in these areas tend a variety of scattered small plots of land. In some places, land reform initiatives have consolidated land-holdings to some degree, but fragmentation is still common in many parts of the world.

Villages

Throughout this book we take note of various core–periphery contrasts which our world presents. Such contrasts are prominent in rural as well as urban areas. Traditional farm–village life is still common in India, Subsaharan Africa, China, and Southeast Asia. In India, farming, much of it subsistence farming, still occupies over 60 percent of the population. As

we have seen, however, in the world's core areas agriculture has taken on a very different form, and true farm villages, in which farming or providing services for farmers are the dominant activities, are disappearing. In the United States, where farming once was the leading economic activity, only some 2 percent of the labor force remains engaged in agriculture, and the population of most rural villages and towns is a mix of farmers and people who commute to work in urban areas.

Traditionally, the people who lived in villages either farmed the surrounding land or provided services to those who did the farming. Thus, they were closely connected to the land, and most of their livelihoods depended, directly or indirectly, on the cultivation of nearby farmland. As such, they tended to reflect historical and environmental conditions. Houses in Japanese farming villages, for example, are so tightly packed together that only the narrowest passageways remain between them. This village form reflects the pressure to allocate every possible square foot of land to farming; villages must not use land where crops could grow.

Unlike Japan, in the United States Midwest individual farm houses lie quite far apart in what we call a *dispersed settlement* pattern; the land is intensively cultivated but by machine rather than by hand. In the populous Indonesian island of Java, villages are located every half mile or so along a rural road, and settlement there is defined as nucleated. Land use is just as intense, but the work is done by people and animals. Hence, when we consider the density of human settlement as it relates to the intensity of land use, we should keep in mind the way the land is cultivated. *Nucleated settlement* is by far the most prevalent rural residential pattern in agricultural areas around the world (Fig. 11.12). When houses are grouped together in tiny clusters or hamlets, or in slightly larger clusters we call villages, their spatial arrangement also has significance.

In the hilly regions of Europe, villages frequently are clustered on hills, leaving the level land for farming. Often an old castle sits atop the hill, so in earlier times the site offered protection as well as land conservation. In many low-lying areas of western Europe, villages are located on dikes and levees, so that they often take on linear characteristics (Fig. 11.13A). Villages oriented along roads also have this characteristic. Where there is space, a house and outbuildings may be surrounded by a small garden; the farms and pasturelands lie just beyond. In other cases, a village may take on the characteristics of a cluster (Fig. 11.13B). It may have begun as a small hamlet at the intersection of two roads and then developed by accretion. The European version of the East African circular village, with its central cattle corral, is the round village or *rundling* (Fig. 11.13C). This layout was first used by Slavic farmer-herdsmen in eastern Europe and was later modified by Germanic settlers.

In many parts of the world, farm villages were fortified to protect their inhabitants against marauders. Ten thousand years ago, the first farmers in the Fertile Crescent faced attacks from the horsemen of Asia's steppes and clustered together to ward off this danger. In Nigeria's Yorubaland, the farmers would go out into the surrounding fields by day but retreat to the protection of walled villages at night. Villages, as well as larger towns and cities in Europe, were frequently walled and surrounded by moats. When the population became so large that people had to build houses outside the original wall, a new wall would be built to protect them as well. *Walled villages* (Fig. 11.13D) still exist in rural areas of many countries—reminders of a turbulent past.

More modern villages, notably planned rural settlements, may be arranged on a grid pattern (Fig. 11.13E). Grid patterns are not, however, a twentieth-century invention. Ancient Rome, Ancient Greece, Indus cities including Mohenjo-Daro and Harappa, ancient cities in central Mexico, and early cities in China all had streets laid out in grid patterns.

Although the twentieth century has witnessed unprecedented urban growth throughout the world, half of the world's people still reside in villages and rural areas. As total world population increases, total population in rural areas is increasing in many parts of the world (even though the proportion of the total population in rural areas may be stagnant or declining). In China alone, approximately 50 percent of the more than 1.3 billion people live in rural areas. In India, with a population of over 1 billion, between 60 and 70 percent of the people live in places the government defines as nonurban. Small rural settlements are home to most of the inhabitants of Indonesia, Bangladesh, Pakistan, and other countries of the global economic periphery, including those in Africa. The agrarian village remains one of the most common forms of settlement on Earth.

In some places, rural villages have changed as the global economy has changed. For example, Mexico has experienced rapid economic change since passage of the North American Free Trade Act (NAFTA) in 1992. Along with major shifts in industrial production (see Chapter 12), major changes in agricultural production and village life have occurred in Mexico. Before the passage of NAFTA, the Mexican government protected corn production

© Barbara A. Weightman

■■ **Figure 11.12**

Aquitaine, France. The agricultural landscape of Aquitaine demonstrates three features of rural France: people living in nucleated villages, a highly fragmented land ownership pattern, and land divided according to the French long-lot system.

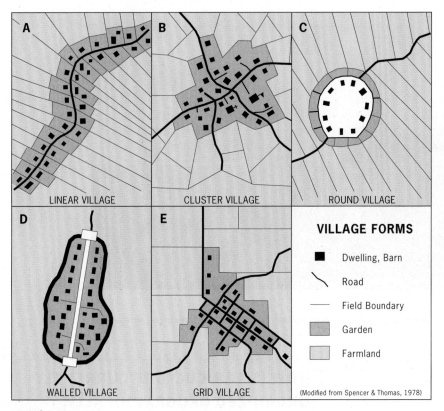

Figure 11.13

Village Forms. Five different representative nucleated village layouts are shown here. *Adapted with permission from*: J. E. Spencer and W. H. Thomas, *Introducing Cultural Geography*. New York: John Wiley & Sons, Inc., 1978, p. 154.

Functional Differentiation Within Villages

Villages everywhere display certain common qualities, including evidence of social stratification and differentiation of buildings. The range in size and quality of houses, representing their owners' wealth and standing in the community, reflects social stratification. Material well-being is the chief determinant of stratification in Western commercial agricultural regions, where it translates into more elaborate homes. In Africa, as in most other places, a higher social position in the community is associated with a more impressive house. The house of the chief or headman may not only be more elaborate than others but may also be in a more prominent location. In India, caste still strongly influences daily life, including village housing; the manors of landlords, often comprising large walled compounds, stand in striking contrast to the modest houses of domestic servants, farm workers, carpenters, and craftspeople. The poorest people of the lowest castes live in small one-room, wattle-and-thatch dwellings. In Cambodia, the buildings in stilt villages built throughout the Mekong Basin look similar (Fig. 11.14).

because white corn is a staple crop used to make tortillas, a principal component of the Mexican diet. Through protection, Mexico's corn prices were higher than those in the United States. With the passage of NAFTA, Mexico entered a 15-year transition away from protecting its corn production. Economists believed the price of corn in Mexico would fall and in turn Mexicans would produce less corn.

What happened instead is that corn prices in Mexico fluctuated over time, tortilla prices rose, and then production of corn in Mexico increased. Tortilla prices rose in response to higher prices for corn in the United States as a result of corn being used for fuel. Mexican farmers increased corn production both because of a higher demand for corn in the United States and Mexico and also because indigenous farmers in the south switched to subsistence farming of corn to provide for their families and to remove themselves from the fluctuating global agriculture market and the uncertainties of NAFTA.

© Alexander B. Murphy

Figure 11.14

Siem Reap, Cambodia. A stilt village along the shores of Tonle Sap, the largest lake in Cambodia. The houses in this village in the Cambodian countryside are designed on stilts or floats to handle seasonal changes in water levels in the Tonle Sap Lake. In the dry fall and winter, the lake reduces in size and the stilts of the houses are exposed. In the wet spring and summer, the lake swells and inundates the village, covering the stilts with water.

© Erin H. Fouberg

■■ **Figure 11.15**
Winthrop, Minnesota.   The modern American farm typically has a two-story farm house surrounded by several outbuildings.

The functional differentiation of buildings within farm villages (like the functional zonation of cities whereby different areas of the village play different roles and function differently) is more elaborate in some societies than in others. Protection of livestock and storage of harvested crops are primary functions of farm villages, and in many villages where subsistence farming is the prevailing way of life, the storage place for grains and other food is constructed with as much care as the best-built house. Moisture and vermin must be kept away from stored food; containers of grain often stand on stilts under a carefully thatched roof or behind walls made of carefully maintained sun-dried mud. In India's villages, the paddy-bin made of mud (in which rice is stored) often stands inside the house. Similarly, livestock pens are often attached to houses, or, as in Africa, dwellings are built in a circle surrounding the corral.

The functional differentiation of buildings is greatest in Western cultures, where a single farmstead may contain as many buildings as an entire hamlet elsewhere in the world. A prosperous North American farm is likely to include a two-story farm house, a stable, a barn, and various outbuildings, including a garage for motorized equipment, a workshop, a shed for tools, and a silo for grain storage (Fig. 11.15). The space these structures occupy can exceed that used by entire villages in Japan, China, and other agrarian regions where space is at a greater premium.

thinking
geographically

Think of an agricultural region where you have visited or lived. Describe the imprint of agriculture on the landscape and consider what the cultural landscape tells you about how agriculture is produced in this region or how production has changed over time.

HOW IS AGRICULTURE CURRENTLY ORGANIZED GEOGRAPHICALLY, AND HOW HAS AGRIBUSINESS INFLUENCED THE CONTEMPORARY GEOGRAPHY OF AGRICULTURE?

Understanding global agricultural patterns requires looking at more than market location, land use, and transportation costs—the factors analyzed by von Thünen. We must also consider the effects of different climate and soil conditions, variations in farming methods and technology, the role of governments and social norms, and the lasting impacts of history.

Commercial farming has come to dominate in the world's economic core, as well as some of the places in the semi-periphery and periphery. Commercial farming is the agriculture of large-scale grain producers and cattle ranches, mechanized equipment, and factory-type labor forces. It is a world apart from the traditional farms of Asia and Africa.

The spatial expansion of modern **commercial agriculture** began in the eighteenth and nineteenth centuries when Europe became a market for agricultural products from around the world: Moreover, European countries manufactured and sold in their colonies the finished products made from imported raw materials. Thus, cotton grown in Egypt, Sudan, India, and other countries colonized by Europe was bought cheaply, imported to European factories, and made into clothes—many of which were then exported and sold, often in the very colonies where the cotton had been grown in the first place.

Major changes in transportation and food storage, especially refrigeration, further intertwined agricultural

FIELD NOTE

"The technology of refrigeration has kept pace with the containerization of seaborne freight traffic. When we sailed into the port of Dunedin, New Zealand, I was unsure of just what those red boxes were. Closer inspection revealed that they are refrigeration units, to which incoming containers are attached. Meats and other perishables can thus be kept frozen until they are transferred to a refrigerator ship."

© H. J. de Blij

■■ **Figure 11.16**
Dunedin, New Zealand.

production and food processing regions around the world during the twentieth century (Fig. 11.16). The beef industry of Argentina, for example, secured a world market when the invention of refrigerated ships made it possible to transport a highly perishable commodity over long distances. European colonial powers required farmers in their colonies to cultivate specific crops. One major impact of colonial agriculture was the establishment of **monoculture** (dependence on a single agricultural commodity) throughout much of the colonial world. Colonies became known for certain crops, and colonizers came to rely on those crops. Ghanaians still raise cacao; Moçambiquans still grow cotton; and Sri Lankans still produce tea. The production of cash crops in poorer countries is perpetuated by loan and aid requirements from lending countries, the World Trade Organization, the International Monetary Fund, and the World Bank (see Chapter 10).

The World Map of Climates

Before we can study the distribution of agriculture in the world today, we need to examine Figure 11.17, the distribution of climate zones. All of the elements of weather, absorption of the sun's energy, rotation of the Earth, circulation of the oceans, movement of weather systems, and the jet stream, produce a pattern of climates represented in the map—and those climate patterns have a profound impact on what can be grown where. We owe this remarkable map to Wladimir Köppen (1846–1940), who devised a scheme called the **Köppen climate classification system** for classifying the world's climates on the basis of temperature and precipitation.

Köppen's map provides one means of understanding the distribution of **climatic regions** (areas with similar climatic characteristics) across the planet. The legend looks complicated, but for present purposes it is enough to get a sense of the distribution of the major types of climate. The letter categories in the legend give a clear indication of the conditions they represent.

The (A) climates are hot or very warm and generally humid. The "no dry season" (Af) regions are *equatorial rainforest* regions. The "short dry season" (Am) climate is known as the *monsoon climate*. And if you can envisage an African savanna, you know what the (Aw, *savanna*) designation means.

Once you realize that the yellow and light brown colors on the map represent dry climates (BW, *desert* and BS, *steppe*), it becomes clear how much of the world has limited water availability. Nonetheless, some very large population clusters have developed in these water-deficient regions, especially at lower (and warmer) latitudes. The world faces a long-term water crisis, and the Köppen map helps show why.

The (C) climates also have familiar names. The (Cf) climate, represented by dark green, prevails over the southeastern United States. If you know the local climate in Atlanta or Nashville or Jacksonville, you understand why this climate is often called "humid temperate." It is moist, and it does not get as cold as it does in Canada or as warm (continuously, anyway) as in the Amazon Basin. If you have experienced this kind of climate, the map gives you a good idea of what it's like in much of eastern China, southeastern Australia, and a large part of southeastern South America.

WORLD CLIMATES
After Köppen–Geiger

A HUMID EQUATORIAL CLIMATE

Af	No dry season
Am	Short dry season
Aw	Dry winter

B DRY CLIMATE

| BS | Semiarid |
| BW | Arid |

h=hot
k=cold

C HUMID TEMPERATE CLIMATE

Cf	No dry season
Cw	Dry winter
Cs	Dry summer

a=hot
  summer
b=cool
  summer
c=short, cool
  summer
d=very cold
  winter

D HUMID COLD CLIMATE

| Df | No dry season |
| Dw | Dry winter |

E COLD POLAR CLIMATE

| E | Tundra and ice |

H HIGHLAND CLIMATE

| H | Unclassified highlands |

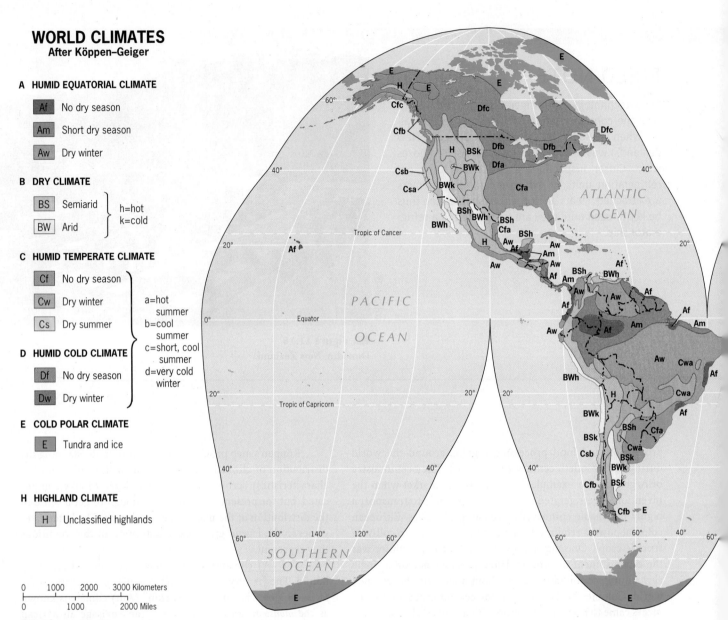

■ **Figure 11.17**
World Climates.   The Köppen map of world climates, as modified by R. Geiger. Climates generally follow lines of latitude because the amount of incoming solar radiation varies by latitude. Climates are shaped further by the presence of mountains, as is seen in western North and South America and by the proximity to warm or cold ocean currents, as is evidenced on the west coast of southern Africa and the east coast of the United States.

The "dry summer" (C) climates are known as *Mediterranean* climates (the small s in Cs means that summers are dry). This mild climate occurs not only around the Mediterranean Sea, and thus in the famous wine countries of France, Italy, and Spain, but also in California, Chile, South Africa's Cape, and southern parts of Australia.

Farther toward the poles, the planet gets rather cold. Note that the (D) climates dominate in the United States' upper Midwest and Canada, but it gets even colder in Siberia. The "milder" (Da) climates (here the key is the small a, which denotes a warm summer) are found only in limited parts of Eurasia. Winters are very cold in all the (D) climates and downright frigid

(and long) in the (Dfb) and (Dfc) regions. (D) climates are generally continental, on the interior of continents, instead of on coasts. Continental locations make (D) climates generally drier than (C) climates. The continentality of (D) climates also contributes to the large range of temperatures found across the year because land heats and cools much faster than water.

Polar climates, where tundra and ice prevail, are found poleward of (D) climates. The polar location of (E) climates means temperatures are cold throughout the year. As a result, plant life does not break down and nourish the soil during the year, and also a layer of permafrost (frozen ground) exists year round.

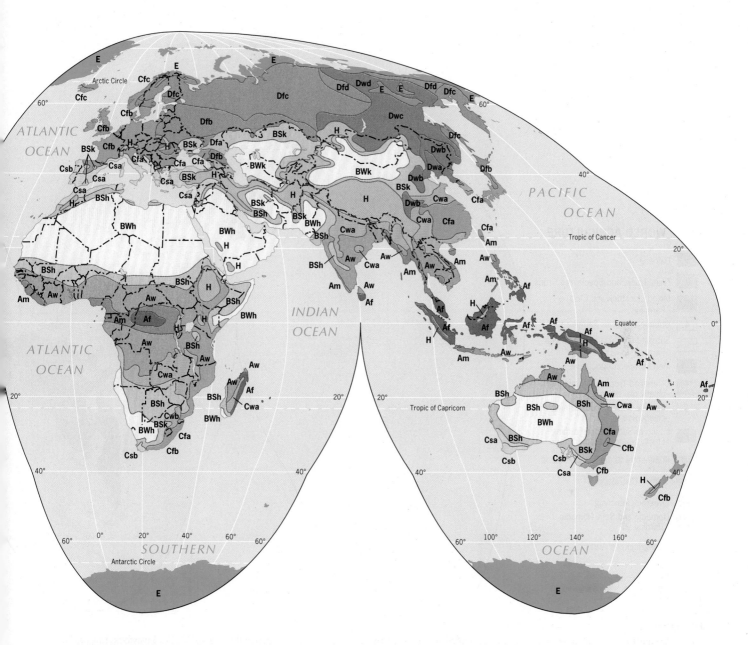

The World Map of Agriculture

When comparing the world map of agriculture (Fig. 11.18) with the distribution of climate types across the world (Fig. 11.17), we can see the correlation between climate and agriculture. For example, drier lands rely on livestock ranching, whereas moister climates are characterized by grain production. Understanding the major agricultural zones shown in Figure 11.18 requires looking at both environmental and social variables.

CASH CROPS AND PLANTATION AGRICULTURE

Colonialism profoundly shaped nonsubsistence farming in many poorer countries. Colonial powers implemented agriculture systems to benefit their needs, a practice that has tended to lock poorer countries into production of one or two "cash" crops. Cash farming continues to provide badly needed money, even if the conditions of sale to the urban-industrial world are unfavorable. In the Caribbean region, for example, whole national economies depend on sugar exports (sugar having been introduced by the European colonists in the 1600s). These island countries wish to sell the sugar at the highest possible price, but they are not in a position to dictate prices. Sugar is produced by many countries in various parts of the world, as well as by farmers in the global economic core (Fig. 11.18). Governments in the core place quotas on imports of agricultural products and subsidize domestic production of the same commodities.

Occasionally, producing countries consider forming a cartel in order to present a united front to the importing countries and to gain a better price, as oil-producing states did during the 1970s. Such collective action is difficult to coordinate, as the wealthy importing countries can buy products from countries that are not members of the cartel.

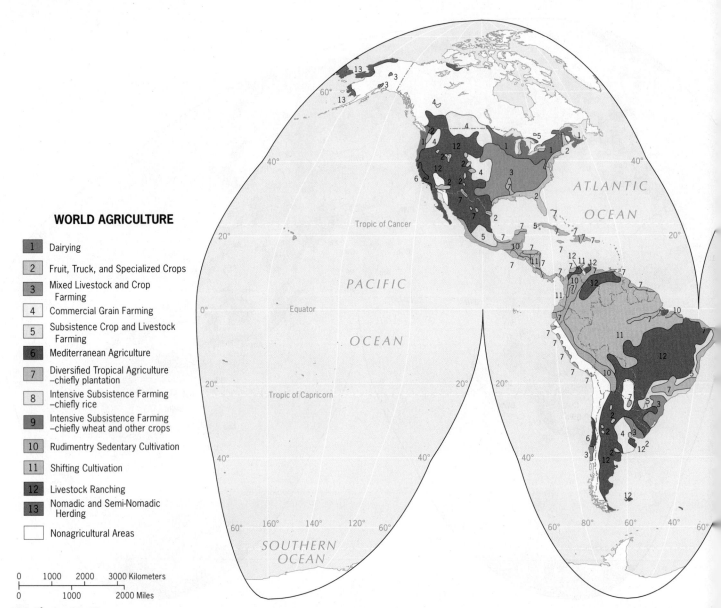

WORLD AGRICULTURE

1	Dairying
2	Fruit, Truck, and Specialized Crops
3	Mixed Livestock and Crop Farming
4	Commercial Grain Farming
5	Subsistence Crop and Livestock Farming
6	Mediterranean Agriculture
7	Diversified Tropical Agriculture –chiefly plantation
8	Intensive Subsistence Farming –chiefly rice
9	Intensive Subsistence Farming –chiefly wheat and other crops
10	Rudimentry Sedentary Cultivation
11	Shifting Cultivation
12	Livestock Ranching
13	Nomadic and Semi-Nomadic Herding
	Nonagricultural Areas

■ **Figure 11.18**

World Agriculture.   The type of agriculture practiced varies with climate. Compare this map with Figure 11.17. Livestock raising is common in semi-arid and savanna climate zones. Crop farming and commercial grain farming are found in places that receive higher rainfall. Dairy production generally occurs where climates are cooler. In addition to climate, land ownership patterns factor into the type of agricultural production globally. Where parcels of land are small, farmers generally focus on subsistence production.   *Adapted with permission from:* Hammond, Inc., 1977.

Also, the withholding of produce by exporting countries may stimulate domestic production among importers. For example, although cane sugar accounts for 75 percent of the commercial world sugar crop each year, farmers in the United States, Europe, and Russia also produce sugar from sugar beets. In Europe and Russia, these beets already yield 25 percent of the annual world sugar harvest.

When cash crops are grown on large estates, we use the term **plantation agriculture** to describe the production system. Plantations are colonial legacies that persist in poorer, primarily tropical, countries along with subsistence farming. Figure 11.18 shows that plantation agriculture (7 in the

legend) continues in Middle and South America, Africa, and South Asia. Laid out to produce bananas, sugar, coffee, and cocoa in Middle and South America, rubber, cocoa, and tea in West and East Africa, tea in South Asia, and rubber in Southeast Asia, these plantations have outlasted the period of decolonization and continue to provide specialized crops to wealthier markets. Many of the most productive plantations are owned by European or American individuals or corporations.

Multinational corporations have tenaciously protected their economic interests in plantations. In the 1940s and 1950s, the Guatemalan government began an agrarian reform

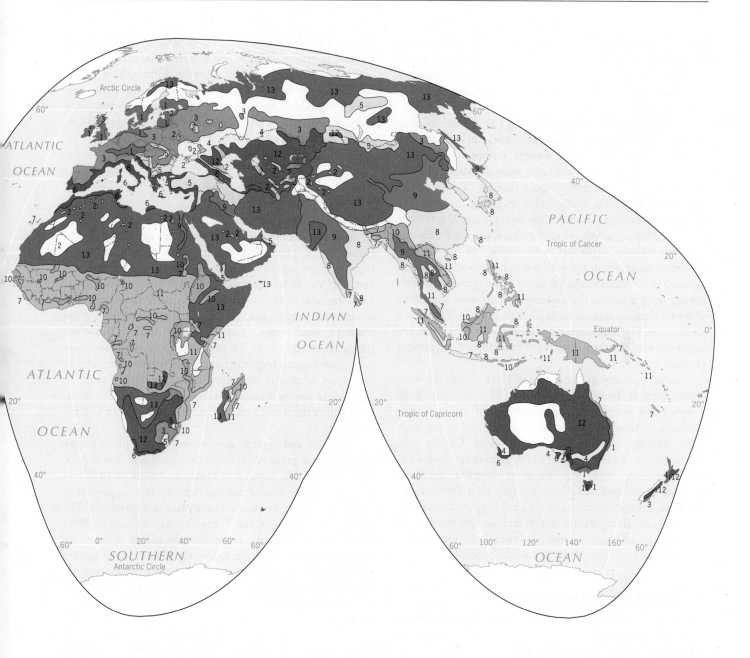

program. The plan entailed renting unused land from foreign corporations to landless citizens at a low appraised value. The United Fruit Company, an American firm with extensive holdings in the country, was greatly concerned by this turn of events. The company had close ties to powerful individuals in the American government, including Secretary of State John Foster Dulles, CIA director Allen Dulles (the two were brothers), and Assistant Secretary of State for Inter-American Affairs John Moors Cabot. In 1954, the United States supported the overthrow of the government of Guatemala because of stated concerns about the spread of communism. This ended all land reform initiatives but led many commentators to question the degree to which the United Fruit Company was behind the coup. Indeed, with the exception of President Dwight Eisenhower, every individual involved in the decision to help topple Guatemala's government had ties

to the company. This example illustrates the inextricable links between economics and political motivations—and it raises questions about the degree to which multinational corporations based in wealthy countries influence decisions about politics, agriculture, and land reform in other parts of the world.

COMMERCIAL LIVESTOCK, FRUIT, AND GRAIN AGRICULTURE

As Figure 11.18 shows, by far the largest areas of commercial agriculture (1 through 4 in the legend) lie outside the tropics. Dairying (1) is widespread at the northern margins of the midlatitudes—particularly in the northeastern United States and in northwestern Europe. Fruit, truck, and specialized crops (2), including the market gardens von Thünen observed around Rostock, are found in the eastern and southeastern United States and in widely dispersed small areas where environments are favorable. In Central Asia and the Sahara, major oases stand out as commercial agriculture on the map.

Mixed livestock and crop farming (3) is widespread in the more humid parts of the midlatitudes, including much of the eastern United States, western Europe, and western Russia, but it is also found in smaller areas in Uruguay, Brazil, and South Africa. Commercial grain farming (4) prevails in the drier parts of the midlatitudes, including the southern Prairie Provinces of Canada, in the Dakotas and Montana in the United States, as well as in Nebraska, Kansas, and adjacent areas. Spring wheat (planted in the spring and harvested in the summer) grows in the northern zone, and winter wheat (planted in the autumn and harvested in the spring of the following year) is used in the southern area. An even larger belt of wheat farming extends from Ukraine through Russia into Kazakhstan. The Argentinean and Australian wheat zones are smaller in area, but their exports are an important component of world trade.

Even a cursory glance at Figure 11.18 reveals the wide distribution of **livestock ranching** (12), the raising of domesticated animals for the production of meat and by-products, such as leather and wool. In addition to the large cattle-ranching areas in the United States, Canada, and Mexico, much of eastern Brazil and Argentina are devoted to ranching, along with large tracts of Australia and New Zealand, as well as South Africa. You may see a Thünian pattern here: livestock ranching on the periphery and consumers in the cities. Refrigeration has overcome the problem of perishability, and high volume has lowered the unit cost of transporting beef, lamb, and other animal products.

SUBSISTENCE AGRICULTURE

The map of world agriculture labels three types of subsistence agriculture: subsistence crop and livestock farming, intensively subsistence farming (chiefly rice), and intensively subsistence farming (chiefly wheat and other crops). In some regions that are labeled as subsistence, that label does not tell the whole story. For example, in Southeast Asia, rice is grown on small plots and is labor-intensive, so that subsistence and export production occur side by side. Despite the region's significant rice exports, most Southeast Asian farmers are subsistence farmers. Thus, Southeast Asia appears on the map as primarily a subsistence grain-growing area.

MEDITERRANEAN AGRICULTURE

Only one form of agriculture mentioned in the legend of Figure 11.18 refers to a particular climatic zone: **Mediterranean agriculture** (6). As the map shows, this kind of specialized farming occurs only in areas where the dry summer Mediterranean climate prevails (Fig. 11.17): along the shores of the Mediterranean Sea, in parts of California and Oregon, in central Chile, at South Africa's Cape, and in parts of southwestern and southern Australia. Farmers here grow a special combination of crops: grapes, olives, citrus fruits, figs, certain vegetables, dates, and others. From these areas come many wines; these and other commodities are exported to distant markets because Mediterranean products tend to be popular and command high prices.

DRUG AGRICULTURE

Certain important agricultural activities cannot easily be mapped at the global scale and therefore do not appear in Figure 11.18. One of those activities is the cultivation of crops that are turned into illegal drugs. Because of the high demand for drugs—particularly in the global economic core—farmers in the periphery often find it more profitable to cultivate poppy, coca, or marijuana plants than to grow standard food crops. Cultivation of these plants has increased steadily over the past several decades, and they now constitute an important source of revenue for parts of the global economic periphery. Coca, the source plant of cocaine, is grown widely in Colombia, Peru, and Bolivia. Over half of the world's cultivation of coca occurs in Colombia alone.

Heroin and opium are derived from opium poppy plants, grown predominantly in Southeast and South Asia, especially in Afghanistan and Myanmar. In the 2013 World Drug Report, the United Nations reported that 74 percent of the world's opium production took place in Afghanistan. The U.S.-led overthrow of the Taliban in Afghanistan in 2001 created a power vacuum in the country and an opportunity for illegal drug production to quickly rebound (the austere Taliban government had virtually eradicated opium production in Afghanistan by 2001). Most opium production in Afghanistan today occurs in five unstable southern provinces.

U.S. government policies have affected production of illegal drugs in Latin America. During the 1980s and 1990s, the U.S. government worked with local authorities to crack down on coca production in Colombia. As a result of this crackdown, much of the drug production and trafficking moved north to northern Mexico. In June 2005, *The Economist* quoted one American official as reporting that "Mexican criminal gangs 'exert more influence over drug trafficking in the U.S. than any other group.' Mexicans now control 11 of the 13 largest drug markets in the United States." Marijuana and opium production in Mexico is on the rise, and the United States Drug Enforcement Agency (DEA) is concerned about the high potency of marijuana coming out of Mexico and Canada. Despite Afghanistan's dominance as a heroin producer, most heroin (which is derived from opium) consumed in the western United States comes from opium grown in Mexico, whereas the heroin consumed in the eastern United States comes from opium grown in Colombia.

Drug cartels that oversee the drug trade have brought crime and violence to the places where they hold sway (Fig. 11.19). There are areas in Rio de Janeiro where the official police have little control, and drug lords have imposed reigns of terror over swaths of the countryside in parts of Central and South America, Southwest Asia, Southeast Asia, and elsewhere. The drug trade depends on the voracious appetite for mind-altering substances in North America and Europe in particular.

The supply of marijuana in the United States traditionally came from Mexico and Canada, as the DEA has reported. But an increasing amount of marijuana consumed in the United States is grown in the United States. Since 1996, a total of 16 states in the United States—mostly in the West—have legalized marijuana for medicinal purposes, and in 2013 Colorado and Washington legalized it entirely (though they forbid consumption in public places and they have placed additional restrictions on cultivation for personal use and the amount of marijuana people can purchase). An April 2011 article in the *New York Times* valued marijuana production at $40 billion, "with California, Tennessee, Kentucky, Hawaii and Washington the top five production states," despite the fact that medicinal marijuana is not legal in Tennessee or Kentucky.

Marijuana production has more than a monetary impact. Marijuana grown indoors consumes massive amounts of electricity. The cost of indoor production includes grow lamps that are the kinds used in operating rooms, dehumidifiers, air conditioners, electric generators, water pumps, heaters, carbon dioxide generators, ventilation systems, and electrical control systems. Energy analyst Evan Mills published a study in April 2011 estimating the energy costs of producing marijuana in the United States costs at about $5 billion a year (i.e., around 1 percent of all power consumed in the United States). Marijuana grown outdoors has much lower energy costs than marijuana grown indoors. Growers plant crops on public lands, especially in the West, because the remote location of public lands makes detection less likely. Also, the land is public and therefore not owned by any one person to whom a crop could be traced.

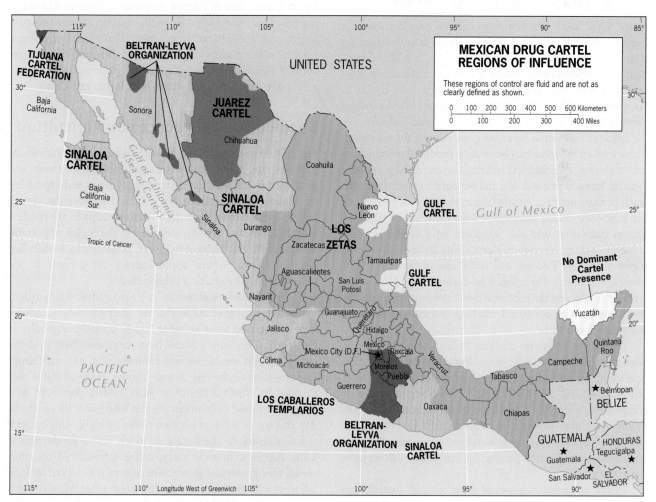

■ **Figure 11.19**

Mexican Drug Cartel Regions of Influence in Mexico.   Mexican drug cartels claim swaths of the country and fight with each other for control of territory. Control of territory is important in order to move cocaine, methamphetamine, and marijuana into the United States. The cartels involved and their territorial control has changed as the Mexican government has worked to disrupt the control of the cartels since their war on drugs began in 2006.   *Courtesy of*: Food and Agriculture Service. http://www.fas.org/sgp/crs/row/RL34215.pdf.

INFORMAL AGRICULTURE

Small-scale informal agricultural activities are also missing from maps of global agricultural patterns, yet these play an important role in the contemporary world. Millions of people cultivate small plots of land in and around their homes for domestic consumption or to trade informally with others. These activities are not captured by formal agricultural statistics, but the food that is grown in this fashion plays a vital role in the lives of literally billions of people. Even city dwellers in many parts of the world are involved in small-scale agricultural activities—cultivating or raising livestock in small plots of land around their dwellings, on rooftop gardens, or in community gardens. Such practices are encouraged in some places—notably China—but more often they are ignored, or even discouraged. Yet the contribution urban agriculture can make to the food security of city dwellers is attracting growing attention, and it is likely to grow in importance in the coming years.

Political Influences on Agriculture

As we noted above, the European colonial period provides a stunning example of the impact of political circumstances on agricultural practices. Consider, for example, one of the most significant contemporary **cash crops**: cotton. The colonial powers encouraged the production of plantation-scale cotton in many regions of the world (e.g., India) and established a trading network that led to the globalization of the cotton industry.

Cotton cultivation expanded greatly during the nineteenth century, when the Industrial Revolution produced machines for cotton ginning, spinning, and weaving that increased productive capacity, brought prices down, and put cotton goods within the reach of mass markets. As with sugar, the colonial powers laid out large-scale cotton plantations, sometimes under irrigation. Cotton cultivation was also promoted on a smaller scale in numerous other countries: in Egypt's Nile Delta, in the Punjab region shared by Pakistan and India, and in Sudan, Uganda, Mexico, and Brazil. The colonial producers received low prices for their cotton, and the European industries prospered as cheap raw materials were converted into large quantities of items for sale at home and abroad.

Wealthier countries continue to buy cotton, and cotton sales remain important for some former colonies. But they now compete with cotton being grown in the United States, northeast China, and Central Asia. Moreover, cotton is in competition today with synthetic fibers such as nylon and rayon. As global supply and demand shift in response to changing markets and new alternatives, economies that have been built around cotton production can go through wrenching adjustments.

Even as countries emerged from colonial control, they were left with a legacy of large landholdings owned or controlled by wealthy individuals or business entities. That legacy contributed to uprisings among the rural poor in places such as Mexico, Cuba, and Guatemala. The efforts of governmental authorities in some former colonies to confront this situation provide a different example of the impact of politics on agriculture. In some cases, governments enacted policies that perpetuated preexisting inequalities; in others, land reforms were introduced that served to redistribute land to individuals or communities. The latter effort was common in parts of Central and South America, leading to a substantial reorganization of the rural landscape—sometimes spreading wealth more broadly. Pressure for land reform continues in many countries, and land issues are at the heart of many social movements in the global economic periphery and semiperiphery.

A more mundane, but common, way in which governments influence agriculture is through tax regulations and subsidies favoring certain land uses. The U.S. government currently spends more than $10 billion subsidizing large-scale farmers. Pushed by a strong farm lobby, these subsidies guarantee floor prices for staple crops and protect farmers in bad years. They give large-scale agriculture an advantage over smaller scale alternatives. But in the past 60 years perhaps the most dramatic examples of politics affecting agriculture have come from the communist world. The governments of the former Soviet Union, eastern Europe, and Maoist China initiated far-reaching land reforms that led to the creation of large collective farms and agricultural communes. This giant experiment resulted in the massive displacement of rural peoples and irrevocably altered traditional rural social systems. Today privatization of farming is under way in both Russia and China.

Sociocultural Influences on Agriculture

Agriculture is also affected by social and cultural factors. As incomes rise, many people start consuming more meat and processed foods, seek out better-quality fruits and vegetables, or demand fresh produce year round. Consider the case of coffee, one the most important **luxury crops** in the modern world. Coffee was first domesticated in the region of present-day Ethiopia, but today it is grown primarily in Middle and South America, where approximately 70 percent of the world's annual production is harvested.

In the early eighteenth century, coffee was virtually unknown in most of the world. Yet, after petroleum, coffee is now the second most valuable legally traded commodity in the world. The United States buys more than half of all the coffee sold on world markets annually, and western Europe imports most of the rest. A well-known image of coffee production in North America is Juan Valdez, portrayed as a simple yet proud Colombian peasant who handpicks beans by day and enjoys a cup of his own coffee by night. This image is quite contrary to the reality of much coffee production in Latin America. In most cases, coffee is produced on enormous, foreign-owned plantations, where it is picked by local laborers who are hired at very low wage rates. Most coffee is sent abroad; and if the coffee pickers drink coffee, it is probably of the imported and instant variety.

In the past few decades, however, coffee production has undergone changes as more consumers demand fair trade coffee and more coffee producers seek fair trade certification.

© Lindsay Naylor

■ **Figure 11.20**
Los Altos, Chiapas, Mexico. A Mayan farmer picks ripe coffee beans for sale to North American customers as fair trade coffee.

The aim of fair trade is to raise the income of certified producers by reducing the number of actors in the supply chain. Coffee producers form democratically run cooperatives that, if certified, can be registered on the International Fair Trade Coffee Register. Coffee importers then purchase the fair trade coffee directly from the registered cooperatives. Being registered guarantees coffee producers a "fair trade price" of $1.40 per pound of coffee (plus bonuses of $0.30 per pound for organic). Over 1.3 million farmers and workers in 70 countries, mainly in the periphery and semiperiphery, are connected to the 1150 fair trade certified producer organizations worldwide (Fig. 11.20). The fair trade campaign pressured Starbucks into selling fair trade coffee. Starbucks buys around 20 million pounds of fair trade coffee each year. That amounts to just 5 percent of its total purchases, but it is the largest purchaser of fair trade coffee in the world. Other retailers have followed suit; for example, all espresso sold at Dunkin' Donuts in North America and Europe is fair trade certified. Fair trade coffee is available at large retail outlets and under corporate brands at Target, Wal-Mart, and Sam's Club. The corporate embrace of fair trade coffee has boosted the movement considerably, though it has also raised concerns about corporate cooptation of fair trade standards.

The push for fair trade production shows how social movements can influence agriculture. And fair trade goes beyond coffee. Dozens of commodities and products, ranging from tea, bananas, fresh cut flowers, and chocolate to soccer balls, can be certified fair trade. According to Fair Trade International, consumers spent more than $6.5 billion on fair trade certified products in 2012.

People's changing tastes also shape the geography of agriculture. Tea is a rather recent addition to the Western diet. It was grown in China perhaps 2000 years ago, but it became popular in Europe only during the nineteenth century. The colonial powers (mainly the British) established enormous tea plantations in Asia and thus began the full-scale flow of tea into European markets. Tea was one of the first plantation-produced products to receive fair trade certification. Both the

fair trade and the traditionally traded varieties are on the rise globally to meet the increasing demand.

Even as social preferences shape agricultural production, the consumption of particular products can have social consequences. Just a few decades ago, city dwellers in West Africa primarily consumed grains grown from nearby fields. Over the past three decades, relatively cheap imported rice from Malaysia and Thailand has become an important food source, and many locals came to prefer the taste of the imported rice. This set of circumstances left West Africa vulnerable when the price of imported grains skyrocketed in 2008. Local riots broke out and a food crisis ensued.

Agribusiness and the Changing Geography of Agriculture

The commercialization of crop production and the associated development of new agricultural technologies have changed how agricultural goods are grown and have sparked the rapid growth of agribusiness. **Agribusiness** is an encompassing term for the businesses that provide a vast array of goods and services to support the agricultural industry. Agribusiness serves to connect local farms to a spatially extensive web of production and exchange. At the same time, it fosters the spatial concentration of agricultural activities. Both of these trends are revealed in the development of the poultry industry in the United States.

Early in the twentieth century, poultry production in the United States was highly disaggregated, with many farmers raising a few chickens as part of a multifaceted farming operation. Over the past 50 years, however, poultry production has fundamentally changed. Today, the farmers on the Delmarva Peninsula east of Washington, D.C., account for 8 percent of poultry production in the United States, and they do so by contracting and working directly with four major poultry companies. In an article on modern agriculture, David Lanegran summarized the impact of this transformation as follows:

> Today, chickens are produced by large agribusiness companies operating hatcheries, feed mills, and processing plants. They supply chicks and feed to the farmers. The farmers are responsible for building a house and maintaining proper temperature and water supply. Once a week the companies fill the feed bins for the farmers, and guarantee them a price for the birds. The companies even collect market-ready birds and take them away for processing and marketing. Most of the nation's poultry supply is handled by a half dozen very large corporations that control the process from chicks to chicken pieces in stores.

Lanegran goes on to show how selective breeding has produced faster growing, bigger chickens, which are housed in enormous broiler houses that are largely mechanized.

Broiler houses are concentrated in northwestern Arkansas, northern Georgia, the Delmarva Peninsula (Delaware, Maryland, and Virginia), the Piedmont areas of North Carolina, and the Shenandoah Valley of Virginia (Fig. 11.21). Lanegran

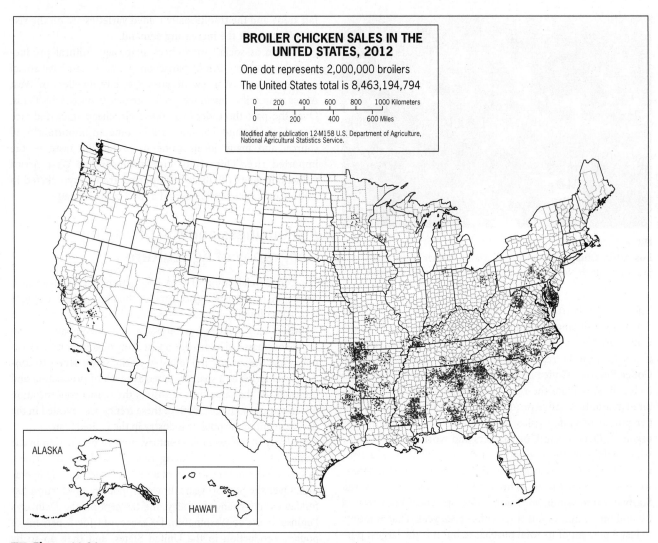

BROILER CHICKEN SALES IN THE UNITED STATES, 2012

One dot represents 2,000,000 broilers

The United States total is 8,463,194,794

0   200   400   600   800   1000 Kilometers

0   200   400   600 Miles

Modified after publication 12-M158 U.S. Department of Agriculture, National Agricultural Statistics Service.

■■ **Figure 11.21**

Broiler Chicken Sales in the United States, 2012.   Broiler chickens are grown for meat, which means they will be processed and consumed once sold. The chickens are produced at the locations on this map that shows sales. Farmers typically sell broiler chickens to one of 40 large processing companies including Tyson and Purdee. Ninty five percent of broiler chickens in the United States are produced by farmers who are under contract with a large processing firm and are required to follow their standards and use their feed from hatched egg to table.   *Courtesy of:* United States Census of Agriculture, National Agricultural Statistics Service.

shows that in many respects the "farmers" who manage these operations are involved in manufacturing as much or more as farming. They are as likely to spend their time talking to bank officers, overseeing the repair of equipment, and negotiating with vendors rather than tending their animals. As such, they symbolize the breakdown between the rural and the urban in wealthier parts of the world—as well as the interconnections between rural places and distant markets.

The poultry example is not unusual. During the 1990s, hog production on the Oklahoma and Texas panhandles increased rapidly with the arrival of corporate hog farms. John Fraser Hart and Chris Mayda described the quick change with statistics. In 1992, the U.S. Census of Agriculture counted just over 31,000 hogs marketed in Texas County, Oklahoma, and just four years later "the panhandle was plastered with proliferating pork places, and Texas County alone produced 2 million hogs. It was the epicenter of an area

that produced 4 million hogs, 4 percent of the national total and one-seventh as many finished hogs as the entire state of Iowa." The availability of both inexpensive water and natural gas on the Oklahoma panhandle was enticing for corporate hog farms, which require both. Hart and Mayda explain that the "reasonable" price of land and the accessibility to "growing metropolitan markets of the South and the West" also made the region attractive for hog production. As in poultry production, a corporation built a processing plant, and production (both by farms owned by the corporation and those owned privately) increased to meet the demand (Fig. 11.22).

Because of agribusiness, the range and variety of products on the shelves of urban supermarkets in the United States is a world apart from the constant quest for sufficient, nutritionally balanced food that exists in some places. A global network of farm production is oriented to the one-fifth of the world's population that is highly urbanized, wealthy, and powerful. Few

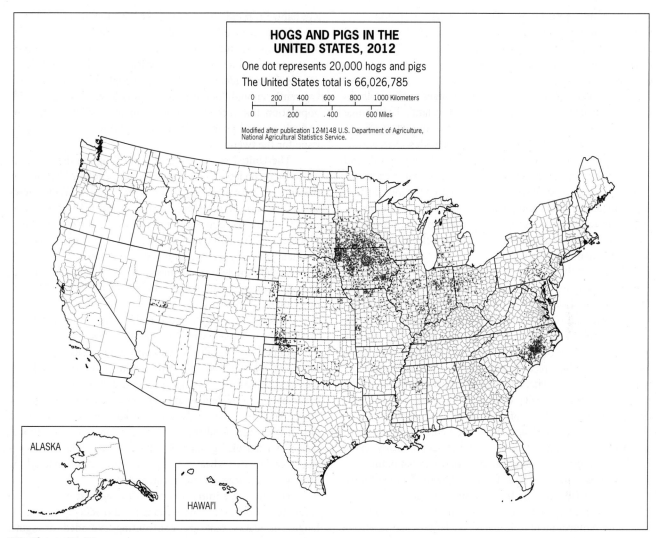

**HOGS AND PIGS IN THE
UNITED STATES, 2012**

One dot represents 20,000 hogs and pigs

The United States total is 66,026,785

Modified after publication 12-M148 U.S. Department of Agriculture,
National Agricultural Statistics Service.

ALASKA

HAWAI'I

■▦ **Figure 11.22**

Hogs and Pigs in the United States, 2012.   Hog and pig production is concentrated in the Corn Belt in and around Iowa and in North Carolina. The earliest stages of hog production are done inside buildings using systems designed to reduce the possibility of disease spreading among the livestock.   *Courtesy of*: United States Census of Agriculture, National Agricultural Statistics Service.

farmers in distant lands have real control over land-use decisions, for the better-off people in the global economic core play a disproportionate role in deciding what will be bought at what price. The colonial era may have come to an end, but as the map of agricultural regions reminds us, its imprint remains strong.

Environmental Impacts of Commercial Agriculture

Commercial agriculture produces significant environmental changes. The growing demand for protein-rich foods and more efficient technologies are leading to overfishing in many regions of the world. In many places fish stocks are declining at an alarming rate. From mid-century to the late 1980s, the fish harvest from oceans and seas increased fivefold, and there seemed to be no limit to it. Countries quarreled over fishing rights, poorer countries leased fishing grounds to richer ones,

and fleets of trawlers plied the oceans. International attempts to regulate fishing industries failed. Then in the 1970s and 1980s, overfishing began destroying fish stocks. The cod fisheries on Canada's Grand Banks off Newfoundland collapsed. In 1975, biologists estimated the Atlantic bluefin tuna population at 250,000; today the western stock is listed as critically endangered, and the stock in the Mediterranean is listed as endangered. From ocean perch and king crabs off Alaska to rock lobsters and roughies off New Zealand, fish and shellfish populations are depleted. The total annual catch is also declining and may already be beyond the point of recovery. Much of the damage has already been done, and fishing industries in many parts of the world have reported dwindling harvests and missing species.

If you travel to Mediterranean Europe today you will see a landscape that reflects the clearing of forests in ancient times to facilitate agriculture and trade. Look carefully at many hillslopes and you will see evidence of terraces cut into the hills many centuries ago. The industrialization and commercialization of agriculture has accelerated the pace and extent of agriculture's impact on the environment in recent times. More land has been cleared, and the land that is under cultivation is ever more intensively used.

Significant agriculturally driven changes to the environment go far beyond the simple clearing of land. They range from soil erosion to changes in the organic content of soils to the presence of chemicals (herbicides, pesticides, even antibiotics and growth hormones from livestock feces) in soils and groundwater. In places where large commercial crop farms dominate, the greatest concerns often center on the introduction of chemical fertilizers and pesticides into the environment—as well as soil erosion. And, as we have seen, the movement toward genetically modified crops carries with it another set of environmental concerns.

The growth of organic farming (discussed at the beginning of the chapter) and the move toward the use of local foods in some communities can benefit the environment. Yet such initiatives have had only modest impacts on the majority of the world's peoples and places. A telling sign is that the organic movement has had little effect on the production of the staple foods on which billions of people depend. Moreover, large corporate entities are playing an increasingly prominent role in the organic movement—raising concerns about standards and rendering illusory the ideal of an independent organic farmer engaged in "sustainable" agriculture. Nonetheless, better regulated organic farming and local food initiatives are clearly on the rise. Their proponents argue that they are priced out of the market by subsidies favoring large farms and by the failure of most agribusiness to incorporate the environmental and health costs of large-scale, intensive farming, into their production costs.

The environmental impacts of large-scale intensive agriculture can be particularly severe when agriculture moves into marginal environments, as has happened with the expansion of livestock herding into arid or semiarid areas (see the map of world climates, Fig. 11.17). The natural vegetation in these areas cannot always sustain the herds, especially during prolonged droughts. As a result, ecological degradation and, in some areas, desertification are the result.

In recent decades, the popularity of fast-food chains that serve hamburgers has led to the deforestation of wooded areas in order to open up additional pastures for beef cattle, notably in Central and South America. Livestock ranching is an extremely land-, water-, and energy-intensive process. Significant land must be turned over to the cultivation of cattle feed, and the animals themselves need extensive grazing areas. By stripping away vegetation, the animals can promote the erosion of river banks, with implications for everything from water quality to wildlife habitat.

The Challenge of Feeding Everyone

Food riots that break out in low-income countries and stories of famine in countries such as Somalia, Sudan, Malawi, and Zimbabwe remind us that food security remains a challenge for millions of people around the globe. Although food production has expanded in some parts of the world, food production per capita has actually declined in Africa over the past decade. Worldwide, nearly 1 billion people are malnourished. Currently, enough food is produced worldwide to feed Earth's population, but in the face of inadequate distribution systems and widespread poverty, food security looms as a significant issue for the twenty-first century.

The United Nations World Food Program defines hunger as living on less than the daily recommended 2100 calories the average person needs to live a healthy life. While news stories focus on starving populations in the wake of wars and natural disasters, acute emergencies account for less than 8 percent of the global hungry. Chronic undernourishment is a much greater problem, impeding childhood development, weakening immune systems, and undermining the social fabric of communities. Malnutrition is a key factor in the death of more than 2.3 million children who do not reach the age of 5.

In response to widespread malnourishment and famine, in 1985 the U.S. Agency for International Development created the Famine Early Warning System, which now collaborates with other organizations worldwide to monitor food stores and predict food insecurity. Many governments and nongovernmental organizations provide food aid to populations in need. The UN World Food Program is the largest source of food aid in the world. It delivers food that is tailored to meet the nutritional needs of particular groups. A typical food basket includes a staple food such as wheat flour or rice; a protein, often lentils or other legumes; vegetable oil; sugar; and salt.

Despite these initiatives, the battle against malnutrition is far from won, and climate change is introducing new challenges in places that are confronting extended droughts, exacerbated threats from new pests, and altered growing conditions for traditional crops (see Chapter 13). For the moment, however, the global food supply remains adequate to meet the needs of the human population, meaning that malnutrition and famine are at heart political and social problems. In their landmark work on vulnerability, geographers Michael Watts and Hans Bohl point to three interrelated causes of food insecurity: declining control over local food resources, lack of political power, and political-economic structures that foster inequality. With government corruption, institutional inefficiencies, and power struggles layered on top of these, the stage is set for the hunger problems described above.

Of course, many people in poorer countries do not suffer from malnutrition, and malnutrition is not limited to the periphery. There are children in virtually every county in the United States who do not have access to adequate food. That reality gave rise to the No Kid Hungry Campaign, which provides breakfasts to children who come to school hungry. Research shows that students who are hungry do not perform well in school, and that breakfast is critical to academic success. No Kid Hungry also helps ensure children receive lunches during the summer, when school is out and children cannot take advantage of school lunch programs.

HIGH QUALITY FARMLAND IN THE PATH OF DEVELOPMENT

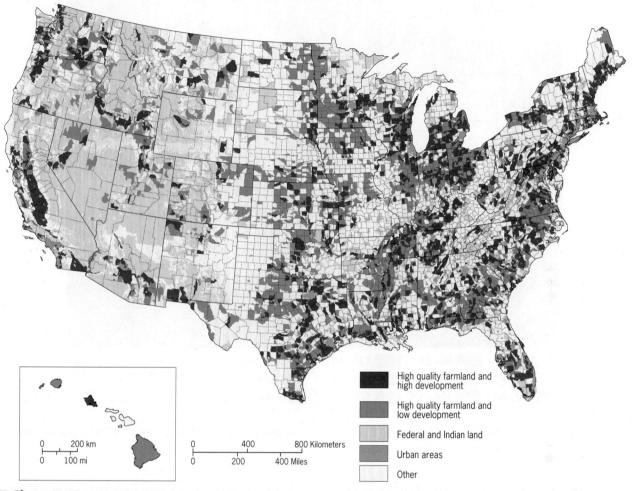

High quality farmland and high development

High quality farmland and low development

Federal and Indian land

Urban areas

Other

■■ **Figure 11.23**

Farming on the Edge: High-Quality Farmland in the Path of Development, 2002.   This map from American Farmland Trust, whose charge is to preserve farmland, highlights farmland that is endangered of being suburbanized as cities expand into neighboring farmlands.   *Courtesy of*: American Farm Trust, http://www.farmland.org/farmingontheedge/maps.htm, last accessed November 2005.

Looking ahead, there is growing concern in the United States and beyond over the loss of fertile, productive farmlands to housing and retail developments (Fig. 11.23). Many cities were established amid productive farmlands that could supply the needs of their inhabitants. Now the cities are absorbing the productive farmlands as they expand. Between 1987 and 1992, China lost more than one million hectares of farmland to urbanization. In the United States, the American Farmland Trust identified 12 U.S. areas where farmland was giving way to urban uses at a rapid rate in the 1990s, including California's Central Valley, South Florida, California's coastal zone, North Carolina's Piedmont, and the Chicago–Milwaukee–Madison triangle in Illinois–Wisconsin. These 12 areas represent only 5 percent of U.S. farmland, but they produce 17 percent of total agricultural sales, 67 percent of all fruit, 55 percent of all vegetables, and one-quarter of all dairy products. Figures for other countries in the richer parts of the world (such as Japan) as well as for poorer countries (such as

Egypt) prove that urban expansion into productive farmland is a global problem with serious implications for the future.

The conversion of farmlands into housing developments is not confined to areas close to major cities that could become suburbs. Expendable wealth and the desire to have a place to "get away from it all" have led highly productive commercial agricultural areas to be converted into regions for second homes. On the Delmarva Peninsula in the United States, for example, where poultry production is concentrated, the price of land rose as urbanites from Pennsylvania, Washington, D.C., Maryland, and New York bought land on the eastern shore to build second homes. Many of the new residents on the peninsula are demanding higher environmental standards. Rising land prices and stricter environmental standards are placing a squeeze on the cost of chicken production. As urban population continues to grow and expendable wealth increases for the wealthiest of the population, more agricultural lands will be converted to housing

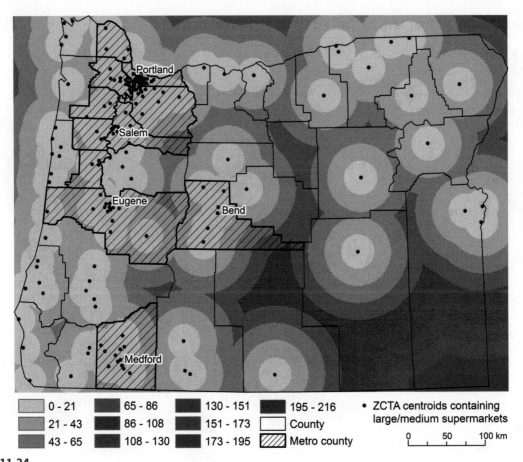

Food Deserts in Oregon, 2010. Mean distance (km) from population-weighted ZIP Code Tabulation Area (ZCTA) centroids containing large or medium supermarkets in Oregon. *Map courtesy of*: Aki Michimi, 2011.

developments, especially lands in beautiful areas with recreational amenities.

Population growth, the loss of agricultural land, and the types of political-economic factors highlighted by Watts and Bohle help explain why global food prices have been on the rise for more than a decade. Further pressure on food prices is coming from consumption increases in countries experiencing rapid development (e.g., China) and from a trend toward using food crops for biofuel production. These factors were behind an almost 50 percent surge in global food prices between April 2007 and March 2008. Food riots broke out in some cities, and the specter of large-scale famine grew. Another more recent spike in food prices was one factor in the outbreak of revolutions in North Africa and Southwest Asia in spring 2011. A convergence of changing land use, increasing use of grains for fuel, corrupt governments, and environmental impacts works against the provision of adequate food at reasonable prices for the world's poor.

Despite the severity of the situation, in today's world it is possible for many people to put farming largely out of their minds. As a result of the industrialization of agriculture and improvements in transportation, consumers come in contact with farmers much less frequently than did previous generations. On a freezing cold winter day in Cincinnati,

Ohio, consumers can purchase fresh strawberries grown in Chile. Consumers can also purchase highly processed foods with long shelf lives and forget where the item was purchased, much less think of the farm work that went into the ingredients.

As a result of the growing distance between farmers and consumers, geographers have sought to draw attention to **food deserts**—areas where people have limited access to fresh, nutritious foods (Fig. 11.24). Urban food deserts are typically found in low-income neighborhoods where medium-size and large grocery stores are largely absent; instead, the only grocery stores within easy reach are small ones filled mainly with processed, energy-dense but nutrient-poor food. British geographer Hilary Shaw (2006) found that consumers in urban food deserts were more likely to purchase unhealthy foods because these foods were cheaper than fresh fruits and vegetables.

Geographers Akihiko Michimi and Michael Wimberly found that rural food deserts lack not only larger grocery stores but also public transportation to reach larger grocery stores. In their study of food deserts and access to fruits and vegetables, the geographers found that since the 1980s in rural areas of the United States a "restructuring of food retail industries has occurred such that local grocery stores that once served small rural communities have been closed" and replaced with larger national chains in regional trade centers. Michimi and Wimberly also found a difference between food deserts in metropolitan and nonmetropolitan areas of the United States. In metropolitan areas, obesity rates increased and the rate of fruit and vegetable consumption decreased with increasing distance from grocery stores. They did not find the same correlation in nonmetropolitan areas.

Summary

Agricultural production has changed drastically since the First Agricultural Revolution. Today, agricultural products, even perishable ones, are shipped around the world. Agriculture has industrialized, and in many places, food production is dominated by large-scale agribusiness. A major commonality between ancient agriculture and modern agriculture remains: the need to change. Trial and error were the norms of early plant and animal domestication; those same processes are at play in the biotechnology-driven agriculture of the contemporary era. Whatever the time period or process involved, agriculture leaves a distinct imprint on the cultural landscape, from land surveys to land ownership to land use. Globalization has made an imprint on landscapes and agribusiness. What is produced where is not simply a product of the environment and locally available plants; the modern geography of agriculture depends on factors ranging from climate and government regulation to technology and shifting global consumption patterns.

Geographic Concepts

organic agriculture
agriculture
primary economic activity
secondary economic activity
tertiary economic activity
quaternary economic activity
quinary economic activity
plant domestication
root crops
seed crops
First Agricultural Revolution
animal domestication
subsistence agriculture

shifting cultivation
slash-and-burn agriculture
Second Agricultural Revolution
von Thünen model
Third Agricultural Revolution
biotechnology
Green Revolution
genetically modified organisms
    (GMOs)
rectangular survey system
township- and range-system
metes-and-bounds system
long-lot survey system

primogeniture
commercial agriculture
monoculture
Köppen climatic classification system
climatic regions
plantation agriculture
livestock ranching
Mediterranean agriculture
cash crops
luxury crops
agribusiness
food desert

Learn More Online

About food production and development
www.foodfirst.org

About the preservation of agricultural lands
www.farmland.org

Watch It Online

Guns, Germs, and Steel
www.pbs.org/gunsgermssteel

Loss of agricultural land to suburbanization in Chicago
www.learner.org/resources/series180.html#program_
descriptions
click on video on demand for program 24

Russia's Farming Revolution
www.learner.org/resources/series180.html#program_
descriptions
click on video on demand for program 7

Sustainable agriculture in India
www.learner.org/resources/series180.html#program_
descriptions
click on video on demand for program 17

INDUSTRY AND SERVICES

Containing the World-Economy

I found myself mesmerized by the loading of a container ship at the port just outside of Copenhagen, Denmark. The crane reached over to the ship, picked up each container, and slowly lowered the container onto the neatly organized dock. Slowly the stack of containers on the ship shrunk, each one emblazoned with a label of a shipping company based in one country or another: Germany, China, the United States, Japan, Sweden, Australia. The crane continued to unload goods produced in Asia. From the port in Copenhagen, the containers will be shipped by road, railroad, and barge to destinations throughout Scandinavia and to countries around the Baltic Sea.

The container ship is the backbone of globalization and has dramatically changed the economic geography of the planet since the first one sailed in 1956. Before containers, a ship would arrive at port with various, odd-sized crates and boxes. Hundreds of longshoremen would flock to the dock to unload the goods by hand. With **containerization**, ports now have relatively few employees who operate the high-tech cranes, moving standard-sized containers from ship to dock or dock to ship with precision. Cranes move containers with the goal of unloading a massive container ship within 24 hours of reaching port.

Nearly 90 percent of long-distance cargo is now shipped in standard containers. With a volume in excess of 2250 cubic feet (more than 65 m³), one container can accommodate goods worth millions of dollars. Steel containers are structurally sound and can be stacked and moved from truck to rail to ship without worrying about how fragile the contents of the containers are.

The container ship in Figure 12.1 is small compared to the *Marco Polo*, the world's largest container ship. Although the *Marco Polo* is the length of four football fields, it was designed to fit through the Suez Canal, making transportation of massive amounts of goods from Asia to Europe possible. The larger the ship, the less expensive it is to transport each container. So, shipbuilders keep going larger. Certain bottlenecks of shipping routes, including the Panama Canal,

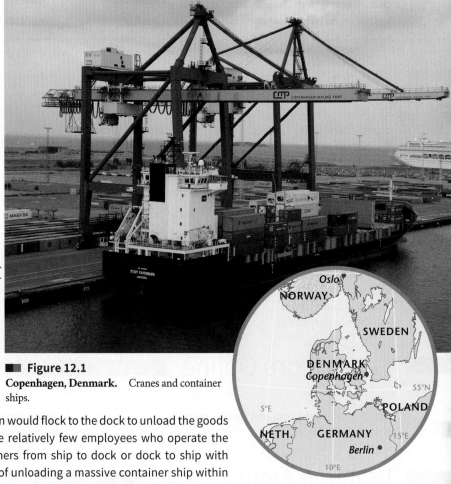

© Alexander B. Murphy

■ **Figure 12.1**
Copenhagen, Denmark. Cranes and container ships.

the Suez Canal, and the Straits of Magellan (at the tip of Malaysia) limit, how large the ships can be built. Most container ships are too large for the Panama Canal, but ships going from Asia to Europe are carefully designed to still use the Straits of Magellan and the Suez Canal.

Containerization has even changed the map of major port cities. Ports have become intermodal hubs, and port authorities and managers are constantly expanding and improving their infrastructure and systems to attract more cargo through their port. Ports don't solely attract cargo, as the cruise ship in the background of Figure 12.1 demonstrates. In 2014, the Copenhagen Malmo Port completed construction on a cruise ship quay with three terminal buildings so that the port can serve more cruise ships and passengers.

Ports such as San Francisco declined because their piers were not well suited to the loading and unloading of containers. Others such as nearby Oakland boomed—capitalizing on a container-friendly port retrofit that made it one of the most important shipping centers along the West Coast of the United States. With proximity to customers less important than it once was, small ports such as Busan, South Korea, expanded dramatically, and previously nonexistent ports such as Tanjun Pelepas, Malaysia, were built. They have emerged as significant port cities because containerization made it economical to sell local goods in New York, London, and Buenos Aires.

The geography of industry and services is a product of shifting developments that have shaped production and consumption over time. In this chapter, we begin by looking at the origins of the Industrial Revolution in Great Britain and its diffusion into mainland Europe. In addition, we look at the rise of manufacturing belts in Europe, Asia, and North America. We then explore how industrialization has changed, focusing on the emergence of global labor networks and such concepts as flexible production and the global division of labor. We also consider how the expanding service economy is changing the nature of employment and the economic bases of many places.

Key Questions FOR CHAPTER 12

1. Where did the Industrial Revolution begin, and how did it diffuse?
2. How have the character and geography of industrial production changed?
3. How have deindustrialization and the rise of service industries altered the economic geography of production?

WHERE DID THE INDUSTRIAL REVOLUTION BEGIN, AND HOW DID IT DIFFUSE?

The manufacturing of goods began long before the Industrial Revolution. In **cottage industries**, families in a community worked together, each creating a component of a finished good or the good itself. For example, in a small town in England, a few families would receive a shipment of wool from a merchant and then prepare the wool and pass it on to families who would spin the wool into yarn. The families who made the wool into yarn passed the yarn to weavers who made blankets and other wool products. Typically, this work was done over the winter, after harvest and before planting the next year's crop. In the spring before planting, the merchants returned to pick up the finished products and pay for the production. Merchants shipped the goods around the world.

In the 1800s, as global trade intensified with the availability of steam-powered ships, goods produced in cottage industries in India were in demand around the world. Indian, cottage industries produced goods made of iron, gold, silver, and brass, Indian woodworkers produced hand-carved items that were in demand wherever they could be bought. India's textiles, made on individual spinning wheels and hand looms, were considered the best in the world. India's textiles were so finely produced that British textile makers rioted in 1721, demanding legislative protection against imports from India. China and Japan also possessed a substantial industrial base of cottage industries, long before the Industrial Revolution.

The transition from cottage industries to the Industrial Revolution happened in the context of changing **economies of scale**. Europeans sought to capitalize on economies of scale, to generate a greater profit by producing larger quantities of the goods in high demand, which in turn decreased the average cost of producing the good. European industries, from the textile makers of Flanders and Britain to the iron smelters of Thüringen, had become substantial operations. However, in price and quality, Europe's products could not match those of other parts of the world. European commercial companies, including the Dutch and British East India Companies, sought to gain control over local industries in Indonesia and India, respectively, in the 1700s and 1800s.

Both the Dutch and British companies were privately owned and operated under the flag of their country. Each company established battalions of soldiers as they sought to politically and economically control the sectors of production in Southeast and South Asia. The European presence on the ground created political chaos, and the Dutch and British companies profited from the political chaos, pitting local factions against one another. British merchants exported tons of raw fiber from India to expand textile industries in northern England, including Liverpool and Manchester.

The wealth brought into the Netherlands and England through trade (Fig. 12.2) funded technological innovations in manufacturing in Europe and fueled the expansion of production through the Industrial Revolution. The wealth was so great that the monarchs of both the Netherlands and England eventually stepped in and directly colonized Indonesia and South Asia in an effort to squelch the political chaos created by the companies and to secure the continued flow of wealth into European coffers. Through the mass production of goods, brought about by the Industrial Revolution, Europe eventually flooded global markets with inexpensive products, burying cottage industries at home and in Asia. Colonies were no longer merely sites of production and resource extraction.

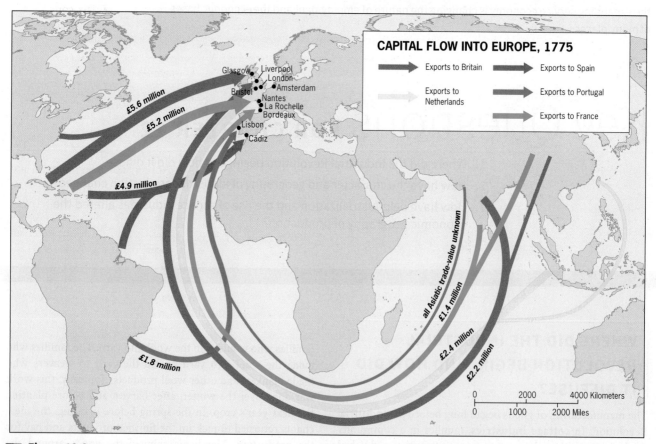

■■ **Figure 12.2**

Capital Flows into Europe During the Period of European Colonialism.   This map shows the major flows of capital into Europe from Europe's colonies. The capital helped fuel Europe's Industrial Revolution at the end of the 1700s and into the 1800s.   *Adapted with permission from*: Geoffrey Barraclough, ed., *The Times Concise Atlas of World History,* 5th ed., Hammond Incorporated, 1998.

When Europe exported inexpensive, mass-produced products globally, colonies became customers, places where European goods were purchased.

The Industrial Revolution

The first steps in industrialization occurred in northern England, where cotton from America and India was shipped to the port of Liverpool. Textile factories in the British Midlands, south of Manchester, took advantage of rivers and hills to power cotton spinning machines by water running downhill.

The hearth of the Industrial Revolution was England in the eighteenth century. Wealth brought to Europe through the colonization of and trade with South Asia, Southeast Asia, the Americas, and Africa funded inventions, including the spinning jenny and the steam engine (Fig. 12.2). James Watt is credited with improving the steam engine by creating a separate chamber to house the steam and by perfecting the pistons and getting them to perform correctly. The invention did not happen overnight: A series of attempts over a few decades finally worked when Watt partnered with toymaker and metal worker Matthew Boulton, who inherited great wealth from his wife (her father had amassed wealth as a global cloth trader). Boulton financed the final trials and errors that made the Boulton & Watt steam engine functional and reliable. Coal powered the steam engine, which fueled water pumps, trains, looms, and eventually ships.

The steam engine, trains, and railroads were all made of iron. Before Boulton and Watt could perfect the steam engine, inventors needed a reliable way to heat up iron so that it could be poured into cast molds to make the same product over and over again. In Coalbrookdale, England, in 1709, iron worker Abraham Darby found a way to *smelt* iron. By burning coal in a vacuum-like environment, the English already knew they could cook off impurities, leaving behind coke, the high-carbon portion of coal. Darby put iron ore and coke in a blast furnace and then pushed air into the furnace. This combination allowed the furnace to burn at a much higher temperature than wood charcoal or coal allowed. Mixing the iron ore with limestone (to attract impurities) and water and smelting it with coke enabled iron workers to pour melted iron ore into molds (instead of shaping it by hammering against anvils), yielding *cast iron*. The use of molds allowed more consistency in iron parts and increased production of iron components. As the toponym indicates, the residents of Ironbridge, a town neighboring Coalbrookdale, still take pride in their town's bridge, the first in the world to be constructed entirely from cast iron in 1779 (Fig. 12.3).

During the early part of the Industrial Revolution, before the railroad connected nodes of industry and reduced the transportation costs of coal, manufacturing needed to be located close to coal fields. Manufacturing plants also needed to be connected to ports, where raw materials could arrive and finished products could depart. In the first decades of the Industrial Revolution, plants were usually connected to ports by a broad canal or river system. In Britain, densely populated and heavily urbanized industrial regions developed near the coal fields (Fig. 12.4). The two largest centers of industry in Britain were an iron-working region in the Midlands, where Birmingham is located, and a textile production region in the Northwest, where Liverpool and Manchester are located.

The steam engine had a dramatic impact on industry and helped concentrate even more industrial production in the Midlands and Northwest. Industrialists used the steam engine to pump water out of coal mines, enabling coal workers to reach deeper coal seams, to power spinning wheels that spun 100 plus spools of thread at a time, to power dozens of looms in a factory all at once, and to create a new mode of transportation: the railroad. The first commercial railway connected Manchester, a center of textile manufacturing, along 35 miles of track to the port of

Figure 12.3
Ironbridge, England. The world's first bridge made entirely of cast iron was constructed in the late eighteenth century near Coalbrookdale, England, reflecting the resources, technology, and available skills in this area at the time.

© John Robertson/Alamy Images

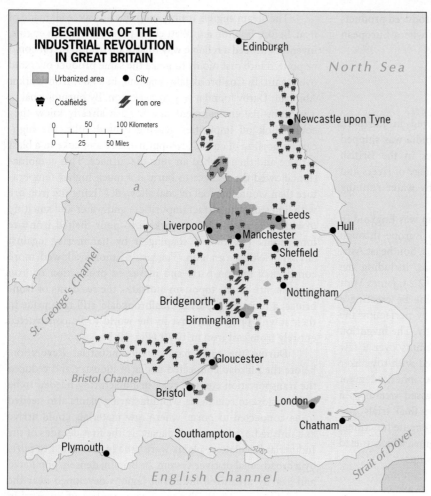

BEGINNING OF THE INDUSTRIAL REVOLUTION IN GREAT BRITAIN

Urbanized area   ● City

Coalfields   Iron ore

0   50   100 Kilometers
0   25   50 Miles

■ **Figure 12.4**

The Origins of the Industrial Revolution. The areas of Great Britain that industrialized earliest were those closest to the resources needed for industrialization: coal, iron ore, and capital. Large areas of urbanization grew near industrial zones and in the port cities where materials came in and from which industrialized products went out. *Adapted with permission from:* Geoffrey Barraclough, ed., *The Times Concise Atlas of World History,* 5th ed., Hammond Incorporated, 1998.

With the advent of the railroad and steamship, Great Britain enjoyed even greater advantages over the rest of the world than it did at the beginning of the Industrial Revolution. British investors and business leaders held a near monopoly over the manufacture of many products that were in demand around the world. The British perfected coal smelting, cast iron, the steam engine, and the steam locomotive. The railroad pioneer George Stephenson, who led the building of the railway between Manchester and Liverpool, set the standard gauge for the railroad track that is still used for about 60 percent of the world's railroads today. The Industrial Revolution increased Britain's influence globally. The British had the know-how, the experience, and the capital to diffuse the Industrial Revolution into the Americas and continental Europe.

Diffusion to Mainland Europe

In the early 1800s, as the innovations of Britain's Industrial Revolution diffused into mainland Europe, the same set of **locational criteria** for industrial zones applied: sites needed to be close to resources and connected to ports by water. Coal and iron ore were heavy, and transportation of both resources was costly. The first manufacturing belts in continental Europe were located close to coal fields and connected by water to a port so that raw materials could be imported from the Americas and Asia and finished products could be exported. A belt of major coal fields extends from west to east through mainland Europe, roughly along the southern margins of the North European Lowland—across northern France and southern Belgium, the Netherlands, the German Rühr, western Bohemia in the Czech Republic, and Silesia in Poland. Colonial empires gave France, Britain, Belgium, the Netherlands, and, later, Germany access to the capital necessary to fuel industrialization and in some cases the raw materials necessary for production. Iron ore is dispersed along a similar belt, and the map showing the pattern of diffusion of the Industrial Revolution into Europe shows industrial production was concentrated along the coal and iron ore belt through the middle of mainland Europe (Fig. 12.6).

When industry developed in one area, economic growth had a **spillover effect** on the port cities to which

Liverpool in 1830. Sited where the River Mersey flows into the Irish Sea, Liverpool faces west, toward Britain's colonies in the Americas. Cotton and tobacco arrived in Liverpool, and were transported by rail or canal to Manchester, which was a center for textile manufacturing. Coal from Leeds, northeast of Manchester, was transported to Manchester. The coal, cotton, and textile plants were located close to each other, helping the area become the center for mechanized textile manufacturing in the Industrial Revolution.

The new transportation system of the railway diffused as thousands of miles of iron and then steel track were laid, fundamentally changing the quantity of and speed at which goods could be transported over land. The steam engine made its mark on sea transportation, as the first steam-powered vessel crossed the Atlantic Ocean in 1819, shrinking the time it took to travel across seas and also enabling shipbuilders to design larger vessels that could transport more goods (Fig. 12.5).

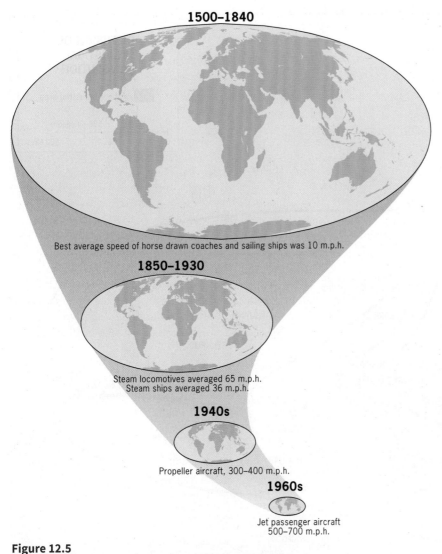

1500–1840

Best average speed of horse drawn coaches and sailing ships was 10 m.p.h.

1850–1930

Steam locomotives averaged 65 m.p.h.
Steam ships averaged 36 m.p.h.

1940s

Propeller aircraft, 300–400 m.p.h.

1960s

Jet passenger aircraft
500–700 m.p.h.

Figure 12.5

The World Shrinks Through Transportation Innovations. This diagram helpfully illuminates how much more quickly goods and people can move over land and sea after 1960 compared to 1650. The maps are slightly misleading, though, because these new transportation technologies do not connect every single place on Earth. Places close to airports and seaports are more connected to each other than places away from transportation nodes. Time–space compression tells us the world is shrinking, but unevenly as some places are closer and some are relatively farther away than ever before. *Figure courtesy of*: Peter Dicken, Global Shift.

sited in the mouth of a delta (Rodrigue 2014).

Over the last 200 years, the Dutch have radically altered the port, expanding it from the mouth of the delta west to the coast of the North Sea. With each change in the situation of the global economy, Rotterdam built new facilities to accommodate the new production and transportation needs. For example, in the 1950s, Rotterdam Municipal Port Management recognized the growth in oil dependency and built the Europoort, extending pipelines and a deep canal to allow the importation of oil, which was then distributed into the port's hinterland. In the 1980s, Rotterdam saw an opportunity to connect the port with the interior of continental Europe by railroad. It extended the port further west and built the Betuweroute rail line, which connects Rotterdam with Genoa, Italy. Rotterdam is both the starting and end point for goods along the corridor. It continues to expand to meet the changing situation of the global economy. In 2007, Rotterdam added land to the western end of the port, constructing a deep seaport to better serve larger container ships. The economic landscape of the port of Rotterdam has changed as the port managers have adjusted to the changing world-economy in order to facilitate transportation and solidify its position as the most important port in Europe and a hub of global commerce.

Once railroads were well established in Great Britain and continental Europe, the factors that determine where to locate, or site, manufacturing facilities changed. Transportation is a major cost in the production of a good, and railroads

they were linked by river or canal. For example, one of the largest industrial centers in continental Europe was the Rühr area of present-day Germany (Germany was not consolidated into a single country until the 1870s). The Rühr is connected to the port of Rotterdam, the Netherlands by the Rhine River. Each port has a **hinterland**, or an area from which goods can be produced, delivered to the port, and then exported. A port also serves its hinterland by importing raw materials that are delivered to manufacturing sites for production. In other words, Rotterdam is the port, and its hinterland includes the region along the Rhine, including the Rühr in Germany. Rotterdam is considered to be a port

lowered the cost of transporting bulk and heavy goods. Companies could locate manufacturing plants away from coal and iron ore and in major cities, like London and Paris. Cities could import raw materials, produce goods drawing from the larger labor supply, and sell the goods to the larger population of consumers found in cities. Industrialization was slow to reach London because it lacked easy access to coal and iron ore until the railway expanded through Great Britain. London became a particularly attractive site for industry at this point because of its port location on the Thames River and, more importantly, because of its major role in the flow of regional and global capital.

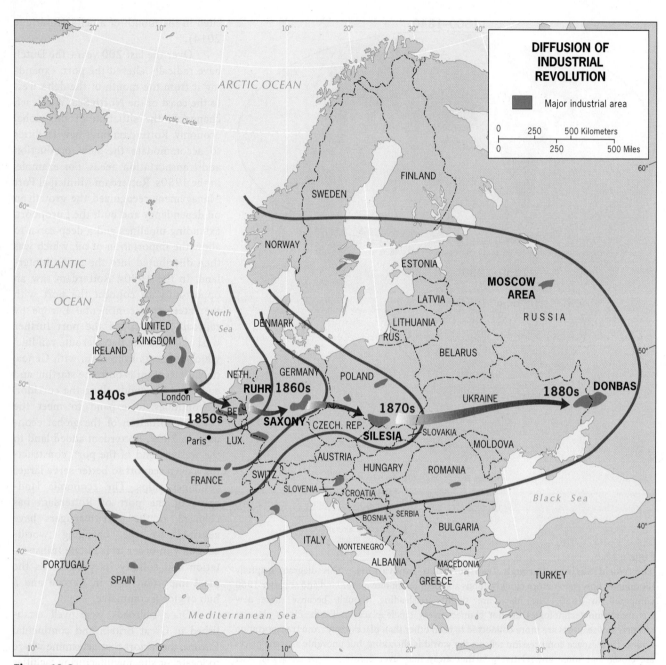

Figure 12.6
Diffusion of the Industrial Revolution. The eastward diffusion of the Industrial Revolution occurred during the second half of the nineteenth century. © H. J. de Blij, P. O. Muller, and John Wiley & Sons, Inc.

By choosing a site, or location, in London, a manufacturing company put itself at the center of Britain's global network of influence. Paris was already continental Europe's greatest city, but like London, it did not have coal or iron deposits in its immediate vicinity. When a railroad system was added to the existing network of road and waterway connections to Paris, however, the city became the largest local market for manufactured products for hundreds of miles. Paris attracted major industries, and the city, long a center for the manufacture of luxury items (jewelry, perfumes, and fashions), experienced substantial growth in such industries as metallurgy and chemical manufacturing. With a ready labor force, an ideal regional position for the distribution of finished products, the presence of governmental agencies, a nearby ocean port (Le Havre), and France's largest domestic market, Paris's development as a major industrial center was no accident.

London and Paris became, and remain, important industrial complexes not because of their coal fields but because of their commercial and political **connectivity** to the rest of the world (Fig. 12.7). Germany still ranks among the world's leading producers of both coal and steel and remains

FIELD NOTE

"Paris and the Paris Basin form the industrial as well as agricultural heart of France. The city and region are served by the Seine River, along which lies a string of ports from Le Havre at the mouth to Rouen at the head of navigation for oceangoing ships. Rouen has become a vital center on France's industrial map. As we approached on the river, you could see the famous cathedral and the city's historic cultural landscape to the left (north), but on the right bank lay a major industrial complex including coal-fired power facilities (although France leads Europe in nuclear energy), petrochemical plants, and oil installations. It is all part of the industrial region centered on Paris."

© H. J. de Blij

■ **Figure 12.7**
Rouen, France.

Europe's leading industrial power (Table 12.1). By the early twentieth century, industry began to diffuse far from the original European hearth to northern Italy (now one of Europe's major industrial regions), Catalonia (anchored by Barcelona) and northern Spain, southern Sweden, and southern Finland.

Diffusion Beyond Europe

Western Europe's early industrialization gave it a huge economic head start, or a **first mover advantage**, putting the region at the center of a quickly growing world-economy in

the nineteenth century. Industrialization began to diffuse from Europe to the Americas and Asia in the nineteenth century, and **secondary hearths** of industrialization were established in eastern North America, western Russia and Ukraine, and East Asia. Each of the primary industrial regions established by the 1950s were close to coal, which was the major energy source, connected by water or railroad to ports, and heavily invested in by wealthy persons already in the region and by merchants from Europe (Fig. 12.8).

NORTH AMERICA

By the beginning of the twentieth century, the only serious rival to Europe was a territory settled predominantly by Europeans and with particularly close links to Britain, which provided links to the capital and innovations that fueled industrialization there: North America. Manufacturing in North America began in New England during the colonial period, but the northeastern States were not especially rich in mineral resources. North America, however, benefited from the ability of its companies to acquire needed raw materials from overseas sources.

Industries developed along the Great Lakes where canal, river, and lakes connected with railroads on land to move resources and goods in and out of industrial centers. The industrial region benefited from a ready supply of energy to fuel industrialization. Coal was the chief fuel for industries at the time, and there was never

TABLE 12.1
World's Largest Oil Producers.

TOP OIL PRODUCERS (BARRELS PER DAY)

1. Saudi Arabia	11,730,000	12. Nigeria	2,524,000
2. United States	11,110,000	13. Venezuela	2,489,000
3. Russia	10,440,000	14. Norway	1,902,000
4. China	4,197,000	15. Algeria	1,875,000
5. Canada	3,856,000	16. Angola	1,872,000
6. Iran	3,594,000	17. Kazakhstan	1,606,000
7. United Arab Emirates	3,213,000	18. Qatar	1,579,000
8. Iraq	2,979,000	19. Libya	1,483,000
9. Mexico	2,936,000	20. India	990,200
10. Kuwait	2,797,000	21. Indonesia	974,300
11. Brazil	2,652,000	22. Colombia	969,100

Data from: United States Central Intelligence Agency, World Factbook, 2014.

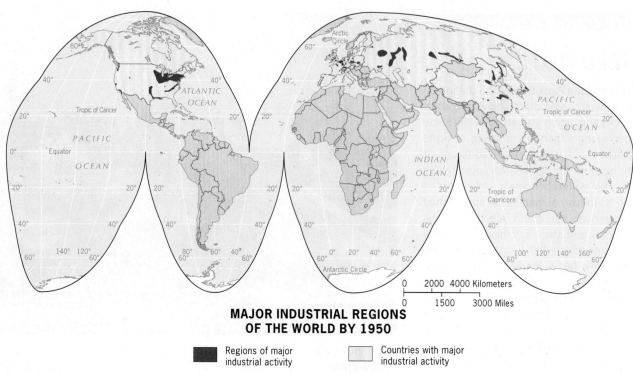

**MAJOR INDUSTRIAL REGIONS
OF THE WORLD BY 1950**

▮ Regions of major
industrial activity

☐ Countries with major
industrial activity

■ **Figure 12.8**
Major Industrial Regions of the World in 1950. This map shows the major industrial districts of Europe, North America, Russia, and East Asia in approximately 1950. © E. H. Fouberg, A. B. Murphy, H. J. de Blij, and John Wiley & Sons, Inc.

any threat of a coal shortage in the United States: U.S. coal reserves are among the world's largest and are widely distributed, being found from Appalachian Pennsylvania to the northwestern Great Plains (Fig. 12.9).

RUSSIA AND UKRAINE

The St. Petersburg region is one of Russia's oldest manufacturing centers. Tsar Peter the Great planned and constructed the city not only to serve as Russia's capital but also to become the country's industrial core. Peter the Great encouraged western European artisans with skills and specializations to migrate to the region, and he imported high-quality machine-building equipment to help fuel industrialization. The St. Petersburg region soon attracted industries including shipbuilding, chemical production, food processing, and textile making. After World War I, the newly formed Soviet Union annexed Ukraine and took advantage of its rich resources and industrial potential, especially in the coal-rich Donbas region, to become an industrial power. The Soviet Union (and Russia today) was resource rich. Soviet leaders directed an economic plan to industrialize the Moscow region. They developed industries in Nizhni Novgorod, a river port located at the confluence of the Volga and Oka rivers, 270 miles southeast of Moscow. Following the Volga River, goods can be imported or exported from Nizhni Nogorod to the Black Sea or the Caspian Sea.

EAST ASIA

After Japan opened its economy through a change in government policy in 1868, the Industrial Revolution diffused to Japan. Japan began industrializing with its military sector and encouraged Japanese men to study sciences in universities abroad so they could bring their knowledge back to Japan and create industries. With limited natural resources, Japan depended on raw materials imported from other parts of the world for manufacturing. In the late 1800s and early 1900s, Japan colonized Korea, Taiwan, and portions of mainland China, which brought capital and resources for industry. Japan's dominant region of industrialization and urbanization is the *Kanto Plain* (Fig. 12.7), which contains about one-third of the nation's population and includes the Tokyo–Yokohama–Kawasaki metropolitan area. Japan's second largest industrial complex extends from the eastern end of the Seto Inland Sea to the Nagoya area and includes the Kobe–Kyoto–Osaka triangle, which is a vast industrial region with steel mills, a major chemical industry, automobile manufacturing, shipbuilding, textile factories, and many other types of production.

Examine the map of diffusion of the Industrial Revolution into Europe (Fig. 12.6) and hypothesize what other variables (aside from the presence of coal) were necessary for industrialization to take hold in these regions.

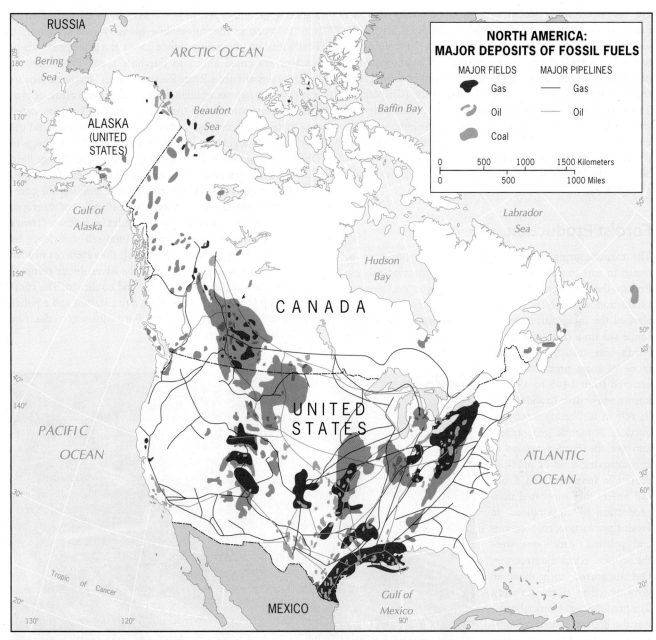

■ Figure 12.9

Major Deposits of Fossil Fuels in North America.   North America is one of the world's largest energy consumers, and the continent is also endowed with substantial energy sources.   © H. J. de Blij, P. O. Muller and John Wiley & Sons, Inc.

HOW HAVE THE CHARACTER AND GEOGRAPHY OF INDUSTRIAL PRODUCTION CHANGED?

Economic geography provides context for understanding a multitude of human geographic developments. In this book, we have already made reference to economic geography to help explain globalization in Chapter 1, local and popular cultures in Chapter 4, identities and scale in Chapter 5, language loss and toponyms in Chapter 7, colonialism and political

disputes in Chapter 8, and the geography of development in Chapter 10. In this section of the chapter, we incorporate economic geography principles we introduced in earlier chapters with other economic geography concepts to provide a context for understanding changes in the character and geography of manufacturing and service industries since World War II.

In Chapter 1, we defined **globalization** as a set of processes that are increasing interactions, deepening relationships, and heightening interdependence without regard to country borders. Globalization is also a set of outcomes that are felt from these global processes—outcomes that are unevenly distributed and differently manifested across the world. Improvements in transportation and communication technologies are at the root of globalization. The improvement of sailing ships and navigation methods helped establish global trade routes and the first wave of colonialism (Chapter 8). The advent of the steam ship, the diffusion of railroads, and the invention of the telegraph and then the telephone quickened global trade and connected empires in the second wave of colonialism. Through colonialism and trade, capitalism became the economic foundation of the world-economy (Chapter 8).

Fordist Production

The manufacturing boom of the twentieth century can be traced in part to early innovations in the production process. Perhaps the most significant of these innovations was the mass-production assembly line pioneered by Henry Ford, which allowed the inexpensive production of consumer goods at a single site on a previously unknown scale. So significant was Ford's idea that the dominant mode of mass production that endured from 1945 to 1970 is known as **Fordist**. In addition to its role in facilitating mass production, economic geographers also see the Fordist system as encompassing a set of political-economic structures and financial orders that supported mass production by corporations. In Fordist production, corporations and political institutions were the political-economic structures that supported each other in growing the world-economy. The predominant financial order was the Bretton Woods arrangement, negotiated in 1944, under which countries adopted the gold standard, agreeing to peg the values of their currency to the price of gold. These structures created a degree of stability in international exchange that encouraged global mass production of goods.

The Fordist period is marked by a surge in both mass production and mass consumption. On the Ford assembly line, machines replaced people, and unskilled workers instead of craftsmen worked on the assembly lines. Ford paid his workers a good wage, and droves of job seekers migrated to the Detroit area to work in the automobile industry (see Chapter 9). Ford's goal was to mass produce goods at a price point where his workers could afford to purchase them. Production of automobiles at Ford's River Rouge plant in Dearborn, Michigan (Fig. 12.10) exemplified the **vertical integration** of production common during the Fordist period. Ford imported raw materials, from coal to rubber to steel, from around the world and brought them to his plant on the River Rouge in Dearborn, just west of Detroit. The massive River Rouge Ford plant is better described as an industrial complex. The Henry Ford Foundation describes Ford's goal in building the complex of 93 buildings with more than 120 miles of conveyor belts that covered an area 1 by 1.5 miles as follows: "Henry Ford's ultimate goal was to achieve total self-sufficiency by owning, operating and coordinating all the resources needed to produce complete automobiles." The River Rouge complex included a power plant, boat docks, and a railroad. The complex had up to 100,000 employees, a fire station and a police department, prompting the Henry Ford Museum to describe it as "a city without residents."

Alamy

■■ Figure 12.10

Dearborn, Michigan.   The industrial complex of the Ford River Rouge Plant as it stood in the 1940s. In Fordist production, the corporation imported raw materials, bringing them by barge and rail to the Ford River Rouge Plant. The complex included a power plant, steel production, and the manufacturing of component parts of automobiles. Nearly everything Ford needed to produce an automobile was brought together at the factory complex where up to 100,000 employees (at its peak in the 1930s) labored to manufacture components and assembled automobiles.

Under Fordist production, distance was a major consideration in the location of industry. For example, in the United States, furniture manufacturing shifted from Boston in 1875 to Cincinnati by 1890 and then Grand Rapids, Michigan, by 1910. Furniture manufacturing took off in North Carolina when northern entrepreneurs built manufacturing plants there in the early 1900s to take advantage of North Carolina's "abundance of lumber, low-cost labor combined with Reconstruction era wood-working skills and attitudes" (Walcott 2011). The presence of infrastructure, nearness to customers, and humid climate (which kept wood from cracking) were also reasons furniture manufacturers located in close proximity to one another in North Carolina. High Point and other furniture centers agglomerated, or clustered together, to take advantage of not only the location and resources but also the services and infrastructure that grew to accommodate and aid furniture manufacturers in the region.

Finished furniture is a bulky commodity. Whenever furniture manufactures have considered locating outside of North Carolina and the Piedmont region or moving operations abroad, one of the key issues has been the **friction of distance**: the increase in time and cost that usually comes with increased distance over which commodities must travel. If a heavy raw material is shipped thousands of miles to a factory, the friction of distance increases. Friction of distance accounts for the raw materials that go into a product and prompts manufacturers to locate their plants close to raw materials if needed raw materials, such as coal and iron ore, are heavy.

A corollary to the concept of the friction of distance focuses on the location of customers instead of on the transport of raw materials. **Distance decay** (see Chapter 4) assumes the impact of a function or an activity will decline as one moves away from its point of origin. Distance decay suggests that manufacturing plants should be more concerned with serving the markets of nearby places than more distant places. This basic principle is important in understanding the locational dynamics of furniture manufacturing. Locating in North Carolina allows furniture manufacturers to reach nearby places, in the Northeast and Southeast, where the vast majority of their customers live, in less than a day.

AGGLOMERATION

British economist Alfred Marshall (1842–1924), a leader in economic theory who is often credited with pioneering the field of industrial **location theory**, argued that a particular industry, whether automobile manufacturing or furniture production, clusters in an area. He called this process *localization*, and later theorists called it agglomeration. Marshall held that localized industries could attract workers with industry-specific skills, be able to share information, and attract support services specific to the industry.

Marshall explained *why* industries would cluster, and German economic geographer Alfred Weber (1868–1958) developed a basic model explaining *where* industries would cluster. Weber helped develop locational studies in economic geography by focusing on the location of manufacturing facilities. In *Theory of the Location of Industries* (1909), Weber focused on specific factors that pull industry to particular locations.

Weber's **least cost theory** focused on a factory owner's desire to minimize three categories of costs. The first and most important of these categories was *transportation*. Weber suggested that the site where transportation costs are lowest is the place where it is least expensive to bring raw materials to the point of production and to distribute finished products to consumers. The second cost was that of *labor*. Higher labor costs tend to reduce the margin of profit, so a factory farther away from raw materials and markets might do better if cheap labor compensates for the added transport costs.

The third factor in Weber's model was similar to Marshall's theory of localization. Weber described the advantages that came about when similar industries clustered together, which he termed **agglomeration**. When a substantial number of companies that produce the same or similar goods cluster in one area, as with furniture manufacturing in North Carolina, Weber held that the industries can assist each other through shared talents, services, and facilities. For example, all the furniture companies will need access to lumber, textiles, ports, and skilled employees. By clustering together in the High Point region of North Carolina, all the furniture manufacturers benefit because the government builds better infrastructure they can all share and business services, like accountants and lawyers who specialize in contracts and trade, will open offices to offer services the companies need. In 2012, local governments in the High Point region invested in a system of wireless Internet access so that the 75,000 furniture buyers who go to market to buy furniture in High Point twice a year can use the wireless systems on their iPads and tablets as they seal deals (Fig. 12.11). Agglomeration can make a location more attractive for a company, potentially overcoming higher transportation or labor costs.

Taking these three factors together, transportation, labor, and localization (agglomeration), Weber determined that the least cost location for a manufacturing plant could be determined by a *location triangle* (Fig. 12.12). Economic geographer Jean-Paul Rodrigue (2014) explains that "solving Weber's location model often implies three stages; finding the least transport cost location, and adjusting this location to consider labor costs and agglomeration economies." Weber reasoned that industry will be located close to raw materials in order to lower transportation costs, but that availability of labor (either particularly skilled or cheap) and agglomeration of industry will "pull" where to locate the industry in two other directions.

Weber's theory of location was written over a century ago and is built on the assumption that a manufacturer will choose where to locate in order to minimize the cost of transportation. The cost of transporting goods has changed a great deal since then with the diffusion of container ships after 1956. When Weber was writing, transportation costs accounted for upwards of 50 percent of the cost of a good; today, transportation costs account for less than 5 percent of

■ **Figure 12.11**
High Point, North Carolina.   Twice a year 75,000 furniture buyers descend on the High Point Furniture Market in North Carolina. Purchasing goods to sell in furniture stores throughout the country and beyond, the buyers are attracted to 180 buildings and 11.5 million square feet of furniture show floor.

over the world, and then quickly shift where they manufacture their products in response to adjustments in production costs or consumer demand. These systems are designed to respond to consumers who want the newest/best/greatest offering or and also to enable manufacturers to lower cost of production by moving around the world.

Capitalism persists as an economic system not only because people consume but also because producers create and respond to consumer demand. Companies adapt to changing consumer preferences and commodify goods. Through the process of **commodification**, goods that were not previously bought, sold, and traded gain a monetary value and are bought, sold, and traded on the market. A new good, such as a mobile tablet, starts at a high price and becomes somewhat of a status symbol because of its high cost. The longer the mobile tablet is on the market and the greater the number of firms producing mobile tablets, the lower the price drops. Eventually, companies move the production of mobile tablets to lower the price of production and the price of

the cost of a good. This shift in transportation cost limits the value of Weber's theory today, except in the case of goods that rely on heavy raw materials (Rodrigue 2014).

Flexible Production and Product Life Cycle

Fordist production was based on both mass production and mass consumption. Money flowed through the world-economy as consumers purchased goods manufactured in large-scale complexes. As the global economy became more integrated and transportation costs decreased, the advantages of concentrating production in large-scale complexes declined. As a result, in the latter third of the twentieth century many enterprises began moving toward a *post-Fordist*, flexible production model. The post-Fordist model refers to a set of production processes in which the components of goods are made in different places around the globe and then brought together as needed to assemble the final product in response to customer demand. The term **flexible production** is used to describe this state of affairs because firms can pick and choose among a multitude of suppliers and production strategies all

WEBER'S LOCATION TRIANGLE

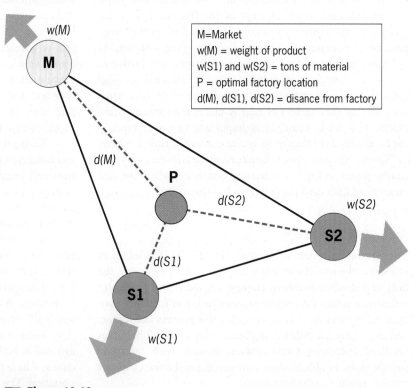

M=Market
w(M) = weight of product
w(S1) and w(S2) = tons of material
P = optimal factory location
d(M), d(S1), d(S2) = disance from factory

■ **Figure 12.12**
Weber's Location Triangle.   Weber assumed that the cost of transporting goods was the same in all directions and increased at an equal rate in all directions. He also assumed that water was available everywhere but that labor was available only in certain population centers.

the good, in order to compete. Changes in the production of a good over time take place as part of a **product life cycle**.

The production of televisions over time and space is a good example of how a product life cycle moves through four states: introduction, growth, maturity, and decline. Commercial production of television sets began after World War II, with a variety of small and medium-sized firms in Europe, Asia, and North America involved in production in the *introduction stage*. Firms in the United States, including Zenith, were the dominant producers of televisions until the 1970s. The cost of producing and purchasing televisions is high in the introductory stage because the company has invested a great deal in developing the technology but has not sold enough units to lower the cost.

During the 1970s and 1980s, in the *growth stage*, a dramatic shift occurred, with a small number of large Asian producers—particularly in Japan—seizing a much larger percentage of the market and with a few European firms increasing their position as well. The growth of television sales and the generation of profits from sales during this stage encouraged companies to focus on economies of scale to produce and sell massive numbers of televisions. During the 1970s, major firms moved the manufacture of components and assembly of televisions out of their home countries. U.S. firms moved these functions to the *maquiladora* of Mexico (discussed in Chapter 10) and the special economic zones of China (described in Chapter 9); Japanese firms moved component manufacturing and assembly to Taiwan, Singapore, Malaysia, and South Korea. Because the assembly stage was the most labor intensive, television manufacturers tapped into the global labor market, locating assembly plants not just in Mexico, China, and Southeast Asia, but also in India and Brazil.

In the *maturity* stage, few manufacturers continue to make small changes to the product and invest in marketing to secure their market share. Manufacturing of televisions became more mechanized, and with more technology and lower wage costs, companies moved production closer to consumers. By 1990, ten large firms were responsible for 80 percent of the world's color television sets; eight of them were Japanese and two European. Only one firm in the United States, Zenith, remained, and its share of the global market was relatively small.

In the *decline* stage, fewer consumers are demanding the product, and manufacturers shift to research and development of new goods or production of other, higher-demand goods. In the twenty-first century, electronics companies, including Samsung and Panasonic, invested in research and development of high-definition and plasma televisions, leading to production of these high-end televisions in Japan—and more recently into China and South Korea. These investments began a new product development cycle for high-definition electronics.

The Global Division of Labor

Tracing the production of televisions throughout the world over time helps us see how the **global division of labor** (also called the new international division of labor) currently works. Production of mass numbers of well-established goods is concentrated in the global economic periphery and semiperiphery to take advantage of lower labor costs, whereas research and development for new products is primarily located in the core. Fewer factors are fixed in flexible production, and as methods of assembly and products themselves change, production may be moved to take advantage of infrastructure, skilled labor, and accessible markets.

Geographically, the concept of **time–space compression** is the easiest way to capture the dramatic temporal and spatial changes taking place in the contemporary global economy. Time–space compression is based on the idea that developments in communication and transportation technologies have accelerated the speed with which things happen and have made the distance between places less significant (see Chapter 4). David Harvey, who coined the term *time–space compression*, argues that modern capitalism has so accelerated the pace of life and so changed the nature of the relationship between places that "the world seems to collapse inwards upon us." Fluctuations in the Tokyo stock market affect New York just hours later. Overnight, marketing campaigns can turn a product innovation into a fad in far-flung corners of the globe. Kiwis picked in New Zealand yesterday can be in the lunch boxes of boys and girls in Canada tomorrow. And decisions made in London can make or break a fast-developing deal over a transport link between Kenya and Tanzania.

Time–space compression shapes the global division of labor. When the world was less interconnected, most goods were produced not just close to raw materials, but close to the point of consumption. Thus, the major industrial belt in the United States was in the Northeast both because of readily available coal and other raw materials and because the major concentration of the North American population was there. With **just-in-time delivery** this has changed. Rather than keeping a large inventory of components or products, companies keep just what they need for short-term production and new parts are shipped quickly when needed. In turn, corporations can draw from labor around the globe for different components of production.

Advances in information technologies and shipping coupled with the global division of labor enable companies to move production from one site to another based on calculations of the "new place-based cost advantages" in a decision process geographer David Harvey has called a **spatial fix** (Walcott 2011, 7). In choosing a production site, location is only one consideration. "Distance is neither determinate nor insignificant as a factor in production location decisions" today (Walcott 2011, 9).

Major global economic players, including General Motors, Philips, Union Carbide, and Exxon, take advantage of low transportation costs, favorable governmental regulations, and expanding information technology to construct vast economic networks in which different facets of production are carried out in different places in order to benefit from the advantages of specific locations. Publicly traded companies, whose stock you can buy or sell on the stock exchange, are pressured by shareholders to grow their profits annually. One way to grow profits is to cut costs, and labor (wages, benefits, insurance) makes up a sizable proportion of production costs. Most multinational corporations have moved labor-intensive manufacturing, particularly assembly activities, to peripheral countries where labor is cheap, regulations are few, and tax rates are low. The manufacturing that remains in the core is usually highly mechanized. Technologically sophisticated manufacturing also tends to be sited in the core or semiperiphery because the expertise, infrastructure, and research and development are there.

Flexible Production of Nike

We can use Weber's location theory to consider the site for a factory producing lightweight consumer goods, including textiles and shoes, during the first half of the twentieth century. In the triangle of factors, the most important for lightweight consumer goods is a ready supply of low-cost *labor*. Being close to the *raw materials* is less of a concern, as shipping low-weight components is relatively inexpensive. *Agglomeration* is drawn for production of lightweight consumer goods so that component producers locate nearby and serve more than one company.

Companies that specialized in manufacturing components would locate close to the manufacturer of the final product. For example, companies that made shoe laces would locate close to shoe manufacturers. In the 1920s in the United States, towns near Boston, Massachusetts—great "shoe towns" including Haverhill, Brockton, and Lynn—were home to shoe factories specializing in both men's and women's shoes. About 300 shoe factories had sales offices "within a few blocks of each other in Boston" (Smith 1925), and in a leather district close to the city, tanneries prepared hides imported from around the world.

Economic geographer J. Russel Smith (1925) described the economic landscape of the shoe factory town of Lynn:

> *Walking the streets of Lynn one realizes what concentration an industry can have; the signs upon the places of business read—heels, welts, insoles, uppers, eyelets, thread, etc., etc. It is an astonishing proof of the degree to which even a simple commodity like a shoe, so long made by one man, can be subdivided and become the work of scores of industries and thousands of people.*

Shoe salespeople periodically flocked to shoe company headquarters in Boston to learn about the company's newest offerings and filled their sample suitcases with shoes to show their clients as they made the rounds of their sales territories.

With flexible production systems and container ships, lightweight consumer goods still need to be located close to low-cost labor, but another important consideration is connectedness to an intermodal port where components can be imported by ship, rail, or truck. The production of shoes is no longer concentrated in a handful of shoe towns on the East Coast. One of the most famous brands of shoes, Nike, demonstrates how selecting manufacturing sites for components and products has changed with the advent of just-in-time production and globalization. The transformation from producing shoes in a few shoe towns to producing shoes through an elaborate global network of international manufacturing and sales did not happen overnight.

University of Oregon track coach Bill Bowerman and one of his former runners, Phil Knight, founded Nike in 1961. Knight designed a trademark waffle sole that would create more traction for runners. Nike sold $8000 in footwear in its first year. The company established headquarters in Beaverton, Oregon, a suburb of Portland. Nike began production in the 1960s by contracting with an Asian firm to manufacture its shoes. In 1974, Nike set up its first domestic shoe manufacturing facility in the small town of Exeter, New Hampshire, just 46 miles from Lynn, Massachusetts. By the end of that year, Nike's workforce was still modest in number. Nike employees in Oregon concentrated on running the company and expanding sales, while employees who worked directly for Nike in New Hampshire and Asia produced shoes.

Nike has grown to be a giant in the shoe and apparel business, with sales of over $27.8 billion in fiscal year 2014. Although several thousand people work for Nike in Beaverton, not a single individual in Oregon is directly involved in the process of putting a shoe together. Worldwide, some 40,000 people work directly for Nike today, and according to Nike, nearly one million workers are employed by Nike's 719 contract factories in 44 countries (Fig. 12.13).

Nike grew to become the world's leading manufacturer of athletic shoes, with an 18.6 percent share of the world's athletic shoe market and up to 60 percent of the U.S. market. Its employment numbers skyrocketed, and many new manufacturing plants were established in Asia and beyond. Today no manufacturing takes place at or near the headquarters in Beaverton. Employees at Nike headquarters are designers, planners, financial administrators, marketing and sales specialists, information technology directors, computer technicians, lawyers, and support personnel. The local social and economic geography of Beaverton bears little resemblance to what one might have expected in a town housing an important shoe company. Each **node**, or connection point in a network, of the Nike network is functionally specialized, dependent on other nodes, and influenced by the niche it occupies in the network.

Distribution in the Commodity Chain

The largest producer of furniture in the world is not located in High Point, North Carolina, but in Sweden. Ikea, a global company with sales of $37.38 billion in 2013, is the world's largest producer, distributor, and seller of furniture. Ingvar Kamprad founded the company in 1943 at the age of 17. Kamprad, a born entrepreneur, first sold matches from door to door in his neighborhood in Sweden. He expanded his

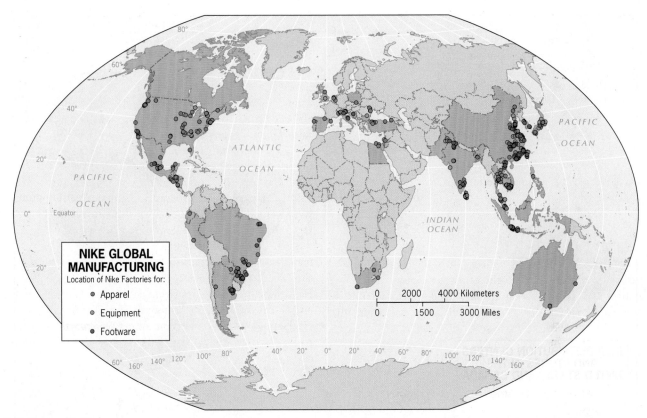

■ **Figure 12.13**

Nike Production Facilities and Contract Factories.   Nike uses flexible production to manufacture shoes and apparel in 719 contract factories around the world. Nike plans short- and long-range contracts with factories, constantly assessing the best possible places to manufacture shoes, apparel, and equipment.

offerings to pens, Christmas decorations, and greeting cards during his teenage years. Pens were one of the main offerings in Ikea when he founded the company in 1943. According to the history told by Ikea, Kamprad first produced and sold furniture in 1948, using wood from Sweden's expansive forests. The company expanded in product offerings and locations since, focusing on producing modern and classic furniture at an affordable price point.

With approximately 300 stores in 26 countries, Ikea created and controls its own commodity chain. Ikea designs the furniture, sources the materials, and produces its famous products, including its best-selling product, the Billy bookcase. The company has over 1200 suppliers located in 55 countries (Krewson 2010). The company's volume of production and sales is so high that it has to consider carefully where to locate distribution centers to serve its stores. In the United States, Ikea has five distribution centers: Port Wentworth, Georgia (near Savannah), Perryville, Maryland (near Baltimore), Tejon, California (near Los Angeles), Westhampton, New Jersey (near Philadelphia, Pennsylvania), and Brossard, Quebec (near Montreal, Canada) (Fig. 12.14). Ikea has plans to build distribution centers in Joliet, Illinois (near Chicago), and Tacoma, Washington (near Seattle).

Ikea chooses the sites for its distribution centers with an eye on where stores are and where store expansion will occur.

The Savannah distribution center is one of its newest, and locating in Georgia allowed Ikea to reduce transportation time and cost from distribution (formerly from Perryville, Maryland) to its stores in Orlando, Tampa, and Atlanta. The new distribution center also enabled Ikea to open more locations in Florida and allows for further expansion in the Southeast. The Savannah distribution center is a model of efficiency. Thirteen computerized robotic cranes move Ikea products into the distribution center and then pull goods out for distribution to stores. The goal is for a crane not to return empty handed. So the same crane that is loading goods into the distribution center from a ship is also finding and loading goods onto truck and rail for transport to stores.

Controlling a large proportion of the commodity chain allows Ikea to operate at incredibly high volume with low prices, generating small profits for the company along each step in the commodity chain. Ikea invests in distribution logistics in order to keep transportation costs as low as possible. According to Ikea, the company is reorganizing its distribution center structure so that low-flow products (products that do not turn over in stores quickly) will be stored in a central distribution center and high-flow products will be stored closer to stores so they can quickly replenish supply.

Ikea is leading innovations in distribution of goods and is also a leader in Green technologies. The company is

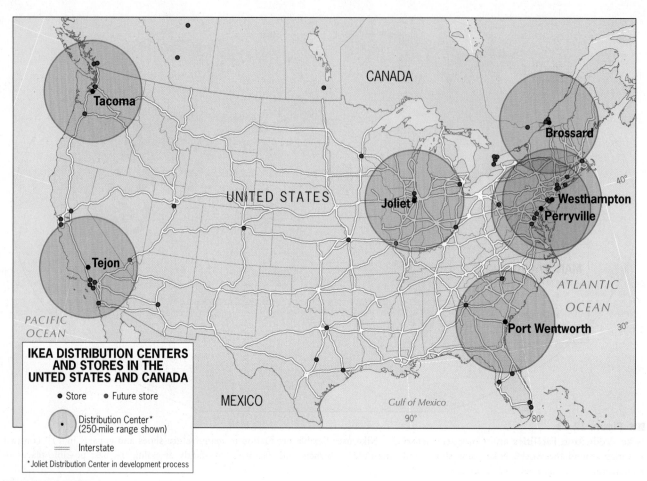

IKEA DISTRIBUTION CENTERS
AND STORES IN THE
UNITED STATES AND CANADA

- ● Store   ● Future store

⊙ Distribution Center*
(250-mile range shown)

══ Interstate

*Joliet Distribution Center in development process

■■ **Figure 12.14**
Ikea Distribution Center and Store Map.

generating its own electricity through solar and wind energy both as a Green initiative and also to manage costs of heating and cooling its buildings. As of 2014, Ikea was producing about half the energy it uses. Ikea is also working with the United Nations High Commissioner on Refugees (UNHCR) to create a new housing system for the world's refugees. The tents the UNHCR currently distributes are designed to last 6 months, and they do little besides providing shelter. Ikea's new house designed for refugees comes in flat boxes and can be assembled in a day. They are made of plastic that keeps the interior cool during the day and allows privacy so people outside the tent cannot see shadows from the tent at night. They include a solar panel that generates enough energy to power one light and a USB charging port. And, they last for about 3 years. The Ikea refugee houses are now being used in Syria and Ethiopia, with hopes of much broader distribution and a better quality of life for the world's refugees (see Chapter 3).

Outsourcing: Business Product Outsourcing and Global Sourcing

Where to produce or assemble a good is only one small aspect of decisions made in a **commodity chain** (see Chapter 10)

for any good produced in an economy based on flexible production. A large part of business decision making today focuses on outsourcing and global sourcing, on where to extend contracts to complete projects and where to have component parts produced and assembled.

Economic geographers originally used the term *outsourcing* to describe a company moving production or services abroad. In the first model of outsourcing, a global corporation moved a certain division of its production, whether assembling the final product or supplying telephone support for software, to another country. In the 1990s and into the twenty-first century, outsourcing implied taking work that would normally be done in America and moving it abroad. The media focused on the outsourcing of manufacturing jobs to China and the outsourcing of call centers to India.

Using this basic concept of outsourcing is misleading in the world-economy. The global division of labor and growing connectivity, accompanied by fundamental shifts by Chinese and Indian companies, have deepened globalization and created a new world-economy. **Outsourcing** is now an umbrella term for globalized production in which a defined segment of the commodity chain is contracted abroad, either through business process outsourcing (BPO) or through global sourcing.

In the world-economy, the new model of outsourcing has developed out of the growth of Indian companies, including Tata, Infosys, and Wipro, who specialize in completing projects and fulfilling contracts by becoming experts in outsourcing themselves. Imagine that a global company, headquartered in the United States, produces and sells accounting software. A major regulation changes in the United States, and the company now needs someone to reprogram the software to account for the complexities of the new regulation. The company can hire an Indian company that specializes in BPO. The two companies contract the work to reprogram the software. The ball is then in the Indian company's court. It has to produce a finished product by the date on the contract in order to get paid, and it can do so however it sees fit. In many cases, the Indian company outsources the work itself, keeping tabs on and testing the product before delivering it to the company in the United States. BPO includes completing projects, as in this example, and it includes turning certain business functions, such as call centers, human resources, accounting, or software engineering, over to the Indian BPO in a longer-term contract.

Maximizing profits when producing goods is no longer as simple as moving around to take advantage of lower labor costs. China has capitalized on the desire of companies to produce goods globally by becoming the world leader in **global sourcing**. Say you are daydreaming and you think of a great new product, like sunglasses with windshield wipers on them. You no longer need to figure out where to make your product. You can mock up a prototype and take it to a global sourcing fair in Las Vegas, Mexico City, Johannesburg, or São Paulo and meet with dozens of Chinese global sourcing firms (Fig. 12.15). They will give you a bid on what it will cost to produce your awesome new product, and they will tell you when it can be done. You sign a contract, and you receive shipment of your product without ever having set foot in China. The Chinese global sourcing firm is connected to manufacturers throughout Asia, Africa, and the Americas, Your windshield wiper sunglasses may be stickered "Made in Mexico" when you receive them. If your product flies off the shelf and you order another shipment, your Chinese global sourcing company may ship the next order with stickers saying "Made in China." The global sourcing firm is connected and nimble so you do not have to be. The global sourcing firm controls a larger part of the commodity chain and can generate more wealth for itself by making the lowest cost production decisions.

Business process outsourcing and global sourcing both fall under the umbrella of outsourcing. Both take a segment of the commodity chain and move it to another country with full responsibility for that segment of the commodity chain in the contracted company's hands. BPO is typically for services, whether tertiary, quaternary, or quinary (Chapter 10). Global sourcing is typically for the secondary, or manufacturing, sector of the economy. However, global sourcing includes quite a bit of service work because the Chinese sourcing company develops the relations with the manufacturers, uses its knowledge of trade regulations, and manages a large sector of the product's commodity chain.

Supporting the global division of labor and global sourcing are elaborate trading networks and intricate financial relations. Trade itself is a tertiary economic activity of considerable importance to the global economy. Regardless of where goods are produced, consumption is still concentrated in the core and, increasingly, among the wealthy and middle classes of the semiperiphery.

■ Figure 12.15
New York. Business people visit booths to find producers at China Textile and Apparel Sourcing Expo.

Made in America or Designed in America?

In 2011, ABC World News featured a segment called "Made in America," where journalists knocked on doors and challenged homeowners to look at every item in their home for the "made in" sticker. The news crew then helped families move all goods not "Made in America" onto the street so the family could visualize how much of what is in their home is made in the United States and how much is made elsewhere in the world. The ABC World News crew then, according to their website, "took on the challenge of trying to fill three rooms in a home entirely with 100 percent American-made products."

Would an iPod get to stay in the house redesigned by ABC World News? When you open a new iPod or other Apple product, a sticker greets you that says "Designed in California." The iPod would not pass the ABC "made in" test, but we should ask whether it is better for the American economy for a good to be made in or designed in America. Three authors asked this exact question in the journal *Communications of the*

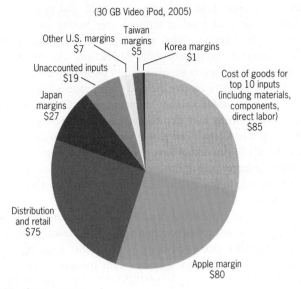

BREAKDOWN OF THE COST OF A $299 IPOD

(30 GB Video iPod, 2005)

- Other U.S. margins $7
- Taiwan margins $5
- Korea margins $1
- Unaccounted inputs $19
- Japan margins $27
- Cost of goods for top 10 inputs (includng materials, components, direct labor) $85
- Distribution and retail $75
- Apple margin $80

■ **Figure 12.16**

Breakdown of the Cost of a $299 iPod. *Courtesy of:* Greg Linden, Kenneth L. Kraemer, and Jason Dedrick. Who captures value in a global innovation network? The case of Apple's iPod. *Communications of the ACM,* 52, 3, March 2009.

ACM in 2009. Linden et al. asked who captures the value in a $299 iPod touch.

Using published sources on computer machinery and component parts, the authors figured out the iPod supply chain and calculated the value added at each step in the commodity chain (Fig. 12.16). The components of an iPod are produced by companies in Japan, Korea, Taiwan, and China. The most expensive component in the iPod is the hard drive, which is produced and designed by Toshiba, a Japanese company. One component that sets the iPod apart from other MP3 players is the microchip that controls access to songs and movies on the iPod. The microchip is housed in a wheel on the iPod classic and is produced by PortalPlayer, a California company with offices in India.

In his piece on PortalPlayer called "The World in an iPod," journalist Andrew Leonard explained that PortalPlayer has a 24-hour development cycle because engineers in California and in India can work around the clock (with time zones 12 hours apart) to design and redesign the microchip. The actual microchips are created in Taiwan. The commodity chain for PortalPlayer (Fig. 12.17) reveals how people and places around the world interconnect to design and create the company's microchip.

Linden et al. estimate that the PortalPlayer component is a small fraction of the cost of an iPod but that the research and

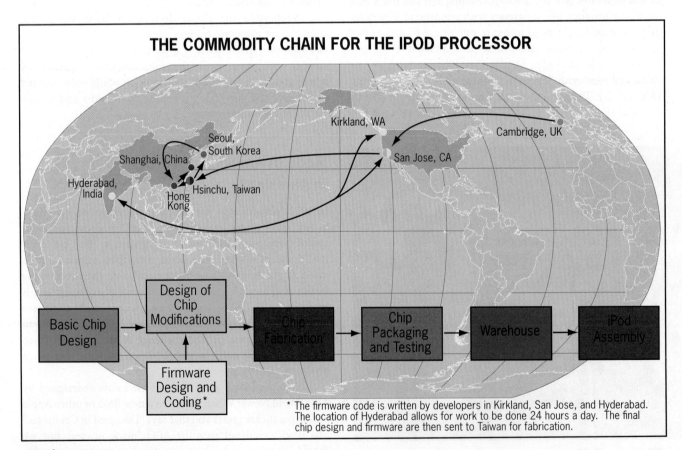

THE COMMODITY CHAIN FOR THE IPOD PROCESSOR

Kirkland, WA · Cambridge, UK · Seoul, South Korea · Shanghai, China · San Jose, CA · Hyderabad, India · Hong Kong · Hsinchu, Taiwan

Basic Chip Design → Design of Chip Modifications → Chip Fabrication → Chip Packaging and Testing → Warehouse → iPod Assembly

Firmware Design and Coding*

* The firmware code is written by developers in Kirkland, San Jose, and Hyderabad. The location of Hyderabad allows for work to be done 24 hours a day. The final chip design and firmware are then sent to Taiwan for fabrication.

■ **Figure 12.17**

Inside an iPod: The PortalPlayer World. *Map designed by Stephen P. Hanna, based on information from:* Andrew Leonard, "The World in the iPod," Spiegel Online, August 8, 2005.

development that go into PortalPlayer and other innovative components that differentiate the iPod from its competitors derive more value from the sale of one iPod than does Invotec, the company that actually assembles the iPod. Linden et al. concluded that "while the iPod is manufactured offshore and has a global roster of suppliers, the greatest benefits from this innovation go to Apple, an American company, with predominantly American employees and stockholders who reap the benefits" (2009, 143) and that the second greatest benefit goes to the two Japanese companies that produce components that help differentiate the iPod, the hard drive, and the display screen.

The act of consumption is an end point of a commodity chain. It is also the beginning of the product's afterlife. What happens when you discard or donate the item? What are the costs or benefits created by the funds (whether funds for a charity or profits for a corporation) generated by your purchase? Corporations such as Apple, which sells the iPod, work to reduce consumer waste by recycling iPods and computers, and by offering discounts to consumers who recycle their old iPods. Nonetheless, in many global cities in poorer parts of the world, adults and children work in garbage dumps to recover valuable copper wire and other components of computers and related electronic devices made by Apple and its competitors.

Tracing the commodity chain of the iPod demonstrates that rarely does the consumption of a particular product have an unambiguous positive or negative consequence. In addition to the fact that components are made all over the world and assembly is only one small part of the commodity chain, we should consider the environmental consequences of steps in commodity chains. Jobs created by industry in one place can cause environmental damage in another. Consumption, or purchasing an item, is the end point in a commodity chain that affects places in a variety of different ways. The importance of studying the geography of commodity chains is that such an undertaking sheds light on the origins of products and helps explain why production occurs where and how it does and how production affects places and peoples at each step in the chain.

Major Influences on the Contemporary Geography of Manufacturing

As the iPod example illustrates, multinational corporations frequently subcontract many of the steps in the production and retailing process to outside companies or subsidiaries, through BPO and global sourcing contracts, including the extraction of raw materials, engineering, manufacturing, marketing, distribution, and customer support. Weber's location theory no longer works for most products, except those that rely on heavy raw materials. With networks of global cities, container ships crossing the oceans in regular patterns, and flexible production, choosing an industrial location depends on labor costs, transportation (as Weber suggested), and also on regulatory constraints, expertise, and access to energy.

TRANSPORTATION

Relatively inexpensive transportation is one of the foundations on which the flexible production system rests. In the early 1900s, the cost of transportation accounted for half or more of the final price of many goods traveling over significant distances. Transportation now accounts for 5 percent or less of the cost of most goods. In an era of vastly improved infrastructure, relatively cheap oil, and container ships, spatially disaggregated production systems are cost effective.

Efficient transportation systems enable manufacturers to purchase raw materials from distant sources and distribute finished products to widely dispersed consumers. Cost is not the only issue. Manufacturers also consider the availability of alternative systems in the event of emergencies (e.g., truck routes when rail service is interrupted). Since World War II, major developments in transportation have focused on improving **intermodal connections**, places where two or more modes of transportation meet (including air, road, rail, barge, and ship), in order to ease the flow of goods and reduce the costs of transportation.

The current volume of resources and goods shipped around the globe daily could not be supported without the invention of the container system, whereby goods are packed in containers that are picked up by special, mechanized cranes from a container ship at an intermodal connection and placed on the back of a semitrailer truck, on a barge, or on a railroad car. This innovation lowered costs and increased flexibility, permitting many manufacturers to pay less attention to transportation in their location decisions. Refrigerated containers also ease the shipment of perishable goods around the globe.

Jacques Charlier has studied the major changes to the Benelux (Belgium, the Netherlands, and Luxembourg) seaport system and the role containerization played in these changes. Charlier stressed the importance of containerization to the growth of sea trade in the Benelux ports and explained the locational advantage of Rotterdam, which is no more than six hours by rail or truck from 85 percent of the population of western Europe.

The container system and the growth in shipping at Rotterdam and other Benelux ports have combined to foster the development of other industries in the region, helping to make the Netherlands, in Charlier's words, a warehouse for Europe. The Netherlands is now home to more than 1800 U.S. firms, including call centers, distribution centers, and production centers, especially for food. Over 50 percent of all goods entering the European Union pass through Rotterdam or Amsterdam (also in the Netherlands).

REGULATORY CIRCUMSTANCES

Regional trade organizations including the Association of Southeast Asian Nations (ASEAN), the North American Free Trade Agreement (NAFTA), and the European Union (EU) have trade agreements that influence where imported goods (and components of goods) are produced. Similarly, governments have individual agreements with each other about production and imports, and most governments (160 as of 2014) are part of the World Trade Organization (WTO), which works to negotiate rules of trade among the member states.

The WTO promotes freer trade by negotiating agreements among member states, typically dismissing import quota systems and discouraging protection by a country of its domestically produced goods. Agreements negotiated under the WTO are typically enacted in steps in order to avoid a major shock to a state's economy. In 2001 when Europe and the United States agreed to allow China to become a member of the WTO, they also agreed to remove the quota system that restricts the importation of Chinese goods into Europe and the United States. Soon after these quotas were eliminated, both the United States and the European Union issued "safeguard quotas" against certain Chinese imports. These quotas buffered the impact of Chinese goods on domestic producers. But most of the quotas have now expired, paving the way for mass importation of Chinese goods in the United States and Europe.

In addition to the growth of the purview of the WTO, the proliferation of regional trade associations in the last two decades is unprecedented. The list of acronyms for regional trade associations is almost overwhelming: EU, NAFTA, MERCOSUR, SAFTA, CARICOM, ANDEAN AFTA, COMESA, to name but a few (see Chapter 8). The World Trade Organization estimates that more than 360 regional trade agreements are in existence. Regional trade agreements are similar to bilateral agreements on trade between two countries, although they involve more than two countries. Most regional trade agreements encourage movement of production within the trade region and promote trade by diminishing (or deleting) trade quotas and tariffs among member countries. A regional trade agreement sets up a special free trade agreement among parties to the association, leaving nonmember countries to trade through the rules of the WTO or an existing bilateral agreement. Whether regional or global, trade agreements directly affect the location of production and even what is produced in a place.

Regulations at the state and local scales also matter. Not infrequently, the location of industrial operations is influenced by a range of state and local regulations that influence the cost of production. These range from tax regulations to environmental and safety standards. In many cases, governments actively seek to recruit industry through incentives that include tax breaks, subsidies, and exemptions from particular bureaucratic requirements. Export processing zones such as the *maquiladoras,* discussed in Chapter 10, provide a case in point. There are now many hundreds of such zones around the world, and they are shaping the global geography of industry.

ENERGY

The role of energy supply as a factor in industrial location decisions has changed over time. Earlier in the chapter, we explained that at the start of the Industrial Revolution manufacturing plants were often established on or near coal fields. During the mid-twentieth century, the use of coal as an energy source in industry increasingly gave way to oil and gas. Today major industrial complexes are not confined to areas near oil fields. Instead, a huge system of pipelines and tankers delivers oil and natural gas to manufacturing regions throughout the world. For some time during and after the global oil supply crises of the 1970s, fears of future spikes in oil costs led some industries that require large amounts of electricity to move to sites where energy costs were low. When the crisis waned, national energy-conservation goals were modified. Energy supply has become a less significant factor in industrial location, but securing an energy supply is an increasingly important national priority.

U.S. consumption of petroleum and natural gas today is about 20 percent of the annual world total. By 2007, the United States required more than 20.6 million barrels of petroleum per day to keep its power plants, machinery, vehicles, aircraft, and ships functioning. However, U.S. production of oil in recent years has averaged about 10 percent of the world total, and even including the known Alaskan potential and the oil and natural gas in shale, U.S. oil reserves are estimated to amount to only about 4 percent of the world total. More so than many countries, the United States taps the oil that it has. In 2009 the country was the third largest oil producer in the world (Fig. 12.18). Even with this level of production, the United States remains heavily dependent on foreign oil supplies, with all the uncertainties that involves. There is, consequently, a push for the United States to begin large-scale fracking of oil and natural gas shale and to expand offshore drilling in the hope of expanding its production of oil. Opposition to the environmental and social consequences of fracking is growing, but the wealth being generated for corporations and state governments is hard to resist. Opposition to offshore drilling is also based on environmental grounds that were heightened by the major BP oil spill that occurred in the Gulf of Mexico in 2010—an example of what can happen when offshore oil resources are exploited without careful safeguards.

The United States leads world demand and consumption not just in oil, but in natural gas as well. As Figure 12.18 shows, natural gas often occurs in association with oil deposits. The use of natural gas has increased enormously since World War II. One result of the increased use of natural gas is the proliferation of pipelines shown on the map. In the United States in 2013, there were 2.4 million miles (over 4 million km) of pipelines, with 2.1 million miles of the pipelines providing local distribution of natural gas. Countries with large reserves of oil and natural gas—Saudi Arabia, Kuwait, Iraq, Russia, and others—occupy a special position in the global economic picture. None of these countries except Russia is a major industrial power, but they all played a key role in the industrial boom of the twentieth century. And while oil has brought wealth to some in Southwest Asia, it has also ensured that outside powers such as the United States and Great

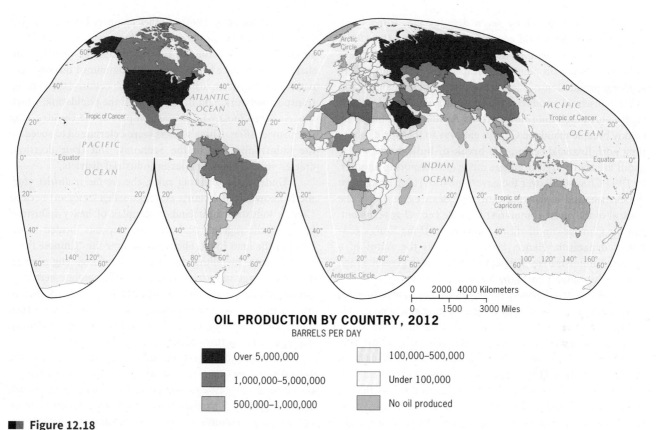

OIL PRODUCTION BY COUNTRY, 2012
BARRELS PER DAY

- Over 5,000,000
- 1,000,000–5,000,000
- 500,000–1,000,000
- 100,000–500,000
- Under 100,000
- No oil produced

■ **Figure 12.18**
Oil Production by Country, 2012. Saudi Arabia, the United States, and Russia each produce more than 10 million barrels of oil per day.
Data from: United States Central Intelligence Agency, World Factbook, 2014.

Britain are involved and invested in what happens in the region. This set of circumstances has produced an uneasy relationship (at best) between countries in the oil-producing region and the major industrial powers of the "West."

New Centers of Industrial Activity

As a result of advances in flexible production, over the last 30 years many older manufacturing regions have experienced **deindustrialization**, a process by which companies move industrial jobs to other regions, leaving the newly deindustrialized region to work through a period of high unemployment and, if possible, switch to a service economy (see the last major section of this chapter). At the same time, the places with lower labor costs and the right mix of laws attractive to businesses (often weak environmental laws and pro-free-trade laws) have become newly industrial regions. The new industrial regions are emerging as shifts in politics, laws, capital flow, and labor availability occur.

East Asia has become a particularly important new region of industrialization. From Taiwan to Guangdong and from South Korea to Singapore, the islands, countries, provinces, and cities fronting the Pacific Ocean have gotten caught up in a frenzy of industrialization that has made the geographic term *Pacific Rim* synonymous with manufacturing.

THE RISE OF EAST ASIA

Throughout the better part of the twentieth century, Japan was the only global economic power in East Asia, and its regional dominance seemed beyond doubt. Other nodes of manufacturing existed, but these were no threat, and certainly no match, for Japan's industrial might. The picture began to change with the rise of the so-called Four Tigers of East and Southeast Asia: South Korea, Taiwan, Hong Kong, and Singapore in the 1960s and 1970s. Benefiting from the shift of labor-intensive industries to areas with lower labor costs, government efforts to protect developing industry, and government investment in education and training, the tigers emerged as **newly industrializing countries (NICs)**.

South Korea developed significant manufacturing districts exporting products ranging from automobiles and grand pianos to calculators and computers. One of these districts is centered on the capital, Seoul (with 10 million inhabitants in the city proper and some 25 million in the metropolitan area), and the two others lie at the southern end of the peninsula, anchored by Pusan and Kwangju, respectively. Taiwan's economic planners promoted high-technology industries, including personal computers, telecommunications equipment, precision electronic instruments, and other high-tech products. More recently, the South Koreans have moved in a similar direction.

Just a trading colony seven decades ago, Hong Kong exploded onto the world economic scene during the 1950s with textiles and light manufactures. The success of these industries, based on plentiful, cheap labor, was followed by growing production of electrical equipment, appliances, and other household products. Hong Kong's situational advantages contributed enormously to its economic fortunes. The colony became mainland China's gateway to the world, a bustling port, financial center, and **break-of-bulk point**, where goods are transferred from one mode of transport to another. In 1997 China took over the government of Hong Kong from the British, and a showplace of capitalism came under the control of the quasi-communist Chinese central government. But the Chinese can ill afford to undercut Hong Kong's economic dynamism. Hence, Hong Kong has the status of a Special Administrative District in China, which gives it a high degree of autonomy from the mainland.

The industrial growth of Singapore also was influenced by its geographical setting and the changing global economic division of labor. Strategically located at the tip of the Malay Peninsula, Singapore is a small island inhabited by a little over 4 million people, mostly ethnic Chinese but with Malay and Indian minorities. Fifty years ago, Singapore was mainly an entrepôt (transshipment point) for such products as rubber, timber, and oil; today, the bulk of its foreign revenues come from exports of manufactured goods and, increasingly, high-technology products. Singapore is also a center for quaternary industries, selling services and expertise to a global market.

Rapid economic growth entails risks, and in 1997 risky lending practices and government investment decisions caused Thailand's currency to collapse, followed by its stock market; banks closed and bankruptcies abounded. Soon Malaysia and Indonesia were affected, and by early 1998 one of the Four Tigers, South Korea, required a massive infusion of dollars (provided by the International Monetary Fund, a Washington-based bank) to prevent economic chaos. But the reforms that allowed the region to overcome these economic troubles served to strengthen East and Southeast Asia's economies, and the Four Tigers continue to exert a powerful regional—and international—economic role.

THE CHINESE JUGGERNAUT

Although some industrial growth occurred in China during the period of European colonial influence, and later during the Japanese occupation, China's major industrial expansion occurred during the Communist period. When communist planners took over in 1949, one of their leading priorities was to develop China's resources and industries as rapidly as possible.

China is a vast country and has a substantial resource base. The quality of its coal is good, the quantity enormous, and many of the deposits are near the surface and easily extracted. China's iron ores are not as productive and are generally of rather low grade, but new finds are regularly being made.

Until the early 1960s, Soviet planners helped promote China's industrial development. China was spatially constrained by the location of raw materials, the development that had taken place before the 1949 communist takeover, the pattern of long-term urbanization in the country, the existing transport network, and the location of the population, which was clustered mostly in the eastern part of the country. Like their Soviet allies, China's rulers were determined to speed up the industrialization of the economy, and their decisions created several major and lesser industrial districts.

Under state planning rules, the *Northeast district* (formerly known as Manchuria and now called Dongbei) became China's industrial heartland, a complex of heavy industries based on the region's coal and iron deposits located in the basin of the Liao River. Shenyang became the "Chinese Pittsburgh," with metallurgical, machine-making, engineering, and other large industries. Anshan, to the south, emerged as China's leading iron- and steel-producing center. Harbin to the north (China's northernmost large city, with more than 5.4 million inhabitants) produced textiles, farm equipment, and light manufactures of many kinds (Fig. 12.19).

The second largest industrial region in China, the *Shanghai and the Chang Jiang district*, developed in and around the country's biggest city, Shanghai. The Chang Jiang district, containing both Shanghai and Wuhan, rose to prominence and, by some measures, exceeded the Northeast as a contributor to the national economy. Another industrial complex that developed farther upstream, along the Chang Jiang River, focused on the city of Chongqing. The Chang Jiang district has become a pacesetter for Chinese industrial growth—if not in terms of iron and steel production, then at least in terms of its diversified production and local specializations. Railroad cars, ships, books, foods, chemicals—an endless variety of products—come from the Chang Jiang district.

In Chinese cities including Dalian, Shanghai, Zhuhai, Xiamen, and Shenzhen, pollution-belching smokestacks rise above the urban landscape. Streets are jammed with traffic ranging from animal-drawn carts and overloaded bicycles to trucks and buses. Bulldozers are sweeping away the vestiges of the old China; cottages with porches and tile roofs on the outskirts of the expanding city must make way for often faceless tenements (Fig. 12.20). Decaying remnants of the old city stand amid the glass-encased towers that symbolize the new economic order. Modern skyscrapers now dominate the skyline of the cities at the top of the Chinese urban-economic and administrative hierarchy—including Beijing, Shanghai, and cities in SEZs. China's major cities now play host to gleaming new airports, daring architecture, spectacular public projects, and the terminuses of efficient high-speed railroads.

At the same time, the Northeast has become China's "Rust Belt." Many of its state-run factories have been sold or closed, or are operating below capacity. Unemployment is high, and economic growth has stalled. Eventually, the Northeast is likely to recover because of its resources and its favorable geographic site, but under the state's new economic policies, the dynamic eastern and southern provinces have

FIELD NOTE

"Humen is one of the Pearl River Delta cities that has been transformed by the rise of China. The small textile factory I visited provided insights into the opportunities and challenges that are confronting China today. The 40 or so employees were mostly young, but there were a few older folks. They were making women's clothes for the French market. Most of them made the clothes from start to finish, although there were a few unskilled laborers who were ironing the fabric, cutting off loose ends of thread, and so on. Into each of the items of clothing was sewn a label with a fancy-sounding Italian name. The clothes are sold in Humen for the equivalent of $1.50–$2.50 each, but most of them were destined for France, where they would be sold for 20 times that amount. The employees work under a contract that stipulates a 9-hour day and a base wage of about $275/month plus basic room and board. They can work more hours, however, and are compensated based on how much they produce during the extra hours. Apparently, almost all employees choose to work extra hours—typically seven days a week, with breaks only on Sunday evenings and one day at the beginning of each month. If they work that hard, they can earn the equivalent of close to $500/month. The main workroom had decent lighting and ventilation (it was hot, of course). The manager told me there had been significant upward pressure on the wages of employees in the last few years, making it harder for him to earn much of a profit. He worried about factories relocating to lower-wage countries. In addition, he said that he was having an increasingly difficult time recruiting employees. He also noted with some mixture of amusement and annoyance that the people who had made out the best in his part of the city were the former farmers, who either had received substantial compensation (in the form of apartments) for being displaced or who were getting some share of rent for buildings constructed on the land they used to farm."

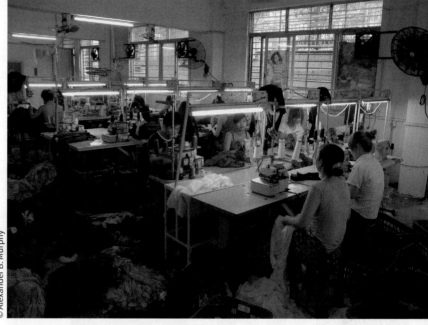

© Alexander B. Murphy

■■ **Figure 12.19**
Humen, China.

grown into major manufacturing belts and have changed the map of this part of the Pacific Rim.

Today, the Chinese government is pushing industrialization into the country's interior, with new investment flowing into poorer parts of the central and western portions of the country. China is also looking to take advantage of its proximity to South and Southeast Asia through efforts to deepen transnational economic cooperation. From a global perspective, what is particularly striking is the magnitude and influence of the Chinese economic juggernaut. On August 15, 2010, China officially surpassed Japan as the world's second largest economy. China has become the world's largest exporter, and its energy and raw materials demands are now affecting the global supply of key resources. Today more passenger vehicles are purchased in China each year than in the United States, and China invests more domestically than any other country in the world.

None of the foregoing means that China will inevitably become the dominant power of the twenty-first century. China's economy still depends heavily on exports and foreign investment, and China's GDP per capita, while on the rise, is 10 times smaller than Japan's and 12.5 times smaller than that of the United States. Moreover, there are potentially destabilizing social and environmental costs to China's rapid rise, and with labor costs growing in China relative to Southeast Asia, China could be vulnerable to some of the very forces that gave it an advantage over other places not long ago.

THE WIDER WORLD

Other newly industrializing countries have become increasingly significant global nodes of production. Over the past decade manufacturing has surged in South and Southeast

FIELD NOTE

"Beijing, Shanghai, and other Chinese cities are being transformed as the old is swept away in favor of the new. Locals, powerless to stop the process, complain that their neighborhoods are being destroyed and that their relocation to remote apartment complexes is a hardship. Urban planners argue that the 'historic' neighborhoods are often dilapidated, decaying, and beyond renovation. The housing shown in Figure 12.20a was demolished to make room for what is going up in Figure 12.20b, a scene repeated countless times throughout urbanizing China."

■ **Figure 12.20a**
Beijing, China.

■ **Figure 12.20b**
Beijing, China.

Asia, in South Africa, and in parts of Central and South America. Brazil, Russia, India, China, and South Africa are increasingly grouped under the acronym BRICS (each letter standing for one of these countries) because these are the countries that demonstrate a shift in global economic power away from the traditional economic core. As we have seen, China is currently leading the way, but India has recently become the world's sixth largest economy. Although industrial production in India is modest in the context of the country's huge size and enormous population, major industrial complexes have developed around Calcutta (the Eastern district, with engineering, chemical, cotton, and jute industries, plus iron and steel based on the Chota Nagpur reserves), Mumbai (the Western district, where cheap electricity helps the cotton and chemical industries), and Chennai (the Southern district, with an emphasis on light engineering and textiles) (Fig. 12.21).

India has no major oil reserves, so it must spend heavily on oil energy. On the other hand, the country has a great deal of hydroelectric potential and access to ample coal. Its Bihar and Karnataka iron ore reserves may be among the largest in the world. With a large labor force, a growing middle class, and a location midway between Europe and the Pacific Rim, India's economic influence is clearly on the rise.

WHERE FROM HERE?

The diffusion of manufacturing activity to the semiperiphery and periphery and the associated sensation of a shrinking world have led a few commentators to suggest that we are entering an era characterized by the "end of geography." Alvin Toffler first suggested this idea in his *Future Shock* (1970). More recently, Richard O'Brien advanced a similar idea in *Global Financial Integration: The End of Geography* (1992) and Thomas Friedman suggested *The World Is Flat* (2005). Each author argues that a combination of technological changes and developments in the global economy have reduced the significance of location and made place differences increasingly insignificant. Geographers who study industrial production recognize that the nature and meaning of location and place have changed greatly in recent times, but they also note that these changes do not create a geographically undifferentiated world. Hence, what is needed is a greater understanding of how places have changed as a

© Viviane Moos/© Corbis

■ **Figure 12.21**
Mumbai, India.   The cotton industry has been a major part of Mumbai's economy since the first cotton mill in India was built in 1854 in the city.

result of new production methods, new corporate structures, and new patterns of industry, as well as an examination of how the interplay between global processes and local places is creating opportunities and constraints for different parts of the planet.

geographically

Think about a cutting-edge, high-technology product that is still quite expensive to purchase and not yet broadly used (perhaps something you have read about but not even seen). Using the Internet, determine where this product is manufactured and assess why the product is manufactured there. Hypothesize where production of the good is in its production cycle, where production may shift to in the future, and how long it might take for production costs (and the price of the product) to decrease substantially.

HOW HAVE DEINDUSTRIALIZATION AND THE RISE OF SERVICE INDUSTRIES ALTERED THE ECONOMIC GEOGRAPHY OF PRODUCTION?

Service industries—tertiary, quaternary, and quinary sectors—produce ideas, advice, innovations, and assistance to businesses and individuals. *Tertiary* services include a broad range of actions that aid people and businesses, including personal services such as cutting hair and giving massages, as well as entertainment, transportation, and retail. Quaternary industries are for the collection, processing, and manipulation of information and capital (finance, administration, insurance, legal services, computer services) and *quinary* industries are for activities that facilitate complex decision making and the advancement of human capacities (scientific research, higher education, and high-level management).

Distinguishing among types of services is useful, given the extraordinary growth in the size and complexity of the service sector. In the global economic core, service industries employ more workers than the primary and secondary industries combined, yet these service industries range from small-scale retailing to tourism services to research on the causes of cancer. Placing all of these activities in a single category seems unwarranted.

Specificity in terminology is also useful in highlighting different phases in the development of the service sector. In the early decades of the twentieth century, the domestic and quasidomestic tertiary industries were experiencing rapid growth in the industrialized world. With the approach of World War II, the quaternary sector began expanding rapidly, and this expansion continued after the war. During the last three decades, both the quaternary and quinary sectors have experienced very rapid growth, giving greater meaning to the term *postindustrial*.

The expanding service sector in the core economies is only one aspect of the changing global economy. Accompanying, and in some cases driving, this expansion are several other developments that have already been mentioned: the increasing mechanization of production, particularly in manufacturing enterprises operating in the core; the growth of large multinational corporations; and the dispersal of the production process.

Not all services contribute to an economy equally. Consider that you can pay $20 for a haircut and $20,000 for a surgery, and both are part of the service industry. An alternative way to think about the wealth generated through the service industries is to think about services in terms of *low cost, low benefit* versus *high cost, high benefit*. When you pay $20 for a haircut, the money goes to the person who cut your hair, and in turn the stylist puts some of the money toward rent to the salon owner and some of the money to buying groceries on the way home. That fraction that went to rent multiplies, as it helps pay the utilities in the salon and the beauty companies where the salon purchases products. With the $20,000 surgery, you are paying part of the income of the surgeon, the anesthesiologist, and the nurses. You are paying the hospital, which in turn purchases utilities and all kinds of medical products. For each service you purchased, think about the persons being paid as having a wake (like that caused by a boat) behind them. The stylist can pay for only a small part of the rent and a couple of groceries from your $20—low cost, low benefit to the economy. The surgeon can pay part of a child's private school tuition, part of a Disney vacation, and an entire month's worth of groceries—high cost, high benefit to the economy.

Geographical Dimensions of the Service Economy

Deindustrialization and the growth of the service economy unfolded in the context of a world-economy that was already characterized by wide socioeconomic disparities. Only areas that had industry could deindustrialize, of course, and at the global scale the wealthier industrial regions were the most successful in establishing a postindustrial service economy. Deindustrialization did little to change the basic disparities between core and periphery that have long characterized the global economy. Even in the manufacturing realm, the availability of capital, mechanization, and innovative production strategies allowed the core industrial regions to retain their dominance. In the first decade of the twenty-first century, eastern Asia, western Russia and Ukraine, western Europe,

and North America still accounted for well over 75 percent of the world's total output of manufactured goods.

Despite its continued dominance in the manufacturing arena, the core has experienced some wrenching changes associated with the economic shifts of the past four decades. Anyone who has ever spent time in Detroit, Michigan, the British Midlands, or Silesia (southern Poland and northeastern Czech Republic) knows that there are pockets of significant hardship in relatively prosperous countries (Fig. 12.22). These are the result of large-scale deindustrialization. In the United Kingdom, the major industrial zones of Newcastle, Liverpool, and Manchester lost much of their industrial bases during the 1960s and 1970s. Similarly, the industrial zone of the northeastern United States (around the Great Lakes) lost much of its industrial base in the same time period, with steel manufacturing jobs moving to areas of the world with lower wages. This region of the United States, which used to be called the Manufacturing Belt, is now commonly called the **Rust Belt**, evoking the image of long-abandoned, rusted-out steel factories (Fig. 12.23). More recently, the global economic downturn that began in 2008 has resulted in devastating job losses in communities dependent on both secondary and tertiary industries. These examples serve to remind us that not all deindustrialized regions find their niche easily in the new service economy and that a tertiary economy, once established, does not necessarily buffer places from recessionary trends.

Nonetheless, some secondary industrial regions have made the transition to a viable service economy fairly successfully. The **Sun Belt** is the southern region of the United States, stretching through the Southeast to the Southwest. Both the population and economy of this region have grown over the last few decades, as service sector businesses have chosen to locate in areas such as Atlanta and Dallas where the climate is warm and the local laws welcome their presence. The eastern part of the Sun Belt served as an early industrial region, with Birmingham developing an iron and steel economy and Atlanta an industrial economy around cotton, tobacco, and furniture. In recent decades, high-tech and financial industries changed the economy and landscape of the Sun Belt, as can be seen in the names of stadiums in the region, such as EverBank Field in Jacksonville, Florida; Bank of America Stadium in Charlotte, North Carolina; and AT&T Center in San Antonio, Texas.

© Richard Klune/Corbis

■ **Figure 12.22**
Liverpool, England.   With the deindustrialization of the Liverpool region, the city has lost thousands of jobs and the city's population has decreased by one-third. Abandoned streets, such as this one, are a reflection of the city's industrial decline.

NEW PATTERNS OF ECONOMIC ACTIVITY

With the striking growth of the service sector and information technologies, new factors have come into play that are affecting patterns of economic activity. Most service industries are not tied to raw materials and

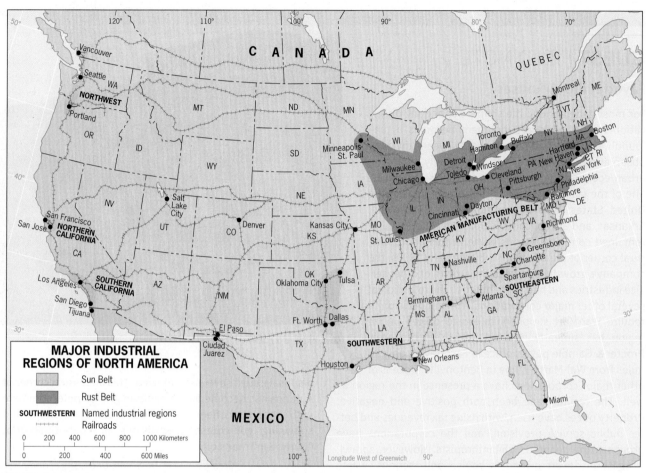

■ Figure 12.23

Major Manufacturing Regions of North America.   North American manufacturing has dispersed to the Sun Belt, and deindustrialization has taken hold in much of the American Manufacturing Belt, now known as the Rust Belt.   © E. H. Fouberg, A. B. Murphy, H. J. de Blij, and John Wiley & Sons, Inc.

do not need large amounts of energy. Market accessibility is more relevant for the service sector, but advances in telecommunications have rendered even that factor less important for some types of service industries.

To understand the influences that shape the location of services, it is useful to go back to our distinction among tertiary, quaternary, and quinary industries. Tertiary services related to transportation and communication are closely tied to population patterns and to the location of primary and secondary industries. As the basic facilitators of interaction, they are strongly linked to the basic geography of production and consumption. Other tertiary services—restaurants, hotels, and retail establishments—are influenced mainly by market considerations. If they are located far from their consumers, they are unlikely to succeed.

Employing technologies such as geographic information systems (GIS) (see Chapter 1), geographers can model the best locations for new businesses, office complexes, government centers, or transportation connections. Major retailers not only shape the landscapes of the places where they choose to put stores, but they also change the economic prospects and physical landscapes of the places where their headquarters

are located. Wal-Mart's headquarters in Bentonville, Arkansas, provides a particularly striking example. If producers of consumer products want to sell their goods in Wal-Mart stores, they must travel to Bentonville, Arkansas, to negotiate deals with Wal-Mart. In order to provide low prices to consumers, Wal-Mart negotiates very low prices with major producers. To create lower-priced products, companies have moved production abroad, and to create good relationships with the world's number one retailer (with sales of $405 billion in fiscal year 2010), a variety of companies have moved into Arkansas (Fig. 12.24). Those companies, along with an array of other businesses supporting their activities (hotels, restaurants, copy centers, delivery services), have fundamentally transformed the city.

The locational influences on quaternary services—high-level services aimed at the collection, processing, and manipulation of information and capital—are more diverse. Some of these services are strongly tied geographically to a particular locus of economic activity. Retail banking and various types of administrative services require a high level of interpersonal contact and therefore tend to be located near the businesses they are serving. Other types of quaternary services can

GUEST FIELD NOTE

Fayetteville, Arkansas

For most geographers, the simple act of daily observation of the world around them becomes a profoundly satisfying habit. For the last 17 years, my daily observations have been of the rapidly changing urban/economic landscape of northwest Arkansas, one of the fastest growing metropolitan areas in the United States. Wal-Mart originated in Bentonville, Arkansas, and as it became increasingly successful, it remained committed to its home in this affordable, rural corner of the mid-South. By the early 1990s, the company's growth had fueled the growth of other service industries and had contributed to the retention of several other major corporations. A recent decision to require Wal-Mart suppliers to locate offices in the region has similarly boosted growth in the area. Procter & Gamble put its office in Fayetteville only 25 miles from Wal-Mart's home in Bentonville. Dozens of other major corporations have a presence in the region as well. The results have been both positive and negative. Property prices have risen, with rising tax revenues and better public service provision, and the corporations have proven to be generous philanthropists. However, sprawl, congestion, overcrowded schools, and serious waste

■ **Figure 12.24**

disposal issues have also followed. This once-rural corner of America has become a metropolitan growth pole, complete with national coffee shops, rush hour congestion, and sprawling golf-course subdivisions of 6000-square-foot "European" mansions.

Credit: Fiona M. Davidson, University of Arkansas.

operate almost anywhere as long as they have access to digital processing equipment and telecommunications. When you send in your credit card bill, it is unlikely to go to the city where the headquarters of the issuing bank is located. Instead, it is likely to go to North Dakota, South Dakota, Nebraska, or Colorado. Similarly, many "back-office" tasks related to insurance are performed in places such as Des Moines, Iowa, not Chicago or Hartford.

Many of the call centers for technical help for computers and related industries (software, hardware) are located in India and the Philippines. Given the relatively high levels of college education and the vast numbers of English speakers in these places, as well as the ease of routing phones through the Internet, "help desks" need not be located down the hall or even down the street. These locational curiosities occur because technological advances in the telecommunications sector have made it possible for all sorts of quaternary industries to be located far away from either producers or consumers. What matters most is infrastructure, a workforce that is sufficiently skilled but not too expensive, and favorable tax rates.

Those who work in the quinary sector tend to be concentrated around governmental seats, universities, and corporate headquarters. Corporate headquarters tend to be located in large metropolitan areas, whereas seats of government and

universities can be found in places that were chosen long ago as appropriate sites for administrative or educational activities based on cultural values or political compromises. The American ideal of the "university town" (which originated in Germany) led to the establishment of many universities at a distance from major commercial and population centers, in such towns as Champaign-Urbana, Illinois; Norman, Oklahoma; and Eugene, Oregon. Political compromises led to the establishment of major seats of government in small towns. Ottawa, Canada, and Canberra, Australia, are examples of this phenomenon. The point is that historical location decisions influence the geography of the quinary sector. And it is not just university professors and government officials who are affected. All sorts of high-level research and development activities are located on the fringes of universities, and a host of specialized consultants are concentrated around governmental centers. These then become major nodes of quinary activity.

High-Technology Clusters

A **high-technology corridor** is an area designated by local or state government to benefit from lower taxes and high-technology infrastructure, with the goal of providing high-technology jobs to the local population. The goal of a high-technology corridor is to attract designers of computers, semiconductors, telecommunications, sophisticated medical equipment, and the like.

California's Silicon Valley is a well-known example of a high-technology corridor. Several decades ago a number of innovative technology companies located their research and development activities in the area around the University of California, Berkeley, and Stanford University, both near San Francisco, California. They were attracted by the prospect of developing links with existing research communities and the availability of a highly educated workforce. Once some high-technology businesses located in the Silicon Valley, others were drawn to the area as well. The area became what geographers call a **growth pole**, not just because other high-technology businesses came to Silicon Valley, but because the concentration of these businesses spurred economic development in the surrounding area.

Today, Silicon Valley is home to dozens of computer companies, many of which are familiar to the computer literate (such as Cisco Systems, Adobe, Hewlett-Packard, Intel, and IBM). The resulting collection of high-technology industries produced what Manuel Castells, Peter Hall, and John Hutriyk call a **technopole**, an area planned for high technology where agglomeration built on a synergy among technological companies occurs. A similar sort of technopole developed outside Boston, where the concentration of technology-based businesses close to Harvard University and the Massachusetts Institute of Technology gave rise to what is called the Route 128 high-technology corridor. The Route 128 corridor has been largely supported by the federal government rather than the local government, which supports many other technopoles.

Technopoles can be found in a number of countries in western Europe, East Asia, North America, and Australia. Few are on the scale of Silicon Valley, but they are noticeable elements of the economic landscape. Many of them have sprung up on the edges of good-sized cities, particularly near airports. In Brussels (Belgium), for example, the route into the city from the airport passes an array of buildings occupied by computer, communication, and electronics firms. In Washington, D.C., the route from Dulles International Airport (located in the Virginia suburbs) to the city passes buildings housing the headquarters of companies such as AOL, MCI, and Orbital Sciences (the Dulles Corridor). In the Telecom Corridor of Plano-Richardson (just outside of Dallas, Texas), telecom companies such as Nortel and Ericsson have taken root, but so too have numerous high-technology companies that are not telecom related (Fig. 12.25). In each of these technopoles, the presence of major multinational companies attracts other startup companies hoping to become major companies, provide services to major companies, or be bought by major companies.

Many of the technology firms are multinationals, and like their counterparts in other countries, they function in an

ASSOCIATED PRESS

■■ **Figure 12.25**

Plano-Richardson, Texas. The Plano-Richardson Telecom Corridor is located just north of Dallas and is home to telecom corporate headquarters, such as Electronic Data Systems Corporation's headquarters in this photograph.

information environment and market their products all over the world. Being near raw materials or even a particular market is unimportant for these firms; what matters to them is proximity to major networks of transportation and communication. High-technology industries have become such an important symbol of the postindustrial world that local, regional, and national governments often pursue aggressive policies to attract firms in this sector. Bidding wars sometimes develop between localities seeking to attract such industries. Although high-technology industries often bring a variety of economic benefits, they have some drawbacks as well. Communities that have attracted production facilities find that the manufacture of computer chips, semiconductors, and the like requires toxic chemicals and large quantities of water. And even more research-oriented establishments sometimes have negative environmental impacts in that land must be cleared and buildings constructed to house them. Despite these drawbacks, the high-technology sector is clearly here to stay, and areas that can tap into it are likely to find themselves in an advantageous economic position in the coming years.

Tourism Services

Every service industry has its own locational characteristics, but tourism is almost in a class by itself due to its geographical extent and economic significance. Once a relatively small activity confined to a set of specialized locations, tourism is now the world's largest service sector industry.

Tourism grew dramatically during the second half of the twentieth century. The tourism boom began in the global economic core as incomes and leisure time increased for a rapidly expanding segment of the population. Over the past three decades, the number of East and Southeast Asian tourists has risen much faster than the global average, reflecting the economic boom in many of the Pacific Rim countries. The combination of a weakening global economy and concerns over political stability caused noticeable dips in travel at the beginning and end of the first decade of the twenty-first century, but absent a major economic or geopolitical crisis, tourism is likely to continue to expand.

In Chapter 10 we looked at some of the social and cultural impacts of tourism, but it is important to recognize that tourism is a major industry as well. Communities all over the world have worked hard to promote tourism, and many are now notably reliant on tourist receipts. The tourist industry has transformed downtowns, ports, hinterlands, parks, and waterfronts. High-rise, ultramodern hotels dominate urban skylines from Boston to Brisbane. The Port of Miami and Fort Lauderdale's Port Everglades have been reconstructed to serve the cruise industry, and many ports from Tokyo to Tampa have added cruise terminals complete with shopping malls and restaurants. Theme parks such as Disney's establishments near Orlando, Paris, Tokyo, Hong Kong, Shanghai, and Los Angeles draw millions of visitors and directly and indirectly employ thousands of workers. Dubai has constructed an indoor ski run in the Mall of the Emirates in an effort to attract more visitors. Once-remote wildlife parks and nature reserves in East Africa and South Asia now receive thousands of visitors, requiring expanded facilities and sometimes causing ecological damage. Formerly isolated beaches are now lined by high-rise hotels and resorts; in the Caribbean and the Pacific, some entire islands have been taken over by tour operators.

The economic impacts of tourist-related development are far-reaching. The monetary value of goods and services associated with tourism is now conservatively estimated at more than $2 trillion—and if spillover effects are taken into consideration, the figure could be twice as large. With the growing middle class in China and India and with increases in average life expectancy, the figure is likely to continue to grow, affecting the prospects of places all over the world.

Place Vulnerabilities in a Service Economy

Every type of economy carries with it potential vulnerabilities. In the early stages of industrialization, the economic destinies of places were tied to their manufacturing operations. As a result, such places were vulnerable to wrenching adjustments when demand shifted for the goods produced by local manufacturers or when the changing costs of transportation or labor led business owners to downscale or shift production elsewhere. Many older industrial areas in the United States and Europe experienced such adjustments, and their best hope for rebuilding often lay in the service economy. Thus, in Duisburg—a city at the heart of Germany's Ruhr Valley—abandoned steel mills were turned into tourist

attractions and warehouses were converted into retail establishments, restaurants, and offices (Fig. 12.26).

Service economies have their own vulnerabilities. Tourism can fall off in the face of economic downturns or natural hazards, and office work can be outsourced to distant places. Mechanization can also have a negative impact. We usually think of manufacturing jobs being affected by mechanization, but service jobs are vulnerable as well. In recent decades, countless jobs in the travel planning industry have been lost to the Internet, scanning machines in supermarkets have reduced the need for employees, and automated answering services have taken the place of live voices in many businesses. Changes of this sort can create the same sorts of hardships and pressures for economic readjustment that communities reliant on secondary industries face.

At a different spatial scale, the very geographical structure of large-scale service economies can affect the fortunes of places, regions, countries, and even the globe. Places dominated by the service sector cannot exist without extensive connections with other places because those living in such places still need food and material products, and they often need a large market to sustain their services. Hence, the dramatic shift away from the primary and secondary sectors that has taken place in some parts of the world is inextricably tied to economic globalization. But economic decision making in a globalized economy can easily become disconnected from the fate of individual places and regions.

The burgeoning financial service industry provides a case in point. That industry has grown explosively over the past few decades with the development of increasingly innovative products and arrangements. Some people made spectacular amounts of money in the process, but in recent

© Alexander B. Murphy

■ Figure 12.26
Duisburg, Germany.   The old industrial canal corridor is being converted to a pedestrian district that local authorities hope will attract locals and tourists.

decades key financial instruments and procedures were developed based on unrealistic assumptions about concrete circumstances. Banks made loans they should not have made, and mortgages were issued to people who were unlikely to be able to meet their payments. These practices helped to bring about the dramatic economic downturn that began in 2008, when a housing slump precipitated high levels of defaults on so-called subprime mortgages. A banking crisis ensued that rippled throughout the economy and, in our interconnected world, affected the fortunes and prospects of places near and far. The crisis serves as a reminder of the continuing vulnerabilities of places in a service economy, even in the absence of any direct challenge to the specific service industries on which particular local economies are based. It also raises a key question with a geographical foundation: What are the consequences of divorcing the development of wealth in a knowledge economy from the fate of individual places, regions, or countries?

How does a place change when deindustrialization occurs? Consider a place that has experienced deindustrialization, and research recent news articles on the Internet to find out how the economy of the place has changed since the loss of industry. What has happened to the place and its economy?

Summary

The Industrial Revolution transformed the world economically, politically, and socially. Many of the places where industrialization first took hold have since become deindustrialized, both with the relocation of manufacturing plants and with the outsourcing of steps of the production process domestically and offshore. With changing economics, places change. Some now look like ghost towns, serving merely as a reminder that industrialization took place there. Others have booming economies and are thriving, having kept industry or having successfully developed a service economy. Still other places are redefining themselves. In the next chapter, we consider another lasting effect of industrialization and deindustrialization: environmental change.

Geographic Concepts

containerization	friction of distance	node
cottage industries	distance decay	commodity chain
economies of scale	location theory	outsourcing
locational criteria	least cost theory	intermodal connections
spillover effect	agglomeration	deindustrialization
hinterland	flexible production	newly industrializing countries
connectivity	commodification	break-of-bulk point
first mover advantage	product life cycle	Rust Belt
secondary hearths	global division of labor	Sun Belt
globalization	time–space compression	high-technology corridor
Fordist	just-in-time delivery	growth pole
vertical integration	spatial fix	technopole

Learn More Online

About the port of Rotterdam:
www.portofrotterdam.com
www.portofrotterdam.com/en/Port/port-in-general/
Documents/20100726_EN/index.html

About Nike
www.nikebiz.com/company_overview

About Global Sourcing in China
http://www.forbes.com/sites/allbusiness/2014/01/06/
sourcing-goods-and-suppliers-in-china-a-how-to-guide-for-
small-businesses/

Watch It Online

About Wal-Mart's influence on Bentonville, Arkansas
www.pbs.org/wgbh/pages/frontline/shows/walmart

THE HUMANIZED ENVIRONMENT

Disaster Along Indian Ocean Shores

Watching the horrors of the tsunami of December 26, 2004, unfold on screen (Fig. 13.1), I found it quite eerie to see such devastation in places where earlier I walked, drove and rode—like that Sri Lankan train on which I took a group of students in 1978—now smashed by the waves, the carriages toppled, killing more than a thousand passengers, some of them tourists. And the beaches near Phuket in Thailand, so serene and beautiful in memory, now proved a fatal attraction leading to disaster for thousands more, tourists and workers alike.

I went online to follow the events of that day and those that followed, horrified by the rising death toll and by the images of destruction and devastation. The in-box of my e-mail began to include messages from former students who remembered my in-field assessment of the tsunami risks in Southeast Asia. But I had not been especially prescient. Just like people farming the fertile soils on the slopes of an active volcano, people living at or near sea level near an earthquake zone live with risk.

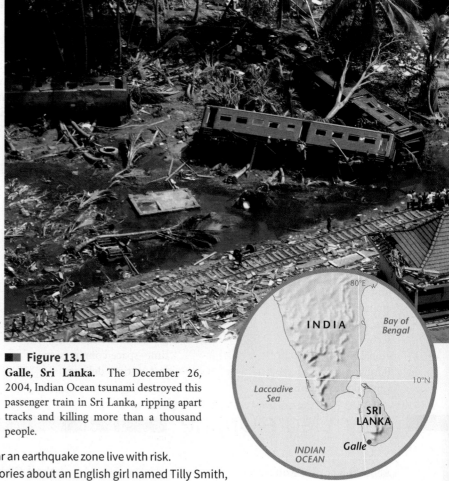

© AP/Wide World Photos

■ **Figure 13.1**
Galle, Sri Lanka. The December 26, 2004, Indian Ocean tsunami destroyed this passenger train in Sri Lanka, ripping apart tracks and killing more than a thousand people.

A few weeks later I began to hear and read stories about an English girl named Tilly Smith, who had been vacationing with her parents at a hotel on the beach at Phuket and was on Maikhao Beach when she saw the water suddenly recede into the distance. Tilly had just taken a geography class in her school not far from London, and her teacher, Mr. Andrew Kearney, had told the class what happens when a tsunami strikes: The huge approaching wave first sucks the water off the beaches, and then the sea foams, rises, and returns as a massive, breaking wall that crashes over and inundates the whole shoreline. Tilly saw what was happening and alerted her parents, her father told hotel security, and they ran back and forth, screaming at beachgoers to seek shelter on higher ground in the hotel behind them. About a hundred people followed the Smith family into the building, and they all survived. Of those who stayed behind, none did.

Being aware of some of the basics of physical geography has its advantages, and Mr. Kearney clearly had the attention of his students.

Newspaper editors could use some of this awareness. Many headlines referred to the tsunami as a tidal wave, but a tsunami has nothing to do with the tides that affect all oceans and seas. A tsunami results from an undersea earthquake involving a large displacement of the Earth's crust. Most submarine earthquakes do not generate tsunamis, but in some cases, fortunately relatively rare ones, a large piece of crust is pushed up or pulled under (or both), and this causes the water overhead to pile up and start rolling away in all directions. If you were on a cruise ship somewhere in the middle of the ocean, nothing catastrophic would mark the passing of this tsunami wave; your ship would be lifted up and then lowered, but it would not overturn. But when such a huge wave reaches a beach, it does what all waves do: It breaks. Most of us have seen this happen with waves several feet (or even tens of feet) high. But imagine a wave over 200 feet high approaching a beach. As it begins to break, it pulls the water away, exposing wide swaths of muddy bottom. Then it comes crashing into the shore, pushing deep inland.

Tsunamis of the magnitude of 2004 are not common, but as the deadly tsunami that struck the northeast coast of Japan in 2011 reminds us, the hazard is continuous. As the Earth's human population has grown, so have the numbers of people vulnerable to such a calamity. And as human land use along and near coasts intensifies, so too can the impacts of tsunamis. In the case of the 2004 tsunami, significant destruction of mangroves to make way for shrimp farms in Southeast Asia exacerbated the impacts of the disaster.

As we learn more about the submarine zones where earthquakes are most likely to occur, and couple that understanding with an appreciation of the human patterns discussed in other chapters, we can begin to determine where the hazards are greatest. Here we combine two major fields of study in geography, physical geography and human geography. Geographers who work in this arena study human-environmental relationships—the reciprocal relationships between human societies and natural environments. The environment is not a passive stage, and environmental change affects human societies. At the same time, humans have an impact on their natural environments. The study of hazards, not just from tsunamis but also from volcanic eruptions, terrestrial earthquakes, landslides, floods, avalanches, and other threats, is a key part of this research.

The tsunami that struck coasts along the Indian Ocean from Indonesia to Somalia and from Thailand to the Maldives resulted from a violent earthquake measuring more than 9.0 on the (10-point) Richter scale off the west coast of the island of Sumatra (Indonesia).

There, two of the planet's tectonic plates are colliding, forcing one beneath the other (Fig. 13.2). A series of tremors and quakes affects the crust in such subduction zones, but sometimes a major shock occurs. In this case, the towering wave generated by the December 26 earthquake had but a short distance to travel to reach northern Sumatra, where it struck in full force. By the time it had done its damage in remote Somalia (in Africa), it had claimed approximately 300,000 lives and ruined the livelihoods of millions more. The 2004 Indian Ocean tsunami illustrated one consequence of the tourist industry: Drawing millions of tourists and workers to coasts makes them more vulnerable to coastal hazards.

Geography is a discipline in which the relationship between humans and environment is a primary concern. One of the most influential nineteenth-century texts on this relationship, *Man and Nature* (1865), was written by the geographer George Perkins Marsh. In 1955, geographers were centrally involved in an international interdisciplinary symposium on "Man's Role in Changing the Face of the Earth." This symposium, like Marsh's earlier book, focused primarily on local and regional changes. More recently, a symposium led by geographers on "The Earth as Transformed by Human Action" picked up where the 1955 discussion left off, addressing global environmental changes. The geographer's concern with how things are organized on Earth and how places are connected provides an analytical platform from which to consider human-induced environmental change.

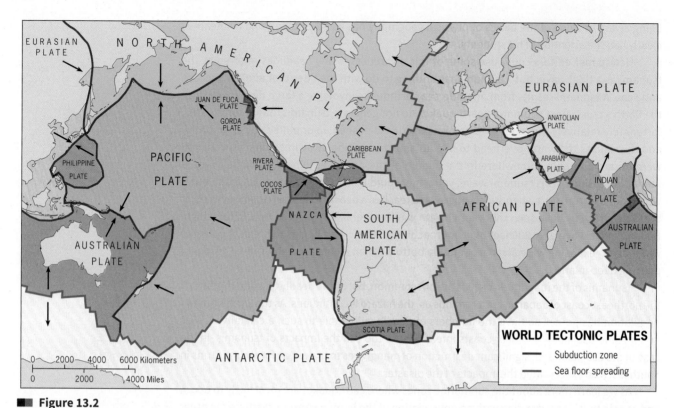

■ **Figure 13.2**
World Tectonic Plates. The places at or near where tectonic plates meet are parts of Earth's surface most susceptible to earthquakes and volcanism. © H. J. de Blij, P. O. Muller, and John Wiley & Sons, Inc.

As the study of environmental change has moved forward, one of the most important lessons we have learned is that global environmental systems are interconnected. For example, the release of **chlorofluorocarbons** (CFCs) in the Northern Hemisphere in past decades contributed to a hole in Earth's ozone layer over Antarctica. Industrial production in the Netherlands and Germany contributes to acid rain in Scandinavia. The use of water from the Rio Grande for irrigation in northern New Mexico affects the amount and quality of the river's water that flows along the Texas–Mexico border. Human actions—the activities we undertake individually and collectively—are increasingly important factors in all sorts of global environmental changes. To confront these changes, we must consider the complex relationship between humans and environment.

Key Questions FOR CHAPTER 13

1. How has Earth's environment changed over time?
2. How have humans altered Earth's environment?
3. What are the major factors contributing to environmental change today?
4. What is the international response to climate change?

HOW HAS EARTH'S ENVIRONMENT CHANGED OVER TIME?

Environmental variation, spatial as well as temporal, is one of Earth's crucial characteristics. Temperatures rise and fall, precipitation waxes and wanes. Forests flourish and wither, deserts expand and contract. Humanity has evolved during a series of alternatively warm and cold phases of an Ice Age that is still in progress. But today humanity itself is part of the process.

Modern *Homo sapiens* emerged less than 200,000 years ago (and possibly not much more than 100,000 years ago). Humans altered their environment from the beginning by setting fires to kill herds of reindeer and bison, or by hunting entire species of large mammals to extinction. The Maori, who arrived in New Zealand not much more than 1000 years ago, greatly altered native species of animals and plants long before the advent of modern technology. Elsewhere in the Pacific realm, Polynesians reduced forest cover to brush and, with their penchant for wearing bird-feather robes, exterminated more than 80 percent of the regional bird species by the time the first Europeans arrived. Europeans ravaged species ranging from Galapagos turtles to Antarctic seals. European fashions had a disastrous impact on African species ranging from snakes to leopards. Traditional as well as modern societies have had devastating impacts on their ecosystems (ecological units consisting of self-regulating associations of living and nonliving natural elements) as well as on ecosystems into which they migrated.

Human alteration of the environment continues in many forms today. For the first time in history, however, the combined impact of humanity's destructive and exploitative actions is capable of producing environmental changes at the global scale. Consider for a moment the history of human life on Earth. Early human societies had relatively small populations, and their impacts on the physical environment were limited in both duration and intensity. With the development of agrarian and preindustrial societies, human alterations of the physical environment increased, yet the effects of these early activities were still limited in scale. Even the onset of urbanization and the development of urban centers, which concentrated large numbers of people in particular places, had relatively limited effects on a global scale.

Over the last 500 years, however, both the rate and the scale at which humans modify Earth have increased dramatically. Particularly during the last half-century, every place on Earth has been transformed, either directly or indirectly, by humans. The twentieth-century surge in the size of the human population, combined with a rapid escalation in consumption, magnifies humanity's impact on Earth in unprecedented ways. To acknowledge the incredible role humans play in shaping Earth's environment, atmospheric chemist Paul Crutzen argues that we have entered a new geologic epoch, the **anthropocene**.

Tectonic Plates

How representative is the short-term present of the long-term past? Over the past century, geographers and other scientists have been engaged in a joint mission to reconstruct our planet's history on the basis of current evidence. One of them, the climatologist–geographer Alfred Wegener, used his spatial view of the world to make a key contribution. Viewing the increasingly accurate maps of the opposite coastlines of the North and South Atlantic oceans, he proposed a hypothesis that would account for the close "fit" of the shapes of the facing continents, which, he argued, would be unlikely to be a matter of chance. His continental drift hypothesis required the preexistence of a supercontinent, which he called **Pangaea**, which broke apart into the fragments we now know as Africa, the Americas, Eurasia, and Australia (Fig. 13.3). Wegener's hypothesis spurred thinking about plate tectonics and crustal spreading. Scientists now know that Pangaea and its fragmentation were only the latest episodes in a cycle of continental coalescence and splintering that spans billions of years. This latest Pangaean breakup, however, began only a little over 200 million years ago and continues to this day.

At plate boundaries, **tectonic plates** either *diverge* (spread apart), *converge* (come together), or *transform* (slide past one another). In the Atlantic Ocean, the North American plate is diverging from the Eurasian plate. Along this plate boundary, new oceanic crust is constantly being created where the plates diverge. A chain of volcanoes called the Mid-Atlantic Ridge has formed on the ocean floor.

Where the Indian plate meets the Eurasian plate, the two plates are converging. The Himalaya Mountains on this plate boundary were built through convergence. The Himalayas are still rising, and earthquakes are relatively common in the region as a result. When an oceanic plate converges with a continental plate, it is called a subduction zone. Along a subduction zone, the denser oceanic plate subducts under the continental plate, creating a trench along the boundary as well as volcanoes and strong earthquakes. Most of the strongest earthquakes that occur, including those in Haiti, Chile, and Japan in 2010 and 2011, happen along subduction zones.

Ocean and Atmosphere

Earth is often called the Blue Planet because more than 70 percent of its surface is covered by water and views from space are dominated by blue hues and swirls of white clouds. The surrounding atmosphere was once loaded with the gas carbon dioxide (CO_2), and if you could have looked up at the sky it would have been bright red because CO_2 scatters red light. Eventually, however, the primitive ocean, still heated from below, began to absorb CO_2 in enormous quantities. A very long time passed before oxygen became a substantial gas in the atmosphere. Around 1500 million years ago, green algae started to spread across Earth's ocean surfaces, and as their colonies grew, their **photosynthesis** (the conversion of carbon dioxide and water into carbohydrates and oxygen

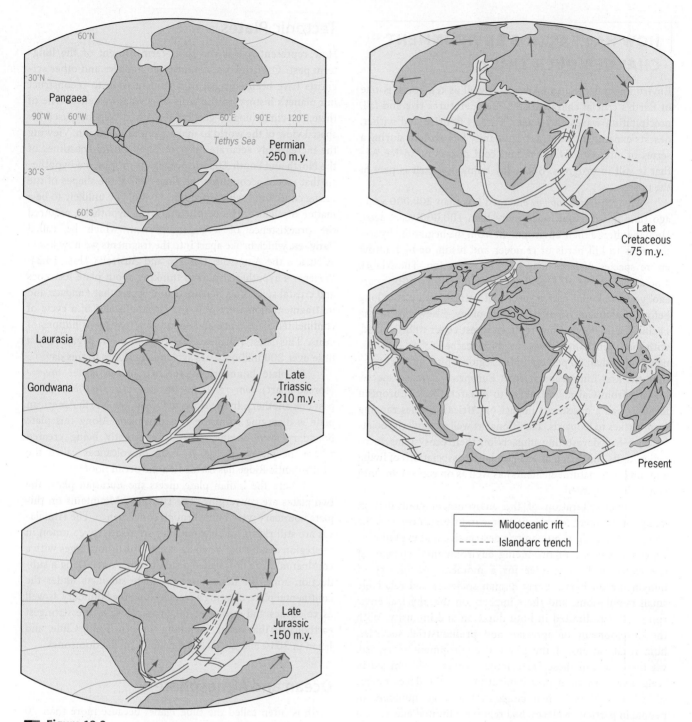

■ Figure 13.3
Breakup of Pangaea.   Pangaea broke up over millions of years, as reflected in this series of diagrams.   *Redrawn and simplified from*: Maps by R. S. Dietz and J. C. Holden, *Journal of Geophysical Research*, vol. 75, pp. 4943–4951, Figures 2 to 6.   © By the American Geophysical Union. Used by permission.

through the absorption of sunlight) raised the atmosphere's oxygen content. About 800 million years ago, the oxygen content in the atmosphere was about one-twentieth of its present strength, or just 1 percent of the total. But that was enough to support the emergence of the first single-celled animals, the protozoa.

Fire and Ice

Today major volcanic eruptions happen infrequently enough that they make the news. Krakatoa (1883), Mount St. Helens (1980), Pinatubo (1991), and Merapi (2010) took many lives, damaged property, and, in the case of Pinatubo, even changed global climate slightly. In 2010, a relatively mild

FIELD NOTE

"Kilauea has been erupting almost continuously since 1983, making it one of Earth's most active volcanoes. After flying over the volcano in a helicopter and looking down at the molten lava, I asked the pilot to take us to the coast where the lava was spilling into the sea. What we saw provided a stirring reminder that the environment is anything but static. Lava had poured across the road that ran along the coast, and the configuration of the coast was being remade before our eyes."

© Alexander B. Murphy

■■ **Figure 13.4**
The Southeast Coast of the Big Island of Hawai'i.

eruption of the Icelandic volcano Eyjafjallajökull spewed enough ash in the air to disrupt air traffic across the northern Atlantic for more than a week. Over the past three decades, ongoing eruptions of the Kilauea volcano have altered the coastline of the Big Island of Hawai'i (Fig. 13.4) and displaced people along the slopes of Mount Etna in Sicily.

Yet such events are relatively minor compared to one billion years ago, when Earth's crust was still immature and subject to huge bursts of volcanic activity. Such episodes poured incalculable volumes of gases and ash into the atmosphere, perhaps contributing to the three **mass extinctions** (mass destruction of most species) known to have occurred over the past 500 million years.

The Earth's most recent experience with mass volcanism took place between 180 and 160 million years ago, when the supercontinent Pangaea was in the process of breaking apart. Lava poured from fissures and vents as South America separated from Africa and India moved northeast. Skies were blackened, the atmosphere choked with ash. Animals responded as they always have in time of crisis: by migrating, fragmenting into smaller groups, and speeding up their adaptive evolutionary response. Physical geographers hypothesize that the earliest phase of Pangaea's fragmentation was also the most violent, that the plate separations that started it all were driven by built-up, extreme heat below the supercontinent, but that the motion of the plates has since slowed down. The **Pacific Ring of Fire**—an ocean-girdling zone of crustal instability, volcanism, and earthquakes—is but a trace of the paroxysm that marked the onset of Pangaea's

breakup (Fig. 13.5). Yet, as we saw with the tsunami in Japan in 2011, modern tectonic events can cost millions of humans lives and alter the course of history.

When Pangaea still was a supercontinent, an Ice Age cooled Earth and may have contributed to, if not caused, the greatest known extinction crisis in the history of life on the planet. Ice Ages are not uniform cooling events: Surges of coldness and advances of glaciers are interrupted by temporary warming spells long enough to reverse much of the glacial impact.

The **Pleistocene** epoch, which began 2 million years ago (Fig. 13.6), was marked by long **glaciations** and short, warm **interglacials**. When the Pleistocene glaciations were most severe, permanent ice advanced deep into the landmasses of the Northern Hemisphere. Plants, animals, and hominids saw their living space diminished, their refuges shrunk, their niches unusable. Such glaciations could last as long as 100,000 years, but eventually a warming spell would arrive, the ice would recede, and space as well as opportunity expanded again. A warming phase of this kind occurred between about 120,000 and 100,000 years ago.

After this warm-up came the most recent glaciation of the Pleistocene, the **Wisconsinan Glaciation**, which left its mark on much of the Northern Hemisphere (Fig. 13.7). But resourceful humans managed to survive where their predecessors could not, and there is ample evidence of human occupation in southern Europe, ranging from cave art to tool kits. Even during a glacial advance brief periods of milder climate emerge. Thus, Figure 13.7 represents a glacial

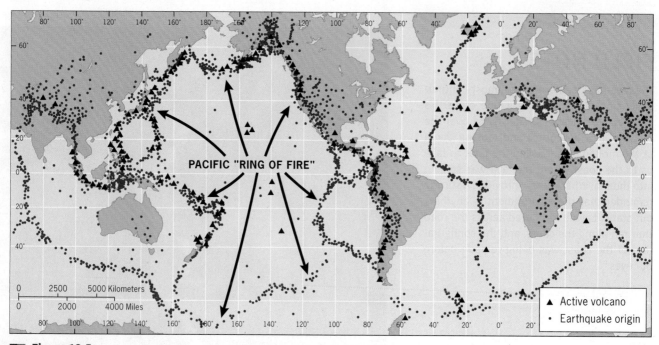

■ **Figure 13.5**
Recent Earthquakes and Volcanic Eruptions. © H. J. de Blij, P. O. Muller, and John Wiley & Sons, Inc.

GEOLOGIC TIME SCALE

Era	Period	Epoch	Age in Millions of Years Before Present
CENOZOIC	Quaternary	Holocene	Present
			0.01
		Pleistocene	
			1.6
	Neogene	Pliocene	
			5.3
		Miocene	
	Tertiary		23.7
	Paleogene	Oligocene	
			36.6
		Eocene	
			57.8
		Paleocene	
			66.4
MESOZOIC	Cretaceous		
			144
	Jurassic		
			208
	Triassic		
			245
PALEOZOIC	Permian		
			286
	Carboniferous — Pennsylvanian		
			320
	Carboniferous — Mississippian		
			360
	Devonian		
			408
	Silurian		
			438
	Ordovician		
			505
	Cambrian		
			570
PRECAMBRIAN			
			4,550

extreme, not the whole picture. So human communities—fishing, hunting and gathering, and using increasingly sophisticated tools (and probably means of verbal communication)—exploited the milder times to expand their frontiers, then hunkered down when it got cold again.

About 73,500 years ago, something happened that appears to have come close to exterminating humanity altogether. A volcano, Mount Toba, erupted on the Indonesian island of Sumatra. This was not just an eruption: The entire mountain exploded, sending millions of tons of debris into orbit, obscuring the sun, creating long-term darkness, and altering global climate. Mount Toba's detonation could hardly have come at a worse time. Earth's habitable zone was already constricted because of glaciation. Anthropologists refer to this event as humanity's "evolutionary bottleneck," suggesting that much genetic diversity was lost. Today, the filled-in caldera marking Toba's cataclysm is 90 kilometers (55 miles) long and 50 kilometers (30 miles) wide, silent witness to the greatest threat to our existence ever to come from any source (Fig. 13.8).

The Wisconsinan Glaciation eventually gave way to a full-scale interglacial, the current warm interlude that has been given its own designation, the **Holocene** (Fig. 13.6). Global warming began about 18,000 years ago, and for the next 6000 years, temperatures rose rapidly. Although the ice sheets were thinning and giant, mud-laden floods sped down the Mississippi Valley, building the river's enormous delta, ice

■ **Figure 13.6**
Stages in Earth History.

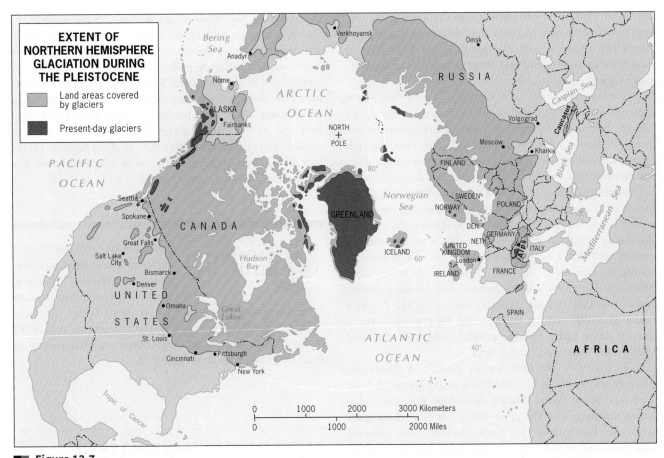

■■ Figure 13.7
Extent of Northern Hemisphere Glaciation. During the Late Pleistocene's Wisconsinan Glaciation, glaciers covered northern North America and Eurasia. The evidence on which this map is based includes glacial deposits and marks on bedrock cut by glaciers. © H. J. de Blij, P. O. Muller, and John Wiley & Sons, Inc.

continued to cover most of northern North America as recently as 13,000 years ago.

To our human ancestors in the Northern Hemisphere, who inhabited much of western and eastern Eurasia and may just have been entering the Americas (some scholars argue that American Indians were here earlier), this warming must have been a welcome experience. So persistent was this most recent warming that people ventured farther and farther poleward.

The Little Ice Age in the Modern Era

To the farmers, winegrowers, and seafarers of the fourteenth century, increasing cold, decreasing rainfall, frigid winds, and shortened growing seasons made for dwindling harvests, failing farms, and seas too stormy for fishing. By the turn of the

TeeJe/Flickr/Getty Images

Figure 13.8
Mount Toba, Indonesia. The lake in this photo fills in the gigantic caldera left from the eruption of Mount Toba on the island of Sumatra in Indonesia.

fourteenth century, alpine glaciers began to advance. Greenland's small settlement had long since disappeared, and many people left Iceland as well. Weather extremes abounded, not only in the form of record cold snaps but also as searing summer heat and raging storms.

Famines struck all over Europe, just at a time when more people were clustered in towns than ever before. The climatic record, pieced together from farmers' diaries (winegrowers' diaries are especially useful), tree ring research (dendochronology), ice cores, contemporary writings, illustrative paintings, and surviving sketches and drawings, justifies the designation of the post–1300 period as a shift in the direction of reglaciation. We now know that this return to colder times, marked by advancing mountain glaciers and thickening subarctic ice, would end in the mid-nineteenth century and that even the worst of it, starting in the late 1600s, did not lead to full-scale Pleistocene glaciation. Only when new methods of analysis became available did scientists realize that this temporary cooling was no ice age: It was a minor glaciation and not the first over the past 6000 years. But the name **Little Ice Age** certainly was more dramatic than "Minor Glaciation," and it stuck.

In his book *The Little Ice Age* (2000), archaeologist Brian Fagan described how the Franz Josef Glacier on New Zealand's South Island "thrust downslope into the valley below, smashing into the great rainforests . . . felling giant trees like matchsticks." In North America, our growing understanding of the Little Ice Age helps explain why the Jamestown colony collapsed so fast, a failure attributed by historians solely to ineptitude and lack of preparation. Geographer David Stahle (1998) and his team, studying tree ring records that go back eight centuries, found that the Jamestown area experienced a seven-year drought between 1606 (the year before the colony's founding) through 1612, the worst in nearly eight centuries. European colonists and American Indians were in the same situation, and their relations worsened as they were forced to compete for dwindling food and falling water tables. The high rate of starvation was not unique to the colonists. They, and their American Indian neighbors, faced the rigors of the Little Ice Age as well.

As the Little Ice Age continued into the 1800s, a large-scale volcano had a major impact on human society. On April 5, 1815, the Tambora volcano on the island of Sumatra in what was then the Dutch East Indies, located not far east of Bali, rumbled to life. Less than a week later it was pulverized in a series of explosions that could be heard a thousand miles away, killing all but 26 of the island's population of 12,000. When it was over, the top 4000 feet of the volcano were gone, and much of what is now Indonesia was covered by debris. Darkness enveloped most of the colony for weeks, and tens of thousands died of famine in the months that followed. Colonial reports describe fields covered by poisonous ash and powder, waters clogged by trees and cinders, and air rendered unbreathable by a fog of acid chemicals.

Since the 1850s, when the Little Ice Age waned and a slow but nearly continuous warming phase began,

climatologists and other scientists have sought answers to crucial questions relating to climate change: What causes alternating cycles of global warming and cooling? Given the enormous quantities of pollution poured into the planet's atmosphere as the Industrial Revolution gathered momentum, how large is the human contribution to the associated **greenhouse effect** (that results when greenhouse gases trap heat and raise temperatures)? This worldwide, effort to answer such questions involves the use of sophisticated computers and complicated models, and as discussed below, has achieved an alarming consensus.

Take time to search the Internet and read about what has happened to Phuket, Thailand, since the Indian Ocean tsunami hit in December 2004. Look for before and after images of Phuket—how did it look before the tsunami hit and after? Research how Phuket has been rebuilt and determine why Phuket has been rebuilt the way it has.

HOW HAVE HUMANS ALTERED EARTH'S ENVIRONMENT?

Biologists estimate that as many as 25 million types of organisms inhabit Earth, perhaps even more. Most have not yet been identified, classified, or studied. No species, not even the powerful dinosaurs, ever affected their environment as much as humans do today. An impact by comets probably made the dinosaurs and many other species extinct. Some biogeographers suggest that the next great extinction is already occurring, and it is caused not by asteroids but by humans, whose numbers and demands are destroying millions of species.

The natural environment is being modified and stressed by human activity in many obvious and some less obvious ways. Some **environmental stress** is more obvious because it takes place around human habitats, such as cutting forests and emitting pollutants into the atmosphere. Less obvious environmental stress takes place away from dense concentrations of humans, including mountain-top mining, burying toxic wastes that contaminate groundwater supplies, and dumping vast amounts of garbage into waterways and the world's oceans. Humans have built seawalls, terraced hillslopes, dammed rivers, cut canals, and modified the environment in many constructive as well as destructive ways. All of these activities have an impact on environment and have given rise to a number of key concerns. Among these concerns are the future of water supplies, the state of the atmosphere, climate change, desertification, deforestation, soil degradation, and the disposal of industrial wastes.

Water

Resources that are replenished even as they are being used are **renewable resources**, and resources that are present in finite quantities are **nonrenewable resources**. Water, essential to life, is a renewable resource. But the available supply of fresh water is not distributed evenly across the globe. Figure 1.11 shows the world distribution of precipitation, with the largest totals recorded in equatorial and tropical areas of Southeast Asia, South Asia, central and coastal West Africa, and Middle and South America. The volume of precipitation in the world as a whole is enormous; spread out evenly, it would cover the land area of the planet with about 33 inches (83 cm) of water each year. Much of that water is lost through runoff and evaporation, but enough of it seeps downward into porous, water-holding rocks called **aquifers** to provide millions of wells with steady flows. In the United States alone, it is estimated that there is 50 times as much water stored in aquifers as there is precipitation falling on the land surface every year.

Despite such favorable data, the supply of water is anything but plentiful (Fig. 13.9). Chronic water shortages afflict tens of millions of farmers in Africa and hundreds of thousands of city dwellers in Southern California; water rationing has been imposed in rainy South Florida and in Spain, which faces the Mediterranean Sea.

In many areas of the world, people have congregated in places where water supplies are insufficient, undependable, or both. In California, people are sometimes not allowed to wash their cars or refill their swimming pools; these are minor inconveniences compared to the fate faced by millions of Sudanese trying to escape violence in their country by fleeing to parched pans of the Sahara. In Florida, where the urban population depends on the Biscayne Aquifer for most of its water, the long-term prospect is troubled; whenever seasonal rainfalls do not reach their projected averages, Floridians overuse the Biscayne Aquifer, and saltwater enters the aquifer from the nearby Atlantic Ocean. The invasion of saltwater over time can permanently destroy a fresh water aquifer.

Hundreds of millions of people still cluster along several of Earth's great rivers. Indeed, nearly three-quarters of all the fresh water used annually is consumed in farming, not in cities. In California, where about 80 percent of available water is used for irrigation, an intense debate has emerged over whether cities should be provided with water at the expense of Central Valley farms, and whether fruits and vegetables should be bought from elsewhere, even overseas, rather than be grown locally?

As human populations have expanded, people have increasingly settled in arid regions. One of the great ecological disasters of the twentieth century occurred in Kazakhstan and Uzbekistan, whose common boundary runs through the Aral Sea. Streams that fed this large body of water were diverted to irrigate the surrounding desert, mainly for commercial cotton production. Heavy use of chemical pesticide ruined the groundwater below, causing a health crisis that some observers describe as an "ecological Chernobyl" (referring to the 1986 nuclear reactor meltdown in the Ukraine). In the meantime the Aral Sea began to dry up, and by the mid-1990s it had lost more than three-quarters of its total surface area (Fig. 13.10). In 2001, the Kazakhstan government, with a loan from the World Bank, began work to restore the lake. A dam was completed in 2005 and leaky irrigation canals have been fixed. As a result, the northern end of the lake is capturing more water from the Syr Darya River and the

FIELD NOTE

"We drove north on Route 89 from Tucson, Arizona, across the desert. Drought rules the countryside here, and dams conserve what water there is. Snaking through the landscape are lifelines such as this, linking Coolidge Dam to distant farms and towns. In the vast, arid landscape, this narrow ribbon of water seems little more than an artificial brook— but to hundreds of thousands of people, this is what makes life possible in the Southwest."

© H. J. de Blij

■■ **Figure 13.9**
Tucson, Arizona.

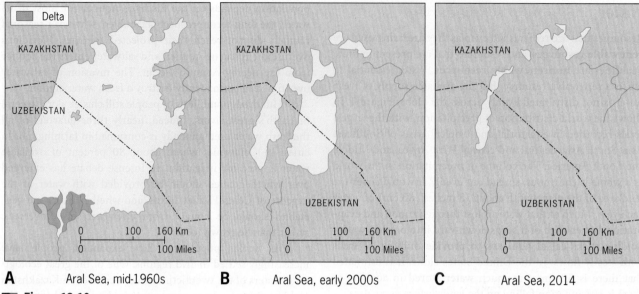

A Aral Sea, mid-1960s   **B** Aral Sea, early 2000s   **C** Aral Sea, 2014

■■ **Figure 13.10**

The Aral Sea. Affected by climatic cycles and afflicted by human interference, the Aral Sea on the border of Kazakhstan and Uzbekistan has shrunk. In a quarter of a century, it lost three-quarters of its surface area and more than 90 percent of its volume.   © E. H. Fouberg, A. B. Murphy, H. J. de Blij, and John Wiley & Sons, Inc.

fishing industry has rebounded slightly. But the general story is one or remarkable shrinkage.

The history of the Aral Sea highlights another aspect of the water story—the environmental concerns generated from damming rivers to generate hydroelectricity and capture water for rural and urban uses. In many of the wealthier parts of the world, dam building reached its peak in the middle of the twentieth century, and some dams are now slated for removal. But many dams are still being built in other parts of the world—along the Tigris and Euphrates, along the Mekong and its tributaries, along China's major rivers, and elsewhere. China's recently completed Three Gorges Dam, now the world's largest hydropower project, reduces the need to burn greenhouse-gas-producing coal, but its construction raised a host of concerns related to its impacts on forest cover, wildlife, sedimentation, and much more. And that dam is but one of many water-related projects in China. The geographical mismatch between population concentrations and available water is behind a decades-long project aimed at building a channel that can send water from the Yangtze River to the north. The project aims to meet the needs of a burgeoning urban population around Beijing and beyond, but the associated environmental alterations are tremendous.

School children are not typically taught to think about the geography of water—how varying precipitation and human uses of water affect its availability and quantity. Textbooks teach that water is a constant whose distribution is sustained through the **hydrologic cycle**, where water from oceans, lakes, soil, rivers, and vegetation evaporates, condenses, and then precipitates on landmasses. The precipitation infiltrates and recharges groundwater or runs off into lakes, rivers, and oceans. Physical geographer Jamie Linton questions the utility of any model of the water cycle that does not take into account the role of humans and culture, suggesting that by "representing water as a constant, cyclical flow, the hydrologic cycle establishes a norm that is at odds with the hydrological reality of much of the world."

Linton argues that the hydrologic cycle does not take into account the norms of water in arid regions of the world, and it also assumes water cycles in a predictable, linear fashion. The amount of water cycling through is not a constant. For instance, land cover changes how much water is in the cycle. In the global south, Linton contends, forests "can actually promote evapotranspiration at rates much higher than for short crops," which has "the overall effect of *reducing* the quantity of water available for runoff or groundwater recharge."

Instead of the hydrologic cycle, Linton advocates thinking of water as a system rather than a cycle (Fig. 13.11). He defines the water system as the "integration of physical, biological, biogeochemical, and human components" of the global water system.

WATER SECURITY

Throughout the world, people have come to depend on water sources with an uncertain future. Rocky Mountain and Sierra Nevada snows feed the Colorado River and the aquifers that irrigate the California Central Valley. Aqueducts snake their way across the desert to urban communities. None of this has slowed the population's move to the Sun Belt, and the water situation there is becoming problematic. In coastal eastern Spain, low water pressure in city pipes sometimes deprives the upper floors of high-rise buildings of water. In Southwest Asia and the Arabian Peninsula, growing populations strain ancient water supply systems, and desalinization plants that convert saltwater to fresh water are a necessity.

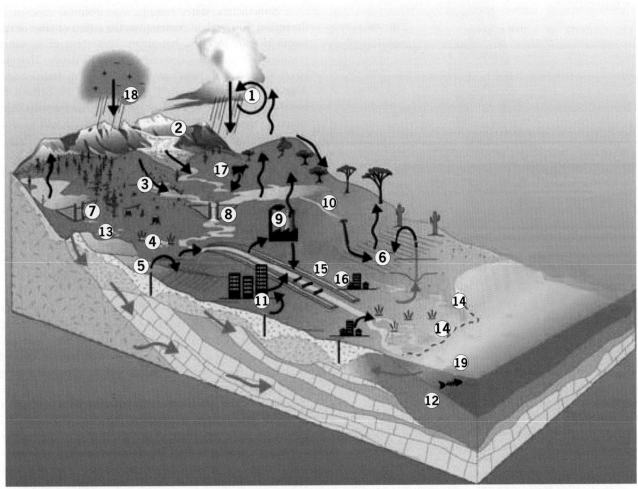

1. Hydrological cycle accelerated
2. Mountain snow and ice lost
3. Tree removal increases runoff, reduces transpiration, affects water table and landscape salinity
4. Wetlands dried up or drained
5,6. Ground- and surface water used for irrigated agriculture

7,8. Dams alter flow and reservoirs increase evaporation
9. Industrial water coolers release water vapor
10. Water transfers between basins
11. Urban, mining, and construction areas alter water flows and quality
12. Coastal saltwater intrudes inland

13. Impoundments reduce flows
14. Siltation, erosion, and nutrient flows change coastlines and affect water quality
15. Levees and locks modify flows and channels
16. Settlements alter floodplain landscapes
17. Grazing affects runoff and water quality
18. Industry causes acid rain
19. Coastal waters polluted and species lost

■■■ **Figure 13.11**

The Global Water System.   The human imprint is reflected in this diagram of the global water system.   *Reproduced with permission from:* American Geophysical Union.

Water also plays a role in regional conflicts in places such as the Darfur region of Sudan. Consider, for example, the situation of Israel and its neighbors. With 8.1 million people, Israel annually consumes nearly three times as much water as Jordan, the West Bank Palestinian areas, and Gaza combined (total population: 11.7 million). As much as half of Israel's water comes from sources outside the Israeli state.

The key sources of water for the entire area are the Jordan River and an aquifer beneath the West Bank. When Israel captured the Golan Heights from Syria and the West Bank from Jordan during the 1967 war, it gained control over both of these sources, including the Jordan River's important tributary, the Yarmuk (Fig. 13.12). As the map shows, the Sea of Galilee forms a large fresh water reservoir in the Jordan River Valley. This is the source of the majority of Israel's water, though desalinization of sea water is increasingly important.

The water situation has the potential to further complicate relations between Israel and its neighbors. The aquifer

■ Figure 13.12
Key Water Resources in the Middle East.   Here, as in many other places, meeting the needs of different populations for water requires cooperation among peoples and governments.   © E. H. Fouberg, A. B. Murphy, H. J. de Blij, and John Wiley & Sons, Inc.

beneath the West Bank yields about 625 million cubic meters (22,071 cubic feet) of water through hundreds of wells linked together by a system of pipelines. Of this total, some 450 million cubic meters go directly to Israel; another 35 million are consumed by Israeli settlers on the West Bank, and only some 140 million are allotted to the West Bank's nearly 2 million Arabs. This is unfair, say the Palestinian Arabs: If the West Bank is to become an independent Palestinian territory, the water below the surface should belong to the Palestinians. But the Israeli cities of Tel Aviv and Jerusalem depend heavily on water from the West Bank, and Israel cannot survive without this source.

There are, however, signs of cooperation over water in the region. In late 2013 Israel, the Palestinian Authority, and Jordan signed an agreement to build the Red Sea–Dead Sea project (Fig. 13.12). A major desalinization plant will convert saltwater from the Red Sea into potable water that will be moved by pipeline to the north, and the briny runoff will be piped through Jordan to the Dead Sea to combat its rapid contraction. Israel and Jordan hope to gain between 8 and 13 billion gallons of water. Israel will also provide Amman with 8–13 billion gallons of fresh water from the Sea of Galilee, and the Palestinians can buy up to 8 billion gallons of

additional water from Israel at "preferential prices." The plan has been in the works for 20 years; it is hailed as a rare success in a region riven by conflict.

Nonetheless, water remains a geopolitical concern in the region. Israel might contemplate the return of most of the Golan Heights to Syria, but about 30 percent of all water reaching the Sea of Galilee comes from the Golan Heights. Israel might support the establishment of an independent state in the West Bank, but approximately 30 percent of Israel's water supply comes from the West Bank aquifer. Any effort to negotiate a lasting peace in the region will have to take these geographical circumstances into account.

Atmosphere

Earth's **atmosphere** is a thin layer of air lying directly above the lands and oceans. We depend on the atmosphere for our survival: We breathe its oxygen; it shields us from the destructive rays of the sun; it moderates temperatures; and it carries moisture from the oceans over the land, sustaining crops and forests and replenishing soils and wells.

Scientists are concerned that human pollution of the atmosphere will result in long-lasting, possibly permanent damage. True, the air disperses even the densest smoke and most acrid chemical gases. However, anthropogenic sources of pollution from two centuries of industrial expansion are pouring into the atmosphere at an unprecedented rate. While the United States remains the world's largest per capita leader in terms of pollutants generated, China has overtaken the United States in total volume, India's share is rising rapidly, and other growing economies are compounding a problem that can only be solved by determined international action. Yet different national priorities, and the unequal distribution of contributors to the problem and beneficiaries of action, have worked against serious coordinated action.

CLIMATE CHANGE

Growing populations and increased human activity, ranging from the burning of tropical forests to pollution of the atmosphere by industry and automobiles, are having an unprecedented impact on the atmosphere. The amounts of key "greenhouse" gases, carbon dioxide (CO_2), methane, and nitrous oxides in the atmosphere have been increasing at a rate of about 2 percent per decade; automobiles, steel mills, refineries, and chemical plants account for a large part of this increase. A simple experiment in a college chemistry lab shows that an increase in the level of CO_2 in the atmosphere traps more heat. Hence, it is not surprising that an overwhelming majority of climate scientists have concluded that *tropospheric* pollution from anthropogenic (human) sources is causing the Earth to retain increasing amounts of heat, with effects that will increase during the course of the twenty-first century and beyond.

While estimates of the degree of human-induced **climate change** differ, climate records from recent decades show that global temperatures are rising, which is why climate change is sometimes called global warming. Climate change is a more accurate term, however, because while the global temperature is rising, the outcome will vary greatly across regions of the world.

Sea-level rise is one aspect of climate change. While the rise in global temperatures will undoubtedly be interrupted by occasional spurts of cooling, computer models predict that warmer temperatures will melt polar and glacial ice and sea levels will rise as much as 50 centimeters or more during the twenty-first century. Certain calculations project an even greater sea-level rise. Low-lying islands in the Indian Ocean and the South Pacific have already disappeared beneath the waves. Alarmed government leaders in low-lying Pacific and Indian Ocean island nations talk of buying higher ground in other countries and of suing the governments of polluting states over lost real estate.

Changes in climate involve alterations in the amount of water vapor in the atmosphere, which affects patterns of precipitation. Changes in precipitation affect where certain types of vegetation can grow, altering everything from agricultural patterns to the location of animal habitats. Predicting exactly where, and in what magnitude, these changes will occur is difficult. What is clear is that those living on the margins of sustainability are facing even riskier futures.

Atmospheric scientists are investigating the relationship between current changes in the climate and extreme weather events. If you follow the news, you have read headlines from around the world about cold snaps that are the worst in the century, floods the highest in memory, and droughts the longest on record. Although the science is not completely settled, there is growing evidence of a link between warming global temperatures and the intensification of regional weather systems.

ACID RAIN

A by-product of the enormous volume of pollutants spewed into the atmosphere is **acid rain**. Acid rain forms when sulfur dioxide and nitrogen oxides are released into the atmosphere by the burning of fossil fuels (coal, oil, and natural gas). These pollutants combine with water vapor in the air to form dilute solutions of sulfuric and nitric acids, which then are washed out of the atmosphere by rain or other types of precipitation, such as fog and snow.

Although acid rain usually consists of relatively mild acids, it can be caustic enough to harm certain natural ecosystems (the mutual interactions between groups of plant and animal organisms and their environment). Acid rain has acidified lakes and streams (with resultant fish kills), stunted growth of forests, and damaged crops in affected areas. In cities it has accelerated corrosion of buildings and monuments.

Areas affected by acid rain are generally downwind from industrial concentrations. In the United States and western Europe, compliance with legislated emission reductions is having positive results. In Canada as well as in Scandinavia, where acid rain from neighboring industrial regions damaged forests and acidified lakes, recovery came faster than most scientists

had predicted. This evidence is now encouraging other countries to impose stricter controls on factory emissions.

The Land

Over the centuries, human population growth has put increasing pressure on land surfaces. More land is cleared and placed under cultivation, trees are cut down, and cities expand. The effects can be seen almost everywhere and are so extensive that it is often difficult even to reconstruct what an area might be like in the absence of humans. The human impact on Earth's land surface has several key aspects, the most significant of which are deforestation, soil erosion, waste disposal, and biodiversity loss.

DEFORESTATION

Forests cover 31 percent of the total surface of the Earth from the tropical Amazon Basin to high-latitude North America and Eurasia. The world's forests, especially those of lower and middle latitudes, play a critical role in the **oxygen cycle**. Atmospheric oxygen is consumed by natural processes as well as by human activities. Forests counteract this loss through photosynthesis and related processes, which release oxygen into the atmosphere. The destruction of vast tracts of forest is called **deforestation**. Ecologists and others warn of unforeseeable and incalculable impacts not only for the affected areas but for the planet as a whole.

In the early 1980s, the Food and Agriculture Organization (FAO) of the United Nations undertook a study of the rate at which forests were being depleted. This analysis showed that 44 percent of the tropical rainforest had already been affected by cutting and that more than 1 percent was being logged every year (Fig. 13.13). A 2014 report revealed that Indonesia lost more than 6 million hectares of primary forest between 2000 and 2012.

In 2014, the FAO released its annual report on the world's forests with good news: The rate of deforestation worldwide declined in the last decade. According to the FAO, during the 1990s humans deforested 16 million hectares a year, mostly by converting tropical rainforests to agriculture land. Between 2000 and 2010, humans deforested 13 million hectares a year. Lower deforestation rates have been coupled with tree planting programs, especially in Brazil. As a result, the "net loss of forests was 5.2 million hectares per year between 2000 and 2010, down from 8.3 million hectares annually in the 1990s."

Deforestation is not a singular process: It has been going on for centuries, and the motivations for deforestation vary vastly. Forests are cut and reforested for wood and paper products; forests are preserved for the maintenance of biodiversity; and other forests are cleared for new agricultural production. The 2014 FAO report suggests that some 1.25 billion people depend on forest resources for their livelihood and argues that local economies need to do a better job at balancing resource extraction and conservation.

The reforestation (and harvesting) of deforested areas is not the whole answer to the problem, even if it could be done

FIELD NOTE

"This was one of the most depressing days of this long South American field trip. We had been briefed and had seen the satellite pictures of the destruction of the rainforest, with ugly gashes of bare ground pointing like rows of arrows into the woods. But walking to the temporary end points of some of these new roads made a lot more impact. From the remaining forest around came the calls of monkeys and other wildlife, their habitat retreating under the human onslaught. Next week this road would push ahead another mile, the logs carted away and burned, the first steps in a process that would clear this land, ending billions of years of nature's dominance."

© H. J. de Blij

Figure 13.13
Para, Brazil.

on a large scale. Forests in the United States, for example, consist mainly of second-growth trees, which replaced the original forest after it was logged. However, the controlled second-growth forest does not (as the natural forest did) have many trees dying of old age after their trunks and limbs become soft from rot. As a result, many animal species that depend on holes in trunks and hollows in tree limbs cannot find places to nest (thus, the spotted owl dispute in the Pacific Northwest of the United States). For them the forest has ceased to be a favorable habitat. Moreover, reforested areas generally do not have the type of rich understory layer that can store substantial amounts of water and provide more organic input to the soil.

SOIL EROSION

Soil erosion is caused by a variety of factors: Livestock are allowed to graze in areas where they destroy the natural vegetation; lands too dry to sustain farming are plowed, and wind erosion follows. Soil is a renewable resource because, with proper care, it can recover. However, it is being "mined" as if it were a nonrenewable resource.

The loss of potentially productive soil to erosion has been described as a "quiet crisis" of global proportions. Ecologists Lester Brown and Edward Wolf point out that the increasing rate of this loss over the past generation is not the result of a decline in the skills of farmers but rather of the pressures on farmers to produce more. In an integrated world food economy, the pressures on land resources are not confined to particular countries; they permeate the entire world.

Why has **soil erosion** increased so much? Part of the answer lies in population pressure: World population is over 7 billion. Associated with population growth is the cultivation of ever-steeper slopes, with hastily constructed terraces

or without any terraces at all (Fig. 13.14). As the pressure on land increases, farmers are less able to leave part of their soil fallow (unused) to allow it to recover its nutrients. Another part of the answer lies in rising levels of consumption accompanying industrialization and development (see below). As socioeconomic circumstances improve and people become more interconnected with the global economy, diets change and the demand for specialty items increases. Those changes in turn increase the pressure to farm marginal areas and to create large, monocropped factory farms that are less conservative of the soil than their small, multicropped counterparts.

Given that 99.7 percent of all human food is grown in soil (some is grown in water), the annual toll that soil erosion takes on the cropland available for agriculture is concerning. The dimensions of the problem are suggested by a 2006 study, which reported that globally about 37,000 square miles (10 million ha) of cropland are lost to soil erosion each year. An even more recent study suggests that soil is being lost at between 10 and 40 times natural replacement levels. International cooperation in food distribution, education of farmers and governments, and worldwide dissemination of soil conservation methods are urgently needed to address this "quiet crisis."

WASTE DISPOSAL

If anything has grown faster than population itself, it is the waste generated by households, communities, and industries—much of it a matter of bulk, some of it a source of danger.

There is a strong correlation between level of socioeconomic well-being and solid waste production. The United States is one of the largest producers of **solid waste**, debris, and garbage discarded by those living in cities, industries, mines, and farms. According to current estimates, the United States produces about 4.5 pounds (2 kg) of solid waste per person per day, which adds up to more than 250 million tons (226 million metric tons) per year. But the United States is not alone. Other high-technology economies with a high ratio of disposable materials (containers, packaging) face the same problems.

Disposal of these wastes is a major worldwide problem. The growing volume of waste must be put somewhere, but space for it is no longer easy to find. In poorer countries, waste is often thrown onto open dumps where vermin multiply, decomposition sends methane gas into the air, rain and waste liquids carry contaminants into the groundwater below, and fires pollute the surrounding atmosphere. In countries that can afford it, such open dumps have been replaced by **sanitary landfills**. The waste is put in a hole that has been dug and prepared for the purpose, including a floor of materials to treat seeping liquids and soil to cover each load as it is compacted and deposited in the fill.

The number of suitable sites for sanitary landfills is decreasing, however, and it is increasingly difficult to design new sites. In the United States landfill capacity has been reached or will soon be reached in about a dozen States, most of them in the Northeast and Mid-Atlantic regions, and those States must now buy space from other States for this purpose. Trucking or sending garbage by rail to distant landfills is very expensive, but there are few alternatives.

Similar problems are evident on a global scale. The United States, the European Union, and Japan export solid (including hazardous) wastes to countries in Africa, Middle and South America, and East Asia. While these countries are paid for accepting the waste, they do not always have the capacity to treat it properly. So the waste often is dumped in open landfills, where it creates the very hazards that the exporters want to avoid. In the late 1980s, the wealthier countries' practice of "managing" waste by exporting it became a controversial issue, and in 1989 a treaty was drawn up to control it. The treaty did not (as many poorer countries wished) prohibit the exporting of hazardous waste, although it did place some restrictions on trade in hazardous materials.

It is useful to draw a distinction between **toxic wastes**, which are dangerous because of chemicals, infectious materials, and the like, and **radioactive wastes**, which are of two types: low-level radioactive wastes, which give off small amounts of radiation and are produced by industry, hospitals, research facilities, and nuclear power plants; and high-level radioactive wastes, which emit strong radiation and are produced by nuclear power plants and nuclear weapons factories.

© H. J. de Blij

■ **Figure 13.14**
Guangxi-Zhuang, China.   Overuse of land in this area of China has led to the collapse of formerly sound terracing systems.

In the United States, low-level radioactive wastes have for many years been disposed of in steel drums placed in six special government-run landfills, three of which are now closed.

High-level radioactive waste is extremely dangerous and difficult to get rid of. Fuel rods from nuclear reactors will remain radioactive for thousands of years and must be stored in remote places where they will not contaminate water, air, or any other part of the environment. In fact, no satisfactory means or place for the disposal of high-level radioactive waste has been found. Among many suggested disposal sites are deep shafts in the bedrock, chambers dug in salt deposits (salt effectively blocks radiation), ice chambers in Antarctica, sediments beneath the ocean floor, and volcanically active midocean trenches. Meanwhile, spent fuel rods (which last only about three years in the reactor) are put in specially designed drums and stored in one of about 100 sites, all of them potentially dangerous.

There is a related problem: transportation of waste. Even if secure and safe storage can be found for high-level radioactive waste, the waste has to be transported from its source to the disposal site. Such transportation presents an additional hazard: a truck or train accident could have disastrous consequences.

The dimensions of the waste-disposal problem are growing and globalizing. The threat to the planet's environment is not just over the short term but can exist for centuries, indeed millennia.

Biodiversity

A significant change that is related to all of the developments discussed so far is the accelerating loss of **biodiversity**. An abbreviation of "biological diversity," biodiversity refers to the diversity of all aspects of life found on Earth. Although the term is commonly used when referring to the diversity of species, it encompasses the entire range of biological diversity, from the genetic variability within individuals of a species to the diversity of ecosystems on the planet.

Species are becoming extinct at a rapid rate. It is difficult to say exactly how quickly extinctions are occurring, since we do not know how many species there are. What is clear, however, is that although extinction is a natural process, humans have dramatically increased rates of extinction, particularly over the last few hundred years. Estimates from the United Nations Environment Program's Global Biodiversity Assessment indicate that 8 percent of plants, 5 percent of fish, 11 percent of birds, and 18 percent of the world's mammal species are currently threatened.

Whether a species is threatened with extinction depends on the range of the species, its scarcity, and its geographic concentration. If a species with a small range, a high degree of scarcity, and a small geographic concentration has its habitat threatened, extinction can follow. Because most species have small ranges, change in a limited area can affect a species. A 2005 report in *Scientific American* explained that "clearing a forest, draining a wetland, damming a river or dynamiting a coral reef to kill its fish can more readily eliminate species with small ranges than more widespread species."

Human impacts on biodiversity have increased over time. The domestication of animals, followed by the agricultural domestication of plant life, caused significant alterations in our relationship with other species. Large vertebrates have always been particularly hard hit by human activities. Many birds and mammals have been hunted not only for food but also for their skins, feathers, and so forth. During the eighteenth and nineteenth centuries, beaver populations in North America were drastically reduced as the beavers were trapped and skinned for their pelts. Many bird species were hunted for their feathers, which were sold to decorate fashionable hats. Worldwide, elephants and walruses continue to be hunted for their ivory tusks. From historical records we know that over 650 species of plants and over 480 animal species have become extinct in just the last 400 years. These represent only the documented extinctions. The actual number of extinctions that occurred during this period is almost certainly much higher.

Humans have also indirectly contributed to extinctions. Human travel, for instance, introduced new species to areas around the globe. Rats are among the more destructive of these; they have had devastating effects on oceanic islands. Introduced species may cause extinctions by preying upon native species or competing with them for resources. A famous example is the dodo bird (*Raphus cuculatus*), which was hunted to extinction by humans, dogs, and rats on the island of Mauritius. Introduced species may also carry new diseases, leading to the decimation and extinction of local populations. Species on islands are particularly susceptible to extinction because of the more insular ecosystems found on

islands. An estimated 2000 species of birds on tropical Pacific islands became extinct following human settlement.

Identifying the nature and extent of environmental changes is only a first step toward understanding the extent of human alteration of the planet. A second, and more complicated step is to consider the forces driving these changes.

What is the greatest environmental concern facing the region where you live, and in what other regions of the world is that concern also present? How do differences between your region and the other regions sharing the concern influence how it is understood and approached?

WHAT ARE THE MAJOR FACTORS CONTRIBUTING TO ENVIRONMENTAL CHANGE TODAY?

Environmental change occurs at all levels of scale, from local to global. For example, deforestation has local effects by reducing the diversity of species even in a small area. It has regional consequences by increasing sediment runoff into streams and rivers. And, globally, it results in the increased release of carbon dioxide in the atmosphere, which affects the planetary climate.

Several interrelated factors influence the escalating impact of human activities on the natural environment. The past two centuries have witnessed dramatic growth in the human population, a fourfold increase (from about 1.5 billion to 6 billion) in the twentieth century alone. Per capita consumption of virtually everything, from water and farm products to metals and energy resources, has increased rapidly as well. Fast-developing technologies allow us to alter the natural environment ever more. Each of these interrelated factors that contribute to environmental change can be studied broadly, focusing on the general impacts of each factor on the global environment. Yet, when we shift scales to the local and regional, and we consider the context of human actions at these scales, we often find that the causes of environmental change vary depending on the local and regional context.

Political Ecology

Leslie Gray and William Moseley describe the field of political ecology, which traces its roots to the 1960s and 1970s, as a way of considering the roles of "political economy, power and history in shaping human–environmental interactions." Political ecologists are interested in how environmental issues such as deforestation are affected by the ways in which political, economic, social, and ecological circumstances play out in individual places. As such, they focus attention on the spatial coalescence of processes operating at different scales on Earth's surface.

GUEST FIELD NOTE

Try, Mali

In this photo, a young man brings home the cotton harvest in the village of Try in southern Mali. Prior to my graduate studies in geography, I spent a number of years as an international development worker concerned with tropical agriculture—both on the ground in Africa and as a policy wonk in Washington, D.C. I drew at least two important lessons from these experiences. First, well-intentioned work at the grassroots level would always be limited if it were not supported by broader scale policies and economics. Second, the people making the policies were often out of touch with the real impacts their decisions were having in the field. As such, geography, and the subfield of political ecology, were appealing to me because of its explicit attention to processes operating at multiple scales, its tradition of fieldwork, and its longstanding attention to human–environment interactions. I employed a political ecology approach during fieldwork for my dissertation in 1999–2000. Here, I sought to test the notion that poor farmers are more likely to degrade soils than their wealthier counterparts (a concept widely proclaimed in the development policy literature of the 1990s). Not only did I interview rich and poor farmers about their management practices, but I tested their soils and questioned policymakers at the provincial, national, and international levels. My findings (and those of others) have led to a questioning of the poverty–environmental degradation paradigm.

Credit: William Moseley, Macalester College.

■ **Figure 13.15**
Try, Mali.

William Moseley, Macalester College

Moseley, for example, has studied the conservation behaviors of farmers in southern Mali (Fig. 13.15). His research directly highlighted a fundamental fallacy in the widely held view that poorer people degrade the land more than wealthier people. Through extensive fieldwork, interviews, and soil surveys, Moseley found that poorer farmers in southern Mali were more likely to use organic materials to preserve topsoil, whereas wealthier farmers were more likely to use inorganic fertilizers and pesticides. The explanation for this outcome lies in the policies and power relationships at play in southern Mali. The government of Mali's agricultural extension service singled out the wealthiest households for cotton farming, which "helped these households become even wealthier in the short term." And the farmers, who (unlike their poorer counterparts) were able to afford inorganic fertilizers, turned to their use in the face of an increasingly competitive global market. Recognizing these points requires looking at the intersection of multi-scale political and economic influences on southern Mali.

Population

Because humans across the world do not consume or pollute in exactly the same ways, we cannot make a simple chart showing that each additional human born on Earth results in a certain amount of consumption or generates a certain amount of pollution. Of course, all humans affect the environment, and a greater number of people on Earth necessarily translates into a greater capacity for environmental change, but the impacts of people in some places are much greater than those in other places.

Similarly, environmental change influences humans differently, depending in part on who they are and where they live. To underscore the spatial differences in environmental impact on humans, we can consider two maps of natural disaster hot spots published by the Earth Institute at Columbia University and the World Bank in a 2005 report. The maps highlight the places in the world most susceptible to natural disasters, whether caused by drought, tectonic activity (earthquakes and volcanoes), or hydrological hazards (floods, cyclones, and landslides) (Fig. 13.16). Comparing the map of

MORTALITY RISKS

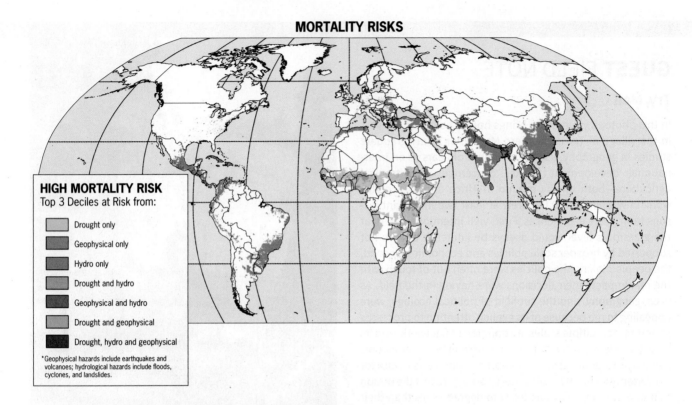

HIGH MORTALITY RISK
Top 3 Deciles at Risk from:

- Drought only
- Geophysical only
- Hydro only
- Drought and hydro
- Geophysical and hydro
- Drought and geophysical
- Drought, hydro and geophysical

*Geophysical hazards include earthquakes and volcanoes; hydrological hazards include floods, cyclones, and landslides.

ECONOMIC LOSS RISKS

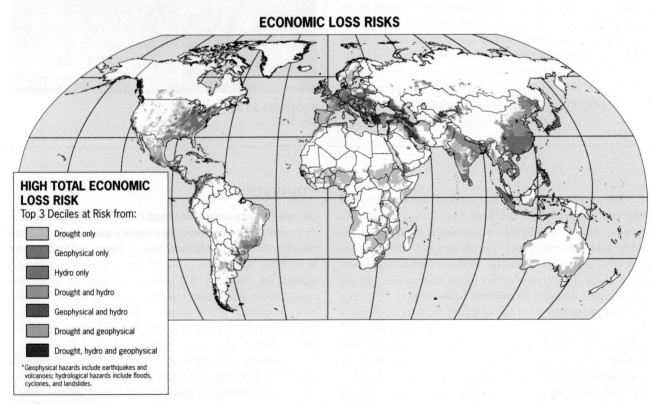

HIGH TOTAL ECONOMIC LOSS RISK
Top 3 Deciles at Risk from:

- Drought only
- Geophysical only
- Hydro only
- Drought and hydro
- Geophysical and hydro
- Drought and geophysical
- Drought, hydro and geophysical

*Geophysical hazards include earthquakes and volcanoes; hydrological hazards include floods, cyclones, and landslides.

■■ **Figure 13.16**

Natural Disaster Hot Spots.   The top map shows the potential mortality risks if major natural disasters occur in global natural disaster hot spots, and the bottom map shows the potential economic risks if major natural disasters occur in natural disaster hot spots.   *Courtesy of*: Center for Hazards and Risk Research at Columbia University and the World Bank, "Natural Disaster Hotspots—A Global Risk Analysis," March 29, 2005.

mortality risk with the map of total economic loss risk demonstrates that when a natural disaster hits a wealthier area, the place will more likely be hit financially, whereas in a poorer area of the world, the place will likely be hit by both financial loss and the loss of lives. Thus, when a devastating earthquake hit the Kobe region in Japan in 1995, there was enormous property damage, but fewer than 6500 people died. By contrast, when an earthquake of a similar magnitude struck Haiti in 2010, well over 100,000 people lost their lives.

Patterns of Consumption

We humans rely on Earth's resources for our very survival. At the most basic level, we consume water, oxygen, and organic and mineral materials. Over time we have developed increasingly complex ways of using resources in pursuit of agricultural intensification and industrial production. Consequently, many societies now consume resources at a level and rate that far exceed basic subsistence needs. In a 1996 article on "Humanity's Resources" in *The Companion Encyclopedia of Geography: The Environment and Humankind*, I. G. Simmons notes that a hunter–gatherer subsisted, on average, on the resources found within an area of about 26 square kilometers (10 square miles). Today many people living in urban centers in the global economic core draw on resources scattered all over the planet.

The wealthier countries account for only a modest fraction of the human population (Chapter 2), but they make far greater demands on Earth's resources than do their counterparts in poorer countries. It has been estimated that a baby born in the United States during the first decade of the twenty-first century, at current rates, consumes about 250 times as much energy over a lifetime as a baby born in Bangladesh over the same lifetime. In terms of food, housing and its components, metals, paper (and thus trees), and many other materials, the consumption of individuals in affluent countries far exceeds that of people in poorer countries. Rapid population growth in poorer parts of the world tends to have local or regional environmental impacts, but expanding resource consumption in wealthier regions has greater global environmental consequences.

The foregoing discussion underscores the importance of thinking geographically about human impacts on the natural world. People living in the global economic periphery tend to affect their immediate environment, putting pressure on soil, natural vegetation, and water supplies, and polluting the local air with the smoke from their fires. The reach of affluent societies is much greater. The demand for low-cost meat for hamburgers in the United States has led to deforestation in Central and South America to make way for pastures and cattle herds. In the process, water demand has increased in such areas (Table 13.1). This example shows just one of the many ways in which the American (and European, Japanese, and Australian) consumer has an impact on distant environments.

The industrialized core has access to a vast array of transportation and communication technologies that allow

TABLE 13.1

Estimated Liters of Water Required to Produce 1 Kilogram of Food.

ESTIMATED LITERS OF WATER REQUIRED TO PRODUCE 1 KILOGRAM OF FOOD	
Food	Liters
Chocolate	17,196
Beef	15,415
Chicken meat	4,325
Rice	2,497
Bread	1,608
Potatoes	287

advertisers to stimulate demand for particular goods around the world and allow manufacturers to bring goods from distant places. The growing wealth over the last two decades in the semiperiphery, especially in India and China, has significantly increased the overall global consumption of consumer goods. The story of the Indian company Tata (which we described at the beginning of Chapter 4), however, illustrates the complexities of meeting growing demand. In 2008 Tata created the Nano, an automobile for the Indian market that was priced below $2500. Tata ramped up plans to produce 250,000 of the "people's car" a year. The Nano did not sell well, however; India's rising middle class wanted low-cost cars but not cars that appeared cheap. Tata initially spent $400 million to develop the vehicle, but it was then forced to spend considerably more to revamp it to meet the increasingly sophisticated tastes of Indian consumers.

As global consumption of consumer goods increases, the market for luxury goods has similarly expanded as more people around the world move into middle-class lifestyles. There is a rapidly growing market for luxury-brand leather handbags (Coach, Louis Vuitton, Gucci, and Chanel), particularly in Asia where American and European high-end brands are popular (and can be more affordable than a designer wardrobe). Japan and Hong Kong have the greatest market share of luxury-brand handbags in the region, and Chinese tourists account for a significant percentage of the designer bags purchased in the United States. In Hong Kong, a local money lender even allows women to hand over their designer bags as collateral to receive loans of up to 80 percent of the bag's value (though the lender only accepts four high-end brands!).

Beyond such stories is a more general growth in demand for natural resources in rapidly developing countries. China provides the most striking example. As recently as the 1980s, China's GDP was smaller than Spain's. Over the past few decades, however, the Chinese economy has surged forward. In 2010 it surpassed Japan to become the world's second largest economy, and in 2013 it became the world's second-biggest consumer country.

Overall consumer spending in the United States still significantly outpaces that in China, but China is gaining ground, and because of the size of its population, China surpasses the United States as a consumer in some areas. In 2010 China became the world's biggest consumer of energy, and it has led the world in the consumption of coal for many years. China has also emerged as one of the world's leading consumers of a wide variety of raw materials, from logs to iron ore to grains.

To meet the growing demand for natural resources, China has greatly expanded its overseas investments. From Africa to South America to other parts of Asia, Chinese firms are increasingly in evidence—extracting resources and shipping them back home. In the process, China's role in consumption-related environmental change now rivals that of the United States and the European Union. China's new international economic clout also carries with it predictable social consequences. In some places, Chinese investment is seen as a boost to the local economy and is welcomed. But there is growing concern that China is acting as a neo-colonial power, altering environmental and social systems while returning relatively little to the local economy.

Industrial Technology

Technological advances have increased rapidly since the Industrial Revolution and today affect all aspects of our lives. We are continually developing technologies that we hope will improve our standard of living, protect us against disease, and allow us to work more efficiently. But these technologies come at a cost. Resource extraction practices such as mining and logging, which provide the materials to produce technologies, have created severe environmental problems. Technological innovations have produced hazardous and toxic by-products, creating pollution and health problems that we are only now beginning to recognize. In short, technology has enabled humans to alter large portions of the planet in a short period of time.

There are many dramatic examples of the role of industrial technology in environmental change. The impacts include degradation of the oceans (oil and gas exploitation and spills, pollution dumping, and massive overfishing), land surfaces (open pit and mountain top mining, dams, and irrigation projects), the biosphere (deforestation, vegetation loss), and the atmosphere (air pollution).

As the first parts of the planet to industrialize, western Europe and North America long led the world in industrial-related pollution. Now attention is turning to rapidly industrializing countries such as China, where the 2008 Beijing Olympics opened the world's eyes to the incredibly high emissions level in that country (Fig. 13.17).

According to the World Health Organization (WHO), anything over 10 micrograms per cubic meter of pollutant particles in the atmosphere represents a threat to human health. The most polluted city in the United States, Bakersfield, California, has days of 18.2 micrograms per cubic meter. By contrast, the ten most heavily polluted Chinese cities regularly see numbers above 100 and 150, and sometimes even above 250 micrograms per cubic meter—well beyond the limit of what the WHO considers "hazardous" air quality. The most polluted hour ever recorded was in Beijing between 11:00 P.M. and midnight on January 23, 2008. Extensive fireworks from Lunar New Year celebrations caused the already high pollution levels to rise to a frightening 994 micrograms per cubic meter.

These sustained levels of pollution, with smog so thick that it can be seen from space on the worst days, are raising alarm in China and beyond. In April 2014, China's national legislature made sweeping reforms to the country's environmental protection law, a sign the country is starting to take environmental issues more seriously.

Transportation

Changing modes of transportation are a product of some of the most important technological advances in human history. Each innovation in transportation has required increased resource use, not only to make the vehicles that move people and goods, but also to build and maintain the related infrastructure—roads, railroad tracks, airports, parking structures, repair facilities, and the like. With each innovation the impacts

David G. McIntyre/epa/ © Corbis

■ **Figure 13.17**

Beijing, China. Smog covers the traffic on a motorway in the central business district of Beijing just a few months before the opening of the 2008 Olympics in Beijing.

seem to widen. As David Headrick points out in a study discussed in the *Companion Encyclopedia of Geography*, Chicago's O'Hare Airport covers a larger area (approximately 28 square kilometers or 17 square miles) than Chicago's central business district (which covers approximately 8 square kilometers or 5 square miles). Moreover, transportation innovations offer access to remote areas of the planet. There are vehicles that allow people to travel through extreme climates, to the bottoms of the ocean, and across the polar ice caps. These places, in turn, have been altered by human activity.

Transportation is also implicated in global environmental change—albeit sometimes indirectly. Advances in transportation have produced significant pollution, as seen in the extent of oil spills along major shipping lanes (Fig. 13.18).

Transportation facilitates the types of global networks necessary to sustain the patterns of consumption outlined earlier. Many of the products available in stores—be they electronics or clothing or food—come from distant places. Resources are required to produce and ship them, and except those that meet basic subsistence needs, they all contribute to the greater strains placed on the environment that come from those living in wealthier parts of the world. This realization has led some individuals to reduce their levels of consumption or to consume more environmentally friendly, locally produced products. These changes have had some effect, but so far their impact on the geography of global consumption has been marginal.

Energy

Consumption of material goods is closely linked to the consumption of energy. It takes energy to produce material goods, energy to deliver them to markets, and, for many products (such as appliances and automobiles), energy to keep them running. The resulting demands for energy are a factor in environmental change. Much of our energy supply comes from nonrenewable fossil fuels, such as coal, oil, and natural gas. Moreover, the evolution of tertiary, quaternary, and quinary economic activities has led to an increase in the consumption of nonrenewable resources. As populations grow, so does the demand for energy, and we can expect that over the coming decades energy production will expand to meet the increased demand. In developing countries in particular, demands for more energy are largely met by the burning of fossil fuels. This helps explain why, according to the United States Energy Information Administration (EIA), global oil production increased from 45.89 million barrels per day in 1970 to 90.1 million barrels per day in 2013.

Oil is a finite resource. It is not a question of *if* the world's oil supply will run out but *when*. Because discoveries of new reserves continue to be made, and because the extraction of fossil fuels is becoming ever more efficient, it is difficult to predict exactly how much longer oil will remain a viable energy source. Many suggest that the current level of oil consumption can be sustained for up to 100 years, although some argue for much shorter or much longer time frames. Despite the range of opinion, the majority of scientists believe that by the middle of this century alternative sources will have to play a much more significant role than they do now.

In recent decades, natural gas has emerged as an increasingly common alternative to oil. Natural gas can be extracted from the oil-refinement process, but major subsurface reservoirs of natural gas also exist, and they are being increasingly

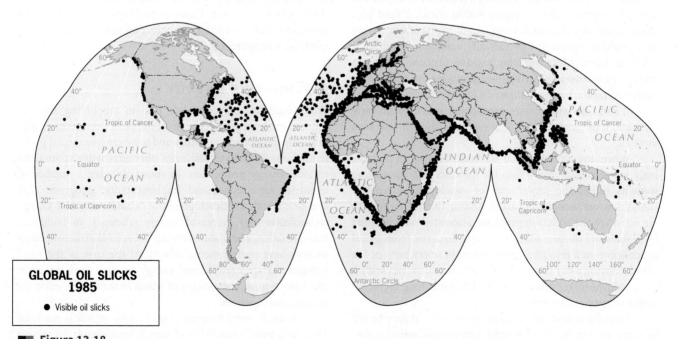

GLOBAL OIL SLICKS 1985

● Visible oil slicks

■■ **Figure 13.18**

Locations of Visible Oil Slicks.   Oil slicks are a problem around the globe. This map was created in the 1980s, but the overall pattern has not greatly changed since then.   *Adapted with permission from:* Organization for Economic Co-operation and Development, *The State of the Environment,* 1985, p. 76.

tapped. Like oil, natural gas is a greenhouse gas, but it burns somewhat more cleanly. Natural gas is becoming increasingly common in energy production, and natural gas vehicles are even coming into wider use, particularly in Iran, Pakistan, Argentina, Brazil, India, and China.

Despite its advantages, natural gas is difficult to store and transport. To address this problem, scientists have figured out how to create liquefied natural gas (LNG), which is achieved by condensing natural gas at a very low temperature. The process is expensive, and LNG is highly flammable, but South Korea, Taiwan, and several European countries now import large volumes of LNG, and Japan turned to LNG after shutting down its nuclear power plants in the wake of the Fukushima nuclear power plant disaster. With countries ranging from Australia to Argentina to Qatar ramping up production, LNG's significance is growing.

In recent years, technological advances have also made it possible to access hard-to-reach pockets of natural gas trapped in shale. Rising energy prices have made it economical to use a costly technique called hydraulic fracturing, or fracking, to reach these pockets. Fracking operations inject a high-pressure fluid (typically water mixed with sand and chemicals) into deep-rock formations to create small fissures and release natural gas. The gas is then transported via pipeline to natural goas processing or LNG facilities.

Shale gas accounted for over 20 percent of natural gas production in the United States in 2010, and the EIA estimates that it will be 46 percent by 2035. Proponents hail the process because it is decreasing America's dependence on foreign oil. But fracking comes at a potentially high environmental cost. The extraction process uses a tremendous amount of water. In addition, the chemicals within fracking fluid may contaminate underground water supplies. Residents living near fracking operations periodically complain about foul-smelling odors. Moreover, the fracking process sometimes produces microseismic activity—earthquakes too small to be easily detectable, but with unknown long-term consequences. Finally, shale gas emits more greenhouse gases, particularly methane, than generic natural gas and oil, though coal tops them all.

When one considers that oil could become an increasingly scarce commodity within the lifetimes of many college students today, the importance of developing alternative energy sources becomes apparent. Adding further urgency to the quest are the pollution problems associated with burning fossil fuels and the geopolitical tensions that arise from global dependence on a resource concentrated in select parts of the world. Moving away from a dependence on oil carries with it some clear positives, but it could lead to wrenching socioeconomic adjustments as well.

The effects of a shift away from oil will certainly be felt to some degree in the industrial and postindustrial countries, where considerable retooling of the economic infrastructure will be necessary. It is the oil-producing countries, however, that will face the greatest adjustments. More than half of the world's oil supply is found in the Middle Eastern countries of Saudi Arabia, Iraq, Kuwait, the United Arab Emirates (UAE), and Iran. In each of these countries, the extraction and exportation of oil account for at least 75 percent of total revenue and 90 percent of export-generated income. What will happen to these countries when their oil reserves run dry?

Consider the case of Kuwait—a country in which the incomes of 80 percent of the wage earners are tied to oil. Kuwait's citizens are currently guaranteed housing, education, and health care, and each adult couple receives a one-time stipend when a child is born. All of these programs are provided tax free, and when workers retire, their pensions are close to the salaries they earned as active members of the workforce.

Concerns over the long-term implications of a decline in oil revenue in Kuwait have led to efforts to find an alternative source of wealth: potable water. In a part of the world that can go for months without rain, water is a most precious resource. Some people in Kuwait joke that for each million dollars spent in the quest for sources of fresh water, all that is found is a billion dollars' worth of oil! But where fresh water cannot be found, it can potentially be made, and Kuwait has positioned itself as one of the world's leaders in the field of desalinization. This is currently a very expensive process, but Kuwait has been able to devote some of its oil revenues to desalinization efforts. As a result, 90 percent of the small country's water supply is now generated from seawater. Absent a major technological breakthrough, in the short term income generated by desalinization will amount to only a tiny fraction of the income provided by oil production. The long term may be a different story, however. If not, Kuwait—and other countries in its position—will be facing a socioeconomic adjustment of enormous proportions.

ALTERNATIVE ENERGY

Technology has played a key role in amplifying human-induced environmental change. At the same time, technologies are being developed to identify and solve environmental problems. Some of these technologies offer alternative approaches to local energy production. In recent decades, a number of countries have established implementation programs that encourage both the development of "clean" renewable energy technologies and increased energy efficiency in buildings, transportation, and manufacturing. Yet even alternative energy sources have environmental effects. At the core of the wind turbines that generate "clean" energy are rare earth minerals, the extraction and processing of which have negative environmental consequences.

A single wind turbine (Fig. 13.19), which is made of fiberglass, weighs hundreds of metric tons, stands 90 meters (196 feet) high, and "fundamentally relies on roughly 300 kilograms of soft, silvery metal known as neodymium—a so called rare earth" (Biello 2010, 16). Neodymium is used for

■ **Figure 13.19**

Lake Benton, Minnesota. The wind park near Lake Benton, Minnesota, was developed beginning in 1994 and now includes more than 600 wind turbines.

"thousands of times because the elements are so chemically similar" in order to separate the neodymium from other rare earth elements (Biello 2010, 17).

The chemical processing of rare earth elements uses electricity and water—leaving behind chemicals and residuals, including thorium (a radioactive metal) and salt. The environmental consequences of rare earth element mining have historically been costly enough that production stopped at Mountain Pass Mine in California in 2002, in part because of the cost of complying with environmental laws in the United States.

A combination of looser environmental laws and labor costs led to increased production of rare earth elements in China during the last decade (Fig. 13.20). In Inner Mongolia, China, the extraction of rare earth elements at the Bayan-Obo mine alone accounts for 40 percent of the world's supply. China closed off access to the mine to all outsiders, but the mine's enormous pits and waste ponds can still be viewed from space and even seen using Google Earth (Fig. 13.21).

Because rare earth elements can be used in weapons systems, the United States military blocked the sale of Mountain Pass Mine to a Chinese company as a matter of national security. Instead, Molycorp bought Mountain Pass Mine and has begun extracting rare earth elements again. China will likely remain the leading producer of rare earth elements in the near term. However, recycling rare earth elements from discarded devices and new mining efforts in the United States, Australia, and Vietnam will likely improve the availability of rare earth elements from sources outside of China in years to come.

the powerful magnets in a wind turbine that generate electricity. It is one of 17 elements on the periodic table that are considered rare earth elements.

Rare earth elements are in demand because they are used not only in wind turbines but also in alternative energy cars, computers, screens, compact fluorescent light bulbs, cell phones, MRI machines, and advanced weapons systems (Biello 2010). Rare earth elements are found in rock, and 97 percent of rare earth elements mined today come from China. Mining is only the first step in the exploitation of rare earth minerals because making them usable requires separating elements that are bound together in the rock. Hence, once the rocks are mined, Chinese companies intensively boil them in acid, repeating the process

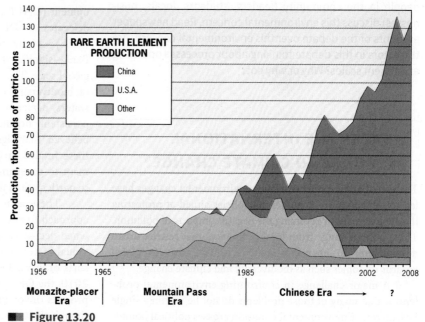

■ **Figure 13.20**

Rare Earth Element Production Since 1964. *Courtesy of:* USGS, http://files.eesi.org/usgs_china_030011.pdf.

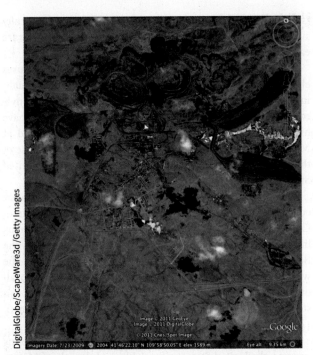

■ **Figure 13.21**

Inner Mongolia, China.   GoogleEarth image of Bayan-Obo mine in Inner Mongolia, China.   *Courtesy of*: Google Earth. © 2011 GeoEye © CNES 2011, Distribution Astrium Services/Spot Images S. A., France, all rights reserved.

Go back to the last Thinking Geographically question: What is the greatest environmental concern facing the region where you live? Now, add to your answer by concentrating on how people in the community (leaders, students, locals, businesses) discuss this environmental concern. Read newspaper accounts of the debate over this environmental concern. Are the actors in this debate thinking about processes operating at different scales? Why or why not?

WHAT IS THE INTERNATIONAL RESPONSE TO CLIMATE CHANGE?

The extent and rapidity of recent environmental changes have led to the adoption of numerous policies aimed at protecting the environment or reversing the negative impacts of pollution. These policies range from local ordinances that restrict urban development in environmentally sensitive areas to global accords on topics such as biodiversity and climate change.

A major challenge in confronting environmental problems is that many of those problems do not lie within a single jurisdiction. Environmental pollution crosses political boundaries, and people sometimes move across those boundaries in response to environmental pressures. Designing policy responses is thus complicated by the fact that the political map does not reflect the geography of environmental issues. The problem is particularly acute when environmental problems cross international boundaries, for there are few international policymaking bodies with significant authority over multinational environmental spaces. Moreover, those that do exist—the European Union, for example—often have limited authority and must heed the concerns of member states. Those concerns, in turn, may not work in the interests of environmental sustainability. Within democracies, politicians with an eye to the next election may hesitate to tackle long-term problems that require short-term sacrifices. Most authoritarian regimes have an even worse record, as can be seen in the policies of the Soviet-dominated governments of eastern Europe during the communist era. Moreover, governmental leaders in poorer countries find it very difficult to take action when, as is often the case, action requires reductions in already marginal standards of living and even greater difficulties in meeting the kinds of debt payments discussed in Chapter 10.

Despite these obstacles, the growing extent and urgency of global environmental changes have led to a number of international agreements to address selected problems. Some of these agreements have been spearheaded by nongovernmental organizations (NGOs) that operate outside of the formal political arena. They tend to focus on specific issues and problems, often in particular places. With the 1972 *United Nations Conference on the Human Environment* in Stockholm, international governmental organizations began playing a major role in environmental policy.

The framework that currently guides international governmental activity in the environmental arena evolved from the United Nations Conference on Environment and Development (UNCED) held in Rio de Janeiro in June 1992. The delegates to UNCED gave the Global Environment Facility (GEF)—a joint project of the United Nations and the World Bank—significant authority over environmental action on a global scale. The GEF funds projects related to six issues: loss of biodiversity, climate change, protection of international waters, depletion of the ozone layer, land degradation, and persistent organic pollutants. The delegates to UNCED believed that significant progress could be made through these funded projects, along with bilateral (that is, government-to-government) aid. They also made it easier for NGOs to participate in international environmental policymaking.

These actions hold the promise of a more coherent approach to environmental problem solving than is possible when decisions are made on a state-by-state basis. Yet individual states continue to influence decision making in all sorts of ways. Take the case of the GEF. Between 1991 and 2010, the GEF provided $4.5 billion in grants, primarily to projects involving climate change or biodiversity. Even though the GEF is charged with protecting key elements of the global environment, it still functions in a state-based

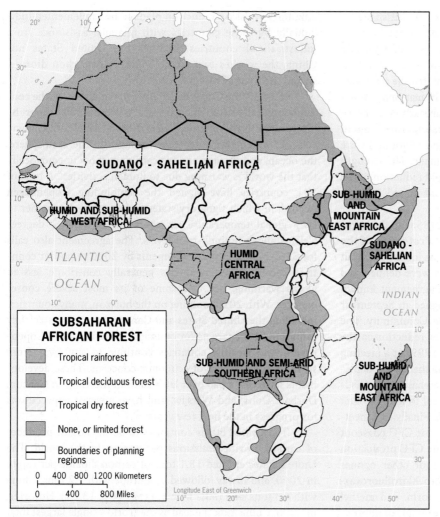

■■ Figure 13.22
Major Regions and Forest Zones in Subsaharan Africa.   This map is based on a figure in a World Bank technical paper on the forest sector in Subsaharan Africa. The map shows major forest regions crossing state boundaries, but planning regions adhere to state boundaries. *Adapted with permission from:* N. P. Sharma, S. Rietbergen, C. R. Heimo, and J. Patel. A Strategy for the Forest Sector in Sub-Saharan Africa, World Bank Technical Paper No. 251, Africa Technical Department Series (Washington, DC: The World Bank, 1994).

world, as suggested by Figure 13.22—a map from a 1994 World Bank technical report on the forest sector in Subsaharan Africa that divides the realm into "major regions" that follow state rather than ecological borders. Nonetheless, the GEF serves the important role of providing financial resources to four major international conventions on the environment: the Convention on Biological Diversity, the United Nations Framework Convention on Climate Change, the United Nations Convention to Combat Desertification, and the Stockholm Convention on Persistent Organic Pollutants.

A few global environmental issues are so pressing that efforts are being made to draw up guidelines for action in the form of international conventions or treaties. The most prominent examples are in the areas of biological diversity,

protection of the ozone layer, and global climate change.

Biological Diversity

International concern over the loss of species led to calls for a global convention (agreement) as early as 1981. By the beginning of the 1990s, a group working under the auspices of the United Nations Environment Program reached agreement on the wording of the convention, and it was submitted to UNCED for approval. It went into effect in late 1993; as of 2011, 168 countries had signed it. The convention calls for establishing a system of protected areas and a coordinated set of national and international regulations on activities that can have significant negative impacts on biodiversity. It also provides funding for developing countries that are trying to meet the terms of the convention.

The biodiversity convention is a step forward in that it both affirms the vital significance of preserving biological diversity and provides a framework for cooperation toward that end. However, the agreement has proved difficult to implement. In particular, there is an ongoing struggle to find a balance between the need of poorer countries to promote local economic development and the need to preserve biodiversity, which happens to be richest in parts of the global economic periphery. Also, there has been controversy over the sharing of costs for conservation programs, which has led to heated debates over ratification of the convention in some countries. Nevertheless, this convention, along with a host of voluntary efforts, has helped to focus attention on the biodiversity issue and to promote the expansion of protected areas. Whether those areas will succeed in providing long-term species protection is an open question that will occupy geographers and biologists for years to come.

Protection of the Ozone Layer

When found in the troposphere (0 to 16 km or 1.0 to 10 mile altitude), ozone (O_3) gas is a harmful pollutant closely associated with the creation of smog. However, a naturally occurring **ozone layer** exists in the stratosphere (between 30 and 45 km altitude). The ozone layer is of vital importance because it protects Earth's surface from the sun's harmful ultraviolet rays. In 1985, a group of British scientists working in Antarctica discovered that the thickness of the ozone layer above the South Pole was dramatically reduced, from 300 Dobson units (DUs) in the 1960s to almost 200 DUs by 1985. Studies revealed that the main culprits in ozone depletion were a group of human-made gases collectively known as CFCs (chlorofluorocarbons). These gases, used mainly as refrigerants in fire extinguishers and in aerosol cans, had only been in use since the 1950s and were thought to be completely harmless to humans. The strength of the scientific evidence pointing to a rapid reduction of the ozone layer led to an unusually rapid and united international response.

International cooperation began in 1985 with the negotiation of the **Vienna Convention for the Protection of the Ozone Layer**. Specific targets and timetables for the phaseout of production and consumption of CFCs were defined and agreed upon as part of the international agreement known as the **Montreal Protocol**, which was signed in September 1987 by 105 countries and the European Community. The original agreement called for a 50 percent reduction in the production and consumption of CFCs by 1999. At a meeting in London in 1990, scientific data showing that ozone depletion would continue for many years after a phaseout of CFCs led the signatories of the Montreal Protocol to agree to halt CFC production entirely by the year 2000. Finally, at a meeting in Copenhagen in 1992, the timetable for CFC phaseout accelerated. Participants agreed to eliminate CFC production by 1996 and to accelerate the phaseout of other ozone-depleting chemicals such as halons, hydrochlorofluorocarbons, carbon tetrachloride, methyl chloroform, and methyl bromide. This response is an encouraging example of international cooperation in the face of a significant, albeit clearly defined, problem.

Global Climate Change

Beginning in the late 1980s, growing concern about climate change led to a series of intergovernmental conferences on the nature and extent of human impacts on climate. In December 1990, the United Nations General Assembly approved the start of treaty negotiations. A draft convention called on developed countries to take measures aimed at reducing their emissions to 1990 levels by the year 2000 and to provide technical and financial support for emission-reduction efforts in the developing countries. The European Community (precursor to the European Union) and 154 other states signed the convention, commonly called the Earth Summit, in Rio de Janeiro.

In 1997, the Kyoto Agreement set a target period of 2008–2012 for the United States, the European Union, and Japan to cut their greenhouse gas emissions by 7, 8, and 6 percent, respectively, below 1990 levels. The agreement reached in Kyoto did not obligate less developed countries to adhere to specific reduction goals; instead it called for voluntary emission reduction plans to be implemented individually by those countries with financial assistance from industrialized countries. Neither the United States nor China, the world's two largest emitters of carbon dioxide, signed the Kyoto Protocol.

In 2009, the Copenhagen Agreement endorsed the continuation of the Kyoto Accord in the wake of a 2007 report by the United Nations Intergovernmental Panel on Climate Change, which concluded that "changes in the atmosphere, the ocean, and glaciers and ice caps now show unequivocally that the world is warming due to human activities." A total of 141 countries have signed the nonbinding Copenhagen Accord, in which signatory states agreed to work together to keep global temperature increases to less than 2 degrees Celsius above preindustrial levels. The agreement also calls for $100 billion in yearly payments by 2020 to poorer countries because those countries generally contribute less to global warming, but face some of its most severe consequences. With 2020 looming on the horizon, many countries, including the United States and Canada, have suggested they cannot meet the targets for emission reduction set in Copenhagen. And wealthy countries continue to shy away from strong action because of economic concerns. These developments have cast a pall over later summit meetings in Cancun, Durban, Doha, and Warsaw, and have lowered expectations for progress in the next few years.

The United States continues to be the largest producer of carbon dioxide emissions per person in the world. The United States emitted 18.1 tons of carbon dioxide per capita in 2010, and it was followed by Europe with 7.2 tons, China with 6.3 tons, and India with 1.4 tons (Fig. 13.23). However, in 2006, China took the lead as the world's single largest total emitter of carbon dioxide, pushing the United States out of the top spot.

With most countries continuing to prioritize economic concerns over efforts to make serious inroads in the reduction of greenhouse gases, there is much doubt as to whether significant progress will be made in confronting the human role in climate change. Hence, policymakers and scientists are increasingly focusing their attention on adaptation strategies.

Water Scarcity

One-fifth of the world's population lives in regions confronting water scarcity. Yet to date there have been few conflicts among states over water. On the contrary, geographer Aaron Wolf has shown that cooperation between states tends to increase in the face of growing water concerns. Cooperation usually takes the form of transboundary or multilateral treaties governing the use and protection of water resources. During the past half century, the world's states have entered into some 150 such agreements. From the Mekong to the Ganges to the Indus to the Niger, treaties have helped to promote the equitable management of river-basin waters.

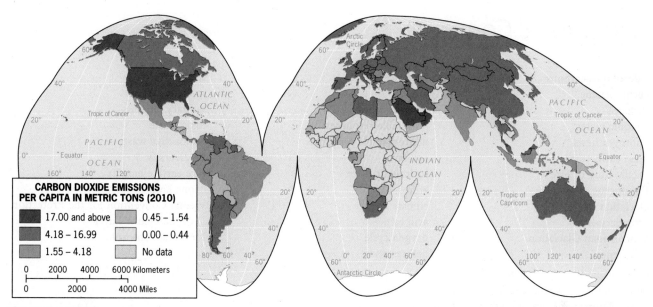

■ **Figure 13.23**

Carbon Dioxide Emissions per Capita, 2004.   Recently, China's total carbon dioxide emissions exceeded those of the United States. However, in per capita emissions of carbon dioxide, mapped here, the United States, Canada, and the United Arab Emirates are the highest.   *Data from*: United Nations Development Programme, Human Development Report, 2007/2008.

Despite the many examples of cooperation, water-management challenges abound. In many cases monitoring is inadequate, enforcement mechanisms are lacking, and provisions do not exist to address more extreme variations in water availability. The last-named issue in particular is looming ever larger because the current structure of agreements may well not be adequate to cope with the more significant shifts in water availability that are likely to occur (indeed, are already occurring) in the face of climate change. Against this backdrop, a 2014 World Bank working paper (Dinar et al.) foresees the potential for growing political tensions over water in the coming years.

Examine the map of global carbon dioxide emissions and explain the pattern you see. What other geographic patterns are correlated with those shown in the map?

Summary

What will the future be like? Many would agree with geographer Robert Kates, who foresees a "warmer, more crowded, more connected but more diverse world." As we consider this prospect, we must acknowledge that global environmental changes are among the most pressing issues facing the world today, but also illustrate the limits of what we know about our planet. Global environmental change is not always anticipated and is often nonlinear. Some changes are "chaotic" in the sense that future conditions cannot be reliably predicted. Nonlinearity means that small actions in certain situations may result in large impacts and may be more important than larger actions in causing change. Thresholds also exist in many systems, which, once past, are irreversible. Irreversible changes occur, for example, when the habitat for a species is diminished to the point where the species quickly dies off.

Unfortunately, we may not be able to identify these thresholds until we pass them. This leaves open the possibility of "surprises"—unanticipated responses by physical systems.

The complexity and urgency of environmental change will tax the energies of the scientific and policy communities for some time to come. Geography must be an essential part of any serious effort to grapple with these challenges. The major changes that are taking place have different origins and spatial expressions, and each results from a unique combination of physical and social processes. We cannot simply focus on system dynamics and generalized causal relationships. We must also consider emerging patterns of environmental change and the impacts of differences from place to place on the operation of general processes. Geography is not the backdrop to the changes taking place; it is at the very heart of the changes themselves.

Geographic Concepts

chlorofluorocarbons
anthropocene
Pangaea
tectonic plates
photosynthesis
mass extinctions
Pacific Ring of Fire
Pleistocene
glaciation
interglacials
Wisconsinan Glaciation
Holocene

Little Ice Age
greenhouse effect
environmental stress
renewable resources
nonrenewable resources
aquifers
hydrologic cycle
atmosphere
climate change
acid rain
oxygen cycle
deforestation

soil erosion
solid waste
sanitary landfills
toxic waste
radioactive waste
biodiversity
rare earth elements
ozone layer
Vienna Convention for the Protection
   of the Ozone Layer
Montreal Protocol

Learn More Online

About geography and environmental hazards
www.bbc.co.uk/scotland/education/int/geog/envhaz/index.shtml

Forest change
http://earthenginepartners.appspot.com/science-2013-global-forest

Oxford's Environmental Change Institute
www.eci.ox.ac.uk/

Time-lapse imagery of environmental change
http://world.time.com/timelapse/

United Nations Framework Convention on Climate Change
http://unfccc.int/2860.php

About Rare Earth Minerals
http://ngm.nationalgeographic.com/2011/06/rare-earth-elements/folger-text

Watch It Online

About Climate Change
http://youtu.be/2JmrmwIyhAE

About Tsunamis
http://video.nationalgeographic.com/video/101-videos/tsunami-101

About Desertification and Climate Change
http://www.ted.com/talks/allan_savory_how_to_green_the_world_s_deserts_and_reverse_climate_change

GLOBALIZATION AND THE GEOGRAPHY OF NETWORKS

Happiness Is in the Eye of the Beholder

Traveling through a rural village in Andhra Pradesh, India, we stopped to take in a weekend morning market. Women sold spices stored in heaps of colored flakes; a man had a chair set up and was cutting a little boy's hair; a group of men sold rebar from shops behind vegetable stands. I was used to seeing the colorful sarees and salwar kameez worn by Indian women. Then, an older woman from one of India's scheduled tribes caught my eye. I first noticed her clothing. The colors were as bright as any saree, but the silver, mirrors, and beads adorning her dress stood out. I looked up at her, our eyes connected, and then she smiled (Fig. 14.1). I asked if I could take her picture, and she nodded yes.

I think of her when I am teaching human geography. Often, students in their first college-level geography class are excited at the end of the semester to have learned so much about the world. Some have had their eyes opened to the world for the first time as an adult. Others have finally understood the roots of a conflict they have only heard about on television. And many feel overwhelmed. Too much information. Too many people. Too little they can do to help.

Everyone feels this frustration to some degree, since no one can understand all of the complexities that govern life on Earth. But the ideas and perspectives set forth in this book give you insight into what it means to think geographically. That type of thinking is critical if you are to raise the types of questions that go beyond the generalizations and stereotypes that can work against deeper understanding. So many books try to simplify the world in an alarmist way. The world is flat (Thomas Friedman)! There's a population

■ Figure 14.1
Andhra Pradesh, India. A woman who is a member of a scheduled tribe in India smiles in the middle of a Saturday morning market. The government has affirmative action programs where they reserve seats in universities and government for Indians in scheduled tribes (also called Adivasis), scheduled castes (known as Dalits and formerly as Untouchables), and the lowest castes (called "other backwards castes"). The scheduled tribes are India's indigenous population, and they comprise an estimated 8.2 percent of India's 1.27 billion people.

bomb (Paul Ehrlich)! We live in a post-American world (Fareed Zakaria)! Such books often start from an interesting observation but then overlook how geography affects what is happening.

Each of us can attest that the world is anything but flat. Millions of people in India may be competing on a more level playing field with those in North America than was true in the past, but many other millions live in a different world that we ignore at our peril. As geographer Yi Fu Tuan said, "People make places." Each place is an imprint of culture, a reflection of diffusion, and a dynamic entity. Each place has its own identity that makes it unique.

It is important not just to understand that the world is diverse, but to appreciate that the uniqueness of places cuts against the stereotypes that circulate about them. The image of the tribal woman in India is the counterbalance to the images of the developing world I saw when I was growing up. I remember seeing pictures of women in remote parts of South America wearing exotic clothing. I also saw television coverage of children in Subsaharan Africa with distended stomachs and hunger in their faces. But in these images of the developing world that I saw as a child, no one was smiling. The images I saw growing up formed the perceptions I had of the developing world and the people who live there. My experiences since then have changed the ways I see the world and my own place in it.

The king of Bhutan, a small country nestled in the foothills of the Himalayas, decided that statistics that calculate the wealth of a country (Chapter 10), from gross national income (GNI) to Internet access, did not accurately measure the state of people's lives. In the 1970s, the preceding king of Bhutan coined the term *gross national happiness*, stating that the government needed to focus on achieving happiness instead of focusing on gross domestic product (GDP). In 2008, the current leader of Bhutan, King Wangchuck, released a new measurement, an index called gross national happiness (GNH) (Fig. 14.2). King Wangchuck explained that measurements such as GDP or GNI emphasize production and consumption instead of conservation of resources and environment.

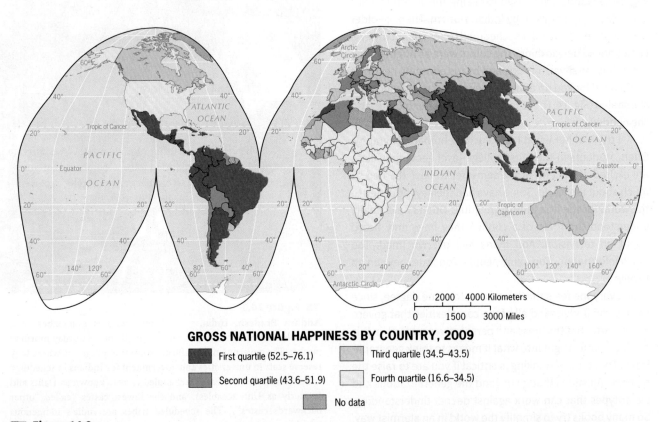

GROSS NATIONAL HAPPINESS BY COUNTRY, 2009

First quartile (52.5–76.1)   Third quartile (34.5–43.5)

Second quartile (43.6–51.9)   Fourth quartile (16.6–34.5)

No data

■ **Figure 14.2**
Gross National Happiness, 2010.   Instead of measuring income, the government of Bhutan measures happiness, how well the people in the country are, using nine markers, including health, education, environment, and governance.   *Data from*: Centre for Bhutan Studies.

The Center for Bhutan Studies measures nine dimensions of happiness and calculates a single numerical index reported as GNH. The nine dimensions include measurements of psychological well-being, time use, community vitality, culture, health, education, environmental diversity, living standard, and governance. Regardless of the accuracy of the GNH index, we welcome a critical and reflective look at how we measure our world.

Our hope is that this book has helped you think through the ways you make sense of the world. In this chapter, we consider how identities have changed in a globalizing world. In an effort to deepen our understanding of globalization, we also examine how networks operate in our world, in order to encourage you to consider the possibilities for tomorrow.

Key Questions FOR CHAPTER 14

1. How have identities changed in a globalized world?
2. What is globalization, and what role do networks play in globalization?
3. How do networks operate in a globalized world?

HOW HAVE IDENTITIES CHANGED IN A GLOBALIZED WORLD?

Gillian Rose defines identity as "how we make sense of ourselves." She explains that we have identities at different scales: We have local, national, regional, and global identities. At each scale, place factors into our identities. We infuse places with meaning and emotions based on our experiences in those places. Relatively few people living in today's globalized world are world travelers. And many of those who have traveled the globe have missed out on the uniqueness of place by visiting only global cities, living the lives of businesspeople (visiting airports, office buildings, and hotels), or staying in luxurious resorts (separated from the "local") as tourists. How, then, can a person have a global identity if he or she has not experienced the globe?

Globalization networks link us with other people and places, and the flow of information technology is a daily way in which we are interlinked. A person may be overwhelmed by the flow of information and choose to ignore it, but even such a person has a global identity. People identify themselves by identifying with or against others at local, regional, and global scales. We make sense of the world by identifying with people and places.

In 1995, *National Geographic* discussed the future of the digital age and argued that as a result of technological advances and the Internet, people were interacting in person less. However, the author (Swerdlow 1995) also claimed that people would continue to have "a need for skin," a desire to interact with other humans in person. As evidence, the author cited how busy a mall is when the people in the mall could just as easily be ordering all of their purchases from home on the Internet.

This discussion of a pull between a faceless Internet and the "need for skin" took place nine years before Mark Zuckerberg created Facebook in 2004. People with Facebook or Twitter accounts (see Chapter 4) can feel connected without sharing skin by posting a quip or thought, which friends around the world can respond to immediately. Psychologists also recognize that the proliferation of reality television shows is connected to declining human interaction. Service organizations and clubs that used to be a major way for young members of a community to connect are generally experiencing membership declines in the United States.

In the 1990s, at the launch of the digital revolution, psychologists predicted that people would have poorer social skills because of the lack of personal or face-to-face interaction in the digital age. We can certainly see evidence of this in our daily lives, from people answering a phone call or text message when they are in the middle of a conversation with someone in person to students texting or multitasking on laptops during a geography lecture. Today, psychologists recognize that the networks created among people through digital technology also enable greater personal interaction and opportunities for empathy. Someone with medical problems can post a journal on a site such as Caring Bridge, and hundreds can follow the person's recovery and offer words of support. A young boy with a medical condition that makes it difficult to leave home can post lip-synched videos on YouTube, develop followers around the world, and end up with recording artists stopping by to lip sync with him. Social networks can be used for good or for ill, but either way, they tend to be a major way by which individuals, in a global, digital age, can develop a sense of belonging and a personal connectedness to people who are separated by computer screens.

Personal Connectedness

Sixteen years before hundreds of millions around the world watched a live feed of the wedding of Price William and Catherine Middleton (Chapter 4) on the Internet and on television, the news that Prince William's mother, Princess Diana, had died traveled quickly from global television, radio, and print media sources among friends, family, and even strangers. Many felt the need to mourn for a princess they had never met in a place they had never been. Some wanted to leave a token offering for the princess: a rose, a note, a candle, a photograph. Impromptu shrines to Princess Diana cropped up at the British embassy in Washington, D.C., and at British embassies and consulates around the world. People in Britain left countless flowers at the royal palace in London, where Princess Diana resided.

In an incredibly divided world, in which the rift between rich and poor is growing at the global scale, what made people feel connected to a woman who was a royal, a member of a family that presides over a modest-sized country? Why do we relate to someone from an elite group of people of wealth and privilege? What, 16 years later, made people want to see how her son turned out and "get to know" who he was marrying by watching television programs and reading stories online and in print about Catherine Middleton leading up to the wedding?

The idea that people who do not personally know each other and likely never will are linked and have shared experiences, including death, tragedy, sorrow, and even joy, draws from Benedict Anderson's concept of the nation as an **imagined community** (see Chapter 8). When massive tragedies such as 9/11, Hurricane Katrina, or the Japan tsunami occur, people often talk about someone they knew who was in the place (or had been at some point), someone who died (even those they did not know but heard about in the news), or an act of bravery or triumph that occurred in the midst of tragedy. The desire to *personalize*, to *localize*, a tragedy or even a joyous event feeds off of the imagined global community in which we live. In the process of personalizing and localizing, events can be *globalized* in an effort to appeal to the humanity of all people with the hope that all will feel or experience the loss or joy tangentially.

In a world where some commentators argue that place and territory are unimportant because things like global superhighways of information transcend place, people continue to recognize territories and create places. In the case of a death or a tragedy, how do people choose a local space in which to express a personal and/or global sorrow? In the case of Princess Diana's death, people created hundreds of spaces of sorrow to mourn the loss of a seemingly magnanimous person whose life was cut short. In the case of September 11, people transformed homes, schools, public spaces, and houses of worship into spaces of reflection by creating human chains, participating in moments of silence, or holding prayer vigils for the victims.

In his book *Shadowed Ground: America's Landscapes of Violence and Tragedy*, Kenneth Foote examines the "spontaneous shrines" created at a place of loss or at a place that represents loss and describes these spontaneous shrines as a "first stage in the commemoration of a disaster." Foote drew from extensive fieldwork that he conducted while visiting hundreds of landscapes of tragedy and violence in the United States to show how people mark or do not mark tragedy, both immediately with spontaneous shrines and in the longer term with permanent memorials (Fig. 14.3). He examines the struggles over whether and how to memorialize significant people or experienced tragedy. His research focuses on the United States, and after tracing and following the stories of hundreds of people and places, Foote concludes that "the debate over what, why, when, and where to build" a memorial for a person or event is "best considered a part of the grieving process."

Foote realized that the ways sites are memorialized or not vary over time and across a multitude of circumstances, depending on whether funding is available, what kind of structure is to be built, who is being remembered (only those who died or also those injured?), whether the site represents a socially contested event (which often happens when racism is involved), and whether people want to remember the site. In recent American history, major terrorist attacks have been memorialized, often with the word "closure" evoked. Oklahoma City permanently memorialized the site of a terrorist attack at the Murrah Federal Building on the five-year anniversary of the tragedy. Other tragedies, such as that experienced at the World Trade Center in New York City on September 11, 2001, take longer to memorialize. Millions of people feel a personal connection to the World Trade Center site, and so choosing a design and building a memorial took longer (Fig. 14.4).

The mass of information coming our way each day is often overwhelming. As people filter through or ignore the flow of information, they may personalize the information and either make a connection or differentiate themselves from particular people or places. In the end, many people's identities are shaped by developments unfolding at the global scale. Living in a world, at a scale we have not experienced previously, changes us and profoundly changes places. Globalization, for good or for ill, has modified how we interact with one another and has shaped how we make sense of ourselves in our world, our state, our region, and our locality.

thinking geographically Think of a national or global-scale tragedy, such as September 11 or World War II. In what ways do memorials of that tragedy reflect both globalization and localization at the same time?

GUEST FIELD NOTE

Columbine, Colorado

I took this photo at the dedication ceremony for the memorial to the victims of the Columbine High School shooting of April 20, 1999. Columbine is located near Littleton, Colorado, in Denver's southern suburbs. The memorial, dedicated on September 21, 2007, provides a quiet place for meditation and reflection in a public park adjacent to the school. Hundreds came to the ceremony to honor those killed and wounded in the attack, one of the deadliest school shootings in U.S. history.

After tragedies like the Columbine shootings, creating a memorial often helps to rebuild a sense of community. Public ceremonies like this can set an example for survivors who may otherwise have difficulty facing their loss in private. A group memorial helps to acknowledge the magnitude of the community's loss and, by so doing, helps assure families and survivors that the victims did not suffer alone—that their deaths and wounds are grieved by the entire community. Memorials are important too because they can serve as a focus for remembrance and commemoration long into the future, even after all other evidence of a tragedy has disappeared.

In my research for *Shadowed Ground*, I have visited hundreds of such places in the United States and Europe. I am still surprised by the power of such places and the fact that shrines and memorials resulting from similar tragedies are tended lovingly for decades, generations, and centuries. They produce strong emotions and sometimes leave visitors—including me—in tears. But by allowing individuals to share loss, tragedy, and sorrow with others, they create a sense of common purpose.

Credit: Kenneth E. Foote, University of Colorado at Boulder.

■ **Figure 14.3**

■■ **Figure 14.4**

New York, New York. The 9/11 Memorial commemorates those who died in the terrorist attacks on the World Trade Center on September 11, 2001. The wall includes the names of those who died in each tower, the first responders, those who died at the Pentagon, and those who died on each flight involved in that day's attacks. Additionally, the memorial includes the names of those who died during the first attack on the World Trade Center, a bomb detonated in the parking garage of the North Tower on February 26, 1993. A total of 2983 names are etched in the walls around the memorial pools of the North and South Towers, the footprints of the former buildings.

© Richard Baker/In Pictures/Corbis

WHAT IS GLOBALIZATION, AND WHAT ROLE DO NETWORKS PLAY IN GLOBALIZATION?

Whether you are in favor of or opposed to globalization, we all must recognize that globalization is "neither an inevitable nor an irreversible set of processes," as John O'Loughlin, Lynn Staeheli, and Edward Greenberg put it. Andrew Kirby explains that globalization is "not proceeding according to any particular playbook. It is not a smoothly evolving state of capitalist development." Rather, it is fragmented, and its flows are "chaotic in terms of origins and destinations."

Globalization is a "chaotic" set of processes and outcomes created by people, whether they are corporate CEOs, university administrators, readers of blogs, electrical engineers, or protesters at a trade meeting. The processes of globalization and the connectedness created through globalization occur across scales and across networks, regardless of state borders.

The backbone of economic globalization is trade; so, debates over globalization typically focus on trade. To visualize how trade fosters globalization, examine a map of shipping routes (Fig. 14.5). The density of the networks on the map tells us how extensively connected the world really is. But what are the consequences of those connections? The arguments in favor of globalization, as explained by economist Keith Maskus (2004), are that "free trade raises the well-being of all countries by inducing them to specialize their resources in those goods they produce relatively most efficiently" in order to lower production costs, and that "competition through trade raises a country's long-term growth rate by expanding access to global technologies and promoting innovation."

The view that free trade raises the wealth of all countries involved underpins a set of neoliberal policies known as the **Washington Consensus**. The World Bank, the International Monetary Fund, the World Trade Organization, and investment banks are all part of the Washington Consensus. Together, these institutions created a set of policies, including structural adjustment loans, that encouraged neoliberalism (Chapter 10). Not everyone accepts this "consensus." Leaders in both the developing and developed countries questioned the underlying assumptions of the Washington Consensus, especially after the global economic downturn began in 2008.

Opponents view this set of policies as part of a Western-dominated effort to get the rest of the world to privatize state-owned entities, to open financial markets, to liberalize trade by removing restrictions on the flow of goods, and to encourage foreign direct investment (Fig. 14.6). They argue that the countries of the global economic core continue to protect their own economies while forcing the countries of the semi-periphery and periphery to open their economies in ways that can have significant negative local consequences. According to Maskus, the rules negotiated for the World Trade Organization "inevitably reflect the economic interest of powerful lobbyists" in places such as the United States and the European Union, and have heightened wealth differences between

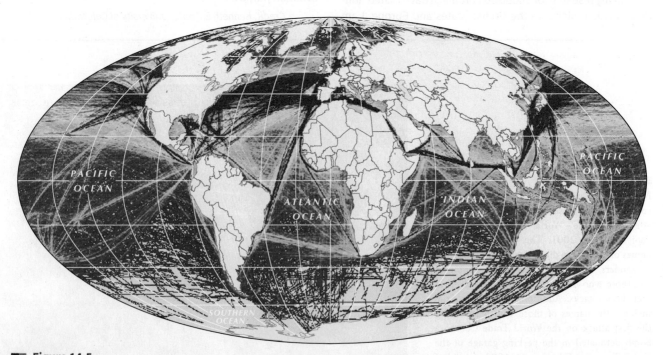

■ **Figure 14.5**

Global Shipping Lanes.   The map traces over 3000 shipping routes used by commercial and government vessels during 2006. The red lines mark the most frequently used shipping lanes.   *Courtesy of*: National Center for Ecological Analysis and Synthesis, http://ebm.nceas.ucsb.edu/ GlobalMarine/impacts/transformed/jpg/shipping.jpg, last accessed August 2008.

FIELD NOTE

"'You cannot come to southern Brazil without seeing our biggest city,' said the vintner who was showing me around the Cooperativa Aurora, the huge winery in Bento Gonçalves, in the State of Rio Grande do Sul. 'Besides, it's January, so they'll be having the big marches, it's almost like carnival time in Rio!' So I headed for Porto Alegre, only to find that a hotel room was not to be had. Tens of thousands of demonstrators had converged on the State's capital, largest port, and leading industrial city—and what united them was opposition to globalization. It was not quite a carnival, but the banners held aloft by the noisy, sometimes singing and dancing demonstrators left no doubt as to their common goals. The World Social Forum has become an annual event held in cities around the world, with ever-larger marches and meetings to protest the actions of the world's dominant states, especially the United States. The World Social Forum is a network of antiglobalizationists—people who seek an alternative economic reality for the globe, one not

Lima Agliberto/Gamma-Presse/Zuma Press

■ **Figure 14.6**
Porto Alegre, Brazil.

centered on accumulation of capital. Socialist economic views, leftist political leanings, and support for minority causes combine each year at the World Social Forum in a show of strength."

more and less prosperous regions, and deepened the inequalities of the global system.

Whether or not you support neoliberalism, the globalizing trends of the last few decades mean that we are, in many respects, living on an unprecedented scale. In Andrew Kirby's words, we are living "not so much in a world without boundaries, or in a world without geography—*but more literally in a world*, as opposed to a neighborhood or a region" (emphasis added).

Networks

Manuel Castells defines **networks** as "a set of interconnected nodes" without a center. A nonhierarchical network is horizontally structured, with power shared among all participants and ideas flowing in all directions. The multitude of networks that exist in the world—financial, transportation, communication, kinship, corporate, nongovernmental, trade, government, media, education, social, and dozens of others—enable globalization to occur and create a higher degree of interaction and interdependence among people than ever before in human history. Deeply entrenched hierarchies in the networks knit together the contemporary world, and these affect the character of different places and the interactions among them.

While networks have always existed, Castells says that they have fundamentally changed since 1995 as a result of

the diffusion of information technology that links places in a global, yet uneven, way. Through information technology networks, Castells argues that globalization has proceeded by "linking up all that, according to dominant interests, has value anywhere in the planet, and discarding anything (people, firms, territories, resources) which has no value or becomes devalued." Information technology networks link some places more than others, helping to create the spatial unevenness of globalization as well as the uneven outcomes of globalization.

Time–Space Compression

Access (or lack of access) to information technology networks creates time–space compression, which means that certain places, such as global cities (especially in the core), are more interconnected than ever through communication and transportation networks, even as other places, such as those in the periphery, are farther removed (Chapters 1 and 4). According to Castells (2000), the age of information technology networks is more revolutionary than the advent of the printing press or the Industrial Revolution. He claims that we are just at the beginning of this age "as the Internet becomes a universal tool of interactive communication, as we shift from computer-centered technologies to network-diffused technologies, (and) as we make progress in nanotechnology (and thus in the diffusion capacity of information devices)."

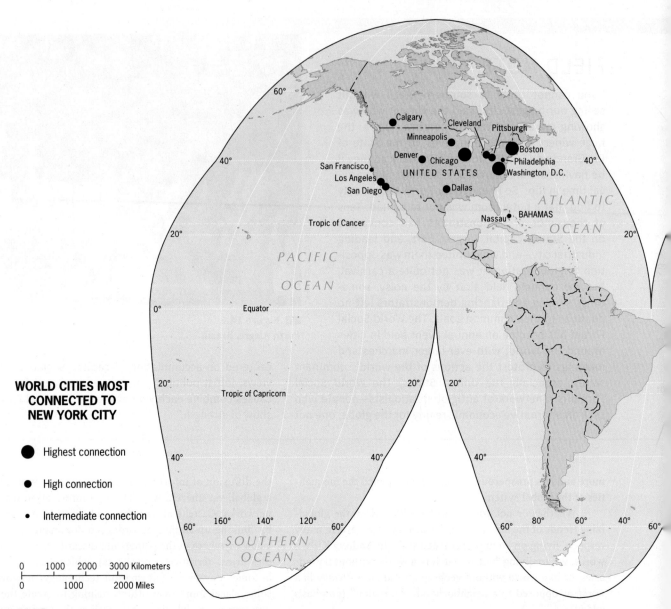

WORLD CITIES MOST CONNECTED TO NEW YORK CITY

● Highest connection

● High connection

• Intermediate connection

0   1000   2000   3000 Kilometers
0   1000   2000 Miles

■■ **Figure 14.7**
World Cities Most Connected to New York City.   This map shows the 30 world cities that are the most connected to New York City, as measured by flows in the service economy.   *Data from*: P. J. Taylor and R. E. Lang, "U.S. Cities in the 'World City Network,'" The Brookings Institution, Survey Series, February 2005. http://wwww.brookings.edu/dybdocroot/metro/pubs/20050222_worldcities.pdf, last accessed September 2005.

A major divide in access to information technology—sometimes called the **Digital Divide**—is both a hallmark of the current world and an example of the uneven outcomes of globalization. The International Telecommunications Union reported the levels of digital access for developing and developed regions of the world. In 2014, the World Bank reported that on average developed (high-income) states had 42 landline telephone connections, 120 mobile cellular connections, and 78.2 Internet users for every 100 people. On average, developing (low- and middle-income) states had 10 landline telephone connections, 86 mobile cellular connections, and 29.1 Internet users for every 100 people.

The quickening pace of technological change is another hallmark of globalization and magnifies the global technological

divide. We may be shocked to see how quickly technology has changed and diffused. In 1992, the highest-income states had on average only 10 cellular subscribers and 2.5 Internet users per 1000 people.

GLOBAL CITIES

Time–space compression has helped to create and reinforce a network of highly linked global cities. In Chapter 9, we discussed the growth of *global cities* in the core, semiperiphery, and periphery and the deepening of their connectedness. We considered research published by geographers in the Globalization and World Cities group based in the United Kingdom, who use network analyses to examine levels of connectivity among

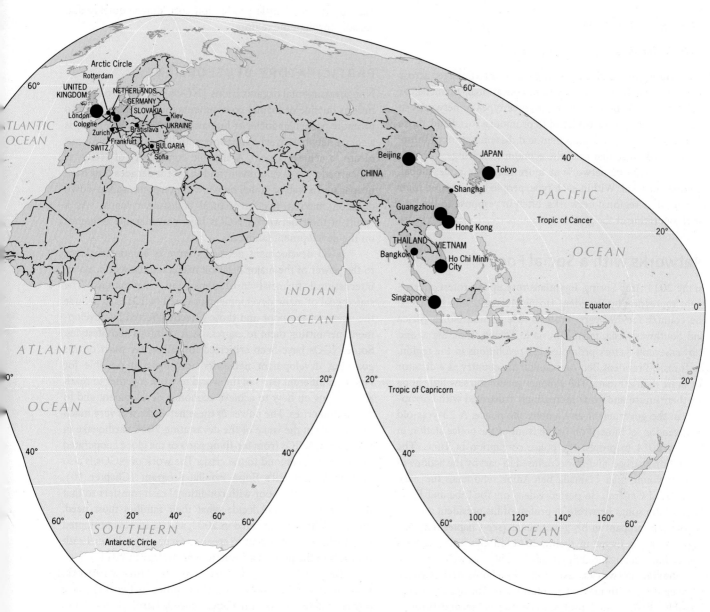

cities, based on such factors as air travel between cities, and the interpenetration of financial and advertising networks.

These researchers generated data for 315 global cities, measuring the information technology flows among the cities by tracking the flow of advanced services among them, focusing on accounting, advertising, banking/finance, insurance, law, and management consulting. Figure 14.7 shows the 30 cities they found to be most connected to New York City, as measured by the flow of producer services. By tracking flows, the authors found that Miami, not Los Angeles, is the U.S. city most closely linked to Latin America and that New York is the second most *globally* linked city in the world (behind London and ahead of Tokyo). Chicago is also a highly ranked member of the global city network, coming in seventh. The researchers found that New York and Chicago stand apart from other world cities in that these American cities have greater domestic linkages than global cities in the Pacific Rim or the European Union.

The linkages among global cities provide insights into the spatial character of the networks that underlie globalized processes. A multitude of globalized processes such as financial transactions and flows (represented here by banking/finance and accounting) occur across the network of global cities. Similarly, this network reflects the flow of advertising and marketing consultation services, which in turn reflects the flow of ideas through the media across the globe.

Castells claims that the age of information technology is more revolutionary than either the advent of the printing press or the Industrial Revolution. Do you agree with him? Write an argument in support of your position, drawing on your understanding of the expansion of the world-economy since 1500.

HOW DO NETWORKS OPERATE IN A GLOBALIZED WORLD?

The term *network* defines any number of interlinkages across the globe, whether transportation, educational, financial, or social. In this section we examine three types of networks in the world today: those designed to promote a social end, those concerned with the development and dissemination of information, and those that underlie economic exchange. We consider each type of network at more than one scale: global, regional, or local. Within each type, people have created their own local or regional networks, often in response to the network operating at the global scale.

Networks with a Social Focus

In the 2011 Arab Spring, Egyptians rose up to protest government repression by President Hosni Mubarak, who had ruled the country for 29 years. Protests rose around North Africa and Southwest Asia, from Tunisia to Yemen, Iran, Syria, and Libya. Several factors prompted the revolutions in the region. In Tunisia, President Ben Ali had run the country as a dictator for more than 20 years. The younger generation saw little hope for their future and grew increasingly frustrated with corruption in the government and among the police. A 23-year-old fruit vendor set himself on fire in front of the police station in January 2011 to protest the police corruption in Tunis. The revolution sparked, and it was diffused in part by the actions of another young man, Hamada Ben Amor, who takes the stage name of El Général. He posted videos on YouTube and Facebook of rap songs he wrote in protest of his president and the corruption rampant in his government (see Chapter 4). During protests in Egypt in spring 2011, El Général's anthems caught hold and inspired Egyptians to protest as well.

Social networks, especially Facebook and Twitter, were credited with making revolutions in Tunisia and Egypt possible—first, through protest rap music and second, through construction and completion of plans for protest. In Egypt, a Google employee anonymously created a Facebook page titled "We are all Khaled Said" in honor of a young Egyptian businessman who was beaten and killed by two police officers. The page garnered 473,000 supporters, and it "helped spread the word about the demonstrations in Egypt, which were ignited after a revolt in neighboring Tunisia toppled the government there" (Preston 2011, 1).

Rap or hiphop music diffused among protesters who shared the Arabic language. Islam, the predominant religion in the region, instructs followers to learn the Arabic language, and most people in the region can speak Arabic (Chapters 6 and 7). El Général's raps, spoken in Arabic, were readily understood by Arabic speakers around the region. He rapped, "My president, your country is dead/People eat garbage/Look at what is happening/Misery everywhere/Nowhere to sleep/I'm speaking for the people who suffer/Ground under feet." The accessibility of social media helped the video of a young man, produced at little production cost, diffuse quickly and broadly through the region.

PARTICIPATORY DEVELOPMENT

Nongovernmental organizations (NGOs) are nonprofit institutions outside of formal governments that are established to promote particular social or humanitarian ends. Each NGO is a social network in which people with like interests communicate to achieve a goal. A sizeable community of NGOs is concerned with development, and in recent decades they have propagated a web of global networks in response to top-down decision making (e.g., structural adjustment loans). As a result of their networks, NGOs have considerable influence on the development landscape.

NGO development networks serve as a counterbalance to the power of the major decision makers in the world, states, international financial institutions, and corporations. The stated goal of many development-oriented NGOs is to include the voices of the poor and those directly affected by development, permitting them to express their opinions and lifestyles. Some NGOs have been criticized for falling far short of this goal, but development networks now make it possible for NGOs in different parts of the world to work together to reach a consensus on how to achieve economic development and to respond to crises. The power of these networks was very much in evidence in the wake of the devastating 2010 earthquake in Haiti, when NGOs from far-flung parts of the globe cooperated in an effort to respond to the crisis. The work of NGOs is also evidenced in Brazil's Bolsa Familia program (Chapter 10), which entrusts the poor with conditional cash transfers so that those in poverty can decide what their families most need. Bolsa Familia was expanded in 2003, and its success prompted the World Bank president to speak in favor of conditional cash transfers to the poor as a development strategy in 2011.

Despite the goal of sharing power across a network, most development networks (like other networks) have power differences within them. Indeed, Leroi Henry, Giles Mohan, and Helen Yanacopulos (2004) find that power relationships exist both within and between networks—often privileging the views of NGOs headquartered in the core, as opposed to those in the periphery.

A growing number of development entities are promoting local solutions to development. **Participatory development**—the idea that locals should be engaged in deciding what development means for them and how to achieve it—is another response to top-down decision making. Stuart Corbridge has studied how the global push for participatory development has encouraged the government of India to enact participatory development programs. Corbridge and his colleague Sanjay Kumar describe the goal of participatory development as giving the people who are directly affected by policies and programs a voice in making the policies and programs—that is, to use local networks to shape development for local goals. Kumar and Corbridge found that "[t]here can be no doubting the sincerity of" participatory development programs "to engage the rural poor" in India. However, they also found that local politics factor into the distribution of poverty alleviation schemes because richer farmers and elites in rural areas tend to be most involved with development program.

This situation is a failure not of development, they maintain, but rather of the definition of success. The goal of the program they studied in India was to get seeds to farmers and to create irrigation schemes. The program has succeeded in this respect for many farmers, though not for the poorest farmers. Their lack of participation is not a reason to abandon the participatory program, however. According to Kumar and Corbridge, the program (like other participatory development programs) has to "operate in an environment that is dominated by better off farmers and particular community groups." They argue that the definition of success must change because development organizations cannot expect the poorest to "participate in groups that have little meaning for them." In other words, Kumar and Corbridge contend that it is worthwhile to invest in participatory development, even if existing political and economic divisions among the poor influence who receives assistance. They conclude that efforts to move decision making to those most affected represent a move in the right direction and should not be cast aside.

The World Bank, the International Monetary Fund, and even state governments are increasingly embracing the ideal of participatory development, loosening demands for trade liberalization in the periphery and semiperiphery. As Kumar and Corbridge explain, politics will enter participatory development, just as it enters the development networks and the global development organizations. The goal of participatory development is worthwhile, even if the short-term results do not mesh with Western concepts of success.

Networks and Information

The diffusion of products and ideas associated with popular culture depends largely on globalized media and retail store networks, as well as the advertising practices in which both engage. Today's media encompass much more than print, radio, and television. With technological advances, media include entertainment, music, video games, streaming media sites, smart phone apps, and social networks. Generation Like (Chapter 4) relies on social networks, and the teenagers and young adults who use them generate and diffuse popular culture.

Through a series of mergers and consolidations occurring mostly in the post–Cold War era, global media are controlled largely by six globe-spanning corporations: Time-Warner, Disney, Bertelsmann, Viacom, News Corporation, and Vivendi Universal. These six media corporations (along with other media corporations) are masters of **vertical integration**. A vertically integrated corporation is one that has ownership in all or most of the points along the production and consumption of a commodity chain.

Media companies compete for three things: *content*, *delivery*, and *consumers* (Pereira 2003). Through consolidation and mergers, vertically integrated global media companies such as the Walt Disney Corporation (Fig. 14.8) control

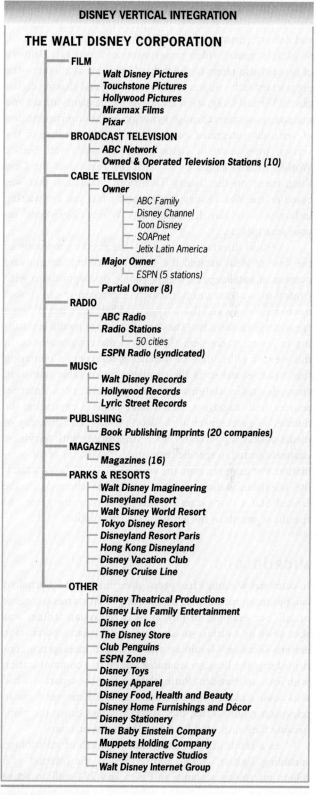

■ **Figure 14.8**

The Walt Disney Corporation. A list of companies that are part of the Walt Disney Company, based on data collected by the Columbia School of Journalism in 2013. By owning film, television, radio, and publishing, Disney can keep its message intact through vertical integration and synergy. *Data from:* Columbia Journalism Review, Who Owns What. http://www.cjrarchives.org/tools/owners/disney.asp

content (through ownership of production companies, radio shows, television stations, film producers, and publishers) and *delivery* (through ownership of radio, television stations, magazines, music, video games, apps, and movies). Delivery of content also refers to the technological infrastructure—the proprietary technologies used for creating and sharing digital media. Vertical integration also helps media giants attract and maintain customers through **synergy**, or the cross promotion of vertically integrated goods. For example, because of the vertical integration of Disney, you can visit Walt Disney World's Animal Kingdom to catch the Festival of the Lion King, based on the Disney Theatrical Production that was based on the Walt Disney Picture, and while you are waiting in line, you can play the Disney app "Where's My Water" on your smartphone.

Vertical integration of media changes the geography of the flow of ideas around the globe by limiting the ultimate number of **gatekeepers**, that is, people or corporations with control over access to information. A gatekeeper can choose not to tell a story, and the story is less likely to be heard. Some are concerned, then, that the consolidation of media is resulting in fewer gatekeepers. The big media conglomerates, in this view, have become the ultimate gatekeepers. Countering this trend, however, is the proliferation of cable television channels, radio stations, streaming media sites, Internet sources, and magazines, which some argue is expanding the number of gatekeepers in the world today. The diversity of media outlets supports the latter proposition, with television channels geared to specific segments (or markets) of the population. For example, both the wide-reaching Al-Jazeera satellite television station and the new cable channels in the United States that target Muslim Americans are geared to specific segments of the global or U.S. population.

MICROBLOGS

In countries without a free press, governments and journalists can be strong gatekeepers by choosing what stories to release or tell. For example, in July 2014, a Malaysian airliner was shot down by a surface-to-air missile by Russian separatists in eastern Ukraine. Ukrainian and American intelligence confirmed that the Russian separatist leader, in a communication with Russian President Putin, claimed that the separatists had shot down a plane (The Economist 2014). However, Russian television reported that the Ukrainians shot down the plane because they suspected President Putin was on board.

As a result of the extraordinary growth of microblogs, including Twitter, Weibo, and Qzone, on the Internet (1.3 billion microblog accounts in China and 271 million active accounts on Twitter), tight gatekeeping is much more difficult. A microblog allows individuals, without cost, to post thoughts, photographs, and experiences, albeit in a limited number of characters, and to spread word about a cause or concern through hashtags. The person or organization behind each account can represent actors and networks at local, regional, national, or global scales.

Networks and Economic Exchange

Unlike traditional vertically integrated media, social media are more often horizontally integrated. A horizontally integrated corporation is one that acquires ownership of other corporations engaged in similar activities. The retail industry may appear to be dominated by a large number of different companies; however, many retail companies bearing different names are in fact owned by the same horizontally integrated parent corporation.

With **horizontal integration**, similar products are owned by one company, but they are branded separately so that consumers may think they are separate companies. Horizontal integration is common in clothing companies and housewares. Williams-Sonoma, West Elm, and Pottery Barn are separate stores in a mall, but they are all owned by the same parent company. Likewise, Athleta, Old Navy, Gap, and Banana Republic are separate stores in a mall but are all owned by Gap, Inc.

The incentive for horizontal integration is that a company successful in producing one good can replicate its success, share costs (like websites), and increase profits at different price points or slightly different genres of the same good. Facebook bought Instagram, another social media network, in 2012. In 2014, the messaging app What's App gained in popularity, and so Facebook purchased it as well. Facebook's goal is to be involved in some way each time Generation Like consumes or shares online.

COMMUNITY-SUPPORTED AGRICULTURE

In the von Thünen model (Chapter 11), farms surrounded urban areas in a regular pattern, and farmers provided fresh food to the people in cities by bringing their products to markets. With the industrialization of agriculture (Chapter 11), the distance between farmers and consumers has increased, figuratively and literally. Consumers often do not consider the source of their food, and some processed foods look so little like natural foods that it is all too easy to forget farmers were involved in producing the food.

Container ships and refrigerated trucking and shipping (Chapter 12) now allow consumers in cold regions of the world in winter months to purchase fresh fruits and vegetables grown thousands of miles away, in warmer climates. In 2007, when the United States conducted its last Census of Agriculture, it found the number of principal operators of farms in the United States had grown by 4 percent, to 2.2 million people. According to geographer Steven Schnell (2007), one of the reasons the number of farmers in the United States has increased is the growth in the number of **community-supported agriculture** groups, known as CSAs (Fig. 14. 9). Schnell explains that CSAs began in Japan in the 1960s when a group of women "dissatisfied with imported, processed, and pesticide-laden food, made arrangements directly with farmers to provide natural, organic, local food for their tables."

From its hearth in Japan, CSAs diffused to Europe and then to the United States. The first CSA in the United States

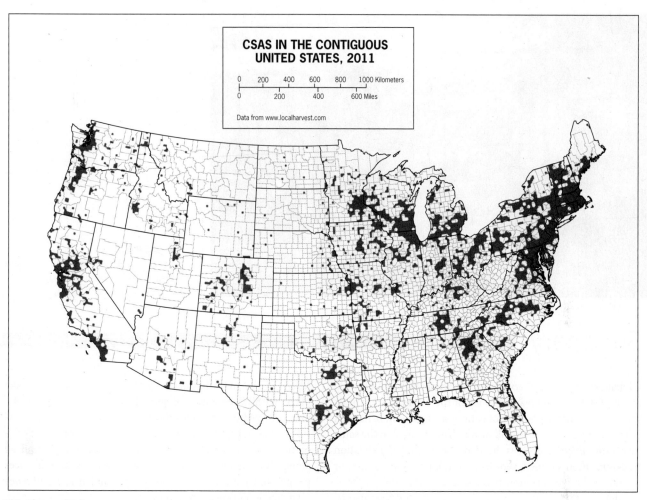

CSAS IN THE CONTIGUOUS UNITED STATES, 2011

0   200   400   600   800   1000 Kilometers

0   200   400   600 Miles

Data from www.localharvest.com

■■ **Figure 14.9**

CSAs in the Contiguous United States, 2011. Schnell (2007) found that CSAs are more likely to be found in urban or suburban areas where people have higher levels of education and are actively involved in discussing politics. *Courtesy of:* Local Harvest.org.

was in the Berkshire Mountains of Massachusetts. By 2011, the number of CSAs in the United States had risen to over 4000, according to Local Harvest, an organization that maps CSAs to help consumers and farmers connect (Fig. 14.10).

Through a CSA, a farmer and consumers create a network whereby both assume risk. Consumers pay for a share of the farmer's harvest, typically fruits and vegetables, before the growing season begins. Farmers use the cash to purchase seeds, then plant, harvest, and deliver goods to consumers over a period of weeks during the growing season. Both Schnell and Local Harvest agree that CSA farmers typically use organic growing standards (Chapter 11) but do not take the time to certify their land and produce as organic.

Analyzing the global consolidation of media, the networking of NGOs concerned with development, and the global presence of retail corporations helps us see the diversity of global networks, with some increasingly centralized and others increasingly disaggregated. Aside from the spatial

characteristics of the network itself, what is interesting for geographers is the impact of these networks on local places, for globalized networks do not affect individual places in the same way. People interact with the global network, shaping it, resisting it, embracing it, and responding to globalization in unique ways.

thinking geographically

Think about the information you are exposed to through the Internet, television, and other social media each day. Make a list of the companies that publish or produce these news sources you use. Go to *Columbia Journalism Review's* website, Who Owns What (http://www.cjr.org/resources/). Determine how many gatekeepers control the information you use to make decisions and understand your world.

Jeff and Meggan Haller/Keyhole Photo/© Corbis

■ **Figure 14.10**
Belforest, Alabama. Buford and Stewart Foster count and bag corn to be sold at a farmers' market.

Summary

Globalization has been compared to a runaway train blowing through stations and leaving much of the world to stare at its caboose. This description is not entirely accurate. Globalization is a series of processes, not all of which are headed in the same direction. Even processes headed down the globalization track are often stopped, sent back to the previous station, or derailed. The globalization track is not "inevitable" or "irreversible" (in the words of O'Loughlin, Staeheli, and Greenberg).

Many of the most important globalization processes take place within networks of global cities (see Chapter 9), places linked by popular culture (see Chapter 4), governments (see Chapter 8), trade (see Chapter 12), and development (see Chapter 10). People and places are found all along these networks, and just as globalization influences people and places, those same people and places influence globalization's trajectory and future.

Geographic Concepts

imagined community
globalization
Washington Consensus
networks

Digital Divide
social networks
participatory development
vertical integration

synergy
gatekeepers
horizontal integration
community-supported agriculture

Learn More Online

About media ownership
Columbia Journalism Review's Who Owns What Website
www.cjr.org/tools/owners/

About the Network of World Cities
www.brook.edu/metro/pubs/20050222_worldcities.pdf

About the World Social Forum
www.forumsocialmundial.org.br/

Watch It Online

About Gross National Happiness in Bhutan
http://youtu.be/CXJwNSkdTH0

About the Growth of the World City of Lagos, Nigeria
http://youtu.be/x5_9m4je3ck

AREA AND DEMOGRAPHIC DATA FOR THE WORLD'S STATES

Appendix B: Area and Demographic Data for the World's States

Country	Land Area sq. km.	Land Area sq. mi.	Arable Land in sq. km.	Population 2013 (millions)	Population 2025 (millions)	Population Density Arithmetic	Population Density Physiologic	Total Fertility Rate (TFR)	Life Expectancy Male (years)	Life Expectancy Female (years)	Infant Mortality per 1,000	Natural Increase (percent)	Net Migration per 1,000	Urban (percent)	Poverty Index	GINI Index	Human Development Index (HDI)	Corruption Index	GNI per Capita	CO_2 Emissions per Capita
WORLD	134,134,451	51,789,601	49,194,729	7,137	8,095	53.21	145.08	2.5	68	73	40	1.2	0	52			0.702		$11,690	
SUBSAHARAN AFRICA	22,434,378	8,661,914	9,591,310	1,100	1,464	49.03	114.69	4.8	57	60	68	2.6	0	40						
Angola	1,246,700	481,351	591,900	21.6	31.6	17.33	36.49	6.3	50	53	98	3.2	1	59	0.401	42.66	0.526	23	4580	1.6
Benin	112,622	43,483	37,000	9.6	13.4	85.24	259.46	5.2	58	60	70	2.9	0	45		43.53	0.476	36	750	0.5
Botswana	581,730	224,606	258,870	1.9	2.1	3.27	7.34	2.7	47	46	33	0.7	2	24	0.508	60.46	0.683		7650	2.7
Burkina Faso	274,200	105,869	120,700	18	25.6	65.65	149.13	6	55	56	73	3.1	-2	27	0.442	39.78	0.388	21	670	0.1
Burundi	27,830	10,745	19,330	10.9	15.5	391.66	563.89	6.2	51	55	89	3.2	1	11	0.260	40.72	0.389	25	240	0
Cameroon	475,440	183,567	97,500	21.5	29.5	45.22	220.51	5.1	53	55	62	2.7	-1	52		43.82	0.504		1170	0.4
Cape Verde	4,033	1,557	750	0.5	0.6	123.98	666.67	2.4	70	78	18	1.5	-9	63			0.636		3830	0.7
Central African Republic	622,984	240,534	50,800	4.7	6.1	7.54	92.52	6.2	47	51	116	3.2	0	39	0.424	56.30	0.341	25	510	0.1
Chad	1,284,000	495,752	499,320	12.2	17.8	9.50	24.43	7	49	51	106	3.6	-2	22		43.30	0.372	19	770	0
Comoros	2,235	863	1,580	0.8	1	357.94	506.33	4.3	59	62	69	2.3	-3	28	0.192		0.488	28	840	0.2
Congo	342,000	132,046	106,000	4.4	5.8	12.87	41.51	5	56	59	66	2.8	-1	64		40.17	0.564	22	2550	0.5
Congo, Dem. Rep.	2,344,858	905,350	260,100	71.1	99.7	30.32	273.36	6.3	48	51	111	2.9	0	34	0.399		0.338	22	230	0
Cote d'Ivoire	322,463	124,503	206,000	21.1	27.5	65.43	102.43	5	49	51	68	2.2	-1	51	0.307	43.19	0.452	27	1220	0.3
Djibouti	23,200	8,958	17,020	0.9	1.1	38.79	52.88	3.7	59	62	58	2	-4	77	0.127		0.467	36	440	0.6
Equatorial Guinea	28,051	10,830	2,840	0.8	1	28.52	281.69	5.1	51	54	65	2.3	6	39			0.556	19	13560	6.7
Eritrea	117,600	45,405	75,920	5.8	8	49.32	76.40	4.9	59	64	46	3.1	2	21			0.381	20	450	0.1
Ethiopia	1,104,300	426,370	364,880	89.2	118.1	80.78	244.46	4.8	61	64	52	2.6	0	17	0.537	33.60	0.435	33	380	0.1
Gabon	267,667	103,346	51,600	1.6	2.1	5.98	31.01	4.1	62	64	43	2.2	1	86	0.073		0.674	34	10040	1.7
Gambia	11,295	4,361	6,050	1.9	2.7	168.22	314.05	5.8	57	60	81	3.3	-2	57	0.329		0.441	28	510	0.3
Ghana	238,533	92,098	157,000	26.1	32.7	109.42	166.24	4.2	60	62	53	2.4	0	52	0.144		0.573	46	1550	0.4
Guinea	245,857	94,925	144,000	11.8	15.7	48.00	81.94	5.1	55	56	67	2.6	-3	35	0.548		0.392	24	440	0.1
Guinea-Bissau	36,125	13,948	16,300	1.7	2.2	47.06	104.29	4.5	52	55	96	2.5	-2	44	0.495	33.68	0.396	19	510	0.2
Kenya	580,367	224,080	274,300	44.2	59.2	76.16	161.14	4.5	59	62	54	2.7	0	24	0.226		0.535	27	860	0.3
Lesotho	30,355	11,720	22,853	2.2	2.5	72.48	96.27	3.1	48	48	65	1.2	-2	28	0.227	54.17	0.486	49	1380	0
Liberia	111,369	43,000	27,100	4.4	6	39.51	162.36	5.7	59	61	63	3.3	2	48	0.459	38.16	0.412		370	0.2
Madagascar	587,041	226,657	414,050	22.5	31.2	38.33	54.34	4.6	62	65	39	2.8	0	33	0.420	40.63	0.498	28	430	0.1
Malawi	118,484	45,747	57,350	16.3	22.7	137.57	284.22	5.6	54	54	89	2.9	0	16	0.332	46.18	0.414		320	0.1
Mali	1,240,192	478,838	416,510	15.5	21.8	12.50	37.21	6.1	52	56	58	3.1	-3	35	0.533	33.02	0.407	28	660	0
Mauritania	1,030,700	397,953	396,610	3.7	4.9	3.59	9.33	4.8	60	63	73	2.6	-1	41	0.362	40.46	0.487	30	1110	0.6
Mauritius	2,040	788	870	1.3	1.3	637.25	1494.25	1.4	70	77	12.9	0.4	0	42			0.771	52	8570	3.2
Mozambique	799,380	308,641	499,500	24.3	33.5	30.40	48.65	5.9	49	50	64	3	0	31	0.390	45.66	0.393	30	510	0.1
Namibia	824,292	318,259	388,090	2.4	3	2.91	6.18	3.2	61	66	36	1.9	-2	38	0.200	61.32	0.624	48	5610	1.5
Niger	1,267,000	489,189	447,820	16.9	27	13.34	37.74	7.6	57	58	71	3.8	0	18	0.584	31.16	0.337	34	390	0.1
Nigeria	923,768	356,667	720,000	173.6	239.9	187.93	241.11	6	51	52	97	2.8	0	50	0.239	42.95	0.504	25	1440	0.5
Reunion	2,510	969	350	0.8	1	318.73	2285.71	2.4	77	83	7	1.2	0	94						
Rwanda	26,338	10,169	18,568	11.1	15	421.44	597.80	4.7	61	65	51	2.9	-1	19	0.352	50.82	0.506	53	600	0.1
São Tomé and Principe	964	372	497	0.2	0.3	207.47	402.41	4.6	64	68	44	3.1	-2	63	0.217	33.87	0.558		1310	0.6
Senegal	196,722	75,954	90,150	13.5	18.5	68.62	149.75	5	62	65	51	3.1	-2	47	0.390	40.31	0.485		1030	0.5
Seychelles	455	176	30	0.1	0.1	219.78	3333.33	2.4	69	78	9.8	1.1	-3	54		65.77	0.756	54	12180	7.8
Sierra Leone	71,740	27,699	40,970	6.2	7.7	86.42	151.33	4.9	45	45	128	2	0	41	0.405	35.35	0.374	30	580	0.1
Somalia	637,657	246,199	441,290	10.4	14.6	16.31	23.57	6.8	53	56	83	3.2	-4	38	0.500			8		0.1
South Africa	1,219,090	470,691	963,410	53	56.9	43.48	55.01	2.4	56	60	45	1	4	62	0.041	65.02	0.658		7460	9.2
South Sudan	644,329	248,775	285,332	9.8	13.5	15.21	34.35	5.1	53	55	81	2.4	16	18		45.53		14	790	..

Appendix B: Area and Demographic Data for the World's States (Continued)

Country	Land Area sq. km.	Land Area sq. mi.	Arable Land in sq. km.	Population 2013 (millions)	Population 2025 (millions)	Population Density Arithmetic	Population Density Physiologic	Total Fertility Rate (TFR)	Life Expectancy Male (years)	Life Expectancy Female (years)	Infant Mortality per 1,000	Natural Increase (percent)	Net Migration per 1,000	Urban (percent)	Poverty Index	GINI Index	Human Development Index (HDI)	Corruption Index	GNI per Capita	CO_2 Emissions per Capita
Swaziland	17,364	6,704	12,220	1.2	1.4	69.11	98.20	3.5	49	48	68	1.6	-1	21	0.113	51.49	0.530		2860	0.9
Tanzania	947,300	365,753	406,500	49.1	69.1	51.83	120.79	5.4	59	61	52	3.1	-1	27	0.335	37.82	0.488	33	570	0.2
Togo	56,785	21,925	38,500	6.2	8.2	109.18	161.04	4.7	55	57	69	2.6	0	38	0.260	45.96	0.473	29	500	0.2
Uganda	241,038	93,065	142,620	36.9	55.4	153.09	258.73	6.2	57	59	54	3.5	1	16	0.359	44.55	0.484	26	480	0.1
Zambia	752,618	290,586	238,360	14.2	21.5	18.87	59.57	5.9	54	57	69	3.3	1	39	0.318	57.49	0.561		1350	0.2
Zimbabwe	390,757	150,871	162,000	13	17.9	33.27	80.25	3.8	55	56	41	2.2	0	39	0.181		0.492	21	650	0.7
NORTH AFRICA AND SOUTHWEST ASIA	12,710,422	4,907,492	4,893,118	251	307	19.75	51.30	2.9	70	75	27	1.8	2	70						
Algeria	2,381,741	919,590	414,320	38.3	46.5	16.08	92.44	3	76	77	23	5	0	73	0.002	30.30		36	3720	1.4
Armenia	29,743	11,484	16,830	3	3	100.86	178.25	1.6	71	78	11	0.4	0	63	0.009	33.06		28	6220	5.1
Azerbaijan	86,600	33,436	47,683	9.4	10.4	108.55	197.14	2.3	71	77	11	1.3	0	53				48	19560	19.3
Bahrain	760	293	86	1.1	1.4	1447.37	12790.70	1.9	75	78	7	1.2	-40	100					26110	7
Cyprus	9,251	3,572	1,249	1.1	1.4	118.91	880.70	1.5	76	81	6	0.6	14	62	0.008	41.35		49	3290	1.4
Egypt	1,001,450	386,660	36,120	84.7	100.1	84.58	2344.96	3	69	72	24	6	-1	43	0.052	29.54		16	6130	3.7
Georgia	69,700	26,911	24,650	4.5	4.2	64.56	182.56	1.7	70	79	13	0.2	5	58					32030	9.3
Iraq	438,317	169,234	76,570	35.1	49.3	80.08	458.40	4.3	66	73	28	2.6	-1	71	0.004	33.69		45	4670	3.4
Israel	20,770	8,019	5,232	8.1	9.8	389.99	1548.17	3	80	84	3.5	1.6	2	91						31.3
Jordan	89,342	34,495	10,423	7.3	9.1	81.71	700.37	3.5	72	74	17	2.4	11	83				28	9190	4.7
Kuwait	17,818	6,880	1,520	3.5	4.3	196.43	2302.63	2.4	74	76	8	1.7	37	98				47		20.4
Lebanon	10,400	4,015	7,330	4.8	5	461.54	654.84	1.5	77	82	9	0.9	18	87	0.007					0.6
Libya	1,759,540	679,358	153,550	6.5	7.5	3.69	42.33	2.5	73	77	15	4	-6	78		41.10			24310	40.3
Morocco	446,550	172,413	304,030	33	38.2	73.90	108.54	2.7	69	72	28	6	-3	59				46		17
Oman	309,500	119,498	14,728	4	5.2	12.92	271.59	2.9	74	78	9	1.8	42	75	0.024			17		2.9
Palestinian Territory	6,260	2,417	3,730	4.4	5.9	702.88	1179.62	4.1	71	74	20	2.9	-2	83		40.04		50	10830	4.1
Qatar	11,586	4,473	657	2.2	2.7	189.88	3348.55	2.2	77	79	7	1.1	49	100				18	38620	19.9
Saudi Arabia	2,149,690	829,995	1,733,900	30.1	36.7	14.00	17.36	2.9	73	75	16	1.8	2	81	0.191			18	1270	1
Sudan	1,861,484	718,719	1,127,020	34.2	44.7	18.37	30.35	4.6	60	63	56	9	-4	33			0.717	36	5020	3.3
Syria	185,180	71,498	139,210	21.9	27.9	118.26	157.32	3.1	72	78	17	2.2	-14	54	0.036	30.75	0.682	32	2980	2.6
Tunisia	163,610	63,170	100,790	10.9	12.1	66.62	108.15	2.2	73	77	16	6	-1	66			0.784	15		9.8
Turkey	783,562	302,533	384,070	76.1	85.5	97.12	198.14	2.1	71	76	21	1.2	0	77		40.88	0.617	37	2960	1.6
United Arab Emirates	83,600	32,278	3,970	9.3	11.5	111.24	2342.57	1.9	76	78	7	1.5	11	83		35.29	0.473	11	1500	0.3
Western Sahara	266,000	102,703	50,040	0.6	0.8	2.26	1199	2.5	65	69	39	6	18	82	0.006	35.79	0.721		4150	2.5
Yemen	527,968	203,848	235,410	25.2	34	47.73	107.05	4.9	61	63	72	2.7	-1	29				37	2920	0.6
SOUTH ASIA	6,779,264	2,617,474	3,098,440	1,779	2,047	3,664	10,631	2.6	65	68	47	1.6	-1	32						
Afghanistan	652,230	251,826	379,100	30.6	39.6	46.92	80.72	5.4	59	61	71	2.8	-5	24	0.293			8	680	0.3
Bangladesh	143,998	55,598	91,250	156.6	177.9	1087.52	1716.16	2.3	69	71	35	1.5	-3	26	0.237	32.12		27	840	0.4
Bhutan	38,394	14,824	5,200	0.70	0.9	18.23	134.62	3.6	65	69	4	1.5	0	36	0.128	38.73			2420	0.7
India	3,287,263	1,269,212	1,793,000	1,276.50	1,443.30	388.32	711.94	2.4	65	68	44	1.5	0	31	0.282	33.60		36	1550	1.7
Iran	1,648,195	636,368	491,310	76.5	87	46.41	155.71	1.9	72	75	19	1.4	-1	71				25	5750	7.7
Maldives	298	115	70	0.4	0.4	1342.28	5714.29	2.3	73	75	9	1.9	0	35	0.008					3.3
Nepal	147,181	56,827	41,210	26.8	30.4	182.09	650.33	2.6	66	69	46	1.7	-5	17	0.197	32.82		31	700	0.1
Pakistan	796,095	307,372	270,400	190.7	245.9	239.54	705.25	3.8	65	67	74	2.3	-2	35	0.237	29.63		28	1260	0.9
Sri Lanka	65,610	25,332	26,900	20.5	22	312.45	762.08	2.1	71	77	12	1.2	-1	15		36.40		37	2920	0.6
SOUTHEAST ASIA	4,494,507	1,735,330	1,285,456	612	699	136.17	476.10	2.4	68	73	28	1.3	-1	47						
Brunei	5,765	2,226	134	0.4	0.5	69.38	2985.07	1.6	77	79	7	1.4	3	72						22.9
Cambodia	181,035	69,898	57,550	14.4	17.2	79.54	250.22	2.8	61	64	45	1.8	-4	20	0.211	31.82		20	880	0.3

Appendix B: Area and Demographic Data for the World's States (Continued)

Country	Land Area sq. km.	Land Area sq. mi.	Arable Land in sq. km.	Population 2013 (millions)	Population 2025 (millions)	Pop. Density Arithmetic	Pop. Density Physiologic	Total Fertility Rate (TFR)	Life Exp. Male (years)	Life Exp. Female (years)	Infant Mortality per 1,000	Natural Increase (percent)	Net Migration per 1,000	Urban (percent)	Poverty Index	GINI Index	Human Development Index (HDI)	Corruption Index	GNI per Capita	CO_2 Emissions per Capita
Indonesia	1,904,569	735,354	565,000	248.5	290.6	130.48	439.82	2.6	68	72	32	1.5	-1	50	0.024	38.14		32	3420	1.8
Laos	236,800	91,428	24,690	6.7	7.9	28.29	271.36	3.2	66	69	68	2	-2	27	0.186	36.22		26	1270	0.3
Malaysia	329,847	127,354	77,495	29.8	34.3	90.34	384.54	2.1	72	77	7	1.3	4	64		46.21		50	9820	7.7
Myanmar	676,590	261,232	105,770	53.3	57.7	78.78	503.92	2	63	67	52	1	-2	31	0.038			21		0.2
Phillippines	300,000	115,830	123,950	96.2	115.8	320.67	776.12	3	66	72	22	1.5	-2	63		43.03		36	2500	0.9
Singapore	697	269	7	5.4	6.4	7747.49	771428.57	1.3	80	84	1.8	0.6	19	100	0.004			86	47210	2.7
Thailand	513,120	198,116	218,600	66.2	67.1	129.01	302.84	1.6	71	78	11	0.4	0	46	0.004	39.37		35	5210	4.4
Timor-Leste	14,874	5,743	3,840	1.1	1.3	73.95	286.46	5.7	65	68	45	2.7	-14	30	0.322	30.41		30	3620	0.2
Vietnam	331,210	127,880	108,420	89.7	100.1	270.83	827.34	2.1	70	76	16	1	0	32	0.026	35.62		31	1550	1.7
EAST ASIA	11,796,361	4,554,575	6,378,919	1,594	1,641	135.13	249.89	1.5	73	78	15	0.4	0	57						
China	9,596,960	3,705,386	5,145,530	1,357.40	1,406.10	141.44	263.80	1.5	73	77	16	0.5	0	53	0.026	37.01			5720	6.2
China, Hong Kong SAR	1,104	426	51	7.2	7.9	6521.74	141176.47	1.3	81	86	1.4	0.7	2	100				75	36560	5.2
China, Macao SAR	28	11	0	0.6	0.7	21428.57	600000.00	1.4	79	86	3	1	34	100						
Japan	377,915	145,913	45,490	127.3	120.7	336.85	2798.42	1.4	79	86	2.2	-0.2	1	91				74	47870	9.2
Korea, North	120,538	46,540	26,300	24.7	26.2	204.91	939.16	2	65	73	27	0.5	0	60				8		2.9
Korea, South	99,720	38,502	17,800	50.2	52	503.41	2820.22	1.3	78	84	3	0.4	1	82					22670	11.5
Mongolia	1,564,116	603,905	1,133,958	2.8	3.3	1.79	2.47	2.8	65	72	36	2.1	-1	63	0.077	36.52			3160	4.2
Taiwan	35,980	13,892	9,790	23.4	23.7	650.36	2390.19	1.3	76	83	4.2	0.3	0	78						
EUROPE	5,992,212	2,313,634	2,541,948	740	746	123.49	291.12	1.6	74	81	5	0	2	71						
Albania	28,748	11,100	12,013	2.8	2.9	97.40	233.08	1.8	74	80	14.4	0.5	-15	54	0.005	28.96		31	4030	1.4
Andorra	468	181	202	0.1	0.1	213.68	495.05	1.2	-	-	1.9	0.5	4	90						6.6
Austria	83,871	32,383	31,600	8.5	8.9	101.35	268.99	1.4	78	83	3.1	0	5	67					47850	8
Belarus	207,600	80,154	87,960	9.5	8.9	45.76	108.00	1.6	67	78	3.4	-0.1	1	76	0.001	26.46		29	6530	6.6
Belgium	30,528	11,787	13,330	11.2	12	366.88	840.21	1.8	78	83	3.3	0.2	6	99				75	44720	10
Bosnia-Herzegovina	51,197	19,767	21,590	3.8	3.8	74.22	176.01	1.2	73	78	5	-0.1	-1	46	0.006	33.04			4750	8.1
Bulgaria	110,879	42,810	51,230	7.3	6.7	65.84	142.49	1.5	71	78	7.8	0.6	-1	73		34.28			6840	5.9
Croatia	56,594	21,851	13,277	4.3	4.1	75.98	323.87	1.5	74	80	4.7	-0.2	1	56		33.61		48	13490	4.7
Czech Republic	78,867	30,451	42,250	10.5	10.7	133.14	248.52	1.5	75	81	2.6	0	1	74		26.39		48	18130	10.6
Denmark	43,094	16,639	26,240	5.6	5.8	129.95	213.41	1.7	78	82	3.4	0.1	4	87					59870	8.3
Estonia	45,228	17,463	9,560	1.3	1.3	28.74	135.98	1.6	71	81	3.6	-0.1	-5	69		32.69			16270	13.7
Finland	338,145	130,558	22,851	5.4	5.7	15.97	236.31	1.8	78	83	2.4	0.1	3	68				89	46490	11.5
France	643,801	248,572	288,390	63.9	67.3	99.25	221.57	2	79	85	3.3	0.4	1	78					41750	5.6
Germany	357,022	137,846	166,640	80.6	80	225.76	483.68	1.4	78	83	3.3	-0.2	5	73				78	45070	9.1
Greece	131,957	50,949	81,600	11.1	11.3	84.12	136.03	1.4	79	83	3.4	0	-1	73					23660	7.7
Hungary	93,028	35,918	53,380	9.9	9.8	106.42	185.46	1.3	71	78	4.9	-0.4	1	69		28.94		54	12410	5.1
Iceland	103,000	39,768	18,722	0.3	0.4	2.91	16.02	2	81	84	1.8	0.8	-1	95				78	38270	6.2
Ireland	70,273	27,132	45,330	4.6	4.9	65.46	101.48	2	78	83	3.5	1	-7	60				72	39020	8.9
Italy	301,340	116,347	137,285	59.8	61.6	198.45	435.59	1.4	79	85	3.2	-0.1	4	68				43	34640	6.7
Kosovo	10,887	4,203	5,700	1.8	2	165.33	315.79	1.9	67	71	10	0.4	-2	38				33	3600	
Latvia	64,589	24,938	18,410	2	1.9	30.97	108.64	1.4	69	79	6.3	-0.5	3	68		36.03		53	14060	3.4
Liechtenstein	160	62	60	0.04	0.04	250.00	666.67	1.4	79	84	1.6	0.4	3	15						..
Lithuania	65,300	25,212	28,422	3	2.8	45.94	105.55	1.4	68	79	3.9	-0.4	-7	67		32.63			13820	4.1
Luxembourg	2,586	998	1,314	0.5	0.6	193.35	380.52	1.5	78	83	3.4	0.4	19	83				80	71640	21.4
Macedonia	25,713	9,928	12,670	2.1	2.1	81.67	165.75	1.5	73	77	10	0.2	0	65	0.007	43.56		44	4620	5.2
Malta	316	122	103	0.4	0.5	1265.82	3883.50	1.5	79	83	6.3	0.3	3	100					19710	6.2
Moldova	33,851	13,070	24,600	4.1	3.8	121.12	166.67	1.3	67	75	10	0	0	42	0.005	30.63		35	2070	1.4

Appendix B: Area and Demographic Data for the World's States (Continued)

Country	Land Area sq. km.	sq. mi.	Arable Land in sq. km.	Population 2013 (millions)	2025 (millions)	Pop. Density Arithmetic	Physiologic	Total Fertility Rate (TFR)	Life Exp. Male (years)	Female (years)	Infant Mortality per 1,000	Natural Increase (percent)	Net Migration per 1,000	Urban (percent)	Poverty Index	GINI Index	Human Development Index (HDI)	Corruption Index	GNI per Capita	CO2 Emissions per Capita
Monaco	2	1	1	0.04	0.04	20000.00	40000.00	1.4	-	-	-	0	13	100						..
Montenegro	13,812	5,333	5,130	0.6	0.7	43.44	116.96	1.7	72	77	5.6	0.3	0	64	0.012	30.63		44	7220	4.2
Netherlands	41,543	16,040	18,417	16.8	17.4	404.40	912.20	1.7	79	83	3.7	0.2	1	66				83	48000	11
Norway	323,802	125,020	9,917	5.1	5.8	15.75	514.27	1.8	79	83	2.4	0.4	9	80				86	98780	11.7
Poland	312,685	120,728	145,290	38.5	38.2	123.13	264.99	1.3	72	81	4.7	0	0	61		32.78			12660	8.3
Portugal	92,090	35,556	36,360	10.5	10	114.02	288.78	1.3	77	83	3.4	-0.2	-4	38					20640	4.9
Romania	238,391	92,043	137,330	21.3	20.7	89.35	155.10	1.4	70	77	9.4	-0.3	0	55		27.33			8560	3.7
San Marino	61	24	10	0.03	0.04	491.80	3000.00	1.5	82	86	3.1	0.2	7	84						..
Serbia	77,474	29,913	50,530	7.1	6.8	91.64	140.51	1.4	72	77	5.4	-0.5	1	59	0.001	29.65			5280	6.3
Slovakia	49,035	18,932	19,274	5.4	5.4	110.13	280.17	1.3	72	79	5.8	0.1	1	54		26.58		47	17190	6.6
Slovenia	20,273	7,827	4,797	2.1	2.1	103.59	437.77	1.5	76	83	1.6	0.1	0	50		24.87			22810	7.5
Spain	505,370	195,123	269,600	46.6	45.2	92.21	172.85	1.3	79	85	3.1	0.1	-3	77					29270	5.9
Sweden	450,295	173,859	30,486	9.6	10.5	21.32	314.90	1.9	80	84	2.6	0.2	5	84				89	56120	5.6
Switzerland	41,277	15,937	15,287	8.1	8.6	196.24	529.86	1.5	80	85	3.8	0.2	8	74				85	80970	5
Ukraine	603,550	233,031	412,970	45.5	41.8	75.39	110.18	1.5	66	76	8.5	-0.3	1	69	0.002	24.82		25	3500	6.6
United Kingdom	243,610	94,058	171,820	64.1	69.8	263.13	373.06	2	80	84	4.2	0.4	2	80				76	38500	7.9
NORTH AND CENTRAL EURASIA	21,101,693	8,147,363	4,983,193	66	78	3.13	13.24	2.6	64	72	38	1.7	-2	47						
Kazakhstan	2,724,900	1,052,084	2,079,750	17	19.4	6.24	8.17	2.6	64	74	28	1.4	0	55	0.004	28.56		26	9780	15.2
Kyrgyzstan	199,951	77,201	105,913	5.7	6.6	28.51	53.82	3.1	66	74	27	2.1	-7	34	0.013	33.39		24	990	1.2
Russia	17,098,242	6,601,631	2,143,500	143.5	143.1	8.39	66.95	1.7	64	76	7.4	0	2	74		39.69		28	12700	12.2
Tajikistan	143,100	55,251	48,750	8.1	10.1	56.60	166.15	3.7	64	71	34	2.5	-1	26	0.031	29.88		22	880	0.4
Turkmenistan	488,100	188,455	338,380	5.2	6	10.65	15.37	2.5	61	69	49	1.4	-2	47				17	5410	10.5
Uzbekistan	447,400	172,741	266,900	30.2	35.7	67.50	113.15	2.3	65	71	46	1.6	-2	51	0.013			17	1720	3.7
NORTH AMERICA	19,811,345	7,649,525	4,740,525	352	386	17.77	74.25	1.9	77	81	6	0.4	-3	81						
Canada	9,984,670	3,855,081	653,460	35.3	39.7	3.54	54.02	1.6	79	83	4.9	0.4	7	80			0.902	81	51570	14.6
United States	9,826,675	3,794,079	4,087,065	316.2	346.4	32.18	77.37	1.9	76	81	5.9	0.5	2	81			0.914	73	52340	17.6
LATIN AMERICA AND THE CARIBBEAN	20,543,351	7,931,787	7,491,294	606	682	29.50	85.98	2.2	72	78	19	1.3	-1	79						
Antigua and Barbuda	443	171	90	0.1	0.1	225.73	1111.11	2.1	74	80	16	0.8	0	30					12480	5.9
Argentina	2,780,400	1,073,512	1,487,910	41.3	46.8	14.85	27.76	2.4	72	80	11.7	1.1	-1	93	0.015	43.57		34		4.5
Bahamas	13,880	5,359	140	0.3	0.4	21.61	2142.86	1.7	72	78	16	0.7	6	84		..		71	20600	6.8
Barbados	430	166	140	0.3	0.3	697.67	2142.86	1.8	73	77	12	0.4	1	44				75	15080	5.4
Belize	22,966	8,867	1,600	0.3	0.4	13.06	187.50	2.6	71	77	14	1.8	5	45	0.030	..	0.732			1.4
Bolivia	1,098,581	424,162	375,150	11	12.5	10.01	29.32	3.2	65	69	40	1.9	0	67	0.097	46.64		34	2220	1.5
Brazil	8,514,877	3,287,594	2,756,050	195.5	214.1	22.96	70.93	1.8	71	78	21	0.9	0	85	0.012	52.67			11630	2.2
Chile	756,102	291,931	158,090	17.6	19.2	23.28	111.33	1.9	76	82	7.4	0.9	0	87		50.84		71	14310	4.2
Colombia	1,138,910	439,733	426,176	48	54.6	42.15	112.63	2.3	70	77	17	1.4	-1	76	0.032	53.53		36	7020	1.6
Costa Rica	51,100	19,730	18,850	4.7	5.4	91.98	249.34	1.9	77	81	9.1	1.2	3	73		48.61		53	8820	1.7
Cuba	110,860	42,803	64,060	11.3	11	101.93	176.40	1.8	76	80	4.9	0.4	-4	75			0.763	46		3.4
Curaçao	444	171	44	0.2	0.2	450.45	4545.45	2.1	72	80	7.6	0.5	19	-						
Dominica	751	290	260	0.1	0.1	133.16	384.62	2	71	77	15	0.5	-6	67					6440	1.9
Dominican Republic	48,670	18,791	24,970	10.3	11.6	211.63	412.49	2.6	70	76	27	1.6	-3	67	0.026	45.68		29	5470	2.1
Ecuador	283,561	109,483	75,069	15.8	18.7	55.72	210.47	2.7	72	78	20	1.7	0	67		46.57		35	5170	2.2
El Salvador	21,041	8,124	15,670	6.3	6.7	299.42	402.04	2.2	67	77	8	1.2	-8	65		41.80			3590	1
French Guiana	88,150	34,034	121	0.2	0.3	2.27	1652.89	3.4	76	83	10	2.3	-1	76						
Grenada	344	133	110	0.1	0.1	290.70	909.09	2	70	75	5	0.8	-8	39					7220	2.5
Guadeloupe	1,690	652	210	0.4	0.4	236.69	1904.76	2.2	77	84	7.9	0.6	-6	98						

Appendix B: Area and Demographic Data for the World's States (Continued)

Country	Land Area sq. km.	Land Area sq. mi.	Arable Land in sq. km.	Population 2013 (millions)	Population 2025 (millions)	Total Fertility Rate (TFR)	Population Density Arithmetic	Population Density Physiologic	Life Expectancy Male (years)	Life Expectancy Female (years)	Infant Mortality per 1,000	Natural Increase (percent)	Net Migration per 1,000	Urban (percent)	Poverty Index	GINI Index	Human Development Index (HDI)	Corruption Index	GNI per Capita	CO_2 Emissions per Capita
Guatemala	108,889	42,042	44,290	15.4	20.3	3.9	141.43	347.71	68	75	25	2.6	-2	50		52.35		29	3120	0.8
Guyana	214,969	83,000	16,780	0.8	0.8	2.6	3.72	47.68	63	69	29	1.4	-8	28	0.031			27	3410	2.2
Haiti	27,750	10,714	17,700	10.4	12.5	3.5	374.77	587.57	61	64	59	1.7	-4	53	0.242			19	760	0.2
Honduras	112,090	43,278	32,350	8.6	10.8	2.9	76.72	265.84	71	76	24	2.2	-2	52	0.098	57.40		26	2120	1.1
Jamaica	10,991	4,244	4,490	2.7	2.9	2.1	245.56	601.34	71	76	22	0.8	-6	52					5130	2.6
Martinique	1,060	409	110	0.4	0.4	1.9	377.36	3636.36	79	85	9	0.4	-5	89						
Mexico	1,964,375	758,445	1,067,050	117.6	132.8	2.2	59.87	110.21	75	79	15	1.5	-2	78	0.024	48.07		34	9640	3.8
Nicaragua	130,370	50,336	50,710	6	7	2.6	46.02	118.32	71	77	18	1.9	-5	58	0.088	45.73		28	1650	0.8
Panama	75,420	29,120	22,650	3.9	4.6	2.6	51.71	172.19	74	80	15	1.5	1	75		51.90		35	8510	2.6
Paraguay	406,752	157,047	215,000	6.8	8.2	2.9	16.72	31.63	70	74	31	1.8	-1	62		48.01		24	3400	0.8
Peru	1,285,216	496,222	243,260	30.5	34.4	2.6	23.73	125.38	72	77	17	15	-3	75	0.043	45.33			6060	2
Puerto Rico	13,790	5,324	1,968	3.6	1.6	1.6	261.06	1829.27	76	83	7.7	0.3	-8	99					18000	
St. Lucia	616	238	106	0.2	0.2	2	324.68	1886.79	72	77	11	0.9	1	18					6890	2.3
St. Kitts-Nevis	261	101	60	0.1	0.1	1.8	383.14	1666.67	72	77	18	0.6	1	32					13610	4.8
St. Vincent and the Grenadines	389	150	100	0.1	0.1	2.2	257.07	1000.00	70	74	17	1.1	-9	49					6400	1.9
Suriname	163,820	63,251	830	0.6	0.6	2.3	3.66	722.89	67	74	19	1.1	-2	70	0.033			36	8680	4.5
Trinidad and Tobago	5,128	1,980	540	1.3	1.3	1.8	253.51	2407.41	68	74	25	0.6	-2	14	0.007				14710	38.2
Uruguay	176,215	68,037	152,590	3.4	3.5	2	19.29	22.28	73	80	8.9	0.4	-2	94		41.32		73	13580	2
Venezuela	912,050	352,143	216,000	29.7	34.4	2.4	32.56	137.50	72	78	11.6	1.7	0	89				20	12460	6.9
PACIFIC AND AUSTRALIA	8,560,172	3,305,083	4,190,526	38	45	2.4	4.44	9.07	75	79	20	1.1	6	66						
Australia	7,741,220	2,988,885	4,054,740	23.1	27.1	1.9	2.98	5.70	80	84	3.4	0.7	10	82				81	59260	16.9
Federated States of Micronesia	702	271	220	0.1	0.1	3.5	142.45	454.55	67	68	36	1.9	-15	22					3230	1
Fiji	18,274	7,056	4,250	0.9	0.9	2.6	49.25	211.76	67	72	26	1.2	-8	51		42.83			4110	1.5
French Polynesia	4,167	1,609	455	0.3	0.3	2.1	71.99	659.34	74	78	5.5	1.1	0	51						
Guam	544	210	180	0.2	0.2	2.9	367.65	1111.11	75	81	10.5	1.5	-10	93						
Kiribati	811	313	340	0.1	0.1	3.6	123.30	294.12	62	67	38	2	-1	54					2520	0.6
Marshall Islands	181	70	130	0.1	0.1	3.9	552.49	769.23	70	74	21	2.5	-18	65					4040	2
New Caledonia	18,575	7,172	1,840	0.3	0.3	2.2	16.15	163.04	74	81	5	1.2	4	58						
New Zeland	267,710	103,363	112,803	4.5	5	2	16.81	39.89	79	83	4.2	0.7	0	86				91	36900	7.2
Palau	459	177	50	0.02	0.02	2.2	43.57	400.00	66	72	20	0.6	0	77					9860	10.6
Papua New Guinea	462,840	178,703	11,900	7.2	9.1	4	15.56	605.04	61	66	45	2.1	0	13				25	1790	0.5
Samoa	2,831	1,093	350	0.2	0.2	4.5	70.65	571.43	72	74	21	2.2	-17	21					3260	0.9
Solomon Islands	28,896	11,157	1,070	0.6	0.8	4.6	20.76	560.75	66	69	40	2.7	0	20					1130	0.4
Tonga	747	288	310	0.1	0.1	3.9	133.87	322.58	70	75	19	2	-17	23					4220	1.5
Tuvalu	26	10	18	0.01	0.01	3.1	384.62	555.56	63	67	17	1.4	-9	47					5650	
Vanuatu	12,189	4,706	1,870	0.3	0.3	4	24.61	160.43	70	73	21	2.6	0	24	0.135				3000	0.5

Sources for Country Data Table

Data for population 2013, population 2025, total fertility rate, life expectancy–female, life expectancy–male, life expectancy, infant mortality rate, natural increase, net migration, and percent urban are from the Population Reference Bureau, 2013 World Population Data Sheet (http://www.prb.org/pdf13/2013-population-data-sheet_eng.pdf). Data for total land area are from the CIA World Factbook, 2014. Data for arable land, GINI Index, GNI per capita, and carbon dioxide emissions per capita are from World Bank, 2013 (http://data.worldbank.org/). Population density data are calculated by dividing total population by land area and arable land, for arithmetic and physiologic density, respectively. Data for poverty index are from Multidimensional Poverty Index, revised specifications are from the United Nations Development Program (http://hdr.undp.org/en/content/multidimensional-poverty-index-mpi). Data for corruption index are from Transparency International (http://www.transparency.org/cpi2013).

GLOSSARY

Absolute location The position or place of a certain item on the surface of the Earth as expressed in degrees, minutes, and seconds of **latitude**, 0° to 90° north or south of the equator, and **longitude**, 0° to 180° east or west of the **Prime Meridian** passing through Greenwich, England (a suburb of London).

Accessibility The degree of ease with which it is possible to reach a certain location from other locations. Accessibility varies from place to place and can be measured.

Acid rain A growing environmental peril whereby acidified rainwater severely damages plant and animal life; caused by the oxides of sulfur and nitrogen that are released into the atmosphere when coal, oil, and natural gas are burned, especially in major manufacturing zones.

Acropolis Literally "high point of the city." The upper fortified part of an ancient Greek city, usually devoted to religious purposes.

Activity (action) space The space within which daily activity occurs.

Agglomeration A process involving the clustering or concentrating of people or activities. The term often refers to manufacturing plants and businesses that benefit from close proximity because they share skilled-labor pools and technological and financial amenities.

Agora In ancient Greece, public spaces where citizens debated, lectured, judged one another, planned military campaigns, socialized, and traded.

Agribusiness General term for the businesses that provide the vast array of goods and services that support the agriculture industry.

Agricultural surplus One of two components, together with **social stratification**, that enable the formation of **cities**; agricultural production in excess of what the producer needs for his or her own sustenance and that of his or her family and that is then sold for consumption by others.

Agricultural village A relatively small, egalitarian village, where most of the population was involved in agriculture. Starting over 10,000 years ago, people began to cluster in agricultural villages as they stayed in one place to tend their crops.

Agriculture The purposeful tending of crops and livestock in order to produce food and fiber.

AIDS (Acquired Immune Deficiency Syndrome) Immune system disease caused by the Human Immunodeficiency Virus (HIV), which over a period of years weakens the capacity of the immune system to fight off infection so that weight loss and weakness set in and other afflictions such as cancer or pneumonia may hasten an infected person's demise.

Animal domestication Genetic modification of an animal such that it is rendered more amenable to human control.

Animistic religion The belief that inanimate objects, such as hills, trees, rocks, rivers, and other elements of the natural landscape, possess souls and can help or hinder human efforts on Earth.

Anthropocene geological epoch defined by atmospheric chemist Paul Crutzen to acknowledge the central role humans play in shaping the Earth's environment.

Aquifers Subterranean, porous, water-holding rocks that provide millions of wells with steady flows of water.

Arable Literally, cultivable; land fit for cultivation by one farming method or another.

Area A term that refers to a part of the Earth's surface with less specificity than **region**. For example, "urban area" alludes very generally to a place where urban development has taken place, whereas "urban region" requires certain specific criteria on which a delimitation is based (e.g., the spatial extent of commuting or the built townscape).

Arithmetic population density The population of a country or region expressed as an average per unit area. The figure is derived by dividing the population of the areal unit by the number of square kilometers or miles that make up the unit.

Assimilation The process through which people lose originally differentiating traits, such as dress, speech particularities or mannerisms, when they come into contact with another society or culture. Often used to describe immigrant adaptation to new places of residence.

Asylum Shelter and protection in one state for refugees from another state.

Atmosphere Blanket of gases surrounding the Earth and located some 350 miles above the Earth's surface.

Authenticity In the context of local cultures or customs, the accuracy with which a single stereotypical or typecast image or experience conveys an otherwise dynamic and complex local culture or its customs.

Backward reconstruction The tracking of **sound shifts** and hardening of consonants "backward" toward the original **language**.

Barrioization Defined by geographer James Curtis as the dramatic increase in Hispanic population in a given neighborhood; referring to *barrio*, the Spanish word for neighborhood.

Biodiversity The total variety of plant and animal species in a particular place; biological diversity.

Biotechnology Technology designed to manipulate seed varieties to increase crop yields.

Blockbusting Rapid change in the racial composition of residential blocks in American cities that occurs when real estate agents and others stir up fears of neighborhood decline after encouraging people of color to move to previously white neighborhoods. In the resulting outmigration, real estate agents profit through the turnover of properties.

Boundary Vertical plane between states that cuts through the rocks below, and the airspace above the surface.

Bracero Program A 1940s-era U.S. government program designed to encourage Mexicans to come to the United States to work as contract laborers.

Break-of-bulk point A **location** along a transport route where goods must be transferred from one carrier to another. In a port, the cargoes of oceangoing ships are unloaded and put on trains, trucks, or perhaps smaller riverboats for inland distribution.

Buddhism Religion founded in the sixth century BCE and characterized by the belief that enlightenment would come through knowledge, especially self-knowledge; elimination of greed, craving, and desire; complete honesty; and never hurting another person or animal. Buddhism splintered from **Hinduism** as a reaction to the strict social hierarchy maintained by Hinduism.

Cadastral map A large-scale map, usually created at the scale of 1:2500, depicting the value, extent, and ownership of land for purposes of taxation.

Capitalism Economic model wherein people, corporations, and **states** produce goods and exchange them on the world market, with the goal of achieving profit.

Cartography The art and science of making maps, including data compilation, layout, and design. Also concerned with the interpretation of mapped patterns.

Caste system The strict social segregation of people—specifically in India's Hindu society—on the basis of ancestry and occupation.

Census A periodic and official count of a country's population.

Central Business District (CBD) The downtown heart of a **central city**, the CBD is marked by high land values, a concentration of business and commerce, and the clustering of the tallest buildings.

Central city The urban area that is not suburban; generally, the older or original **city** that is surrounded by newer **suburbs**.

Central place Any point or place in the urban hierarchy, such as a town or city, having a certain economic reach or hinterland.

Central Place Theory Theory proposed by Walter Christaller that explains how and where **central places** in the **urban hierarchy** should be functionally and spatially distributed with respect to one another.

Centrality The strength of an urban center in its capacity to attract producers and consumers to its facilities; a city's "reach" into the surrounding region.

Centrifugal Forces that tend to divide a country—such as internal religious, linguistic, ethnic, or ideological differences.

Centripetal Forces that tend to unify a country—such as widespread commitment to a national culture, shared ideological objectives, and a common faith.

Chain migration Pattern of **migration** that develops when migrants move along and through kinship links (i.e. one migrant settles in a place and then writes, calls, or communicates through others to describe this place to family and friends who in turn then migrate there).

Child dependency ratio The number of people between the ages of 0 and 14 for every 100 people between the ages of 15-64.

Child mortality rate A figure that describes the number of children that die between the first and fifth years of their lives in a given population.

Chlorofluorocarbons (CFCs) Synthetic organic compounds first created in the 1950s and used primarily as refrigerants and as propellants. The role of CFCs in the destruction of the ozone layer led to the signing of an international agreement (the **Montreal Protocol**).

Christianity Religion based on the teachings of Jesus. According to Christian teaching, Jesus is the son of God, placed on Earth to teach people how to live according to God's plan.

Chronic (or degenerative) diseases Generally long-lasting afflictions now more common because of higher life expectancies.

City Conglomeration of people and buildings clustered together to serve as a center of politics, culture, and economics.

Climatic regions Areas of the world with similar climatic characteristics.

Cognate A word that has the same linguistic derivation as another word (i.e., the word comes from the same root as another word).

Colonialism Rule by an autonomous power over a subordinate and alien people and place. Although often established and maintained through political structures, colonialism also creates unequal cultural and economic relations. Because of the magnitude and impact of the European colonial project of the last few centuries, the term is generally understood to refer to that particular colonial endeavor.

Colonization Physical process whereby the colonizer takes over another place, putting its own government in charge and either moving its own people into the place or bringing in indentured outsiders to gain control of the people and the land.

Commercial agriculture Term used to describe large-scale farming and ranching operations that employ vast land bases, large mechanized equipment, factory-type labor forces, and the latest technology.

Commercialization The transformation of an area of a **city** into an area attractive to residents and tourists alike in terms of economic activity.

Commodification The process through which something is given monetary value. Commodification occurs when a good or idea that previously was not regarded as an object to be bought and sold is turned into something that has a particular price and that can be traded in a market economy.

Commodity chain Series of links connecting the many places of production and distribution and resulting in a commodity that is then exchanged on the world market.

Complementarity A condition that exists when two regions, through an exchange of raw materials and/or finished products, can specifically satisfy each other's demands.

Community-supported agriculture (CSA) Network between agricultural producers and consumers whereby consumers pledge support to a farming operation in order to receive a share of the output from the farming operation.

Concentric zone model A structural model of the American **central city** that suggests the existence of five concentric land-use rings arranged around a common center.

Confucianism A philosophy of ethics, education, and public service based on the writings of Confucius and traditionally thought of as one of the core elements of Chinese culture.

Connectivity Connectedness of a node in the world economy to other nodes along networks.

Conquest theory One major theory of how **Proto-Indo-European** diffused into Europe which holds that the early speakers of Proto-Indo-European spread westward on horseback, overpowering earlier inhabitants and beginning the **diffusion** and differentiation of Indo-European tongues.

Contagious diffusion The distance-controlled spreading of an idea, innovation, or some other item through a local population by contact from person to person—analogous to the communication of a contagious illness.

Context The geographical situation in which something occurs; the combination of what is happening at a variety of **scales** concurrently.

Core Processes that incorporate higher levels of education, higher salaries, and more technology; generate more wealth than **periphery** processes in the world-economy.

Core area In geography, a term with several connotations. Core refers to the center, heart, or focus. The core area of a **nation-state** is constituted by the national heartland—the largest population cluster, the most productive region, the area with greatest **centrality** and **accessibility**, probably containing the capital city as well.

Cottage industries Small-scale production of goods, typically by hand or with low technology In a home or small workshop.

Creole language A language that began as a **pidgin language** but was later adopted as the mother tongue by a people in place of the mother tongue.

Critical geopolitics Process by which geopoliticians deconstruct and focus on explaining the underlying spatial assumptions and territorial perspectives of politicians.

Crude Birth Rate (CBR) The number of live births yearly per thousand people in a population.

Crude Death Rate (CDR) The number of deaths yearly per thousand people in a population.

Cultural appropriation The process by which cultures adopt customs and knowledge from other cultures and use them for their own benefit.

Cultural barrier Prevailing cultural attitude rendering certain innovations, ideas or practices unacceptable or unadoptable in that particular **culture**.

Cultural complex A related set of **cultural traits**, such as prevailing dress codes and cooking and eating utensils.

Cultural diffusion The expansion and adoption of a cultural element, from its place of origin to a wider area.

Cultural ecology The multiple interactions and relationships between a culture and the natural environment.

Cultural hearth Heartland, source area, innovation center; place of origin of a major **culture**.

Cultural landscape The visible imprint of of human activity and culture on the landscape. The layers of buildings, forms, and artifacts sequentially imprinted on the landscape by the activities of various human occupants.

Cultural trait A single element of normal practice in a **culture**, such as the wearing of a turban.

Culture The sum total of the knowledge, attitudes, and habitual behavior patterns shared and transmitted by the members of a society. This is anthropologist Ralph Linton's definition; hundreds of others exist.

Custom Practice routinely followed by a group of people.

Cyclic movement Movement—for example, nomadic migration—that has a closed route and is repeated annually or seasonally.

Definition In political geography, the written legal description (in a treaty-like document) of a boundary between two countries or territories. See also **delimitation**.

Deforestation The clearing and destruction of forests to harvest wood for consumption, clear land for agricultural uses, and make way for expanding settlement frontiers.

Deglomeration The process of industrial deconcentration in response to technological advances and/or increasing costs due to congestion and competition.

Deindustrialization Process by which companies move industrial jobs to other regions with cheaper labor, leaving the newly deindustrialized region to switch to a service economy and to work through a period of high unemployment.

Delimitation In political geography, the translation of the written terms of a boundary treaty (the **definition**) into an official cartographic representation.

Demarcation In political geography, the actual placing of a political boundary on the landscape by means of barriers, fences, walls, or other markers.

Democracy Government based on the principle that the people are the ultimate sovereign and have the final say over what happens within the state.

Demographic transition Multistage model, based on Western Europe's experience, of changes in population growth exhibited by countries undergoing industrialization. High birth rates and death rates are followed by plunging death rates, producing a huge net population gain; this is followed by the convergence of birth rates and death rates at a low overall level.

Dependency theory A structuralist theory that offers a critique of the **modernization model** of development. Based on the idea that certain types of political and economic relations (especially **colonialism**) between countries and regions of the world have created arrangements that both control and limit the extent to which regions can develop.

Deportation The act of a government sending a migrant out of its country and back to the migrant's home country.

Desertification The encroachment of desert conditions on moister zones along the desert margins, where plant cover and soils are threatened by desiccation—through overuse, in part by humans and their domestic animals, and, possibly, in part because of inexorable shifts in the Earth's environmental zones.

Deterritorialization the movement of economic, social and cultural processes out of the hands of states.

Devolution The process whereby regions within a **state** demand and gain political strength and growing autonomy at the expense of the central government.

Dialect Local or regional characteristics of a **language**. While *accent* refers to the pronunciation differences of a standard language, a dialect, in addition to pronunciation variation, has distinctive grammar and vocabulary.

Dialect chains A set of contiguous dialects in which the dialects nearest to each other at any place in the chain are most closely related.

Diaspora From the Greek "to disperse," a term describing forceful or voluntary dispersal of a people from their homeland to a new place. Originally denoting the dispersal of Jews, it is increasingly applied to other population dispersals, such as the involuntary relocation of Black peoples during the slave trade or Chinese peoples outside of Mainland China, Taiwan and Hong Kong.

Diffusion The spatial spreading or dissemination of a culture element (such as a technological innovation) or some other phenomenon (e.g., a disease outbreak). See also **contagious, expansion, hierarchical, relocation**, and **stimulus diffusion**.

Diffusion routes The spatial trajectory through which **cultural traits** or other phenomena spread.

Digital divide The gap in access to telecommunications between developed and developing regions.

Disamenity sector The very poorest parts of **cities** that in extreme cases are not even connected to regular city services and are controlled by gangs or drug lords.

Distance Measurement of the physical space between two places.

Distance decay The effects of distance on interaction, generally the greater the distance the less interaction.

Dollarization When a poorer country ties the value of its currency to that of a wealthier country, or when it abandons its currency and adopts the wealthier country's currency as its own.

Dot map Maps where one dot represents a certain number of a phenomenon, such as a population.

Doubling time The time required for a population to double in size.

Dowry death In the context of arranged marriages in India, disputes over the price to be paid by the family of the bride to the father of the groom (the dowry) have, in some extreme cases, led to the death of the bride.

Eastern Orthodox Church One of three major branches of **Christianity**, the Eastern Orthodox Church, together with the **Roman Catholic Church**, a second of the three major branches of Christianity, arose out of the division of the Roman Empire by Emperor Diocletian into four governmental regions: two western regions centered in Rome, and two eastern regions centered in Constantinople (now Istanbul, Turkey). In 1054 CE, Christianity was divided along that same line when the Eastern Orthodox Church, centered in Constantinople; and the Roman Catholic Church, centered in Rome, split.

Economies of scale Increasing production of a good so that the average cost of the good declines.

Edge cities A term introduced by American journalist Joel Garreau in order to describe the shifting focus of **urbanization** in the United States away from the **Central Business District (CBD)** toward new loci of economic activity at the urban fringe. These cities are characterized by extensive amounts of office and retail space, few residential areas, and modern buildings (less than 30 years old).

Emigrant A person migrating away from a country or area; an out-migrant.

Emigration The act of a person leaving a country or area to settle elsewhere.

Endemic A disease that is particular to a locality or region. See also **pandemic**.

Environmental determinism The view that the natural environment has a controlling influence over various aspects of human life, including cultural development. Also referred to as environmentalism.

Environmental stress The threat to environmental security by human activity such as atmospheric and groundwater pollution, deforestation, oil spills, and ocean dumping.

Epidemic Regional outbreak of a disease.

Ethnic religion A religion that is particular to one, culturally distinct, group of people. Unlike **universalizing religions**, adherents of ethnic religions do not actively seek converts through evangelism or missionary work.

Ethnic neighborhood   Neighborhood, typically situated in a larger metropolitan city and constructed by or comprised of a **local culture**, in which a local culture can practice its customs.

Ethnicity   Affiliation or identity within a group of people bound by common ancestry and culture.

Eugenic population policies   Government policies designed to favor one racial sector over others.

Expansion diffusion   The spread of an innovation or an idea through a population in an area in such a way that the number of those influenced grows continuously larger, resulting in an expanding area of dissemination.

Expansive population policies   Government policies that encourage large families and raise the rate of population growth.

Export Processing Zones (EPZs)   Zones established by many countries in the **periphery** and **semi-periphery** where they offer favorable tax, regulatory, and trade arrangements to attract foreign trade and investment.

Extinct language   **Language** without any native speakers.

Extremism see **religious extremism**

Federal (state)   A political-territorial system wherein a central government represents the various entities within a **nation-state** where they have common interests—defense, foreign affairs, and the like—yet allows these various entities to retain their own identities and to have their own laws, policies, and customs in certain spheres.

Feng Shui   Literally "wind-water." The Chinese art and science of placement and orientation of tombs, dwellings, buildings, and cities. Structures and objects are positioned in an effort to channel flows of *sheng-chi* ("life-breath") in favorable ways.

Fertile Crescent   Crescent-shaped zone of productive lands extending from near the southeastern Mediterranean coast through Lebanon and Syria to the alluvial lowlands of Mesopotamia (in Iraq). Once more fertile than today, this is one of the world's great source areas of agricultural and other innovations.

Fieldwork   The study of phenomena by visiting places and observing how people interact with and thereby change those places.

First Agricultural Revolution   Dating back 10,000 years, the First Agricultural Revolution achieved **plant domestication** and **animal domestication**.

First mover advantage   The benefit first innovators or first in a market have over later entries.

First Urban Revolution   The innovation of the **city**, which occurred independently in five separate **hearths**.

Five themes (of geography)   Developed by the **Geography Educational National Implementation Project (GENIP)**, the five themes of geography are **location, human-environment, region, place**, and **movement**.

Flexible production system   a system of industrial production characterized by a set of processes in which the components of goods are made in different places around the globe and then brought together as needed to meet consumer demand.

Folk culture   **Cultural traits** such as dress modes, dwellings, traditions, and institutions of usually small, **traditional** communities.

Folk-housing region   A region in which the housing stock predominantly reflects styles of building that are particular to the culture of the people who have long inhabited the area.

Food desert   An area characterized by a lack of affordable, fresh and nutritious food.

Forced migration   Human **migration** flows in which the movers have no choice but to relocate.

Fordist   A highly organized and specialized system for organizing industrial production and labor. Named after automobile producer Henry Ford, Fordist production features assembly-line production of standardized components for mass consumption.

Formal economy   The legal economy that is taxed and monitored by a government and is included in a government's **Gross National Product (GNP)**; as opposed to an **informal economy**.

Formal region   A type of **region** marked by a certain degree of homogeneity in one or more phenomena; also called uniform region or homogeneous region.

Forum   The focal point of ancient Roman life combining the functions of the ancient Greek *acropolis* and *agora*.

Friction of distance   The increase in time and cost that usually comes with increasing **distance**.

Functional region   A **region** defined by the particular set of activities or interactions that occur within it.

Functional zonation   The division of a **city** into different regions or **zones** (e.g. residential or industrial) for certain purposes or functions (e.g. housing or manufacturing).

Fundamentalism   see **religious fundamentalism**

Galactic city   A modern city in which the old downtown plays the role of a festival or recreational area, and widely dispersed industrial parks, shopping centers, high-tech industrial spaces, edge-city downtowns, and industrial suburbs are the new centers of economic activity.

Gated communities   Restricted neighborhoods or subdivisions, often literally fenced in, where entry is limited to residents and their guests. Although predominantly high-income based, in North America gated communities are increasingly a middle-class phenomenon.

Gatekeepers   People or corporations who control access to information.

Gender   Social differences between men and women, rather than the anatomical, biological differences between the sexes. Notions of gender differences—that is, what is considered "feminine" or "masculine"—vary greatly over time and space.

Gendered   In terms of a place, whether the place is designed for or claimed by men or women.

Genetic or inherited diseases   Diseases caused by variation or mutation of a gene or group of genes in a human.

Genetically modified organisms (GMOs)   Crops that carry new traits that have been inserted through advanced genetic engineering methods.

Gentrification   The rehabilitation of deteriorated, often abandoned, housing of low-income inner-city residents.

Geocaching   A hunt for a cache, the **Global Positioning System (GPS)** coordinates which are placed on the Internet by other geocachers.

Geographic concept   Ways of seeing the world spatially that are used by geographers in answering research questions.

Geographic Information System (GIS)   A collection of computer hardware and software that permits spatial data to be collected, recorded, stored, retrieved, manipulated, analyzed, and displayed to the user.

Geography   From the Greek meaning "to write about the Earth." As a modern academic discipline, geography is concerned with the analysis of the physical and human characteristics of the Earth's surface from a **spatial** perspective. "Why are things located where they are?" and "What does it mean for things to be located in particular places?" are central questions that geographical scholarship seeks to answer.

Geography Educational National Implementation Project (GENIP)   Joint effort undertaken in the 1980s by the American Geographical Society, the Association of American Geographers, the National Council for Geographic Education and the National Geographic Society designed to bring together the many subfields of human geography and to explain to nongeographers the discipline of geography; developed the **five themes** of geography: **location, human-environment, region, place**, and **movement**.

Geometric boundary   Political boundary **defined** and **delimited** (and occasionally **demarcated**) as a straight line or an arc.

Germanic languages   Languages (English, German, Danish, Norwegian, and Swedish) that reflect the expansion of peoples out of Northern Europe to the west and south.

Gerrymandering   Redistricting for advantage, or the practice of dividing areas into electoral districts to give one political party an electoral majority in a large number of districts while concentrating the voting strength of the opposition in as few districts as possible.

Glaciation   A period of global cooling during which continental ice sheets and mountain glaciers expand.

Global division of labor   Phenomenon whereby corporations and others can draw from labor markets around the world, made possible by the compression of time and space through innovation in communication and transportation systems.

Global language   The **language** used most commonly around the world; defined on the basis of either the number of speakers of the language, or prevalence of use in commerce and trade.

Global-local continuum   The notion that what happens at the global scale has a direct effect on what happens at the local scale, and vice versa. This idea posits that the world is comprised of an interconnected series of relationships that extend across space.

Global positioning system (GPS)   Satellite-based system for determining the **absolute location** of **places** or geographic features.

Global scale   Interactions occurring at the scale of the world, in a global setting.

Global warming   Theory that the Earth is gradually warming as a result of an enhanced **greenhouse effect** in the Earth's **atmosphere** caused by ever-increasing amounts of carbon dioxide produced by various human activities.

Globalization   The expansion of economic, political, and cultural processes to the point that they become global in scale and impact. The processes of globalization transcend state boundaries and have outcomes that vary across places and scales.

Glocalization   The process by which people in a local place mediate and alter regional, national, and global processes.

Gondwana   The southern portion of the primeval supercontinent, Pangaea.

Gravity model   A mathematical prediction of the interaction of places, the interaction being a function of population size of the respective places and the distance between them.

Green Revolution   The recently successful development of higher-yield, fast-growing varieties of rice and other cereals in certain developing countries, which led to increased production per unit area and a dramatic narrowing of the gap between population growth and food needs.

Greenhouse effect   The widely used analogy describing the blanket-like effect of the atmosphere in the heating of the Earth's surface; shortwave insolation passes through the "glass" of the atmospheric "greenhouse," heats the surface, is converted to long-wave radiation that cannot penetrate the "glass," and thereby results in trapping heat, which raises the temperature inside the "greenhouse."

Griffin-Ford model   Developed by geographers Ernst Griffin and Larry Ford, a model of the Latin American city showing a blend of traditional elements of Latin American culture with the forces of globalization that are reshaping the urban scene.

Gross Domestic Product (GDP)   The total value of all goods and services produced within a country during a given year.

Gross National Income (GNI)   The total value of what is produced in a country in addition to the income received from investments outside of the country and minus payments to other countries around the world.

Gross National Product (GNP)   The total value of all goods and services produced by a country's economy in a given year. It includes all goods and services produced by corporations and individuals of a country, whether or not they are located within the country.

Guest worker   Legal **immigrant** who has a work visa, usually short term.

Hajj   The Muslim **pilgrimage** to Mecca, the birthplace of Muhammad.

Hearth   The area where an idea or cultural trait originates.

Heartland theory   A geopolitical hypothesis, proposed by British geographer Halford Mackinder during the first two decades of the twentieth century, that any political power based in the heart of Eurasia could gain sufficient strength to eventually dominate the world. Mackinder further proposed that since Eastern Europe controlled access to the Eurasian interior, its ruler would command the vast "heartland" to the east.

Hierarchical diffusion   A form of **diffusion** in which an idea or innovation spreads by passing first among the most connected places or peoples. An **urban hierarchy** is usually involved, encouraging the leapfrogging of innovations over wide areas, with geographic distance a less important influence.

High-technology corridors   Areas along or near major transportation arteries that are devoted to the research, development, and sale of high-technology products. These areas develop because of the networking and synergistic advantages of concentrating high-technology enterprises in close proximity to one another. "Silicon Valley" is a prime example of a high-technology corridor in the United States.

Hinduism   One of the oldest **religions** in the modern world, dating back over 4000 years, and originating in the Indus River Valley of what is today part of Pakistan. Hinduism is unique among the world's religions in that it does not have a single founder, a single theology, or agreement on its origins.

Hinterland   An area of economic production that is located inland and is connected to the world by a port.

Holocene   The current **interglaciation** period, extending from 10,000 years ago to the present on the geologic time scale.

Homo sapiens   The only living species of the genus *Homo*; modern humans.

Horizontal integration   Ownership by the same firm of a number of companies that exist at the same point on a **commodity chain**.

Huang He (Yellow) and Wei (Yangtzi) River Valleys   Rivers in present-day China; it was at the confluence of the Huang He and Wei Rivers where chronologically the fourth urban **hearth** was established around 1500 BCE.

Human-environment   The second theme of geography as defined by the **Geography Educational National Implementation Project**; reciprocal relationship between humans and environment.

Human geography   One of the two major divisions of **geography**; the spatial analysis of human population, its cultures, activities, and landscapes.

Human territoriality   A term associated with the work of Robert Sack that describes the efforts of human societies to influence events and achieve social goals by exerting, and attempting to enforce, control over specific geographical areas.

Human trafficking   A form of **forced migration** in which organized criminal elements move people illegally from one place to another, typically either to work as involuntary laborers or to participate in the commercial sex trade.

Hydrologic cycle   The system of exchange involving water in its various forms as it continually circulates among the atmosphere, the oceans, and above and below the land surface.

Identifying against   Constructing an **identity** by first defining the "other" and then defining ourselves as "not the other."

Identity   Defined by geographer Gillian Rose as "how we make sense of ourselves;" how people see themselves at different scales.

Imam   The political head of the Muslim community or the person who leads prayer services. In **Shiite** Islam the Imam is immune from sin or error.

Immigrant   A person migrating into a particular country or area; an in-migrant.

Immigration   The act of a person migrating into a new country or area.

Immigration laws   Laws and regulations of a state designed specifically to control immigration into that **state**.

Immigration wave   Phenomenon whereby different patterns of **chain migration** build upon one another to create a swell in **migration** from one origin to the same destination.

Independent invention   The term for a trait with many **cultural hearths** that developed independent of each other.

Indigenous religions   Belief systems and philosophies practiced and traditionally passed from generation to generation among peoples within an indigenous tribe or group.

Indus River Valley   Chronologically, the third urban **hearth**, dating to 2200 BCE.

Industrial Revolution   The term applied to the social and economic changes in agriculture, commerce and manufacturing that resulted from technological innovations and specialization in late-eighteenth-century Europe.

Infant Mortality Rate (IMR)   A figure that describes the number of babies that die within the first year of their lives in a given population.

Infectious diseases   Diseases that are spread by bacteria, viruses, or parasites. Infectious diseases diffuse directly or indirectly from human to human.

Informal economy   Economic activity that is neither taxed nor monitored by a government and is not included in that government's **Gross National Product (GNP)**; as opposed to a formal economy.

Interface areas   Places where neighborhoods associated with different religions meet.

Interfaith boundaries   Boundaries between the world's major faiths.

Interglacials   Warm periods during an ice age.

Interglaciation   Sustained warming phase between glaciations during an ice age.

Intermodal (connections)   Places where two or more modes of transportation meet (including air, road, rail, barge, and ship).

Internal migration   Human movement within a **nation-state**, such as ongoing westward and southward movements in the United States.

Internal displaced persons   People who have been displaced within their own countries and do not cross international borders as they flee.

International migration   Human movement involving movement across international boundaries.

Intervening opportunity   The presence of a nearer opportunity that greatly diminishes the attractiveness of sites farther away.

Intrafaith boundaries   Boundaries within a single major faith.

Islam   The youngest of the major world **religions**, Islam is based on the teachings of Muhammad, born in Mecca in 571 CE. According to Islamic teaching, Muhammad received the truth directly from Allah in a series of revelations during which Muhammad spoke the verses of the *Qu'ran* (*Koran*), the Islamic holy book.

Island of development   Place built up by a government or corporation to attract foreign investment and which has relatively high concentrations of paying jobs and infrastructure.

Isogloss   A geographic **boundary** within which a particular linguistic feature occurs.

Isotherm   Line on a map connecting points of equal temperature values.

Jihad   A doctrine within **Islam**. Commonly translated as "Holy War," jihad represents either a personal or collective struggle on the part of Muslims to live up to the religious standards set by the *Qu'ran*.

Judaism   Religion with its roots in the teachings of Abraham (from Ur), who is credited with uniting his people to worship only one god. According to Jewish teaching, Abraham and God have a covenant in which the Jews agree to worship only one God, and God agrees to protect his chosen people, the Jews.

Just-in-time delivery   Method of inventory management made possible by efficient transportation and communication systems, whereby companies keep on hand just what they need for near-term production, planning that what they need for longer-term production will arrive when needed.

Kinship links   Types of **push factors** or **pull factors** that influence a migrant's decision to go where family or friends have already found success.

Köppen climate classification system   Developed by Wladimir Köppen, a system for classifying the world's climates on the basis of temperature and precipitation.

Landscape   The overall appearance of an area. Most landscapes are comprised of a combination of natural and human-induced influences.

Language   A set of sounds, combination of sounds, and symbols that are used for communication.

Language convergence   The collapsing of two **languages** into one resulting from the consistent **spatial interaction** of peoples with different languages; the opposite of **language divergence**.

Language divergence   The opposite of **language convergence**; a process suggested by German linguist August Schleicher whereby new **languages** are formed when a language breaks into dialects due to a lack of **spatial interaction** among speakers of the language and continued isolation eventually causes the division of the language into discrete new languages.

Language family   Group of **languages** with a shared but fairly distant origin.

Latitude   An imaginary line running parallel to the equator that is used to measure distance in degrees north or south from the equator.

Laws of migration   Developed by British demographer Ernst Ravenstein, five laws that predict the flow of migrants.

Leadership class   Group of decision-makers and organizers in early **cities** who controlled the resources, and often the lives, of others.

Least Cost Theory   Model developed by Alfred Weber according to which the location of manufacturing establishments is determined by the minimization of three critical expenses: labor, transportation, and **agglomeration**.

Life expectancy   A figure indicating how long, on average, a person may be expected to live. Normally expressed in the context of a particular state.

Lingua franca   A term deriving from "Frankish language" and applying to a tongue spoken in ancient Mediterranean ports that consisted of a mixture of Italian, French, Greek, Spanish, and even some Arabic. Today it refers to a "common language," a language used among speakers of different languages for the purposes of trade and commerce.

Little Ice Age   Temporary but significant cooling period between the fourteenth and the nineteenth centuries; accompanied by wide temperature fluctuations, droughts, and storms, causing famines and dislocation.

Livestock ranching   The raising of domesticated animals for the production of meat and other byproducts such as leather and wool.

Local culture   Group of people in a particular **place** who see themselves as a collective or a community, who share experiences, customs, and traits, and who work to preserve those traits and customs in order to claim uniqueness and to distinguish themselves from others.

Local Exchange Trading System (LETS)   A barter system whereby a local currency is created through which members trade services or goods in a local **network** separated from the **formal economy**.

Location   The first theme of geography as defined by the **Geography Educational National Implementation Project**; the geographical **situation** of people and things.

Location theory   A logical attempt to explain the locational pattern of an economic activity and the manner in which its producing areas are interrelated. The agricultural location theory contained in the **von Thünen** model is a leading example.

Locational interdependence   Theory developed by economist Harold Hotelling that suggests competitors, in trying to maximize sales, will seek to constrain each other's territory as much as possible, which will therefore lead them to locate adjacent to one another in the middle of their collective customer base.

Longitude   An imaginary line circling the Earth and running through the poles. Used to determine the location of things by measurement of the angular distance, in degrees east or west, from the **Prime Meridian**.

Long-lot survey system Distinct regional approach to land surveying found in the Canadian Maritimes, parts of Quebec, Louisiana, and Texas whereby land is divided into narrow parcels stretching back from rivers, roads, or canals.

Luxury crops Non-subsistence crops such as tea, cacao, coffee, and tobacco.

Majority-minority districts In the context of determining representative districts, the process by which a majority of the population is from the minority.

Malaria Vectored disease spread by mosquitoes that carry the malaria parasite in their saliva and which kills approximately 150,000 children in the global **periphery** each month.

Manufacturing export zones A feature of economic development in peripheral countries whereby the host country establishes areas with favorable tax, regulatory, and trade arrangements in order to attract foreign manufacturing operations. The goods manufactured in these export zones are primarily destined for the global market.

Maquiladora The term given to zones in northern Mexico with factories supplying manufactured goods to the U.S. market. The low-wage workers in the primarily foreign-owned factories assemble imported components and/or raw materials and then export finished goods.

Mass extinctions Mass destruction of most species.

Material culture The art, housing, clothing, sports, dances, foods, and other similar items constructed or created by a group of people.

McGee model Developed by geographer T.G. McGee, a model showing similar land-use patterns among the medium-sized cities of Southeast Asia.

McMansions Homes referred to as such because of their "super size" and similarity in appearance to other such homes; homes often built in place of **tear-downs** in American suburbs.

Medical geography The study of health and disease within a geographic context and from a geographical perspective. Among other things, medical geography looks at sources, diffusion routes, and distributions of diseases.

Mediterranean agriculture Specialized farming that occurs only in areas where the dry-summer Mediterranean climate prevails.

Megacities cities with 10 million or more residents.

Megalopolis Term used to designate large coalescing supercities that are forming in diverse parts of the world; formerly used specifically with an uppercase "M" to refer to the Boston—Washington multimetropolitan corridor on the northeastern seaboard of the United States, but now used generically with a lower-case "m" as a synonym for conurbation.

Mental map Image or picture of the way space is organized as determined by an individual's perception, impression, and knowledge of that space.

Mercantilism In a general sense, associated with the promotion of commercialism and trade. More specifically, a protectionist policy of European **states** during the sixteenth to the eighteenth centuries that promoted a state's economic position in the contest with other countries. The acquisition of gold and silver and the maintenance of a favorable trade balance (more exports than imports) were central to the policy.

Mesoamerica Chronologically the fifth urban hearth, dating to 200 BCE.

Mesopotamia Region of great cities (e.g. Ur and Babylon) located between the Tigris and Euphrates Rivers; chronologically the first urban **hearth**, dating to 3500 BCE, and founded in the **Fertile Crescent**.

Metes and bounds system A system of land surveying east of the Appalachian Mountains. It is a system that relies on descriptions of land ownership and natural features such as streams or trees. Because of the imprecise nature of metes and bounds surveying, the U.S. Land Office Survey abandoned the technique in favor of the **rectangular survey system**.

Microcredit program Program that provides small loans to poor people, especially women, to encourage development of small businesses.

Migration A change in residence intended to be permanent. See also **chain, forced, internal, international, step**, and **voluntary migration**.

Millennium Development Goals A set of markers outlined by the United Nations with the aim of improving quality of life and the economy in developing countries.

Minaret Tower attached to a Muslim mosque, having one or more projecting balconies from which a crier calls Muslims to prayer.

Modernization model A model of economic development most closely associated with the work of economist Walter Rostow. The modernization model (sometimes referred to as modernization theory) maintains that all countries go through five interrelated stages of development, which culminate in an economic state of self-sustained economic growth and high levels of mass consumption.

Monoculture Dependence on a single agricultural commodity.

Monolingual states Countries in which only one **language** is spoken.

Monotheistic religion Belief system in which one supreme being is revered as creator and arbiter of all that exists in the universe.

Montreal Protocol An international agreement signed in 1987 by 105 countries and the European Community (now European Union). The protocol called for a reduction in the production and consumption of chlorofluorocarbons (CFCs) of 50 percent by 2000. Subsequent meetings in London (1990) and Copenhagen (1992) accelerated the timing of CFC phaseout, and a worldwide complete ban has been in effect since 1996.

Movement The fifth theme of geography as defined by the **Geography Educational National Implementation Project**: the mobility of people, goods and ideas across the surface of the planet

Multilingual states Countries in which more than one **language** is spoken.

Multinational state **State** with more than one nation within its borders.

Multiple nuclei model A structural model of the American city that suggests a decline in significance of the **central business district** and the concomitant rise in significance of regions within metropolitan areas with their own nuclei.

Multistate nation Nation that stretches across borders and across states.

Mutual intelligibility The ability of two people to understand each other when speaking.

Nation Legally, a term encompassing all the citizens of a state. Most definitions now tend to refer to a tightly knit group of people possessing bonds of language, ethnicity, religion, and other shared cultural attributes. Such homogeneity actually prevails within very few states.

Nation-state Theoretically, a recognized member of the modern state system possessing formal **sovereignty** and occupied by a people who see themselves as a single, united **nation**. Most nations and states aspire to this form, though it is realized almost nowhere. Nonetheless, in common parlance, nation-state is used as a synonym for country or state.

Natural increase Population growth measured as the excess of live births over deaths. Natural increase of a population does not reflect either **emigrant** or **immigrant** movements.

Natural resource Any valued element of (or means to an end using) the environment; includes minerals, water, vegetation, and soil.

Neocolonialism The entrenchment of the colonial order, such as trade and investment, under a new guise. See also **postcolonialism**.

Neoliberalism Policies based on the economic theory that government should not intervene in markets.

Neolocalism The seeking out of the regional culture and reinvigoration of it in response to the uncertainty of the modern world.

Networks Defined by Manuel Castells as a set of interconnected nodes without a center.

Newborn mortality rate The number of infants who die within the first month of life per 1,000 live births.

New urbanism Outlined by a group of architects, urban planners, and developers from over 20 countries, an urban design that calls for development, urban revitalization, and suburban reforms that create walkable neighborhoods with a diversity of housing and jobs.

Newly industrializing countries States that underwent industrialization after World War II and whose economies have grown at a rapid pace.

Nile River Valley Chronologically the second urban **hearth**, dating to 3200 BCE.

Node Connection point in a network, where goods and ideas flow in, out, and through the network.

Nomadism Movement among a definite set of places—often **cyclic movement**.

Nongovernmental organizations (NGOs) International organizations that operate outside of the formal political arena but that are nevertheless influential in spearheading international initiatives on social, economic, and environmental issues.

Non-material culture The beliefs, practices, aesthics, and values of a group of people.

Nonrenewable resources Resources that are present in finite quantities because they are not self-replenishing or take an extraordinarily long time to replenish.

North American Free Trade Agreement (NAFTA) Agreement entered into by Canada, Mexico, and the United States in December, 1992 and taking effect on January 1, 1994, to eliminate the barriers to trade in, and facilitate the cross-border movement of goods and services between the countries.

Official language In multilingual countries the **language** selected, often by the educated and politically powerful elite, to promote internal cohesion; usually the language of the courts and government.

Offshore With reference to production, to **outsource** to a third party located outside of the country.

Old age dependency ratio The number of people 65 years of age for every 100 people between the ages of 15-64.

One-child policy A program established by the Chinese government in 1979 to slow population growth in China.

Opinion leaders People in social networks who have millions of followers and help diffuse new ideas and products hierarchically.

Organic agriculture Approach to farming and ranching that avoids the use of herbicides, pesticides, growth hormones, and other similar synthetic inputs.

Outsource With reference to production, to turn over in part or in total to a third party.

Oxygen cycle Cycle whereby natural processes and human activity consume atmospheric oxygen and produce carbon dioxide and the Earth's forests and other flora, through **photosynthesis**, consume carbon dioxide and produce oxygen.

Ozone layer The layer in the upper atmosphere located between 30 and 45 kilometers above the Earth's surface where stratospheric ozone is most densely concentrated. The ozone layer acts as a filter for the Sun's harmful ultraviolet rays.

Pacific Ring of Fire Ocean-girdling zone of crustal instability, volcanism, and earthquakes resulting from the tectonic activity along plate boundaries in the region.

Pandemic An outbreak of a disease that spreads worldwide. See also **endemic**.

Pangaea The primeval supercontinent, hypothesized by Alfred Wegener, that broke apart and formed the continents and oceans as we know them today; consisted of two parts—a northern Laurasia and a southern **Gondwana**.

Participatory development The notion that locals should be engaged in deciding what development means for them and how it should be achieved.

Pastoralist Person involved in a form of agricultural activity that involves the raising of livestock. Many peoples described as herders actually pursue mixed agriculture, in that they may also fish, hunt, or even grow a few crops. But pastoral peoples' lives revolve around their animals.

Pattern The design of a **spatial distribution** (e.g. scattered or concentrated).

Peace of Westphalia Peace negotiated in 1648 to end the Thirty Years' War, Europe's most destructive internal struggle over religion. The treaties contained new language recognizing statehood and nationhood, clearly defined borders, and guarantees of security.

Per capita GNI The **Gross National Income (GNI)** of a given country divided by its population.

Perception of place Belief or "understanding" about a place developed through books, movies, stories or pictures.

Perceptual region A **region** that only exists as a conceptualization or an idea and not as a physically demarcated entity. For example, in the United States, "the South" and "the Mid-Atlantic region" are perceptual regions.

Periphery Processes that incorporate lower levels of education, lower salaries, and less technology; and generate less wealth than core processes in the world-economy.

Periodic Movement Movement—for example, college attendence or military service—that involves temporary, recurrent relocation.

Photosynthesis The formation of carbohydrates in living plants from water and carbon dioxide, through the action of sunlight on chlorophyll in those plants, including algae.

Physical geography One of the two major divisions of systematic geography; the spatial analysis of the structure, processes, and location of the Earth's natural phenomena such as climate, soil, plants, animals, and topography.

Physical-political (natural-political) boundary Political boundary **defined** and **delimited** (and occasionally **demarcated**) by a prominent physical feature in the natural landscape—such as a river or the crest ridges of a mountain range.

Physiologic population density The number of people per unit area of **arable** land.

Pidgin language When parts of two or more languages are combined in a simplified structure and vocabulary.

Pilgrimage Voluntary travel by an adherent to a **sacred site** to pay respects or participate in a ritual at the site.

Place The fourth theme of geography as defined by the **Geography Educational National Implementation Project**: uniqueness of a **location**.

Placelessness Defined by geographer Edward Relph as the loss of uniqueness of **place** in the **cultural landscape** so that one place looks like the next.

Plant domestication Genetic modification of a plant such that its reproductive success depends on human intervention.

Plantation agriculture Production system based on a large estate owned by an individual, family, or corporation and organized to produce a cash crop. Almost all plantations were established within the tropics; in recent decades, many have been divided into smaller holdings or reorganized as cooperatives.

Pleistocene The most recent epoch of the Late Cenozoic Ice Age, beginning about 1.8 million years ago and marked by as many as **20 glaciations and interglaciations** of which the current warm phase, the Holocene epoch, has witnessed the rise of human civilization.

Political ecology An approach to studying nature-society relations that is concerned with the ways in which environmental issues both reflect, and are the result of, the political and socioeconomic contexts in which they are situated.

Political geography A subdivision of **human geography** focused on the nature and implications of the evolving spatial organization of political governance and formal political practice on the Earth's surface. It is concerned with why political spaces emerge in the places that they do and with how the character of those spaces affects social, political, economic, and environmental understandings and practices.

Polytheistic religion Belief system in which multiple deities are revered as creators and arbiters of all that exists in the universe.

Popular culture Cultural traits such as dress, diet, and music that identify and are part of today's changeable, urban-based, media-influenced western societies.

Population composition   Structure of a population in terms of age, sex and other properties such as marital status and education.

Population density   A measurement of the number of people per given unit of land.

Population distribution   Description of locations on the Earth's surface where populations live.

Population explosion   The rapid growth of the world's human population during the past century, attended by ever-shorter **doubling times** and accelerating rates of increase.

Population pyramids   Visual representations of the age and sex composition of a population whereby the percentage of each age group (generally five-year increments) is represented by a horizontal bar the length of which represents its relationship to the total population. The males in each age group are represented to the left of the center line of each horizontal bar; the females in each age group are represented to the right of the center line.

Possibilism   Geographic viewpoint—a response to determinism—that holds that human decision making, not the environment, is the crucial factor in cultural development. Nonetheless, possibilists view the environment as providing a set of broad constraints that limits the possibilities of human choice.

Post-Fordist   World economic system characterized by a more flexible set of production practices in which goods are not mass-produced; instead, production has been accelerated and dispersed around the globe by multinational companies that shift production, outsourcing it around the world and bringing places closer together in time and space than would have been imaginable at the beginning of the twentieth century.

Postcolonialism   A recent intellectual movement concerned with examining the enduring impacts of **colonialism**, not just in economic and political relations (the focus of **neocolonialism**), but especially in cultural terms. Postcolonial studies examine the ways in which basic concepts of culture and forms of cultural interaction continue to be shaped by the hegemonic ideas and practices of colonialism.

Primary economic activity   Economic activity concerned with the direct extraction of **natural resources** from the environment—such as mining, fishing, lumbering, and especially **agriculture**.

Primary industrial regions   Western and Central Europe; Eastern North America; Russia and Ukraine; and Eastern Asia, each of which consists of one or more core areas of industrial development with subsidiary clusters.

Primate city   A country's largest city—ranking atop the **urban hierarchy**—most expressive of the national culture and usually (but not always) the capital city as well.

Prime Meridian   An imaginary north-south line of **longitude** on the Earth grid, passing through the Royal Observatory at Greenwich in London, defined as having a longitude of 0°.

Primogeniture   System which the eldest son in a family—or, in exceptional cases, daughter—inherits all of a dying parent's land.

Product life cycle   The introduction, growth, maturation and decline of a product.

Protestant   One of three major branches of **Christianity** (together with the **Eastern Orthodox Church** and the **Roman Catholic Church**). Following the widespread societal changes in Europe starting in the 1300s CE, many adherents of the Roman Catholic Church began to question the role of religion in their lives and opened the door to the Protestant Reformation wherein John Huss, Martin Luther, John Calvin, and others challenged many of the fundamental teachings of the Roman Catholic Church.

Proto-Eurasiatic   Linguistic hypothesis proposing the existence of a language or group of languages that predated, and gave rise to, **Proto-Indo-European** and other language families with Eurasian origins.

Proto-Indo-European (language)   Linguistic hypothesis proposing the existence of an ancestral Indo-European **language** that is the **hearth** of the ancient Latin, Greek, and Sanskrit languages; this hearth would link modern languages from Scandinavia to North Africa and from North America through parts of Asia to Australia.

Pull factor   Positive conditions and perceptions that effectively attract people to new locales from other areas.

Push factor   Negative conditions and perceptions that induce people to leave their abode and migrate to a new locale.

Quaternary economic activity   Service sector industries concerned with the collection, processing, and manipulation of information and capital. Examples include finance, administration, insurance, and legal services.

Queer theory   Theory defined by geographers Glen Elder, Lawrence Knopp, and Heidi Nast that highlights the contextual nature of opposition to the heteronormative and focuses on the political engagement of "queers" with the heteronormative.

Quinary economic activity   Service sector industries that require a high level of specialized knowledge or technical skill. Examples include scientific research and high-level management.

Race   A categorization of humans based on skin color and other physical characteristics. Racial categories are social and political constructions because they are based on ideas that some biological differences (especially skin color) are more important than others (e.g., height, etc.), even though the latter might have more significance in terms of human activity. With its roots in sixteenth-century England, the term is closely associated with European **colonialism** because of the impact of that development on global understandings of racial differences.

Racism   Frequently referred to as a system or attitude toward visible differences in individuals, racism is an ideology of difference that ascribes (predominantly negative) significance and meaning to culturally, socially, and politically constructed ideas based on phenotypical features.

Radioactive waste   Hazardous-waste-emitting radiation from nuclear power plants, nuclear weapons factories, and nuclear equipment in hospitals and industry.

Rank-size rule   In a model urban hierarchy, the idea that the population of a **city** or town will be inversely proportional to its rank in the hierarchy.

Rare earth elements   Seventeen chemical elements that commonly occur together but are difficult to separate. They are commonly used to make high tech electronics and weapons systems.

Reapportionment   Process by which representative districts are switched according to population shifts, so that each district encompasses approximately the same number of people.

Rectangular survey system   Also called the Public Land Survey, the system was used by the U.S. Land Office Survey to parcel land west of the Appalachian Mountains. The system divides land into a series of rectangular parcels.

Redlining   A discriminatory real estate practice in North America in which members of minority groups are prevented from obtaining money to purchase homes or property in predominantly white neighborhoods. The practice derived its name from the red lines depicted on **cadastral maps** used by real estate agents and developers. Today, redlining is officially illegal.

Reference maps   Maps that show the absolute location of places and geographic features determined by a frame of reference, typically latitude and longitude.

Refugees   People who have fled their country because of political persecution and seek asylum in another country.

Refugee camps   Temporary settlements set up to accommodate people who flee their homelands in the face of civil unrest, oppression, or warfare.

Region   The third theme of geography as defined by the **Geography Educational National Implementation Project**: an **area** on the Earth's surface marked by a degree of formal, functional, or perceptual homogeneity of some phenomenon.

Regional scale   Interactions occurring within a **region**, in a regional setting.

Relative location   The regional position or **situation** of a place relative to the position of other places. Distance, **accessibility**, and connectivity affect relative location.

Religion   Defined by geographers Robert Stoddard and Carolyn Prorak in the book *Geography in America* as "a system of beliefs and practices that attempts to order life in terms of culturally perceived ultimate priorities."

Religious extremism   **Religious fundamentalism** carried to the point of violence.

Religious fundamentalism   Religious movement whose objectives are to return to the foundations of the faith and to influence state policy.

Relocation diffusion   Sequential **diffusion** process in which the items being diffused are transmitted by their carrier agents as they evacuate the old areas and relocate to new ones. The most common form of relocation diffusion involves the spreading of innovations by a migrating population.

Remittances   Money migrants send back to family and friends in their home countries, often in cash, forming an important part of the economy in many poorer countries.

Remote sensing   A method of collecting data or information through the use of instruments (e.g., satellites) that are physically distant from the area or object of study.

Renewable resources   Resources that can regenerate as they are exploited.

Renfrew hypothesis   Hypothesis developed by British scholar Colin Renfrew wherein he proposed that three areas in and near the first agricultural hearth, the **Fertile Crescent**, gave rise to three language families: Europe's Indo-European languages (from Anatolia [present-day Turkey]); North African and Arabian languages (from the western arc of the Fertile Crescent); and the languages in present-day Iran, Afghanistan, Pakistan, and India (from the eastern arc of the Fertile Crescent).

Repatriation   A refugee or group of refugees returning to their home country, usually with the assistance of government or a non-governmental organization.

Rescale   Involvement of players at other scales to generate support for a position or an initiative (e.g., use of the Internet to generate interest on a national or global scale for a local position or initiative).

Residential segregation   Defined by geographers Douglas Massey and Nancy Denton as the degree to which two or more groups live separately from one another, in different parts of an urban environment.

Restrictive population policies   Government policies designed to reduce the rate of natural population increase.

Reterritorialization   With respect to popular culture, when people within a place start to produce an aspect of popular culture themselves, doing so in the context of their local culture and making it their own.

Roman Catholic Church   One of three major branches of **Christianity**, the Roman Catholic Church, together with the **Eastern Orthodox Church**, a second of the three major branches of Christianity, arose out of the division of the Roman Empire by Emperor Diocletian into four governmental regions: two western regions centered in Rome, and two eastern regions centered in Constantinople (now Istanbul, Turkey). In 1054 CE, Christianity was divided along that same line when the Eastern Orthodox Church, centered in Constantinople; and the Roman Catholic Church, centered in Rome, split.

Romance languages   Languages (French, Spanish, Italian, Romanian, and Portuguese) that lie in the areas that were once controlled by the Roman Empire but were not subsequently overwhelmed.

Root crop   Crop that is reproduced by cultivating the roots of or the cuttings from the plants.

Russification   the Soviet policy to promote the diffusion of Russian culture throughout the republics of the former Soviet Union.

Rust belt   a region in the northeastern United States that was once characterized by industry. Now so-called because of the heavy deindustrialization of the area.

Sacred site   **Place** or **space** people infuse with religious meaning.

Sanitary landfills   Disposal sites for non-hazardous solid waste that is spread in layers and compacted to the smallest practical volume. The sites are typically designed with floors made of materials to treat seeping liquids and are covered by soil as the wastes are compacted and deposited into the landfill.

Scale   Representation of a real-world phenomenon at a certain level of reduction or generalization. In **cartography**, the ratio of map distance to ground distance; indicated on a map as a bar graph, representative fraction, and/or verbal statement.

Second Agricultural Revolution   Dovetailing with and benefiting from the **Industrial Revolution**, the Second Agricultural Revolution witnessed improved methods of cultivation, harvesting, and storage of farm produce.

Secondary economic activity   Economic activity involving the processing of raw materials and their transformation into finished industrial products; the manufacturing sector.

Secondary hearth   An area to which an innovation diffuses and from which the innovation diffuses more broadly.

Sector model   A structural model of the American city that suggests that low-rent and other types of areas can extend from the **central business district** to the city's outer edge, creating zones that are shaped like a piece of pie.

Secularism   The idea that ethical and moral standards should be formulated and adhered to for life on Earth, not to accommodate the prescriptions of a deity and promises of a comfortable afterlife. A secular state is the opposite of a **theocracy**.

Seed crop   Crop that is reproduced by cultivating the seeds of the plants.

Selective immigration   Process to control immigration in which individuals with certain backgrounds (i.e. criminal records, poor health, or subversive activities) are barred from immigrating.

Semi-periphery   Places where **core** and **periphery** processes are both occurring; places that are exploited by the core but in turn exploit the periphery.

Sense of place   State of mind derived through the infusion of a place with meaning and emotion by remembering important events that occurred in that place or by labeling a place with a certain character.

Sequent occupance   The notion that successive societies leave their cultural imprints on a place, each contributing to the cumulative **cultural landscape**.

Shamanism   Community faith in traditional societies in which people follow their shaman—a religious leader, teacher, healer, and visionary. At times, an especially strong shaman might attract a regional following. However, most shamans remain local figures.

Shantytown   Unplanned slum development on the margins of cities, dominated by crude dwellings and shelters made mostly of scrap wood, iron, and even pieces of cardboard.

Sharia law   The system of Islamic law, sometimes called *Qu'ranic law*. Unlike most Western systems of law that are based on legal precedents, Sharia is based on varying degrees of interpretation of the *Qu'ran*.

Shifting cultivation   Cultivation of crops in tropical forest clearings in which the forest vegetation has been removed by cutting and burning. These clearings are usually abandoned after a few years in favor of newly cleared forestland. Also known as **slash-and-burn agriculture**.

Shintoism   **Religion** located in Japan and related to **Buddhism**. Shintoism focuses particularly on nature and ancestor worship.

Shi'ites   Adherents of one of the two main divisions of Islam. Also known as Shiahs, the Shiites represent the Persian (Iranian) variation of Islam and believe in the infallibility and divine right to authority of the **Imams**, descendants of Ali.

Site   The internal physical attributes of a **place**, including its absolute location, its spatial character and physical setting.

Situation   The external locational attributes of a place; its **relative location** or regional position with reference to other nonlocal places.

Slash-and-burn agriculture   See **shifting cultivation**.

Slavic languages   Languages (Russian, Polish, Czech, Slovak, Ukrainian, Slovenian, Serbo-Croatian, and Bulgarian) that developed as Slavic people migrated from a base in present-day Ukraine close to 2000 years ago.

Social networks   Interconnections among individuals that foster social interaction.

Social stratification   One of two components, together with **agricultural surplus**, which enables the formation of **cities**; the differentiation of society into classes based on wealth, power, production, and prestige.

Soil erosion   The wearing away of the land surface by wind and moving water.

Solid waste   Non-liquid, non-soluble materials ranging from municipal garbage to sewage sludge, agricultural refuse, and mining residues.

Sound shift   Slight change in a word across **languages** within a **subfamily** or through a language family from the present backward toward its origin.

Sovereignty   A principle of international relations that holds that final authority over social, economic, and political matters should rest with the legitimate rulers of independent states.

Space   Defined by Doreen Massey and Pat Jess as "social relations stretched out."

Spaces of consumption   Areas of a **city**, the main purpose of which is to encourage people to consume goods and services; driven primarily by the global media industry.

Spatial   Pertaining to space on the Earth's surface; sometimes used as a synonym for *geographic*.

Spatial distribution   Physical location of geographic phenomena across **space**.

Spatial fix   The movement of production from one site to another based on the place-based cost advantages of the new site.

Spatial interaction   The degree of flow of people, ideas, and goods among places. See **complementarity** and **intervening opportunity**.

Spatial perspective   Observing variations in geographic phenomena across **space**.

Special Economic Zone (SEZ)   Specific **area** within a country in which tax incentives and less stringent environmental regulations are implemented to attract foreign business and investment.

Splitting   In the context of determining representative districts, the process by which the majority and minority populations are spread evenly across each of the districts to be created therein, ensuring control by the majority of each of the districts; as opposed to the result of **majority-minority districts**.

Standard language   The variant of a **language** that a country's political and intellectual elite seek to promote as the norm for use in schools, government, the media, and other aspects of public life.

State   A politically organized territory that is administered by a sovereign government and is recognized by a significant portion of the international community. A state has a defined territory, a permanent population, a government, and is recognized by other states.

Stateless nation   **Nation** that does not have a state.

Stationary population level   The level at which a national population ceases to grow.

Step migration   **Migration** to a distant destination that occurs in stages, for example, from farm to nearby village and later to town and city.

Stimulus diffusion   A form of diffusion in which a cultural adaptation is created as a result of the introduction of a **cultural trait** from another **place**.

Structural adjustment loans   Loans granted by international financial institutions such as the World Bank and the International Monetary Fund to countries in the **periphery** and the **semi-periphery** in exchange for certain economic and governmental reforms in that country (e.g. privatization of certain government entities and opening the country to foreign trade and investment).

Structuralist theory   A general term for a model of economic development that treats economic disparities among countries or regions as the result of historically derived power relations within the global economic system.

Subfamilies (language)   Divisions within a **language** family where the commonalities are more definite and the origin is more recent.

Subsistence agriculture   Self-sufficient **agriculture** that is small scale and low technology and emphasizes food production for local consumption, not for trade.

Suburb   A subsidiary urban area surrounding and connected to the central city. Many are exclusively residential; others have their own commercial centers or shopping malls.

Suburban downtown   Significant concentration of diversified economic activities around a highly **accessible** suburban location, including retailing, light industry, and a variety of major corporate and commercial operations. Late-twentieth-century coequal to the American central city's **Central Business District (CBD)**.

Suburbanization   Movement of upper- and middle-class people from urban **core areas** to the surrounding outskirts to escape pollution as well as deteriorating social conditions (perceived and actual). In North America, the process began in the early nineteenth century and became a mass phenomenon by the second half of the twentieth century.

Succession   Process by which new **immigrants** to a **city** move to and dominate or take over areas or neighborhoods occupied by older immigrant groups. For example, in the early twentieth century, Puerto Ricans "invaded" the immigrant Jewish neighborhood of East Harlem and successfully took over the neighborhood or "succeeded" the immigrant Jewish population as the dominant immigrant group in the neighborhood.

Sunbelt   The South and Southwest regions of the United States

Sunnis   Adherents to the largest branch of Islam, called the orthodox or traditionalist. They believe in the effectiveness of family and community in the solution of life's problems, and they differ from the **Shiites** in accepting the traditions (*sunna*) of Muhammad as authoritative.

Supranational organization   A venture involving three or more **nation-states** involving formal political, economic, and/or cultural cooperation to promote shared objectives. The European Union is one such organization.

Syncretic   A blend of religious beliefs and traditions, often forming a new religion.

Synekism   The possibility of change that results from people living together in cities.

Synergy   The cross-promotion of vertically-integrated goods.

Taoism   **Religion** believed to have been founded by Lao-Tsu and based upon his book entitled "Tao-te-ching," or "Book of the Way." Lao-Tsu focused on the proper form of political rule and on the oneness of humanity and nature.

Tear-downs   Homes bought in many American suburbs with the intent of tearing them down and replacing them with much larger homes, often referred to as **McMansions**.

Technopole   Centers or nodes of high-technology research and activity around which a **high-technology corridor** is sometimes established.

Tectonic plates   Large pieces of rock that form portions of the Earth's mantle and crust and which are in motion.

Terra incognita   Areas on maps that are not well defined because they are off limits or unknown to the map maker.

Territorial integrity   The right of a **state** to defend soverign territory against incursion from other states.

Territorial representation   System wherein each representative is elected from a territorially defined district.

Territoriality   In **political geography**, a country's or more local community's sense of property and attachment toward its territory, as expressed by its determination to keep it inviolable and strongly defended. See more generally **human territoriality**.

Tertiary economic activity   Economic activity associated with the provision of services—such as transportation, banking, retailing, education, and routine office-based jobs.

Thematic maps　Maps that tell stories, typically showing the degree of some attribute or the movement of a geographic phenomenon.

Theocracy　A **state** whose government is under the control of a ruler who is deemed to be divinely guided, or of a group of religious leaders, as in post-Khomeini Iran. The opposite of a theocracy is a secular state.

Third Agricultural Revolution　Currently in progress, the Third Agricultural Revolution has as its principal orientation the development of **genetically modified organisms (GMOs)**.

Three-tier structure　With reference to Immanuel Wallerstein's **world-systems theory**, the division of the world into the **core**, the **periphery**, and the **semi-periphery** as a means to help explain the interconnections between places in the global economy.

Thunian pattern　See **Von Thünen Model**.

Time-Distance decay　The declining degree of acceptance of an idea or innovation with increasing time and distance from its point of origin or source.

Time-space compression　A term associated with the work of David Harvey that refers to the social and psychological effects of living in a world in which **time-space convergence** has rapidly reached a high level of intensity.

Time-space convergence　A term coined by Donald Janelle that refers to the greatly accelerated movement of goods, information, and ideas during the twentieth century made possible by technological innovations in transportation and communications.

Toponym　Place name.

Total Fertility Rate (TFR)　The average number of children born to a woman during her childbearing years.

Township-and-range system　A rectangular land division scheme designed by Thomas Jefferson to disperse settlers evenly across farmlands of the U.S. interior. See also **rectangular survey system**.

Toxic waste　Hazardous waste causing danger from chemicals and infectious organisms.

Trade area　**Region** adjacent to every town and **city** within which its influence is dominant.

Traditional　Term used in various contexts (e.g., traditional religion) to indicate originality within a culture or long-term part of an indigenous society. It is the opposite of modernized, superimposed, or changed; it denotes continuity and historic association.

Trafficking　When a family sends a child or an adult to a labor recruiter in hopes that the labor recruiter will send money, and the family member will earn money to send home.

Transhumance　A seasonal periodic movement of **pastoralists** and their livestock between highland and lowland pastures.

Unilateralism　World order in which one state is in a position of dominance with allies following rather than joining the political decision-making process.

Unitary (state)　A **nation-state** that has a centralized government and administration that exercises power equally over all parts of the state.

Universalizing religion　A belief system that espouses the idea that there is one true religion that is universal in scope. Adherents of universalizing religious systems often believe that their religion represents universal truths, and in some cases great effort is undertaken in evangelism and missionary work.

Urban (area)　The entire built-up, nonrural area and its population, including the most recently constructed suburban appendages. Provides a better picture of the dimensions and population of such an area than the delimited municipality (central city) that forms its heart.

Urban hierarchy　A ranking of settlements (hamlet, village, town, city, metropolis) according to their size and economic functions.

Urban morphology　The study of the physical form and structure of urban **places**.

Urban realm　A **spatial** generalization of the large, late-twentieth-century **city** in the United States. It is shown to be a widely dispersed, multicentered metropolis consisting of increasingly independent zones or realms, each focused on its own **suburban downtown**; the only exception is the shrunken central realm, which is focused on the **central business district (CBD)**.

Urban sprawl　Unrestricted growth in many American **urban** areas of housing, commercial development, and roads over large expanses of land, with little concern for urban planning.

Urbanization　A term with several connotations. The proportion of a country's population living in urban places is its level of urbanization. The process of urbanization involves the movement of people to, and the clustering of people in, towns and cities—a major force in every geographic realm today. Another kind of urbanization occurs when an expanding city absorbs the rural countryside and transforms it into suburbs; in the case of cities in the developing world, this also generates peripheral **shantytowns**.

Urbicide　The deliberate killing of a city, as happens, for example, when cities are targeted for destruction during wars.

Variable costs　Costs that change directly with the amount of production (e.g. energy supply and labor costs).

Vectored disease　A disease carried from one host to another by an intermediate host.

Vertical integration　Ownership by the same firm of a number of companies that exist along a variety of points on a **commodity chain**.

Vienna Convention for the Protection of the Ozone Layer　The first international convention aimed at addressing the issue of ozone depletion. Held in 1985, the Vienna Convention was the predecessor to the **Montreal Protocol**.

Voluntary migration　**Movement** in which people relocate in response to perceived opportunity, not because they are forced to move.

Von Thünen Model　A model that explains the location of agricultural activities in a commercial, profit-making economy. A process of spatial competition allocates various farming activities into rings around a central market city, with profit-earning capability the determining force in how far a crop locates from the market.

Washington Consensus　Label used to refer to the following fundamental principles of free trade: 1) that free trade raises the well-being of all countries by inducing them to devote their resources to production of those goods they produce relatively most efficiently; and 2) that competition through trade raises a country's long-term growth rate by expanding access to global technologies and promoting innovation.

Wisconsinian Glaciation　The most recent glacial period of the Pleistocene, enduring about 100,000 years and giving way, beginning about 18,000 years ago, to the current interglacial, the Holocene.

World city　Dominant **city** in terms of its role in the global political economy. Not the world's biggest city in terms of population or industrial output, but rather centers of strategic control of the world economy.

World-systems theory　Theory originated by Immanuel Wallerstein and illuminated by his **three-tier structure**, proposing that social change in the developing world is inextricably linked to the economic activities of the developed world.

Zero population growth　a state in which a population is maintained at a constant level because the number of deaths is exactly offset by the number of births.

Zionism　The movement to unite the Jewish people of the **diaspora** and to establish a national homeland for them in the promised land.

Zone　Area of a **city** with a relatively uniform land use (e.g. an industrial zone or a residential zone).

Zoning laws　Legal restrictions on land use that determine what types of building and economic activities are allowed to take place in certain areas. In the United States, areas are most commonly divided into separate zones of residential, retail, or industrial use.

INDEX